2002

J11

8-3554

DATA STRUCTURES & ALGORITHM ANALYSIS IN JAVA™

DATA STRUCTURES & ALGORITHM ANALYSIS IN JAVA™

MARK ALLEN WEISS

Florida International University

 ADDISON-WESLEY

An imprint of Addison Wesley Longman, Inc.

Reading, Massachusetts • Harlow, England • Menlo Park, California
Berkeley, California • Don Mills, Ontario • Sydney • Bonn • Amsterdam
Tokyo • Mexico City

Acquisitions Editor: Susan Hartman
Associate Editor: Katherine Harutunian
Production Editor: Patricia A. O. Unubun
Production Management: Publication Services, Inc.
Composition: Publication Services, Inc.
Cover Design: Trudi Gershenov Design

This book was typeset in TEX on a UNIX system. The fonts used were Syntax and Berkeley, and mathsy for math. It was printed on New Era Matte.

Library of Congress Cataloging-in-Publication Data
Weiss, Mark Allen.
    Data structures and algorithm analysis in Java / Mark Allen Weiss.
        p.   cm.
    Includes bibliographical references and index.
    ISBN 0-201-35754-2
        1. Java (Computer program language) 2. Data structures (Computer
    science) 3. Computer algorithms. I. Title.
    QA76.73.J38W448   1999   98-38827
    005.7'3–dc21   CIP

1 2 3 4 5 6 7 8 9 10–MA–0201009998

Preface

Purpose/Goals

This new Java edition describes *data structures,* methods of organizing large amounts of data, and *algorithm analysis,* the estimation of the running time of algorithms. As computers become faster and faster, the need for programs that can handle large amounts of input becomes more acute. Paradoxically, this requires more careful attention to efficiency, since inefficiencies in programs become most obvious when input sizes are large. By analyzing an algorithm before it is actually coded, students can decide if a particular solution will be feasible. For example, in this text students look at specific problems and see how careful implementations can reduce the time constraint for large amounts of data from 16 years to less than a second. Therefore, no algorithm or data structure is presented without an explanation of its running time. In some cases, minute details that affect the running time of the implementation are explored.

Once a solution method is determined, a program must still be written. As computers have become more powerful, the problems they must solve have become larger and more complex, requiring development of more intricate programs. The goal of this text is to teach students good programming and algorithm analysis skills simultaneously so that they can develop such programs with the maximum amount of efficiency.

This book is suitable for either an advanced data structures (CS7) course or a first-year graduate course in algorithm analysis. Students should have some knowledge of intermediate programming, including such topics as object-based programming and recursion, and some background in discrete math.

Approach

Although the material in this text is largely language independent, programming requires the use of a specific language. As the title implies, we have chosen Java for this book.

Java is a relatively new language that is often examined in comparison with C++. Java offers many benefits, and programmers often view Java as a safer, more portable, and easier-to-use language than C++. As such, it makes a fine core language for discussing and implementing fundamental data structures. Other important parts of Java, such as threads and its GUI, although important, are not needed in this text and thus are not discussed.

As with every programming language, Java has some disadvantages. It does not directly support generic programming; a workaround is required that is discussed in Chapter 1. I/O support using Java is minimal, but there are now many I/O classes available on the Internet that make things simpler. In any event, the examples in the text make minimal use of the Java I/O facilities.

Java's advantage—that it simplifies C++'s (sometimes confusing) syntax—is also a liability. Programmers who eventually code in C++ will find hidden traps in what should be a straightforward conversion of Java code to C++ code. To help alleviate this problem, the accompanying website contains a chapter that describes C++ and illustrates many of C++'s subtleties and nuances that would not be obvious to many.

Complete versions of the data structures, in both Java and C++, are available on the Internet. We use similar coding conventions to make the parallels between the two languages more evident.

Overview

Chapter 1 contains review material on discrete math and recursion. I believe the only way to be comfortable with recursion is to see good uses over and over. Therefore, recursion is prevalent in this text, with examples in every chapter except Chapter 5. Chapter 1 also presents material that serves as a review of basic Java. Included is a discussion of the Java workaround needed for generic algorithms and data structures.

Chapter 2 deals with algorithm analysis. This chapter explains asymptotic analysis and its major weaknesses. Many examples are provided, including an in-depth explanation of logarithmic running time. Simple recursive programs are analyzed by intuitively converting them into iterative programs. More complicated divide-and-conquer programs are introduced, but some of the analysis (solving recurrence relations) is implicitly delayed until Chapter 7, where it is performed in detail.

Chapter 3 covers lists, stacks, and queues. The emphasis here is on coding these data structures using ADTS, fast implementation of these data structures, and an exposition of some of their uses. There are almost no complete programs, but the exercises contain plenty of ideas for programming assignments.

Chapter 4 covers trees, with an emphasis on search trees, including external search trees (B-trees). The UNIX file system and expression trees are used as examples. AVL trees and splay trees are introduced. More careful treatment of search tree implementation details is found in Chapter 12. Additional coverage of trees, such as file compression and game trees, is deferred until Chapter 10. Data structures for an external medium are considered as the final topic in several chapters.

Chapter 5 is a relatively short chapter concerning hash tables. Some analysis is performed, and extendible hashing is covered at the end of the chapter.

Chapter 6 is about priority queues. Binary heaps are covered, and there is additional material on some of the theoretically interesting implementations of priority queues. The Fibonacci heap is discussed in Chapter 11, and the pairing heap is discussed in Chapter 12.

Chapter 7 covers sorting. It is very specific with respect to coding details and analysis. All the important general-purpose sorting algorithms are covered and compared. Four algorithms are analyzed in detail: insertion sort, Shellsort, heapsort, and quicksort. External sorting is covered at the end of the chapter.

Chapter 8 discusses the disjoint set algorithm with proof of the running time. This is a short and specific chapter that can be skipped if Kruskal's algorithm is not discussed.

Chapter 9 covers graph algorithms. Algorithms on graphs are interesting, not only because they frequently occur in practice but also because their running time is so heavily dependent on the proper use of data structures. Virtually all of the standard algorithms are presented along with appropriate data structures, pseudocode, and analysis of running time. To place these problems in a proper context, a short discussion on complexity theory (including *NP*-completeness and undecidability) is provided.

Chapter 10 covers algorithm design by examining common problem-solving techniques. This chapter is heavily fortified with examples. Pseudocode is used in these later chapters so that the student's appreciation of an example algorithm is not obscured by implementation details.

Chapter 11 deals with amortized analysis. Three data structures from Chapters 4 and 6 and the Fibonacci heap, introduced in this chapter, are analyzed.

Chapter 12 covers search tree algorithms, the *k*-d tree, and the pairing heap. This chapter departs from the rest of the text by providing complete and careful implementations for the search trees and pairing heap. The material is structured so that the instructor can integrate sections into discussions from other chapters. For example, the top-down red-black tree in Chapter 12 can be discussed along with AVL trees (in Chapter 4).

Appendix A lists some commonly used Java classes. Appendix B discusses the Java Collections package. This standard package (as of Java 1.2) contains implementations of several data structures discussed in the text.

Chapters 1–9 provide enough material for most one-semester data structures courses. If time permits, then Chapter 10 can be covered. A graduate course on algorithm analysis could cover Chapters 7–11. The advanced data structures analyzed in Chapter 11 can easily be referred to in the earlier chapters. The discussion of *NP*-completeness in Chapter 9 is far too brief to be used in such a course. Garey and Johnson's book on *NP*-completeness can be used to augment this text.

Exercises

Exercises, provided at the end of each chapter, match the order in which material is presented. The last exercises may address the chapter as a whole rather than a specific section. Difficult exercises are marked with an asterisk, and more challenging exercises have two asterisks.

A solutions manual containing solutions to almost all the exercises is available to instructors from the Addison Wesley Longman Publishing Company.

References

References are placed at the end of each chapter. Generally the references either are historical, representing the original source of the material, or they represent extensions and improvements to the results given in the text. Some references represent solutions to exercises.

Code Availability

The example program code in this book is available via anonymous ftp at `aw.com`. It is also accessible through the World Wide Web; the URL is `http://www.awl.com/cseng/` (follow the links from there). The exact location of this material may change.

Acknowledgments

Many, many people have helped me in the preparation of books in this series. Some are listed in other versions of the book; thanks to all.

As usual, the writing process was made easier by the professionals at Addison Wesley Longman. I'd like to thank my editor, Susan Hartman; associate editor, Katherine Harutunian; and production editor, Pat Unubun. I'd also like to thank Kris Engberg and her staff at Publication Services for their usual fine work putting the final pieces together.

I would like to thank the reviewers, who provided valuable comments, many of which have been incorporated into the text. For this edition, they are Chris Brown (University of Rochester), Thang N. Bui (Pennsylvania State University at Harrisburg), G. H. Hedrick (Oklahoma State University), Sampath Kannan (University of Pennsylvania), and Gurdip Singh (Kansas State University).

Finally, I'd like to thank the numerous readers who have sent e-mail messages and pointed out errors or inconsistencies in earlier versions. My World Wide Web page http://www.cs.fiu.edu/~weiss will contain updated source code (in Java, C, and C++), an errata list, and a link to submit bug reports.

M.A.W.

Contents

Chapter 1   Introduction   1

1.1.   What's the Book About?   1

1.2.   Mathematics Review   2

    1.2.1. Exponents   2

    1.2.2. Logarithms   3

    1.2.3. Series   3

    1.2.4. Modular Arithmetic   5

    1.2.5. The P Word   5

1.3.   A Brief Introduction to Recursion   7

1.4.   Generic Objects in Java   11

    1.4.1. The `IntCell` Class   11

    1.4.2. The `MemoryCell` Class   13

    1.4.3. Implementing Generic `findMax`   15

1.5.   Exceptions   16

1.6.   Input and Output   19

    1.6.1. Basic Stream Operations   19

    1.6.2. The `StringTokenizer` Object   20

    1.6.3. Sequential Files   20

1.7.   Code Organization   24

    1.7.1. Packages   24

    1.7.2. The `MyInteger` Class   24

    1.7.3. Efficiency Considerations   24

    Summary   25

Exercises   25
References   27

Chapter 2 Algorithm Analysis   29

2.1. Mathematical Background   29

2.2. Model   32

2.3. What to Analyze   32

2.4. Running Time Calculations   35

2.4.1. A Simple Example   35

2.4.2. General Rules   35

2.4.3. Solutions for the Maximum Subsequence Sum Problem   37

2.4.4. Logarithms in the Running Time   43

2.4.5. Checking Your Analysis   47

2.4.6. A Grain of Salt   48

Summary   48

Exercises   49

References   54

Chapter 3 Lists, Stacks, and Queues   55

3.1. Abstract Data Types (ADTs)   55

3.2. The List ADT   56

3.2.1. Simple Array Implementation of Lists   56

3.2.2. Linked Lists   57

3.2.3. Programming Details   58

3.2.4. Doubly Linked Lists   63

3.2.5. Circular Linked Lists   63

3.2.6. Examples   64

3.2.7. Cursor Implementation of Linked Lists   69

3.3. The Stack ADT   75

3.3.1. Stack Model   75

3.3.2. Implementation of Stacks   76

3.3.3. Applications   81

3.4.   The Queue ADT   88

3.4.1. Queue Model   88

3.4.2. Array Implementation of Queues   89

3.4.3. Applications of Queues   92

Summary   94

Exercises   94

Chapter 4   Trees   99

4.1.   Preliminaries   99

4.1.1. Implementation of Trees   100

4.1.2. Tree Traversals with an Application   101

4.2.   Binary Trees   105

4.2.1. Implementation   105

4.2.2. An Example: Expression Trees   106

4.3.   The Search Tree ADT—Binary Search Trees   109

4.3.1. find   110

4.3.2. findMin and findMax   111

4.3.3. insert   112

4.3.4. remove   113

4.3.5. Average-Case Analysis   116

4.4.   AVL Trees   118

4.4.1. Single Rotation   120

4.4.2. Double Rotation   123

4.5.   Splay Trees   130

4.5.1. A Simple Idea (That Does Not Work)   130

4.5.2. Splaying   132

4.6.   Tree Traversals (Revisited)   138

4.7.   B-Trees   139

Summary   144

Exercises   145

References   152

Chapter 5 Hashing   155

5.1. General Idea   155

5.2. Hash Function   156

5.3. Separate Chaining   158

5.4. Open Addressing   162

    5.4.1. Linear Probing   162

    5.4.2. Quadratic Probing   164

    5.4.3. Double Hashing   170

5.5. Rehashing   171

5.6. Extendible Hashing   174

    Summary   176

    Exercises   178

    References   181

Chapter 6 Priority Queues (Heaps)   183

6.1. Model   183

6.2. Simple Implementations   184

6.3. Binary Heap   184

    6.3.1. Structure Property   185

    6.3.2. Heap Order Property   186

    6.3.3. Basic Heap Operations   188

    6.3.4. Other Heap Operations   192

6.4. Applications of Priority Queues   195

    6.4.1. The Selection Problem   195

    6.4.2. Event Simulation   196

6.5. d-Heaps   198

6.6. Leftist Heaps   198

    6.6.1. Leftist Heap Property   199

    6.6.2. Leftist Heap Operations   200

6.7. Skew Heaps   206

6.8. Binomial Queues   208

    6.8.1. Binomial Queue Structure   208

6.8.2. Binomial Queue Operations   208

6.8.3. Implementation of Binomial Queues   213

Summary   215

Exercises   218

References   222

Chapter 7   Sorting   225

7.1. Preliminaries   225

7.2. Insertion Sort   226

    7.2.1. The Algorithm   226

    7.2.2. Analysis of Insertion Sort   226

7.3. A Lower Bound for Simple Sorting Algorithms   227

7.4. Shellsort   228

    7.4.1. Worst-Case Analysis of Shellsort   229

7.5. Heapsort   232

    7.5.1. Analysis of Heapsort   232

7.6. Mergesort   235

    7.6.1. Analysis of Mergesort   237

7.7. Quicksort   240

    7.7.1. Picking the Pivot   241

    7.7.2. Partitioning Strategy   243

    7.7.3. Small Arrays   245

    7.7.4. Actual Quicksort Routines   245

    7.7.5. Analysis of Quicksort   246

    7.7.6. A Linear-Expected-Time Algorithm for Selection   250

7.8. A General Lower Bound for Sorting   252

    7.8.1. Decision Trees   252

7.9. Bucket Sort   254

7.10. External Sorting   255

    7.10.1. Why We Need New Algorithms   255

    7.10.2. Model for External Sorting   255

    7.10.3. The Simple Algorithm   255

7.10.4. Multiway Merge   257

7.10.5. Polyphase Merge   258

7.10.6. Replacement Selection   259

Summary   260

Exercises   261

References   265

Chapter 8 The Disjoint Set ADT   269

8.1. Equivalence Relations   269

8.2. The Dynamic Equivalence Problem   270

8.3. Basic Data Structure   271

8.4. Smart Union Algorithms   274

8.5. Path Compression   276

8.6. Worst Case for Union-by-Rank and Path Compression   279

8.6.1. Analysis of the Union/Find Algorithm   279

8.7. An Application   285

Summary   287

Exercises   287

References   289

Chapter 9 Graph Algorithms   291

9.1. Definitions   291

9.1.1. Representation of Graphs   292

9.2. Topological Sort   294

9.3. Shortest-Path Algorithms   297

9.3.1. Unweighted Shortest Paths   299

9.3.2. Dijkstra's Algorithm   304

9.3.3. Graphs with Negative Edge Costs   310

9.3.4. Acyclic Graphs   311

9.3.5. All-Pairs Shortest Path   314

9.4. Network Flow Problems   314

9.4.1. A Simple Maximum-Flow Algorithm   315

9.5. Minimum Spanning Tree   319

    9.5.1. Prim's Algorithm   320

    9.5.2. Kruskal's Algorithm   323

9.6. Applications of Depth-First Search   325

    9.6.1. Undirected Graphs   326

    9.6.2. Biconnectivity   327

    9.6.3. Euler Circuits   331

    9.6.4. Directed Graphs   334

    9.6.5. Finding Strong Components   336

9.7. Introduction to NP-Completeness   337

    9.7.1. Easy vs. Hard   338

    9.7.2. The Class NP   339

    9.7.3. NP-Complete Problems   339

    Summary   341

    Exercises   341

    References   349

Chapter 10   Algorithm Design Techniques   353

10.1. Greedy Algorithms   353

    10.1.1. A Simple Scheduling Problem   354

    10.1.2. Huffman Codes   357

    10.1.3. Approximate Bin Packing   362

10.2. Divide and Conquer   370

    10.2.1. Running Time of Divide
and Conquer Algorithms   371

    10.2.2. Closest-Points Problem   373

    10.2.3. The Selection Problem   377

    10.2.4. Theoretical Improvements
for Arithmetic Problems   380

10.3. Dynamic Programming   384

    10.3.1. Using a Table Instead of Recursion   384

    10.3.2. Ordering Matrix Multiplications   387

10.3.3. Optimal Binary Search Tree   389

10.3.4. All-Pairs Shortest Path   393

10.4. Randomized Algorithms   395

10.4.1. Random Number Generators   396

10.4.2. Skip Lists   399

10.4.3. Primality Testing   402

10.5. Backtracking Algorithms   403

10.5.1. The Turnpike Reconstruction Problem   405

10.5.2. Games   409

Summary   415

Exercises   415

References   423

Chapter 11 Amortized Analysis   429

11.1. An Unrelated Puzzle   430

11.2. Binomial Queues   430

11.3. Skew Heaps   435

11.4. Fibonacci Heaps   437

11.4.1. Cutting Nodes in Leftist Heaps   438

11.4.2. Lazy Merging for Binomial Queues   440

11.4.3. The Fibonacci Heap Operations   443

11.4.4. Proof of the Time Bound   443

11.5. Splay Trees   446

Summary   449

Exercises   450

References   452

**Chapter 12 Advanced Data Structures
                  and Implementation   453**

12.1. Top-Down Splay Trees   453

12.2. Red-Black Trees   460

12.2.1. Bottom-Up Insertion   461

    12.2.2. Top-Down Red-Black Trees   462

    12.2.3. Top-Down Deletion   467

12.3. Deterministic Skip Lists   468

12.4. AA-Trees   474

12.5. Treaps   481

12.6. *k*-d Trees   483

12.7. Pairing Heaps   486

    Summary   492

    Exercises   492

    References   495

Appendix A Some Library Routines   499

A.1. Classes in Package `java.lang`   499

    A.1.1. `Character`   499

    A.1.2. `Integer`   500

    A.1.3. `Object`   501

    A.1.4. `String`   502

    A.1.5. `StringBuffer`   503

    A.1.6. `System`   505

    A.1.7. `Throwable`   506

A.2. Classes in Package `java.io`   506

    A.2.1. `BufferedReader`   506

    A.2.2. `BufferedWriter`   507

    A.2.3. `File`   507

    A.2.4. `FileReader`   508

    A.2.5. `FileWriter`   508

    A.2.6. `InputStreamReader`   509

    A.2.7. `PrintWriter`   509

    A.2.8. `PushbackReader`   509

A.3. Classes in Package `java.util`   510

    A.3.1. `Random`   510

    A.3.2. `StringTokenizer`   511

Appendix B The Collections Library   513

B.1. Introduction   513

B.2. Basic Classes   514

    B.2.1. `Collection`   514

    B.2.2. `Iterator`   514

    B.2.3. `Comparable`   515

    B.2.4. `Comparator`   515

B.3. Lists   516

    B.3.1. `ArrayList` vs. `LinkedList`   516

    B.3.2. Stacks and Queues   517

    B.3.3. `ListIterator`   517

B.4. Sets   517

B.5. Maps   517

    B.5.1. `put`, `get`, `remove`, and `contains`   518

    B.5.2. Getting a `Collection` from the Map   518

    B.5.3. `Map.Entry` Pairs   518

B.6. Example: Generating a Concordance   519

    B.6.1. Collections API Version   519

    B.6.2. Version Using Package `DataStructures`   519

B.7. Example: Shortest-Path Calculation   523

    B.7.1. Collections API Implementation   523

    B.7.2. Version Using Package `DataStructures`   526

B.8. Priority Queues   530

    Summary   530

Index   531

Introduction

In this chapter, we discuss the aims and goals of this text and briefly review programming concepts and discrete mathematics. We will

- See that how a program performs for reasonably large input is just as important as its performance on moderate amounts of input.
- Summarize the basic mathematical background needed for the rest of the book.
- Briefly review recursion.
- Summarize some important features of Java that are used throughout the text.

1.1. What's the Book About?

Suppose you have a group of N numbers and would like to determine the kth largest. This is known as the *selection problem*. Most students who have had a programming course or two would have no difficulty writing a program to solve this problem. There are quite a few "obvious" solutions.

One way to solve this problem would be to read the N numbers into an array, sort the array in decreasing order by some simple algorithm such as bubblesort, and then return the element in position k.

A somewhat better algorithm might be to read the first k elements into an array and sort them (in decreasing order). Next, each remaining element is read one by one. As a new element arrives, it is ignored if it is smaller than the kth element in the array. Otherwise, it is placed in its correct spot in the array, bumping one element out of the array. When the algorithm ends, the element in the kth position is returned as the answer.

Both algorithms are simple to code, and you are encouraged to do so. The natural questions, then, are which algorithm is better and, more important, is either algorithm good enough? A simulation using a random file of 1 million elements and $k = 500,000$ will show that neither algorithm finishes in a reasonable amount of time; each requires several days of computer processing to terminate (albeit eventually with a correct answer). An alternative method, discussed in Chapter 7, gives a solution in about a second. Thus, although our proposed algorithms work, they cannot be considered good algorithms, because they are entirely impractical for input sizes that a third algorithm can handle in a reasonable amount of time.

A second problem is to solve a popular word puzzle. The input consists of a two-dimensional array of letters and a list of words. The object is to find the words in the puzzle.

	1	2	3	4
1	t	h	i	s
2	w	a	t	s
3	o	a	h	g
4	f	g	d	t

Figure 1.1 Sample word puzzle

These words may be horizontal, vertical, or diagonal in any direction. As an example, the puzzle shown in Figure 1.1 contains the words *this, two, fat,* and *that.* The word *this* begins at row 1, column 1, or (1,1), and extends to (1,4); *two* goes from (1,1) to (3,1); *fat* goes from (4,1) to (2,3); and *that* goes from (4,4) to (1,1).

Again, there are at least two straightforward algorithms that solve the problem. For each word in the word list, we check each ordered triple (*row, column, orientation*) for the presence of the word. This amounts to lots of nested **for** loops but is basically straightforward.

Alternatively, for each ordered quadruple (*row, column, orientation, number of characters*) that doesn't run off an end of the puzzle, we can test whether the word indicated is in the word list. Again, this amounts to lots of nested **for** loops. It is possible to save some time if the maximum number of characters in any word is known.

It is relatively easy to code up either method of solution and solve many of the real-life puzzles commonly published in magazines. These typically have 16 rows, 16 columns, and 40 or so words. Suppose, however, we consider the variation where only the puzzle board is given and the word list is essentially an English dictionary. Both of the solutions proposed require considerable time to solve this problem and therefore are not acceptable. However, it is possible, even with a large word list, to solve the problem in a matter of seconds.

An important concept is that, in many problems, writing a working program is not good enough. If the program is to be run on a large data set, then the running time becomes an issue. Throughout this book we will see how to estimate the running time of a program for large inputs and, more important, how to compare the running times of two programs without actually coding them. We will see techniques for drastically improving the speed of a program and for determining program bottlenecks. These techniques will enable us to find the section of the code on which to concentrate our optimization efforts.

1.2. Mathematics Review

This section lists some of the basic formulas you need to memorize or be able to derive and reviews basic proof techniques.

1.2.1. Exponents

$$X^A X^B = X^{A+B}$$

$$\frac{X^A}{X^B} = X^{A-B}$$

$$(X^A)^B = X^{AB}$$

$$X^N + X^N = 2X^N \neq X^{2N}$$

$$2^N + 2^N = 2^{N+1}$$

1.2.2. Logarithms

In computer science, all logarithms are to the base 2 unless specified otherwise.

DEFINITION: $X^A = B$ if and only if $\log_X B = A$

$X^A = B \qquad \log_X B = A$

Several convenient equalities follow from this definition.

THEOREM 1.1.

$$\log_A B = \frac{\log_C B}{\log_C A}; \quad A, B, C > 0, A \neq 1$$

$\log_A B = \dfrac{\log_C B}{\log_C A}$

PROOF:

Let $X = \log_C B$, $Y = \log_C A$, and $Z = \log_A B$. Then, by the definition of logarithms, $C^X = B$, $C^Y = A$, and $A^Z = B$. Combining these three equalities yields $C^X = B = (C^Y)^Z$. Therefore, $X = YZ$, which implies $Z = X/Y$, proving the theorem.

THEOREM 1.2.

$$\log AB = \log A + \log B; \quad A, B > 0$$

PROOF:

Let $X = \log A$, $Y = \log B$, and $Z = \log AB$. Then, assuming the default base of 2, $2^X = A$, $2^Y = B$, and $2^Z = AB$. Combining the last three equalities yields $2^X 2^Y = AB = 2^Z$. Therefore, $X + Y = Z$, which proves the theorem.

Some other useful formulas, which can all be derived in a similar manner, follow.

$$\log A/B = \log A - \log B$$

$$\log(A^B) = B \log A$$

$$\log X < X \quad \text{for all } X > 0$$

$$\log 1 = 0, \qquad \log 2 = 1, \qquad \log 1{,}024 = 10, \qquad \log 1{,}048{,}576 = 20$$

1.2.3. Series

The easiest formulas to remember are

$$\sum_{i=0}^{N} 2^i = 2^{N+1} - 1$$

and the companion,

$$\sum_{i=0}^{N} A^i = \frac{A^{N+1} - 1}{A - 1}$$

In the latter formula, if $0 < A < 1$, then

$$\sum_{i=0}^{N} A^i \leq \frac{1}{1 - A}$$

and as N tends to ∞, the sum approaches $1/(1 - A)$. These are the "geometric series" formulas.

We can derive the last formula for $\sum_{i=0}^{\infty} A^i$ $(0 < A < 1)$ in the following manner. Let S be the sum. Then

$$S = 1 + A + A^2 + A^3 + A^4 + A^5 + \cdots$$

Then

$$AS = A + A^2 + A^3 + A^4 + A^5 + \cdots$$

If we subtract these two equations (which is permissible only for a convergent series), virtually all the terms on the right side cancel, leaving

$$S - AS = 1$$

which implies that

$$S = \frac{1}{1 - A}$$

We can use this same technique to compute $\sum_{i=1}^{\infty} i/2^i$, a sum that occurs frequently. We write

$$S = \frac{1}{2} + \frac{2}{2^2} + \frac{3}{2^3} + \frac{4}{2^4} + \frac{5}{2^5} + \cdots$$

and multiply by 2, obtaining

$$2S = 1 + \frac{2}{2} + \frac{3}{2^2} + \frac{4}{2^3} + \frac{5}{2^4} + \frac{6}{2^5} + \cdots$$

Subtracting these two equations yields

$$S = 1 + \frac{1}{2} + \frac{1}{2^2} + \frac{1}{2^3} + \frac{1}{2^4} + \frac{1}{2^5} + \cdots$$

Thus, $S = 2$.

Another type of common series in analysis is the arithmetic series. Any such series can be evaluated from the basic formula.

$$\sum_{i=1}^{N} i = \frac{N(N + 1)}{2} \approx \frac{N^2}{2}$$

For instance, to find the sum $2 + 5 + 8 + \cdots + (3k - 1)$, rewrite it as $3(1 + 2 + 3 + \cdots + k) - (1 + 1 + 1 + \cdots + 1)$, which is clearly $3k(k + 1)/2 - k$. Another way to remember this is to add the first and last terms (total $3k + 1$), the second and next to last terms (total $3k + 1$), and so on. Since there are $k/2$ of these pairs, the total sum is $k(3k + 1)/2$, which is the same answer as before.

The next two formulas pop up now and then but are fairly uncommon.

$$\sum_{i=1}^{N} i^2 = \frac{N(N + 1)(2N + 1)}{6} \approx \frac{N^3}{3}$$

$$\sum_{i=1}^{N} i^k \approx \frac{N^{k+1}}{|k + 1|} \qquad k \neq -1$$

When $k = -1$, the latter formula is not valid. We then need the following formula, which is used far more in computer science than in other mathematical disciplines. The numbers H_N are known as the harmonic numbers, and the sum is known as a harmonic sum. The error in the following approximation tends to $\gamma \approx 0.57721566$, which is known as *Euler's constant*.

$$H_N = \sum_{i=1}^{N} \frac{1}{i} \approx \log_e N$$

These two formulas are just general algebraic manipulations.

$$\sum_{i=1}^{N} f(N) = N f(N)$$

$$\sum_{i=n_0}^{N} f(i) = \sum_{i=1}^{N} f(i) - \sum_{i=1}^{n_0-1} f(i)$$

1.2.4. Modular Arithmetic

We say that A is congruent to B modulo N, written $A \equiv B \pmod{N}$, if N divides $A - B$. Intuitively, this means that the remainder is the same when either A or B is divided by N. Thus, $81 \equiv 61 \equiv 1 \pmod{10}$. As with equality, if $A \equiv B \pmod{N}$, then $A + C \equiv B + C \pmod{N}$ and $AD \equiv BD \pmod{N}$.

There are many theorems that apply to modular arithmetic, and some of them require extraordinary proofs in number theory. We will use modular arithmetic sparingly, and the preceding theorems will suffice.

1.2.5. The *P* Word

The two most common ways of proving statements in data structure analysis are proof by induction and proof by contradiction (and occasionally proof by intimidation, used by professors only). The best way of proving that a theorem is false is by exhibiting a counter-example.

Proof by Induction

A proof by induction has two standard parts. The first step is proving a *base case,* that is, establishing that a theorem is true for some small (usually degenerate) value(s); this step is almost always trivial. Next, an *inductive hypothesis* is assumed. Generally this means that the theorem is assumed to be true for all cases up to some limit k. Using this assumption, the theorem is then shown to be true for the next value, which is typically $k + 1$. This proves the theorem (as long as k is finite).

As an example, we prove that the Fibonacci numbers, $F_0 = 1, F_1 = 1, F_2 = 2, F_3 = 3, F_4 = 5, \ldots, F_i = F_{i-1} + F_{i-2}$, satisfy $F_i < (5/3)^i$, for $i \geq 1$. (Some definitions have $F_0 = 0$, which shifts the series.) To do this, we first verify that the theorem is true for the trivial cases. It is easy to verify that $F_1 = 1 < 5/3$ and $F_2 = 2 < 25/9$; this proves the basis. We assume that the theorem is true for $i = 1, 2, \ldots, k$; this is the inductive hypothesis. To prove the theorem, we need to show that $F_{k+1} < (5/3)^{k+1}$. We have

$$F_{k+1} = F_k + F_{k-1}$$

by the definition, and we can use the inductive hypothesis on the right-hand side, obtaining

$$F_{k+1} < (5/3)^k + (5/3)^{k-1}$$
$$< (3/5)(5/3)^{k+1} + (3/5)^2(5/3)^{k+1}$$
$$< (3/5)(5/3)^{k+1} + (9/25)(5/3)^{k+1}$$

which simplifies to

$$F_{k+1} < (3/5 + 9/25)(5/3)^{k+1}$$
$$< (24/25)(5/3)^{k+1}$$
$$< (5/3)^{k+1}$$

proving the theorem.

As a second example, we establish the following theorem.

THEOREM 1.3.

If $N \geq 1$, then $\displaystyle\sum_{i=1}^{N} i^2 = \frac{N(N + 1)(2N + 1)}{6}$

PROOF:

The proof is by induction. For the basis, it is readily seen that the theorem is true when $N = 1$. For the inductive hypothesis, assume that the theorem is true for $1 \leq k \leq N$. We will establish that, under this assumption, the theorem is true for $N + 1$. We have

$$\sum_{i=1}^{N+1} i^2 = \sum_{i=1}^{N} i^2 + (N + 1)^2$$

Applying the inductive hypothesis, we obtain

$$\sum_{i=1}^{N+1} i^2 = \frac{N(N + 1)(2N + 1)}{6} + (N + 1)^2$$

$$= (N + 1)\left[\frac{N(2N + 1)}{6} + (N + 1)\right]$$

$$= (N + 1)\frac{2N^2 + 7N + 6}{6}$$

$$= \frac{(N + 1)(N + 2)(2N + 3)}{6}$$

Thus,

$$\sum_{i=1}^{N+1} i^2 = \frac{(N + 1)[(N + 1) + 1][2(N + 1) + 1]}{6}$$

proving the theorem.

Proof by Counterexample

The statement $F_k \leq k^2$ is false. The easiest way to prove this is to compute $F_{11} = 144 > 11^2$.

Proof by Contradiction

Proof by contradiction proceeds by assuming that the theorem is false and showing that this assumption implies that some known property is false, and hence the original assumption was erroneous. A classic example is the proof that there is an infinite number of primes. To prove this, we assume that the theorem is false, so that there is some largest prime P_k. Let $P_1, P_2, \ldots, P_k$ be all the primes in order and consider

$$N = P_1 P_2 P_3 \cdots P_k + 1$$

Clearly, N is larger than P_k, so by assumption N is not prime. However, none of P_1, P_2, $\ldots$, P_k divides N exactly, because there will always be a remainder of 1. This is a contradiction, because every number is either prime or a product of primes. Hence, the original assumption, that P_k is the largest prime, is false, which implies that the theorem is true.

1.3. A Brief Introduction to Recursion

Most mathematical functions that we are familiar with are described by a simple formula. For instance, we can convert temperatures from Fahrenheit to Celsius by applying the formula

$$C = 5(F - 32)/9$$

Given this formula, it is trivial to write a Java method; with declarations and braces removed, the one-line formula translates to one line of Java.

Mathematical functions are sometimes defined in a less standard form. As an example, we can define a function f, valid on nonnegative integers, that satisfies $f(0) = 0$ and $f(x) = 2f(x-1) + x^2$. From this definition we see that $f(1) = 1, f(2) = 6, f(3) = 21$, and $f(4) = 58$. A function that is defined in terms of itself is called *recursive*. Java allows functions to be recursive.* It is important to remember that what Java provides is merely an attempt to follow the recursive spirit. Not all mathematically recursive functions are efficiently (or correctly) implemented by Java's simulation of recursion. The idea is that the recursive function f ought to be expressible in only a few lines, just like a nonrecursive function. Figure 1.2 shows the recursive implementation of f.

Lines 1 and 2 handle what is known as the *base case,* that is, the value for which the function is directly known without resorting to recursion. Just as declaring $f(x) = 2f(x-1) + x^2$ is meaningless, mathematically, without including the fact that $f(0) = 0$, the

```
        public static int f( int x )
        {
/* 1*/      if( x == 0 )
/* 2*/          return 0;
            else
/* 3*/          return 2 * f( x - 1 ) + x * x;
        }
```

Figure 1.2 A recursive method

---

*Using recursion for numerical calculations is usually a bad idea. We have done so to illustrate the basic points.

recursive Java method doesn't make sense without a base case. Line 3 makes the recursive call.

There are several important and possibly confusing points about recursion. A common question is: Isn't this just circular logic? The answer is that although we are defining a method in terms of itself, we are not defining a particular instance of the method in terms of itself. In other words, evaluating $f(5)$ by computing $f(5)$ would be circular. Evaluating $f(5)$ by computing $f(4)$ is not circular—unless, of course, $f(4)$ is evaluated by eventually computing $f(5)$. The two most important issues are probably the *how* and *why* questions. In Chapter 3, the *how* and *why* issues are formally resolved. We will give an incomplete description here.

It turns out that recursive calls are handled no differently from any others. If f is called with the value of 4, then line 3 requires the computation of $2 * f(3) + 4 * 4$. Thus, a call is made to compute $f(3)$. This requires the computation of $2 * f(2) + 3 * 3$. Therefore, another call is made to compute $f(2)$. This means that $2 * f(1) + 2 * 2$ must be evaluated. To do so, $f(1)$ is computed as $2 * f(0) + 1 * 1$. Now, $f(0)$ must be evaluated. Since this is a base case, we know a priori that $f(0) = 0$. This enables the completion of the calculation for $f(1)$, which is now seen to be 1. Then $f(2)$, $f(3)$, and finally $f(4)$ can be determined. All the bookkeeping needed to keep track of pending calls (those started but waiting for a recursive call to complete), along with their variables, is done by the computer automatically. An important point, however, is that recursive calls will keep on being made until a base case is reached. For instance, an attempt to evaluate $f(-1)$ will result in calls to $f(-2)$, $f(-3)$, and so on. Since this will never get to a base case, the program won't be able to compute the answer (which is undefined anyway). Occasionally, a much more subtle error is made, which is exhibited in Figure 1.3. The error in Figure 1.3 is that bad(1) is defined, by line 3, to be bad(1). Obviously, this doesn't give any clue as to what bad(1) actually is. The computer will thus repeatedly make calls to bad(1) in an attempt to resolve its values. Eventually, its bookkeeping system will run out of space, and the program will terminate abnormally. Generally, we would say that this method doesn't work for one special case but is correct otherwise. This isn't true here, since bad(2) calls bad(1). Thus, bad(2) cannot be evaluated either. Furthermore, bad(3), bad(4), and bad(5) all make calls to bad(2). Since bad(2) is unevaluable, none of these values are either. In fact, this program doesn't work for any value of n, except 0. With recursive programs, there is no such thing as a "special case."

These considerations lead to the first two fundamental rules of recursion:

1. *Base cases.* You must always have some base cases, which can be solved without recursion.

2. *Making progress.* For the cases that are to be solved recursively, the recursive call must always be to a case that makes progress toward a base case.

```
        public static int bad( int n )
        {
/* 1*/      if( n == 0 )
/* 2*/          return 0;
            else
/* 3*/          return bad( n / 3 + 1 ) + n - 1;
        }
```

Figure 1.3 A nonterminating recursive method

Throughout this book, we will use recursion to solve problems. As an example of a nonmathematical use, consider a large dictionary. Words in dictionaries are defined in terms of other words. When we look up a word, we might not always understand the definition, so we might have to look up words in the definition. Likewise, we might not understand some of those, so we might have to continue this search for a while. Because the dictionary is finite, eventually either (1) we will come to a point where we understand all of the words in some definition (and thus understand that definition and retrace our path through the other definitions) or (2) we will find that the definitions are circular and we are stuck, or that some word we need to understand for a definition is not in the dictionary.

Our recursive strategy to understand words is as follows: If we know the meaning of a word, then we are done; otherwise, we look the word up in the dictionary. If we understand all the words in the definition, we are done; otherwise, we figure out what the definition means by *recursively* looking up the words we don't know. This procedure will terminate if the dictionary is well defined but can loop indefinitely if a word is either not defined or circularly defined.

Printing Out Numbers

Suppose we have a positive integer, n, that we wish to print out. Our routine will have the heading printOut(n). Assume that the only I/O routines available will take a single-digit number and output it to the terminal. We will call this routine printDigit; for example, printDigit(4) will output a 4 to the terminal.

Recursion provides a very clean solution to this problem. To print out 76234, we need to first print out 7623 and then print out 4. The second step is easily accomplished with the statement printDigit(n%10), but the first doesn't seem any simpler than the original problem. Indeed it is virtually the same problem, so we can solve it recursively with the statement printOut(n/10).

This tells us how to solve the general problem, but we still need to make sure that the program doesn't loop indefinitely. Since we haven't defined a base case yet, it is clear that we still have something to do. Our base case will be printDigit(n) if $0 \le n < 10$. Now printOut(n) is defined for every positive number from 0 to 9, and larger numbers are defined in terms of a smaller positive number. Thus, there is no cycle. The entire procedure* is shown in Figure 1.4.

We have made no effort to do this efficiently. We could have avoided using the mod routine (which can be very expensive) because $n\%10 = n - \lfloor n/10 \rfloor * 10$.[†]

```
public static void printOut( int n )  /* Print nonnegative n */
{
    if( n >= 10 )
        printOut( n / 10 );
    printDigit( n % 10 );
}
```

Figure 1.4 Recursive routine to print an integer

*The term *procedure* refers to a method that returns void.
[†] $\lfloor x \rfloor$ is the largest integer that is less than or equal to x.

Recursion and Induction

Let us prove (somewhat) rigorously that the recursive number-printing program works. To do so, we'll use a proof by induction.

THEOREM 1.4.
The recursive number-printing algorithm is correct for n $\geq$ 0.

PROOF (BY INDUCTION ON THE NUMBER OF DIGITS IN n):
First, if n has one digit, then the program is trivially correct, since it merely makes a call to `printDigit`. Assume then that `printOut` works for all numbers of k or fewer digits. A number of $k + 1$ digits is expressed by its first k digits followed by its least significant digit. But the number formed by the first k digits is exactly $\lfloor n/10 \rfloor$, which, by the inductive hypothesis, is correctly printed, and the last digit is n mod 10, so the program prints out any $(k + 1)$-digit number correctly. Thus, by induction, all numbers are correctly printed.

This proof probably seems a little strange in that it is virtually identical to the algorithm description. It illustrates that in designing a recursive program, all smaller instances of the same problem (which are on the path to a base case) may be *assumed* to work correctly. The recursive program needs only to combine solutions to smaller problems, which are "magically" obtained by recursion, into a solution for the current problem. The mathematical justification for this is proof by induction. This gives the third rule of recursion:

3. *Design rule.* Assume that all the recursive calls work.

This rule is important because it means that when designing recursive programs, you generally don't need to know the details of the bookkeeping arrangements, and you don't have to try to trace through the myriad of recursive calls. Frequently, it is extremely difficult to track down the actual sequence of recursive calls. Of course, in many cases this is an indication of a good use of recursion, since the computer is being allowed to work out the complicated details.

The main problem with recursion is the hidden bookkeeping costs. Although these costs are almost always justifiable, because recursive programs not only simplify the algorithm design but also tend to give cleaner code, recursion should never be used as a substitute for a simple `for` loop. We'll discuss the overhead involved in recursion in more detail in Section 3.3.

When writing recursive routines, it is crucial to keep in mind the four basic rules of recursion:

1. *Base cases.* You must always have some base cases, which can be solved without recursion.
2. *Making progress.* For the cases that are to be solved recursively, the recursive call must always be to a case that makes progress toward a base case.
3. *Design rule.* Assume that all the recursive calls work.
4. *Compound interest rule.* Never duplicate work by solving the same instance of a problem in separate recursive calls.

The fourth rule, which will be justified (along with its nickname) in later sections, is the reason that it is generally a bad idea to use recursion to evaluate simple mathematical functions, such as the Fibonacci numbers. As long as you keep these rules in mind, recursive programming should be straightforward.

1.4. Generic Objects in Java

Consider the problem of finding the largest item in any array of items. A simple algorithm is the *sequential scan,* in which we examine each item in order, keeping track of the maximum. As is typical of many algorithms, the sequential scan algorithm is *type-independent,* which means that the logic of the algorithm does not depend on the type of items that are stored in the array. The same logic works for an array of integers, floating-point numbers, or any type for which comparison can be meaningfully defined.

Throughout this text, we will describe algorithms and data structures that are type-independent. When we write Java code for a type-independent algorithm or data structure, we prefer to write the code just once, rather than recode it for each different type.

In this section we describe how type-independent algorithms (also known as *generic algorithms*) are written in Java. We begin by *reviewing* some basic Java features in a non-generic class called the `IntCell`. The `IntCell` will store an `int` and allow a `read` and `write` operation, thus simulating (a single `int` worth of) memory. We then illustrate a generic class called the `MemoryCell`, which will store any type of object. Finally we illustrate the generic sequential scan for the maximum element described above.

1.4.1. The `IntCell` Class

Figure 1.5 is the `IntCell` class. A class consists of data and operations; these are its members. In the `IntCell` class, each instance of the `IntCell`—an `IntCell` object—contains a single data member named `storedValue`. Data members are known as *fields.* Everything else in the class is a *method.* Methods are operations; these are generally operations that can be applied to instances of the class. In our example, there are four methods. Two of these methods are `read` and `write`; the other two are special methods known as *constructors.* Let us describe four key features:

1. `public` *and* `private`. Each member can be declared with a *visibility specifier.* The two most common specifiers are `public` and `private`. A member that is `public` may be accessed by any method in any class. A member that is `private` may only be accessed by methods in its class. Typically, data members are declared `private`, thus restricting access to internal details of the class. This is known as *information hiding.* Typically, users of the class do not need to know internal details of how the class is implemented. In many cases, having this access leads to trouble. For instance, in a class that stores dates using month, day, and year, we might want to make the month, day, and year `private` to prevent an outsider from setting these fields to illegal dates, such as Feb. 29, 2001. Conversely, methods intended for general use are made `public`.

2. *Constructors.* A class may define methods that describe how an instance of the class is constructed; these are called *constructors.* If no constructor is explicitly defined, one that initializes the fields using language defaults is automatically

```
/**
 * A class for simulating an integer memory cell.
 * @author Mark A. Weiss
 */
public class IntCell
{
    /**
     * Construct the IntCell.
     * Initial value is 0.
     */
    public IntCell( )
      { this( 0 ); }

    /**
     * Construct the IntCell.
     * @param initialValue the initial value.
     */
    public IntCell( int initialValue )
      { storedValue = initialValue; }

    /**
     * Get the stored value.
     * @return the stored value.
     */
    public int read( )
      { return storedValue; }

    /**
     * Store a value.
     * @param x the number to store.
     */
    public void write( int x )
      { storedValue = x; }

    private int storedValue;
}
```

Figure 1.5 IntCell class

generated. The IntCell class defines two constructors. The first is called if no parameter is specified. The second is called if an int parameter is provided, and uses that int to initialize the storedValue field.

3. this. In many cases, the zero-parameter constructor can be implemented by calling another constructor. In the IntCell example, the zero-parameter constructor is implemented by initializing storedValue to 0. By using this, we avoid replicating code logic in separate constructors. (A different use of this is as a reference to the object being acted upon, and is used in Section 6.6.)

4. *javadoc*. The methods in the IntCell class are commented by using a special syntax that can be recognized by a program called *javadoc*. *javadoc* automatically generates HTML documentation for the class, using tags such as @author, @param,

```
//  Exercise the IntCell class
public class TestIntCell
{
    public static void main( String [ ] args )
    {
        IntCell m = new IntCell( );

        m.write( 5 );
        System.out.println( "Cell contents: " + m.read( ) );
        // The next line would be illegal if uncommented
    //  m.storedValue = 0;
    }
}
```

Figure 1.6 TestIntCell class that uses IntCell

and @return. You can see the result of *javadoc* by looking in the Documentation subdirectory in the online code.

Now that IntCell is written, it can be used (see Fig. 1.6). In it, we embed a simple test program inside a class. There are three features of interest:

1. static *methods and* main. TestIntCell contains a single method called main. The method must be static, meaning that it applies to the TestIntCell class instead of a single instance of the class. Each class may declare a main method that will be used when the Java interpreter is called for that class. Thus IntCell may also have a main, which is very useful for providing testing routines for each class. Data members can also be static; in that case, there is one instance of the data member that is shared amongst all instances of the class. static data members are less widely used; we use them in Chapter 12.

2. *Object creation.* Objects are created by using new. In TestIntCell, m references an IntCell object, which is constructed using the zero-parameter IntCell constructor (thus it has an initial state corresponding to 0). Java performs automatic garbage collection; when an object is no longer referenced, it is available for reclamation, and no explicit action (such as delete or free) is required on the part of the programmer.

3. *Method calls.* Members of any object are accessed by using the dot operator (.). In TestIntCell, this is illustrated by calls to the write and read methods. Data members can also be accessed using the dot operator. However, if members are private, then the compiler will disallow access to members from other classes. Thus in TestIntCell, the access to the storedValue field of m would be illegal if it were not commented out.

1.4.2. The MemoryCell Class

To generalize the IntCell class, we can design a class that works for any type of object. The standard mechanism for doing this in Java is to use inheritance (we assume familiarity with the general principles of inheritance). The idea is to write the class for the most general

```
// MemoryCell class
//  Object read( )         --> Returns the stored value
//  void write( Object x ) -->  x is stored

public class MemoryCell
{
        // Public methods
    public Object read( )
      { return storedValue; }
    public void write( Object x )
      { storedValue = x; }

        // Private internal data representation
    private Object storedValue;
}
```

Figure 1.7 The generic MemoryCell class

type of object. In Java, every object is a subclass of the predefined class Object. Thus, in principle, the code in Figure 1.7 is all we need. (Note that to shorten the code, we use fewer comments and accept a default constructor that leaves storedValue uninitialized.)

Although this seems fine in theory, when using the generic MemoryCell class, we run into two problems if we try to use primitive types.

The first problem is that although all objects are subclasses of Object, the primitive types boolean, short, char, byte, int, long, float, and double are not objects. Thus we cannot directly use MemoryCell to store a primitive value. Instead we must use *wrapper classes* provided by Java. Wrapper classes store a single primitive value and can be used wherever an Object is needed. The wrapper class provides a method that can be used to access the primitive value it stores (however, the value can never be changed). For the Integer wrapper, this method is named intValue.

The second problem is that the read method for MemoryCell returns an Object. To get the int value that is hidden inside the Integer object, we must convert the result of read back to an Integer, and then access the int value. This involves using a type conversion.

```
    public class TestMemoryCell
    {
        public static void main( String [ ] args )
        {
            MemoryCell m = new MemoryCell( );

/* 1*/      m.write( new Integer( 5 ) );
/* 2*/      System.out.println( "Contents are: " +
/* 3*/                          ( (Integer) m.read( ) ).intValue( ) );
        }
    }
```

Figure 1.8 Using the generic MemoryCell class

Figure 1.8 illustrates the use of the `Integer` wrapper class that stores a single `int` value. Line 1 shows how an `Integer` wrapper is placed in the `MemoryCell`. Line 3 shows the type conversion that is done prior to the call to `intValue`. The parentheses will be necessary in general. In this particular case (since `Integer` objects have a built-in conversion to `String`), the call to `m.read` would have been sufficient for printing purposes; however, we illustrate the more general case, where the `int` value is required.

1.4.3 Implementing Generic findMax

The `MemoryCell` class required no special properties of `Object`; the only operations performed were reference assignments, which are always available. Finding the maximum item in an array of items does require a special property; we must be able to compare two items and decide which is larger.

Figure 1.9 illustrates a generic `findMax` algorithm. Notice that the objects that are manipulated are not `Object`, but instead are `Comparable`. The algorithm is straightforward; the only interesting syntactic part is on line 3, where we compare `maxValue` and `a[i]` using a `lessThan` method. So what exactly is `Comparable`?

As Figure 1.10 illustrates, `Comparable` is an *interface*. In Java, an interface declares a set of methods that must be implemented. In this example, any class that is `Comparable` must provide an implementation of `lessThan`. A class that is `Comparable` must also declare so by using the **implements** clause. A class is then said to *implement the interface*. Thus in Figure 1.10, we are certain that the call to the `lessThan` method on line 3 is meaningful.

Java 1.2 (but not earlier releases) provides an interface named `Comparable`, but it has different semantics than the one described above. In particular, it assumes a three-way comparison function `compareTo`, which has the same semantics as the `String` version. `compareTo` returns either a negative number, zero, or a positive number, depending on whether the controlling `Comparable` is less than, equal to, or greater than the parameter. It does not provide `lessThan`. The Appendix describes that version of `Comparable`. Thus, line 3 of `findMax` would be rewritten as

```
/* 3*/          if( maxValue.compareTo( a[ i ] ) < 0 )
```

Predefined wrapper classes such as `Integer` implement `Comparable` in Java 1.2. However, they do not do that in earlier releases. To use `findMax` for integers, in an earlier release, we have to write our own wrapper class. A minimal example of this is the `MyInteger` class

```
        Comparable findMax( Comparable [ ] a )
        {
/* 1*/      Comparable maxValue = a[ 0 ];

/* 2*/      for( int i = 1; i < a.length; i++ )
/* 3*/          if( maxValue.lessThan( a[ i ] ) )
/* 4*/              maxValue = a[ i ];

/* 5*/      return maxValue;
        }
```

Figure 1.9 A generic `findMax` method

```
public interface Comparable
{
    int compareTo( Comparable rhs );
}
```

Figure 1.10 The Comparable interface

```
public class MyInteger implements Comparable
{
        // Constructor
    public MyInteger( int x )
      { value = x; }

    public int intValue( )
      { return value; }

        // Implement the interface
    public boolean compareTo( Comparable rhs )
      { return value < ((MyInteger)rhs).value ? -1 :
              value == ((MyInteger)rhs).value ? 0 : 1; }

        // Data field
    private int value;
}
```

Figure 1.11 The MyInteger class

shown in Figure 1.11. MyInteger provides a constructor and an intValue method. It also provides the compareTo method, which is required to implement the Comparable interface. MyInteger also illustrates the implements clause.

1.5. Exceptions

Exceptions are objects that store information and are transmitted outside the normal return sequence. They are propagated back through the calling sequence until some routine "catches" the exception. In other words, if main calls function f, which then calls function g, which somehow generates an exception, then either the exception will be caught in g, or it will propagate back to f and be caught there, or it will propagate back to main and be caught there, or possibly (but this is poor design), it propagates past main, causing an abnormal program termination. Exceptions are used to handle *exceptional occurrences,* such as errors. Thus in many cases, exceptions are allowed to propagate back to main, at which point a graceful exit can be performed. In less serious cases (for instance, if a file fails to open correctly), error recovery can be attempted.

The code in Figure 1.12 illustrates the use of exceptions. It uses some terminal I/O that will be discussed in Section 1.6. Suffice it to say that the code in lines 1, 7, and 8 attempts

```
         import java.io.*;

         public class DivideByTwo
         {
             public static void main( String [ ] args )
             {
/* 1*/          BufferedReader in = new BufferedReader( new
                                       InputStreamReader( System.in ) );
/* 2*/          int x;
/* 3*/          String oneLine;

/* 4*/          System.out.println( "Enter an integer: " );
/* 5*/          try
/* 6*/          {
/* 7*/              oneLine = in.readLine( );
/* 8*/              x = Integer.parseInt( oneLine );
/* 9*/              System.out.println( "Half of x is " + ( x / 2 ) );
/*10*/          }
/*11*/          catch( Exception e )
/*12*/             { System.out.println( e ); }
            }
         }
```

Figure 1.12 Simple program to illustrate exceptions

to read a line of input (as a **String**) from the terminal, and then uses **parseInt** to generate an integer from the **String**. Code that might result in an exception's being propagated is enclosed in a **try** *block*. The exceptions that might occur are **IOException**, generated by **readLine** if some unexpected error occurs, and the **NumberFormatException**, generated by **parseInt** if **oneLine** is not convertible to an **int**. The **try** block extends from lines 6 to 10.

Immediately following the **try** block are the exception handlers, which are enclosed in **catch** blocks. This part of the code is jumped to only if an exception is raised; at the point where the exception is raised, the **try** block from which it came is considered terminated. Each **catch** block is attempted in order until a matching handler is found. Since **Exception** matches all exceptions that are of interest to us, it will match whatever exception is generated in the **try** block. The code in the **catch** block—in this case line 12—is executed if the exception occurs. Then the **catch** block and the block containing the **try/catch** combination are considered terminated. (Note that both **try** and **catch** require a block and not simply a single statement. Thus braces are not optional.) A meaningful message is printed from the **Exception** object **e**. Alternatively, additional processing and more detailed error messages might be given.

There are several types of *standard exceptions* in Java. The *standard run-time exceptions* include events such as integer divide-by-zero and illegal array access. Since these events can happen virtually anywhere, it would be burdensome to require exception handlers for them. If a **catch** block is provided, these exceptions behave like any other exception. If a **catch** block is not provided for a standard exception, and a standard exception is thrown, then it propagates as usual, possibly past **main**. In this case, it causes an abnormal program termination with an error message. Some of the common standard run-time exceptions are `ArithmeticException`, `NumberFormatException`, and `IndexOutOfBoundsException`.

Checked exceptions must be handled by a `catch` block or listed in a **throws** *clause* (which will be described shortly). Most exceptions are of the *standard checked exception* variety. If a method is called that may either directly or indirectly throw a standard checked exception, then the programmer must either provide a `catch` block for it, or explicitly indicate that the exception is to be propagated by use of a **throws** clause in the method declaration. Note that eventually it should be handled, because `main` should not have a **throws** clause. Some of the common standard checked exceptions are `java.io.EOFException`, `java.io.IOException`, and `InterruptedException`.

Errors are unrecoverable exceptions; yet although they are exceptions, they are not matched by `Exception`. The most common error is `OutOfMemoryError`. To catch every possible exception, catch a `Throwable` object.

The programmer can generate an exception by use of the **throw** *clause,* which we will illustrate shortly.

As mentioned earlier, standard checked exceptions must either be caught or explicitly propagated to the calling routine; but they should, as a last resort, eventually be handled in `main`. To do the latter, the method that is unwilling to catch the exception must indicate, via a **throws** clause, which exceptions it may propagate. The **throws** clause is attached at the end of the method header.

Almost all of the data structures in this text store collections of objects and then provide methods to insert, remove, or access items from the collection. Consider, for instance, the abstract collection we call a *box*. Suppose a box allows for the access or removal of an arbitrary item in the collection; these are the `getAny` and `removeAny` operations. Suppose the collection is empty. How should the removal be handled?

There are several plausible alternatives:

1. Do nothing. A remove in an empty container is simply a no-op (no operation).
2. Have `removeAny` return a `boolean` that indicates if the remove was successful.
3. Throw an exception.

This text defines two exception objects, `Underflow` and `Overflow`. `Underflow` is used to signal an illegal attempt to extract from an empty collection. `Overflow` signals that a capacity has been exceeded. (These classes are easily implemented by extending `Exception`; look online to see how.) The method for `removeAny` would look something like

```
public void removeAny( ) throws Underflow
{
    if( isEmpty( ) )
        throw new Underflow( );
    // Rest of the code follows ...
}
```

The use of the exception has both advantages and disadvantages. One of the advantages is that it tends to simplify the code that implements the data structures. On the other hand, it potentially complicates the code that uses the data structures, because that code must be prepared to handle the exception. For instance, the code

```
// Does not compile; Underflow must be caught
public void makeEmpty( )
{
    while( !isEmpty( ) )
        removeAny( );
}
```

does not compile, because the compiler thinks that **removeAny** might throw an exception. Some compiler implementations are also very inefficient when an exception is actually thrown. In other words, on these compilers, there is little run-time penalty in using exceptions as long as the exception does not happen. But when it happens, the cost is prohibitive. This cost is justifiable, as long as exceptions are used for exceptional, and thus rare, circumstances. But when exceptions are used in place of return statements, there can be a severe performance penalty.

As a result, we try to avoid gratuitous use of exceptions in our container classes. Instead, operations that access the data structure typically return an item. For instance, we would write a method named **getAndRemoveAny**, which not only removes an arbitrary item, but also returns the item that is removed. We can return the **null** reference if the box is empty:

```
public Object getAndRemoveAny( )
{
    if( isEmpty( ) )
        return null;
    // Rest of the code follows ...
}
```

One disadvantage of this strategy is that error checking is now optional. The compiler will not require that the programmer verify that the return value is not **null**, but the program will generate an exception, when run, if the **null** reference is used as if it were an object. The advantage is that, as described earlier, it is probably faster; and in cases such as the above, it avoids introducing unnecessary **try** and **catch** blocks.

1.6. Input and Output

Input and output (I/O) in Java is achieved through the use of the **java.io** package. The statement

```
import java.io.*;
```

should appear in any program that makes more than trivial use of the I/O routines. The Java library is very sophisticated and has a host of options. We examine only the most basic uses, concentrating entirely on formatted I/O.

1.6.1. Basic Stream Operations

Three streams are predefined for terminal I/O: **System.in**, the standard input; **System.out**, the standard output; and **System.err**, the standard error.

As already mentioned, the `print` and `println` methods are used for formatted output. Any type can be converted to a `String` suitable for printing by calling an appropriate `toString` method; in many cases, this is done automatically. Unlike with C and C++, which have an enormous number of formatting options, output in Java is done almost exclusively by `String` concatenation, with no built-in formatting.

A simple method for reading formatted input is to read a single line into a `String` object using `readLine`. The `readLine` method reads until it encounters a line terminator or end of file. The characters that are read, minus the line terminator (if read), are returned as a newly constructed `String`. To use `readLine`, we must first construct a `BufferedReader` object from an `InputStreamReader` object that is itself constructed from `System.in`.

If an immediate end of file is encountered, then `null` is returned. If a read error occurs for some reason other than end of file, then some `IOException` is generated. Note that the `IOException`, which is a standard checked exception, must eventually be caught. In many instances, the `IOException` is allowed to propagate back to a `catch` block in the `main` method.

1.6.2. The `StringTokenizer` Object

Recall that to read a single primitive type, such as an `int`, we use `readLine` to read the line as a `String` and then apply a method to generate the primitive type from the `String`. For `int`, we can use `parseInt`.

Sometimes we have several items on a line. For instance, suppose each line has two `int`s. Java provides the `StringTokenizer` object to separate a `String` into tokens. To use it, provide the `import` directive

```
import java.util.*;
```

Use of the string tokenizer is illustrated in Figure 1.13. First, at line 9, we construct a `StringTokenizer` object by providing the `String` representing the line of input. The `countTokens` method, shown on line 10, will provide the number of tokens in the `String`; in this example, this should be two, or else the input is in error. Then, the `nextToken` method returns the next token as a `String`. This method throws `NoSuchElementException` if there is no token, but this is an `Error` and does not have to be caught. At lines 12 and 13, we use `nextToken` followed by `parseInt` to obtain an `int`. All errors, including the failure to provide exactly two tokens, are handled in the `catch` block. Of course, more effort could go into better error messages.

By default, tokens are separated by white space. The `StringTokenizer` can be constructed to recognize other characters as delimiters and to include these delimiters as tokens.

1.6.3. Sequential Files

One of the basic rules of Java is that what works for terminal I/O also works for files. To deal with a file, we do not construct a `BufferedReader` object from an `InputStreamReader`. Instead, we construct it from a `FileReader` object, which itself can be constructed by providing a filename.

```
         import java.io.*;
         import java.util.*;

         // Read two integers and output the maximum.

         public class MaxTest
         {
             public static void main( String [ ] args )
             {
/* 1*/           BufferedReader in = new BufferedReader( new
                                   InputStreamReader( System.in ) );
/* 2*/           String oneLine;
/* 3*/           StringTokenizer str;
/* 4*/           int x;
/* 5*/           int y;

/* 6*/           System.out.println( "Enter 2 ints on one line: " );
/* 7*/           try
                 {
/* 8*/               oneLine = in.readLine( );
/* 9*/               str = new StringTokenizer( oneLine );
/*10*/               if( str.countTokens( ) != 2 )
/*11*/                   throw new NumberFormatException( );
/*12*/               x = Integer.parseInt( str.nextToken( ) );
/*13*/               y = Integer.parseInt( str.nextToken( ) );
/*14*/               System.out.println( "Max: " + Math.max( x, y ) );
                 }
/*15*/           catch( Exception e )
/*16*/             { System.err.println( "Error: need two ints" ); }
             }
         }
```

Figure 1.13 Program that demonstrates the string tokenizer

An example that illustrates these basic ideas is shown in Figure 1.14 on page 22. Here, we have a program that will list the contents of the text files that are specified as command-line arguments. The main routine simply steps through the command-line arguments (stored in args, which is an array of String), passing each one to listFile. In listFile, we construct the FileReader object at line 7, and then use it to construct a BufferedReader object—fileIn—at line 8. At that point, reading is identical to what we have already seen.

After we are done with the file, we must close it; otherwise, we could eventually run out of streams. Note that this cannot be done at the end of the try block, since an exception could cause a premature exit from the block. Thus we close the file after the try/catch sequence.

Formatted file output is similar to file input, with the FileWriter class corresponding to FileReader and the BufferedWriter class corresponding to BufferedReader. However, there is an extra level of abstraction needed: the PrintWriter class. (Appendix A lists these classes with some of their methods.) All of this is best illustrated with an example.

```
          import java.io.*;
          public class ListFiles
          {
              public static void main( String [ ] args )
              {
/* 1*/            if( args.length == 0 )
/* 2*/                System.out.println( "No files specified" );
/* 3*/            for( int i = 0; i < args.length; i++ )
/* 4*/                listFile( args[ i ] );
              }

              public static void listFile( String fileName )
              {
                  FileReader theFile;
                  BufferedReader fileIn = null;
                  String oneLine;

/* 5*/            System.out.println( "FILE: " + fileName );
/* 6*/            try
                  {
/* 7*/                theFile = new FileReader( fileName );
/* 8*/                fileIn  = new BufferedReader( theFile );
/* 9*/                while( ( oneLine = fileIn.readLine( ) ) != null )
/*10*/                    System.out.println( oneLine );
                  }
/*11*/            catch( Exception e )
/*12*/              { System.out.println( e ); }

                  // Close the stream
/*13*/            try
                  {
/*14*/                if( fileIn != null )
/*15*/                    fileIn.close( );
                  }
/*16*/            catch( IOException e ) { }
              }
          }
```

Figure 1.14 Program to list contents of a file

The program in Figure 1.15 copies the file given by the first command-line argument into a file given by the second command-line argument. As is common with most languages, if the target file does not exist, it is created; otherwise, it is truncated prior to the copy. To make the program moderately interesting, the copy will include line numbering. Furthermore, if the target file is not specified, the copy is made to the standard output. This will illustrate that there is little difference between files and terminal I/O.

fileOut will store a reference to a PrintWriter object. Lines 1 and 2 tell us that if there is no target file, System.out will be used. Otherwise, we expect a target file. Lines 5 and 6 perform an *alias test*: if we were to attempt to copy a file to itself, it would be truncated prior to the copy; thus we test to avoid this case. (This test is not perfect, because a file can

```
         import java.io.*;

         public class NumberLines
         {
             public static void main( String [ ] args )
             {
                 PrintWriter fileOut = null;
                 BufferedReader fileIn = null;

                 try
                 {
/* 1*/               if( args.length == 1 )
/* 2*/                   fileOut = new PrintWriter( System.out );
/* 3*/               else if( args.length == 0 || args.length > 2 )
/* 4*/                   throw new Exception( "Usage: java NumberLines sourceFile destFile" );
/* 5*/               else if( args[ 0 ].equals( args[ 1 ] ) )
/* 6*/                   throw new Exception( "Cannot copy to self" );
/* 7*/               else
/* 8*/                   fileOut = new PrintWriter( new BufferedWriter(
                                         new FileWriter( args[ 1 ] ) ) );

/* 9*/               fileIn = new BufferedReader( new FileReader( args[ 0 ] ) );
/*10*/               String oneLine;
/*11*/               int lineNum = 0;

/*12*/               while( ( oneLine = fileIn.readLine( ) ) != null )
                     {
/*13*/                   fileOut.print( ++lineNum + "\t" );
/*14*/                   fileOut.println( oneLine );
                     }
                 }
/*15*/           catch( Exception e )
/*16*/             { System.out.println( e ); }
/*17*/           try
/*18*/           {
/*19*/               if( fileIn != null )
/*20*/                   fileIn.close( );
/*21*/               if( fileOut != null )
/*22*/                   fileOut.close( );
/*23*/           }
/*24*/           catch( IOException e )
/*25*/             { }
             }
         }
```

Figure 1.15 Program that copies from one text file to another, with the target file containing line numbers. With only one command-line argument, output is sent to System.out.

be known by several names.) At line 8, the PrintWriter object is constructed if a target file is specified, and at line 9 the BufferedReader object is constructed. These constructions are a bit convoluted. Once this is done, however, we use readLine, print, and println, just as we did for the terminal I/O streams, so the rest of the program illustrates nothing new.

1.7. Code Organization

Except for a few scattered fragments, all of the code in this text is available online. This section describes how the code is organized.

1.7.1. Packages

Java allows the programmer to group related classes into packages. The classes in a package have slightly more visibility amongst each other than do classes in different packages. Specifically, we will occasionally use the fact that a data member whose visibility specifier is omitted is visible to other classes in the same package (but invisible outside of the package). This is referred to as *package-friendly visibility*.

Most of our classes will be found in a package named `DataStructures`. This includes the `Overflow` and `Underflow` exception classes. These classes must be placed in a directory named `DataStructures` that is a subdirectory of a directory listed in the `CLASSPATH` variable. (For further details, consult a Java reference.) These classes will declare that they are members of the `DataStructures` package by using a **package** *statement*:

```
package DataStructures;
```

The code in the text will omit the **package** statements.

1.7.2. The MyInteger Class

Package `DataStructures` contains a `MyInteger` class (somewhat enhanced from Fig. 1.11) that is used to test many of the other classes. As mentioned earlier, users of Java 1.2 or higher can use `Integer` instead of `MyInteger` for routines that require a `Comparable`.

1.7.3. Efficiency Considerations

Many years ago, it was common for programmers to rewrite portions of code in the hope that the compiler would generate more efficient code. Consider, for instance, the following loop:

```
for( int angle = 0; angle < 180; angle++ )
    s[ angle ] = Math.sin( angle * Math.PI / 180.0 ) +
                 Math.cos( angle * Math.PI / 180.0 );
```

In the old days, it would be common to store the value of `angle*Math.PI/180.0` in a temporary variable, rather than compute it twice. (One might even have stored `Math.PI/180.0` prior to entering the loop.) Modern optimizing compilers, however, have made most of the tricks obsolete.

Unfortunately, many Java compilers have not implemented modern optimizers. And for various reasons, some "obvious" optimizations are difficult. We will list two cases of code that can be mechanically optimized, if needed, but which are not optimized in our implementations.

Comparable

We frequently have code of the form

```
        if( x.compareTo( y ) < 0 )
          { /* Some stuff */ }
        else if( x.compareTo( y ) > 0 )
          { /* More stuff */ }
```

In this fragment, `x.compareTo( y )` is evaluated twice, even though the result is (presumably) the same. Precomputing it cuts the number of calls to `compareTo` in half. Note that the compiler cannot perform this optimization itself, because it is possible that a bizarre implementation of `compareTo` could return different values (if the answer depends on values other than `x` and `y`, and these other values are somehow altered by calling `compareTo`).

We leave the code as above, because it is clearer than using a temporary variable. Furthermore, it corresponds to the two-way comparisons (the first is <, the second is >) that are common in other languages. `compareTo` actually implements a three-way comparison, because it differentiates among less than, greater than, and equal to.

Three-way comparisons are often implemented as two two-way comparisons, but in some cases `compareTo` can be implemented using a subtraction trick. For instance, if `x` and `y` are both *positive* integers, the value of `x-y` satisfies the usual properties of `compareTo` (if `x` and `y` are arbitrary integers, the trick fails because of the possibility of overflow).

final Classes

Declaring classes `final` can improve performance, because it allows the compiler to perform *inline optimizations*. In an inline optimization, the body of a trivial method is logically used in place of the method call, thus saving the overhead of the method call. For instance, you will find that if `str` is a `String`, the call to `str.length()` is typically inlined, and logically replaced with `str.theLength`, where `theLength` is the `private String` data member that maintains the actual length. Thus, although calls to `length` look like expensive method calls, the optimizer can avoid the overhead of the method call. Not all compilers aggressively inline, but those that do, often get large speedups. You cannot declare a class `final` if you intend to derive a new class from it using inheritance. But since we do not discuss or use general inheritance in this text, it is safe to assume that this won't be a problem.

Important Disclaimer

These optimizations are only worth performing in the critical part of the program. Otherwise, you are wasting development time and possibly writing code that is harder to read, maintain, and modify. In future chapters we'll see how to determine these critical parts.

SUMMARY

This chapter sets the stage for the rest of the book. The time taken by an algorithm confronted with large amounts of input will be an important criterion for deciding if it is a good algorithm. (Of course, correctness is most important.) Speed is relative. What is fast for one problem on one machine might be slow for another problem or a different machine. We will begin to address these issues in the next chapter and will use the mathematics discussed here to establish a formal model.

EXERCISES

1.1 Write a program to solve the selection problem. Let $k = N/2$. Draw a table showing the running time of your program for various values of N.

1.2 Write a program to solve the word puzzle problem.

1.3 Write a method to output an arbitrary **double** number (which might be negative) using only `printDigit` for I/O.

1.4 C allows statements of the form

   #include *filename*

   which reads *filename* and inserts its contents in place of the *include* statement. *Include* statements may be nested; in other words, the file *filename* may itself contain an *include* statement, but, obviously, a file can't include itself in any chain. Write a program that reads in a file and outputs the file as modified by the *include* statements.

1.5 Write a recursive method that returns the number of 1's in the binary representation of N. Use the fact that this is equal to the number of 1's in the representation of $N/2$, plus 1, if N is odd.

1.6 Write the routines with the following declarations:

```
public  void permute( String str );
private void permute( char [ ] str, int low, int high );
```

   The first routine is a driver that calls the second and prints all the permutations of the characters in **String str**. If **str** is `"abc"`, then the strings that are output are **abc**, **acb**, **bac**, **bca**, **cab**, and **cba**. Use recursion for the second routine.

1.7 Prove the following formulas:

   a. $\log X < X$ for all $X > 0$

   b. $\log(A^B) = B \log A$

1.8 Evaluate the following sums:

   a. $\displaystyle\sum_{i=0}^{\infty} \frac{1}{4^i}$

   b. $\displaystyle\sum_{i=0}^{\infty} \frac{i}{4^i}$

   *c. $\displaystyle\sum_{i=0}^{\infty} \frac{i^2}{4^i}$

   **d. $\displaystyle\sum_{i=0}^{\infty} \frac{i^N}{4^i}$

1.9 Estimate

$$\sum_{i=\lfloor N/2 \rfloor}^{N} \frac{1}{i}$$

*1.10 What is $2^{100} (\bmod\ 5)$?

1.11 Let F_i be the Fibonacci numbers as defined in Section 1.2. Prove the following:

   a. $\displaystyle\sum_{i=1}^{N-2} F_i = F_N - 2$

    b. $F_N < \phi^N$, with $\phi = (1 + \sqrt{5})/2$

**c. Give a precise closed-form expression for F_N.

1.12 Prove the following formulas:

    a. $\displaystyle\sum_{i=1}^{N} (2i - 1) = N^2$

    b. $\displaystyle\sum_{i=1}^{N} i^3 = \left(\sum_{i=1}^{N} i\right)^2$

1.13 Design a generic class, `Collection`, that stores a collection of `Object`s (in an array), along with the current size of the collection. Provide `public` methods `isEmpty`, `makeEmpty`, `insert`, `remove`, and `isPresent`. `isPresent(x)` returns `true` if and only if an `Object` that is equal to `x` (as defined by `equals`) is present in the collection.

1.14 Design a generic class, `OrderedCollection`, that stores a collection of `Comparable`s (in an array), along with the current size of the collection. Provide `public` methods `isEmpty`, `makeEmpty`, `insert`, `remove`, `findMin`, and `findMax`. `findMin` and `findMax` return references to the smallest and largest, respectively, `Comparable` in the collection (or `null` if the collection is empty).

REFERENCES

There are many good textbooks covering the mathematics reviewed in this chapter. A small subset is [1], [2], [3], [11], [13], and [14]. Reference [11] is specifically geared toward the analysis of algorithms. It is the first volume of a three-volume series that will be cited throughout this text. More advanced material is covered in [8].

Throughout this book we will assume a knowledge of Java [4], [6], [7], [12]. The material in Sections 1.4–1.7 is meant to serve as an overview of the features that we will use in this text. We also assume familiarity with recursion (the recursion summary in this chapter is meant to be a quick review). We will attempt to provide hints on its use where appropriate throughout the textbook. Readers not familiar with recursion should consult [15] or any good intermediate programming textbook.

General programming style is discussed in several books. Some of the classics are [5], [9], and [10].

1. M. O. Albertson and J. P. Hutchinson, *Discrete Mathematics with Algorithms,* John Wiley & Sons, New York, 1988.
2. Z. Bavel, *Math Companion for Computer Science,* Reston Publishing Co., Reston, Va., 1982.
3. R. A. Brualdi, *Introductory Combinatorics,* North-Holland, New York, 1977.
4. G. Cornell and C. S. Horstmann, *Core Java,* 3d ed., Prentice Hall, Englewood Cliffs, N.J., 1998.
5. E. W. Dijkstra, *A Discipline of Programming,* Prentice Hall, Englewood Cliffs, N.J., 1976.
6. D. Flanagan, *Java in a Nutshell,* 2d ed., O'Reilly and Associates, Sebastopol, Calif., 1997.
7. J. Gosling, B. Joy, and G. Steele, *The Java Language Specification,* 2d ed., Addison-Wesley, Reading, Mass., 1998.
8. R. L. Graham, D. E. Knuth, and O. Patashnik, *Concrete Mathematics,* Addison-Wesley, Reading, Mass., 1989.
9. D. Gries, *The Science of Programming,* Springer-Verlag, New York, 1981.

10. B. W. Kernighan and P. J. Plauger, *The Elements of Programming Style,* 2d ed., McGraw-Hill, New York, 1978.

11. D. E. Knuth, *The Art of Computer Programming, Vol. 1: Fundamental Algorithms,* 3d ed., Addison-Wesley, Reading, Mass., 1997.

12. J. Lewis and W. Loftus, *Java Software Solutions: Foundations of Program Design,* Addison-Wesley, Reading, Mass., 1997.

13. F. S. Roberts, *Applied Combinatorics,* Prentice Hall, Englewood Cliffs, N.J., 1984.

14. A. Tucker, *Applied Combinatorics,* 2d ed., John Wiley & Sons, New York, 1984.

15. M. A. Weiss, *Data Structures and Problem Solving Using Java,* Addison-Wesley, Reading, Mass., 1998.

Algorithm Analysis

An *algorithm* is a clearly specified set of simple instructions to be followed to solve a problem. Once an algorithm is given for a problem and decided (somehow) to be correct, an important step is to determine how much in the way of resources, such as time or space, the algorithm will require. An algorithm that solves a problem but requires a year is hardly of any use. Likewise, an algorithm that requires several gigabytes of main memory is not (currently) useful on most machines.

In this chapter, we shall discuss

- How to estimate the time required for a program.
- How to reduce the running time of a program from days or years to fractions of a second.
- The results of careless use of recursion.
- Very efficient algorithms to raise a number to a power and to compute the greatest common divisor of two numbers.

2.1. Mathematical Background

The analysis required to estimate the resource use of an algorithm is generally a theoretical issue, and therefore a formal framework is required. We begin with some mathematical definitions.

Throughout the book we will use the following four definitions:

DEFINITION: $T(N) = O(f(N))$ if there are positive *constants* c and n_0 such that $T(N) \leq cf(N)$ when $N \geq n_0$. $T(N) \leq cf(N)$ when $N \geq n_0$

DEFINITION: $T(N) = \Omega(g(N))$ if there are positive *constants* c and n_0 such that $T(N) \geq cg(N)$ when $N \geq n_0$.

DEFINITION: $T(N) = \Theta(h(N))$ if and only if $T(N) = O(h(N))$ and $T(N) = \Omega(h(N))$.

DEFINITION: $T(N) = o(p(N))$ if $T(N) = O(p(N))$ and $T(N) \neq \Theta(p(N))$.

The idea of these definitions is to establish a relative order among functions. Given two functions, there are usually points where one function is smaller than the other function, so it does not make sense to claim, for instance, $f(N) < g(N)$. Thus, we compare their *relative rates of growth.* When we apply this to the analysis of algorithms, we shall see why this is the important measure.

Although 1,000N is larger than N^2 for small values of N, N^2 grows at a faster rate, and thus N^2 will eventually be the larger function. The turning point is $N = 1,000$ in this case. The first definition says that eventually there is some point n_0 past which $c \cdot f(N)$ is always at least as large as $T(N)$, so that if constant factors are ignored, $f(N)$ is at least as big as $T(N)$. In our case, we have $T(N) = 1,000N$, $f(N) = N^2$, $n_0 = 1,000$, and $c = 1$. We could also use $n_0 = 10$ and $c = 100$. Thus, we can say that $1,000N = O(N^2)$ (order N-squared). This notation is known as *Big-Oh* notation. Frequently, instead of saying "order...," one says "Big-Oh...."

If we use the traditional inequality operators to compare growth rates, then the first definition says that the growth rate of $T(N)$ is less than or equal to ($\leq$) that of $f(N)$. The second definition, $T(N) = \Omega(g(N))$ (pronounced "omega"), says that the growth rate of $T(N)$ is greater than or equal to ($\geq$) that of $g(N)$. The third definition, $T(N) = \Theta(h(N))$ (pronounced "theta"), says that the growth rate of $T(N)$ equals ($=$) the growth rate of $h(N)$. The last definition, $T(N) = o(p(N))$ (pronounced "little-oh"), says that the growth rate of $T(N)$ is less than ($<$) the growth rate of $p(N)$. This is different from Big-Oh, because Big-Oh allows the possibility that the growth rates are the same.

To prove that some function $T(N) = O(f(N))$, we usually do not apply these definitions formally but instead use a repertoire of known results. In general, this means that a proof (or determination that the assumption is incorrect) is a very simple calculation and should not involve calculus, except in extraordinary circumstances (not likely to occur in an algorithm analysis).

When we say that $T(N) = O(f(N))$, we are guaranteeing that the function $T(N)$ grows at a rate no faster than $f(N)$; thus $f(N)$ is an *upper bound* on $T(N)$. Since this implies that $f(N) = \Omega(T(N))$, we say that $T(N)$ is a *lower bound* on $f(N)$.

As an example, N^3 grows faster than N^2, so we can say that $N^2 = O(N^3)$ or $N^3 = \Omega(N^2)$. $f(N) = N^2$ and $g(N) = 2N^2$ grow at the same rate, so both $f(N) = O(g(N))$ and $f(N) = \Omega(g(N))$ are true. When two functions grow at the same rate, then the decision of whether or not to signify this with $\Theta()$ can depend on the particular context. Intuitively, if $g(N) = 2N^2$, then $g(N) = O(N^4)$, $g(N) = O(N^3)$, and $g(N) = O(N^2)$ are all technically correct, but the last option is the best answer. Writing $g(N) = \Theta(N^2)$ says not only that $g(N) = O(N^2)$, but also that the result is as good (tight) as possible.

The important things to know are

RULE 1:
If $T_1(N) = O(f(N))$ and $T_2(N) = O(g(N))$, then
  (a) $T_1(N) + T_2(N) = \max(O(f(N)), O(g(N)))$,
  (b) $T_1(N) * T_2(N) = O(f(N) * g(N))$.

RULE 2:
If $T(N)$ is a polynomial of degree k, then $T(N) = \Theta(N^k)$.

RULE 3:
$\log^k N = O(N)$ *for any constant k. This tells us that logarithms grow very slowly.*

This information is sufficient to arrange most of the common functions by growth rate (see Fig. 2.1).

Function	Name
c	Constant
$\log N$	Logarithmic
$\log^2 N$	Log-squared
N	Linear
$N \log N$	
N^2	Quadratic
N^3	Cubic
2^N	Exponential

Figure 2.1 Typical growth rates

Several points are in order. First, it is very bad style to include constants or low-order terms inside a Big-Oh. Do not say $T(N) = O(2N^2)$ or $T(N) = O(N^2 + N)$. In both cases, the correct form is $T(N) = O(N^2)$. This means that in any analysis that will require a Big-Oh answer, all sorts of shortcuts are possible. Lower-order terms can generally be ignored, and constants can be thrown away. Considerably less precision is required in these cases.

Second, we can always determine the relative growth rates of two functions $f(N)$ and $g(N)$ by computing $\lim_{N \to \infty} f(N)/g(N)$, using L'Hôpital's rule if necessary.* The limit can have four possible values:

- The limit is 0: This means that $f(N) = o(g(N))$.
- The limit is $c \neq 0$: This means that $f(N) = \Theta(g(N))$.
- The limit is ∞: This means that $g(N) = o(f(N))$.
- The limit oscillates: There is no relation (this will not happen in our context).

Using this method almost always amounts to overkill. Usually the relation between $f(N)$ and $g(N)$ can be derived by simple algebra. For instance, if $f(N) = N \log N$ and $g(N) = N^{1.5}$, then to decide which of $f(N)$ and $g(N)$ grows faster, one really needs to determine which of $\log N$ and $N^{0.5}$ grows faster. This is like determining which of $\log^2 N$ or N grows faster. This is a simple problem, because it is already known that N grows faster than any power of a log. Thus, $g(N)$ grows faster than $f(N)$.

One stylistic note: It is bad to say $f(N) \leq O(g(N))$, because the inequality is implied by the definition. It is wrong to write $f(N) \geq O(g(N))$, which does not make sense.

As an example of the typical kinds of analysis that are performed, consider the problem of downloading a file over the Internet. Suppose there is an initial 3-sec delay (to set up a connection), after which the download proceeds at 1.5 K(bytes)/sec. Then it follows that if the file is N kilobytes, the time to download is described by the formula $T(N) = N/1.5 + 3$. This is a *linear function*. Notice that the time to download a 1,500K file (1,003 sec) is approximately (but not exactly) twice the time to download a 750K file (503 sec). This is typical of a linear function. Notice, also, that if the speed of the connection doubles, both times decrease, but the 1,500K file still takes approximately twice the time to download as a 750K file. This is the typical characteristic of linear-time algorithms, and it is why we

---

*L'Hôpital's rule states that if $\lim_{N \to \infty} f(N) = \infty$ and $\lim_{N \to \infty} g(N) = \infty$, then $\lim_{N \to \infty} f(N)/g(N) = \lim_{N \to \infty} f'(N)/g'(N)$, where $f'(N)$ and $g'(N)$ are the derivatives of $f(N)$ and $g(N)$, respectively.

write $T(N) = O(N)$, ignoring constant factors. (Although using Big-Theta would be more precise, Big-Oh answers are typically given.)

Observe, too, that this behavior is not true of all algorithms. For the first selection algorithm described in Section 1.1, the running time is controlled by the time it takes to perform a sort. For a simple sorting algorithm, such as the suggested bubble sort, when the amount of input doubles, the running time increases by a factor of four for large amounts of input. This is because those algorithms are not linear. Instead, as we will see when we discuss sorting, trivial sorting algorithms are $O(N^2)$, or quadratic.

2.2. Model

In order to analyze algorithms in a formal framework, we need a model of computation. Our model is basically a normal computer, in which instructions are executed sequentially. Our model has the standard repertoire of simple instructions, such as addition, multiplication, comparison, and assignment, but, unlike the case with real computers, it takes exactly one time unit to do anything (simple). To be reasonable, we will assume that, like a modern computer, our model has fixed-size (say, 32-bit) integers and that there are no fancy operations, such as matrix inversion or sorting, that clearly cannot be done in one time unit. We also assume infinite memory.

This model clearly has some weaknesses. Obviously, in real life, not all operations take exactly the same time. In particular, in our model one disk read counts the same as an addition, even though the addition is typically several orders of magnitude faster. Also, by assuming infinite memory, we never worry about page faulting, which can be a real problem, especially for efficient algorithms.

2.3. What to Analyze

The most important resource to analyze is generally the running time. Several factors affect the running time of a program. Some, such as the compiler and computer used, are obviously beyond the scope of any theoretical model, so, although they are important, we cannot deal with them here. The other main factors are the algorithm used and the input to the algorithm.

Typically, the size of the input is the main consideration. We define two functions, $T_{avg}(N)$ and $T_{worst}(N)$, as the average and worst-case running time, respectively, used by an algorithm on input of size N. Clearly, $T_{avg}(N) \leq T_{worst}(N)$. If there is more than one input, these functions may have more than one argument.

Occasionally the best-case performance of an algorithm is analyzed. However, this is often of little interest, because it does not represent typical behavior. Average-case performance often reflects typical behavior, while worst-case performance represents a guarantee for performance on any possible input. Notice, also, that, although in this chapter we analyze Java code, these bounds are really bounds for the algorithms rather than programs. Programs are an implementation of the algorithm in a particular programming language, and almost always the details of the programming language do not affect a Big-Oh answer. If a program is running much more slowly than the algorithm analysis suggests, there may be an implementation inefficiency. This is more common in languages (like C++) where arrays can be inadvertently copied in their entirety, instead of passed with references. However, this can occur in Java, too; an extremely subtle example of this is in the last two paragraphs of Section 12.7. Thus in future chapters we will analyze the algorithms rather than the programs.

Generally, the quantity required is the worst-case time, unless otherwise specified. One reason for this is that it provides a bound for all input, including particularly bad input, which an average-case analysis does not provide. The other reason is that average-case bounds are usually much more difficult to compute. In some instances, the definition of "average" can affect the result. (For instance, what is average input for the following problem?)

As an example, in the next section, we shall consider the following problem:

MAXIMUM SUBSEQUENCE SUM PROBLEM:

Given (possibly negative) integers $A_1, A_2, \ldots, A_N$, find the maximum value of $\sum_{k=i}^{j} A_k$. (For convenience, the maximum subsequence sum is 0 if all the integers are negative.)

Example:

For input $-2, 11, -4, 13, -5, -2$, the answer is 20 (A_2 through A_4).

This problem is interesting mainly because there are so many algorithms to solve it, and the performance of these algorithms varies drastically. We will discuss four algorithms to solve this problem. The running time on some computer (the exact computer is unimportant) for these algorithms is given in Figure 2.2.

There are several important things worth noting in this table. For a small amount of input, the algorithms all run in a blink of the eye, so if only a small amount of input is expected, it might be silly to expend a great deal of effort to design a clever algorithm. On the other hand, there is a large market these days for rewriting programs that were written five years ago based on a no-longer-valid assumption of small input size. These programs are now too slow, because they used poor algorithms. For large amounts of input, algorithm 4 is clearly the best choice (although algorithm 3 is still usable).

Second, the times given do not include the time required to read the input. For algorithm 4, the time merely to read in the input from a disk is likely to be an order of magnitude larger than the time required to solve the problem. This is typical of many efficient algorithms. Reading the data is generally the bottleneck; once the data are read, the

Algorithm		1	2	3	4
Time		$O(N^3)$	$O(N^2)$	$O(N \log N)$	$O(N)$
Input Size	$N = 10$	0.00103	0.00045	0.00066	0.00034
	$N = 100$	0.47015	0.01112	0.00486	0.00063
	$N = 1,000$	448.77	1.1233	0.05843	0.00333
	$N = 10,000$	NA	111.13	0.68631	0.03042
	$N = 100,000$	NA	NA	8.0113	0.29832

Figure 2.2 Running times of several algorithms for maximum subsequence sum (in seconds)

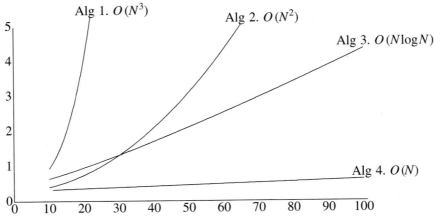

Figure 2.3 Plot (N vs. milliseconds) of various maximum subsequence sum algorithms

problem can be solved quickly. For inefficient algorithms this is not true, and significant computer resources must be used. Thus it is important that, whenever possible, algorithms be efficient enough not to be the bottleneck of a problem.

Figure 2.3 shows the growth rates of the running times of the four algorithms. Even though this graph encompasses only values of N ranging from 10 to 100, the relative growth rates are still evident. Although the graph for algorithm 3 seems linear, it is easy to verify that it is not by using a straight-edge (or piece of paper). Figure 2.4 shows the performance for larger values. It dramatically illustrates how useless inefficient algorithms are for even moderately large amounts of input.

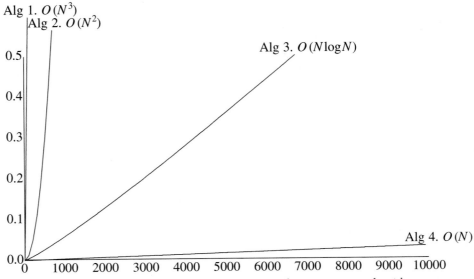

Figure 2.4 Plot (N vs. seconds) of various maximum subsequence sum algorithms

2.4. Running Time Calculations

There are several ways to estimate the running time of a program. The previous table was obtained empirically. If two programs are expected to take similar times, probably the best way to decide which is faster is to code them both up and run them!

Generally, there are several algorithmic ideas, and we would like to eliminate the bad ones early, so an analysis is usually required. Furthermore, the ability to do an analysis usually provides insight into designing efficient algorithms. The analysis also generally pinpoints the bottlenecks, which are worth coding carefully.

To simplify the analysis, we will adopt the convention that there are no particular units of time. Thus, we throw away leading constants. We will also throw away low-order terms, so what we are essentially doing is computing a Big-Oh running time. Since Big-Oh is an upper bound, we must be careful never to underestimate the running time of the program. In effect, the answer provided is a guarantee that the program will terminate within a certain time period. The program may stop earlier than this, but never later.

2.4.1. A Simple Example

Here is a simple program fragment to calculate $\sum_{i=1}^{N} i^3$:

```
        public static int sum( int n )
        {
            int partialSum;

/* 1*/      partialSum = 0;
/* 2*/      for( int i = 1; i <= n; i++ )
/* 3*/          partialSum += i * i * i;
/* 4*/      return partialSum;
        }
```

The analysis of this fragment is simple. The declarations count for no time. Lines 1 and 4 count for one unit each. Line 3 counts for four units per time executed (two multiplications, one addition, and one assignment) and is executed N times, for a total of $4N$ units. Line 2 has the hidden costs of initializing i, testing $i \leq N$, and incrementing i. The total cost of all these is 1 to initialize, $N + 1$ for all the tests, and N for all the increments, which is $2N + 2$. We ignore the costs of calling the method and returning, for a total of $6N + 4$. Thus, we say that this method is $O(N)$.

If we had to perform all this work every time we needed to analyze a program, the task would quickly become infeasible. Fortunately, since we are giving the answer in terms of Big-Oh, there are lots of shortcuts that can be taken without affecting the final answer. For instance, line 3 is obviously an $O(1)$ statement (per execution), so it is silly to count precisely whether it is two, three, or four units; it does not matter. Line 1 is obviously insignificant compared with the **for** loop, so it is silly to waste time here. This leads to several general rules.

2.4.2. General Rules

RULE 1---*FOR* LOOPS:
*The running time of a **for** loop is at most the running time of the statements inside the **for** loop (including tests) times the number of iterations.*

RULE 2—NESTED LOOPS:

Analyze these inside out. The total running time of a statement inside a group of nested loops is the running time of the statement multiplied by the product of the sizes of all the loops.

As an example, the following program fragment is $O(N^2)$:

```
for( i = 0; i < n; i++ )
    for( j = 0; j < n; j++ )
        k++;
```

RULE 3—CONSECUTIVE STATEMENTS:

These just add (which means that the maximum is the one that counts; see rule 1(a) on page 30).

As an example, the following program fragment, which has $O(N)$ work followed by $O(N^2)$ work, is also $O(N^2)$:

```
for( i = 0; i < n; i++ )
    a[ i ] = 0;
for( i = 0; i < n; i++ )
    for( j = 0; j < n; j++ )
        a[ i ] += a[ j ] + i + j;
```

RULE 4—*IF/ELSE*:

For the fragment

```
if( condition )
    S1
else
    S2
```

the running time of an **if/else** *statement is never more than the running time of the test plus the larger of the running times of S1 and S2.*

Clearly, this can be an overestimate in some cases, but it is never an underestimate.

Other rules are obvious, but a basic strategy of analyzing from the inside (or deepest part) out works. If there are method calls, these must be analyzed first. If there are recursive methods, there are several options. If the recursion is really just a thinly veiled **for** loop, the analysis is usually trivial. For instance, the following method is really just a simple loop and is $O(N)$:

```
public static long factorial( int n )
{
    if( n <= 1 )
        return 1;
    else
        return n * factorial( n - 1 );
}
```

This example is really a poor use of recursion. When recursion is properly used, it is difficult to convert the recursion into a simple loop structure. In this case, the analysis will involve a recurrence relation that needs to be solved. To see what might happen, consider the following program, which turns out to be a horrible use of recursion:

```
        public static long fib( int n )
        {
/* 1*/      if( n <= 1 )
/* 2*/          return 1;
            else
/* 3*/          return fib( n - 1 ) + fib( n - 2 );
        }
```

At first glance, this seems like a very clever use of recursion. However, if the program is coded up and run for values of N around 30, it becomes apparent that this program is terribly inefficient. The analysis is fairly simple. Let $T(N)$ be the running time for the method call fib(n). If $N = 0$ or $N = 1$, then the running time is some constant value, which is the time to do the test at line 1 and return. We can say that $T(0) = T(1) = 1$ because constants do not matter. The running time for other values of N is then measured relative to the running time of the base case. For $N > 2$, the time to execute the method is the constant work at line 1 plus the work at line 3. Line 3 consists of an addition and two method calls. Since the method calls are not simple operations, they must be analyzed by themselves. The first method call is fib(n - 1) and hence, by the definition of T, requires $T(N - 1)$ units of time. A similar argument shows that the second method call requires $T(N - 2)$ units of time. The total time required is then $T(N - 1) + T(N - 2) + 2$, where the 2 accounts for the work at line 1 plus the addition at line 3. Thus, for $N \geq 2$, we have the following formula for the running time of fib(n):

$$T(N) = T(N - 1) + T(N - 2) + 2$$

Since $fib(N) = fib(N - 1) + fib(N - 2)$, it is easy to show by induction that $T(N) \geq fib(N)$. In Section 1.2.5, we showed that $fib(N) < (5/3)^N$. A similar calculation shows that (for $N > 4$) $fib(N) \geq (3/2)^N$, and so the running time of this program grows *exponentially*. This is about as bad as possible. By keeping a simple array and using a **for** loop, the running time can be reduced substantially.

This program is slow because there is a huge amount of redundant work being performed, violating the fourth major rule of recursion (the compound interest rule), which was presented in Section 1.3. Notice that the first call on line 3, fib(n - 1), actually computes fib(n - 2) at some point. This information is thrown away and recomputed by the second call on line 3. The amount of information thrown away compounds recursively and results in the huge running time. This is perhaps the finest example of the maxim "Don't compute anything more than once" and should not scare you away from using recursion. Throughout this book, we shall see outstanding uses of recursion.

2.4.3. Solutions for the Maximum Subsequence Sum Problem

We will now present four algorithms to solve the maximum subsequence sum problem posed earlier. The first algorithm, which merely exhaustively tries all possibilities, is depicted in Figure 2.5. The indices in the **for** loop reflect the fact that in Java, arrays begin at 0, instead of 1. Also, the algorithm does not compute the actual subsequences; additional code is required to do this.

```
         /**
          * Cubic maximum contiguous subsequence sum algorithm.
          */
         public static int maxSubSum1( int [ ] a )
         {
/* 1*/       int maxSum = 0;

/* 2*/       for( int i = 0; i < a.length; i++ )
/* 3*/           for( int j = i; j < a.length; j++ )
             {
/* 4*/               int thisSum = 0;

/* 5*/               for( int k = i; k <= j; k++ )
/* 6*/                   thisSum += a[ k ];

/* 7*/               if( thisSum > maxSum )
/* 8*/                   maxSum = thisSum;
             }

/* 9*/       return maxSum;
         }
```

Figure 2.5 Algorithm 1

Convince yourself that this algorithm works (this should not take much convincing). The running time is $O(N^3)$ and is entirely due to lines 5 and 6, which consist of an $O(1)$ statement buried inside three nested **for** loops. The loop at line 2 is of size N.

The second loop has size $N - i$ which could be small but could also be of size N. We must assume the worst, with the knowledge that this could make the final bound a bit high. The third loop has size $j - i + 1$, which, again, we must assume is of size N. The total is $O(1 \cdot N \cdot N \cdot N) = O(N^3)$. Statement 1 takes only $O(1)$ total, and statements 7 and 8 take only $O(N^2)$ total, since they are easy expressions inside only two loops.

It turns out that a more precise analysis, taking into account the actual size of these loops, shows that the answer is $\Theta(N^3)$ and that our estimate above was a factor of 6 too high (which is all right, because constants do not matter). This is generally true in these kinds of problems. The precise analysis is obtained from the sum $\sum_{i=0}^{N-1} \sum_{j=i}^{N-1} \sum_{k=i}^{j} 1$, which tells how many times line 6 is executed. The sum can be evaluated inside out, using formulas from Section 1.2.3. In particular, we will use the formulas for the sum of the first N integers and first N squares. First we have

$$\sum_{k=i}^{j} 1 = j - i + 1$$

Next we evaluate

$$\sum_{j=i}^{N-1} (j - i + 1) = \frac{(N - i + 1)(N - i)}{2}$$

This sum is computed by observing that it is just the sum of the first $N - i$ integers. To complete the calculation, we evaluate

$$\sum_{i=0}^{N-1} \frac{(N-i+1)(N-i)}{2} = \sum_{i=1}^{N} \frac{(N-i+1)(N-i+2)}{2}$$

$$= \frac{1}{2}\sum_{i=1}^{N} i^2 - \left(N + \frac{3}{2}\right)\sum_{i=1}^{N} i + \frac{1}{2}(N^2 + 3N + 2)\sum_{i=1}^{N} 1$$

$$= \frac{1}{2}\frac{N(N+1)(2N+1)}{6} - \left(N + \frac{3}{2}\right)\frac{N(N+1)}{2} + \frac{N^2 + 3N + 2}{2}N$$

$$= \frac{N^3 + 3N^2 + 2N}{6}$$

We can avoid the cubic running time by removing a **for** loop. This is not always possible, but in this case there are an awful lot of unnecessary computations present in the algorithm. The inefficiency that the improved algorithm corrects can be seen by noticing that $\sum_{k=i}^{j} A_k = A_j + \sum_{k=i}^{j-1} A_k$, so the computation at lines 5 and 6 in algorithm 1 is unduly expensive. Figure 2.6 shows an improved algorithm. Algorithm 2 is clearly $O(N^2)$; the analysis is even simpler than before.

There is a recursive and relatively complicated $O(N \log N)$ solution to this problem, which we now describe. If there didn't happen to be an $O(N)$ (linear) solution, this would be an excellent example of the power of recursion. The algorithm uses a "divide-and-conquer" strategy. The idea is to split the problem into two roughly equal subproblems, which are then solved recursively. This is the "divide" part. The "conquer" stage consists of patching together the two solutions of the subproblems, and possibly doing a small amount of additional work, to arrive at a solution for the whole problem.

```
        /**
         * Quadratic maximum contiguous subsequence sum algorithm.
         */
        public static int maxSubSum2( int [ ] a )
        {
/* 1*/      int maxSum = 0;

/* 2*/      for( int i = 0; i < a.length; i++ )
            {
/* 3*/          int thisSum = 0;
/* 4*/          for( int j = i; j < a.length; j++ )
                {
/* 5*/              thisSum += a[ j ];

/* 6*/              if( thisSum > maxSum )
/* 7*/                  maxSum = thisSum;
                }
            }

/* 8*/      return maxSum;
        }
```

Figure 2.6 Algorithm 2

In our case, the maximum subsequence sum can be in one of three places. Either it occurs entirely in the left half of the input, or entirely in the right half, or it crosses the middle and is in both halves. The first two cases can be solved recursively. The last case can be obtained by finding the largest sum in the first half that includes the last element in the first half, and the largest sum in the second half that includes the first element in the second half. These two sums can then be added together. As an example, consider the following input:

First Half				Second Half			
4	−3	5	−2	−1	2	6	−2

The maximum subsequence sum for the first half is 6 (elements A_1 through A_3) and for the second half is 8 (elements A_6 through A_7).

The maximum sum in the first half that includes the last element in the first half is 4 (elements A_1 through A_4), and the maximum sum in the second half that includes the first element in the second half is 7 (elements A_5 though A_7). Thus, the maximum sum that spans both halves and goes through the middle is $4 + 7 = 11$ (elements A_1 through A_7).

We see, then, that among the three ways to form a large maximum subsequence, for our example, the best way is to include elements from both halves. Thus, the answer is 11. Figure 2.7 shows an implementation of this strategy.

The code for algorithm 3 deserves some comment. The general form of the call for the recursive method is to pass the input array along with the left and right borders, which delimit the portion of the array that is operated upon. A one-line driver program sets this up by passing the borders 0 and $N - 1$ along with the array.

Lines 1 to 4 handle the base case. If `left == right`, there is one element, and it is the maximum subsequence if the element is nonnegative. The case `left > right` is not possible unless N is negative (although minor perturbations in the code could mess this up). Lines 6 and 7 perform the two recursive calls. We can see that the recursive calls are always on a smaller problem than the original, although minor perturbations in the code could destroy this property. Lines 8 to 12 and 13 to 17 calculate the two maximum sums that touch the center divider. The sum of these two values is the maximum sum that spans both halves. The routine `max3` (not shown) returns the largest of the three possibilities.

Algorithm 3 clearly requires more effort to code than either of the two previous algorithms. However, shorter code does not always mean better code. As we have seen in the earlier table showing the running times of the algorithms, this algorithm is considerably faster than the other two for all but the smallest of input sizes.

The running time is analyzed in much the same way as for the program that computes the Fibonacci numbers. Let $T(N)$ be the time it takes to solve a maximum subsequence sum problem of size N. If $N = 1$, then the program takes some constant amount of time to execute lines 1 to 4, which we shall call one unit. Thus, $T(1) = 1$. Otherwise, the program must perform two recursive calls, the two **for** loops between lines 9 and 17, and some small amount of bookkeeping, such as lines 5 and 18. The two **for** loops combine to touch every element in the subarray, and there is constant work inside the loops, so the time expended in lines 9 to 17 is $O(N)$. The code in lines 1 to 5, 8, 13, and 18 is all a constant amount of work and can thus be ignored compared with $O(N)$. The remainder of

```
        /**
         * Recursive maximum contiguous subsequence sum algorithm.
         * Finds maximum sum in subarray spanning a[left..right].
         * Does not attempt to maintain actual best sequence.
         */
        private static int maxSumRec( int [ ] a, int left, int right )
        {
/* 1*/      if( left == right )  // Base case
/* 2*/          if( a[ left ] > 0 )
/* 3*/              return a[ left ];
                else
/* 4*/              return 0;

/* 5*/      int center = ( left + right ) / 2;
/* 6*/      int maxLeftSum  = maxSumRec( a, left, center );
/* 7*/      int maxRightSum = maxSumRec( a, center + 1, right );

/* 8*/      int maxLeftBorderSum = 0, leftBorderSum = 0;
/* 9*/      for( int i = center; i >= left; i-- )
            {
/*10*/          leftBorderSum += a[ i ];
/*11*/          if( leftBorderSum > maxLeftBorderSum )
/*12*/              maxLeftBorderSum = leftBorderSum;
            }

/*13*/      int maxRightBorderSum = 0, rightBorderSum = 0;
/*14*/      for( int i = center + 1; i <= right; i++ )
            {
/*15*/          rightBorderSum += a[ i ];
/*16*/          if( rightBorderSum > maxRightBorderSum )
/*17*/              maxRightBorderSum = rightBorderSum;
            }

/*18*/      return max3( maxLeftSum, maxRightSum,
                        maxLeftBorderSum + maxRightBorderSum );
        }

        /**
         * Driver for divide-and-conquer maximum contiguous
         * subsequence sum algorithm.
         */
        public static int maxSubSum3( int [ ] a )
        {
            return maxSumRec( a, 0, a.length - 1 );
        }
```

Figure 2.7 Algorithm 3

the work is performed in lines 6 and 7. These lines solve two subsequence problems of size $N/2$ (assuming N is even). Thus, these lines take $T(N/2)$ units of time each, for a total of $2T(N/2)$. The total time for the algorithm then is $2T(N/2) + O(N)$. This gives the equations

$$T(1) = 1$$
$$T(N) = 2T(N/2) + O(N)$$

To simplify the calculations, we can replace the $O(N)$ term in the equation above with N; since $T(N)$ will be expressed in Big-Oh notation anyway, this will not affect the answer. In Chapter 7, we shall see how to solve this equation rigorously. For now, if $T(N) = 2T(N/2) + N$, and $T(1) = 1$, then $T(2) = 4 = 2 * 2$, $T(4) = 12 = 4 * 3$, $T(8) = 32 = 8 * 4$, and $T(16) = 80 = 16 * 5$. The pattern that is evident, and can be derived, is that if $N = 2^k$, then $T(N) = N * (k + 1) = N \log N + N = O(N \log N)$.

This analysis assumes N is even, since otherwise $N/2$ is not defined. By the recursive nature of the analysis, it is really valid only when N is a power of 2, since otherwise we eventually get a subproblem that is not an even size, and the equation is invalid. When N is not a power of 2, a somewhat more complicated analysis is required, but the Big-Oh result remains unchanged.

In future chapters, we will see several clever applications of recursion. Here, we present a fourth algorithm to find the maximum subsequence sum. This algorithm is simpler to implement than the recursive algorithm and also is more efficient. It is shown in Figure 2.8.

It should be clear why the time bound is correct, but it takes a little thought to see why the algorithm actually works. To sketch the logic, note that, like Algorithms 1 and 2, j is representing the end of the current sequence, while i is representing the start of the current sequence. It happens that the use of i can be optimized out of the program if we do not need to know where the actual best subsequence is, so in designing the algorithm, let's

```
         /**
          * Linear-time maximum contiguous subsequence sum algorithm.
          */
         public static int maxSubSum4( int [ ] a )
         {
/* 1*/       int maxSum = 0, thisSum = 0;

/* 2*/       for( int j = 0; j < a.length; j++ )
             {
/* 3*/           thisSum += a[ j ];

/* 4*/           if( thisSum > maxSum )
/* 5*/               maxSum = thisSum;
/* 6*/           else if( thisSum < 0 )
/* 7*/               thisSum = 0;
             }

/* 8*/       return maxSum;
         }
```

Figure 2.8 Algorithm 4

pretend that i is needed, and that we are trying to improve Algorithm 2. One observation is that if a[i] is negative, then it cannot possibly represent the start of the optimal sequence, since any subsequence that begins by including a[i] would be improved by beginning with a[i+1]. Similarly, any negative subsequence cannot possibly be a prefix of the optimal subsequence (same logic). If, in the inner loop, we detect that the subsequence from a[i] to a[j] is negative, then we can advance i. The crucial observation is that not only can we advance i to i+1, but we can also actually advance it all the way to j+1. To see this, let p be any index between i+1 and j. Any subsequence that starts at index p is not larger than the corresponding subsequence that starts at index i and includes the subsequence from a[i] to a[p-1], since the latter subsequence is not negative (j is the first index that causes the subsequence starting at index i to become negative). Thus advancing i to j+1 is risk free: we cannot miss an optimal solution.

This algorithm is typical of many clever algorithms: the running time is obvious, but the correctness is not. For these algorithms, formal correctness proofs (more formal than the sketch above) are almost always required; even then, however, many people still are not convinced. In addition, many of these algorithms require trickier programming, leading to longer development. But when these algorithms work, they run quickly, and we can test much of the code logic by comparing it with an inefficient (but easily implemented) brute-force algorithm using small input sizes.

An extra advantage of this algorithm is that it makes only one pass through the data, and once a[i] is read and processed, it does not need to be remembered. Thus, if the array is on a disk or tape, it can be read sequentially, and there is no need to store any part of it in main memory. Furthermore, at any point in time, the algorithm can correctly give an answer to the subsequence problem for the data it has already read (the other algorithms do not share this property). Algorithms that can do this are called *on-line algorithms*. An on-line algorithm that requires only constant space and runs in linear time is just about as good as possible.

2.4.4. Logarithms in the Running Time

The most confusing aspect of analyzing algorithms probably centers around the logarithm. We have already seen that some divide-and-conquer algorithms will run in $O(N \log N)$ time. Besides divide-and-conquer algorithms, the most frequent appearance of logarithms centers around the following general rule: *An algorithm is $O(\log N)$ if it takes constant $(O(1))$ time to cut the problem size by a fraction (which is usually $\frac{1}{2}$).* On the other hand, if constant time is required to merely reduce the problem by a constant *amount* (such as to make the problem smaller by 1), then the algorithm is $O(N)$.

It should be obvious that only special kinds of problems can be $O(\log N)$. For instance, if the input is a list of N numbers, an algorithm must take $\Omega(N)$ merely to read the input in. Thus, when we talk about $O(\log N)$ algorithms for these kinds of problems, we usually presume that the input is preread. We provide three examples of logarithmic behavior.

Binary Search
The first example is usually referred to as binary search.

BINARY SEARCH:

Given an integer X and integers $A_0, A_1, \ldots, A_{N-1}$, which are presorted and already in memory, find i such that $A_i = X$, or return $i = -1$ if X is not in the input.

```
/**
 * Performs the standard binary search.
 * @return index where item is found, or -1 if not found.
 */
public static int binarySearch( Comparable [ ] a, Comparable x )
{
/* 1*/      int low = 0, high = a.length - 1;

/* 2*/      while( low <= high )
            {
/* 3*/          int mid = ( low + high ) / 2;

/* 4*/          if( a[ mid ].compareTo( x ) < 0 )
/* 5*/              low = mid + 1;
/* 6*/          else if( a[ mid ].compareTo( x ) > 0 )
/* 7*/              high = mid - 1;
                else
/* 8*/              return mid;    // Found
            }
/* 9*/      return NOT_FOUND;        // NOT_FOUND is defined as -1
}
```

Figure 2.9 Binary search

The obvious solution consists of scanning through the list from left to right and runs in linear time. However, this algorithm does not take advantage of the fact that the list is sorted, and is thus not likely to be best. A better strategy is to check if X is the middle element. If so, the answer is at hand. If X is smaller than the middle element, we can apply the same strategy to the sorted subarray to the left of the middle element; likewise, if X is larger than the middle element, we look to the right half. (There is also the case of when to stop.) Figure 2.9 shows the code for binary search (the answer is mid). As usual, the code reflects Java's convention that arrays begin with index 0.

Clearly, all the work done inside the loop takes $O(1)$ per iteration, so the analysis requires determining the number of times around the loop. The loop starts with high - low = $N - 1$ and finishes with high - low ≥ -1. Every time through the loop the value high - low must be at least halved from its previous value; thus, the number of times around the loop is at most $\lceil \log(N - 1) \rceil + 2$. (As an example, if high - low = 128, then the maximum values of high - low after each iteration are 64, 32, 16, 8, 4, 2, 1, 0, -1.) Thus, the running time is $O(\log N)$. Equivalently, we could write a recursive formula for the running time, but this kind of brute-force approach is usually unnecessary when you understand what is really going on and why.

Binary search can be viewed as our first data structure implementation. It supports the find operation in $O(\log N)$ time, but all other operations (in particular insert) require $O(N)$ time. In applications where the data are static (that is, insertions and deletions are not allowed), this could be very useful. The input would then need to be sorted once, but afterward accesses would be fast. An example is a program that needs to maintain information about the periodic table of elements (which arises in chemistry and physics). This table is relatively stable, as new elements are added infrequently. The element names could be kept sorted. Since there are only about 110 elements, at most eight accesses would be required to find an element. Performing a sequential search would require many more accesses.

Euclid's Algorithm

A second example is Euclid's algorithm for computing the greatest common divisor. The greatest common divisor (*gcd*) of two integers is the largest integer that divides both. Thus, $gcd(50, 15) = 5$. The algorithm in Figure 2.10 computes $gcd(M, N)$, assuming $M \geq N$. (If $N > M$, the first iteration of the loop swaps them.)

The algorithm works by continually computing remainders until 0 is reached. The last nonzero remainder is the answer. Thus, if $M = 1,989$ and $N = 1,590$, then the sequence of remainders is 399, 393, 6, 3, 0. Therefore, $gcd(1989, 1590) = 3$. As the example shows, this is a fast algorithm.

As before, estimating the entire running time of the algorithm depends on determining how long the sequence of remainders is. Although $\log N$ seems like a good answer, it is not at all obvious that the value of the remainder has to decrease by a constant factor, since we see that the remainder went from 399 to only 393 in the example. Indeed, the remainder *does not* decrease by a constant factor in one iteration. However, we can prove that after two iterations, the remainder is at most half of its original value. This would show that the number of iterations is at most $2 \log N = O(\log N)$ and establish the running time. This proof is easy, so we include it here. It follows directly from the following theorem.

THEOREM 2.1.
If $M > N$, then $M \bmod N < M/2$.

PROOF:
There are two cases. If $N \leq M/2$, then since the remainder is smaller than N, the theorem is true for this case. The other case is $N > M/2$. But then N goes into M once with a remainder $M - N < M/2$, proving the theorem.

One might wonder if this is the best bound possible, since $2 \log N$ is about 20 for our example, and only seven operations were performed. It turns out that the constant can be improved slightly, to roughly $1.44 \log N$, in the worst case (which is achievable if M and N are consecutive Fibonacci numbers). The average-case performance of Euclid's algorithm requires pages and pages of highly sophisticated mathematical analysis, and it turns out that the average number of iterations is about $(12 \ln 2 \ln N)/\pi^2 + 1.47$.

```
        public static long gcd( long m, long n )
            {
/* 1*/          while( n != 0 )
                {
/* 2*/              long rem = m % n;
/* 3*/              m = n;
/* 4*/              n = rem;
                }
/* 5*/          return m;
            }
```

Figure 2.10 Euclid's algorithm

Exponentiation

Our last example in this section deals with raising an integer to a power (which is also an integer). Numbers that result from exponentiation are generally quite large, so an analysis works only if we can assume that we have a machine that can store such large integers (or a compiler that can simulate this). We will count the number of multiplications as the measurement of running time.

The obvious algorithm to compute X^N uses $N-1$ multiplications. The recursive algorithm in Figure 2.11* does better. Lines 1 to 4 handle the base case of the recursion. Otherwise, if N is even, we have $X^N = X^{N/2} \cdot X^{N/2}$, and if N is odd, $X^N = X^{(N-1)/2} \cdot X^{(N-1)/2} \cdot X$.

For instance, to compute X^{62}, the algorithm does the following calculations, which involves only nine multiplications:

$$X^3 = (X^2)X, \quad X^7 = (X^3)^2X, \quad X^{15} = (X^7)^2X, \quad X^{31} = (X^{15})^2X, \quad X^{62} = (X^{31})^2$$

The number of multiplications required is clearly at most $2\log N$, because at most two multiplications (if N is odd) are required to halve the problem. Again, a recurrence formula can be written and solved. Simple intuition obviates the need for a brute-force approach.

It is sometimes interesting to see how much the code can be tweaked without affecting correctness. In Figure 2.11, lines 3 to 4 are actually unnecessary, because if N is 1, then line 7 does the right thing. Line 7 can also be rewritten as

```
/* 7*/            return pow( x, n - 1 ) * x;
```

without affecting the correctness of the program. Indeed, the program will still run in $O(\log N)$, because the sequence of multiplications is the same as before. However, all of the following alternatives for line 6 are bad, even though they look correct:

```
/* 6a*/           return pow( pow( x, 2 ), n / 2 );
/* 6b*/           return pow( pow( x, n / 2 ), 2 );
/* 6c*/           return pow( x, n / 2 ) * pow( x, n / 2 );
```

Both lines 6a and 6b are incorrect because when N is 2, one of the recursive calls to pow has 2 as the second argument. Thus no progress is made, and an infinite loop results (in an eventual abnormal termination).

```
          public static long pow( long x, int n )
          {
/* 1*/        if( n == 0 )
/* 2*/            return 1;
/* 3*/        if( n == 1 )
/* 4*/            return x;
/* 5*/        if( isEven( n ) )
/* 6*/            return pow( x * x, n / 2 );
              else
/* 7*/            return pow( x * x, n / 2 ) * x;
          }
```

Figure 2.11 Efficient exponentiation

*Java provides a BigDecimal class that can be used to manipulate arbitrarily large integers. Translating Figure 2.11 to use BigDecimal instead of long is straightforward.

Using line 6c affects the efficiency, because there are now two recursive calls of size $N/2$ instead of only one. An analysis will show that the running time is no longer $O(\log N)$. We leave it as an exercise to the reader to determine the new running time.

2.4.5. Checking Your Analysis

Once an analysis has been performed, it is desirable to see if the answer is correct and as good as possible. One way to do this is to code up the program and see if the empirically observed running time matches the running time predicted by the analysis. When N doubles, the running time goes up by a factor of 2 for linear programs, 4 for quadratic programs, and 8 for cubic programs. Programs that run in logarithmic time take only an additive constant longer when N doubles, and programs that run in $O(N \log N)$ take slightly more than twice as long to run under the same circumstances. These increases can be hard to spot if the lower-order terms have relatively large coefficients and N is not large enough. An example is the jump from $N = 10$ to $N = 100$ in the running time for the various implementations of the maximum subsequence sum problem. It also can be very difficult to differentiate linear programs from $O(N \log N)$ programs purely on empirical evidence.

Another commonly used trick to verify that some program is $O(f(N))$ is to compute the values $T(N)/f(N)$ for a range of N (usually spaced out by factors of 2), where $T(N)$ is the empirically observed running time. If $f(N)$ is a tight answer for the running time, then the computed values converge to a positive constant. If $f(N)$ is an overestimate, the values converge to zero. If $f(N)$ is an underestimate and hence wrong, the values diverge.

As an example, the program fragment in Figure 2.12 computes the probability that two distinct positive integers, less than or equal to N and chosen randomly, are relatively prime. (As N gets large, the answer approaches $6/\pi^2$.)

You should be able to do the analysis for this program instantaneously. Figure 2.13 shows the actual observed running time for this routine on a real computer. The table shows that the last column is most likely, and thus the analysis that you should have gotten is probably correct. Notice that there is not a great deal of difference between $O(N^2)$ and $O(N^2 \log N)$, since logarithms grow so slowly.

```
public static double probRelPrime( int n )
{
    int rel = 0, tot = 0;

    for( int i = 1; i <= n; i++ )
        for( int j = i + 1; j <= n; j++ )
        {
            tot++;
            if( gcd( i, j ) == 1 )
                rel++;
        }

    return (double) rel / tot;
}
```

Figure 2.12 Estimate the probability that two random numbers are relatively prime

N	CPU time (T)	T/N^2	T/N^3	$T/(N^2 \log N)$
100	022	.002200	.000022000	.0004777
200	056	.001400	.000007000	.0002642
300	118	.001311	.000004370	.0002299
400	207	.001294	.000003234	.0002159
500	318	.001272	.000002544	.0002047
600	466	.001294	.000002157	.0002024
700	644	.001314	.000001877	.0002006
800	846	.001322	.000001652	.0001977
900	1,086	.001341	.000001490	.0001971
1,000	1,362	.001362	.000001362	.0001972
1,500	3,240	.001440	.000000960	.0001969
2,000	5,949	.001482	.000000740	.0001947
4,000	25,720	.001608	.000000402	.0001938

Figure 2.13 Empirical running times for the routine in Figure 2.12

2.4.6. A Grain of Salt

Sometimes the analysis is shown empirically to be an overestimate. If this is the case, then either the analysis needs to be tightened (usually by a clever observation), or it may be that the *average* running time is significantly less than the worst-case running time and no improvement in the bound is possible. For many complicated algorithms the worst-case bound is achievable by some bad input but is usually an overestimate in practice. Unfortunately, for most of these problems, an average-case analysis is extremely complex (in many cases still unsolved), and a worst-case bound, even though overly pessimistic, is the best analytical result known.

SUMMARY

This chapter gives some hints on how to analyze the complexity of programs. Unfortunately, it is not a complete guide. Simple programs usually have simple analyses, but this is not always the case. As an example, later in the text we shall see a sorting algorithm (Shellsort, Chapter 7) and an algorithm for maintaining disjoint sets (Chapter 8), each of which requires about 20 lines of code. The analysis of Shellsort is still not complete, and the disjoint set algorithm has an analysis that is extremely difficult and requires pages and pages of intricate calculations. Most of the analyses that we will encounter here will be simple and involve counting through loops.

An interesting kind of analysis, which we have not touched upon, is lower-bound analysis. We will see an example of this in Chapter 7, where it is proved that any algorithm that sorts by using only comparisons requires $\Omega(N \log N)$ comparisons in the worst case. Lower-bound proofs are generally the most difficult, because they apply not to an algorithm but to a class of algorithms that solve a problem.

We close by mentioning that some of the algorithms described here have real-life application. The *gcd* algorithm and the exponentiation algorithm are both used in cryptography. Specifically, a 200-digit number is raised to a large power (usually another 200-digit number), with only the low 200 or so digits retained after each multiplication. Since the calculations require dealing with 200-digit numbers, efficiency is obviously important. The straightforward algorithm for exponentiation would require about 10^{200} multiplications, whereas the algorithm presented requires only about 1,300, in the worst case.

EXERCISES

2.1 Order the following functions by growth rate: N, $\sqrt{N}$, $N^{1.5}$, N^2, $N \log N$, $N \log \log N$, $N \log^2 N$, $N \log(N^2)$, $2/N$, 2^N, $2^{N/2}$, 37, $N^2 \log N$, N^3. Indicate which functions grow at the same rate.

2.2 Suppose $T_1(N) = O(f(N))$ and $T_2(N) = O(f(N))$. Which of the following are true?

   a. $T_1(N) + T_2(N) = O(f(N))$

   b. $T_1(N) - T_2(N) = o(f(N))$

   c. $\dfrac{T_1(N)}{T_2(N)} = O(1)$

   d. $T_1(N) = O(T_2(N))$

2.3 Which function grows faster: $N \log N$ or $N^{1+\epsilon/\sqrt{\log N}}$, $\epsilon > 0$?

2.4 Prove that for any constant, k, $\log^k N = o(N)$.

2.5 Find two functions $f(N)$ and $g(N)$ such that neither $f(N) = O(g(N))$ nor $g(N) = O(f(N))$.

2.6 In a recent court case, a judge cited a city for contempt and ordered a fine of $2 for the first day. Each subsequent day, until the city followed the judge's order, the fine was squared (that is, the fine progressed as follows: $2, $4, $16, $256, $65,536, ...).

   a. What would be the fine on day N?

   b. How many days would it take the fine to reach D dollars? (A Big-Oh answer will do.)

2.7 For each of the following six program fragments:

   a. Give an analysis of the running time (Big-Oh will do).

   b. Implement the code in the language of your choice, and give the running time for several values of N.

   c. Compare your analysis with the actual running times.

```
(1)     sum = 0;
        for( i = 0; i < n; i++ )
            sum++;
```

```
(2)     sum = 0;
        for( i = 0; i < n; i++ )
            for( j = 0; j < n; j++ )
                sum++;
```

```
(3)     sum = 0;
        for( i = 0; i < n; i++ )
            for( j = 0; j < n * n; j++ )
                sum++;
```

```
(4)     sum = 0;
        for( i = 0; i < n; i++ )
            for( j = 0; j < i; j++ )
                sum++;
```

```
(5)     sum = 0;
        for( i = 0; i < n; i++ )
            for( j = 0; j < i * i; j++ )
                for( k = 0; k < j; k++ )
                    sum++;
```

```
(6)     sum = 0;
        for( i = 1; i < n; i++ )
            for( j = 1; j < i * i; j++ )
                if( j % i == 0 )
                    for( k = 0; k < j; k++ )
                        sum++;
```

2.8 Suppose you need to generate a *random* permutation of the first N integers. For example, $\{4, 3, 1, 5, 2\}$ and $\{3, 1, 4, 2, 5\}$ are legal permutations, but $\{5, 4, 1, 2, 1\}$ is not, because one number (1) is duplicated and another (3) is missing. This routine is often used in simulation of algorithms. We assume the existence of a random number generator, r, with method randInt(i, j), that generates integers between i and j with equal probability. Here are three algorithms:

1. Fill the array a from a[0] to a[n-1] as follows: To fill a[i], generate random numbers until you get one that is not already in a[0], a[1], ..., a[i-1].

2. Same as algorithm (1), but keep an extra array called the **used** array. When a random number, **ran**, is first put in the array a, set **used[ran]** = **true**. This means that when filling a[i] with a random number, you can test in one step to see whether the random number has been used, instead of the (possibly) i steps in the first algorithm.

3. Fill the array such that a[i] = i + 1. Then

   ```
   for( i = 1; i < n; i++ )
       swapReferences( a[ i ], a[ randInt( 0, i ) ] );
   ```

   a. Prove that all three algorithms generate only legal permutations and that all permutations are equally likely.
   b. Give as accurate (Big-Oh) an analysis as you can of the *expected* running time of each algorithm.
   c. Write (separate) programs to execute each algorithm 10 times, to get a good average. Run program (1) for N = 250, 500, 1,000, 2,000; program (2) for N = 2,500, 5,000, 10,000, 20,000, 40,000, 80,000; and program (3) for N = 10,000, 20,000, 40,000, 80,000, 160,000, 320,000, 640,000.
   d. Compare your analysis with the actual running times.
   e. What is the worst-case running time of each algorithm?

2.9 Complete the table in Figure 2.2 with estimates for the running times that were too long to simulate. Interpolate the running times for these algorithms and estimate the time required to compute the maximum subsequence sum of 1 million numbers. What assumptions have you made?

2.10 Determine, for the typical algorithms that you use to perform calculations by hand, the running time to do the following:

    a. Add two N-digit integers.

    b. Multiply two N-digit integers.

    c. Divide two N-digit integers.

2.11 An algorithm takes 0.5 ms for input size 100. How long will it take for input size 500 if the running time is the following (assume low-order terms are negligible):

    a. linear

    b. $O(N \log N)$

    c. quadratic

    d. cubic

2.12 An algorithm takes 0.5 ms for input size 100. How large a problem can be solved in 1 min if the running time is the following (assume low-order terms are negligible):

    a. linear

    b. $O(N \log N)$

    c. quadratic

    d. cubic

2.13 How much time is required to compute $f(x) = \sum_{i=0}^{N} a_i x^i$:

    a. Using a simple routine to perform exponentiation?

    b. Using the routine in Section 2.4.4?

2.14 Consider the following algorithm (known as *Horner's rule*) to evaluate $f(x) = \sum_{i=0}^{N} a_i x^i$:

```
poly = 0;
for( i = n; i >= 0; i-- )
    poly = x * poly + a[i];
```

    a. Show how the steps are performed by this algorithm for $x = 3$, $f(x) = 4x^4 + 8x^3 + x + 2$.

    b. Explain why this algorithm works.

    c. What is the running time of this algorithm?

2.15 Give an efficient algorithm to determine if there exists an integer i such that $A_i = i$ in an array of integers $A_1 < A_2 < A_3 < \cdots < A_N$. What is the running time of your algorithm?

2.16 Write an alternative **gcd** algorithm based on the following observations (arrange so that $a > b$):

    • $gcd(a, b) = 2gcd(a/2, b/2)$ if a and b are both even.

    • $gcd(a, b) = gcd(a/2, b)$ if a is even and b is odd.

    • $gcd(a, b) = gcd(a, b/2)$ if a is odd and b is even.

    • $gcd(a, b) = gcd((a + b)/2), (a - b)/2)$ if a and b are both odd.

2.17 Give efficient algorithms (along with running time analyses) to:

    a. Find the minimum subsequence sum.

   *b. Find the minimum *positive* subsequence sum.

   *c. Find the maximum subsequence *product*.

2.18 An important problem in numerical analysis is to find a solution to the equation $f(X) = 0$ for some arbitrary f. If the function is continuous and has two points *low* and *high* such that $f(low)$ and $f(high)$ have opposite signs, then a root must exist between *low* and *high* and can be found by a binary search. Write a function that takes as parameters f, *low*, and *high* and solves for a zero. (To implement a generic function as a parameter, pass an object that implements the `Function` interface. The `Function` interface has a single method `f`.) What must you do to ensure termination?

2.19 The maximum contiguous subsequence sum algorithms in the text do not give any indication of the actual sequence. Modify them so that they return in a single object the value of the maximum subsequence and the indices of the actual sequence.

2.20 a. Write a program to determine if a positive integer, N, is prime.

 b. In terms of N, what is the worst-case running time of your program? (You should be able to do this in $O(\sqrt{N})$.)

 c. Let B equal the number of bits in the binary representation of N. What is the value of B?

 d. In terms of B, what is the worst-case running time of your program?

 e. Compare the running times to determine if a 20-bit number and a 40-bit number are prime.

 f. Is it more reasonable to give the running time in terms of N or B? Why?

*2.21 The Sieve of Eratosthenes is a method used to compute all primes less than N. We begin by making a table of integers 2 to N. We find the smallest integer, i, that is not crossed out, print i, and cross out i, $2i$, $3i$, ... When $i > \sqrt{N}$, the algorithm terminates. What is the running time of this algorithm?

2.22 Show that X^{62} can be computed with only eight multiplications.

2.23 Write the fast exponentiation routine without recursion.

2.24 Give a precise count on the number of multiplications used by the fast exponentiation routine. (*Hint:* Consider the binary representation of N.)

2.25 Programs A and B are analyzed and found to have worst-case running times no greater than $150N \log_2 N$ and N^2, respectively. Answer the following questions, if possible:

 a. Which program has the better guarantee on the running time, for large values of N ($N > 10,000$)?

 b. Which program has the better guarantee on the running time, for small values of N ($N < 100$)?

 c. Which program will run faster *on average* for $N = 1,000$?

 d. Is it possible that program B will run faster than program A on *all* possible inputs?

2.26 A majority element in an array, A, of size N is an element that appears more than $N/2$ times (thus, there is at most one). For example, the array

$$3, 3, 4, 2, 4, 4, 2, 4, 4$$

has a majority element (4), whereas the array

$$3, 3, 4, 2, 4, 4, 2, 4$$

does not. If there is no majority element, your program should indicate this. Here is a sketch of an algorithm to solve the problem:

First, a *candidate* majority element is found (this is the harder part). This candidate is the only element that could possibly be the majority element. The second step determines if this candidate is actually the majority. This is just a sequential search through the array. To find a candidate in the array, A, form a second array, B. Then compare A_1 and A_2. If they are equal, add one of these to B; otherwise do nothing. Then compare A_3 and A_4. Again if they are equal, add one of these to B; otherwise do nothing. Continue in this fashion until the entire array is read. Then recursively find a candidate for B; this is the candidate for A (why?).

   a. How does the recursion terminate?

 *b. How is the case where N is odd handled?

 *c. What is the running time of the algorithm?

   d. How can we avoid using an extra array B?

 *e. Write a program to compute the majority element.

2.27 The input is an N by N matrix of numbers that is already in memory. Each individual row is increasing from left to right. Each individual column is increasing from top to bottom. Give an $O(N)$ worst-case algorithm that decides if a number X is in the matrix.

2.28 Design efficient algorithms that take an array of positive numbers **a**, and determine:

   a. the maximum value of **a[j]+a[i]**, with **j** $\geq$ **i**.

   b. the maximum value of **a[j]-a[i]**, with **j** $\geq$ **i**.

   c. the maximum value of **a[j]*a[i]**, with **j** $\geq$ **i**.

   d. the maximum value of **a[j]/a[i]**, with **j** $\geq$ **i**.

*2.29 Why is it important to assume that integers in our computer model have a fixed size?

2.30 Consider the word puzzle problem described in Chapter 1. Suppose we fix the size of the longest word to be 10 characters.

   a. In terms of R and C, which are the number of rows and columns in the puzzle, and W, which is the number of words, what are the running times of the algorithms described in Chapter 1?

   b. Suppose the word list is presorted. Show how to use binary search to obtain an algorithm with significantly better running time.

2.31 Suppose that line 5 in the binary search routine had the statement **low = mid** instead of **low = mid + 1**. Would the routine still work?

2.32 Implement the binary search so that only one two-way comparison is performed in each iteration. (The text implementation uses three-way comparisons. Assume that only a **lessThan** method is available.)

2.33 Suppose that lines 6 and 7 in algorithm 3 (Fig. 2.7) are replaced by

```
/* 6*/    maxLeftSum  = maxSubSum( a, left, center - 1 );
/* 7*/    maxRightSum = maxSubSum( a, center, right );
```

Would the routine still work?

*2.34 The inner loop of the cubic maximum subsequence sum algorithm performs $N(N + 1)(N + 2)/6$ iterations of the innermost code. The quadratic version performs $N(N + 1)/2$ iterations. The linear version performs N iterations. What pattern is evident? Can you give a combinatoric explanation of this phenomenon?

REFERENCES

Analysis of the running time of algorithms was first made popular by Knuth in the three-part series [5], [6], and [7]. Analysis of the *gcd* algorithm appears in [6]. Another early text on the subject is [1].

Big-Oh, big-omega, big-theta, and little-oh notation were advocated by Knuth in [8]. There is still not uniform agreement on the matter, especially when it comes to using $\Theta()$. Many people prefer to use $O()$, even though it is less expressive. Additionally, $O()$ is still used in some corners to express a lower bound, when $\Omega()$ is called for.

The maximum subsequence sum problem is from [3]. The series of books [2], [3], and [4] show how to optimize programs for speed.

1. A. V. Aho, J. E. Hopcroft, and J. D. Ullman, *The Design and Analysis of Computer Algorithms,* Addison-Wesley, Reading, Mass., 1974.
2. J. L. Bentley, *Writing Efficient Programs,* Prentice Hall, Englewood Cliffs, N.J., 1982.
3. J. L. Bentley, *Programming Pearls,* Addison-Wesley, Reading, Mass., 1986.
4. J. L. Bentley, *More Programming Pearls,* Addison-Wesley, Reading, Mass., 1988.
5. D. E. Knuth, *The Art of Computer Programming, Vol 1: Fundamental Algorithms,* 3d ed., Addison-Wesley, Reading, Mass., 1997.
6. D. E. Knuth, *The Art of Computer Programming, Vol 2: Seminumerical Algorithms,* 3d ed., Addison-Wesley, Reading, Mass., 1998.
7. D. E. Knuth, *The Art of Computer Programming, Vol 3: Sorting and Searching,* 2d ed., Addison-Wesley, Reading, Mass., 1998.
8. D. E. Knuth, "Big Omicron and Big Omega and Big Theta," *ACM SIGACT News,* 8 (1976), 18–23.

CHAPTER 3

Lists, Stacks, and Queues

This chapter discusses three of the most simple and basic data structures. Virtually every significant program will use at least one of these structures explicitly, and a stack is always implicitly used in a program, whether or not you declare one. Among the highlights of this chapter, we will

- Introduce the concept of Abstract Data Types (ADTs).
- Show how to efficiently perform operations on lists.
- Introduce the stack ADT and its use in implementing recursion.
- Introduce the queue ADT and its use in operating systems and algorithm design.

Because these data structures are so important, one might expect that they are hard to implement. In fact, they are extremely easy to code up; the main difficulty is maintaining enough discipline to write good general-purpose code for routines that are generally only a few lines long.

3.1. Abstract Data Types (ADTs)

An *abstract data type* (ADT) is a set of objects together with a set of operations. Abstract data types are mathematical abstractions; nowhere in an ADT's definition is there any mention of *how* the set of operations is implemented. Objects such as lists, sets, and graphs, along with their operations, can be viewed as abstract data types, just as integers, reals, and booleans are data types. Integers, reals, and booleans have operations associated with them, and so do abstract data types. For the set ADT, we might have such operations as *union, intersection, size,* and *complement.* Alternatively, we might only want the two operations *union* and *find,* which would define a different ADT on the set.

The Java class allows for the implementation of ADTs, with appropriate hiding of implementation details. Thus any other part of the program that needs to perform an operation on the ADT can do so by calling the appropriate method. If for some reason implementation details need to be changed, it should be easy to do so by merely changing the routines that perform the ADT operations. This change, in a perfect world, would be completely transparent to the rest of the program.

There is no rule telling us which operations must be supported for each ADT; this is a design decision. Error handling and tie breaking (where appropriate) are also generally up to the program designer. Some of the Java alternatives for error handling were outlined in Section 1.5. The three data structures that we will study in this chapter are primary examples of ADTs. We will see how each can be implemented in several ways, but if they are done correctly, the programs that use them will not need to know which implementation was used.*

3.2. The List ADT

We will deal with a general list of the form $A_1, A_2, A_3, \ldots, A_N$. We say that the size of this list is N. We will call the special list of size 0 an *empty list.*

For any list except the empty list, we say that A_{i+1} follows (or succeeds) A_i ($i < N$) and that A_{i-1} precedes A_i ($i > 1$). The first element of the list is A_1, and the last element is A_N. We will not define the predecessor of A_1 or the successor of A_N. The *position* of element A_i in a list is i. Throughout this discussion, we will assume, to simplify matters, that the elements in the list are integers, but in general, arbitrarily complex elements are allowed (and easily handled by a generic Java class).

Associated with these "definitions" is a set of operations that we would like to perform on the list ADT. Some popular operations are `printList` and `makeEmpty`, which do the obvious things; `find`, which returns the position of the first occurrence of an item; `insert` and `remove`, which generally insert and remove some element from some position in the list; and `findKth`, which returns the element in some position (specified as an argument). If the list is 34, 12, 52, 16, 12, then `find(52)` might return 3; `insert(x,3)` might make the list into 34, 12, 52, x, 16, 12 (if we insert after the position given); and `remove(52)` might turn that list into 34, 12, x, 16, 12.

Of course, the interpretation of what is appropriate for a method is entirely up to the programmer, as is the handling of special cases (for example, what does `find(1)` return above?). We could also add operations such as `next` and `previous`, which would take a position as argument and return the position of the successor and predecessor, respectively.

3.2.1. Simple Array Implementation of Lists

All of these instructions can be implemented just by using an array. Even if the array is dynamically allocated, an estimate of the maximum size of the list is required. Usually this requires a high overestimate, which wastes considerable space. This could be a serious limitation, especially if there are many lists of unknown size.

An array implementation allows `printList` and `find` to be carried out in linear time, which is as good as can be expected, and the `findKth` operation takes constant time. However, insertion and deletion are expensive. For example, inserting at position 0 (which amounts to making a new first element) requires first pushing the entire array down one spot to make room, whereas deleting the first element requires shifting all the elements in the list up one, so the worst case of these operations is $O(N)$. On average, half of the list needs to be moved for either operation, so linear time is still required. Merely building a list by N successive inserts would require quadratic time.

---

*Each implementation has a different class name, so the code that uses the ADT will need a minor change to switch implementations. This is required because classes must be declared in a file of the same name, and the online code resides in one directory.

Because the running time for insertions and deletions is so slow and the list size must be known in advance, simple arrays are generally not used to implement lists. The rest of this section deals with the alternative: the *linked list*.

3.2.2. Linked Lists

In order to avoid the linear cost of insertion and deletion, we need to ensure that the list is not stored contiguously, since otherwise entire parts of the list will need to be moved. Figure 3.1 shows the general idea of a *linked list*.

The linked list consists of a series of nodes, which are not necessarily adjacent in memory. Each node contains the element and a link to a node containing its successor. We call this the **next** link. The last cell's **next** link references **null**.

To execute **printList** or **find(x)** we merely start at the first node in the list and then traverse the list by following the **next** links. This operation is clearly linear-time, although the constant is likely to be larger than if an array implementation were used. The **findKth** operation is no longer quite as efficient as an array implementation; **findKth(i)** takes $O(i)$ time and works by traversing down the list in the obvious manner. In practice, this bound is pessimistic, because frequently the calls to **findKth** are in sorted order (by i). As an example, **findKth(2)**, **findKth(3)**, **findKth(4)**, and **findKth(6)** can all be executed in one scan down the list.

The **remove** method can be executed in one **next** reference change. Figure 3.2 shows the result of deleting the third element in the original list.

The **insert** method requires obtaining a new node from the system by using a **new** call and then executing two reference maneuvers. The general idea is shown in Figure 3.3. The dashed line represents the old **next** reference.

Figure 3.1 A linked list

Figure 3.2 Deletion from a linked list

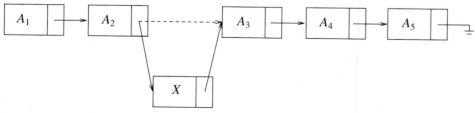

Figure 3.3 Insertion into a linked list

3.2.3. Programming Details

The description above is actually enough to get everything working, but there are several places where you are likely to go wrong. First of all, there is no really obvious way to insert at the front of the list from the definitions given. Second, removing from the front of the list is a special case, because it changes the start of the list; careless coding will lose the list. A third problem concerns deletion in general. Although the link moves above are simple, the deletion algorithm requires us to keep track of the node *before* the one that we want to delete.

It turns out that one simple change solves all three problems. We will keep a sentinel node, which is sometimes referred to as a *header* or *dummy* node. This is a common practice, which we will see several times in the future. Our convention will be that the header is in position 0. Figure 3.4 shows a linked list with a header representing the list $A_1, A_2, \ldots, A_5$. Figure 3.5 shows an empty linked list.

To avoid the problems associated with deletions, we need to write a routine `findPrevious`, which will return the position of the predecessor of the cell we wish to delete. If we use a header, then if we wish to delete the first element in the list, `findPrevious` will return the position of the header. The use of a header node is somewhat controversial. Some people argue that avoiding special cases is not sufficient justification for adding fictitious cells; they view the use of header nodes as little more than old-style hacking. Even so, we will use them here, precisely because they allow us to show the basic link manipulations without obscuring the code with special cases. Otherwise, whether or not a header should be used is a matter of personal preference.

As examples, we will illustrate a complete list ADT (for one subset of operations). As suggested in the above description, the (linked) list ADT is implemented as three separate classes: one class is the list itself (`LinkedList`), another represents the node (`ListNode`), and the third represents the position (`LinkedListItr`). These classes will all be part of the `DataStructures` package, which will allow them to look at each other's internal details without having to grant this access to nonpackage classes.

Figure 3.6 is the node class, `ListNode`. The class consists of two fields: the stored element and the link to the next node. The only methods are the constructors. Notice that `ListNode` is not a public class; instead, the lack of a visibility specifier means that it is

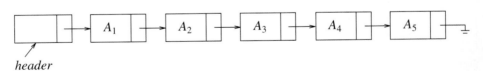

header

Figure 3.4 Linked list with a header

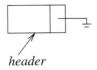

header

Figure 3.5 Empty list with header

```
package DataStructures;

class ListNode
{
        // Constructors
    ListNode( Object theElement )
    {
        this( theElement, null );
    }

    ListNode( Object theElement, ListNode n )
    {
        element = theElement;
        next    = n;
    }

        // Friendly data; accessible by other package routines
    Object    element;
    ListNode next;
}
```

Figure 3.6 Type declaration for linked list node

```
package DataStructures;

public class LinkedListItr
{
    LinkedListItr( ListNode theNode )
    {
        current = theNode;
    }

    public boolean isPastEnd( )
    {
        return current == null;
    }

    public Object retrieve( )
    {
        return isPastEnd( ) ? null : current.element;
    }

    public void advance( )
    {
        if( !isPastEnd( ) )
            current = current.next;
    }

    ListNode current;     // Current position
}
```

Figure 3.7 Iterator class for linked lists

package friendly. This means that `ListNode` is a type that is visible only inside the `DataStructures` package. Similarly, its methods and data fields are also package friendly.

Next, in Figure 3.7, is the class that implements the concept of position, namely `LinkedListItr`. This class is also known as an *iterator class*, because, as we will see shortly, it provides methods that can be used to iterate through the list. `LinkedListItr` stores a reference to a `ListNode`, which represents the current position of the iterator. `isPastEnd` is `true` if the position is past the end of the list, `retrieve` returns the element stored in the current position, and `advance` advances the current position to the next node. The constructor for `LinkedListItr` requires a node that is to be the current node. Notice that this constructor is package friendly; thus `LinkedListItr` objects cannot be constructed by client methods. Instead, the general idea is that the `LinkedList` class returns preconstructed `LinkedListItr` objects, as appropriate.

The `LinkedList` class skeleton is shown in Figure 3.8 (some of its methods are implemented in later figures, while others are implemented in a compressed form to save space). The single data field is a reference to the header node that is allocated by the constructor. `makeEmpty` and `isEmpty` are easily implemented short one-liners. The methods `zeroth` and `first` return iterators corresponding to the header and first element, respectively. Other routines will either search the list for some item or change the list via insertion or deletion.

Figure 3.9 illustrates how the `LinkedList` and `LinkedListItr` classes interact. The `printList` method outputs the contents of a list. This method can be implemented in

```
package DataStructures;

public class LinkedList
{
    public LinkedList( )
      { header = new ListNode( null ); }

    public boolean isEmpty( )
      { return header.next == null; }
    public void makeEmpty( )
      { header.next = null; }

    public LinkedListItr zeroth( )
      { return new LinkedListItr( header ); }
    public LinkedListItr first( )
      { return new LinkedListItr( header.next ); }

    public LinkedListItr find( Object x )
      { /* Figure 3.10 */ }
    public void remove( Object x )
      { /* Figure 3.11 */ }
    public LinkedListItr findPrevious( Object x )
      { /* Figure 3.12 */ }
    public void insert( Object x, LinkedListItr p )
      { /* Figure 3.13 */ }

    private ListNode header;
}
```

Figure 3.8 `LinkedList` class skeleton

```
        // Simple print method
        public static void printList( LinkedList theList )
        {
            if( theList.isEmpty( ) )
                System.out.print( "Empty list" );
            else
            {
                LinkedListItr itr = theList.first( );
                for( ; !itr.isPastEnd( ); itr.advance( ) )
                    System.out.print( itr.retrieve( ) + " " );
            }

            System.out.println( );
        }
```

Figure 3.9 Method to print a list

any class, because it uses only public methods and also uses a typical iteration sequence of obtaining a starting point (via **first**), testing that we have not gone past the ending point (via **isPastEnd**), and advancing in each iteration (via **advance**).

An important issue is whether all three classes are really necessary. For instance, couldn't we just have the **LinkedList** class maintain a notion of a current position? Although this is a feasible option, and will work for many applications, using a separate iterator class expresses the abstraction that the position and list are really separate objects. Further, it allows for a list to be accessed in several places simultaneously. For instance, to remove a sublist from a list, we can easily add a **remove** operation to the list class that uses two iterators to specify the starting and ending points of the sublist that is to be removed. Without the iterator class, this would be more difficult to express.

We can now implement the remaining **LinkedList** methods. First is **find**, shown in Figure 3.10, which returns the position in the list of some element. Line 2 takes advantage of the fact that the *and (&&)* operation is *short-circuited:* if the first half of the *and* is false, the result is automatically false and the second half is not executed.

```
        /**
         * Return iterator corresponding to the first node containing an item.
         * @param x the item to search for.
         * @return an iterator; iterator isPastEnd if item is not found.
         */
        public LinkedListItr find( Object x )
        {
/* 1*/      ListNode itr = header.next;

/* 2*/      while( itr != null && !itr.element.equals( x ) )
/* 3*/          itr = itr.next;

/* 4*/      return new LinkedListItr( itr );
        }
```

Figure 3.10 find routine

```
/**
 * Remove the first occurrence of an item.
 * @param x the item to remove.
 */
public void remove( Object x )
{
    LinkedListItr p = findPrevious( x );

    if( p.current.next != null )
        p.current.next = p.current.next.next;   // Bypass deleted node
}
```

Figure 3.11 Deletion routine for linked lists

```
         /**
          * Return iterator prior to the first node containing an item.
          * @param x the item to search for.
          * @return appropriate iterator if the item is found. Otherwise, the
          * iterator corresponding to the last element in the list is returned.
          */
         public LinkedListItr findPrevious( Object x )
         {
/* 1*/       ListNode itr = header;

/* 2*/       while( itr.next != null && !itr.next.element.equals( x ) )
/* 3*/           itr = itr.next;

/* 4*/       return new LinkedListItr( itr );
         }
```

Figure 3.12 findPrevious—the find routine for use with remove

Some programmers find it tempting to code the **find** routine recursively, possibly because it avoids the sloppy termination condition. We shall see later that this is a very bad idea and should be avoided at all costs.

Our next routine will remove some element **x** from the list. We need to decide what to do if **x** occurs more than once or not at all. Our routine removes the first occurrence of **x** and does nothing if **x** is not in the list. To do this, we find **p**, which is the cell prior to the one containing **x**, via a call to **findPrevious**. The code to implement this is shown in Figure 3.11. The **findPrevious** routine is similar to **find** and is shown in Figure 3.12.

The last routine we will write is an insertion routine. We will pass an element to be inserted and a position **p**. Our particular insertion routine will insert an element *after* the position implied by **p**. This decision is arbitrary and is meant to show that there are no set rules for what insertion does. It is quite possible to insert the new element into position **p** (which means before the element currently in position **p**), but doing this requires knowledge of the element before position **p**. This could be obtained by a call to **findPrevious**. It is thus important to comment what you are doing. This has been done in Figure 3.13.

Notice that the **insert** routine makes no use of the list it is in; it depends only on **p**. The exercises ask you to add tests to ensure that the iterator corresponds to the list. This is done by adding a reference to the list as an extra data member for the list iterator.

```
/**
 * Insert after p.
 * @param x the item to insert.
 * @param p the position prior to the newly inserted item.
 */
public void insert( Object x, LinkedListItr p )
{
    if( p != null && p.current != null )
        p.current.next = new ListNode( x, p.current.next );
}
```

Figure 3.13 Insertion routine for linked lists

   With the exception of the `find` and `findPrevious` routines (and `remove`, which calls `findPrevious`), all of the operations we have coded take $O(1)$ time. This is because in all cases only a fixed number of instructions are performed, no matter how large the list is. For the `find` and `findPrevious` routines, the running time is $O(N)$ in the worst case, because the entire list might need to be traversed if the element either is not found or is last in the list. On average, the running time is $O(N)$, because on average, half the list must be traversed.

3.2.4. Doubly Linked Lists

Sometimes it is convenient to traverse lists backwards. The standard implementation does not help here, but the solution is simple. Merely add to the node an extra field that stores a link to the previous node. The cost of this extra link is an increase in the space requirement and a doubling of the cost of insertions and deletions because there are more links to fix. On the other hand, it simplifies deletion, because you no longer have to refer to an item by using a reference to the previous node; this information is now at hand. Figure 3.14 shows a doubly linked list.

3.2.5. Circular Linked Lists

A popular convention is to have the last node keep a link back to the first. This can be done with or without a header (if the header is present, the last node links to it) and can also be done with doubly linked lists (the first cell's previous link is to the last cell). This clearly affects some of the tests, but the structure is popular in some applications. Figure 3.15 shows a double circular linked list with no header.

Figure 3.14 A doubly linked list

Figure 3.15 A double circular linked list

3.2.6. Examples

We provide three examples that use linked lists. The first is a simple way to represent single-variable polynomials. The second is a method to sort in linear time, for some special cases. Finally, we show a complicated example of how linked lists might be used to keep track of course registration at a university.

The Polynomial ADT

We can define an abstract data type for single-variable polynomials (with nonnegative exponents) by using a list. Let $f(x) = \sum_{i=0}^{N} a_i x^i$. If most of the coefficients a_i are nonzero, we can use a simple array to store the coefficients. We could then write routines to perform addition, subtraction, multiplication, differentiation, and other operations on these polynomials. In this case, we might use the type declarations given in Figure 3.16. We could then write routines to perform various operations. Two possibilities are addition and multiplication; these are shown in Figures 3.17 to 3.19. Ignoring the time to initialize the output polynomials to zero, the running time of the multiplication routine is proportional to the product of the degree of the two input polynomials. This is adequate for dense

```
public class Polynomial
{
    public Polynomial( )
      { zeroPolynomial( ); }
    public void insertTerm( int coef, int exp )
      { /* Exercise */ }

    public void zeroPolynomial( )
      { /* Figure 3.17 */ }
    public Polynomial add( Polynomial rhs )
      { /* Figure 3.18 */ }
    public Polynomial multiply( Polynomial rhs ) throws Overflow
      { /* Figure 3.19 */ }
    public void print( )
      { /* See online code */ }

    public static final int MAX_DEGREE = 100;
    private int coeffArray[ ] = new int [ MAX_DEGREE + 1 ];
    private int highPower = 0;
}
```

Figure 3.16 Type declarations for array implementation of the polynomial ADT

```
public void zeroPolynomial( )
{
    for( int i = 0; i <= MAX_DEGREE; i++ )
        coeffArray[ i ] = 0;
    highPower = 0;
}
```

Figure 3.17 Method to initialize a polynomial to zero

```
public Polynomial add( Polynomial rhs )
{
    Polynomial sum = new Polynomial( );

    sum.highPower = max( highPower, rhs.highPower );
    for( int i = sum.highPower; i >= 0; i-- )
        sum.coeffArray[ i ] = coeffArray[ i ] + rhs.coeffArray[ i ];
    return sum;
}
```

Figure 3.18 Method to add two polynomials

```
public Polynomial multiply( Polynomial rhs ) throws Overflow
{
    Polynomial product = new Polynomial( );

    product.highPower = highPower + rhs.highPower;
    if( product.highPower > MAX_DEGREE )
        throw new Overflow( );
    for( int i = 0; i <= highPower; i++ )
        for( int j = 0; j <= rhs.highPower; j++ )
            product.coeffArray[ i + j ] +=
                    coeffArray[ i ] * rhs.coeffArray[ j ];
    return product;
}
```

Figure 3.19 Method to multiply two polynomials

polynomials, where most of the terms are present, but if $P_1(x) = 10x^{1000} + 5x^{14} + 1$ and $P_2(x) = 3x^{1990} - 2x^{1492} + 11x + 5$, then the running time is likely to be unacceptable. One can see that most of the time is spent multiplying zeros and stepping through what amounts to nonexistent parts of the input polynomials. This is always undesirable.

An alternative is to use a singly linked list. Each term in the polynomial is contained in one cell, and the cells are sorted in decreasing order of exponents. For instance, the linked lists in Figure 3.20 represent $P_1(x)$ and $P_2(x)$. We could then use the declarations in Figure 3.21.

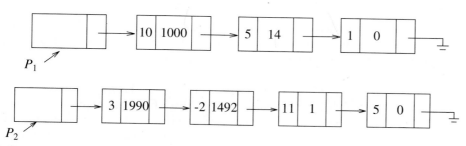

Figure 3.20 Linked list representations of two polynomials

```
public class Literal
{
    // Various constructors (not shown)

    int coefficient;
    int exponent;
}


public class Polynomial
{
    public Polynomial( )
      { /* Exercise */ }
    public void insertTerm( int coef, int exp )
      { /* Exercise */ }

    public void zeroPolynomial( )
      { /* Exercise */ }
    public Polynomial add( Polynomial rhs )
      { /* Exercise */ }
    public Polynomial multiply( Polynomial rhs )
      { /* Exercise */ }
    public void print( )
      { /* Exercise */ }

    private List terms;    // A List of Literals, sorted by exponent
}
```

Figure 3.21 Class skeletons for linked list implementation of the Polynomial ADT

The operations would then be straightforward to implement. The only potential difficulty is that when two polynomials are multiplied, the resultant polynomial will have to have like terms combined. There are several ways to do this, but we leave this as an exercise.

Radix Sort

A second example where linked lists are used is called *radix sort*. Radix sort is sometimes known as *card sort,* because it was used, until the advent of modern computers, to sort old-style punch cards.

If we have N integers in the range 1 to M (or 0 to $M - 1$), we can use this information to obtain a fast sort known as *bucket sort*. We keep an array called **count**, of size M, which is initialized to zero. Thus, **count** has M cells (or buckets), which are initially empty. When A_i is read, increment (by 1) **count**$[A_i]$. After all the input is read, scan the **count** array, printing out a representation of the sorted list. This algorithm takes $O(M + N)$; the proof is left as an exercise. If $M = \Theta(N)$, then bucket sort is $O(N)$.

Radix sort is a generalization of this. The easiest way to see what happens is by example. Suppose we have 10 numbers, in the range 0 to 999, that we would like to sort. In general, this is N numbers in the range 0 to $N^P - 1$ for some constant P. Obviously, we cannot use bucket sort; there would be too many buckets. The trick is to use several passes of bucket sort. The natural algorithm would be to bucket-sort by the most significant "digit" (digit

0	1	512	343	64	125	216	27	8	729
0	1	2	3	4	5	6	7	8	9

Figure 3.22 Buckets after first step of radix sort

is taken to base N), then the next most significant, and so on. That algorithm does not work because recursively bucket sorting each bucket would require keeping track of too many bucket boundaries. However, if we perform bucket sorts by the least significant "digit" first, then the algorithm works. Of course, more than one number could fall into the same bucket and, unlike the original bucket sort, these numbers could be different, so we keep them in a list. Notice that all the numbers could have some digit in common, so if a simple array were used for the lists, each array would have to be of size N, for a total space requirement of $\Theta(N^2)$.

The following example shows the action of radix sort on 10 numbers. The input is 64, 8, 216, 512, 27, 729, 0, 1, 343, 125 (the first 10 cubes, arranged randomly). The first step bucket-sorts by the least significant digit. In this case the math is in base 10 (to make things simple), but do not assume this in general. The buckets are as shown in Figure 3.22, so the list, sorted by least significant digit, is 0, 1, 512, 343, 64, 125, 216, 27, 8, 729. These are now sorted by the next least significant digit (the tens digit here) (see Fig. 3.23). Pass 2 gives output 0, 1, 8, 512, 216, 125, 27, 729, 343, 64. This list is now sorted with respect to the two least significant digits. The final pass, shown in Figure 3.24, bucket-sorts by the most significant digit. The final list is 0, 1, 8, 27, 64, 125, 216, 343, 512, 729.

To see that the algorithm works, notice that the only possible failure would occur if two numbers came out of the same bucket in the wrong order. But the previous passes ensure

| 8 | | 729 | | | | | | | |
| 1 | 216 | 27 | | | | | | | |
0	512	125		343		64			
0	1	2	3	4	5	6	7	8	9

Figure 3.23 Buckets after the second pass of radix sort

64									
27									
8									
1									
0	125	216	343		512		729		
0	1	2	3	4	5	6	7	8	9

Figure 3.24 Buckets after the last pass of radix sort

that when several numbers enter a bucket, they enter in sorted order. The running time is $O(P(N + B))$ where P is the number of passes, N is the number of elements to sort, and B is the number of buckets. In our case, $B = N$; typically $B \ll N$, and P is constant, yielding $O(N)$.

As an example, we could sort all 32-bit integers by radix sort, if we did three passes over a bucket size of 2^{11}. This algorithm would always be $O(N)$ on this computer, but probably still not as efficient as some of the algorithms we shall see in Chapter 7, because of the high constant involved. (Remember that a factor of $\log N$ is not all that high, and this algorithm would have the overhead of maintaining linked lists.)

Multilists

Our last example shows a more complicated use of linked structures. A university with 40,000 students and 2,500 courses needs to be able to generate two types of reports. The first report lists the registration for each class, and the second report lists, by student, the classes that each student is registered for.

The obvious implementation might be to use a two-dimensional array. Such an array would have 100 million entries. The average student registers for about three courses, so only 120,000 of these entries, or roughly 0.1 percent, would actually have meaningful data.

What is needed is a list for each class containing the students in the class. We also need a list for each student containing the classes the student is registered for. Figure 3.25 shows our implementation.

As the figure shows, we have combined two lists into one. We call the result a *multilist*. All lists use a header and are circular. To list all of the students in class C3, we start at C3 and traverse its list (by going right). The first cell belongs to student S1. Although there

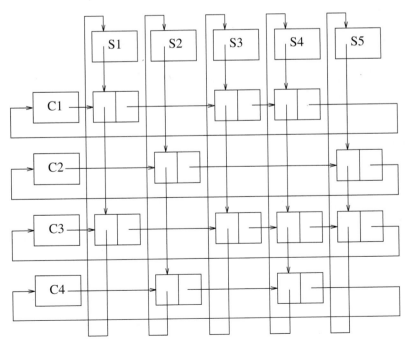

Figure 3.25 Multilist implementation for registration problem

is no explicit information to this effect, this can be determined by following the student's linked list until the header is reached. Once this is done, we return to C3's list (we stored the position we were at in the course list before we traversed the student's list) and find another cell, which can be determined to belong to S3. We can continue and find that S4 and S5 are also in this class. In a similar manner, we can determine, for any student, all of the classes in which the student is registered.

Using a circular list saves space but does so at the expense of time. In the worst case, if the first student was registered for every course, then every entry would need to be examined to determine all the course names for that student. Because in this application there are relatively few courses per student and few students per course, this is not likely to happen. If it were suspected that this could cause a problem, then each of the (nonheader) cells could have links directly back to the student and class header. This would double the space requirement but would simplify and speed the implementation.

3.2.7. Cursor Implementation of Linked Lists

Many languages, such as BASIC and FORTRAN, do not support dynamic linked structures. Those, such as C and C++ that do, occasionally find that the repeated calls to **new** are expensive. Sometimes an alternative implementation must be used. The method we will describe is known as a *cursor* implementation.

The two important features present in our implementation of linked lists are as follows:

1. The data are stored in a collection of nodes. Each node contains data and a link to the next node.

2. A new node can be obtained from the system's memory by a call to **new** and is automatically reclaimed when it is no longer referenced.

Our cursor implementation must be able to simulate this. The logical way to satisfy condition 1 is to have a **static** array of nodes. For any cell in the array, its array index can be used in place of a node reference.* Figure 3.26 gives the declarations for the node and iterator classes in the cursor implementation of linked lists. The code parallels that for the linked list class seen earlier in this chapter.

Figure 3.27 gives the class skeleton for the **CursorList** class. Notice that the array of nodes is stored in the **cursorSpace** array. To simulate condition 2, we must allow the equivalent of **new** for cells in the **cursorSpace** array. We will call this the **alloc** method. To do this, we will keep a list (the freelist) of cells that are not in any list. The freelist will use cell 0 as a header. The initial configuration is shown in Figure 3.28 (on page 72).

A value of 0 for **next** is the equivalent of a **null** reference. The initialization of **cursorSpace** is a straightforward loop and is done by a *static initializer*. The static initializer is called once, when the class is first loaded, and the array is shared amongst all instances of **CursorList**. To perform **alloc**, the first element (after the header) is removed from the freelist. Automatic reclamation of dereferenced nodes, however, is not easily done. Instead, we resort to a technique seen in many other languages: we provide a method that must be called by the programmer. This method is **free**. To implement **free**, we place the cell at the front of the freelist. Figure 3.29 (on page 72) shows the implementation of **alloc** and **free**. Notice that if there is no space available, we throw an **OutOfMemoryError**.

---

*Although we could still use a node reference, using the array index is a more general method for other languages.

```
class CursorNode
{
        // Constructors
    CursorNode( Object theElement )
    {
        this( theElement, 0 );
    }

    CursorNode( Object theElement, int n )
    {
        element = theElement;
        next    = n;
    }

        // Friendly data; accessible by other package routines
    Object element;
    int    next;
}


public class CursorListItr
{
    CursorListItr( int theNode )
    {
        current = theNode;
    }

    public boolean isPastEnd( )
    {
        return current == 0;
    }

    public Object retrieve( )
    {
        return isPastEnd( ) ? null
                            : CursorList.cursorSpace[ current ].element;
    }

    public void advance( )
    {
        if( !isPastEnd( ) )
            current = CursorList.cursorSpace[ current ].next;
    }

    int current;      // Current position
}
```

Figure 3.26 Node and iterator for cursor implementation of linked lists

```java
public class CursorList
{
    private static int alloc( )
      { /* Figure 3.29 */ }
    private static void free( int p )
      { /* Figure 3.29 */ }

    public CursorList( )
      { header = alloc( ); cursorSpace[ header ].next = 0; }

    public boolean isEmpty( )
      {  return cursorSpace[ header ].next == 0; }
    public void makeEmpty( )
      { /* Figure 3.34 */ }
    public CursorListItr zeroth( )
      { return new CursorListItr( header ); }
    public CursorListItr first( )
      { return new CursorListItr( cursorSpace[ header ].next ); }

    public CursorListItr find( Object x )
      { /* Figure 3.31 */ }
    public void insert( Object x, CursorListItr p )
      { /* Figure 3.32 */ }
    public void remove( Object x )
      { /* Figure 3.33 */ }
    public CursorListItr findPrevious( Object x )
      { /* See online code */ }

    private int header;
    static CursorNode [ ] cursorSpace;

    private static final int SPACE_SIZE = 100;

    static
    {
        cursorSpace = new CursorNode[ SPACE_SIZE ];
        for( int i = 0; i < SPACE_SIZE; i++ )
            cursorSpace[ i ] = new CursorNode( null, i + 1 );
        cursorSpace[ SPACE_SIZE - 1 ].next = 0;
    }
}
```

Figure 3.27 Class skeleton for CursorList

Slot	element	next
0		1
1		2
2		3
3		4
4		5
5		6
6		7
7		8
8		9
9		10
10		0

Figure 3.28 An initialized
cursorSpace

```
private static int alloc( )
{
    int p = cursorSpace[ 0 ].next;
    cursorSpace[ 0 ].next = cursorSpace[ p ].next;
    if( p == 0 )
        throw new OutOfMemoryError( );
    return p;
}

private static void free( int p )
{
    cursorSpace[ p ].element = null;
    cursorSpace[ p ].next = cursorSpace[ 0 ].next;
    cursorSpace[ 0 ].next = p;
}
```

Figure 3.29 Routines: alloc and free

Given this, the cursor implementation of linked lists is straightforward. For consistency, we will implement our lists with a header node. As an example, in Figure 3.30, if the value of L is 5 and the value of M is 3, then L represents the list a, b, e, and M represents the list c, d, f.

To write the methods for a cursor implementation of linked lists, we must pass and return the same parameters as the previous linked implementation.* The routines are straightforward. The function **find** in Figure 3.31 returns the position of **x** in the list. Figure 3.32 shows a cursor implementation of **insert**. The code to implement deletion is shown in Figure 3.33. Notice that we must save the index of the deleted node so it can be reclaimed

---

*The types are different so that both CursorList and LinkedList can be in the same online directory.

Slot	element	next
0	–	6
1	b	9
2	f	0
3	header	7
4	–	0
5	header	10
6	–	4
7	c	8
8	d	2
9	e	0
10	a	1

Figure 3.30 Example of a cursor implementation of linked lists

```
        /**
         * Return iterator corresponding to the first node containing an item.
         * @param x the item to search for.
         * @return an iterator; iterator isPastEnd if item is not found.
         */
        public CursorListItr find( Object x )
        {
/* 1*/      int itr = cursorSpace[ header ].next;

/* 2*/      while( itr != 0 && !cursorSpace[ itr ].element.equals( x ) )
/* 3*/          itr = cursorSpace[ itr ].next;

/* 4*/      return new CursorListItr( itr );
        }
```

Figure 3.31 find routine—cursor implementation

by a call to **free**. Finally, the code for **makeEmpty**, which must make sure the cells are reclaimed, is shown in Figure 3.34. Again, the interface for the cursor implementation is identical to the original implementation.

The crucial point is that these routines follow the ADT specification. They take specific arguments and perform specific operations. The implementation is transparent to the user. The cursor implementation could be used instead of the original linked list implementation, with virtually no change required in the rest of the code. If relatively few **finds** are performed, the cursor implementation could be significantly faster because of the lack of memory management routines. This trade-off, however, is very language and compiler dependent.

The freelist represents an interesting data structure in its own right. The cell that is removed from the freelist is the one that was most recently placed there by virtue of **free**.

```
/**
 * Insert after p.
 * @param x the item to insert.
 * @param p the position prior to the newly inserted item.
 */
public void insert( Object x, CursorListItr p )
{
    if( p != null && p.current != 0 )
    {
        int pos = p.current;
        int tmp = alloc( );

        cursorSpace[ tmp ].element = x;
        cursorSpace[ tmp ].next = cursorSpace[ pos ].next;
        cursorSpace[ pos ].next = tmp;
    }
}
```

Figure 3.32 Insertion routine for linked lists—cursor implementation

```
/**
 * Remove the first occurrence of an item.
 * @param x the item to remove.
 */
public void remove( Object x )
{
    CursorListItr p = findPrevious( x );
    int pos = p.current;

    if( cursorSpace[ pos ].next != 0 )
    {
        int tmp = cursorSpace[ pos ].next;
        cursorSpace[ pos ].next = cursorSpace[ tmp ].next;
        free( tmp );
    }
}
```

Figure 3.33 Deletion routine for linked lists—cursor implementation

```
/**
 * Make the list logically empty.
 */
public void makeEmpty( )
{
    while( !isEmpty( ) )
        remove( first( ).retrieve( ) );
}
```

Figure 3.34 makeEmpty for cursor implementation

Thus, the last cell placed on the freelist is the first cell taken off. The data structure that also has this property is known as a *stack*, and is the topic of the next section.

3.3. The Stack ADT

3.3.1. Stack Model

A *stack* is a list with the restriction that insertions and deletions can be performed in only one position, namely, the end of the list, called the *top*. The fundamental operations on a stack are **push**, which is equivalent to an insert, and **pop**, which deletes the most recently inserted element. The most recently inserted element can be examined prior to performing a **pop** by use of the **top** routine. A **pop** or **top** on an empty stack is generally considered an error in the stack ADT. On the other hand, running out of space when performing a **push** is an implementation limit but not an ADT error.

Stacks are sometimes known as LIFO (last in, first out) lists. The model depicted in Figure 3.35 signifies only that **push**es are input operations and **pop**s and **top**s are output. The usual operations to make empty stacks and test for emptiness are part of the repertoire, but essentially all that you can do to a stack is **push** and **pop**.

Figure 3.36 shows an abstract stack after several operations. The general model is that there is some element that is at the top of the stack, and it is the only element that is visible.

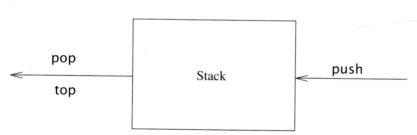

Figure 3.35 Stack model: input to a stack is by **push**, output is by **pop** and **top**

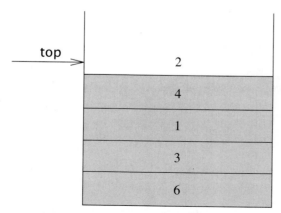

Figure 3.36 Stack model: only the top element is accessible

3.3.2. Implementation of Stacks

Since a stack is a list, any list implementation will do. We will give two popular implementations. One uses a linked structure and the other uses an array, but, as we saw in the previous section, if we use good programming principles, the calling routines do not need to know which method is being used.

Linked List Implementation of Stacks

The first implementation of a stack uses a singly linked list. We perform a **push** by inserting at the front of the list. We perform a **pop** by deleting the element at the front of the list. A **top** operation merely examines the element at the front of the list, returning its value. Sometimes the **pop** and **top** operations are combined into one. We could use calls to the linked list routines of the previous section, but we will rewrite the stack routines from scratch for the sake of clarity.

First, we give the class skeleton in Figure 3.37. We implement the stack without using a header. Several trivial routines, including the constructor, are implemented. Notice that the stack is never full.

The **push** is implemented as an insertion into the front of a linked list, where the front of the list serves as the top of the stack (see Fig. 3.38). **top** is performed by examining the element in the first position of the list (see Fig. 3.39). We implement **pop** as a deletion from the front of the list (see Fig. 3.40); we simply advance **topOfStack**. **pop** throws an exception if the stack is empty. An alternative is **topAndPop**, shown in Figure 3.41, which returns a reference to the removed item, or **null** if the stack was empty.

```
public class StackLi
{
    public StackLi( )
      { topOfStack = null; }

    public boolean isFull( )
      { return false; }
    public boolean isEmpty( )
      { return topOfStack == null; }
    public void makeEmpty( )
      { topOfStack = null; }

    public void push( Object x )
      { /* Figure 3.38 */ }
    public Object top( )
      { /* Figure 3.39 */ }
    public void pop( ) throws Underflow
      { /* Figure 3.40 */ }
    public Object topAndPop( )
      { /* Figure 3.41 */ }

    private ListNode topOfStack;
}
```

Figure 3.37 Class skeleton for linked list implementation of the stack ADT

```
/**
 * Insert a new item into the stack.
 * @param x the item to insert.
 */
public void push( Object x )
{
    topOfStack = new ListNode( x, topOfStack );
}
```

Figure 3.38 Routine to push onto a stack—linked list implementation

```
/**
 * Get the most recently inserted item in the stack.
 * Does not alter the stack.
 * @return the most recently inserted item in the stack, or null if empty.
 */
public Object top( )
{
    if( isEmpty( ) )
        return null;
    return topOfStack.element;
}
```

Figure 3.39 Routine to return top element in a stack—linked list implementation

```
/**
 * Remove the most recently inserted item from the stack.
 * @exception Underflow if the stack is empty.
 */
public void pop( ) throws Underflow
{
    if( isEmpty( ) )
        throw new Underflow( );
    topOfStack = topOfStack.next;
}
```

Figure 3.40 Routine to pop from a stack—linked list implementation

```
/**
 * Return and remove the most recently inserted item from the stack.
 * @return the most recently inserted item in the stack, or null if empty.
 */
public Object topAndPop( )
{
    if( isEmpty( ) )
        return null;

    Object topItem = topOfStack.element;
    topOfStack = topOfStack.next;
    return topItem;
}
```

Figure 3.41 Routine to give top element and pop a stack—list implementation

It should be clear that all the operations take constant time, because nowhere in any of the routines is there even a reference to the size of the stack (except for emptiness), much less a loop that depends on this size. The drawback of this implementation is that (in some languages) the calls to **new** can be expensive, especially in comparison to the simple link manipulations. Some of this can be avoided by using a second stack, which is initially empty. When a cell is to be dropped from the first stack, it is merely placed on the second stack. Then, when new cells are needed for the first stack, the second stack is checked first.

Array Implementation of Stacks

An alternative implementation avoids links and is probably the more popular solution. The only potential hazard with this strategy is that we need to declare an array size ahead of time. Generally this is not a problem, because in typical applications, even if there are quite a few stack operations, the actual number of elements in the stack at any time never gets too large. It is usually easy to declare the array to be large enough without wasting too much space. If this is not possible, we can either use the linked list implementation or use a technique, suggested in Exercise 3.29, that expands the capacity dynamically.

If we use an array implementation, the implementation is trivial. Associated with each stack is **theArray** and **topOfStack**, which is -1 for an empty stack (this is how an empty stack is initialized). To push some element **x** onto the stack, we increment **topOfStack** and then set **theArray[topOfStack]** = **x**. To pop, we set the return value to **theArray[topOfStack]** and then decrement **topOfStack**.

Notice that these operations are performed in not only constant time, but very fast constant time. On some machines, **push**es and **pop**s (of integers) can be written in one machine instruction, operating on a register with auto-increment and auto-decrement addressing. The fact that most modern machines have stack operations as part of the instruction set enforces the idea that the stack is probably the most fundamental data structure in computer science, after the array.

One problem that affects the efficiency of implementing stacks is error testing. Our linked list implementation carefully checked for errors. As described above, a **pop** on an empty stack or a **push** on a full stack will overflow the array bounds and cause an abnormal termination. This is obviously undesirable, but if checks for these conditions were put in the array implementation, they would likely take as much time as the actual stack manipulation. For this reason, it has become a common practice to skimp on error checking in the stack routines, except where error handling is crucial (as in operating systems). Although you can probably get away with this in most cases by declaring the stack to be large enough not to overflow and ensuring that routines that use **pop** never attempt to **pop** an empty stack, this can lead to code that barely works at best, especially when programs are large and are written by more than one person or at more than one time. Because stack operations take such fast constant time, it is rare that a significant part of the running time of a program is spent in these routines. This means that it is generally not justifiable to omit error checks. You should always write the error checks; if they are redundant, you can always comment them out if they really cost too much time. Having said all this, we can now write routines to implement a general stack using arrays.

A stack class, **StackAr** is shown, partially implemented, in Figure 3.42. The remaining stack routines are very simple and follow the written description exactly (see Figs. 3.43 to 3.47). Notice that in both **pop** and **topAndPop**, we *dereference* (that is, make **null**) the array reference to the object being removed. This is not required, since it will

```java
public class StackAr
{
    public StackAr( )
      { /* Figure 3.43 */ }
    public StackAr( int capacity )
      { /* Figure 3.43 */ }

    public boolean isEmpty( )
      { return topOfStack == -1; }
    public boolean isFull( )
      { return topOfStack == theArray.length - 1; }
    public void makeEmpty( )
      { topOfStack = -1; }

    public void push( Object x ) throws Overflow
      { /* Figure 3.44 */ }
    public Object top( )
      { /* Figure 3.45 */ }
    public void pop( ) throws Underflow
      { /* Figure 3.46 */ }
    public Object topAndPop( )
      { /* Figure 3.47 */ }

    private Object [ ] theArray;
    private int        topOfStack;

    static final int DEFAULT_CAPACITY = 10;
}
```

Figure 3.42 Stack class skeleton—array implementation

```java
/**
 * Construct the stack.
 */
public StackAr( )
{
    this( DEFAULT_CAPACITY );
}

/**
 * Construct the stack.
 * @param capacity the capacity.
 */
public StackAr( int capacity )
{
    theArray = new Object[ capacity ];
    topOfStack = -1;
}
```

Figure 3.43 Stack construction—array implementation

```
/**
 * Insert a new item into the stack, if not already full.
 * @param x the item to insert.
 * @exception Overflow if stack is already full.
 */
public void push( Object x ) throws Overflow
{
    if( isFull( ) )
        throw new Overflow( );
    theArray[ ++topOfStack ] = x;
}
```

Figure 3.44 Routine to push onto a stack—array implementation

```
/**
 * Get the most recently inserted item in the stack.
 * Does not alter the stack.
 * @return the most recently inserted item, or null, if empty.
 */
public Object top( )
{
    if( isEmpty( ) )
        return null;
    return theArray[ topOfStack ];
}
```

Figure 3.45 Routine to return top of stack—array implementation

```
/**
 * Remove the most recently inserted item from the stack.
 * @exception Underflow if stack is already empty.
 */
public void pop( ) throws Underflow
{
    if( isEmpty( ) )
        throw new Underflow( );
    theArray[ topOfStack-- ] = null;
}
```

Figure 3.46 Routine to pop from a stack—array implementation

```
/**
 * Return and remove most recently inserted item from the stack.
 * @return most recently inserted item, or null, if stack is empty.
 */
public Object topAndPop( )
{
    if( isEmpty( ) )
        return null;
    Object topItem = top( );
    theArray[ topOfStack-- ] = null;
    return topItem;
}
```

Figure 3.47 Routine to give top element and pop a stack—array implementation be dereferenced when either the array entry gets a new reference or the stack itself is dereferenced.

3.3.3. Applications

It should come as no surprise that if we restrict the operations allowed on a list, those operations can be performed very quickly. The big surprise, however, is that the small number of operations left are so powerful and important. We give three of the many applications of stacks. The third application gives a deep insight into how programs are organized.

Balancing Symbols

Compilers check your programs for syntax errors, but frequently a lack of one symbol (such as a missing brace or comment starter) will cause the compiler to spill out a hundred lines of diagnostics without identifying the real error. (Fortunately, most Java compilers are pretty good about this. But not all languages and compilers are as responsible.)

A useful tool in this situation is a program that checks whether everything is balanced. Thus, every right brace, bracket, and parenthesis must correspond to its left counterpart. The sequence [()] is legal, but [(]) is wrong. Obviously, it is not worthwhile writing a huge program for this, but it turns out that it is easy to check these things. For simplicity, we will just check for balancing of parentheses, brackets, and braces and ignore any other character that appears.

The simple algorithm uses a stack and is as follows:

Make an empty stack. Read characters until end of file. If the character is an opening symbol, push it onto the stack. If it is a closing symbol, then if the stack is empty report an error. Otherwise, pop the stack. If the symbol popped is not the corresponding opening symbol, then report an error. At end of file, if the stack is not empty report an error.

You should be able to convince yourself that this algorithm works. It is clearly linear and actually makes only one pass through the input. It is thus on-line and quite fast. Extra work can be done to attempt to decide what to do when an error is reported—such as identifying the likely cause.

Postfix Expressions

Suppose we have a pocket calculator and would like to compute the cost of a shopping trip. To do so, we add a list of numbers and multiply the result by 1.06; this computes the purchase price of some items with local sales tax added. If the items are 4.99, 5.99, and 6.99, then a natural way to enter this would be the sequence

$$4.99 + 5.99 + 6.99 * 1.06 =$$

Depending on the calculator, this produces either the intended answer, 19.05, or the scientific answer, 18.39. Most simple four-function calculators will give the first answer, but many advanced calculators know that multiplication has higher precedence than addition.

On the other hand, some items are taxable and some are not, so if only the first and last items were actually taxable, then the sequence

$$4.99 * 1.06 + 5.99 + 6.99 * 1.06 =$$

would give the correct answer (18.69) on a scientific calculator and the wrong answer (19.37) on a simple calculator. A scientific calculator generally comes with parentheses, so we can always get the right answer by parenthesizing, but with a simple calculator we need to remember intermediate results.

A typical evaluation sequence for this example might be to multiply 4.99 and 1.06, saving this answer as A_1. We then add 5.99 and A_1, saving the result in A_1. We multiply 6.99 and 1.06, saving the answer in A_2, and finish by adding A_1 and A_2, leaving the final answer in A_1. We can write this sequence of operations as follows:

$$4.99 \ 1.06 * 5.99 + 6.99 \ 1.06 * +$$

This notation is known as *postfix* or *reverse Polish* notation and is evaluated exactly as we have described above. The easiest way to do this is to use a stack. When a number is seen, it is pushed onto the stack; when an operator is seen, the operator is applied to the two numbers (symbols) that are popped from the stack, and the result is pushed onto the stack. For instance, the postfix expression

$$6 \ 5 \ 2 \ 3 + 8 * +3 + *$$

is evaluated as follows: The first four symbols are placed on the stack. The resulting stack is

topOfStack	→	3
		2
		5
		6

Next a '+' is read, so 3 and 2 are popped from the stack and their sum, 5, is pushed.

topOfStack	→	5
		5
		6

Next 8 is pushed.

topOfStack	→	8
		5
		5
		6

Now a '*' is seen, so 8 and 5 are popped and $5 * 8 = 40$ is pushed.

```
topOfStack  →   40
                 5
                 6
```

Next a '+' is seen, so 40 and 5 are popped and 5 + 40 = 45 is pushed.

```
topOfStack  →   45
                 6
```

Now, 3 is pushed.

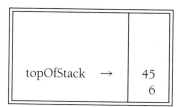

```
topOfStack  →   3
                45
                 6
```

Next '+' pops 3 and 45 and pushes 45 + 3 = 48.

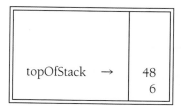

```
topOfStack  →   48
                 6
```

Finally, a '*' is seen and 48 and 6 are popped; the result, 6 * 48 = 288, is pushed.

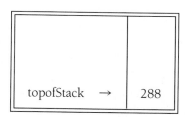

```
topofStack  →   288
```

The time to evaluate a postfix expression is $O(N)$, because processing each element in the input consists of stack operations and thus takes constant time. The algorithm to do so is very simple. Notice that when an expression is given in postfix notation, there is no need to know any precedence rules; this is an obvious advantage.

Infix to Postfix Conversion

Not only can a stack be used to evaluate a postfix expression, but we can also use a stack to convert an expression in standard form (otherwise known as *infix*) into postfix. We will concentrate on a small version of the general problem by allowing only the operators +, *, (,), and insisting on the usual precedence rules. We will further assume that the expression is legal. Suppose we want to convert the infix expression

a + b * c + (d * e + f) * g

into postfix. A correct answer is a b c * + d e * f + g * +.

When an operand is read, it is immediately placed onto the output. Operators are not immediately output, so they must be saved somewhere. The correct thing to do is to place operators that have been seen, but not placed on the output, onto the stack. We will also stack left parentheses when they are encountered. We start with an initially empty stack.

If we see a right parenthesis, then we pop the stack, writing symbols until we encounter a (corresponding) left parenthesis, which is popped but not output.

If we see any other symbol (+, *, (), then we pop entries from the stack until we find an entry of lower priority. One exception is that we never remove a (from the stack except when processing a). For the purposes of this operation, + has lowest priority and (highest. When the popping is done, we push the operator onto the stack.

Finally, if we read the end of input, we pop the stack until it is empty, writing symbols onto the output.

The idea of this algorithm is that when an operator is seen, it is placed on the stack. The stack represents pending operators. However, some of the operators on the stack that have high precedence are now known to be completed, and should be popped, as they will no longer be pending. Thus prior to placing the operator on the stack, operators that are on the stack and are to be completed prior to the current operator, are popped. This is illustrated in the following table:

Expression	Stack When Third Operator Is Processed	Action
a*b-c+d	-	- is completed, + is pushed
a/b+c*d	+	Nothing is completed, * is pushed
a-b*c/d	- *	* is completed, / is pushed
a-b*c+d	- *	* and - are completed, + is pushed

Parentheses simply add an additional complication. We can view a left parenthesis as a high-precedence operator when it is an input symbol (so that pending operators remain pending), and a low-precedence operator when it is on the stack (so that it is not accidentally removed by an operator). Right parentheses are treated as the special case.

To see how this algorithm performs, we will convert the long infix expression above into its postfix form. First, the symbol a is read, so it is passed through to the output. Then

+ is read and pushed onto the stack. Next **b** is read and passed through to the output. The state of affairs at this juncture is as follows:

Next a * is read. The top entry on the operator stack has lower precedence than *, so nothing is output and * is put on the stack. Next, **c** is read and output. Thus far, we have

The next symbol is a **+**. Checking the stack, we find that we will pop a * and place it on the output; pop the other **+**, which is not of *lower* but equal priority, on the stack; and then push the **+**.

The next symbol read is a **(**, which, being of highest precedence, is placed on the stack. Then **d** is read and output.

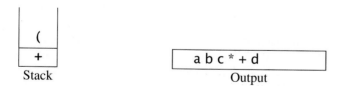

We continue by reading a *. Since open parentheses do not get removed except when a closed parenthesis is being processed, there is no output. Next, **e** is read and output.

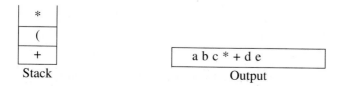

The next symbol read is a +. We pop and output * and then push +. Then we read and output f.

Now we read a), so the stack is emptied back to the (. We output a +.

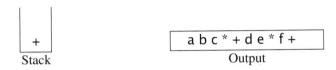

We read a * next; it is pushed onto the stack. Then g is read and output.

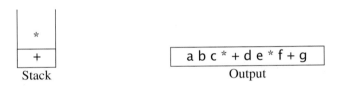

The input is now empty, so we pop and output symbols from the stack until it is empty.

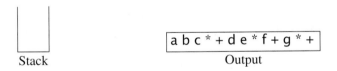

As before, this conversion requires only $O(N)$ time and works in one pass through the input. We can add subtraction and division to this repertoire by assigning subtraction and addition equal priority and multiplication and division equal priority. A subtle point is that the expression a-b-c will be converted to ab-c- and not abc--. Our algorithm does the right thing, because these operators associate from left to right. This is not necessarily the case in general, since exponentiation associates right to left: $2^{2^3} = 2^8 = 256$, not $4^3 = 64$. We leave as an exercise the problem of adding exponentiation to the repertoire of operators.

Method Calls

The algorithm to check balanced symbols suggests a way to implement method calls in compiled procedural and object-oriented languages.* The problem here is that when a call

---

*Since Java is interpreted, rather than compiled, some details in this section may not apply to Java, but the general concepts still do in Java and many other languages.

is made to a new method, all the variables local to the calling routine need to be saved by the system, since otherwise the new method will overwrite the memory used by the calling routine's variables. Furthermore, the current location in the routine must be saved so that the new method knows where to go after it is done. The variables have generally been assigned by the compiler to machine registers, and there are certain to be conflicts (usually all methods get some variables assigned to register #1), especially if recursion is involved. The reason that this problem is similar to balancing symbols is that a method call and method return are essentially the same as an open parenthesis and closed parenthesis, so the same ideas should work.

When there is a method call, all the important information that needs to be saved, such as register values (corresponding to variable names) and the return address (which can be obtained from the program counter, which is typically in a register), is saved "on a piece of paper" in an abstract way and put at the top of a pile. Then the control is transferred to the new method, which is free to replace the registers with its values. If it makes other method calls, it follows the same procedure. When the method wants to return, it looks at the "paper" at the top of the pile and restores all the registers. It then makes the return jump.

Clearly, all of this work can be done using a stack, and that is exactly what happens in virtually every programming language that implements recursion. The information saved is called either an *activation record* or *stack frame*. Typically, a slight adjustment is made: The current environment is represented at the top of the stack. Thus, a return gives the previous environment (without copying). The stack in a real computer frequently grows from the high end of your memory partition downward, and on many non-Java systems there is no checking for overflow. There is always the possibility that you will run out of stack space by having too many simultaneously active methods. Needless to say, running out of stack space is always a fatal error.

In languages and systems that do not check for stack overflow, programs crash without an explicit explanation. In Java, an exception is thrown.

In normal events, you should not run out of stack space; doing so is usually an indication of runaway recursion (forgetting a base case). On the other hand, some perfectly legal and seemingly innocuous programs can cause you to run out of stack space. The routine in Figure 3.48, which prints out a linked list (starting at some node), is perfectly legal and actually correct. It properly handles the base case of an empty list, and the recursion is fine. This program can be *proven* correct. Unfortunately, if the list contains 20,000 elements to

```
          /**
           * Print List from ListNode p onwards.
           */
          public static void printList( ListNode p )
          {
/* 1*/        if( p == null )
/* 2*/            return;

/* 3*/        System.out.println( p.element );
/* 4*/        printList( p.next );
          }
```

Figure 3.48 A bad use of recursion: printing a linked list

```
/**
 * Print List from ListNode p onwards.
 */
public static void printList( ListNode p )
{
  while( true )
  {
    if( p == null )
        return;

    System.out.println( p.element );
    p = p.next;
  }
}
```

Figure 3.49 Printing a list without recursion; a compiler might do this

print, there will be a stack of 20,000 activation records representing the nested calls of line 4. Activation records are typically large because of all the information they contain, so this program is likely to run out of stack space. (If 20,000 elements are not enough to make the program crash, replace the number with a larger one.)

This program is an example of an extremely bad use of recursion known as *tail recursion*. Tail recursion refers to a recursive call at the last line. Tail recursion can be mechanically eliminated by enclosing the body in a `while` loop and replacing the recursive call with one assignment per method argument. This simulates the recursive call because nothing needs to be saved; after the recursive call finishes, there is really no need to know the saved values. Because of this, we can just go to the top of the method with the values that would have been used in a recursive call. The method in Figure 3.49 shows the mechanically improved version. Removal of tail recursion is so simple that some compilers do it automatically. Even so, it is best not to find out that yours does not.

Recursion can always be completely removed (compilers do so in converting to assembly language), but doing so can be quite tedious. The general strategy requires using a stack and is worthwhile only if you can manage to put the bare minimum on the stack. We will not dwell on this further, except to point out that although nonrecursive programs are certainly generally faster than equivalent recursive programs, the speed advantage rarely justifies the lack of clarity that results from removing the recursion.

3.4. The Queue ADT

Like stacks, *queues* are lists. With a queue, however, insertion is done at one end, whereas deletion is performed at the other end.

3.4.1. Queue Model

The basic operations on a queue are enqueue, which inserts an element at the end of the list (called the rear), and dequeue, which deletes (and returns) the element at the start of the list (known as the front). Figure 3.50 shows the abstract model of a queue.

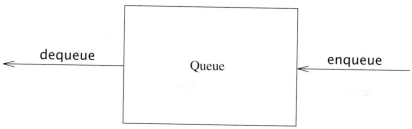

Figure 3.50 Model of a queue

3.4.2. Array Implementation of Queues

As with stacks, any list implementation is legal for queues. Like stacks, both the linked list and array implementations give fast $O(1)$ running times for every operation. The linked list implementation is straightforward and left as an exercise. We will now discuss an array implementation of queues.

For each queue data structure, we keep an array, `theArray`, and the positions `front` and `back`, which represent the ends of the queue. We also keep track of the number of elements that are actually in the queue, `currentSize`. The following figure shows a queue in some intermediate state.

The operations should be clear. To `enqueue` an element `x`, we increment `currentSize` and `back`, then set `theArray[back]=x`. To `dequeue` an element, we set the return value to `theArray[front]`, decrement `currentSize`, and then increment `front`. Other strategies are possible (this is discussed later). We will comment on checking for errors presently.

There is one potential problem with this implementation. After 10 `enqueue`s, the queue appears to be full, since `back` is now at the last array index, and the next `enqueue` would be in a nonexistent position. However, there might only be a few elements in the queue, because several elements may have already been dequeued. Queues, like stacks, frequently stay small even in the presence of a lot of operations.

The simple solution is that whenever `front` or `back` gets to the end of the array, it is wrapped around to the beginning. The following figures show the queue during some operations. This is known as a *circular array* implementation.

Initial State

						2	4
						front	back

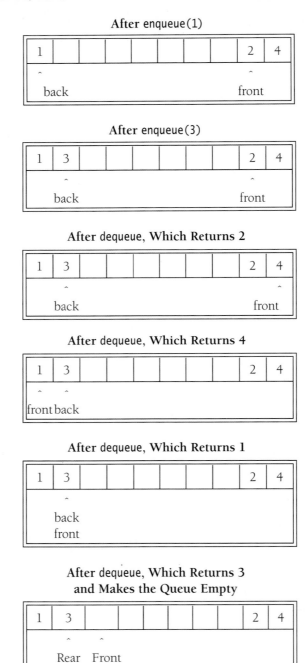

After enqueue(1)

After enqueue(3)

After dequeue, Which Returns 2

After dequeue, Which Returns 4

After dequeue, Which Returns 1

After dequeue, Which Returns 3
and Makes the Queue Empty

The extra code required to implement the wraparound is minimal (although it probably doubles the running time). If incrementing either **back** or **front** causes it to go past the array, the value is reset to the first position in the array.

Some programmers use different ways of representing the front and back of a queue. For instance, some do not use an entry to keep track of the size, because they rely on the base case that when the queue is empty, **back** = **front-1**. The size is computed implicitly by comparing back and front. This is a very tricky way to go, because there are some special cases, so be very careful if you need to modify code written this way. If the currentSize is not maintained as an explicit data field, then the queue is full when there are theArray.length-1 elements, since only theArray.length different sizes can be differentiated, and one of these is 0. Pick any style you like and make sure that all your routines are consistent. Since there are a few options for implementation, it is probably worth a comment or two in the code, if you don't use the currentSize field.

In applications where you are sure that the number of **enqueue**s is not larger than the size of the queue, the wraparound is not necessary. As with stacks, **dequeue**s are rarely performed unless the calling routines are certain that the queue is not empty. Thus error calls are frequently skipped for this operation, except in critical code. This is generally not justifiable, because the time savings that you are likely to achieve are minimal.

We finish this section by writing some of the queue routines. Others can be found in the online code. First, we give the queue class skeleton in Figure 3.51. The constructors

front -1

```java
public class QueueAr
{
    public QueueAr( )
      { /* Figure 3.52 */ }
    public QueueAr( int capacity )
      { /* Figure 3.52 */ }

    public boolean isEmpty( )
      { return currentSize == 0; }
    public boolean isFull( )
      { return currentSize == theArray.length; }
    public void makeEmpty( )
      { /* Figure 3.52 */ }

    public Object getFront( )
      { /* See online code */ }

    public void enqueue( Object x ) throws Overflow
      { /* Figure 3.53 */ }
    private int increment( int x )
      { /* Figure 3.53 */ }
    public Object dequeue( )
      { /* Figure 3.54 */ }

    private Object [ ] theArray;
    private int       currentSize;
    private int       front;
    private int       back;

    static final int DEFAULT_CAPACITY = 10;
}
```

Figure 3.51 Class skeleton for queue—array implementation

```
/**
 * Construct the queue.
 */
public QueueAr( )
{
    this( DEFAULT_CAPACITY );
}

/**
 * Construct the queue.
 */
public QueueAr( int capacity )
{
    theArray = new Object[ capacity ];
    makeEmpty( );
}

/**
 * Make the queue logically empty.
 */
public void makeEmpty( )
{
    currentSize = 0;
    front = 0;
    back = -1;
}
```

Figure 3.52 Constructors and routine to make an empty queue—array implementation

and makeEmpty are in Figure 3.52. Notice that back is preinitialized to 1 before front. The next operation we will write is the enqueue routine. Following the exact description above, we arrive at the implementation in Figure 3.53. Finally, dequeue is shown in Figure 3.54.

3.4.3. Applications of Queues

There are many algorithms that use queues to give efficient running times. Several of these are found in graph theory, and we will discuss them in Chapter 9. For now, we will give some simple examples of queue usage.

When jobs are submitted to a printer, they are arranged in order of arrival. Thus, essentially, jobs sent to a line printer are placed on a queue.*

Virtually every real-life line is (supposed to be) a queue. For instance, lines at ticket counters are queues, because service is first-come first-served.

Another example concerns computer networks. There are many network setups of personal computers in which the disk is attached to one machine, known as the *file server*. Users on other machines are given access to files on a first-come first-served basis, so the data structure is a queue.

---

*We say *essentially* because jobs can be killed. This amounts to a deletion from the middle of the queue, which is a violation of the strict definition.

```java
/**
 * Insert a new item into the queue.
 * @param x the item to insert.
 * @exception Overflow if queue is full.
 */
public void enqueue( Object x ) throws Overflow
{
    if( isFull( ) )
        throw new Overflow( );
    back = increment( back );
    theArray[ back ] = x;
    currentSize++;
}


/**
 * Internal method to increment with wraparound.
 * @param x any index in theArray's range.
 * @return x+1, or 0, if x is at the end of theArray.
 */
private int increment( int x )
{
    if( ++x == theArray.length )
        x = 0;
    return x;
}
```

Figure 3.53 Routines to enqueue—array implementation

```java
/**
 * Return and remove the least recently inserted item from the queue.
 * @return the least recently inserted item, or null, if empty.
 */
public Object dequeue( )
{
    if( isEmpty( ) )
        return null;
    currentSize--;

    Object frontItem = theArray[ front ];
    theArray[ front ] = null;
    front = increment( front );
    return frontItem;
}
```

Figure 3.54 Routine to dequeue—array implementation

Further examples include the following:

- Calls to large companies are generally placed on a queue when all operators are busy.
- In large universities, where resources are limited, students must sign a waiting list if all terminals are occupied. The student who has been at a terminal the longest is forced off first, and the student who has been waiting the longest is the next user to be allowed on.

A whole branch of mathematics, known as *queuing theory*, deals with computing, probabilistically, how long users expect to wait on a line, how long the line gets, and other such questions. The answer depends on how frequently users arrive to the line and how long it takes to process a user once the user is served. Both of these parameters are given as probability distribution functions. In simple cases, an answer can be computed analytically. An example of an easy case would be a phone line with one operator. If the operator is busy, callers are placed on a waiting line (up to some maximum limit). This problem is important for businesses, because studies have shown that people are quick to hang up the phone.

If there are k operators, then this problem is much more difficult to solve. Problems that are difficult to solve analytically are often solved by a simulation. In our case, we would need to use a queue to perform the simulation. If k is large, we also need other data structures to do this efficiently. We shall see how to do this simulation in Chapter 6. We could then run the simulation for several values of k and choose the minimum k that gives a reasonable waiting time.

Additional uses for queues abound, and as with stacks, it is staggering that such a simple data structure can be so important.

SUMMARY

This chapter describes the concept of ADTs and illustrates the concept with three of the most common abstract data types. The primary objective is to separate the implementation of the abstract data types from their function. The program must know what the operations do, but it is actually better off not knowing how it is done.

Lists, stacks, and queues are perhaps the three fundamental data structures in all of computer science, and their use is documented through a host of examples. In particular, we saw how stacks are used to keep track of method calls and how recursion is actually implemented. This is important to understand, not just because it makes procedural languages possible, but because knowing how recursion is implemented removes a good deal of the mystery that surrounds its use. Although recursion is very powerful, it is not an entirely free operation; misuse and abuse of recursion can result in programs crashing.

EXERCISES

3.1 You are given a linked list, L, and another linked list, P, containing integers sorted in ascending order. The operation printLots(L,P) will print the elements in L that are in positions specified by P. For instance, if P = 1,3,4,6, the first, third, fourth, and sixth elements in L are printed. Write the procedure printLots(L,P). You may use only the public list operations. What is the running time of your procedure?

3.2 Swap two adjacent elements by adjusting only the links (and not the data) using:
   a. Singly linked lists.
   b. Doubly linked lists.

3.3 For the LinkedListItr class, add a reference to the LinkedList as a data member that is set when it is constructed. Then modify the LinkedList class routines to check that for insert, the LinkedListItr parameter is referencing the correct list.

3.4 When a remove method is applied to a LinkedList, it invalidates any LinkedListItr that is referencing the removed node. Such an iterator is called *stale*. Describe a constant-time algorithm that guarantees that any operation on a stale iterator acts as if the iterator's current field is null. Note that there may be many stale iterators. You must explain which classes need to be rewritten in order to implement your algorithm.

3.5 Suppose we want to splice part of one linked list into another (a so-called *cut and paste* operation). Assume three LinkedListItr parameters representing the starting point of the cut, the ending point of the *cut,* and the point at which the *paste* is to be attached. Assume all iterators are valid, and the number of items cut is not zero.
   a. Write a method to cut and paste that is not part of DataStructures package. What is the running time of the algorithm?
   b. Write a method in class LinkedList to do the cut and paste. What is the running time of the algorithm?

3.6 Implement retreat for singly linked lists (retreat moves the iterator one node backwards). Notice that it will take linear time.

3.7 Implement a doubly linked list class with an iterator that supports the retreat method (to go backwards). Include a tail that corresponds to the header (at the end of the list). Provide methods that return iterators corresponding to the tail and last node, and provide both insertBefore and insertAfter methods.

3.8 Add the routine removeNext to the LinkedList class. removeNext removes the item after the position given by the LinkedListItr parameter. How are errors handled?

3.9 Given two sorted lists, L_1 and L_2, write a procedure to compute $L_1 \cap L_2$ using only the basic list operations.

3.10 Given two sorted lists, L_1 and L_2, write a procedure to compute $L_1 \cup L_2$ using only the basic list operations.

3.11 Write a method to add two polynomials. Do not destroy the input. Use a linked list implementation. If the polynomials have M and N terms, respectively, what is the time complexity of your program?

3.12 Write a method to multiply two polynomials, using a linked list implementation. You must make sure that the output polynomial is sorted by exponent and has at most one term of any power.
   a. Give an algorithm to solve this problem in $O(M^2N^2)$ time.
   *b. Write a program to perform the multiplication in $O(M^2N)$ time, where M is the number of terms in the polynomial of fewer terms.
   *c. Write a program to perform the multiplication in $O(MN \log(MN))$ time.
   d. Which time bound above is the best?

3.13 Write a program that takes a polynomial, $f(x)$, and computes $(f(x))^p$. What is the complexity of your program? Propose at least one alternative solution that could be competitive for some plausible choices of $f(x)$ and p.

3.14 Write an arbitrary-precision integer arithmetic package. You should use a strategy similar to polynomial arithmetic. Compute the distribution of the digits 0 to 9 in $2^{4,000}$.

3.15 The *Josephus problem* is the following game: N people, numbered 1 to N, are sitting in a circle. Starting at person 1, a hot potato is passed. After M passes, the person holding the hot potato is eliminated, the circle closes ranks, and the game continues with the person who was sitting after the eliminated person picking up the hot potato. The last remaining person wins. Thus, if $M = 0$ and $N = 5$, players are eliminated in order, and player 5 wins. If $M = 1$ and $N = 5$, the order of elimination is 2, 4, 1, 5.

    a. Write a program to solve the Josephus problem for general values of M and N. Try to make your program as efficient as possible. Make sure you dispose of cells.

    b. What is the running time of your program?

3.16 Write a program to find a particular element in a singly linked list. Do this both recursively and nonrecursively, and compare the running times. How big does the list have to be before the recursive version terminates abnormally?

3.17 a. Write a nonrecursive method to reverse a singly linked list in $O(N)$ time.

    *b. Write a method to reverse a singly linked list in $O(N)$ time using constant extra space.

3.18 You have to sort an array of student records by social security number. Write a program to do this, using radix sort with 1,000 buckets and three passes.

3.19 a. Write an array implementation of self-adjusting lists. A *self-adjusting* list is like a regular list, except that all insertions are performed at the front, and when an element is accessed by a **find**, it is moved to the front of the list without changing the relative order of the other items.

    b. Write a linked list implementation of self-adjusting lists.

    *c. Suppose each element has a fixed probability, p_i, of being accessed. Show that the elements with highest access probability are expected to be close to the front.

3.20 An alternative to the deletion strategy we have given is to use *lazy deletion*. To delete an element, we merely mark it deleted (using either an extra bit field or setting the **element** reference to **null**). The number of deleted and nondeleted elements in the list is kept as part of the data structure. If there are as many deleted elements as nondeleted elements, we traverse the entire list, performing the standard deletion algorithm on all marked nodes.

    a. List the advantages and disadvantages of lazy deletion.

    b. Write routines to implement the standard linked list operations using lazy deletion.

3.21 Write a program to check for balancing symbols in the following languages:

    a. Pascal (**begin/end**, ( ), [ ], { }).

    b. Java (/* */, ( ), [ ], { }).

    *c. Explain how to print out an error message that is likely to reflect the probable cause.

3.22 Write a program to evaluate a postfix expression.

3.23 a. Write a program to convert an infix expression which includes (,), +, -, *, and / to postfix.

　　b. Add the exponentiation operator to your repertoire.

　　c. Write a program to convert a postfix expression to infix.

3.24 Write routines to implement two stacks using only one array. Your stack routines should not declare an overflow unless every slot in the array is used.

3.25*a. Propose a data structure that supports the stack **push** and **pop** operations and a third operation **findMin**, which returns the smallest element in the data structure, all in $O(1)$ worst case time.

　　*b. Prove that if we add the fourth operation **deleteMin** which finds and removes the smallest element, then at least one of the operations must take $\Omega(\log N)$ time. (This requires reading Chapter 7.)

*3.26 Show how to implement three stacks in one array.

3.27 If the recursive routine in Section 2.4 used to compute Fibonacci numbers is run for $N = 50$, is stack space likely to run out? Why or why not?

3.28 A *deque* is a data structure consisting of a list of items, on which the following operations are possible:

push(x): Insert item **x** on the front end of the deque.

pop(): Remove the front item from the deque and return it.

inject(x): Insert item **x** on the rear end of the deque.

eject(): Remove the rear item from the deque and return it.

Write routines to support the deque that take $O(1)$ time per operation.

3.29 The array-based stack throws an exception when the array's capacity has been reached. Consider the following alternative: Create a larger array, copy the elements in the current array over to it, and have **array** reference the larger array.

　　a. Suppose we expand the array's capacity by one element. What is the worst-case running time for a sequence of N insertions?

　　b. Suppose we expand the array's capacity by five elements. What is the worst-case running time for a sequence of N insertions?

　　c. Suppose we double the array's capacity (assume the capacity is not zero). What is the worst-case running time for a sequence of N insertions?

　　d. Implement the most efficient of the alternatives above.

*3.30 Redo Exercise 3.29 for queues.

3.31 Implement an efficient stack class by using a **LinkedList** as a data member.

3.32 Implement a queue using a linked list with no header. Store references to the front and back **ListNode**. Be careful to handle the special case of empty queues.

3.33 Implement an efficient queue class by using a **LinkedList** as a data member and a **LinkedListItr** that represents the last position in the **LinkedList**.

3.34 When a **CursorList** is no longer referenced, all of the **CursorNodes** it used are lost, because **free** is not called. Design a **public** method, **reclaim**, that reclaims all **CursorNodes** in the list.

3.35 A linked list contains a cycle if, starting from some node p, it is true that following a sufficient number of **next** links brings us back to node p. p does not have to be the first node in the list. Assume that you are given a linked list that contains N nodes; however, the value of N is unknown.

    a. Design an $O(N)$ algorithm to determine if the list contains a cycle. You may use $O(N)$ extra space.

   *b. Repeat part (a), but use only $O(1)$ extra space. (*Hint:* Use two iterators that are initially at the start of the list, but advance at different speeds.)

3.36 One way to implement a queue is to use a circular linked list. Assume that the list does not contain a header, and that we can maintain, at most, one iterator corresponding to a node in the list. For which of the following representations can all basic queue operations be performed in constant worst-case time? Justify your answers.

    a. Maintain an iterator that corresponds to the first item in the list.

    b. Maintain an iterator that corresponds to the last item in the list.

3.37 Suppose we have a reference to a node in a singly linked list that is guaranteed *not to be the last node* in the list. We do not have references to any other nodes (except by following links). Describe an $O(1)$ algorithm that logically removes the value stored in such a node from the linked list, maintaining the integrity of the linked list. (*Hint:* Involve the next node.)

3.38 Suppose that a singly linked list is implemented with both a header and a tail node. Describe constant-time algorithms to

    a. Insert item x before position p (given by an iterator).

    b. Remove the item stored at position p (given by an iterator).

Trees

For large amounts of input, the linear access time of linked lists is prohibitive. In this chapter we look at a simple data structure for which the running time of most operations is $O(\log N)$ on average. We also sketch a conceptually simple modification to this data structure that guarantees the above time bound in the worst case and discuss a second modification that essentially gives an $O(\log N)$ running time per operation for a long sequence of instructions.

The data structure that we are referring to is known as a *binary search tree*. *Trees* in general are very useful abstractions in computer science, so we will discuss their use in other, more general applications. In this chapter, we will

- See how trees are used to implement the file system of several popular operating systems.

- See how trees can be used to evaluate arithmetic expressions.

- Show how to use trees to support searching operations in $O(\log N)$ average time, and how to refine these ideas to obtain $O(\log N)$ worst-case bounds. We will also see how to implement these operations when the data are stored on a disk.

4.1. Preliminaries

A *tree* can be defined in several ways. One natural way to define a tree is recursively. A tree is a collection of nodes. The collection can be empty; otherwise, a tree consists of a distinguished node r, called the *root*, and zero or more nonempty (sub)trees $T_1, T_2, \ldots, T_k$, each of whose roots are connected by a directed *edge* from r.

The root of each subtree is said to be a *child* of r, and r is the *parent* of each subtree root. Figure 4.1 shows a typical tree using the recursive definition.

From the recursive definition, we find that a tree is a collection of N nodes, one of which is the root, and $N - 1$ edges. That there are $N - 1$ edges follows from the fact that each edge connects some node to its parent, and every node except the root has one parent (see Fig. 4.2).

In the tree of Figure 4.2, the root is A. Node F has A as a parent and K, L, and M as children. Each node may have an arbitrary number of children, possibly zero. Nodes with no children are known as *leaves*; the leaves in the tree above are $B, C, H, I, P, Q, K, L, M$, and N. Nodes with the same parent are *siblings*; thus K, L, and M are all siblings. *Grandparent* and *grandchild* relations can be defined in a similar manner.

Figure 4.1 Generic tree

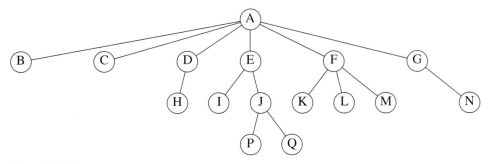

Figure 4.2 A tree

A *path* from node n_1 to n_k is defined as a sequence of nodes $n_1, n_2, \ldots, n_k$ such that n_i is the parent of n_{i+1} for $1 \le i < k$. The *length* of this path is the number of edges on the path, namely $k - 1$. There is a path of length zero from every node to itself. Notice that in a tree there is exactly one path from the root to each node.

For any node n_i, the *depth* of n_i is the length of the unique path from the root to n_i. Thus, the root is at depth 0. The *height* of n_i is the length of the longest path from n_i to a leaf. Thus all leaves are at height 0. The height of a tree is equal to the height of the root. For the tree in Figure 4.2, E is at depth 1 and height 2; F is at depth 1 and height 1; the height of the tree is 3. The depth of a tree is equal to the depth of the deepest leaf; this is always equal to the height of the tree.

If there is a path from n_1 to n_2, then n_1 is an *ancestor* of n_2 and n_2 is a *descendant* of n_1. If $n_1 \ne n_2$, then n_1 is a *proper ancestor* of n_2 and n_2 is a *proper descendant* of n_1.

4.1.1. Implementation of Trees

One way to implement a tree would be to have in each node, besides its data, a link to each child of the node. However, since the number of children per node can vary so greatly and is not known in advance, it might be infeasible to make the children direct links in the data structure, because there would be too much wasted space. The solution is simple: Keep the children of each node in a linked list of tree nodes. The declaration in Figure 4.3 is typical.

```
class TreeNode
{
    Object   element;
    TreeNode firstChild;
    TreeNode nextSibling;
}
```

Figure 4.3 Node declarations for trees

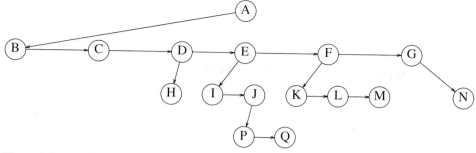

Figure 4.4 First child/next sibling representation of the tree shown in Figure 4.2

Figure 4.4 shows how a tree might be represented in this implementation. Arrows that point downward are `firstChild` links. Horizontal arrows are `nextSibling` links. Null links are not drawn, because there are too many.

In the tree of Figure 4.4, node *E* has both a link to a sibling (*F*) and a link to a child (*I*), while some nodes have neither.

4.1.2. Tree Traversals with an Application

There are many applications for trees. One of the popular uses is the directory structure in many common operating systems, including UNIX, VAX/VMS, and DOS. Figure 4.5 is a typical directory in the UNIX file system.

The root of this directory is */usr*. (The asterisk next to the name indicates that */usr* is itself a directory.) */usr* has three children, *mark, alex,* and *bill*, which are themselves directories. Thus, */usr* contains three directories and no regular files. The filename */usr/mark/book/ch1.r* is obtained by following the leftmost child three times. Each / after the first indicates an edge; the result is the full *pathname*. This hierarchical file system is very popular, because it allows users to organize their data logically. Furthermore, two files in different directories can share the same name, because they must have different paths from the root and thus have different pathnames. A directory in the UNIX file system is just a file with a list of all its children, so the directories are structured almost exactly in accordance with the type declaration above.* Indeed, on some versions of UNIX, if the normal command

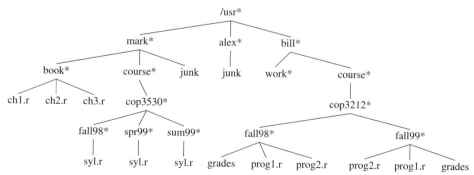

Figure 4.5 UNIX directory

---

*Each directory in the UNIX file system also has one entry that points to itself and another entry that points to the parent of the directory. Thus, technically, the UNIX file system is not a tree, but is treelike.

```
         private void listAll( int depth )
         {
/* 1*/       printName( depth );  // Print the name of the object
/* 2*/       if( isDirectory( ) )
/* 3*/           for each file c in this directory (for each child)
/* 4*/               c.listAll( depth + 1 );
         }

         public void listAll( )
         {
             listAll( 0 );
         }
```

Figure 4.6 Pseudocode to list a directory in a hierarchical file system

to print a file is applied to a directory, then the names of the files in the directory can be seen in the output (along with other non-ASCII information).

Suppose we would like to list the names of all of the files in the directory. Our output format will be that files that are depth d_i will have their names indented by d_i tabs. Our algorithm is given in Figure 4.6 as pseudocode.*

The heart of the algorithm is the recursive method listAll. This routine needs to be started with a depth of 0, to signify no indenting for the root. This depth is an internal bookkeeping variable, and is hardly a parameter that a calling routine should be expected to know about. Thus the driver routine is used to interface the recursive routine to the outside world.

The logic of the algorithm is simple to follow. The name of the file object is printed out with the appropriate number of tabs. If the entry is a directory, then we process all children recursively, one by one. These children are one level deeper, and thus need to be indented an extra space. The output is in Figure 4.7.

This traversal strategy is known as a *preorder* traversal. In a preorder traversal, work at a node is performed before (*pre*) its children are processed. When this program is run, it is clear that line 1 is executed exactly once per node, since each name is output once. Since line 1 is executed at most once per node, line 2 must also be executed once per node. Furthermore, line 4 can be executed at most once for each child of each node. But the number of children is exactly one less than the number of nodes. Finally, the **for** loop iterates once per execution of line 4, plus once each time the loop ends. Thus, the total amount of work is constant per node. If there are N file names to be output, then the running time is $O(N)$.

Another common method of traversing a tree is the *postorder* traversal. In a postorder traversal, the work at a node is performed after (*post*) its children are evaluated. As an example, Figure 4.8 represents the same directory structure as before, with the numbers in parentheses representing the number of disk blocks taken up by each file.

Since the directories are themselves files, they have sizes too. Suppose we would like to calculate the total number of blocks used by all the files in the tree. The most natural way to do this would be to find the number of blocks contained in the subdirectories */usr/mark* (30), */usr/alex* (9), and */usr/bill* (32). The total number of blocks is then the total

---

*The Java code to implement this is provided in the file *FileSystem.java* online. It uses Java features that have not been discussed in the text.

```
/usr
    mark
        book
            ch1.r
            ch2.r
            ch3.r
        course
            cop3530
                fall98
                    syl.r
                spr99
                    syl.r
                sum99
                    syl.r
        junk
    alex
        junk
    bill
        work
        course
            cop3212
                fall98
                    grades
                    prog1.r
                    prog2.r
                fall99
                    prog2.r
                    prog1.r
                    grades
```

Figure 4.7 The (preorder) directory listing

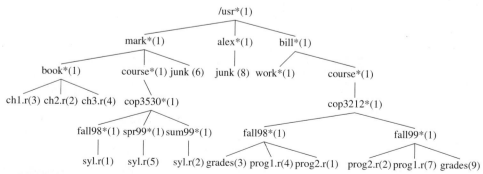

Figure 4.8 UNIX directory with file sizes obtained via postorder traversal

in the subdirectories (71) plus the one block used by */usr*, for a total of 72. The pseudocode method `size` in Figure 4.9 implements this strategy.

If the current object is not a directory, then `size` merely returns the number of blocks it uses. Otherwise, the number of blocks used by the directory is added to the number of blocks (recursively) found in all of the children. To see the difference between the postorder traversal strategy and the preorder traversal strategy, Figure 4.10 shows how the size of each directory or file is produced by the algorithm.

```
        public int size( )
        {
/* 1*/      int totalSize = sizeOfThisFile( );

/* 2*/      if( isDirectory( ) )
/* 3*/          for each file c in this directory (for each child)
/* 4*/              totalSize += c.size( );

/* 5*/      return totalSize;
        }
```

Figure 4.9 Pseudocode to calculate the size of a directory

```
            ch1.r           3
            ch2.r           2
            ch3.r           4
        book               10
                    syl.r   1
                fall98      2
                    syl.r   5
                spr99       6
                    syl.r   2
                sum99       3
            cop3530        12
        course             13
        junk                6
    mark                   30
        junk                8
    alex                    9
        work                1
                    grades  3
                    prog1.r 4
                    prog2.r 1
                fall98      9
                    prog2.r 2
                    prog1.r 7
                    grades  9
                fall99     19
            cop3212        29
        course             30
    bill                   32
/usr                       72
```

Figure 4.10 Trace of the `size` function

4.2. Binary Trees

A binary tree is a tree in which no node can have more than two children.

Figure 4.11 shows that a binary tree consists of a root and two subtrees, T_L and T_R, both of which could possibly be empty.

A property of a binary tree that is sometimes important is that the depth of an average binary tree is considerably smaller than N. An analysis shows that the average depth is $O(\sqrt{N})$, and that for a special type of binary tree, namely the *binary search tree*, the average value of the depth is $O(\log N)$. Unfortunately, the depth can be as large as $N - 1$, as the example in Figure 4.12 shows.

4.2.1. Implementation

Because a binary tree has at most two children, we can keep direct links to them. The declaration of tree nodes is similar in structure to that for doubly linked lists in that a node is a structure consisting of the `element` information plus two references (`left` and `right`) to other nodes (see Fig. 4.13).

We could draw the binary trees using the rectangular boxes that are customary for linked lists, but trees are generally drawn as circles connected by lines, because they are actually graphs. We also do not explicitly draw `null` links when referring to trees, because every binary tree with N nodes would require $N + 1$ `null` links.

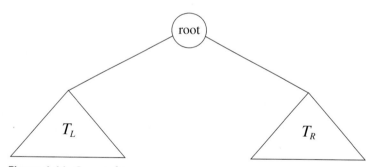

Figure 4.11 Generic binary tree

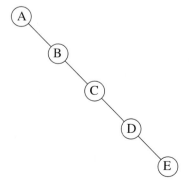

Figure 4.12 Worst-case binary tree

```
class BinaryNode
{
        // Friendly data; accessible by other package routines
    Object     element;      // The data in the node
    BinaryNode left;         // Left child
    BinaryNode right;        // Right child
}
```

Figure 4.13 Binary tree node class

Binary trees have many important uses not associated with searching. One of the principal uses of binary trees is in the area of compiler design, which we will now explore.

4.2.2. An Example: Expression Trees

Figure 4.14 shows an example of an *expression tree*. The leaves of an expression tree are *operands*, such as constants or variable names, and the other nodes contain *operators*. This particular tree happens to be binary, because all of the operators are binary, and although this is the simplest case, it is possible for nodes to have more than two children. It is also possible for a node to have only one child, as is the case with the *unary minus* operator. We can evaluate an expression tree, T, by applying the operator at the root to the values obtained by recursively evaluating the left and right subtrees. In our example, the left subtree evaluates to a + (b * c) and the right subtree evaluates to ((d * e) + f) * g. The entire tree therefore represents (a + (b * c)) + (((d * e) + f) * g).

We can produce an (overly parenthesized) infix expression by recursively producing a parenthesized left expression, then printing out the operator at the root, and finally recursively producing a parenthesized right expression. This general strategy (left, node, right) is known as an *inorder* traversal; it is easy to remember because of the type of expression it produces.

An alternate traversal strategy is to recursively print out the left subtree, the right subtree, and then the operator. If we apply this strategy to our tree above, the output is a b c * + d e * f + g * +, which is easily seen to be the postfix representation of Section 3.3.3. This traversal strategy is generally known as a *postorder* traversal. We have seen this traversal strategy earlier in Section 4.1.

A third traversal strategy is to print out the operator first and then recursively print out the left and right subtrees. The resulting expression, + + a * b c * + * d e f g, is

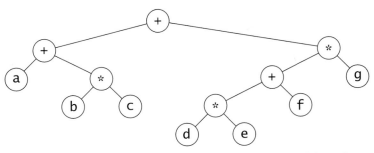

Figure 4.14 Expression tree for (a + b * c) + ((d * e + f) * g)

the less useful *prefix* notation and the traversal strategy is a *preorder* traversal, which we have also seen earlier in Section 4.1. We will return to these traversal strategies later in the chapter.

Constructing an Expression Tree

We now give an algorithm to convert a postfix expression into an expression tree. Since we already have an algorithm to convert infix to postfix, we can generate expression trees from the two common types of input. The method we describe strongly resembles the postfix evaluation algorithm of Section 3.2.3. We read our expression one symbol at a time. If the symbol is an operand, we create a one-node tree and push it onto a stack. If the symbol is an operator, we pop two trees T_1 and T_2 from the stack (T_1 is popped first) and form a new tree whose root is the operator and whose left and right children are T_2 and T_1, respectively. This new tree is then pushed onto the stack.

As an example, suppose the input is

$$a \ b \ + \ c \ d \ e \ + \ * \ *$$

The first two symbols are operands, so we create one-node trees and push them onto a stack.*

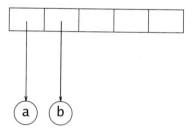

Next, a + is read, so two trees are popped, a new tree is formed, and it is pushed onto the stack.

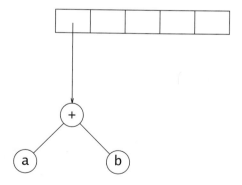

Next, **c**, **d**, and **e** are read, and for each a one-node tree is created and the corresponding tree is pushed onto the stack.

---

*For convenience, we will have the stack grow from left to right in the diagrams.

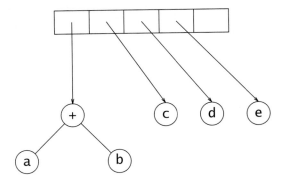

Now a + is read, so two trees are merged.

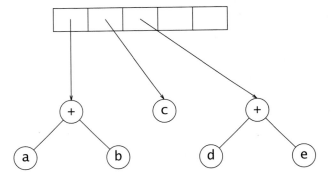

Continuing, a * is read, so we pop two trees and form a new tree with a * as root.

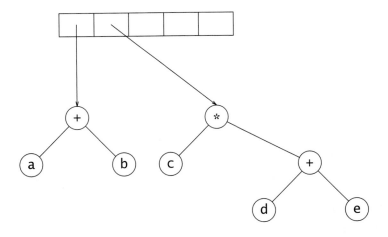

Finally, the last symbol is read, two trees are merged, and the final tree is left on the stack.

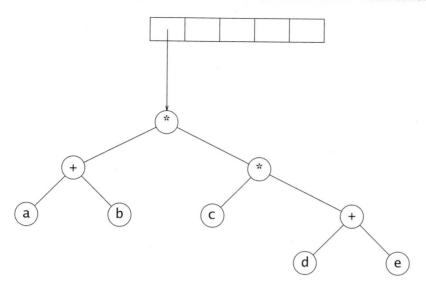

4.3. The Search Tree ADT— Binary Search Trees

An important application of binary trees is their use in searching. Let us assume that each node in the tree stores an item. In our examples, we will assume for simplicity that these are integers, although arbitrarily complex items are easily handled in Java. We will also assume that all the items are distinct, and deal with duplicates later.

The property that makes a binary tree into a binary search tree is that for every node, X, in the tree, the values of all the items in its left subtree are smaller than the item in X, and the values of all the items in its right subtree are larger than the item in X. Notice that this implies that all the elements in the tree can be ordered in some consistent manner. In Figure 4.15, the tree on the left is a binary search tree, but the tree on the right is not. The tree on the right has a node with item 7 in the left subtree of a node with item 6 (which happens to be the root).

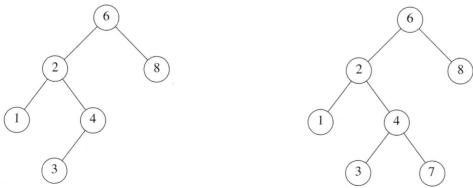

Figure 4.15 Two binary trees (only the left tree is a search tree)

We now give brief descriptions of the operations that are usually performed on binary search trees. Note that because of the recursive definition of trees, it is common to write these routines recursively. Because the average depth of a binary search tree is $O(\log N)$, we generally do not need to worry about running out of stack space.

The binary search tree requires that all the items can be ordered. To write a generic class, we need to provide an **interface** type that represents this property. This interface is **Comparable**, as described in Chapter 1. The interface tells us that two items in the tree can always be compared using a **compareTo** method. From this, we can determine all other possible relationships. Specifically, we do not use the **equals** method. Instead, two items are equal if and only if the **compareTo** method returns 0. Figure 4.16 also shows the **BinaryNode** class that, like the **ListNode** class, is only visible inside the **DataStructures** package.

Figure 4.17 shows the **BinarySearchTree** class skeleton. The single data field is a reference to the root node; this reference is **null** for empty trees. The **public** methods use the general technique of calling **private** recursive methods. The **private** method **elementAt** returns a reference to the item stored in the node referenced by **t**, or **null** if **t** is **null**.

We can now describe some of the private methods.

4.3.1. find

This operation requires returning a reference to the node in tree T that has item X, or **null** if there is no such node. The structure of the tree makes this simple. If T is empty, then we can just return **null**. Otherwise, if the item stored at T is X, we can return T. Otherwise, we make a recursive call on a subtree of T, either left or right, depending on the relationship of X to the item stored in T. The code in Figure 4.18 is an implementation of this strategy.

Notice the order of the tests. It is crucial that the test for an empty tree be performed first, since otherwise, we would generate a **NullPointerException** attempting to access a data field through a **null** reference. The remaining tests are arranged with the least likely case last. Also note that both recursive calls are actually tail recursions and can be easily removed with a **while** loop. The use of tail recursion is justifiable here because the simplicity of algorithmic expression compensates for the decrease in speed, and the amount of stack space used is expected to be only $O(\log N)$.

```
class BinaryNode
{
        // Constructors
    BinaryNode( Comparable theElement )
      { this( theElement, null, null ); }

    BinaryNode( Comparable theElement, BinaryNode lt, BinaryNode rt )
      { element = theElement; left = lt; right = rt; }

        // Friendly data; accessible by other package routines
    Comparable element;        // The data in the node
    BinaryNode left;           // Left child
    BinaryNode right;          // Right child
}
```

Figure 4.16 The BinaryNode class

```java
public class BinarySearchTree
{
    public BinarySearchTree( )
      { root = null; }

    public void makeEmpty( )
      { root = null; }
    public boolean isEmpty( )
      { return root == null; }

    public Comparable find( Comparable x )
      { return elementAt( find( x, root ) ); }
    public Comparable findMin( )
      { return elementAt( findMin( root ) ); }
    public Comparable findMax( )
      { return elementAt( findMax( root ) ); }
    public void insert( Comparable x )
      { root = insert( x, root ); }
    public void remove( Comparable x )
      { root = remove( x, root ); }
    public void printTree( )
      { /* Figure 4.56 */ }

    private BinaryNode root;     // The root

        // Various private methods; mostly recursive
    private Comparable elementAt( BinaryNode t )
      { return t == null ? null : t.element; }
    private BinaryNode find( Comparable x, BinaryNode t )
      { /* Figure 4.18 */ }
    private BinaryNode findMin( BinaryNode t )
      { /* Figure 4.19 */ }
    private BinaryNode findMax( BinaryNode t )
      { /* Figure 4.20 */ }
    private BinaryNode insert( Comparable x, BinaryNode t )
      { /* Figure 4.22 */ }
    private BinaryNode remove( Comparable x, BinaryNode t )
      { /* Figure 4.23 */ }
    private BinaryNode removeMin( BinaryNode t )
      { /* Figure 4.23 */ }
    private void printTree( BinaryNode t )
      { /* Figure 4.56 */ }
}
```

Figure 4.17 Binary search tree class skeleton

4.3.2. findMin and findMax

These private routines return a reference to the node containing the smallest and largest elements in the tree, respectively. To perform a findMin, start at the root and go left as long as there is a left child. The stopping point is the smallest element. The findMax routine is the same, except that branching is to the right child.

```
/**
 * Internal method to find an item in a subtree.
 * @param x is item to search for.
 * @param t the node that roots the tree.
 * @return node containing the matched item.
 */
private BinaryNode find( Comparable x, BinaryNode t )
{
    if( t == null )
        return null;
    if( x.compareTo( t.element ) < 0 )
        return find( x, t.left );
    else if( x.compareTo( t.element ) > 0 )
        return find( x, t.right );
    else
        return t;     // Match
}
```

Figure 4.18 find operation for binary search trees

This is so easy that many programmers do not bother using recursion. We will code the routines both ways by doing **findMin** recursively and **findMax** nonrecursively (see Figs. 4.19 and 4.20).

Notice how we carefully handle the degenerate case of an empty tree. Although this is always important to do, it is especially crucial in recursive programs. Also notice that it is safe to change **t** in **findMax**, since we are only working with a copy of a reference. Always be extremely careful, however, because a statement such as **t.right = t.right.right** will make changes.

4.3.3. insert

The insertion routine is conceptually simple. To insert X into tree T, proceed down the tree as you would with a **find**. If X is found, do nothing (or "update" something). Otherwise, insert X at the last spot on the path traversed. Figure 4.21 shows what happens. To insert

```
/**
 * Internal method to find the smallest item in a subtree.
 * @param t the node that roots the tree.
 * @return node containing the smallest item.
 */
private BinaryNode findMin( BinaryNode t )
{
    if( t == null )
        return null;
    else if( t.left == null )
        return t;
    return findMin( t.left );
}
```

Figure 4.19 Recursive implementation of findMin for binary search trees

```
/**
 * Internal method to find the largest item in a subtree.
 * @param t the node that roots the tree.
 * @return node containing the largest item.
 */
private BinaryNode findMax( BinaryNode t )
{
    if( t != null )
        while( t.right != null )
            t = t.right;

    return t;
}
```

Figure 4.20 Nonrecursive implementation of `findMax` for binary search trees

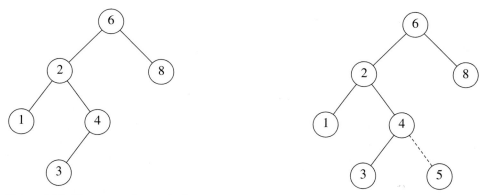

Figure 4.21 Binary search trees before and after inserting 5

5, we traverse the tree as though a `find` were occurring. At the node with item 4, we need to go right, but there is no subtree, so 5 is not in the tree, and this is the correct spot.

Duplicates can be handled by keeping an extra field in the node record indicating the frequency of occurrence. This adds some extra space to the entire tree, but is better than putting duplicates in the tree (which tends to make the tree very deep). Of course, this strategy does not work if the key that guides the `compareTo` method is only part of a larger structure. If that is the case, then we can keep all of the structures that have the same key in an auxiliary data structure, such as a list or another search tree.

Figure 4.22 shows the code for the insertion routine. Since `t` references the root of the tree, and the root changes on the first insertion, `insert` is written as a method that returns a reference to the root of the new tree. Lines 4 and 6 recursively insert and attach `x` into the appropriate subtree.

4.3.4. remove

As is common with many data structures, the hardest operation is deletion. Once we have found the node to be deleted, we need to consider several possibilities.

```
        /**
         * Internal method to insert into a subtree.
         * @param x the item to insert.
         * @param t the node that roots the tree.
         * @return the new root.
         */
        private BinaryNode insert( Comparable x, BinaryNode t )
        {
/* 1*/      if( t == null )
/* 2*/          t = new BinaryNode( x, null, null );
/* 3*/      else if( x.compareTo( t.element ) < 0 )
/* 4*/          t.left = insert( x, t.left );
/* 5*/      else if( x.compareTo( t.element ) > 0 )
/* 6*/          t.right = insert( x, t.right );
/* 7*/      else
/* 8*/          ;  // Duplicate; do nothing
/* 9*/      return t;
        }
```

Figure 4.22 Insertion into a binary search tree

If the node is a leaf, it can be deleted immediately. If the node has one child, the node can be deleted after its parent adjusts a link to bypass the node (we will draw the link directions explicitly for clarity). See Figure 4.23.

The complicated case deals with a node with two children. The general strategy is to replace the data of this node with the smallest data of the right subtree (which is easily found) and recursively delete that node (which is now empty). Because the smallest node in the right subtree cannot have a left child, the second **remove** is an easy one. Figure 4.24 shows an initial tree and the result of a deletion. The node to be deleted is the left child of the root; the key value is 2. It is replaced with the smallest data in its right subtree (3), and then that node is deleted as before.

The code in Figure 4.25 performs deletion. It is inefficient, because it makes two passes down the tree to find and delete the smallest node in the right subtree when this is appro-

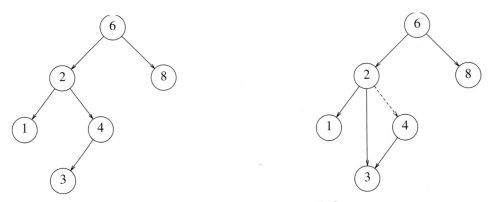

Figure 4.23 Deletion of a node (4) with one child, before and after

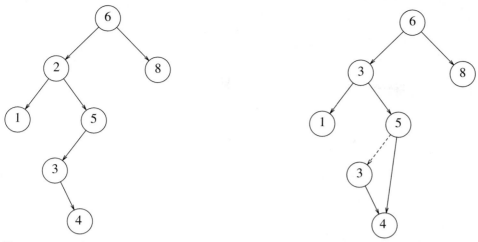

Figure 4.24 Deletion of a node (2) with two children, before and after

```
/**
 * Internal method to remove from a subtree.
 * @param x the item to remove.
 * @param t the node that roots the tree.
 * @return the new root.
 */
private BinaryNode remove( Comparable x, BinaryNode t )
{
    if( t == null )
        return t;    // Item not found; do nothing
    if( x.compareTo( t.element ) < 0 )
        t.left = remove( x, t.left );
    else if( x.compareTo( t.element ) > 0 )
        t.right = remove( x, t.right );
    else if( t.left != null && t.right != null ) // Two children
    {
        t.element = findMin( t.right ).element;
        t.right = remove( x, t.right );
    }
    else
        t = ( t.left != null ) ? t.left : t.right;
    return t;
}
```

Figure 4.25 Deletion routine for binary search trees

priate. It is easy to remove this inefficiency by writing a special **removeMin** method, and we have left it in only for simplicity.

If the number of deletions is expected to be small, then a popular strategy to use is *lazy deletion:* When an element is to be deleted, it is left in the tree and merely *marked* as being deleted. This is especially popular if duplicate items are present, because then the field that keeps count of the frequency of appearance can be decremented. If the number of real nodes in the tree is the same as the number of "deleted" nodes, then the depth of the tree is only expected to go up by a small constant (why?), so there is a very small time penalty associated with lazy deletion. Also, if a deleted item is reinserted, the overhead of allocating a new cell is avoided.

4.3.5. Average-Case Analysis

Intuitively, we expect that all of the operations of the previous section should take $O(\log N)$ time, because in constant time we descend a level in the tree, thus operating on a tree that is now roughly half as large. Indeed, the running time of all the operations is $O(d)$, where d is the depth of the node containing the accessed item.

We prove in this section that the average depth over all nodes in a tree is $O(\log N)$ on the assumption that all insertion sequences are equally likely.

The sum of the depths of all nodes in a tree is known as the *internal path length*. We will now calculate the average internal path length of a binary search tree, where the average is taken over all possible insertion sequences into binary search trees.

Let $D(N)$ be the internal path length for some tree T of N nodes. $D(1) = 0$. An N-node tree consists of an i-node left subtree and an $(N - i - 1)$-node right subtree, plus a root at depth zero for $0 \le i < N$. $D(i)$ is the internal path length of the left subtree with respect to its root. In the main tree, all these nodes are one level deeper. The same holds for the right subtree. Thus, we get the recurrence

$$D(N) = D(i) + D(N - i - 1) + N - 1$$

If all subtree sizes are equally likely, which is true for binary search trees (since the subtree size depends only on the relative rank of the first element inserted into the tree), but not binary trees, then the average value of both $D(i)$ and $D(N - i - 1)$ is $(1/N)\sum_{j=0}^{N-1} D(j)$. This yields

$$D(N) = \frac{2}{N}\left[\sum_{j=0}^{N-1} D(j)\right] + N - 1$$

This recurrence will be encountered and solved in Chapter 7, obtaining an average value of $D(N) = O(N \log N)$. Thus, the expected depth of any node is $O(\log N)$. As an example, the randomly generated 500-node tree shown in Figure 4.26 has nodes at expected depth 9.98.

It is tempting to say immediately that this result implies that the average running time of all the operations discussed in the previous section is $O(\log N)$, but this is not entirely true. The reason for this is that because of deletions, it is not clear that all binary search trees are equally likely. In particular, the deletion algorithm described above favors making the left subtrees deeper than the right, because we are always replacing a deleted node with a node from the right subtree. The exact effect of this strategy is still unknown, but it seems only to be a theoretical novelty. It has been shown that if we alternate insertions and deletions $\Theta(N^2)$ times, then the trees will have an expected depth of $\Theta(\sqrt{N})$. After a quarter-million random **insert/remove** pairs, the tree that was somewhat right-heavy in Figure 4.26 looks decidedly unbalanced (average depth = 12.51). See Figure 4.27.

We could try to eliminate the problem by randomly choosing between the smallest element in the right subtree and the largest in the left when replacing the deleted element. This apparently eliminates the bias and should keep the trees balanced, but nobody has

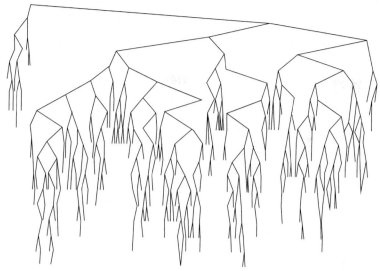

Figure 4.26 A randomly generated binary search tree

actually proved this. In any event, this phenomenon appears to be mostly a theoretical novelty, because the effect does not show up at all for small trees, and stranger still, if $o(N^2)$ insert/remove pairs are used, then the tree seems to gain balance!

The main point of this discussion is that deciding what "average" means is generally extremely difficult and can require assumptions that may or may not be valid. In the absence of deletions, or when lazy deletion is used, we can conclude that the average running times of the operations above are $O(\log N)$. Except for strange cases like the one discussed above, this result is very consistent with observed behavior.

If the input comes into a tree presorted, then a series of inserts will take quadratic time and give a very expensive implementation of a linked list, since the tree will consist only of

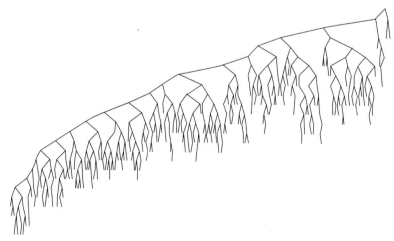

Figure 4.27 Binary search tree after $\Theta(N^2)$ insert/remove pairs

nodes with no left children. One solution to the problem is to insist on an extra structural condition called *balance:* no node is allowed to get too deep.

There are quite a few general algorithms to implement balanced trees. Most are quite a bit more complicated than a standard binary search tree, and all take longer on average for updates. They do, however, provide protection against the embarrassingly simple cases. Below, we will sketch one of the oldest forms of balanced search trees, the AVL tree.

A second, newer method is to forgo the balance condition and allow the tree to be arbitrarily deep, but after every operation, a restructuring rule is applied that tends to make future operations efficient. These types of data structures are generally classified as *self-adjusting.* In the case of a binary search tree, we can no longer guarantee an $O(\log N)$ bound on any single operation, but can show that any *sequence* of M operations takes total time $O(M \log N)$ in the worst case. This is generally sufficient protection against a bad worst case. The data structure we will discuss is known as a *splay tree;* its analysis is fairly intricate and is discussed in Chapter 11.

4.4. AVL Trees

An AVL (Adelson-Velskii and Landis) tree is a binary search tree with a *balance* condition. The balance condition must be easy to maintain, and it ensures that the depth of the tree is $O(\log N)$. The simplest idea is to require that the left and right subtrees have the same height. As Figure 4.28 shows, this idea does not force the tree to be shallow.

Another balance condition would insist that every node must have left and right subtrees of the same height. If the height of an empty subtree is defined to be -1 (as is usual), then only perfectly balanced trees of $2^k - 1$ nodes would satisfy this criterion. Thus, although this guarantees trees of small depth, the balance condition is too rigid to be useful and needs to be relaxed.

An AVL tree is identical to a binary search tree, except that for every node in the tree, the height of the left and right subtrees can differ by at most 1. (The height of an empty tree is defined to be -1.) In Figure 4.29 the tree on the left is an AVL tree, but the tree on the right is not. Height information is kept for each node (in the node structure). It can be shown that the height of an AVL tree is at most roughly $1.44 \log(N + 2) - .328$, but in practice it is only slightly more than $\log N$. As an example, the AVL tree of height 9 with the fewest nodes (143) is shown in Figure 4.30. This tree has as a left subtree an AVL tree

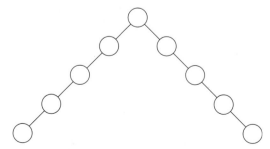

Figure 4.28 A bad binary tree. Requiring balance at the root is not enough.

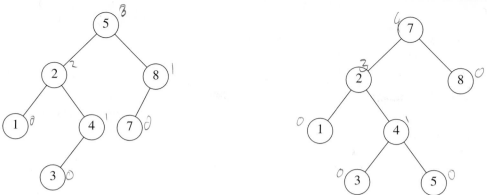

Figure 4.29 Two binary search trees. Only the left tree is AVL.

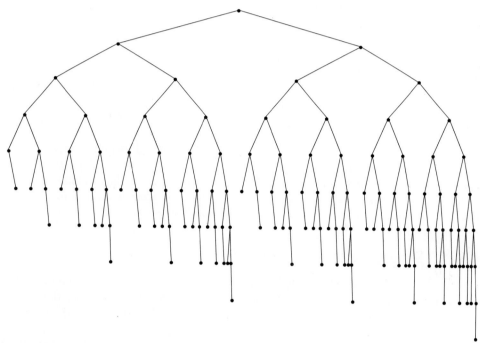

Figure 4.30 Smallest AVL tree of height 9

of height 7 of minimum size. The right subtree is an AVL tree of height 8 of minimum size. This tells us that the minimum number of nodes, $S(h)$, in an AVL tree of height h is given by $S(h) = S(h-1) + S(h-2) + 1$. For $h = 0, S(h) = 1$. For $h = 1, S(h) = 2$. The function $S(h)$ is closely related to the Fibonacci numbers, from which the bound claimed above on the height of an AVL tree follows.

Thus, all the tree operations can be performed in $O(\log N)$ time, except possibly insertion (we will assume lazy deletion). When we do an insertion, we need to update all the balancing information for the nodes on the path back to the root, but the reason that insertion is potentially difficult is that inserting a node could violate the AVL tree property. (For instance, inserting 6 into the AVL tree in Figure 4.29 would destroy the balance condition at the node with key 8.) If this is the case, then the property has to be restored before the insertion step is considered over. It turns out that this can always be done with a simple modification to the tree, known as a *rotation*.

After an insertion, only nodes that are on the path from the insertion point to the root might have their balance altered because only those nodes have their subtrees altered. As we follow the path up to the root and update the balancing information, we may find a node whose new balance violates the AVL condition. We will show how to rebalance the tree at the first (i.e., deepest) such node, and we will prove that this rebalancing guarantees that the entire tree satisfies the AVL property.

Let us call the node that must be rebalanced α. Since any node has at most two children, and a height imbalance requires that α's two subtrees' height differ by two, it is easy to see that a violation might occur in four cases:

1. An insertion into the left subtree of the left child of α.
2. An insertion into the right subtree of the left child of α.
3. An insertion into the left subtree of the right child of α.
4. An insertion into the right subtree of the right child of α.

Cases 1 and 4 are mirror image symmetries with respect to α, as are cases 2 and 3. Consequently, as a matter of theory, there are two basic cases. From a programming perspective, of course, there are still four cases.

The first case, in which the insertion occurs on the "outside" (i.e., left–left or right–right), is fixed by a *single rotation* of the tree. The second case, in which the insertion occurs on the "inside" (i.e., left–right or right–left) is handled by the slightly more complex *double rotation*. These are fundamental operations on the tree that we'll see used several times in balanced-tree algorithms. The remainder of this section describes these rotations, proves that they suffice to maintain balance, and gives a casual implementation of the AVL tree. Chapter 12 describes other balanced-tree methods with an eye toward a more careful implementation.

4.4.1. Single Rotation

Figure 4.31 shows the *single rotation* that fixes case 1. The before picture is on the left, and the after is on the right. Let us analyze carefully what is going on. Node k_2 violates the AVL balance property because its left subtree is two levels deeper than its right subtree (the dashed lines in the middle of the diagram mark the levels). The situation depicted is the only possible case 1 scenario that allows k_2 to satisfy the AVL property before an insertion but violate it afterwards. Subtree X has grown to an extra level, causing it to be exactly two

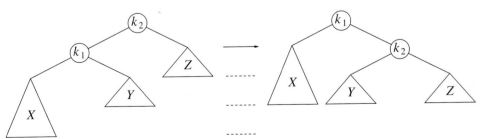

Figure 4.31 Single rotation to fix case 1

levels deeper than Z. Y cannot be at the same level as the new X because then k_2 would have been out of balance *before* the insertion, and Y cannot be at the same level as Z because then k_1 would be the first node on the path toward the root that was in violation of the AVL balancing condition.

To ideally rebalance the tree, we would like to move X up a level and Z down a level. Note that this is actually more than the AVL property would require. To do this, we rearrange nodes into an equivalent tree as shown in the second part of Figure 4.31. Here is an abstract scenario: visualize the tree as being flexible, grab the child node k_1, close your eyes, and shake it, letting gravity take hold. The result is that k_1 will be the new root. The binary search tree property tells us that in the original tree $k_2 > k_1$, so k_2 becomes the right child of k_1 in the new tree. X and Z remain as the left child of k_1 and right child of k_2, respectively. Subtree Y, which holds items that are between k_1 and k_2 in the original tree, can be placed as k_2's left child in the new tree and satisfy all the ordering requirements.

As a result of this work, which requires only a few link changes, we have another binary search tree that is an AVL tree. This happens because X moves up one level, Y stays at the same level, and Z moves down one level. k_2 and k_1 not only satisfy the AVL requirements, but they also have subtrees that are exactly the same height. Furthermore, the new height of the entire subtree is *exactly the same* as the height of the original subtree prior to the insertion that caused X to grow. Thus no further updating of heights on the path to the root is needed, and consequently *no further rotations are needed*. Figure 4.32 shows that after the insertion of 6 into the original AVL tree on the left, node 8 becomes unbalanced. Thus, we do a single rotation between 7 and 8, obtaining the tree on the right.

As we mentioned earlier, case 4 represents a symmetric case. Figure 4.33 shows how a single rotation is applied. Let us work through a rather long example. Suppose we start with

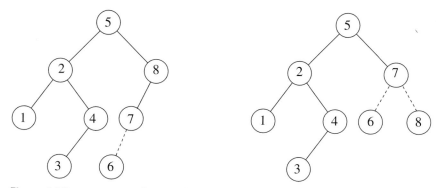

Figure 4.32 AVL property destroyed by insertion of 6, then fixed by a single rotation

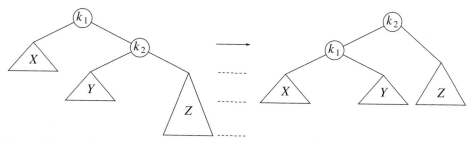

Figure 4.33 Single rotation fixes case 4

an initially empty AVL tree and insert the items 3, 2, 1, and then 4 through 7 in sequential order. The first problem occurs when it is time to insert 1 because the AVL property is violated at the root. We perform a single rotation between the root and its left child to fix the problem. Here are the before and after trees:

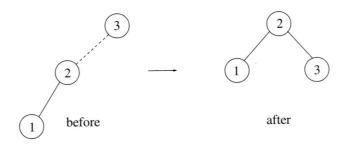

A dashed line joins the two nodes that are the subject of the rotation. Next we insert 4, which causes no problems, but the insertion of 5 creates a violation at node 3 that is fixed by a single rotation. Besides the local change caused by the rotation, the programmer must remember that the rest of the tree has to be informed of this change. Here this means that 2's right child must be reset to link to 4 instead of 3. Forgetting to do so is easy and would destroy the tree (4 would be inaccessible).

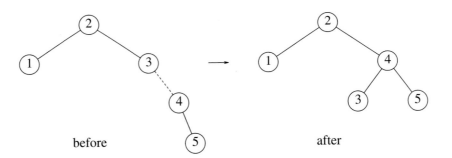

Next we insert 6. This causes a balance problem at the root, since its left subtree is of height 0 and its right subtree would be height 2. Therefore, we perform a single rotation at the root between 2 and 4.

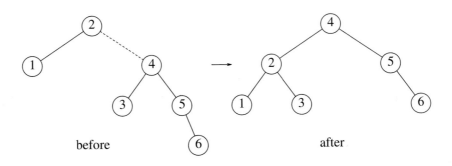

The rotation is performed by making 2 a child of 4 and 4's original left subtree the new right subtree of 2. Every item in this subtree must lie between 2 and 4, so this transformation makes sense. The next item we insert is 7, which causes another rotation:

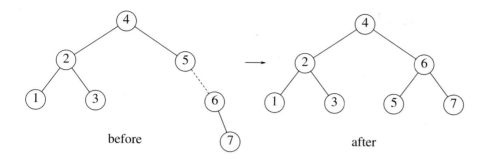

4.4.2. Double Rotation

The algorithm described above has one problem: as Figure 4.34 shows, it does not work for cases 2 or 3. The problem is that subtree Y is too deep, and a single rotation does not make it any less deep. The *double rotation* that solves the problem is shown in Figure 4.35.

The fact that subtree Y in Figure 4.34 has had an item inserted into it guarantees that it is nonempty. Thus, we may assume that it has a root and two subtrees. Consequently, the tree may be viewed as four subtrees connected by three nodes. As the diagram suggests, exactly one of tree B or C is two levels deeper than D (unless all are empty), but we cannot be sure which one. It turns out not to matter; in Figure 4.35, both B and C are drawn at $1\frac{1}{2}$ levels below D.

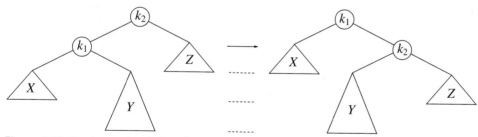

Figure 4.34 Single rotation fails to fix case 2

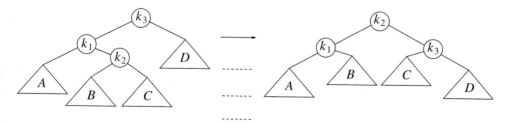

Figure 4.35 Left–right double rotation to fix case 2

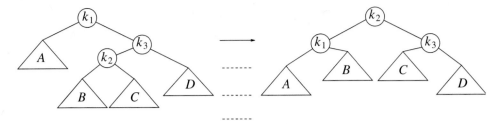

Figure 4.36 Right–left double rotation to fix case 3

To rebalance, we see that we cannot leave k_3 as the root, and a rotation between k_3 and k_1 was shown in Figure 4.34 to not work, so the only alternative is to place k_2 as the new root. This forces k_1 to be k_2's left child and k_3 to be its right child, and it also completely determines the resulting locations of the four subtrees. It is easy to see that the resulting tree satisfies the AVL tree property, and as was the case with the single rotation, it restores the height to what it was before the insertion, thus guaranteeing that all rebalancing and height updating is complete. Figure 4.36 shows that the symmetric case 3 can also be fixed by a double rotation. In both cases the effect is the same as rotating between α's child and grandchild, and then between α and its new child.

We will continue our previous example by inserting 10 through 16 in reverse order, followed by 8 and then 9. Inserting 16 is easy, since it does not destroy the balance property, but inserting 15 causes a height imbalance at node 7. This is case 3, which is solved by a right–left double rotation. In our example, the right–left double rotation will involve 7, 16, and 15. In this case, k_1 is the node with item 7, k_3 is the node with item 16, and k_2 is the node with item 15. Subtrees A, B, C, and D are empty.

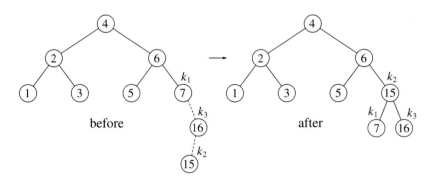

Next we insert 14, which also requires a double rotation. Here the double rotation that will restore the tree is again a right–left double rotation that will involve 6, 15, and 7. In this case, k_1 is the node with item 6, k_2 is the node with item 7, and k_3 is the node with item 15. Subtree A is the tree rooted at the node with item 5; subtree B is the empty subtree that was originally the left child of the node with item 7, subtree C is the tree rooted at the node with item 14, and finally, subtree D is the tree rooted at the node with item 16.

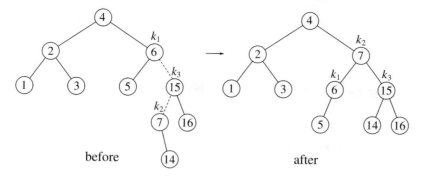

before   after

If 13 is now inserted, there is an imbalance at the root. Since 13 is not between 4 and 7, we know that the single rotation will work.

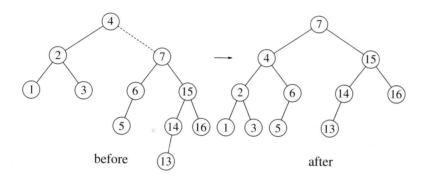

before   after

Insertion of 12 will also require a single rotation:

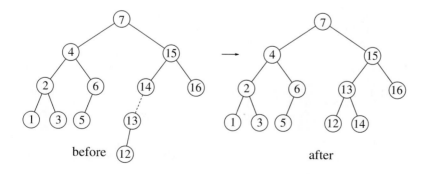

before   after

To insert 11, a single rotation needs to be performed, and the same is true for the subsequent insertion of 10. We insert 8 without a rotation creating an almost perfectly balanced tree:

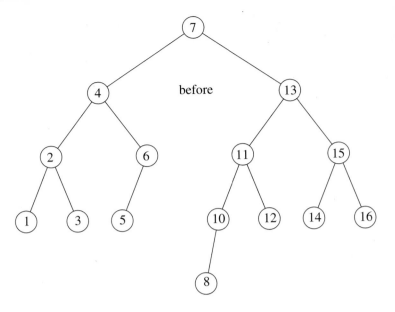

Finally, we will insert 9 to show the symmetric case of the double rotation. Notice that 9 causes the node containing 10 to become unbalanced. Since 9 is between 10 and 8 (which is 10's child on the path to 9), a double rotation needs to be performed, yielding the following tree:

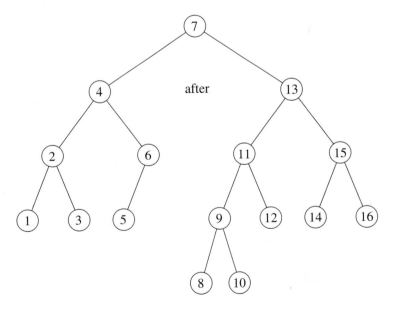

Let us summarize what happens. The programming details are fairly straightforward except that there are several cases. To insert a new node with item X into an AVL tree T, we recursively insert X into the appropriate subtree of T (let us call this T_{LR}). If the height of T_{LR} does not change, then we are done. Otherwise, if a height imbalance appears in T, we do the appropriate single or double rotation depending on X and the items in T and T_{LR}, update the heights (making the connection from the rest of the tree above), and are done. Since one rotation always suffices, a carefully coded nonrecursive version generally turns out to be significantly faster than the recursive version. However, nonrecursive versions are quite difficult to code correctly, so many programmers implement AVL trees recursively.

Another efficiency issue concerns storage of the height information. Since all that is really required is the difference in height, which is guaranteed to be small, we could get by with two bits (to represent $+1$, 0, -1) if we really try. Doing so will avoid repetitive calculation of balance factors but results in some loss of clarity. The resulting code is some-what more complicated than if the height were stored at each node. If a recursive routine is written, then speed is probably not the main consideration. In this case, the slight speed advantage obtained by storing balance factors hardly seems worth the loss of clarity and relative simplicity. Furthermore, since most machines will align this to at least an 8-bit boundary anyway, there is not likely to be any difference in the amount of space used. An eight-bit **byte** will allow us to store absolute heights of up to 127. Since the tree is balanced, it is inconceivable that this would be insufficient (see the exercises).

With all this, we are ready to write the AVL routines. We show some of the code here; the rest is online. First, we need the **AvlNode** class. This is given in Figure 4.37. We also need a quick method to return the height of a node. This method is necessary to handle the annoying case of a **null** reference. This is shown in Figure 4.38. The basic insertion routine is easy to write, since it consists mostly of method calls (see Fig. 4.39).

```
class AvlNode
{
        // Constructors
    AvlNode( Comparable theElement )
      { this( theElement, null, null ); }

    AvlNode( Comparable theElement, AvlNode lt, AvlNode rt )
      { element = theElement; left = lt; right = rt; height = 0; }

        // Friendly data; accessible by other package routines
    Comparable element;      // The data in the node
    AvlNode    left;         // Left child
    AvlNode    right;        // Right child
    int        height;       // Height
}
```

Figure 4.37 Node declaration for AVL trees

```
/**
 * Return the height of node t, or -1, if null.
 */
private static int height( AvlNode t )
{
    return t == null ? -1 : t.height;
}
```

Figure 4.38 Method to compute height of an AVL node

```
/**
 * Internal method to insert into a subtree.
 * @param x the item to insert.
 * @param t the node that roots the tree.
 * @return the new root.
 */
private AvlNode insert( Comparable x, AvlNode t )
{
    if( t == null )
        t = new AvlNode( x, null, null );
    else if( x.compareTo( t.element ) < 0 )
    {
        t.left = insert( x, t.left );
        if( height( t.left ) - height( t.right ) == 2 )
            if( x.compareTo( t.left.element ) < 0 )
                t = rotateWithLeftChild( t );
            else
                t = doubleWithLeftChild( t );
    }
    else if( x.compareTo( t.element ) > 0 )
    {
        t.right = insert( x, t.right );
        if( height( t.right ) - height( t.left ) == 2 )
            if( x.compareTo( t.right.element ) > 0 )
                t = rotateWithRightChild( t );
            else
                t = doubleWithRightChild( t );
    }
    else
        ;    // Duplicate; do nothing
    t.height = max( height( t.left ), height( t.right ) ) + 1;
    return t;
}
```

Figure 4.39 Insertion into an AVL tree

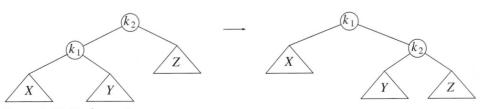

Figure 4.40 Single rotation

For the trees in Figure 4.40, `rotateWithLeftChild` converts the tree on the left to the tree on the right, returning a reference to the new root. `rotateWithLeftChild` is symmetric. The code is shown in Figure 4.41.

The last method we will write will perform the double rotation pictured in Figure 4.42, for which the code is shown in Figure 4.43.

```
/**
 * Rotate binary tree node with left child.
 * For AVL trees, this is a single rotation for case 1.
 * Update heights, then return new root.
 */
private static AvlNode rotateWithLeftChild( AvlNode k2 )
{
    AvlNode k1 = k2.left;
    k2.left = k1.right;
    k1.right = k2;
    k2.height = max( height( k2.left ), height( k2.right ) ) + 1;
    k1.height = max( height( k1.left ), k2.height ) + 1;
    return k1;
}
```

Figure 4.41 Routine to perform single rotation

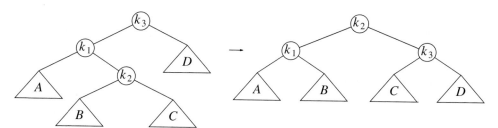

Figure 4.42 Double rotation

```
/**
 * Double rotate binary tree node: first left child
 * with its right child; then node k3 with new left child.
 * For AVL trees, this is a double rotation for case 2.
 * Update heights, then return new root.
 */
private static AvlNode doubleWithLeftChild( AvlNode k3 )
{
    k3.left = rotateWithRightChild( k3.left );
    return rotateWithLeftChild( k3 );
}
```

Figure 4.43 Routine to perform double rotation

Deletion in AVL trees is somewhat more complicated than insertion, and is left as an exercise. Lazy deletion is probably the best strategy if deletions are relatively infrequent.

4.5. Splay Trees

We now describe a relatively simple data structure, known as a *splay tree*, that guarantees that any M consecutive tree operations starting from an empty tree take at most $O(M \log N)$ time. Although this guarantee does not preclude the possibility that any *single* operation might take $O(N)$ time, and thus the bound is not as strong as an $O(\log N)$ worst-case bound per operation, the net effect is the same: There are no bad input sequences. Generally, when a sequence of M operations has total worst-case running time of $O(Mf(N))$, we say that the *amortized* running time is $O(f(N))$. Thus, a splay tree has an $O(\log N)$ amortized cost per operation. Over a long sequence of operations, some may take more, some less.

Splay trees are based on the fact that the $O(N)$ worst-case time per operation for binary search trees is not bad, as long at it occurs relatively infrequently. Any one access, even if it takes $O(N)$, is still likely to be extremely fast. The problem with binary search trees is that it is possible, and not uncommon, for a whole sequence of bad accesses to take place. The cumulative running time then becomes noticeable. A search tree data structure with $O(N)$ worst-case time, but a *guarantee* of at most $O(M \log N)$ for any M consecutive operations, is certainly satisfactory, because there are no bad sequences.

If any particular operation is allowed to have an $O(N)$ worst-case time bound, and we still want an $O(\log N)$ amortized time bound, then it is clear that whenever a node is accessed, it must be moved. Otherwise, once we find a deep node, we could keep performing **find**s on it. If the node does not change location, and each access costs $O(N)$, then a sequence of M accesses will cost $O(M \cdot N)$.

The basic idea of the splay tree is that after a node is accessed, it is pushed to the root by a series of AVL tree rotations. Notice that if a node is deep, there are many nodes on the path that are also relatively deep, and by restructuring we can make future accesses cheaper on all these nodes. Thus, if the node is unduly deep, then we want this restructuring to have the side effect of balancing the tree (to some extent). Besides giving a good time bound in theory, this method is likely to have practical utility, because in many applications, when a node is accessed, it is likely to be accessed again in the near future. Studies have shown that this happens much more often than one would expect. Splay trees also do not require the maintenance of height or balance information, thus saving space and simplifying the code to some extent (especially when careful implementations are written).

4.5.1. A Simple Idea (That Does Not Work)

One way of performing the restructuring described above is to perform single rotations, bottom up. This means that we rotate every node on the access path with its parent. As an example, consider what happens after an access (a **find**) on k_1 in the following tree.

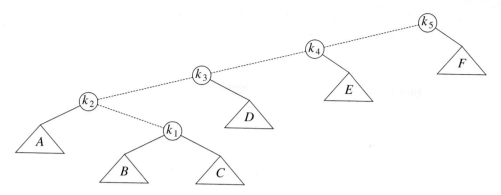

The access path is dashed. First, we would perform a single rotation between k_1 and its parent, obtaining the following tree.

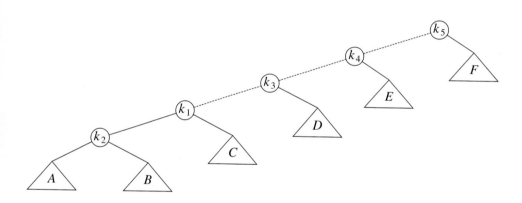

Then, we rotate between k_1 and k_3, obtaining the next tree.

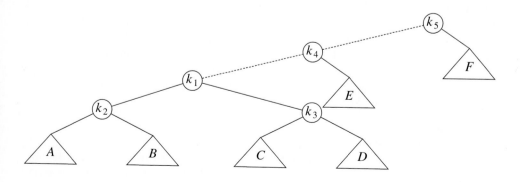

Then two more rotations are performed until we reach the root.

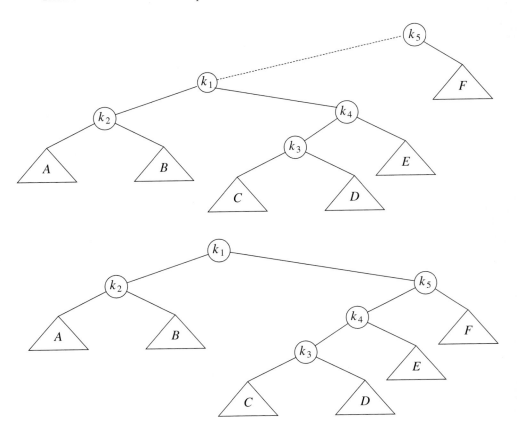

These rotations have the effect of pushing k_1 all the way to the root, so that future accesses on k_1 are easy (for a while). Unfortunately, it has pushed another node (k_3) almost as deep as k_1 used to be. An access on that node will then push another node deep, and so on. Although this strategy makes future accesses of k_1 cheaper, it has not significantly improved the situation for the other nodes on the (original) access path. It turns out that it is possible to prove that using this strategy, there is a sequence of M operations requiring $\Omega(M \cdot N)$ time, so this idea is not quite good enough. The simplest way to show this is to consider the tree formed by inserting keys $1, 2, 3, \ldots, N$ into an initially empty tree (work this example out). This gives a tree consisting of only left children. This is not necessarily bad, though, since the time to build this tree is $O(N)$ total. The bad part is that accessing the node with key 1 takes $N - 1$ units of time. After the rotations are complete, an access of the node with key 2 takes $N - 2$ units of time. The total for accessing all the keys in order is $\sum_{i=1}^{N-1} i = \Omega(N^2)$. After they are accessed, the tree reverts to its original state, and we can repeat the sequence.

4.5.2. Splaying

The splaying strategy is similar to the rotation idea above, except that we are a little more selective about how rotations are performed. We will still rotate bottom up along the access

Figure 4.44 Zig-zag

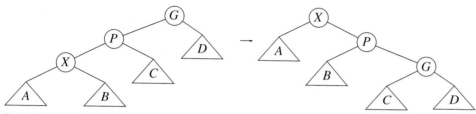

Figure 4.45 Zig-zig

path. Let X be a (nonroot) node on the access path at which we are rotating. If the parent of X is the root of the tree, we merely rotate X and the root. This is the last rotation along the access path. Otherwise, X has both a parent (P) and a grandparent (G), and there are two cases, plus symmetries, to consider. The first case is the *zig-zag* case (see Fig. 4.44). Here, X is a right child and P is a left child (or vice versa). If this is the case, we perform a double rotation, exactly like an AVL double rotation. Otherwise, we have a *zig-zig* case: X and P are both left children (or, in the symmetric case, both right children). In that case, we transform the tree on the left of Figure 4.45 to the tree on the right.

As an example, consider the tree from the last example, with a **find** on k_1:

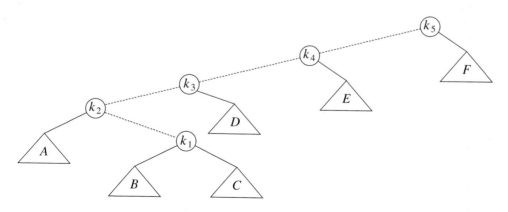

The first splay step is at k_1, and is clearly a *zig-zag*, so we perform a standard AVL double rotation using k_1, k_2, and k_3. The resulting tree follows.

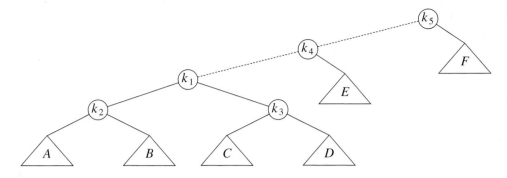

The next splay step at k_1 is a *zig-zig*, so we do the *zig-zig* rotation with k_1, k_4, and k_5, obtaining the final tree.

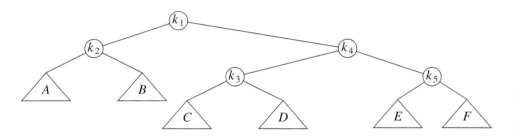

Although it is hard to see from small examples, splaying not only moves the accessed node to the root, but also has the effect of roughly halving the depth of most nodes on the access path (some shallow nodes are pushed down at most two levels).

To see the difference that splaying makes over simple rotation, consider again the effect of inserting items 1, 2, 3, ..., N into an initially empty tree. This takes a total of $O(N)$, as before, and yields the same tree as simple rotations. Figure 4.46 shows the result of splaying at the node with item 1. The difference is that after an access of the node with item 1, which

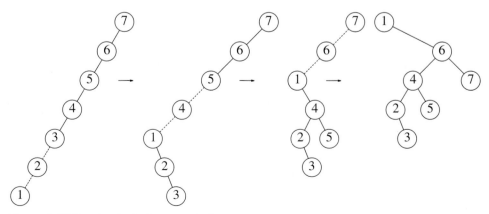

Figure 4.46 Result of splaying at node 1

takes $N - 1$ units, the access on the node with item 2 will only take about $N/2$ units instead of $N - 2$ units; there are no nodes quite as deep as before.

An access on the node with item 2 will bring nodes to within $N/4$ of the root, and this is repeated until the depth becomes roughly $\log N$ (an example with $N = 7$ is too small to see the effect well). Figures 4.47 to 4.55 show the result of accessing items 1 through 9 in a 32-node tree that originally contains only left children. Thus we do not get the same bad behavior from splay trees that is prevalent in the simple rotation strategy. (Actually, this turns out to be a very good case. A rather complicated proof shows that for this example, the N accesses take a total of $O(N)$ time.)

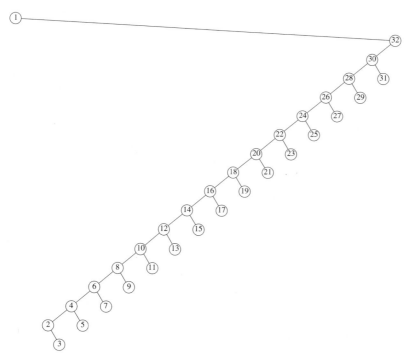

Figure 4.47 Result of splaying at node 1 a tree of all left children

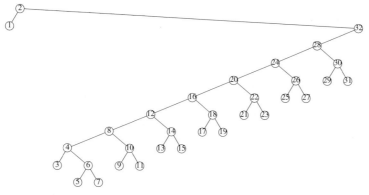

Figure 4.48 Result of splaying previous tree at node 2

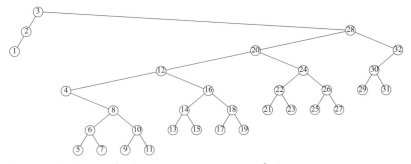

Figure 4.49 Result of splaying previous tree at node 3

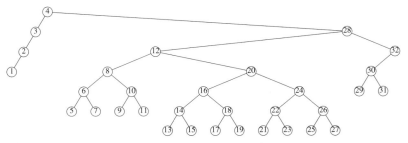

Figure 4.50 Result of splaying previous tree at node 4

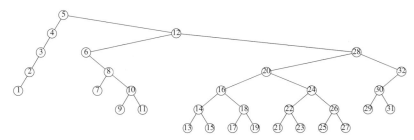

Figure 4.51 Result of splaying previous tree at node 5

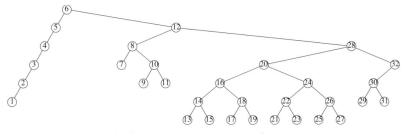

Figure 4.52 Result of splaying previous tree at node 6

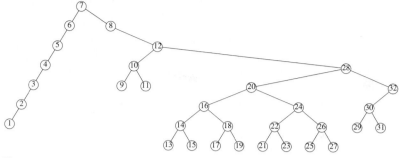

Figure 4.53 Result of splaying previous tree at node 7

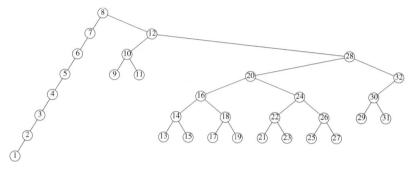

Figure 4.54 Result of splaying previous tree at node 8

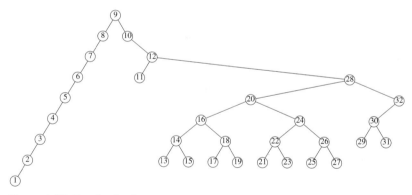

Figure 4.55 Result of splaying previous tree at node 9

These figures highlight the fundamental and crucial property of splay trees. When access paths are long, thus leading to a longer-than-normal search time, the rotations tend to be good for future operations. When accesses are cheap, the rotations are not as good and can be bad. The extreme case is the initial tree formed by the insertions. All the insertions were constant-time operations leading to a bad initial tree. At that point in time, we had a very bad tree, but we were running ahead of schedule and had the compensation of less total running time. Then a couple of really horrible accesses left a nearly balanced tree, but the cost was that we had to give back some of the time that had been saved. The main theorem, which we will prove in Chapter 11, is that we never fall behind a pace of $O(\log N)$ per operation: We are always on schedule, even though there are occasionally bad operations.

We can perform deletion by accessing the node to be deleted. This puts the node at the root. If it is deleted, we get two subtrees T_L and T_R (left and right). If we find the largest element in T_L (which is easy), then this element is rotated to the root of T_L, and T_L will now have a root with no right child. We can finish the deletion by making T_R the right child.

The analysis of splay trees is difficult, because it must take into account the ever-changing structure of the tree. On the other hand, splay trees are much simpler to program than AVL trees, since there are fewer cases to consider and no balance information to maintain. Some empirical evidence suggests that this translates into faster code in practice, although the case for this is far from complete. Finally, we point out that there are several variations of splay trees that can perform even better in practice. One variation is completely coded in Chapter 12.

4.6. Tree Traversals (Revisited)

Because of the ordering information in a binary search tree, it is simple to list all the items in sorted order. The recursive method in Figure 4.56 does the real work.

Convince yourself that this method works. As we have seen before, this kind of routine when applied to trees is known as an *inorder* traversal (which makes sense, since it lists the items in order). The general strategy of an inorder traversal is to process the left subtree

```java
/**
 * Print the tree contents in sorted order.
 */
public void printTree( )
{
    if( isEmpty( ) )
        System.out.println( "Empty tree" );
    else
        printTree( root );
}

/**
 * Internal method to print a subtree in sorted order.
 * @param t the node that roots the tree.
 */
private void printTree( BinaryNode t )
{
    if( t != null )
    {
        printTree( t.left );
        System.out.println( t.element );
        printTree( t.right );
    }
}
```

Figure 4.56 Routine to print a binary search tree in order

```
/**
 * Internal method to compute height of a subtree.
 * @param t the node that roots the tree.
 */
private int height( BinaryNode t )
{
    if( t == null )
        return -1;
    else
        return 1 + max( height( t.left ), height( t.right ) );
}
```

Figure 4.57 Routine to compute the height of a tree using a postorder traversal

first, then perform processing at the current node, and finally process the right subtree. The interesting part about this algorithm, aside from its simplicity, is that the total running time is $O(N)$. This is because there is constant work being performed at every node in the tree. Each node is visited once, and the work performed at each node is testing against `null`, setting up two method calls, and doing a `println`. Since there is constant work per node and N nodes, the running time is $O(N)$.

Sometimes we need to process both subtrees first before we can process a node. For instance, to compute the height of a node, we need to know the height of the subtrees first. The code in Figure 4.57 computes this. Since it is always a good idea to check the special cases—and crucial when recursion is involved—notice that the routine will declare the height of a leaf to be zero, which is correct. This general order of traversal, which we have also seen before, is known as a *postorder* traversal. Again, the total running time is $O(N)$, because constant work is performed at each node.

The third popular traversal scheme that we have seen is *preorder* traversal. Here, the node is processed before the children. This could be useful, for example, if you wanted to label each node with its depth.

The common idea in all of these routines is that you handle the `null` case first, and then the rest. Notice the lack of extraneous variables. These routines pass only the reference to the node that roots the subtree, and do not declare or pass any extra variables. The more compact the code, the less likely that a silly bug will turn up. A fourth, less often used, traversal (which we have not seen yet) is *level-order* traversal. In a level-order traversal, all nodes at depth d are processed before any node at depth $d + 1$. Level-order traversal differs from the other traversals in that it is not done recursively; a queue is used, instead of the implied stack of recursion.

4.7. B-Trees

Thus far, we have assumed that we can store an entire data structure in the main memory of a computer. Suppose, however, that we have more data than can fit in main memory, meaning that we must have the data structure reside on disk. When this happens, the rules of the game change because the Big-Oh model is no longer meaningful.

The problem is that a Big-Oh analysis assumes that all operations are equal. However, this is not true, especially when disk I/O is involved. For example, a 25-MIPS machine allegedly executes 25 million instructions per second. That is pretty fast, mainly because the speed depends largely on electrical properties. On the other hand, a disk is mechanical. Its speed depends largely on the time it takes to spin the disk and to move a disk head. Many disks spin at 3,600 RPM (faster disks spin at 7,200 RPM). Thus in 1 min, it makes 3,600 revolutions; hence, one revolution occurs in 1/60 of a second, or 16.7 ms. On average, we might expect that we have to spin a disk halfway to find what we are looking for; so if we ignore other factors, we get an access time of 8.3 ms. (This is a very charitable estimate; 9–11 ms access times are more common.) Consequently, we can do approximately 120 disk accesses per second. This sounds pretty good, until we compare it with the processor speed. What we have is 25 million instructions equal to 120 disk accesses. Put another way, one disk access is worth about 200,000 instructions. Of course, everything here is a rough calculation, but the relative speeds are pretty clear: Disk accesses are incredibly expensive. Furthermore, processor speeds are increasing at a much faster rate than disk speeds (it is disk *sizes* that are increasing quite quickly). So we are willing to do lots of calculations just to save a disk access. In almost all cases, it is the number of disk accesses that will dominate the running time. Thus, if we halve the number of disk accesses, the running time will also halve.

Here is how the typical search tree performs on disk. Suppose we want to access the driving records for citizens in the State of Florida. We assume that we have 10 million items, that each key is 32 bytes (representing a name), and that a record is 256 bytes. We assume this does not fit in main memory and that we are 1 of 20 users on a system (so we have 1/20 of the resources). Thus, in 1 sec, we can execute a million instructions or perform six disk accesses.

The unbalanced binary search tree is a disaster. In the worst case, it has linear depth and thus could require 10 million disk accesses. On average, a successful search would require $1.38 \log N$ disk accesses, and since $\log 10000000 \approx 24$, an average search would require 32 disk accesses, or 5 sec. In a typical randomly constructed tree, we would expect that a few nodes are three times deeper; these would require about 100 disk accesses, or 16 sec. An AVL tree is somewhat better. The worst case of $1.44 \log N$ is unlikely to occur, and the typical case is very close to $\log N$. Thus an AVL tree would use about 25 disk accesses on average, requiring 4 sec.

We want to reduce the number of disk accesses to a very small constant, such as three or four; and we are willing to write complicated code to do this because machine instructions are essentially free, as long as we are not ridiculously unreasonable. It should probably be clear that a binary search tree will not work, since the typical AVL tree is close to optimal height. We cannot go below $\log N$ using a binary search tree. The solution is intuitively simple: If we have more branching, we have less height. Thus, while a perfect binary tree of 31 nodes has five levels, a 5-ary tree of 31 nodes has only three levels, as shown in Figure 4.58. An *M-ary search tree* allows M-way branching. As branching increases, the depth decreases. Whereas a complete binary tree has height that is roughly $\log_2 N$, a complete M-ary tree has height that is roughly $\log_M N$.

We can create an M-ary search tree in much the same way as a binary search tree. In a binary search tree, we need one key to decide which of two branches to take. In an M-ary search tree, we need $M - 1$ keys to decide which branch to take. To make this scheme efficient in the worst case, we need to ensure that the M-ary search tree is balanced in some

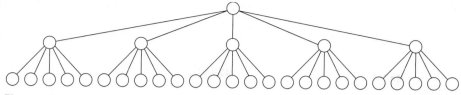

Figure 4.58 5-ary tree of 31 nodes has only three levels

way. Otherwise, like a binary search tree, it could degenerate into a linked list. Actually, we want an even more restrictive balancing condition. That is, we do not want an M-ary search tree to degenerate to even a binary search tree, because then we would be stuck with $\log N$ accesses.

One way to implement this is to use a *B-tree*. The basic B-tree* is described here. Many variations and improvements are possible, and an implementation is somewhat complex because there are quite a few cases. However, it is easy to see that, in principle, a B-tree guarantees only a few disk accesses.

A B-tree of order M is an M-ary tree with the following properties:[†]

1. The data items are stored at leaves.
2. The nonleaf nodes store up to $M - 1$ keys to guide the searching; key i represents the smallest key in subtree $i + 1$.
3. The root is either a leaf or has between two and M children.
4. All nonleaf nodes (except the root) have between $\lceil M/2 \rceil$ and M children.
5. All leaves are at the same depth and have between $\lceil L/2 \rceil$ and L children, for some L (the determination of L is described shortly).

An example of a B-tree of order 5 is shown in Figure 4.59. Notice that all nonleaf nodes have between three and five children (and thus between two and four keys); the root could possibly have only two children. Here, we have $L = 5$. (It happens that L and M are the same in this example, but this is not necessary.) Since L is 5, each leaf has between three and five data items. Requiring nodes to be half full guarantees that the B-tree does not

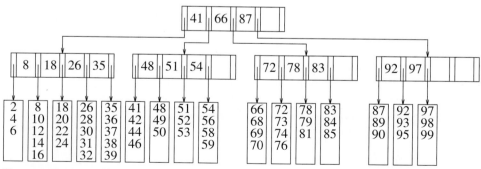

Figure 4.59 B-tree of order 5

---

degenerate into a simple binary tree. Although there are various definitions of B-trees that change this structure, mostly in minor ways, this definition is one of the popular forms.

Each node represents a disk block, so we choose M and L on the basis of the size of the items that are being stored. As an example, suppose one block holds 8,192 bytes. In our Florida example, each key uses 32 bytes. In a B-tree of order M, we would have $M - 1$ keys, for a total of $32M - 32$ bytes, plus M branches. Since each branch is essentially a number of another disk block, we can assume that a branch is 4 bytes. Thus the branches use $4M$ bytes. The total memory requirement for a nonleaf node is thus $36M - 32$. The largest value of M for which this is no more than 8,192 is 228. Thus we would choose $M = 228$. Since each data record is 256 bytes, we would be able to fit 32 records in a block. Thus we would choose $L = 32$. We are guaranteed that each leaf has between 16 and 32 data records and that each internal node (except the root) branches in at least 114 ways. Since there are 10 million records, there are at most 625,000 leaves. Consequently, in the worst case, leaves would be on level 4. In more concrete terms, the worst-case number of accesses is given by approximately $\log_{M/2} N$, give or take 1 (for example, the root and the first level could be cached in main memory, so that, over the long run, disk accesses would be needed only for level 3 and deeper).

The remaining issue is how to add and remove items from the B-tree; the ideas involved are sketched next. Note that many of the themes seen before recur.

We begin by examining insertion. Suppose we want to insert 57 into the B-tree in Figure 4.59. A search down the tree reveals that it is not already in the tree. We can then add it to the leaf as a fifth child. Note that we may have to reorganize all the data in the leaf to do this. However, the cost of doing this is negligible when compared to that of the disk access, which in this case also includes a disk write.

Of course, that was relatively painless because the leaf was not already full. Suppose we now want to insert 55. Figure 4.60 shows a problem: The leaf where 55 wants to go is already full. The solution is simple, however: Since we now have $L + 1$ items, we split them into two leaves, both guaranteed to have the minimum number of data records needed. We form two leaves with three items each. Two disk accesses are required to write these leaves, and a third disk access is required to update the parent. Note that in the parent, both keys and branches change, but they do so in a controlled way that is easily calculated. The resulting B-tree is shown in Figure 4.61. Although splitting nodes is time-consuming because it requires at least two additional disk writes, it is a relatively rare occurrence. If L is 32, for example, then when a node is split, two leaves with 16 and 17 items, respectively,

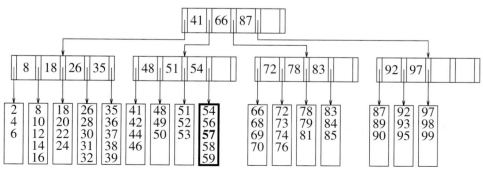

Figure 4.60 B-tree after insertion of 57 into the tree in Figure 4.59

Figure 4.61 Insertion of 55 into the B-tree in Figure 4.60 causes a split into two leaves

are created. For the leaf with 17 items, we can perform 15 more insertions without another split. Put another way, for every split, there are roughly $L/2$ nonsplits.

The node splitting in the previous example worked because the parent did not have its full complement of children. But what would happen if it did? Suppose, for example, that we were to insert 40 into the B-tree in Figure 4.61. We would then have to split the leaf containing the keys 35 through 39, and now 40, into two leaves. But doing this would give the parent six children, and it is allowed only five. Hence, the solution is to split the parent. The result of this is shown in Figure 4.62. When the parent is split, we must update the values of the keys and also the parent's parent, thus incurring an additional two disk writes (so this insertion costs five disk writes). However, once again, the keys change in a very controlled manner, although the code is certainly not simple because of a host of cases.

When a nonleaf node is split, as is the case here, its parent gains a child. What if the parent already has reached its limit of children? In that case, we continue splitting nodes up the tree until either we find a parent that does not need to be split or we reach the root. If we split the root, then we have two roots. Obviously, this is unacceptable, but we can create a new root that has the split roots as its two children. This is why the root is granted the special two-child minimum exemption. It also is the only way that a B-tree gains height. Needless to say, splitting all the way up to the root is an exceptionally rare event, because a tree with four levels indicates that the root has been split three times throughout the entire sequence of insertions (assuming no deletions have occurred). In fact, splitting of any nonleaf node is also quite rare.

There are other ways to handle the overflowing of children. One technique is to put a child up for adoption should a neighbor have room. To insert 29 into the B-tree in Figure

Figure 4.62 Insertion of 40 into the B-tree in Figure 4.61 causes a split into two leaves and then a split of the parent node

Figure 4.63 B-tree after the deletion of 99 from the B-tree in Figure 4.62

4.62, for example, we could make room by moving 32 to the next leaf. This technique requires a modification of the parent because the keys are affected. However, it tends to keep nodes fuller and thus saves space in the long run.

We can perform deletion by finding the item that needs to be removed and then removing it. The problem is that if the leaf it was in had the minimum number of data items, then it is now below the minimum. We can rectify this situation by adopting a neighboring item, if the neighbor is not itself at its minimum. If it is, then we can combine with the neighbor to form a full leaf. Unfortunately, this means that the parent has lost a child. If this loss causes the parent to fall below its minimum, then it follows the same strategy. This process could percolate all the way up to the root. The root cannot have just one child (and even if this were allowed, it would be silly). If a root is left with one child as a result of the adoption process, then we remove the root and make its child the new root of the tree. This is the only way for a B-tree to lose height. For example, suppose we want to remove 99 from the B-tree in Figure 4.62. Since the leaf has only two items, and its neighbor is already at its minimum of three, we combine the items into a new leaf of five items. As a result, the parent has only two children. However, it can adopt from a neighbor because the neighbor has four children. As a result, both have three children. The result is shown in Figure 4.63.

SUMMARY

We have seen uses of trees in operating systems, compiler design, and searching. Expression trees are a small example of a more general structure known as a *parse tree,* which is a central data structure in compiler design. Parse trees are not binary, but are relatively simple extensions of expression trees (although the algorithms to build them are not quite so simple).

Search trees are of great importance in algorithm design. They support almost all the useful operations, and the logarithmic average cost is very small. Nonrecursive implementations of search trees are somewhat faster, but the recursive versions are sleeker, more elegant, and easier to understand and debug. The problem with search trees is that their performance depends heavily on the input being random. If this is not the case, the running time increases significantly, to the point where search trees become expensive linked lists.

We saw several ways to deal with this problem. AVL trees work by insisting that all nodes' left and right subtrees differ in heights by at most one. This ensures that the tree cannot get too deep. The operations that do not change the tree, as insertion does, can all use the standard binary search tree code. Operations that change the tree must restore the tree. This can be somewhat complicated, especially in the case of deletion. We showed how to restore the tree after insertions in $O(\log N)$ time.

We also examined the splay tree. Nodes in splay trees can get arbitrarily deep, but after every access the tree is adjusted in a somewhat mysterious manner. The net effect is that any sequence of M operations takes $O(M \log N)$ time, which is the same as a balanced tree would take.

B-trees are balanced M-way (as opposed to 2-way or binary) trees, which are well suited for disks; a special case is the 2–3 tree ($M = 3$), which is another way to implement balanced search trees.

In practice, the running time of all the balanced tree schemes, while slightly faster for searching, is worse (by a constant factor) for insertions and deletions than the simple binary search tree, but this is generally acceptable in view of the protection being given against easily obtained worst-case input. Chapter 12 discusses some additional search tree data structures and provides detailed implementations.

A final note: By inserting elements into a search tree and then performing an inorder traversal, we obtain the elements in sorted order. This gives an $O(N \log N)$ algorithm to sort, which is a worst-case bound if any sophisticated search tree is used. We shall see better ways in Chapter 7, but none that have a lower time bound.

EXERCISES

Questions 4.1 to 4.3 refer to the tree in Figure 4.64.

4.1 For the tree in Figure 4.64:
    a. Which node is the root?
    b. Which nodes are leaves?

4.2 For each node in the tree of Figure 4.64:
    a. Name the parent node.
    b. List the children.
    c. List the siblings.
    d. Compute the depth.
    e. Compute the height.

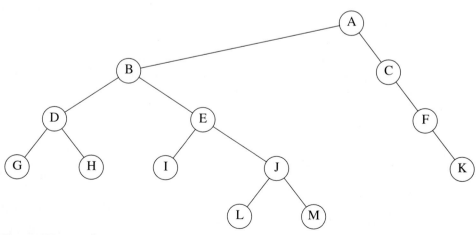

Figure 4.64 Tree for Exercises 4.1 to 4.3

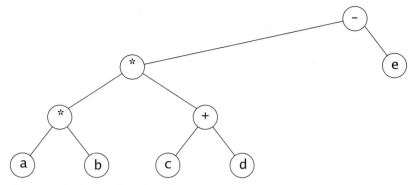

Figure 4.65 Tree for Exercise 4.8

4.3 What is the depth of the tree in Figure 4.64?

4.4 Show that in a binary tree of N nodes, there are $N+1$ **null** links representing children.

4.5 Show that the maximum number of nodes in a binary tree of height h is $2^{h+1} - 1$.

4.6 A *full node* is a node with two children. Prove that the number of full nodes plus one is equal to the number of leaves in a nonempty binary tree.

4.7 Suppose a binary tree has leaves $l_1, l_2, \ldots, l_M$ at depths $d_1, d_2, \ldots, d_M$, respectively. Prove that $\sum_{i=1}^{M} 2^{-d_i} \leq 1$ and determine when the equality is true.

4.8 Give the prefix, infix, and postfix expressions corresponding to the tree in Figure 4.65.

4.9 a. Show the result of inserting 3, 1, 4, 6, 9, 2, 5, 7 into an initially empty binary search tree.

b. Show the result of deleting the root.

4.10 Write a program that lists all files in a directory and their sizes. Mimic the routing in the online code.

4.11 Binary search trees can be implemented with cursors, using a strategy similar to a cursor linked list implementation. Write the basic binary search tree routines using a cursor implementation.

4.12 Modify the binary search tree by defining an iterator to return the result of **find** (and **findMin** and **findMax**), as was done with the linked list class. The iterator stores **current**. The corresponding value can be accessed by **retrieve**. Have the iterator provide **isValid**, which is true if **current** is not **null**.

4.13 Extend the iterator in Exercise 4.12, by adding a stack that stores the access path to the current node. In this way, you can implement **first** and **advance**.

4.14 Suppose you want to perform an experiment to verify the problems that can be caused by random **insert/remove** pairs. Here is a strategy that is not perfectly random, but close enough. You build a tree with N elements by inserting N elements chosen at random from the range 1 to $M = \alpha N$. You then perform N^2 pairs of insertions followed by deletions. Assume the existence of a routine, **randomInteger(a, b)**, which returns a uniform random integer between **a** and **b** inclusive.

   a. Explain how to generate a random integer between 1 and M that is not already in the tree (so a random insertion can be performed). In terms of N and α, what is the running time of this operation?

   b. Explain how to generate a random integer between 1 and M that is already in the tree (so a random deletion can be performed). What is the running time of this operation?

   c. What is a good choice of α? Why?

4.15 Write a program to evaluate empirically the following strategies for removing nodes with two children:

   a. Replace with the largest node, X, in T_L and recursively remove X.

   b. Alternately replace with the largest node in T_L and the smallest node in T_R, and recursively remove the appropriate node.

   c. Replace with either the largest node in T_L or the smallest node in T_R (recursively removing the appropriate node), making the choice randomly.

   Which strategy seems to give the most balance? Which takes the least CPU time to process the entire sequence?

4.16 Redo the binary search tree class to implement lazy deletion. Note carefully that this affects all of the routines. Especially challenging are `findMin` and `findMax`, which must now be done recursively.

**4.17 Prove that the depth of a random binary search tree (depth of the deepest node) is $O(\log N)$, on average.

4.18 *a. Give a precise expression for the minimum number of nodes in an AVL tree of height h.

   b. What is the minimum number of nodes in an AVL tree of height 15?

4.19 Show the result of inserting 2, 1, 4, 5, 9, 3, 6, 7 into an initially empty AVL tree.

*4.20 Keys $1, 2, \ldots, 2^k - 1$ are inserted in order into an initially empty AVL tree. Prove that the resulting tree is perfectly balanced.

4.21 Write the remaining procedures to implement AVL single and double rotations.

4.22 Design a linear-time algorithm that verifies that the height information in an AVL tree is correctly maintained and that the balance property is in order.

4.23 Write a nonrecursive method to insert into an AVL tree.

*4.24 How can you implement (nonlazy) deletion in AVL trees?

4.25 a. How many bits are required per node to store the height of a node in an N-node AVL tree?

   b. What is the smallest AVL tree that overflows an 8-bit height counter?

4.26 Write the methods to perform the double rotation without the inefficiency of doing two single rotations.

4.27 Show the result of accessing the keys 3, 9, 1, 5 in order in the splay tree in Figure 4.66.

4.28 Show the result of deleting the element with key 6 in the resulting splay tree for the previous exercise.

4.29 a. Show that if all nodes in a splay tree are accessed in sequential order, the resulting tree consists of a chain of left children.

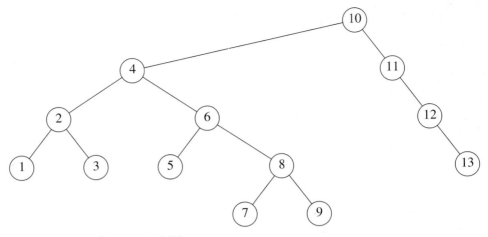

Figure 4.66 Tree for exercise 4.27

**b. Show that if all nodes in a splay tree are accessed in sequential order, then the total access time is $O(N)$, regardless of the initial tree.

4.30 Write a program to perform random operations on splay trees. Count the total number of rotations performed over the sequence. How does the running time compare to AVL trees and unbalanced binary search trees?

4.31 Write efficient methods that take only a reference to the root of a binary tree, T, and compute:
   a. The number of nodes in T.
   b. The number of leaves in T.
   c. The number of full nodes in T.
   What is the running time of your routines?

4.32 Design a recursive linear-time algorithm that tests whether a binary tree satisfies the search tree order property at every node.

4.33 Write a recursive method that takes a reference to the root node of a tree T and returns a reference to the root node of the tree that results from removing all leaves from T.

4.34 Write a method to generate an N-node random binary search tree with distinct keys 1 through N. What is the running time of your routine?

4.35 Write a method to generate the AVL tree of height h with fewest nodes. What is the running time of your method?

4.36 Write a method to generate a perfectly balanced binary search tree of height h with keys 1 through $2^{h+1} - 1$. What is the running time of your method?

4.37 Write a method that takes as input a binary search tree, T, and two keys k_1 and k_2, which are ordered so that $k_1 \leq k_2$, and prints all elements X in the tree such that $k_1 \leq Key(X) \leq k_2$. Do not assume any information about the type of keys except that they can be ordered (consistently). Your program should run in $O(K + \log N)$ average time, where K is the number of keys printed. Bound the running time of your algorithm.

4.38 The larger binary trees in this chapter were generated automatically by a program. This was done by assigning an (x, y) coordinate to each tree node, drawing a circle around each coordinate (this is hard to see in some pictures), and connecting each node to its parent. Assume you have a binary search tree stored in memory (perhaps generated by one of the routines above) and that each node has two extra fields to store the coordinates.

  a. The x coordinate can be computed by assigning the inorder traversal number. Write a routine to do this for each node in the tree.

  b. The y coordinate can be computed by using the negative of the depth of the node. Write a routine to do this for each node in the tree.

  c. In terms of some imaginary unit, what will the dimensions of the picture be? How can you adjust the units so that the tree is always roughly two-thirds as high as it is wide?

  d. Prove that using this system no lines cross, and that for any node, X, all elements in X's left subtree appear to the left of X and all elements in X's right subtree appear to the right of X.

4.39 Write a general-purpose tree-drawing program that will convert a tree into the following graph-assembler instructions:

  a. $Circle(X, Y)$

  b. $DrawLine(i, j)$

  The first instruction draws a circle at (X, Y), and the second instruction connects the ith circle to the jth circle (circles are numbered in the order drawn). You should either make this a program and define some sort of input language or make this a method that can be called from any program. What is the running time of your routine?

4.40 (This exercise assumes familiarity with the Java AWT Library.) Write a program that reads graph-assembler instructions and generates Java code that draws into a canvas. (Note that you have to scale the stored coordinates into pixels.)

4.41 Write a routine to list out the nodes of a binary tree in *level-order*. List the root, then nodes at depth 1, followed by nodes at depth 2, and so on. You must do this in linear time. Prove your time bound.

4.42 *a. Write a routine to perform insertion into a B-tree.

  *b. Write a routine to perform deletion from a B-tree. When an item is deleted, is it necessary to update information in the internal nodes?

  *c. Modify your insertion routine so that if an attempt is made to add into a node that already has M entries, a search is performed for a sibling with less than M children before the node is split.

4.43 A B^*-*tree* of order M is a B-tree in which each interior node has between $2M/3$ and M children. Describe a method to perform insertion into a B^*-tree.

4.44 Show how the tree in Figure 4.67 is represented using a child/sibling link implementation.

4.45 Write a procedure to traverse a tree stored with child/sibling links.

4.46 Two binary trees are similar if they are both empty or both nonempty and have similar left and right subtrees. Write a method to decide whether two binary trees are similar. What is the running time of your method?

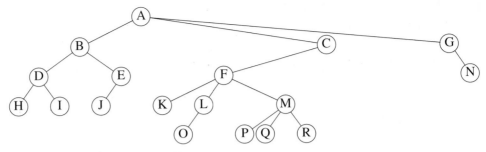

Figure 4.67 Tree for Exercise 4.44

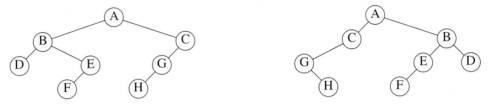

Figure 4.68 Two isomorphic trees

4.47 Two trees, T_1 and T_2, are *isomorphic* if T_1 can be transformed into T_2 by swapping left and right children of (some of the) nodes in T_1. For instance, the two trees in Figure 4.68 are isomorphic because they are the same if the children of A, B, and G, but not the other nodes, are swapped.

  a. Give a polynomial time algorithm to decide if two trees are isomorphic.

  *b. What is the running time of your program (there is a linear solution)?

4.48 *a. Show that via AVL single rotations, any binary search tree T_1 can be transformed into another search tree T_2 (with the same items).

  *b. Give an algorithm to perform this transformation using $O(N \log N)$ rotations on average.

  **c. Show that this transformation can be done with $O(N)$ rotations, worst-case.

4.49 Suppose we want to add the operation findKth to our repertoire. The operation findKth(k) returns the kth smallest item in the tree. Assume all items are distinct. Explain how to modify the binary search tree to support this operation in $O(\log N)$ average time, without sacrificing the time bounds of any other operation.

4.50 Since a binary search tree with N nodes has $N + 1$ null references, half the space allocated in a binary search tree for link information is wasted. Suppose that if a node has a null left child, we make its left child link to its inorder predecessor, and if a node has a null right child, we make its right child link to its inorder successor. This is known as a *threaded tree,* and the extra link are called *threads.*

  a. How can we distinguish threads from real children links?

  b. Write routines to perform insertion and deletion into a tree threaded in the manner described above.

  c. What is the advantage of using threaded trees?

4.51 Let $f(N)$ be the average number of full nodes in a binary search tree.
    a. Determine the values of $f(0)$ and $f(1)$.
    b. Show that for $N > 1$

$$f(N) = \frac{N-2}{N} + \frac{1}{N}\sum_{i=0}^{N-1}(f(i) + f(N - i - 1))$$

    c. Show (by induction) that $f(N) = (N - 2)/3$ is a solution to the equation in part (b), with the initial conditions in part (a).
    d. Use the results of Exercise 4.6 to determine the average number of leaves in a binary search tree.

4.52 Write a program that reads a Java source code file and outputs a list of all identifiers (that is, variable names but not keywords, not found in comments or string constants) in alphabetical order. Each identifier should be output with a list of line numbers on which it occurs.

4.53 Generate an index for a book. The input file consists of a set of index entries. Each line consists of the string IX:, followed by an index entry name enclosed in braces, followed by a page number that is enclosed in braces. Each ! in an index entry name represents a sub-level. A | (represents the start of a range, and a) | represents the end of the range. Occasionally, this range will be the same page. In that case, output only a single page number. Otherwise, do not collapse or expand ranges on your own. As an example, Figure 4.69 shows sample input, and Figure 4.70 shows the corresponding output.

```
IX: {Series |(}              {2}
IX: {Series!geometric|(}     {4}
IX: {Euler's constant}       {4}
IX: {Series!geometric|)}     {4}
IX: {Series!arithmetic|(}    {4}
IX: {Series!arithmetic|)}    {5}
IX: {Series!harmonic|(}      {5}
IX: {Euler's constant}       {5}
IX: {Series!harmonic|)}      {5}
IX: {Series|)}               {5}
```

Figure 4.69 Sample input for Exercise 4.53

```
Euler's constant: 4, 5
Series: 2-5
    arithmetic: 4-5
    geometric: 4
    harmonic: 5
```

Figure 4.70 Sample output for Exercise 4.53

REFERENCES

More information on binary search trees, and in particular the mathematical properties of trees, can be found in the two books by Knuth, [22] and [23].

Several papers deal with the lack of balance caused by biased deletion algorithms in binary search trees. Hibbard's paper [19] proposed the original deletion algorithm and established that one deletion preserves the randomness of the trees. A complete analysis has been performed only for trees with three nodes [20] and four nodes [5]. Eppinger's paper [14] provided early empirical evidence of nonrandomness, and the papers by Culberson and Munro [10], [11] provided some analytical evidence (but not a complete proof for the general case of intermixed insertions and deletions).

AVL trees were proposed by Adelson-Velskii and Landis [1]. Simulation results for AVL trees, and variants in which the height imbalance is allowed to be at most k for various values of k, are presented in [21]. A deletion algorithm for AVL trees can be found in [23]. Analysis of the average search cost in AVL trees is incomplete, but some results are contained in [24].

[3] and [8] considered self-adjusting trees like the type in Section 4.5.1. Splay trees are described in [28].

B-trees first appeared in [6]. The implementation described in the original paper allows data to be stored in internal nodes as well as leaves. The data structure we have described is sometimes known as a B^+-tree. A survey of the different types of B-trees is presented in [9]. Empirical results of the various schemes are reported in [17]. Analysis of 2–3 trees and B-trees can be found in [4], [13], and [32].

Exercise 4.17 is deceptively difficult. A solution can be found in [15]. Exercise 4.29 is from [31]. Information on B*-trees, described in Exercise 4.43, can be found in [12]. Exercise 4.47 is from [2]. A solution to Exercise 4.48 using $2N - 6$ rotations is given in [29]. Using threads, à la Exercise 4.50, was first proposed in [27]. k-d trees, which handle multidimensional data, were first proposed in [7] and are discussed in Chapter 12.

Other popular balanced search trees are red-black trees [18] and weight-balanced trees [26]. More balanced tree schemes can be found in Chapter 12, as well as in the books [16], [25], and [30].

1. G. M. Adelson-Velskii and E. M. Landis, "An Algorithm for the Organization of Information," *Soviet. Mat. Doklady,* 3 (1962), 1259–1263.
2. A. V. Aho, J. E. Hopcroft, and J. D. Ullman, *The Design and Analysis of Computer Algorithms,* Addison-Wesley, Reading, Mass., 1974.
3. B. Allen and J. I. Munro, "Self Organizing Search Trees," *Journal of the ACM,* 25 (1978), 526–535.
4. R. A. Baeza-Yates, "Expected Behaviour of B^+-trees under Random Insertions," *Acta Informatica,* 26 (1989), 439–471.
5. R. A. Baeza-Yates, "A Trivial Algorithm Whose Analysis Isn't: A Continuation," *BIT,* 29 (1989), 88–113.
6. R. Bayer and E. M. McCreight, "Organization and Maintenance of Large Ordered Indices," *Acta Informatica,* 1 (1972), 173–189.
7. J. L. Bentley, "Multidimensional Binary Search Trees Used for Associative Searching," *Communications of the ACM,* 18 (1975), 509–517.
8. J. R. Bitner, "Heuristics that Dynamically Organize Data Structures," *SIAM Journal on Computing,* 8 (1979), 82–110.

9. D. Comer, "The Ubiquitous B-tree," *Computing Surveys,* 11 (1979), 121–137.

10. J. Culberson and J. I. Munro, "Explaining the Behavior of Binary Search Trees under Prolonged Updates: A Model and Simulations," *Computer Journal,* 32 (1989), 68–75.

11. J. Culberson and J. I. Munro, "Analysis of the Standard Deletion Algorithms in Exact Fit Domain Binary Search Trees," *Algorithmica,* 5 (1990) 295–311.

12. K. Culik, T. Ottman, and D. Wood, "Dense Multiway Trees," *ACM Transactions on Database Systems,* 6 (1981), 486–512.

13. B. Eisenbath, N. Ziviana, G. H. Gonnet, K. Melhorn, and D. Wood, "The Theory of Fringe Analysis and its Application to 2–3 Trees and B-trees," *Information and Control,* 55 (1982), 125–174.

14. J. L. Eppinger, "An Empirical Study of Insertion and Deletion in Binary Search Trees," *Communications of the ACM,* 26 (1983), 663–669.

15. P. Flajolet and A. Odlyzko, "The Average Height of Binary Trees and Other Simple Trees," *Journal of Computer and System Sciences,* 25 (1982), 171–213.

16. G. H. Gonnet and R. Baeza-Yates, *Handbook of Algorithms and Data Structures,* 2d ed., Addison-Wesley, Reading, Mass., 1991.

17. E. Gudes and S. Tsur, "Experiments with B-tree Reorganization," *Proceedings of ACM SIGMOD Symposium on Management of Data* (1980), 200–206.

18. L. J. Guibas and R. Sedgewick, "A Dichromatic Framework for Balanced Trees," *Proceedings of the Nineteenth Annual IEEE Symposium on Foundations of Computer Science* (1978), 8–21.

19. T. H. Hibbard, "Some Combinatorial Properties of Certain Trees with Applications to Searching and Sorting," *Journal of the ACM,* 9 (1962), 13–28.

20. A. T. Jonassen and D. E. Knuth, "A Trivial Algorithm Whose Analysis Isn't," *Journal of Computer and System Sciences,* 16 (1978), 301–322.

21. P. L. Karlton, S. H. Fuller, R. E. Scroggs, and E. B. Kaehler, "Performance of Height Balanced Trees," *Communications of the ACM,* 19 (1976), 23–28.

22. D. E. Knuth, *The Art of Computer Programming: Vol. 1: Fundamental Algorithms,* 3d ed., Addison-Wesley, Reading, Mass., 1997.

23. D. E. Knuth, *The Art of Computer Programming: Vol. 3: Sorting and Searching,* 2d ed., Addison-Wesley, Reading, Mass., 1998.

24. K. Melhorn, "A Partial Analysis of Height-Balanced Trees under Random Insertions and Deletions," *SIAM Journal of Computing,* 11 (1982), 748–760.

25. K. Melhorn, *Data Structures and Algorithms 1: Sorting and Searching,* Springer-Verlag, Berlin, 1984.

26. J. Nievergelt and E. M. Reingold, "Binary Search Trees of Bounded Balance," *SIAM Journal on Computing,* 2 (1973), 33–43.

27. A. J. Perlis and C. Thornton, "Symbol Manipulation in Threaded Lists," *Communications of the ACM,* 3 (1960), 195–204.

28. D. D. Sleator and R. E. Tarjan, "Self-adjusting Binary Search Trees," *Journal of ACM,* 32 (1985), 652–686.

29. D. D. Sleator, R. E. Tarjan, and W. P. Thurston, "Rotation Distance, Triangulations, and Hyperbolic Geometry," *Journal of AMS* (1988), 647–682.

30. H. F. Smith, *Data Structures—Form and Function,* Harcourt Brace Jovanovich, Orlando, Fla., 1987.

31. R. E. Tarjan, "Sequential Access in Splay Trees Takes Linear Time," *Combinatorica,* 5 (1985), 367–378.

32. A. C. Yao, "On Random 2–3 Trees," *Acta Informatica,* 9 (1978), 159–170.

Hashing

In Chapter 4, we discussed the search tree ADT, which allowed various operations on a set of elements. In this chapter, we discuss the *hash table* ADT, which supports only a subset of the operations allowed by binary search trees.

The implementation of hash tables is frequently called *hashing*. Hashing is a technique used for performing insertions, deletions, and finds in constant average time. Tree operations that require any ordering information among the elements are not supported efficiently. Thus, operations such as `findMin`, `findMax`, and the printing of the entire table in sorted order in linear time are not supported.

The central data structure in this chapter is the *hash table*. We will

- See several methods of implementing the hash table.
- Compare these methods analytically.
- Show numerous applications of hashing.
- Compare hash tables with binary search trees.

5.1. General Idea

The ideal hash table data structure is merely an array of some fixed size, containing the items. As discussed in Chapter 4, generally a search is performed on some part (that is, data field) of the item. This is called the *key*. For instance, an item could consist of a string (that serves as the key) and additional data fields (for instance, a name that is part of a large employee structure). We will refer to the table size as *TableSize*, with the understanding that this is part of a hash data structure and not merely some variable floating around globally. The common convention is to have the table run from 0 to *TableSize* − 1; we will see why shortly.

Each key is mapped into some number in the range 0 to *TableSize* − 1 and placed in the appropriate cell. The mapping is called a *hash function*, which ideally should be simple to compute and should ensure that any two distinct keys get different cells. Since there are a finite number of cells and a virtually inexhaustible supply of keys, this is clearly impossible, and thus we seek a hash function that distributes the keys evenly among the cells. Figure 5.1 is typical of a perfect situation. In this example, *john* hashes to 3, *phil* hashes to 4, *dave* hashes to 6, and *mary* hashes to 7.

This is the basic idea of hashing. The only remaining problems deal with choosing a function, deciding what to do when two keys hash to the same value (this is known as a *collision*), and deciding on the table size.

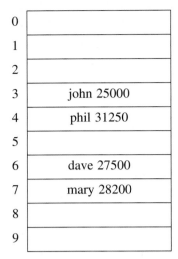

0	
1	
2	
3	john 25000
4	phil 31250
5	
6	dave 27500
7	mary 28200
8	
9	

Figure 5.1 An ideal hash table

5.2. Hash Function

If the input keys are integers, then simply returning *Key* mod *TableSize* is generally a reasonable strategy, unless *Key* happens to have some undesirable properties. In this case, the choice of hash function needs to be carefully considered. For instance, if the table size is 10 and the keys all end in zero, then the standard hash function is a bad choice. For reasons we shall see later, and to avoid situations like the one above, it is usually a good idea to ensure that the table size is prime. When the input keys are random integers, then this function is not only very simple to compute but also distributes the keys evenly.

Usually, the keys are strings; in this case, the hash function needs to be chosen carefully.

One option is to add up the ASCII (or Unicode) values of the characters in the string. The routine in Figure 5.2 implements this strategy.

The hash function depicted in Figure 5.2 is simple to implement and computes an answer quickly. However, if the table size is large, the function does not distribute the keys well. For instance, suppose that *TableSize* = 10,007 (10,007 is a prime number). Suppose all the keys are eight or fewer characters long. Since an ASCII character has an integer value

```
public static int hash( String key, int tableSize )
{
    int hashVal = 0;

    for( int i = 0; i < key.length( ); i++ )
        hashVal += key.charAt( i );

    return hashVal % tableSize;
}
```

Figure 5.2 A simple hash function

```
public static int hash( String key, int tableSize )
{
    return ( key.charAt( 0 ) + 27 * key.charAt( 1 ) +
               729 * key.charAt( 2 ) ) % tableSize;
}
```

Figure 5.3 Another possible hash function—not too good

that is always at most 127, the hash function typically can only assume values between 0 and 1,016, which is 127 * 8. This is clearly not an equitable distribution!

Another hash function is shown in Figure 5.3. This hash function assumes that *Key* has at least three characters. The value 27 represents the number of letters in the English alphabet, plus the blank, and 729 is 27^2. This function examines only the first three characters, but if these are random and the table size is 10,007, as before, then we would expect a reasonably equitable distribution. Unfortunately, English is not random. Although there are $26^3 = 17,576$ possible combinations of three characters (ignoring blanks), a check of a reasonably large on-line dictionary reveals that the number of different combinations is actually only 2,851. Even if none of *these* combinations collide, only 28 percent of the table can actually be hashed to. Thus this function, although easily computable, is also not appropriate if the hash table is reasonably large.

Figure 5.4 shows a third attempt at a hash function. This hash function involves all characters in the key and can generally be expected to distribute well (it computes $\sum_{i=0}^{KeySize-1} Key[KeySize - i - 1] \cdot 37^i$, and brings the result into proper range). The code computes a polynomial function (of 37) by use of Horner's rule. For instance, another way of computing $h_k = k_0 + 37k_1 + 37^2k_2$ is by the formula $h_k = ((k_2) * 37 + k_1) * 37 + k_0$. Horner's rule extends this to an *n*th degree polynomial.

```
/**
 * A hash routine for String objects.
 * @param key the String to hash.
 * @param tableSize the size of the hash table.
 * @return the hash value.
 */
public static int hash( String key, int tableSize )
{
    int hashVal = 0;

    for( int i = 0; i < key.length( ); i++ )
        hashVal = 37 * hashVal + key.charAt( i );

    hashVal %= tableSize;
    if( hashVal < 0 )
        hashVal += tableSize;

    return hashVal;
}
```

Figure 5.4 A good hash function

The hash function takes advantage of the fact that overflow is allowed. This may introduce a negative number; thus the extra test at the end.

The hash function described in Figure 5.4 is not necessarily the best with respect to table distribution, but does have the merit of extreme simplicity and is reasonably fast. If the keys are very long, the hash function will take too long to compute. A common practice in this case is not to use all the characters. The length and properties of the keys would then influence the choice. For instance, the keys could be a complete street address. The hash function might include a couple of characters from the street address and perhaps a couple of characters from the city name and ZIP code. Some programmers implement their hash function by using only the characters in the odd spaces, with the idea that the time saved computing the hash function will make up for a slightly less evenly distributed function.*

The main programming detail left is collision resolution. If, when an element is inserted, it hashes to the same value as an already inserted element, then we have a *collision* and need to resolve it. There are several methods for dealing with this. We will discuss two of the simplest: separate chaining and open addressing.

5.3. Separate Chaining

The first strategy, commonly known as *separate chaining,* is to keep a list of all elements that hash to the same value. We can use the list implementations from Chapter 3. If space is tight, it might be preferable to avoid their use (since the headers waste space). We assume, for this section, that the keys are the first 10 perfect squares and that the hashing function

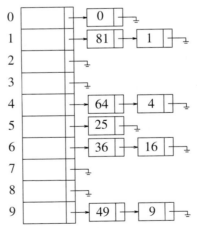

Figure 5.5 A separate chaining hash table

---

*As described in the Appendix, objects in Java automatically have a hashcode method defined. The method returns an int (presumably the HashSet and HashMap classes defined in Java then apply the mod operator). Early versions of hashcode for Strings performed poorly. The current version uses the function we suggest, with 31 instead of 37.

is simply $hash(x) = x$ mod 10. (The table size is not prime but is used here for simplicity.) Figure 5.5 should make this clear.

To perform a `find`, we use the hash function to determine which list to traverse. We then perform a `find` in this list. To perform an `insert`, we check the appropriate list to see whether the element is already in place (if duplicates are expected, an extra field is usually kept, and this field would be incremented in the event of a match). If the element turns out to be new, it is inserted at the front of the list, since it is convenient and also because frequently it happens that recently inserted elements are the most likely to be accessed in the near future.

The class skeleton required to implement separate chaining is shown in Figure 5.6. The hash table structure contains an array of linked lists, which are allocated in the constructor.

Just as the binary search tree works only for objects that are `Comparable`, the hash tables in this chapter work only for objects that implement the `Hashable` interface. The `Hashable` interface contains a single method, shown in Figure 5.7. Figure 5.7 also illustrates an `Employee` class that can be stored in the generic hash table. The `Employee` class implements the `Hashable` interface by using the hash function of Figure 5.5, which is a method in the `SeparateChainingHashTable` class.

Figure 5.8 shows the constructors and `makeEmpty`.

```
public class SeparateChainingHashTable
{
    public SeparateChainingHashTable( )
      { /* Figure 5.8 */ }
    public SeparateChainingHashTable( int size )
      { /* Figure 5.8 */ }

    public void insert( Hashable x )
      { /* Figure 5.10 */ }
    public void remove( Hashable x )
      { /* Figure 5.9 */ }
    public Hashable find( Hashable x )
      { /* Figure 5.9 */ }
    public void makeEmpty( )
      { /* Figure 5.8 */ }
    public static int hash( String key, int tableSize )
      { /* Figure 5.4 */ }

    private static final int DEFAULT_TABLE_SIZE = 101;

      /** The array of Lists. */
    private LinkedList [ ] theLists;

    private static int nextPrime( int n )
      { /* See online code */ }
    private static boolean isPrime( int n )
      { /* See online code */ }
}
```

Figure 5.6 Class skeleton for separate chaining hash table

```
public interface Hashable
{
    int hash( int tableSize );
}

// Example of an Employee class.
public class Employee implements Hashable
{
    public int hash( int tableSize )
      { return SeparateChainingHashTable.hash( name, tableSize ); }
    public boolean equals( Object rhs )
      { return name.equals( ((Employee)rhs).name ); }

    private String name;
    private double salary;
    private int    seniority;
       // Additional fields and methods
}
```

Figure 5.7 The Hashable interface

```
/**
 * Construct the hash table.
 */
public SeparateChainingHashTable( )
{
    this( DEFAULT_TABLE_SIZE );
}

/**
 * Construct the hash table.
 * @param size approximate table size.
 */
public SeparateChainingHashTable( int size )
{
    theLists = new LinkedList[ nextPrime( size ) ];
    for( int i = 0; i < theLists.length; i++ )
        theLists[ i ] = new LinkedList( );
}

/**
 * Make the hash table logically empty.
 */
public void makeEmpty( )
{
    for( int i = 0; i < theLists.length; i++ )
        theLists[ i ].makeEmpty( );
}
```

Figure 5.8 Constructors and makeEmpty for separate chaining hash table

```
/**
 * Remove from the hash table.
 * @param x the item to remove.
 */
public void remove( Hashable x )
{
    theLists[ x.hash( theLists.length ) ].remove( x );
}

/**
 * Find an item in the hash table.
 * @param x the item to search for.
 * @return the matching item, or null if not found.
 */
public Hashable find( Hashable x )
{
    return (Hashable)theLists[ x.hash( theLists.length ) ].
                                    find( x ).retrieve( );
}
```

Figure 5.9 find and remove routines for separate chaining hash table

```
/**
 * Insert into the hash table. If the item is
 * already present, then do nothing.
 * @param x the item to insert.
 */
public void insert( Hashable x )
{
    LinkedList whichList = theLists[ x.hash( theLists.length ) ];
    LinkedListItr itr = whichList.find( x );

    if( itr.isPastEnd( ) )
        whichList.insert( x, whichList.zeroth( ) );
}
```

Figure 5.10 insert routine for separate chaining hash table

The call find(x) will return a reference to the object that matches x. The code to implement both find and remove is shown in Figure 5.9.

Next comes the insertion routine. If the item to be inserted is already present, then we do nothing; otherwise, we place it at the front of the list (see Fig. 5.10). The element can be placed anywhere in the list; this is most convenient in our case.

If the repertoire of hash routines does not include deletions, it is probably best to not use headers, since their use would provide no simplification and would waste considerable space.

Any scheme could be used besides linked lists to resolve the collisions; a binary search tree or even another hash table would work, but we expect that if the table is large and the hash function is good, all the lists should be short, so it is not worthwhile to try anything complicated.

We define the load factor, λ, of a hash table to be the ratio of the number of elements in the hash table to the table size. In the example above, $\lambda = 1.0$. The average length of a list is λ. The effort required to perform a search is the constant time required to evaluate the hash function plus the time to traverse the list. In an unsuccessful search, the number of nodes to examine is λ on average. A successful search requires that about $1 + (\lambda/2)$ links be traversed. To see this, notice that the list that is being searched contains the one node that stores the match plus zero or more other nodes. The expected number of "other nodes" in a table of N elements and M lists is $(N - 1)/M = \lambda - 1/M$, which is essentially λ, since M is presumed to be large. On average, half the "other nodes" are searched, so combined with the matching node, we obtain an average search cost of $1 + \lambda/2$ nodes. This analysis shows that the table size is not really important, but the load factor is. The general rule for separate chaining hashing is to make the table size about as large as the number of elements expected (in other words, let $\lambda \approx 1$). It is also a good idea, as mentioned before, to keep the table size prime to ensure a good distribution.

5.4. Open Addressing

Separate chaining hashing has the disadvantage of using linked lists. This tends to slow the algorithm down a bit because of the time required to allocate new cells (especially in other languages), and also essentially requires the implementation of a second data structure. *Open addressing hashing* is an alternative to resolving collisions with linked lists. In an open addressing hashing system, if a collision occurs, alternative cells are tried until an empty cell is found. More formally, cells $h_0(x), h_1(x), h_2(x), \ldots$ are tried in succession, where $h_i(x) = (hash(x) + f(i)) \bmod TableSize$, with $f(0) = 0$. The function, f, is the collision resolution strategy. Because all the data go inside the table, a bigger table is needed for open addressing hashing than for separate chaining hashing. Generally, the load factor should be below $\lambda = 0.5$ for open addressing hashing. We now look at three common collision resolution strategies.

5.4.1. Linear Probing

In linear probing, f is a linear function of i, typically $f(i) = i$. This amounts to trying cells sequentially (with wraparound) in search of an empty cell. Figure 5.11 shows the result of inserting keys {89, 18, 49, 58, 69} into a hash table using the same hash function as before and the collision resolution strategy, $f(i) = i$.

The first collision occurs when 49 is inserted; it is put in the next available spot, namely, spot 0, which is open. The key 58 collides with 18, 89, and then 49 before an empty cell is found three away. The collision for 69 is handled in a similar manner. As long as the table is big enough, a free cell can always be found, but the time to do so can get quite large. Worse, even if the table is relatively empty, blocks of occupied cells start forming. This effect, known as *primary clustering*, means that any key that hashes into the cluster will require several attempts to resolve the collision, and then it will add to the cluster.

	Empty Table	After 89	After 18	After 49	After 58	After 69
0				49	49	49
1					58	58
2						69
3						
4						
5						
6						
7						
8			18	18	18	18
9		89	89	89	89	89

Figure 5.11 Open addressing hash table with linear probing, after each insertion

Although we will not perform the calculations here, it can be shown that the expected number of probes using linear probing is roughly $\frac{1}{2}(1 + 1/(1 - \lambda)^2)$ for insertions and unsuccessful searches, and $\frac{1}{2}(1 + 1/(1 - \lambda))$ for successful searches. The calculations are somewhat involved. It is easy to see from the code that insertions and unsuccessful searches require the same number of probes. A moment's thought suggests that, on average, successful searches should take less time than unsuccessful searches.

The corresponding formulas, if clustering is not a problem, are fairly easy to derive. We will assume a very large table and that each probe is independent of the previous probes. These assumptions are satisfied by a *random* collision resolution strategy and are reasonable unless λ is very close to 1. First, we derive the expected number of probes in an unsuccessful search. This is just the expected number of probes until we find an empty cell. Since the fraction of empty cells is $1 - \lambda$, the number of cells we expect to probe is $1/(1 - \lambda)$. The number of probes for a successful search is equal to the number of probes required when the particular element was inserted. When an element is inserted, it is done as a result of an unsuccessful search. Thus, we can use the cost of an unsuccessful search to compute the average cost of a successful search.

The caveat is that λ changes from 0 to its current value, so that earlier insertions are cheaper and should bring the average down. For instance, in the table above, $\lambda = 0.5$, but the cost of accessing 18 is determined when 18 is inserted. At that point, $\lambda = 0.2$. Since 18 was inserted into a relatively empty table, accessing it should be easier than accessing a recently inserted element such as 69. We can estimate the average by using an integral to calculate the mean value of the insertion time, obtaining

$$I(\lambda) = \frac{1}{\lambda} \int_0^\lambda \frac{1}{1 - x} dx = \frac{1}{\lambda} \ln \frac{1}{1 - \lambda}$$

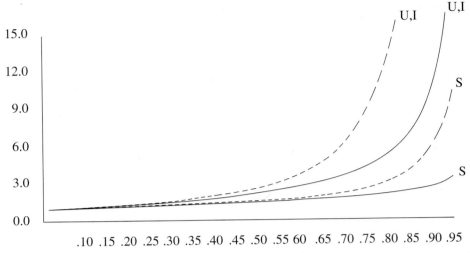

Figure 5.12 Number of probes plotted against load factor for linear probing (dashed) and random strategy (*S* is successful search, *U* is unsuccessful search, and *I* is insertion)

These formulas are clearly better than the corresponding formulas for linear probing. Clustering is not only a theoretical problem but actually occurs in real implementations. Figure 5.12 compares the performance of linear probing (dashed curves) with what would be expected from more random collision resolution. Successful searches are indicated by an *S*, and unsuccessful searches and insertions are marked with *U* and *I*, respectively.

If $\lambda = 0.75$, then the formula above indicates that 8.5 probes are expected for an insertion in linear probing. If $\lambda = 0.9$, then 50 probes are expected, which is unreasonable. This compares with 4 and 10 probes for the respective load factors if clustering were not a problem. We see from these formulas that linear probing can be a bad idea if the table is expected to be more than half full. If $\lambda = 0.5$, however, only 2.5 probes are required on average for insertion, and only 1.5 probes are required, on average, for a successful search.

5.4.2. Quadratic Probing

Quadratic probing is a collision resolution method that eliminates the primary clustering problem of linear probing. Quadratic probing is what you would expect—the collision function is quadratic. The popular choice is $f(i) = i^2$. Figure 5.13 shows the resulting open addressing hash table with this collision function on the same input used in the linear probing example.

When 49 collides with 89, the next position attempted is one cell away. This cell is empty, so 49 is placed there. Next 58 collides at position 8. Then the cell one away is tried, but another collision occurs. A vacant cell is found at the next cell tried, which is $2^2 = 4$ away. The key 58 is thus placed in cell 2. The same thing happens for 69.

For linear probing it is a bad idea to let the hash table get nearly full, because performance degrades. For quadratic probing, the situation is even more drastic: There is no guarantee of finding an empty cell once the table gets more than half full, or even before

	Empty Table	After 89	After 18	After 49	After 58	After 69
0				49	49	49
1						
2					58	58
3						69
4						
5						
6						
7						
8			18	18	18	18
9		89	89	89	89	89

Figure 5.13 Open addressing hash table with quadratic probing, after each insertion

the table gets half full if the table size is not prime. This is because at most half of the table can be used as alternative locations to resolve collisions.

Indeed, we prove now that if the table is half empty and the table size is prime, then we are always guaranteed to be able to insert a new element.

THEOREM 5.1.

If quadratic probing is used, and the table size is prime, then a new element can always be inserted if the table is at least half empty.

PROOF:

Let the table size, *TableSize*, be an (odd) prime greater than 3. We show that the first $\lceil TableSize/2 \rceil$ alternative locations (including the initial location $h_0(x)$) are all distinct. Two of these locations are $h(x)+i^2 \pmod{TableSize}$ and $h(x)+j^2 \pmod{TableSize}$, where $0 \le i,j \le \lfloor TableSize/2 \rfloor$. Suppose, for the sake of contradiction, that these locations are the same, but $i \ne j$. Then

$$h(x) + i^2 = h(x) + j^2 \qquad (\text{mod } TableSize)$$
$$i^2 = j^2 \qquad (\text{mod } TableSize)$$
$$i^2 - j^2 = 0 \qquad (\text{mod } TableSize)$$
$$(i - j)(i + j) = 0 \qquad (\text{mod } TableSize)$$

Since *TableSize* is prime, it follows that either $(i - j)$ or $(i + j)$ is equal to 0 (mod *TableSize*). Since i and j are distinct, the first option is not possible. Since $0 \le i,j \le \lfloor TableSize/2 \rfloor$, the second option is also impossible. Thus, the first $\lceil TableSize/2 \rceil$ alternative locations are distinct. If at most $\lfloor TableSize/2 \rfloor$ positions are taken, then an empty spot can always be found.

If the table is even one more than half full, the insertion could fail (although this is extremely unlikely). Therefore, it is important to keep this in mind. It is also crucial that the table size be prime.* If the table size is not prime, the number of alternative locations can be severely reduced. As an example, if the table size were 16, then the only alternative locations would be at distances 1, 4, or 9 away.

Standard deletion cannot be performed in an open addressing hash table, because the cell might have caused a collision to go past it. For instance, if we remove 89, then virtually all of the remaining **find** operations will fail. Thus, open addressing hash tables require lazy deletion, although in this case there really is no laziness implied.

The class skeleton required to implement open addressing hashing is shown in Figure 5.14. Instead of an array of lists, we have an array of hash table entry cells, which are also shown in Figure 5.14. Each entry in the array of **HashEntry** references is either

1. **null**.
2. Not **null**, and the entry is *active* (**isActive** is **true**).
3. Not **null**, and the entry is *marked deleted* (**isActive** is **false**).

Constructing the table (Fig. 5.15) consists of allocating space and then setting each **HashEntry** reference to **null**.

As with separate chaining hashing, **find(x)**, shown in Figure 5.16 (on page 169), will return a reference to an object that matches **x** in the hash table. If **x** is not present, then **find** will return **null**. The **private** method **findPos** performs the collision resolution. We assume for convenience that the hash table is at least twice as large as the number of elements in the table, so quadratic resolution will always work. Otherwise, we would need to test *i* (**collisionNum**) before line 4. In the implementation in Figure 5.16, elements that are marked as deleted count as being in the table. This can cause problems, because the table can get too full prematurely. We shall discuss this item presently.

Lines 4 through 6 represent the fast way of doing quadratic resolution. From the definition of the quadratic resolution function, $f(i) = f(i-1) + 2i - 1$, so the next cell to try can be determined with a multiplication by 2 (really a bit shift) and a decrement. If the new location is past the array, it can be put back in range by subtracting *TableSize*. This is faster than the obvious method, because it avoids the multiplication and division that seem to be required. An important warning: The order of testing at line 3 is important. Don't switch it!

The final routine is insertion. As with separate chaining hashing, we do nothing if **x** is already present. It is a simple modification to do something else. Otherwise, we place it at the spot suggested by the **findPos** routine. The code is shown in Figure 5.17 (on page 170). If the load factor exceeds 0.5, the table is full. We could throw an exception, but instead, we use an alternative that enlarges the hash table. This is called rehashing, and is discussed in Section 5.5.

Although quadratic probing eliminates primary clustering, elements that hash to the same position will probe the same alternative cells. This is known as *secondary clustering*. Secondary clustering is a slight theoretical blemish. Simulation results suggest that it generally causes less than an extra half probe per search. The following technique eliminates this, but does so at the cost of extra multiplications and divisions.

---

*If the table size is a prime of the form $4k + 3$, and the quadratic collision resolution strategy $F(i) = \pm i^2$ is used, then the entire table can be probed. The cost is a slightly more complicated routine.

```
class HashEntry
{
    Hashable element;   // the element
    boolean  isActive;  // false is deleted

    public HashEntry( Hashable e )
      { this( e, true ); }

    public HashEntry( Hashable e, boolean i )
    {
        element  = e;
        isActive = i;
    }
}

public class QuadraticProbingHashTable
{
    public QuadraticProbingHashTable( )
      { /* Figure 5.15 */ }
    public QuadraticProbingHashTable( int size )
      { /* Figure 5.15 */ }
    public void makeEmpty( )
      { /* Figure 5.15 */ }

    public Hashable find( Hashable x )
      { /* Figure 5.16 */ }
    public void insert( Hashable x )
      { /* Figure 5.17 */ }
    public void remove( Hashable x )
      { /* Figure 5.17 */ }

    public static int hash( String key, int tableSize )
      { /* Figure 5.4 */ }

    private static final int DEFAULT_TABLE_SIZE = 11;

    protected HashEntry [ ] array; // The array of elements
    private int currentSize;        // The number of occupied cells

    private void allocateArray( int arraySize )
      { /* Figure 5.15 */ }
    private boolean isActive( int currentPos )
      { /* Figure 5.16 */ }
    private int findPos( Hashable x )
      { /* Figure 5.16 */ }
    private void rehash( )
      { /* Figure 5.22 */ }
    private static int nextPrime( int n )
      { /* See online code */ }
    private static boolean isPrime( int n )
      { /* See online code */ }
}
```

Figure 5.14 Class skeleton for open addressing hash tables, plus HashEntry class

```
/**
 * Construct the hash table.
 */
public QuadraticProbingHashTable( )
{
    this( DEFAULT_TABLE_SIZE );
}

/**
 * Construct the hash table.
 * @param size the approximate initial size.
 */
public QuadraticProbingHashTable( int size )
{
    allocateArray( size );
    makeEmpty( );
}

/**
 * Make the hash table logically empty.
 */
public void makeEmpty( )
{
    currentSize = 0;
    for( int i = 0; i < array.length; i++ )
        array[ i ] = null;
}

/**
 * Internal method to allocate array.
 * @param arraySize the size of the array.
 */
private void allocateArray( int arraySize )
{
    array = new HashEntry[ arraySize ];
}
```

Figure 5.15 Routines to initialize open addressing hash table

```
         /**
          * Find an item in the hash table.
          * @param x the item to search for.
          * @return the matching item.
          */
         public Hashable find( Hashable x )
         {
             int currentPos = findPos( x );
             return isActive( currentPos ) ? array[ currentPos ].element : null;
         }

         /**
          * Method that performs quadratic probing resolution.
          * @param x the item to search for.
          * @return the position where the search terminates.
          */
         private int findPos( Hashable x )
         {
/* 1*/       int collisionNum = 0;
/* 2*/       int currentPos = x.hash( array.length );

/* 3*/       while( array[ currentPos ] != null &&
                    !array[ currentPos ].element.equals( x ) )
             {
/* 4*/           currentPos += 2 * ++collisionNum - 1;   // Compute ith probe
/* 5*/           if( currentPos >= array.length )         // Implement the mod
/* 6*/               currentPos -= array.length;
             }

/* 7*/       return currentPos;
         }

         /**
          * Return true if currentPos exists and is active.
          * @param currentPos the result of a call to findPos.
          * @return true if currentPos is active.
          */
         private boolean isActive( int currentPos )
         {
             return array[ currentPos ] != null && array[ currentPos ].isActive;
         }
```

Figure 5.16 find routine (and **private** helpers) for hashing with quadratic probing

```
/**
 * Insert into the hash table. If the item is
 * already present, do nothing.
 * @param x the item to insert.
 */
public void insert( Hashable x )
{
        // Insert x as active
    int currentPos = findPos( x );
    if( isActive( currentPos ) )
        return;

    array[ currentPos ] = new HashEntry( x, true );

        // Rehash; see Section 5.5
    if( ++currentSize > array.length / 2 )
        rehash( );
}

/**
 * Remove from the hash table.
 * @param x the item to remove.
 */
public final void remove( Hashable x )
{
    int currentPos = findPos( x );
    if( isActive( currentPos ) )
        array[ currentPos ].isActive = false;
}
```

Figure 5.17 insert routine for hash tables with quadratic probing

5.4.3. Double Hashing

The last collision resolution method we will examine is *double hashing*. For double hashing, one popular choice is $f(i) = i \cdot hash_2(x)$. This formula says that we apply a second hash function to x and probe at a distance $hash_2(x), 2hash_2(x), \ldots$, and so on. A poor choice of $hash_2(x)$ would be disastrous. For instance, the obvious choice $hash_2(x) = x \bmod 9$ would not help if 99 were inserted into the input in the previous examples. Thus, the function must never evaluate to zero. It is also important to make sure all cells can be probed (this is not possible in the example below, because the table size is not prime). A function such as $hash_2(x) = R - (x \bmod R)$, with R a prime smaller than *TableSize,* will work well. If we choose $R = 7$, then Figure 5.18 shows the results of inserting the same keys as before.

	Empty Table	After 89	After 18	After 49	After 58	After 69
0						69
1						
2						
3					58	58
4						
5						
6				49	49	49
7						
8			18	18	18	18
9		89	89	89	89	89

Figure 5.18 Open addressing hash table with double hashing, after each insertion

The first collision occurs when 49 is inserted. $hash_2(49) = 7 - 0 = 7$, so 49 is inserted in position 6. $hash_2(58) = 7 - 2 = 5$, so 58 is inserted at location 3. Finally, 69 collides and is inserted at a distance $hash_2(69) = 7 - 6 = 1$ away. If we tried to insert 60 in position 0, we would have a collision. Since $hash_2(60) = 7 - 4 = 3$, we would then try positions 3, 6, 9, and then 2 until an empty spot is found. It is generally possible to find some bad case, but there are not too many here.

As we have said before, the size of our sample hash table is not prime. We have done this for convenience in computing the hash function, but it is worth seeing why it is important to make sure the table size is prime when double hashing is used. If we attempt to insert 23 into the table, it would collide with 58. Since $hash_2(23) = 7 - 2 = 5$, and the table size is 10, we essentially have only one alternative location, and it is already taken. Thus, if the table size is not prime, it is possible to run out of alternative locations prematurely. However, if double hashing is correctly implemented, simulations imply that the expected number of probes is almost the same as for a random collision resolution strategy. This makes double hashing theoretically interesting. Quadratic probing, however, does not require the use of a second hash function and is thus likely to be simpler and faster in practice.

5.5. Rehashing

If the table gets too full, the running time for the operations will start taking too long and insertions might fail for open addressing hashing with quadratic resolution. This can

0	6
1	15
2	
3	24
4	
5	
6	13

Figure 5.19 Open addressing hash table with linear probing with input 13, 15, 6, 24

0	6
1	15
2	23
3	24
4	
5	
6	13

Figure 5.20 Open addressing hash table with linear probing after 23 is inserted

happen if there are too many removals intermixed with insertions. A solution, then, is to build another table that is about twice as big (with an associated new hash function) and scan down the entire original hash table, computing the new hash value for each (non-deleted) element and inserting it in the new table.

As an example, suppose the elements 13, 15, 24, and 6 are inserted into an open addressing hash table of size 7. The hash function is $h(x) = x \bmod 7$. Suppose linear probing is used to resolve collisions. The resulting hash table appears in Figure 5.19.

If 23 is inserted into the table, the resulting table in Fig. 5.20 will be over 70 percent full. Because the table is so full, a new table is created. The size of this table is 17, because this is the first prime that is twice as large as the old table size. The new hash function is then $h(x) = x \bmod 17$. The old table is scanned, and elements 6, 15, 23, 24, and 13 are inserted into the new table. The resulting table appears in Figure 5.21.

This entire operation is called *rehashing*. This is obviously a very expensive operation; the running time is $O(N)$, since there are N elements to rehash and the table size is roughly 2N, but it is actually not all that bad, because it happens very infrequently. In particular, there must have been N/2 insertions prior to the last rehash, so it essentially adds a constant cost to each insertion.* If this data structure is part of the program, the effect is not noticeable. On the other hand, if the hashing is performed as part of an interactive system, then the unfortunate user whose insertion caused a rehash could see a slowdown.

Rehashing can be implemented in several ways with quadratic probing. One alternative is to rehash as soon as the table is half full. The other extreme is to rehash only when an insertion fails. A third, middle-of-the-road strategy is to rehash when the table reaches a certain load factor. Since performance does degrade as the load factor increases, the third strategy, implemented with a good cutoff, could be best.

---

*This is why the new table is made twice as large as the old table.

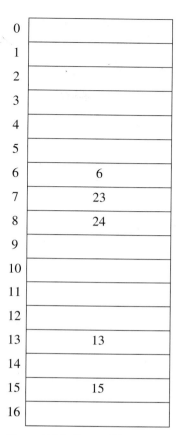

Figure 5.21 Open addressing hash table after rehashing

```
/**
 * Expand the hash table.
 */
private void rehash( )
{
    HashEntry [ ] oldArray = array;

        // Create a new double-sized, empty table
    allocateArray( nextPrime( 2 * oldArray.length ) );
    currentSize = 0;

        // Copy table over
    for( int i = 0; i < oldArray.length; i++ )
        if( oldArray[ i ] != null && oldArray[ i ].isActive )
            insert( oldArray[ i ].element );
}
```

Figure 5.22 Rehashing for open addressing hash tables

Rehashing frees the programmer from worrying about the table size and is important because hash tables cannot be made arbitrarily large in complex programs. The exercises ask you to investigate the use of rehashing in conjunction with lazy deletion. Rehashing can be used in other data structures as well. For instance, if the queue data structure of Chapter 3 became full, we could declare a double-sized array and (carefully) copy everything over, freeing the original.

Figure 5.22 shows that rehashing is simple to implement.

5.6. Extendible Hashing

Our last topic in this chapter deals with the case where the amount of data is too large to fit in main memory. As we saw in Chapter 4, the main consideration then is the number of disk accesses required to retrieve data.

As before, we assume that at any point we have N records to store; the value of N changes over time. Furthermore, at most M records fit in one disk block. We will use $M = 4$ in this section.

If either open addressing hashing or separate chaining hashing is used, the major problem is that collisions could cause several blocks to be examined during a find, even for a well-distributed hash table. Furthermore, when the table gets too full, an extremely expensive rehashing step must be performed, which requires $O(N)$ disk accesses.

A clever alternative, known as extendible hashing, allows a find to be performed in two disk accesses. Insertions also require few disk accesses.

We recall from Chapter 4 that a B-tree has depth $O(\log_{M/2} N)$. As M increases, the depth of a B-tree decreases. We could in theory choose M to be so large that the depth of the B-tree would be 1. Then any find after the first would take one disk access, since, presumably, the root node could be stored in main memory. The problem with this strategy is that the branching factor is so high that it would take considerable processing to determine which leaf the data was in. If the time to perform this step could be reduced, then we would have a practical scheme. This is exactly the strategy used by extendible hashing.

Let us suppose, for the moment, that our data consists of several six-bit integers. Figure 5.23 shows an extendible hashing scheme for these data. The root of the "tree" contains four links determined by the leading two bits of the data. Each leaf has up to $M = 4$ elements. It happens that in each leaf the first two bits are identical; this is indicated by the number in parentheses. To be more formal, D will represent the number of bits used by the root, which is sometimes known as the *directory*. The number of entries in the directory is thus 2^D. d_L is the number of leading bits that all the elements of some leaf L have in common. d_L will depend on the particular leaf, and $d_L \leq D$.

Suppose that we want to insert the key 100100. This would go into the third leaf, but as the third leaf is already full, there is no room. We thus split this leaf into two leaves, which are now determined by the first *three* bits. This requires increasing the directory size to 3. These changes are reflected in Figure 5.24.

Notice that all of the leaves not involved in the split are now pointed to by two adjacent directory entries. Thus, although an entire directory is rewritten, none of the other leaves is actually accessed.

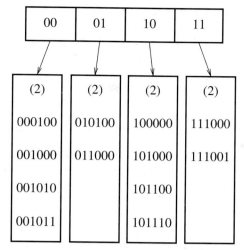

Figure 5.23 Extendible hashing: original data

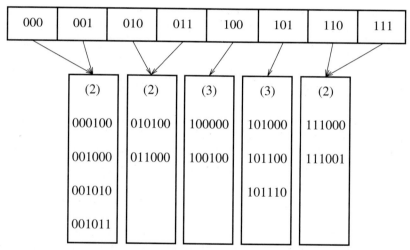

Figure 5.24 Extendible hashing: after insertion of 100100 and directory split

If the key 000000 is now inserted, then the first leaf is split, generating two leaves with $d_L = 3$. Since $D = 3$, the only change required in the directory is the updating of the 000 and 001 links. See Figure 5.25.

This very simple strategy provides quick access times for **insert** and **find** operations on large databases. There are a few important details we have not considered.

First, it is possible that several directory splits will be required if the elements in a leaf agree in more than $D + 1$ leading bits. For instance, starting at the original example, with $D = 2$, if 111010, 111011, and finally 111100 are inserted, the directory size must be increased to 4 to distinguish between the five keys. This is an easy detail to take care of,

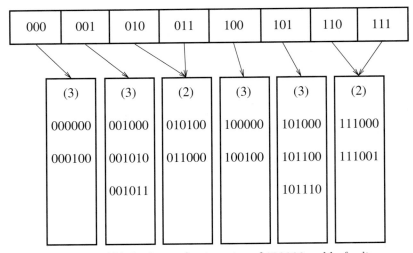

Figure 5.25 Extendible hashing: after insertion of 000000 and leaf split

but must not be forgotten. Second, there is the possibility of duplicate keys; if there are more than M duplicates, then this algorithm does not work at all. In this case, some other arrangements need to be made.

These possibilities suggest that it is important for the bits to be fairly random. This can be accomplished by hashing the keys into a reasonably long integer—hence the name.

We close by mentioning some of the performance properties of extendible hashing, which are derived after a very difficult analysis. These results are based on the reasonable assumption that the bit patterns are uniformly distributed.

The expected number of leaves is $(N/M)\log_2 e$. Thus the average leaf is $\ln 2 = 0.69$ full. This is the same as for B-trees, which is not entirely surprising, since for both data structures new nodes are created when the $(M + 1)$th entry is added.

The more surprising result is that the expected size of the directory (in other words, 2^D) is $O(N^{1+1/M}/M)$. If M is very small, then the directory can get unduly large. In this case, we can have the leaves contain links to the records instead of the actual records, thus increasing the value of M. This adds a second disk access to each **find** operation in order to maintain a smaller directory. If the directory is too large to fit in main memory, the second disk access would be needed anyway.

SUMMARY

Hash tables can be used to implement the **insert** and **find** operations in constant average time. It is especially important to pay attention to details such as load factor when using hash tables, since otherwise the time bounds are not valid. It is also important to choose the hash function carefully when the key is not a short string or integer.

For separate chaining hashing, the load factor should be close to 1, although performance does not significantly degrade unless the load factor becomes very large. For open addressing hashing, the load factor should not exceed 0.5, unless this is completely unavoidable. If linear probing is used, performance degenerates rapidly as the load factor approaches 1. Rehashing can be implemented to allow the table to grow (and shrink), thus maintaining a reasonable load factor. This is important if space is tight and it is not possible just to declare a huge hash table.

Binary search trees can also be used to implement **insert** and **find** operations. Although the resulting average time bounds are $O(\log N)$, binary search trees also support routines that require order and are thus more powerful. Using a hash table, it is not possible to find the minimum element. It is not possible to search efficiently for a string unless the exact string is known. A binary search tree could quickly find all items in a certain range; this is not supported by hash tables. Furthermore, the $O(\log N)$ bound is not necessarily that much more than $O(1)$, especially since no multiplications or divisions are required by search trees.

On the other hand, the worst case for hashing generally results from an implementation error, whereas sorted input can make binary trees perform poorly. Balanced search trees are quite expensive to implement, so if no ordering information is required and there is any suspicion that the input might be sorted, then hashing is the data structure of choice.

Hashing applications are abundant. Compilers use hash tables to keep track of declared variables in source code. The data structure is known as a *symbol table*. Hash tables are the ideal application for this problem because only **inserts** and **finds** are performed. Identifiers are typically short, so the hash function can be computed quickly.

A hash table is useful for any graph theory problem where the nodes have real names instead of numbers. Here, as the input is read, vertices are assigned integers from 1 onward by order of appearance. Again, the input is likely to have large groups of alphabetized entries. For example, the vertices could be computers. Then if one particular installation lists its computers as *ibm1, ibm2, ibm3, . . .* , there could be a dramatic effect on efficiency if a search tree is used.

A third common use of hash tables is in programs that play games. As the program searches through different lines of play, it keeps track of positions it has seen by computing a hash function based on the position (and storing its move for that position). If the same position reoccurs, usually by a simple transposition of moves, the program can avoid expensive recomputation. This general feature of all game-playing programs is known as the *transposition table*.

Yet another use of hashing is in on-line spelling checkers. If misspelling detection (as opposed to correction) is important, an entire dictionary can be prehashed and words can be checked in constant time. Hash tables are well suited for this, because it is not important to alphabetize words; printing out misspellings in the order they occurred in the document is certainly acceptable.

We close this chapter by returning to the word puzzle problem of Chapter 1. If the second algorithm described in Chapter 1 is used, and we assume that the maximum word size is some small constant, then the time to read in the dictionary containing W words and put it in a hash table is $O(W)$. This time is likely to be dominated by the disk I/O and not the hashing routines. The rest of the algorithm would test for the presence of a word for each ordered quadruple (*row, column, orientation, number of characters*). As each lookup would be $O(1)$, and there are only a constant number of orientations (8) and characters per word, the running time of this phase would be $O(R \cdot C)$. The total running time would be $O(R \cdot C + W)$, which is a distinct improvement over the original $O(R \cdot C \cdot W)$. We could make further optimizations, which would decrease the running time in practice; these are described in the exercises.

EXERCISES

5.1 Given input $\{4371, 1323, 6173, 4199, 4344, 9679, 1989\}$ and a hash function $h(x) = x \pmod{10}$, show the resulting:

a. Separate chaining hash table.

b. Open addressing hash table using linear probing.

c. Open addressing hash table using quadratic probing.

d. Open addressing hash table with second hash function $h_2(x) = 7 - (x \bmod 7)$.

5.2 Show the result of rehashing the hash tables in Exercise 5.1.

5.3 Write a program to compute the number of collisions required in a long random sequence of insertions using linear probing, quadratic probing, and double hashing.

5.4 A large number of deletions in a separate chaining hash table can cause the table to be fairly empty, which wastes space. In this case, we can rehash to a table half as large. Assume that we rehash to a larger table when there are twice as many elements as the table size. How empty should the table be before we rehash to a smaller table?

5.5 The `isEmpty` routine for quadratic probing has not been written. Can you implement it by returning the expression `currentSize==0`?

5.6 In the quadratic probing hash table, suppose that instead of inserting a new item into the location suggested by `findPos`, we insert it into the first inactive cell on the search path (thus, it is possible to reclaim a cell that is marked "deleted," potentially saving space).

a. Rewrite the insertion algorithm to use this observation. Do this by having `findPos` maintain, with an additional variable, the location of the first inactive cell it encounters.

b. Explain the circumstances under which the revised algorithm is faster than the original algorithm. Can it be slower?

5.7 The hash function in Figure 5.4 makes repeated calls to `key.length( )` in the `for` loop. Is it worth computing this once prior to entering the loop?

5.8 What are the advantages and disadvantages of the various collision resolution strategies?

5.9 Write a program to implement the following strategy for multiplying two sparse polynomials P_1, P_2 of size M and N, respectively. Each polynomial is represented as a linked list of objects consisting of a coefficient and an exponent (Exercise 3.12). We multiply each term in P_1 by a term in P_2 for a total of MN operations. One method is to sort these terms and combine like terms, but this requires sorting MN records, which could be expensive, especially in small-memory environments. Alternatively, we could merge terms as they are computed and then sort the result.

a. Write a program to implement the alternative strategy.

b. If the output polynomial has about $O(M + N)$ terms, what is the running time of both methods?

5.10 A spelling checker reads an input file and prints out all words not in some on-line dictionary. Suppose the dictionary contains 30,000 words and the file is large, so that the algorithm can make only one pass through the input file. A simple strategy is to read the dictionary into a hash table and look for each input word as it is read.

Assuming that an average word is seven characters and that it is possible to store words of length L in $L + 1$ bytes (so space waste is not much of a consideration), and assuming a quadratic probing hash table, how much space does this require?

5.11 If memory is limited and the entire dictionary cannot be stored in a hash table, we can still get an efficient algorithm that almost always works. We declare an array `table` of `boolean` (initialized to `false`) from 0 to *TableSize* $- 1$. As we read in a word, we set `table[hash(word)]` = `false`. Which of the following is true?

   a. If a word hashes to a location with value `false`, the word is not in the dictionary.

   b. If a word hashes to a location with value `true`, then the word is in the dictionary.

   Suppose we choose *TableSize* = 300,007.

   c. How much memory does this require?

   d. What is the probability of an error in this algorithm?

   e. A typical document might have about three actual misspellings per page of 500 words. Is this algorithm usable?

*5.12 Describe a procedure that avoids initializing a hash table (at the expense of memory).

5.13 Suppose we want to find the first occurrence of a string $P_1 P_2 \cdots P_k$ in a long input string $A_1 A_2 \cdots A_N$. We can solve this problem by hashing the pattern string, obtaining a hash value H_P, and comparing this value with the hash value formed from $A_1 A_2 \cdots A_k, A_2 A_3 \cdots A_{k+1}, A_3 A_4 \cdots A_{k+2}$, and so on until $A_{N-k+1} A_{N-k+2} \cdots A_N$. If we have a match of hash values, we compare the strings character by character to verify the match. We return the position (in A) if the strings actually do match, and we continue in the unlikely event that the match is false.

   *a. Show that if the hash value of $A_i A_{i+1} \cdots A_{i+k-1}$ is known, then the hash value of $A_{i+1} A_{i+2} \cdots A_{i+k}$ can be computed in constant time.

   b. Show that the running time is $O(k + N)$ plus the time spent refuting false matches.

   *c. Show that the expected number of false matches is negligible.

   d. Write a program to implement this algorithm.

   **e. Describe an algorithm that runs in $O(k + N)$ worst-case time.

   **f. Describe an algorithm that runs in $O(N/k)$ average time.

5.14 A BASIC program consists of a series of statements numbered in ascending order. Control is passed by use of a *goto* or *gosub* and a statement number. Write a program that reads in a legal BASIC program and renumbers the statements so that the first starts at number F and each statement has a number D higher than the previous statement. You may assume an upper limit of N statements, but the statement numbers in the input might be as large as a 32-bit integer. Your program must run in linear time.

5.15 a. Implement the word puzzle program using the algorithm described at the end of the chapter.

   b. We can get a big speed increase by storing, in addition to each word W, all of W's prefixes. (If one of W's prefixes is another word in the dictionary, it is stored as a real word.) Although this may seem to increase the size of the hash table drastically, it does not, because many words have the same prefixes. When a scan is performed in a particular direction, if the word that is looked up is not even in the hash table as a prefix, then the scan in that direction can be terminated early. Use this idea to write an improved program to solve the word puzzle.

c. If we are willing to sacrifice the sanctity of the hash table ADT, we can speed up the program in part (b) by noting that if, for example, we have just computed the hash function for "excel," we do not need to compute the hash function for "excels" from scratch. Adjust your hash function so that it can take advantage of its previous calculation.

d. In Chapter 2, we suggested using binary search. Incorporate the idea of using prefixes into your binary search algorithm. The modification should be simple. Which algorithm is faster?

5.16 Under certain assumptions, the expected cost of an insertion into a hash table with secondary clustering is given by $1/(1 - \lambda) - \lambda - \ln(1 - \lambda)$. Unfortunately, this formula is not accurate for quadratic probing. However, assuming that it is, determine the following:

a. The expected cost of an unsuccessful search.

b. The expected cost of an successful search.

5.17 Implement a generic **Dictionary** that supports the **insert** and **lookup** operations. The implementation will store a hash table of pairs (key, definition). You will **lookup** a definition by providing a key. Figure 5.26 provides the **Dictionary** specification (minus some details).

5.18 Implement a spelling checker by using a hash table. Assume that the dictionary comes from two sources: an existing large dictionary and a second file containing a personal dictionary. Output all misspelled words and the line numbers in which they occur. Also, for each misspelled word, list any words in the dictionary that are obtainable by applying any of the following rules:

a. Add one character.

b. Remove one character.

c. Exchange adjacent characters.

```
class Pair implements Hashable
{
    Hashable key;
    Object   def;
    // Appropriate Constructors, etc.
}

class Dictionary
{
    public Dictionary( )

    public void insert( Hashable key, Object definition )
    public Object lookup( Hashable key )
    public boolean isEmpty( )
    public void makeEmpty( )

    private QuadraticProbingHashTable items;
}
```

Figure 5.26 Dictionary skeleton for Exercise 5.17

5.19 Show the result of inserting the keys 10111101, 00000010, 10011011, 10111110, 01111111, 01010001, 10010110, 00001011, 11001111, 10011110, 11011011, 00101011, 01100001, 11110000, 01101111 into an initially empty extendible hashing data structure with $M = 4$.

5.20 Write a program to implement extendible hashing. If the table is small enough to fit in main memory, how does its performance compare with separate chaining and open addressing hashing?

REFERENCES

Despite the apparent simplicity of hashing, much of the analysis is quite difficult and there are still many unresolved questions. There are also many interesting theoretical issues, which generally attempt to make it unlikely that the worst-case possibilities of hashing arise.

An early paper on hashing is [16]. A wealth of information on the subject, including an analysis of hashing with linear probing, can be found in [11]. An excellent survey on the subject is [14]; [15] contains suggestions, and pitfalls, for choosing hash functions. Precise analytic and simulation results for all of the methods described in this chapter can be found in [8].

An analysis of double hashing can be found in [9] and [13]. Yet another collision resolution scheme is coalesced hashing, described in [17]. Yao [19] has shown that uniform hashing, in which no clustering exists, is optimal with respect to cost of a successful search.

If the input keys are known in advance, then perfect hash functions, which do not allow collisions, exist [2], [7]. Some more complicated hashing schemes, for which the worst case depends not on the particular input but on random numbers chosen by the algorithm, appear in [3] and [4].

Extendible hashing appears in [5], with analysis in [6] and [18].

Exercise 5.13 (a–d) is from [10]. Part (e) is from [12], and part (f) is from [1].

1. R. S. Boyer and J. S. Moore, "A Fast String Searching Algorithm," *Communications of the ACM,* 20 (1977), 762–772.

2. J. L. Carter and M. N. Wegman, "Universal Classes of Hash Functions," *Journal of Computer and System Sciences,* 18 (1979), 143–154.

3. M. Dietzfelbinger, A. R. Karlin, K. Melhorn, F. Meyer auf der Heide, H. Rohnert, and R. E. Tarjan, "Dynamic Perfect Hashing: Upper and Lower Bounds," *SIAM Journal on Computing,* 23 (1994), 738–761.

4. R. J. Enbody and H. C. Du, "Dynamic Hashing Schemes," *Computing Surveys,* 20 (1988), 85–113.

5. R. Fagin, J. Nievergelt, N. Pippenger, and H. R. Strong, "Extendible Hashing—A Fast Access Method for Dynamic Files," *ACM Transactions on Database Systems,* 4 (1979), 315–344.

6. P. Flajolet, "On the Performance Evaluation of Extendible Hashing and Trie Searching," *Acta Informatica,* 20 (1983), 345–369.

7. M. L. Fredman, J. Komlos, and E. Szemeredi, "Storing a Sparse Table with $O(1)$ Worst Case Access Time," *Journal of the ACM,* 31 (1984), 538–544.

8. G. H. Gonnet and R. Baeza-Yates, *Handbook of Algorithms and Data Structures,* 2nd ed., Addison-Wesley, Reading, Mass., 1991.

9. L. J. Guibas and E. Szemeredi, "The Analysis of Double Hashing," *Journal of Computer and System Sciences,* 16 (1978), 226–274.

10. R. M. Karp and M. O. Rabin, "Efficient Randomized Pattern-Matching Algorithms," *Aiken Computer Laboratory Report TR-31-81,* Harvard University, Cambridge, Mass., 1981.

11. D. E. Knuth, *The Art of Computer Programming, Vol 3: Sorting and Searching,* 2nd ed., Addison-Wesley, Reading, Mass., 1998.

12. D. E. Knuth, J. H. Morris, and V. R. Pratt, "Fast Pattern Matching in Strings," *SIAM Journal on Computing,* 6 (1977), 323–350.

13. G. Lueker and M. Molodowitch, "More Analysis of Double Hashing," *Proceedings of the Twentieth ACM Symposium on Theory of Computing* (1988), 354–359.

14. W. D. Maurer and T. G. Lewis, "Hash Table Methods," *Computing Surveys,* 7 (1975), 5–20.

15. B. J. McKenzie, R. Harries, and T. Bell, "Selecting a Hashing Algorithm," *Software—Practice and Experience,* 20 (1990), 209–224.

16. W. W. Peterson, "Addressing for Random Access Storage," *IBM Journal of Research and Development,* 1 (1957), 130–146.

17. J. S. Vitter, "Implementations for Coalesced Hashing," *Communications of the ACM,* 25 (1982), 911–926.

18. A. C. Yao, "A Note on The Analysis of Extendible Hashing," *Information Processing Letters,* 11 (1980), 84–86.

19. A. C. Yao, "Uniform Hashing Is Optimal," *Journal of the ACM,* 32 (1985), 687–693.

CHAPTER **6**

Priority Queues (Heaps)

Although jobs sent to a printer are generally placed on a queue, this might not always be the best thing to do. For instance, one job might be particularly important, so it might be desirable to allow that job to be run as soon as the printer is available. Conversely, if, when the printer becomes available, there are several 1-page jobs and one 100-page job, it might be reasonable to make the long job go last, even if it is not the last job submitted. (Unfortunately, most systems do not do this, which can be particularly annoying at times.)

Similarly, in a multiuser environment, the operating system scheduler must decide which of several processes to run. Generally a process is allowed to run only for a fixed period of time. One algorithm uses a queue. Jobs are initially placed at the end of the queue. The scheduler will repeatedly take the first job on the queue, run it until either it finishes or its time limit is up, and place it at the end of the queue if it does not finish. This strategy is generally not appropriate, because very short jobs will seem to take a long time because of the wait involved to run. Generally, it is important that short jobs finish as fast as possible, so these jobs should have precedence over jobs that have already been running. Furthermore, some jobs that are not short are still very important and should also have precedence.

This particular application seems to require a special kind of queue, known as a *priority queue*. In this chapter, we will discuss

- Efficient implementation of the priority queue ADT.
- Uses of priority queues.
- Advanced implementations of priority queues.

The data structures we will see are among the most elegant in computer science.

6.1. Model

A priority queue is a data structure that allows at least the following two operations: `insert`, which does the obvious thing; and `deleteMin`, which finds, returns, and removes the minimum element in the priority queue. The `insert` operation is the equivalent of `enqueue`, and `deleteMin` is the priority queue equivalent of the queue's `dequeue` operation.

As with most data structures, it is sometimes possible to add other operations, but these are extensions and not part of the basic model depicted in Figure 6.1.

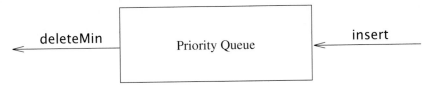

Figure 6.1 Basic model of a priority queue

Priority queues have many applications besides operating systems. In Chapter 7, we will see how priority queues are used for external sorting. Priority queues are also important in the implementation of *greedy algorithms,* which operate by repeatedly finding a minimum; we will see specific examples in Chapters 9 and 10. In this chapter we will see a use of priority queues in discrete event simulation.

6.2. Simple Implementations

There are several obvious ways to implement a priority queue. We could use a simple linked list, performing insertions at the front in $O(1)$ and traversing the list, which requires $O(N)$ time, to delete the minimum. Alternatively, we could insist that the list be kept always sorted; this makes insertions expensive ($O(N)$) and deleteMins cheap ($O(1)$). The former is probably the better idea of the two, based on the fact that there are never more deleteMins than insertions.

Another way of implementing priority queues would be to use a binary search tree. This gives an $O(\log N)$ average running time for both operations. This is true in spite of the fact that although the insertions are random, the deletions are not. Recall that the only element we ever delete is the minimum. Repeatedly removing a node that is in the left subtree would seem to hurt the balance of the tree by making the right subtree heavy. However, the right subtree is random. In the worst case, where the deleteMins have depleted the left subtree, the right subtree would have at most twice as many elements as it should. This adds only a small constant to its expected depth. Notice that the bound can be made into a worst-case bound by using a balanced tree; this protects one against bad insertion sequences.

Using a search tree could be overkill because it supports a host of operations that are not required. The basic data structure we will use will not require links and will support both operations in $O(\log N)$ worst-case time. Insertion will actually take constant time on average, and our implementation will allow building a priority queue of N items in linear time, if no deletions intervene. We will then discuss how to implement priority queues to support efficient merging. This additional operation seems to complicate matters a bit and apparently requires the use of a linked structure.

6.3. Binary Heap

The implementation we will use is known as a *binary heap.* Its use is so common for priority queue implementations that, in the context of priority queues, when the word *heap* is used without a qualifier, it is generally assumed to be referring to this implementation of the data structure. In this section, we will refer to binary heaps merely as *heaps*. Like binary search trees, heaps have two properties, namely, a structure property and a heap-order property. As with AVL trees, an operation on a heap can destroy one of the properties, so a heap operation must not terminate until all heap properties are in order. This turns out to be simple to do.

6.3.1. Structure Property

A heap is a binary tree that is completely filled, with the possible exception of the bottom level, which is filled from left to right. Such a tree is known as a *complete binary tree*. Figure 6.2 shows an example.

It is easy to show that a complete binary tree of height h has between 2^h and $2^{h+1} - 1$ nodes. This implies that the height of a complete binary tree is $\lfloor \log N \rfloor$, which is clearly $O(\log N)$.

An important observation is that because a complete binary tree is so regular, it can be represented in an array and no links are necessary. The array in Figure 6.3 corresponds to the heap in Figure 6.2.

For any element in array position i, the left child is in position $2i$, the right child is in the cell after the left child $(2i + 1)$, and the parent is in position $\lfloor i/2 \rfloor$. Thus not only are links not required, but the operations required to traverse the tree are extremely simple and likely to be very fast on most computers. The only problem with this implementation is that an estimate of the maximum heap size is required in advance, but typically this is

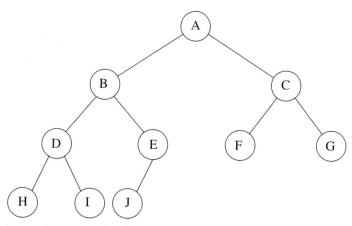

Figure 6.2 A complete binary tree

	A	B	C	D	E	F	G	H	I	J			
0	1	2	3	4	5	6	7	8	9	10	11	12	13

Figure 6.3 Array implementation of complete binary tree

```
public class BinaryHeap
{
    public BinaryHeap( )
      { /* Figure 6.4a */ }
    public BinaryHeap( int capacity )
      { /* Figure 6.4a */ }
    public void insert( Comparable x ) throws Overflow
      { /* Figure 6.8 */ }
    public Comparable findMin( )
      { /* See online code */ }
    public Comparable deleteMin( )
      { /* Figure 6.12 */ }

    public boolean isEmpty( )
      { /* See online code */ }
    public boolean isFull( )
      { /* See online code */ }
    public void makeEmpty( )
      { /* Figure 6.4a */ }

    private static final int DEFAULT_CAPACITY = 100;

    private int currentSize;      // Number of elements in heap
    private Comparable [ ] array; // The heap array

    private void percolateDown( int hole )
      { /* Figure 6.12 */ }
    private void buildHeap( )
      { /* Figure 6.14 */ }
}
```

Figure 6.4 Class skeleton for priority queue

not a problem (and we can resize if necessary). In Figure 6.3, the limit on the heap size is 13 elements. The array has a position 0; more on this later.

A heap data structure will, then, consist of an array (of Comparable objects) and an integer representing the current heap size. Figure 6.4 shows a priority queue skeleton. Figure 6.4a contains the constructors and a makeEmpty method.

Throughout this chapter, we shall draw the heaps as trees, with the implication that an actual implementation will use simple arrays.

6.3.2. Heap Order Property

The property that allows operations to be performed quickly is the *heap-order* property. Since we want to be able to find the minimum quickly, it makes sense that the smallest element should be at the root. If we consider that any subtree should also be a heap, then any node should be smaller than all of its descendants.

Applying this logic, we arrive at the heap order property. In a heap, for every node X, the key in the parent of X is smaller than (or equal to) the key in X, with the exception of

```
/**
 * Construct the binary heap.
 */
public BinaryHeap( )
{
    this( DEFAULT_CAPACITY );
}

/**
 * Construct the binary heap.
 * @param capacity the capacity of the binary heap.
 */
public BinaryHeap( int capacity )
{
    currentSize = 0;
    array = new Comparable[ capacity + 1 ];
}

/**
 * Make the priority queue logically empty.
 */
public void makeEmpty( )
{
    currentSize = 0;
}
```

Figure 6.4a Constructors and makeEmpty for priority queue

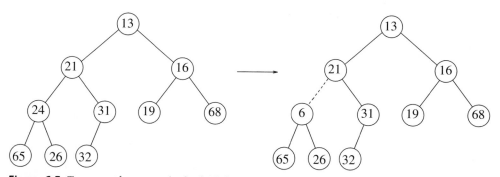

Figure 6.5 Two complete trees (only the left tree is a heap)

the root (which has no parent).* In Figure 6.5 the tree on the left is a heap, but the tree on the right is not (the dashed line shows the violation of heap order).

By the heap order property, the minimum element can always be found at the root. Thus, we get the extra operation, findMin, in constant time.

---

*Analogously, we can declare a (*max*) heap, which enables us to efficiently find and remove the maximum element, by changing the heap order property. Thus, a priority queue can be used to find *either* a minimum or a maximum, but this needs to be decided ahead of time.

6.3.3. Basic Heap Operations

It is easy (both conceptually and practically) to perform the two required operations. All the work involves ensuring that the heap-order property is maintained.

insert

To insert an element X into the heap, we create a hole in the next available location, since otherwise the tree will not be complete. If X can be placed in the hole without violating heap order, then we do so and are done. Otherwise we slide the element that is in the hole's parent node into the hole, thus bubbling the hole up toward the root. We continue this process until X can be placed in the hole. Figure 6.6 shows that to insert 14, we create a hole in the next available heap location. Inserting 14 in the hole would violate the heap-order property, so 31 is slid down into the hole. This strategy is continued in Figure 6.7 until the correct location for 14 is found.

This general strategy is known as a *percolate up;* the new element is percolated up the heap until the correct location is found. Insertion is easily implemented with the code shown in Figure 6.8.

We could have implemented the percolation in the **insert** routine by performing repeated swaps until the correct order was established, but a swap requires three assignment statements. If an element is percolated up d levels, the number of assignments performed by the swaps would be $3d$. Our method uses $d + 1$ assignments.

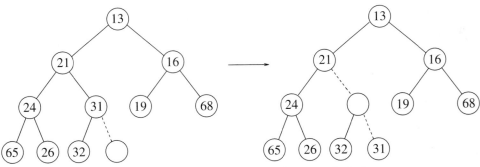

Figure 6.6 Attempt to insert 14: creating the hole, and bubbling the hole up

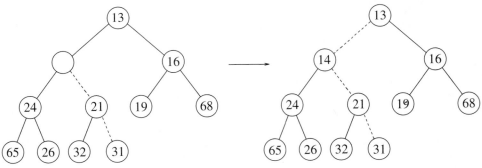

Figure 6.7 The remaining two steps to insert 14 in previous heap

```
/**
 * Insert into the priority queue, maintaining heap order.
 * Duplicates are allowed.
 * @param x the item to insert.
 * @exception Overflow if container is full.
 */
public void insert( Comparable x ) throws Overflow
{
    if( isFull( ) )
        throw new Overflow( );

        // Percolate up
    int hole = ++currentSize;
    for( ; hole > 1 && x.compareTo( array[ hole / 2 ] ) < 0; hole /= 2 )
        array[ hole ] = array[ hole / 2 ];
    array[ hole ] = x;
}
```

Figure 6.8 Procedures to insert into a binary heap

If the element to be inserted is the new minimum, it will be pushed all the way to the top. At some point, `hole` will be 1 and we will want to break out of the loop. We could do this with an explicit test, or we can put a very small value in position 0 in order to make the loop terminate. This value must be guaranteed to be smaller than (or equal to) any element in the heap; it is known as a *sentinel*. This idea is similar to the use of header nodes in linked lists. By adding a dummy piece of information, we could avoid a test that is executed once per loop iteration, thus saving some time. We elect not to use a sentinel in our implementation.

The time to do the insertion could be as much as $O(\log N)$, if the element to be inserted is the new minimum and is percolated all the way to the root. On average, the percolation terminates early; it has been shown that 2.607 comparisons are required on average to perform an insert, so the average **insert** moves an element up 1.607 levels.

deleteMin

`deleteMin`s are handled in a similar manner as insertions. Finding the minimum is easy; the hard part is removing it. When the minimum is removed, a hole is created at the root. Since the heap now becomes one smaller, it follows that the last element X in the heap must move somewhere in the heap. If X can be placed in the hole, then we are done. This is unlikely, so we slide the smaller of the hole's children into the hole, thus pushing the hole down one level. We repeat this step until X can be placed in the hole. Thus, our action is to place X in its correct spot along a path from the root containing *minimum* children.

In Figure 6.9 the left figure shows a heap prior to the **deleteMin**. After 13 is removed, we must now try to place 31 in the heap. The value 31 cannot be placed in the hole, because this would violate heap order. Thus, we place the smaller child (14) in the hole, sliding the hole down one level (see Fig. 6.10). We repeat this again, and since 31 is larger than 19, we place 19 into the hole and create a new hole one level deeper. We then place 26 in the hole and create a new hole on the bottom level since once again, 31 is too large. Finally, we are able to place 31 in the hole (Fig. 6.11). This general strategy is known as a *percolate*

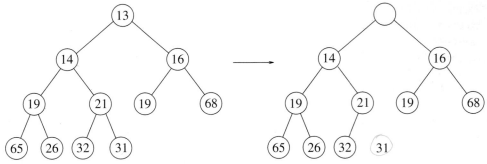

Figure 6.9 Creation of the hole at the root

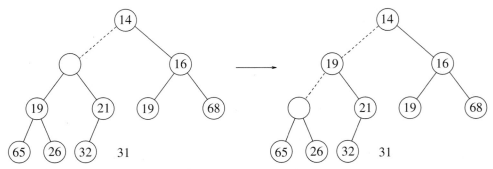

Figure 6.10 Next two steps in `deleteMin`

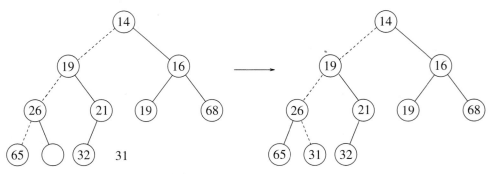

Figure 6.11 Last two steps in `deleteMin`

down. We use the same technique as in the **insert** routine to avoid the use of swaps in this routine.

A frequent implementation error in heaps occurs when there are an even number of elements in the heap, and the one node that has only one child is encountered. You must make sure not to assume that there are always two children, so this usually involves an extra test. In the code depicted in Figure 6.12, we've done this test at line 5. One extremely tricky solution is always to ensure that your algorithm *thinks* every node has two children.

```
/**
 * Remove the smallest item from the priority queue.
 * @return the smallest item, or null, if empty.
 */
public Comparable deleteMin( )
{
    if( isEmpty( ) )
        return null;

    Comparable minItem = findMin( );
    array[ 1 ] = array[ currentSize-- ];
    percolateDown( 1 );

    return minItem;
}

/**
 * Internal method to percolate down in the heap.
 * @param hole the index at which the percolate begins.
 */
private void percolateDown( int hole )
{
/* 1*/      int child;
/* 2*/      Comparable tmp = array[ hole ];

/* 3*/      for( ; hole * 2 <= currentSize; hole = child )
            {
/* 4*/          child = hole * 2;
/* 5*/          if( child != currentSize &&
/* 6*/              array[ child + 1 ].compareTo( array[ child ] ) < 0 )
/* 7*/              child++;
/* 8*/          if( array[ child ].compareTo( tmp ) < 0 )
/* 9*/              array[ hole ] = array[ child ];
                else
/*10*/              break;
            }
/*11*/      array[ hole ] = tmp;
}
```

Figure 6.12 Method to perform deleteMin in a binary heap

Do this by placing a sentinel, of value higher than any in the heap, at the spot after the heap ends, at the start of each *percolate down* when the heap size is even. You should think very carefully before attempting this, and you must put in a prominent comment if you do use this technique. Although this eliminates the need to test for the presence of a right child, you cannot eliminate the requirement that you test when you reach the bottom, because this would require a sentinel for every leaf.

The worst-case running time for this operation is $O(\log N)$. On average, the element that is placed at the root is percolated almost to the bottom of the heap (which is the level it came from), so the average running time is $O(\log N)$.

6.3.4. Other Heap Operations

Notice that although finding the minimum can be performed in constant time, a heap designed to find the minimum element (also known as a (*min*)heap) is of no help whatsoever in finding the maximum element. In fact, a heap has very little ordering information, so there is no way to find any particular element without a linear scan through the entire heap. To see this, consider the large heap structure (the elements are not shown) in Figure 6.13, where we see that the only information known about the maximum element is that it is at one of the leaves. Half the elements, though, are contained in leaves, so this is practically useless information. For this reason, if it is important to know where elements are, some other data structure, such as a hash table, must be used in addition to the heap. (Recall that the model does not allow looking inside the heap.)

If we assume that the position of every element is known by some other method, then several other operations become cheap. The first three operations below all run in logarithmic worst-case time.

decreaseKey

The decreaseKey(p,Δ) operation lowers the value of the item at position **p** by a positive amount Δ. Since this might violate the heap order, it must be fixed by a *percolate up*. This operation could be useful to system administrators: They can make their programs run with highest priority.

increaseKey

The increaseKey(p,Δ) operation increases the value of the item at position **p** by a positive amount Δ. This is done with a *percolate down*. Many schedulers automatically drop the priority of a process that is consuming excessive CPU time.

delete

The delete(p) operation removes the node at position **p** from the heap. This is done by first performing decreaseKey(p,∞) and then performing deleteMin(). When a process is

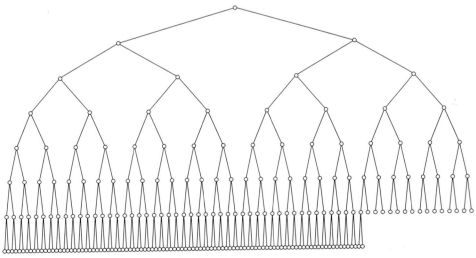

Figure 6.13 A very large complete binary tree

terminated by a user (instead of finishing normally), it must be removed from the priority queue.

buildHeap

The buildHeap operation takes as input N items and places them into an empty heap. Obviously, this can be done with N successive inserts. Since each insert will take $O(1)$ average and $O(\log N)$ worst-case time, the total running time of this algorithm would be $O(N)$ average but $O(N \log N)$ worst-case. Since this is a special instruction and there are no other operations intervening, and we already know that the instruction can be performed in linear average time, it is reasonable to expect that with reasonable care a linear time bound can be guaranteed.

The general algorithm is to place the N items into the tree in any order, maintaining the structure property. Then, if percolateDown(i) percolates down from node i, perform the algorithm in Figure 6.14 to create a heap-ordered tree.*

The first tree in Figure 6.15 is the unordered tree. The seven remaining trees in Figures 6.15 through 6.18 show the result of each of the seven percolateDowns. Each dashed line corresponds to two comparisons: one to find the smaller child and one to compare the smaller child with the node. Notice that there are only 10 dashed lines in the entire algorithm (there could have been an 11th—where?) corresponding to 20 comparisons.

```
/**
 * Establish heap order property from an arbitrary
 * arrangement of items. Runs in linear time.
 */
private void buildHeap( )
{
    for( int i = currentSize / 2; i > 0; i-- )
        percolateDown( i );
}
```

Figure 6.14 Sketch of buildHeap

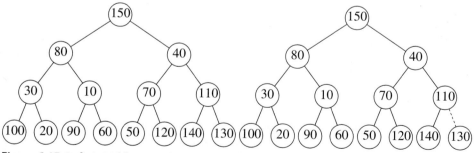

Figure 6.15 Left: initial heap; right: after percolateDown(7)

---

*This code is pseudocode because there are no public methods that could cause a heap-order violation. One possible way to do this is to pass an array containing the N items, and have buildHeap copy these into the array and then perform the percolations.

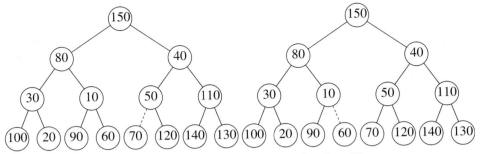

Figure 6.16 Left: after `percolateDown(6)`; right: after `percolateDown(5)`

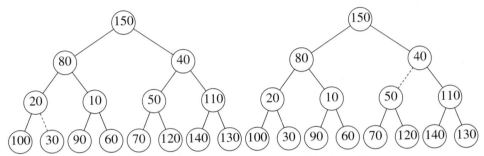

Figure 6.17 Left: after `percolateDown(4)`; right: after `percolateDown(3)`

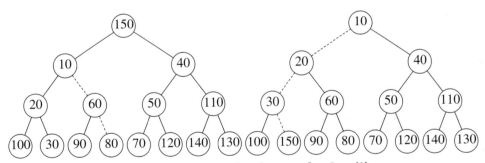

Figure 6.18 Left: after `percolateDown(2)`; right: after `percolateDown(1)`

To bound the running time of **buildHeap**, we must bound the number of dashed lines. This can be done by computing the sum of the heights of all the nodes in the heap, which is the maximum number of dashed lines. What we would like to show is that this sum is $O(N)$.

THEOREM 6.1.
For the perfect binary tree of height h containing $2^{h+1} - 1$ nodes, the sum of the heights of the nodes is $2^{h+1} - 1 - (h + 1)$.

PROOF:

It is easy to see that this tree consists of 1 node at height h, 2 nodes at height $h - 1$, 2^2 nodes at height $h - 2$, and in general 2^i nodes at height $h - i$. The sum of the heights of all the nodes is then

$$S = \sum_{i=0}^{h} 2^i (h - i)$$

$$= h + 2(h - 1) + 4(h - 2) + 8(h - 3) + 16(h - 4) + \cdots + 2^{h-1}(1) \quad (6.1)$$

Multiplying by 2 gives the equation

$$2S = 2h + 4(h - 1) + 8(h - 2) + 16(h - 3) + \cdots + 2^h(1) \quad\quad (6.2)$$

We subtract these two equations and obtain Equation (6.3). We find that certain terms almost cancel. For instance, we have $2h - 2(h - 1) = 2$, $4(h - 1) - 4(h - 2) = 4$, and so on. The last term in Equation (6.2), 2^h, does not appear in Equation (6.1); thus, it appears in Equation (6.3). The first term in Equation (6.1), h, does not appear in Equation (6.2); thus, $-h$ appears in Equation (6.3). We obtain

$$S = -h + 2 + 4 + 8 + \cdots + 2^{h-1} + 2^h = (2^{h+1} - 1) - (h + 1) \quad (6.3)$$

which proves the theorem.

A complete tree is not a perfect binary tree, but the result we have obtained is an upper bound on the the sum of the heights of the nodes in a complete tree. Since a complete tree has between 2^h and 2^{h+1} nodes, this theorem implies that this sum is $O(N)$, where N is the number of nodes.

Although the result we have obtained is sufficient to show that `buildHeap` is linear, the bound on the sum of the heights is not as strong as possible. For a complete tree with $N = 2^h$ nodes, the bound we have obtained is roughly $2N$. The sum of the heights can be shown by induction to be $N - b(N)$, where $b(N)$ is the number of 1s in the binary representation of N.

6.4. Applications of Priority Queues

We have already mentioned how priority queues are used in operating systems design. In Chapter 9, we will see how priority queues are used to implement several graph algorithms efficiently. Here we will show how to use priority queues to obtain solutions to two problems.

6.4.1. The Selection Problem

The first problem we will examine is the *selection problem* from Chapter 1. Recall that the input is a list of N elements, which can be totally ordered, and an integer k. The selection problem is to find the kth largest element.

Two algorithms were given in Chapter 1, but neither is very efficient. The first algorithm, which we shall call algorithm 1A, is to read the elements into an array and sort them, returning the appropriate element. Assuming a simple sorting algorithm, the running time is $O(N^2)$. The alternative algorithm, 1B, is to read k elements into an array and sort them. The smallest of these is in the kth position. We process the remaining elements one by one. As an element arrives, it is compared with the kth element in the array. If it is larger, then the kth element is removed, and the new element is placed in the correct place among the remaining $k - 1$ elements. When the algorithm ends, the element in the kth position is the answer. The running time is $O(N \cdot k)$ (why?). If $k = \lceil N/2 \rceil$, then both algorithms are $O(N^2)$. Notice that for any k, we can solve the symmetric problem of finding the $(N - k + 1)$th smallest element, so $k = \lceil N/2 \rceil$ is really the hardest case for these algorithms. This also happens to be the most interesting case, since this value of k is known as the *median*.

We give two algorithms here, both of which run in $O(N \log N)$ in the extreme case of $k = \lceil N/2 \rceil$, which is a distinct improvement.

Algorithm 6A

For simplicity, we assume that we are interested in finding the kth *smallest* element. The algorithm is simple. We read the N elements into an array. We then apply the `buildHeap` algorithm to this array. Finally, we perform k `deleteMin` operations. The last element extracted from the heap is our answer. It should be clear that by changing the heap-order property, we could solve the original problem of finding the kth *largest* element.

The correctness of the algorithm should be clear. The worst-case timing is $O(N)$ to construct the heap, if `buildHeap` is used, and $O(\log N)$ for each `deleteMin`. Since there are k `deleteMin`s, we obtain a total running time of $O(N + k \log N)$. If $k = O(N / \log N)$, then the running time is dominated by the `buildHeap` operation and is $O(N)$. For larger values of k, the running time is $O(k \log N)$. If $k = \lceil N/2 \rceil$, then the running time is $\Theta(N \log N)$.

Notice that if we run this program for $k = N$ and record the values as they leave the heap, we will have essentially sorted the input file in $O(N \log N)$ time. In Chapter 7, we will refine this idea to obtain a fast sorting algorithm known as *heapsort*.

Algorithm 6B

For the second algorithm, we return to the original problem and find the kth *largest* element. We use the idea from algorithm 1B. At any point in time we will maintain a set S of the k largest elements. After the first k elements are read, when a new element is read it is compared with the kth largest element, which we denote by S_k. Notice that S_k is the smallest element in S. If the new element is larger, then it replaces S_k in S. S will then have a new smallest element, which may or may not be the newly added element. At the end of the input, we find the smallest element in S and return it as the answer.

This is essentially the same algorithm described in Chapter 1. Here, however, we will use a heap to implement S. The first k elements are placed into the heap in total time $O(k)$ with a call to `buildHeap`. The time to process each of the remaining elements is $O(1)$, to test if the element goes into S, plus $O(\log k)$, to delete S_k and insert the new element if this is necessary. Thus, the total time is $O(k + (N - k) \log k) = O(N \log k)$. This algorithm also gives a bound of $\Theta(N \log N)$ for finding the median.

In Chapter 7, we will see how to solve this problem in $O(N)$ average time. In Chapter 10, we will see an elegant, albeit impractical, algorithm to solve this problem in $O(N)$ worst-case time.

6.4.2. Event Simulation

In Section 3.4.3, we described an important queuing problem. Recall that we have a system, such as a bank, where customers arrive and wait in a line until one of k tellers is available.

Customer arrival is governed by a probability distribution function, as is the service time (the amount of time to be served once a teller is available). We are interested in statistics such as how long on average a customer has to wait or how long the line might be.

With certain probability distributions and values of k, these answers can be computed exactly. However, as k gets larger, the analysis becomes considerably more difficult, so it is appealing to use a computer to simulate the operation of the bank. In this way, the bank officers can determine how many tellers are needed to ensure reasonably smooth service.

A simulation consists of processing events. The two events here are (a) a customer arriving and (b) a customer departing, thus freeing up a teller.

We can use the probability functions to generate an input stream consisting of ordered pairs of arrival time and service time for each customer, sorted by arrival time. We do not need to use the exact time of day. Rather, we can use a quantum unit, which we will refer to as a *tick*.

One way to do this simulation is to start a simulation clock at zero ticks. We then advance the clock one tick at a time, checking to see if there is an event. If there is, then we process the event(s) and compile statistics. When there are no customers left in the input stream and all the tellers are free, then the simulation is over.

The problem with this simulation strategy is that its running time does not depend on the number of customers or events (there are two events per customer), but instead depends on the number of ticks, which is not really part of the input. To see why this is important, suppose we changed the clock units to milliticks and multiplied all the times in the input by 1,000. The result would be that the simulation would take 1,000 times longer!

The key to avoiding this problem is to advance the clock to the next event time at each stage. This is conceptually easy to do. At any point, the next event that can occur is either (a) the next customer in the input file arrives or (b) one of the customers at a teller leaves. Since all the times when the events will happen are available, we just need to find the event that happens nearest in the future and process that event.

If the event is a departure, processing includes gathering statistics for the departing customer and checking the line (queue) to see whether there is another customer waiting. If so, we add that customer, process whatever statistics are required, compute the time when that customer will leave, and add that departure to the set of events waiting to happen.

If the event is an arrival, we check for an available teller. If there is none, we place the arrival on the line (queue); otherwise we give the customer a teller, compute the customer's departure time, and add the departure to the set of events waiting to happen.

The waiting line for customers can be implemented as a queue. Since we need to find the event *nearest* in the future, it is appropriate that the set of departures waiting to happen be organized in a priority queue. The next event is thus the next arrival or next departure (whichever is sooner); both are easily available.

It is then straightforward, although possibly time-consuming, to write the simulation routines. If there are C customers (and thus $2C$ events) and k tellers, then the running time of the simulation would be $O(C \log(k + 1))$* because computing and processing each event takes $O(\log H)$, where $H = k + 1$ is the size of the heap.

---

*We use $O(C \log(k + 1))$ instead of $O(C \log k)$ to avoid confusion for the $k = 1$ case.

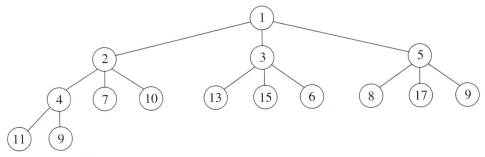

Figure 6.19 A d-heap

6.5. d-Heaps

Binary heaps are so simple that they are almost always used when priority queues are needed. A simple generalization is a *d-heap*, which is exactly like a binary heap except that all nodes have d children (thus, a binary heap is a 2-heap).

Figure 6.19 shows a 3-heap. Notice that a d-heap is much shallower than a binary heap, improving the running time of **insert**s to $O(\log_d N)$. However, for large d, the **deleteMin** operation is more expensive, because even though the tree is shallower, the minimum of d children must be found, which takes $d - 1$ comparisons using a standard algorithm. This raises the time for this operation to $O(d \log_d N)$. If d is a constant, both running times are, of course, $O(\log N)$. Although an array can still be used, the multiplications and divisions to find children and parents are now by d, which, unless d is a power of 2, seriously increases the running time, because we can no longer implement division by a bit shift. d-heaps are interesting in theory, because there are many algorithms where the number of insertions is much greater than the number of **deleteMin**s (and thus a theoretical speedup is possible). They are also of interest when the priority queue is too large to fit entirely in main memory. In this case, a d-heap can be advantageous in much the same way as B-trees. Finally, there is evidence suggesting that 4-heaps may outperform binary heaps in practice.

The most glaring weakness of the heap implementation, aside from the inability to perform **find**s, is that combining two heaps into one is a hard operation. This extra operation is known as a **merge**. There are quite a few ways of implementing heaps so that the running time of a **merge** is $O(\log N)$. We will now discuss three data structures, of various complexity, that support the **merge** operation efficiently. We will defer any complicated analysis until Chapter 11.

6.6. Leftist Heaps

It seems difficult to design a data structure that efficiently supports merging (that is, processes a **merge** in $O(N)$ time) and uses only an array, as in a binary heap. The reason for this is that merging would seem to require copying one array into another, which would take $\Theta(N)$ time for equal-sized heaps. For this reason, all the advanced data structures that support efficient merging require the use of a linked data structure. In practice, we can expect that this will make all the other operations slower.

Like a binary heap, a *leftist heap* has both a structural property and an ordering property. Indeed, a leftist heap, like virtually all heaps used, has the same heap-order property we have already seen. Furthermore, a leftist heap is also a binary tree. The only difference between a leftist heap and a binary heap is that leftist heaps are not perfectly balanced, but actually attempt to be very unbalanced.

6.6.1. Leftist Heap Property

We define the *null path length, npl(X),* of any node X to be the length of the shortest path from X to a node without two children. Thus, the *npl* of a node with zero or one child is 0, while $npl(\text{null}) = -1$. In the tree in Figure 6.20, the null path lengths are indicated inside the tree nodes.

Notice that the null path length of any node is 1 more than the minimum of the null path lengths of its children. This applies to nodes with less than two children because the null path length of null is -1.

The leftist heap property is that for every node X in the heap, the null path length of the left child is at least as large as that of the right child. This property is satisfied by only one of the trees in Figure 6.20, namely, the tree on the left. This property actually goes out of its way to ensure that the tree is unbalanced, because it clearly biases the tree to get deep toward the left. Indeed, a tree consisting of a long path of left nodes is possible (and actually preferable to facilitate merging)—hence the name *leftist heap*.

Because leftist heaps tend to have deep left paths, it follows that the right path ought to be short. Indeed, the right path down a leftist heap is as short as any in the heap. Otherwise, there would be a path that goes through some node X and takes the left child. Then X would violate the leftist property.

THEOREM 6.2.
A leftist tree with r nodes on the right path must have at least $2^r - 1$ nodes.

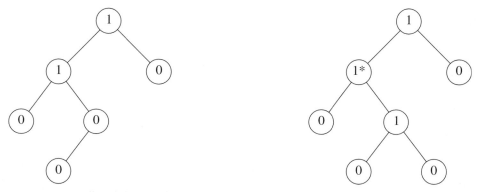

Figure 6.20 Null path lengths for two trees; only the left tree is leftist

PROOF:

The proof is by induction. If $r = 1$, there must be at least one tree node. Otherwise, suppose that the theorem is true for $1, 2, \ldots, r$. Consider a leftist tree with $r + 1$ nodes on the right path. Then the root has a right subtree with r nodes on the right path, and a left subtree with at least r nodes on the right path (otherwise it would not be leftist). Applying the inductive hypothesis to these subtrees yields a minimum of $2^r - 1$ nodes in each subtree. This plus the root gives at least $2^{r+1} - 1$ nodes in the tree, proving the theorem.

From this theorem, it follows immediately that a leftist tree of N nodes has a right path containing at most $\lfloor \log(N + 1) \rfloor$ nodes. The general idea for the leftist heap operations is to perform all the work on the right path, which is guaranteed to be short. The only tricky part is that performing **insert**s and **merge**s on the right path could destroy the leftist heap property. It turns out to be extremely easy to restore the property.

6.6.2. Leftist Heap Operations

The fundamental operation on leftist heaps is merging. Notice that insertion is merely a special case of merging, since we may view an insertion as a **merge** of a one-node heap with a larger heap. We will first give a simple recursive solution and then show how this might be done nonrecursively. Our input is the two leftist heaps, H_1 and H_2, in Figure 6.21. You should check that these heaps really are leftist. Notice that the smallest elements are at the roots. In addition to space for the data and left and right references, each node will have an entry that indicates the null path length.

If either of the two heaps is empty, then we can return the other heap. Otherwise, to merge the two heaps, we compare their roots. First, we recursively merge the heap with the larger root with the right subheap of the heap with the smaller root. In our example, this means we recursively merge H_2 with the subheap of H_1 rooted at 8, obtaining the heap in Figure 6.22.

Since this tree is formed recursively, and we have not yet finished the description of the algorithm, we cannot at this point show how this heap was obtained. However, it is reasonable to assume that the resulting tree is a leftist heap, because it was obtained via a recursive step. This is much like the inductive hypothesis in a proof by induction. Since we can handle the base case (which occurs when one tree is empty), we can assume that the recursive step works as long as we can finish the merge; this is rule 3 of recursion, which we discussed in Chapter 1. We now make this new heap the right child of the root of H_1 (see Figure 6.23).

Although the resulting heap satisfies the heap-order property, it is not leftist because the left subtree of the root has a null path length of 1 whereas the right subtree has a null path length of 2. Thus, the leftist property is violated at the root. However, it is easy to see that the remainder of the tree must be leftist. The right subtree of the root is leftist, because of the recursive step. The left subtree of the root has not been changed, so it too must still be leftist. Thus, we need only to fix the root. We can make the entire tree leftist by merely swapping the root's left and right children (Figure 6.24) and updating the null path length— the new null path length is 1 plus the null path length of the new right child—completing the **merge**. Notice that if the null path length is not updated, then all null path lengths will be 0, and the heap will not be leftist but merely random. In this case, the algorithm will work, but the time bound we will claim will no longer be valid.

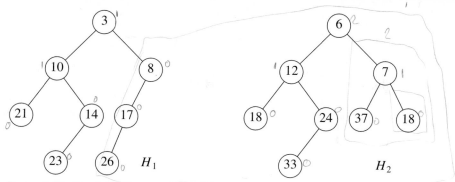

Figure 6.21 Two leftist heaps H_1 and H_2

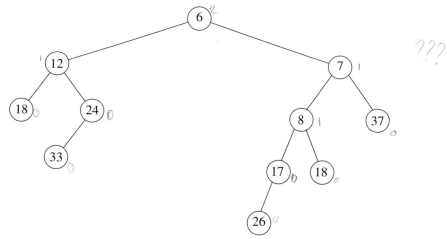

Figure 6.22 Result of merging H_2 with H_1's right subheap

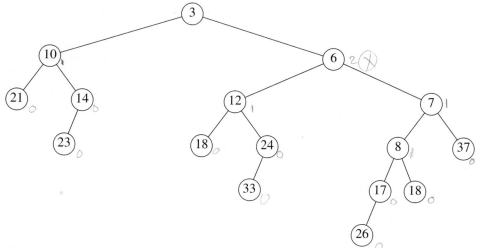

Figure 6.23 Result of attaching leftist heap of previous figure as H_1's right child

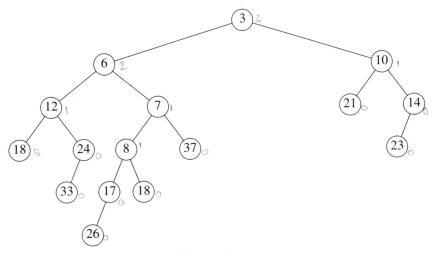

Figure 6.24 Result of swapping children of H_1's root

The description of the algorithm translates directly into code. The node class (Fig. 6.25) is the same as the binary tree, except that it is augmented with the **npl** (null path length) field. The leftist heap stores a reference to the root as its data member. We have seen in Chapter 4 that when an element is inserted into an empty binary tree, the node referenced by the root will need to change. We use the usual technique of implementing **private** recursive methods to do the merging. The class skeleton is also shown in Figure 6.25.

The two **merge** routines (Fig. 6.26) are drivers designed to remove special cases and ensure that H_1 has the smaller root. The actual merging is performed in **merge1** (Fig. 6.27). The public **merge** method merges **rhs** into the controlling heap. **rhs** becomes empty. The alias test in the public method disallows **h.merge(h)**.

The time to perform the merge is proportional to the sum of the length of the right paths, because constant work is performed at each node visited during the recursive calls. Thus we obtain an $O(\log N)$ time bound to merge two leftist heaps. We can also perform this operation nonrecursively by essentially performing two passes. In the first pass, we create a new tree by merging the right paths of both heaps. To do this, we arrange the nodes on the right paths of H_1 and H_2 in sorted order, keeping their respective left children. In our example, the new right path is 3, 6, 7, 8, 18 and the resulting tree is shown in Figure 6.28. A second pass is made up the heap, and child swaps are performed at nodes that violate the leftist heap property. In Figure 6.28, there is a swap at nodes 7 and 3, and the same tree as before is obtained. The nonrecursive version is simpler to visualize but harder to code. We leave it to the reader to show that the recursive and nonrecursive procedures do the same thing.

As mentioned above, we can carry out insertions by making the item to be inserted a one-node heap and performing a **merge**. To perform a **deleteMin,** we merely destroy the root, creating two heaps, which can then be merged. Thus, the time to perform a **deleteMin** is $O(\log N)$. These two routines are coded in Figure 6.29 and Figure 6.30.

Finally, we can build a leftist heap in $O(N)$ time by building a binary heap (obviously using a linked implementation). Although a binary heap is clearly leftist, this is not neces-

```
class LeftHeapNode
{
        // Constructors
    LeftHeapNode( Comparable theElement )
    {
        this( theElement, null, null );
    }

    LeftHeapNode( Comparable theElement, LeftHeapNode lt, LeftHeapNode rt )
    {
        element = theElement;
        left    = lt;
        right   = rt;
        npl     = 0;
    }

        // Friendly data; accessible by other package routines
    Comparable    element;      // The data in the node
    LeftHeapNode left;          // Left child
    LeftHeapNode right;         // Right child
    int          npl;           // null path length
}

public class LeftistHeap
{
    public LeftistHeap( )
      { /* See online code */ }

    public void merge( LeftistHeap rhs )
      { /* Figure 6.26 */ }
    public void insert( Comparable x )
      { /* Figure 6.29 */ }
    public Comparable findMin( )
      { /* See online code */ }
    public Comparable deleteMin( )
      { /* Figure 6.30 */ }

    public boolean isEmpty( )
      { /* See online code */ }
    public boolean isFull( )
      { /* See online code */ }
    public void makeEmpty( )
      { /* See online code */ }

    private LeftHeapNode root;    // root

    private static LeftHeapNode merge( LeftHeapNode h1, LeftHeapNode h2 )
      { /* Figure 6.26 */ }
    private static LeftHeapNode merge1( LeftHeapNode h1, LeftHeapNode h2 )
      { /* Figure 6.27 */ }
    private static void swapChildren( LeftHeapNode t )
      { /* See online code */ }
}
```

Figure 6.25 Leftist heap type declarations

```
/**
 * Merge rhs into the priority queue.
 * rhs becomes empty. rhs must be different from this.
 * @param rhs the other leftist heap.
 */
public void merge( LeftistHeap rhs )
{
    if( this == rhs )      // Avoid aliasing problems
        return;

    root = merge( root, rhs.root );
    rhs.root = null;
}


/**
 * Internal static method to merge two roots.
 * Deals with deviant cases and calls recursive merge1.
 */
private static LeftHeapNode merge( LeftHeapNode h1, LeftHeapNode h2 )
{
    if( h1 == null )
        return h2;
    if( h2 == null )
        return h1;
    if( h1.element.compareTo( h2.element ) < 0 )
        return merge1( h1, h2 );
    else
        return merge1( h2, h1 );
}
```

Figure 6.26 Driving routines for merging leftist heaps

```
/**
 * Internal static method to merge two roots.
 * Assumes trees are not empty, and h1's root contains smallest item.
 */
private static LeftHeapNode merge1( LeftHeapNode h1, LeftHeapNode h2 )
{
    if( h1.left == null )   // Single node
        h1.left = h2;       // Other fields in h1 are already accurate
    else
    {
        h1.right = merge( h1.right, h2 );
        if( h1.left.npl < h1.right.npl )
            swapChildren( h1 );
        h1.npl = h1.right.npl + 1;
    }
    return h1;
}
```

Figure 6.27 Actual routine to merge leftist heaps

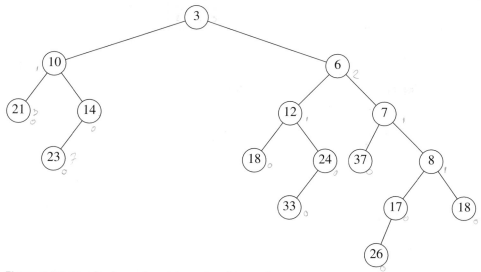

Figure 6.28 Result of merging right paths of H_1 and H_2

```
/**
 * Insert into the priority queue, maintaining heap order.
 * @param x the item to insert.
 */
public void insert( Comparable x )
{
    root = merge( new LeftHeapNode( x ), root );
}
```

Figure 6.29 Insertion routine for leftist heaps

```
/**
 * Remove the smallest item from the priority queue.
 * @return the smallest item, or null if empty.
 */
public Comparable deleteMin( )
{
    if( isEmpty( ) )
        return null;

    Comparable minItem = root.element;
    root = merge( root.left, root.right );

    return minItem;
}
```

Figure 6.30 deleteMin routine for leftist heaps

sarily the best solution, because the heap we obtain is the worst possible leftist heap. Furthermore, traversing the tree in reverse-level order is not as easy with links. The `buildHeap` effect can be obtained by recursively building the left and right subtrees and then percolating the root down. The exercises contain an alternative solution.

6.7. Skew Heaps

A *skew heap* is a self-adjusting version of a leftist heap that is incredibly simple to implement. The relationship of skew heaps to leftist heaps is analogous to the relation between splay trees and AVL trees. Skew heaps are binary trees with heap order, but there is no structural constraint on these trees. Unlike leftist heaps, no information is maintained about the null path length of any node. The right path of a skew heap can be arbitrarily long at any time, so the worst-case running time of all operations is $O(N)$. However, as with splay trees, it can be shown (see Chapter 11) that for any M consecutive operations, the total worst-case running time is $O(M \log N)$. Thus, skew heaps have $O(\log N)$ amortized cost per operation.

As with leftist heaps, the fundamental operation on skew heaps is merging. The `merge` routine is once again recursive, and we perform the exact same operations as before, with one exception. The difference is that for leftist heaps, we check to see whether the left and right children satisfy the leftist heap structure property and swap them if they do not. For skew heaps, the swap is unconditional; we *always* do it, with the one exception that the largest of all the nodes on the right paths does not have its children swapped. This one exception is what happens in the natural recursive implementation, so it is not really a special case at all. Furthermore, it is not necessary to prove the bounds, but since this node is guaranteed not to have a right child, it would be silly to perform the swap and give it one. (In our example, there are no children of this node, so we do not worry about it.) Again, suppose our input is the same two heaps as before, Figure 6.31.

If we recursively merge H_2 with the subheap of H_1 rooted at 8, we will get the heap in Figure 6.32.

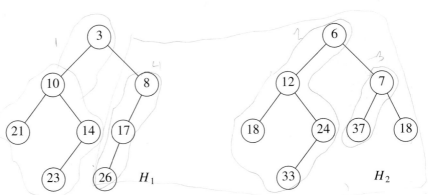

Figure 6.31 Two skew heaps H_1 and H_2

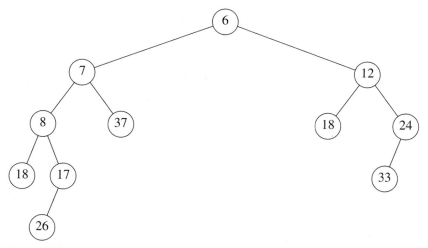

Figure 6.32 Result of merging H_2 with H_1's right subheap

Again, this is done recursively, so by the third rule of recursion (Section 1.3) we need not worry about how it was obtained. This heap happens to be leftist, but there is no guarantee that this is always the case. We make this heap the new left child of H_1, and the old left child of H_1 becomes the new right child (see Fig. 6.33).

The entire tree is leftist, but it is easy to see that that is not always true: Inserting 15 into this new heap would destroy the leftist property.

We can perform all operations nonrecursively, as with leftist heaps, by merging the right paths and swapping left and right children for every node on the right path, with the exception of the last. After a few examples, it becomes clear that since all but the last node on the right path have their children swapped, the net effect is that this becomes the new

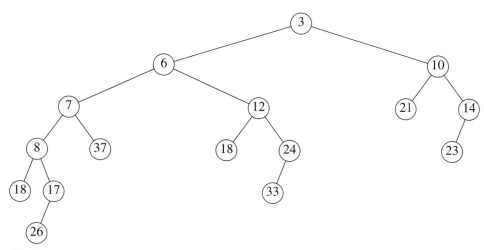

Figure 6.33 Result of merging skew heaps H_1 and H_2

left path (see the preceding example to convince yourself). This makes it very easy to merge two skew heaps visually.*

The implementation of skew heaps is left as a (trivial) exercise. Note that because a right path could be long, a recursive implementation could fail because of lack of stack space, even though performance would otherwise be acceptable. Skew heaps have the advantage that no extra space is required to maintain path lengths and no tests are required to determine when to swap children. It is an open problem to determine precisely the expected right path length of both leftist and skew heaps (the latter is undoubtedly more difficult). Such a comparison would make it easier to determine whether the slight loss of balance information is compensated by the lack of testing.

6.8. Binomial Queues

Although both leftist and skew heaps support merging, insertion, and `deleteMin` all effectively in $O(\log N)$ time per operation, there is room for improvement because we know that binary heaps support insertion in *constant average* time per operation. Binomial queues support all three operations in $O(\log N)$ worst-case time per operation, but insertions take constant time on average.

6.8.1. Binomial Queue Structure

Binomial queues differ from all the priority queue implementations that we have seen in that a binomial queue is not a heap-ordered tree but rather a *collection* of heap-ordered trees, known as a *forest*. Each of the heap-ordered trees is of a constrained form known as a *binomial tree* (the reason for the name will be obvious later). There is at most one binomial tree of every height. A binomial tree of height 0 is a one-node tree; a binomial tree, B_k, of height k is formed by attaching a binomial tree, B_{k-1}, to the root of another binomial tree, B_{k-1}. Figure 6.34 shows binomial trees B_0, B_1, B_2, B_3, and B_4.

From the diagram we see that a binomial tree, B_k, consists of a root with children B_0, B_1, . . . , B_{k-1}. Binomial trees of height k have exactly 2^k nodes, and the number of nodes at depth d is the binomial coefficient $\binom{k}{d}$. If we impose heap order on the binomial trees and allow at most one binomial tree of any height, we can uniquely represent a priority queue of any size by a collection of binomial trees. For instance, a priority queue of size 13 could be represented by the forest B_3, B_2, B_0. We might write this representation as 1101, which not only represents 13 in binary but also represents the fact that B_3, B_2, and B_0 are present in the representation and B_1 is not.

As an example, a priority queue of six elements could be represented as in Figure 6.35.

6.8.2. Binomial Queue Operations

The minimum element can then be found by scanning the roots of all the trees. Since there are at most $\log N$ different trees, the minimum can be found in $O(\log N)$ time. Alternatively,

---

*This is not exactly the same as the recursive implementation (but yields the same time bounds). If we only swap children for nodes on the right path that are above the point where the merging of right paths terminated due to exhaustion of one heap's right path, we get the same result as the recursive version.

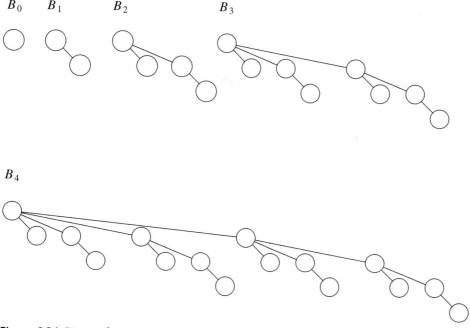

Figure 6.34 Binomial trees B_0, B_1, B_2, B_3, and B_4

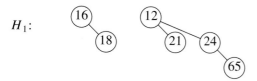

Figure 6.35 Binomial queue H_1 with six elements

we can maintain knowledge of the minimum and perform the operation in $O(1)$ time, if we remember to update the minimum when it changes during other operations.

Merging two binomial queues is a conceptually easy operation, which we will describe by example. Consider the two binomial queues, H_1 and H_2, with six and seven elements, respectively, pictured in Figure 6.36.

The merge is performed by essentially adding the two queues together. Let H_3 be the new binomial queue. Since H_1 has no binomial tree of height 0 and H_2 does, we can just use the binomial tree of height 0 in H_2 as part of H_3. Next, we add binomial trees of height 1. Since both H_1 and H_2 have binomial trees of height 1, we merge them by making the larger root a subtree of the smaller, creating a binomial tree of height 2, shown in Figure 6.37. Thus, H_3 will not have a binomial tree of height 1. There are now three binomial trees of height 2, namely, the original trees of H_1 and H_2 plus the tree formed by the previous step. We keep one binomial tree of height 2 in H_3 and merge the other two, creating a binomial tree of height 3. Since H_1 and H_2 have no trees of height 3, this tree becomes part of H_3 and we are finished. The resulting binomial queue is shown in Figure 6.38.

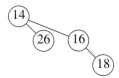

Figure 6.36 Two binomial queues H_1 and H_2

Figure 6.37 Merge of the two B_1 trees in H_1 and H_2

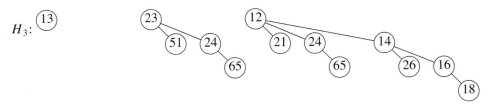

Figure 6.38 Binomial queue H_3: the result of merging H_1 and H_2

Since merging two binomial trees takes constant time with almost any reasonable implementation, and there are $O(\log N)$ binomial trees, the merge takes $O(\log N)$ time in the worst case. To make this operation efficient, we need to keep the trees in the binomial queue sorted by height, which is certainly a simple thing to do.

Insertion is just a special case of merging, since we merely create a one-node tree and perform a merge. The worst-case time of this operation is likewise $O(\log N)$. More precisely, if the priority queue into which the element is being inserted has the property that the smallest nonexistent binomial tree is B_i, the running time is proportional to $i + 1$. For example, H_3 (Fig. 6.38) is missing a binomial tree of height 1, so the insertion will terminate in two steps. Since each tree in a binomial queue is present with probability $\frac{1}{2}$, it follows that we expect an insertion to terminate in two steps, so the average time is constant. Furthermore, an analysis will show that performing N **insert**s on an initially empty binomial queue will take $O(N)$ worst-case time. Indeed, it is possible to do this operation using only $N - 1$ comparisons; we leave this as an exercise.

As an example, we show in Figures 6.39 through 6.45 the binomial queues that are formed by inserting 1 through 7 in order. Inserting 4 shows off a bad case. We merge 4 with

Figure 6.39 After 1 is inserted

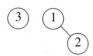

Figure 6.40 After 2 is inserted

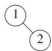

Figure 6.41 After 3 is inserted

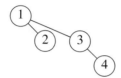

Figure 6.42 After 4 is inserted

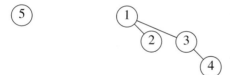

Figure 6.43 After 5 is inserted

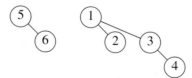

Figure 6.44 After 6 is inserted

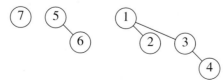

Figure 6.45 After 7 is inserted

B_0, obtaining a new tree of height 1. We then merge this tree with B_1, obtaining a tree of height 2, which is the new priority queue. We count this as three steps (two tree merges plus the stopping case). The next insertion after 7 is inserted is another bad case and would require three tree merges.

A `deleteMin` can be performed by first finding the binomial tree with the smallest root. Let this tree be B_k, and let the original priority queue be H. We remove the binomial tree B_k from the forest of trees in H, forming the new binomial queue H'. We also remove the root of B_k, creating binomial trees $B_0, B_1, \ldots, B_{k-1}$, which collectively form priority queue H''. We finish the operation by merging H' and H''.

As an example, suppose we perform a `deleteMin` on H_3, which is shown again in Figure 6.46. The minimum root is 12, so we obtain the two priority queues H' and H'' in Figure 6.47 and Figure 6.48. The binomial queue that results from merging H' and H'' is the final answer and is shown in Figure 6.49.

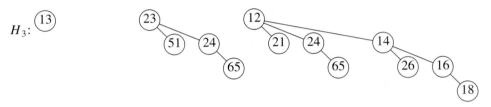

Figure 6.46 Binomial queue H_3

Figure 6.47 Binomial queue H', containing all the binomial trees in H_3 except B_3

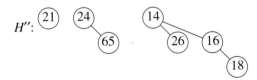

Figure 6.48 Binomial queue H'': B_3 with 12 removed

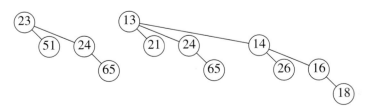

Figure 6.49 Result of applying `deleteMin` to H_3

For the analysis, note first that the `deleteMin` operation breaks the original binomial queue into two. It takes $O(\log N)$ time to find the tree containing the minimum element and to create the queues H' and H''. Merging these two queues takes $O(\log N)$ time, so the entire `deleteMin` operation takes $O(\log N)$ time.

6.8.3. Implementation of Binomial Queues

The `deleteMin` operation requires the ability to find all the subtrees of the root quickly, so the standard representation of general trees is required: The children of each node are kept in a linked list, and each node has a reference to its first child (if any). This operation also requires that the children be ordered by the size of their subtrees. We also need to make sure that it is easy to merge two trees. When two trees are merged, one of the trees is added as a child to the other. Since this new tree will be the largest subtree, it makes sense to maintain the subtrees in decreasing sizes. Only then will we be able to merge two binomial trees, and thus two binomial queues, efficiently. The binomial queue will be an array of binomial trees.

To summarize, then, each node in a binomial tree will contain the data, first child, and right sibling. The children in a binomial tree are arranged in decreasing rank.

Figure 6.51 shows how the binomial queue in Figure 6.50 is represented. Figure 6.52 shows the type declarations for a node in the binomial tree, and the binomial queue class skeleton.

In order to merge two binomial queues, we need a routine to merge two binomial trees of the same size. Figure 6.53 shows how the links change when two binomial trees are merged. The code to do this is simple and is shown in Figure 6.54.

We provide a simple implementation of the **merge** routine. H_1 is represented by the current object and H_2 is represented by **rhs**. The routine combines H_1 and H_2, placing the result in H_1 and making H_2 empty. At any point we are dealing with trees of rank i. **t1** and

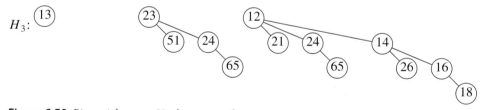

Figure 6.50 Binomial queue H_3 drawn as a forest

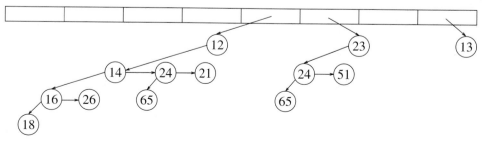

Figure 6.51 Representation of binomial queue H_3

```java
class BinomialNode
{
        // Constructors
    BinomialNode( Comparable theElement )
      { this( theElement, null, null ); }

    BinomialNode( Comparable theElement, BinomialNode lt, BinomialNode nt )
    {
        element     = theElement;
        leftChild   = lt;
        nextSibling = nt;
    }

        // Friendly data; accessible by other package routines
    Comparable   element;      // The data in the node
    BinomialNode leftChild;    // Left child
    BinomialNode nextSibling;  // Right child
}

public class BinomialQueue
{
    public BinomialQueue( )
      { /* See online code */ }
    public void merge( BinomialQueue rhs ) throws Overflow
      { /* Figure 6.55 */ }
    public void insert( Comparable x ) throws Overflow
      { /* See online code */ }
    public Comparable findMin( )
      { /* See online code */ }
    public Comparable deleteMin( )
      { /* Figure 6.56 */ }

    public boolean isEmpty( )
      { /* See online code */ }
    public boolean isFull( )
      { /* See online code */ }
    public void makeEmpty( )
      { /* See online code */ }

    private static final int MAX_TREES = 14;

    private int currentSize;          // # items in priority queue
    private BinomialNode [ ] theTrees; // An array of tree roots

    private static BinomialNode combineTrees( BinomialNode t1,
                                              BinomialNode t2 )

      { /* Figure 6.54 */ }

    private int capacity( )
      { /* See online code */ }
    private int findMinIndex( )
      { /* See online code */ }
}
```

Figure 6.52 Binomial queue class skeleton and node definition

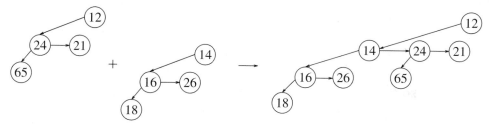

Figure 6.53 Merging two binomial trees

```
/**
 * Return the result of merging equal-sized t1 and t2.
 */
private static BinomialNode combineTrees( BinomialNode t1,
                                          BinomialNode t2 )
{
    if( t1.element.compareTo( t2.element ) > 0 )
        return combineTrees( t2, t1 );
    t2.nextSibling = t1.leftChild;
    t1.leftChild = t2;
    return t1;
}
```

Figure 6.54 Routine to merge two equal-sized binomial trees

t2 are the trees in H_1 and H_2, respectively, and **carry** is the tree carried from a previous step (it might be **null**). Depending on each of the eight possible cases, the tree that results for rank i and the **carry** tree of rank $i + 1$ is formed. This process proceeds from rank 0 to the last rank in the resulting binomial queue. The code is shown in Figure 6.55.

The **deleteMin** routine for binomial queues is given in Figure 6.56.

We can extend binomial queues to support some of the nonstandard operations that binary heaps allow, such as **decreaseKey** and **delete**, when the position of the affected element is known. A **decreaseKey** is a **percolateUp**, which can be performed in $O(\log N)$ time if we add a field to each node that stores a parent link. An arbitrary **delete** can be performed by a combination of **decreaseKey** and **deleteMin** in $O(\log N)$ time.

SUMMARY

In this chapter we have seen various implementations and uses of the priority queue ADT. The standard binary heap implementation is elegant because of its simplicity and speed. It requires no links and only a constant amount of extra space, yet supports the priority queue operations efficiently.

We considered the additional **merge** operation and developed three implementations, each of which is unique in its own way. The leftist heap is a wonderful example of the power of recursion. The skew heap represents a remarkable data structure because of the lack of balance criteria. Its analysis, which we will perform in Chapter 11, is interesting in its own right. The binomial queue shows how a simple idea can be used to achieve a good time bound.

We have also seen several uses of priority queues, ranging from operating systems scheduling to simulation. We will see their use again in Chapters 7, 9, and 10.

Figure 6.55 Routine to merge two priority queues

```
/**
 * Merge rhs into the priority queue.
 * rhs becomes empty. rhs must be different from this.
 * @param rhs the other binomial queue.
 * @exception Overflow if result exceeds capacity.
 */
public void merge( BinomialQueue rhs ) throws Overflow
{
    if( this == rhs )      // Avoid aliasing problems
        return;

    if( currentSize + rhs.currentSize > capacity( ) )
        throw new Overflow( );

    currentSize += rhs.currentSize;

    BinomialNode carry = null;
    for( int i = 0, j = 1; j <= currentSize; i++, j *= 2 )
    {
        BinomialNode t1 = theTrees[ i ];
        BinomialNode t2 = rhs.theTrees[ i ];

        int whichCase = t1 == null ? 0 : 1;
        whichCase += t2 == null ? 0 : 2;
        whichCase += carry == null ? 0 : 4;

        switch( whichCase )
        {
          case 0: /* No trees */
          case 1: /* Only this */
            break;
          case 2: /* Only rhs */
            theTrees[ i ] = t2;
            rhs.theTrees[ i ] = null;
            break;
          case 4: /* Only carry */
            theTrees[ i ] = carry;
            carry = null;
            break;
          case 3: /* this and rhs */
            carry = combineTrees( t1, t2 );
            theTrees[ i ] = rhs.theTrees[ i ] = null;
            break;
          case 5: /* this and carry */
            carry = combineTrees( t1, carry );
            theTrees[ i ] = null;
            break;
          case 6: /* rhs and carry */
            carry = combineTrees( t2, carry );
            rhs.theTrees[ i ] = null;
            break;
```

(continues)

(continued)

```
                    case 7: /* All three */
                        theTrees[ i ] = carry;
                        carry = combineTrees( t1, t2 );
                        rhs.theTrees[ i ] = null;
                        break;
                }
            }

            for( int k = 0; k < rhs.theTrees.length; k++ )
                rhs.theTrees[ k ] = null;
            rhs.currentSize = 0;
    }
```

Figure 6.55 Routine to merge two priority queues

Figure 6.56 deleteMin for binomial queues, with findMinIndex method

```
        /**
         * Remove the smallest item from the priority queue.
         * @return the smallest item, or null, if empty.
         */
        public Comparable deleteMin( )
        {
            if( isEmpty( ) )
                return null;

            int minIndex = findMinIndex( );
            Comparable minItem = theTrees[ minIndex ].element;

            BinomialNode deletedTree = theTrees[ minIndex ].leftChild;

              // Construct H''
            BinomialQueue deletedQueue = new BinomialQueue( );
            deletedQueue.currentSize = ( 1 << minIndex ) - 1;
            for( int j = minIndex - 1; j >= 0; j-- )
            {
                deletedQueue.theTrees[ j ] = deletedTree;
                deletedTree = deletedTree.nextSibling;
                deletedQueue.theTrees[ j ].nextSibling = null;
            }

              // Construct H'
            theTrees[ minIndex ] = null;
            currentSize -= deletedQueue.currentSize + 1;

            try
              { merge( deletedQueue ); }
            catch( Overflow e ) { }
            return minItem;
        }
```

(*continued*)

```
/**
 * Find index of the tree containing the smallest item in the
 * priority queue. The priority queue must not be empty.
 * @return the index of the tree containing the smallest item.
 */
private int findMinIndex( )
{
    int i;
    int minIndex;

    for( i = 0; theTrees[ i ] == null; i++ )
        ;

    for( minIndex = i; i < theTrees.length; i++ )
        if( theTrees[ i ] != null && theTrees[ i ].element.
                    compareTo( theTrees[ minIndex ].element ) < 0 )
            minIndex = i;

    return minIndex;
}
```

Figure 6.56 `deleteMin` for binomial queues, with `findMinIndex` method

EXERCISES

6.1 Can both `insert` and `findMin` be implemented in constant time?

6.2 a. Show the result of inserting 10, 12, 1, 14, 6, 5, 8, 15, 3, 9, 7, 4, 11, 13, and 2, one at a time, into an initially empty binary heap.

   b. Show the result of using the linear-time algorithm to build a binary heap using the same input.

6.3 Show the result of performing three `deleteMin` operations in the heap of the previous exercise.

6.4 A complete binary tree of N elements uses array positions 1 to N. Suppose we try to use an array representation of a binary tree that is not complete. Determine how large the array must be for the following:

   a. a binary tree that has two extra levels (that is, it is very slightly unbalanced)

   b. a binary tree that has a deepest node at depth $2 \log N$

   c. a binary tree that has a deepest node at depth $4.1 \log N$

   d. the worst-case binary tree

6.5 Rewrite the `BinaryHeap` class using the `negInf` sentinel.

6.6 How many nodes are in the large heap in Figure 6.13?

6.7 a. Prove that for binary heaps, `buildHeap` does at most $2N - 2$ comparisons between elements.

   b. Show that a heap of eight elements can be constructed in eight comparisons between heap elements.

   **c. Give an algorithm to build a binary heap in $\frac{13}{8}N + O(\log N)$ element comparisons.

6.8 Show the following regarding the maximum item in the heap:

    a. It must be at one of the leaves.

    b. There are exactly $\lceil N/2 \rceil$ leaves.

    c. Every leaf must be examined to find it.

**6.9 Show that the expected depth of the kth smallest element in a large complete heap (you may assume $N = 2^k - 1$) is bounded by $\log k$.

6.10*a. Give an algorithm to find all nodes less than some value, X, in a binary heap. Your algorithm should run in $O(K)$, where K is the number of nodes output.

    b. Does your algorithm extend to any of the other heap structures discussed in this chapter?

   *c. Give an algorithm that finds an arbitrary item X in a binary heap using at most roughly $3N/4$ comparisons.

**6.11 Propose an algorithm to insert M nodes into a binary heap on N elements in $O(M + \log N \log \log N)$ time. Prove your time bound.

6.12 Write a program to take N elements and do the following:

    a. Insert them into a heap one by one.

    b. Build a heap in linear time.

    Compare the running time of both algorithms for sorted, reverse-ordered, and random inputs.

6.13 Each `deleteMin` operation uses $2 \log N$ comparisons in the worst case.

   *a. Propose a scheme so that the `deleteMin` operation uses only $\log N + \log \log N + O(1)$ comparisons between elements. This need not imply less data movement.

  **b. Extend your scheme in part (a) so that only $\log N + \log \log \log N + O(1)$ comparisons are performed.

  **c. How far can you take this idea?

    d. Do the savings in comparisons compensate for the increased complexity of your algorithm?

6.14 If a d-heap is stored as an array, for an entry located in position i, where are the parents and children?

6.15 Suppose we need to perform M `percolateUp`s and N `deleteMin`s on a d-heap that initially has N elements.

    a. What is the total running time of all operations in terms of M, N, and d?

    b. If $d = 2$, what is the running time of all heap operations?

    c. If $d = \Theta(N)$, what is the total running time?

   *d. What choice of d minimizes the total running time?

6.16 Suppose that binary heaps are represented using explicit links. Give a simple algorithm to find the tree node that is at implicit position i.

6.17 Suppose that binary heaps are represented using explicit links. Consider the problem of merging binary heap `lhs` with `rhs`. Assume both heaps are full complete trees, containing $2^l - 1$ and $2^r - 1$ nodes, respectively.

    a. Give an $O(\log N)$ algorithm to merge the two heaps if $l = r$.

    b. Give an $O(\log N)$ algorithm to merge the two heaps if $|l - r| = 1$.

    c. Give an $O(\log^2 N)$ algorithm to merge the two heaps regardless of l and r.

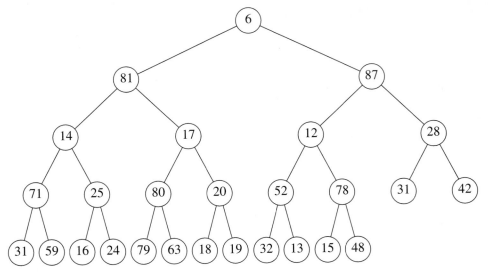

Figure 6.57 Min-max heap

6.18 A *min-max heap* is a data structure that supports both `deleteMin` and `deleteMax` in $O(\log N)$ per operation. The structure is identical to a binary heap, but the heap-order property is that for any node, X, at even depth, the element stored at X is smaller than the parent but larger than the grandparent (where this makes sense), and for any node X at odd depth, the element stored at X is larger than the parent but smaller than the grandparent. See Figure 6.57.

    a. How do we find the minimum and maximum elements?

  *b. Give an algorithm to insert a new node into the min-max heap.

  *c. Give an algorithm to perform `deleteMin` and `deleteMax`.

  *d. Can you build a min-max heap in linear time?

 **e. Suppose we would like to support `deleteMin`, `deleteMax`, and `merge`. Propose a data structure to support all operations in $O(\log N)$ time.

6.19 Merge the two leftist heaps in Figure 6.58.

6.20 Show the result of inserting keys 1 to 15 in order into an initially empty leftist heap.

6.21 Prove or disprove: A perfectly balanced tree forms if keys 1 to $2^k - 1$ are inserted in order into an initially empty leftist heap.

6.22 Give an example of input that generates the best leftist heap.

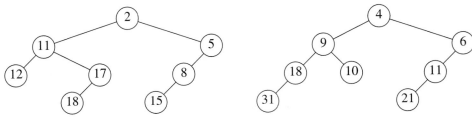

Figure 6.58 Input for Exercises 6.19 and 6.26

6.23 a. Can leftist heaps efficiently support decreaseKey?

b. What changes, if any (if possible), are required to do this?

6.24 One way to delete nodes from a known position in a leftist heap is to use a lazy strategy. To delete a node, merely mark it deleted. When a findMin or deleteMin is performed, there is a potential problem if the root is marked deleted, since then the node has to be actually deleted and the real minimum needs to be found, which may involve deleting other marked nodes. In this strategy, deletes cost one unit, but the cost of a deleteMin or findMin depends on the number of nodes that are marked deleted. Suppose that after a deleteMin or findMin there are k fewer marked nodes than before the operation.

*a. Show how to perform the deleteMin in $O(k \log N)$ time.

**b. Propose an implementation, with an analysis to show that the time to perform the deleteMin is $O(k \log(2N/k))$.

6.25 We can perform buildHeap in linear time for leftist heaps by considering each element as a one-node leftist heap, placing all these heaps on a queue, and performing the following step: Until only one heap is on the queue, dequeue two heaps, merge them, and enqueue the result.

a. Prove that this algorithm is $O(N)$ in the worst case.

b. Why might this algorithm be preferable to the algorithm described in the text?

6.26 Merge the two skew heaps in Figure 6.58.

6.27 Show the result of inserting keys 1 to 15 in order into a skew heap.

6.28 Prove or disprove: A perfectly balanced tree forms if the keys 1 to $2^k - 1$ are inserted in order into an initially empty skew heap.

6.29 A skew heap of N elements can be built using the standard binary heap algorithm. Can we use the same merging strategy described in Exercise 6.25 for skew heaps to get an $O(N)$ running time?

6.30 Prove that a binomial tree B_k has binomial trees $B_0, B_1, \ldots, B_{k-1}$ as children of the root.

6.31 Prove that a binomial tree of height k has $\binom{k}{d}$ nodes at depth d.

6.32 Merge the two binomial queues in Figure 6.59.

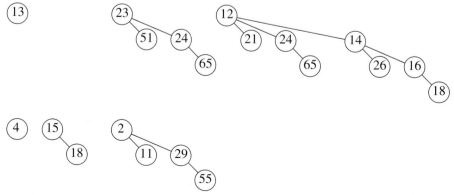

Figure 6.59 Input for Exercise 6.32

6.33 a. Show that N inserts into an initially empty binomial queue takes $O(N)$ time in the worst case.

  b. Give an algorithm to build a binomial queue of N elements, using at most $N - 1$ comparisons between elements.

  *c. Propose an algorithm to insert M nodes into a binomial queue of N elements in $O(M + \log N)$ worst-case time. Prove your bound.

6.34 Write an efficient routine to perform insert using binomial queues. Do not call merge.

6.35 For the binomial queue:

  a. Modify the merge routine to terminate merging if there are no trees left in H_2 and the carry tree is null.

  b. Modify the merge so that the smaller tree is always merged into the larger.

**6.36 Suppose we extend binomial queues to allow at most two trees of the same height per structure. Can we obtain $O(1)$ worst-case time for insertion while retaining $O(\log N)$ for the other operations?

6.37 Suppose you have a number of boxes, each of which can hold total weight C and items $i_1, i_2, i_3, \ldots, i_N$, which weigh $w_1, w_2, w_3, \ldots, w_N$, respectively. The object is to pack all the items without placing more weight in any box than its capacity and using as few boxes as possible. For instance, if $C = 5$, and the items have weights 2, 2, 3, 3, then we can solve the problem with two boxes.

  In general, this problem is very hard, and no efficient solution is known. Write programs to implement efficiently the following approximation strategies:

  *a. Place the weight in the first box for which it fits (creating a new box if there is no box with enough room). (This strategy and all that follow would give three boxes, which is suboptimal.)

  b. Place the weight in the box with the most room for it.

  *c. Place the weight in the most filled box that can accept it without overflowing.

  **d. Are any of these strategies enhanced by presorting the items by weight?

6.38 Suppose we want to add the decreaseAllKeys(Δ) operation to the heap repertoire. The result of this operation is that all keys in the heap have their value decreased by an amount Δ. For the heap implementation of your choice, explain the necessary modifications so that all other operations retain their running times and decreaseAllKeys runs in $O(1)$.

6.39 Which of the two selection algorithms has the better time bound?

REFERENCES

The binary heap was first described in [28]. The linear-time algorithm for its construction is from [14].

  The first description of d-heaps was in [19]. Recent results suggest that 4-heaps may improve binary heaps in some circumstances [22]. Leftist heaps were invented by Crane [11] and described in Knuth [21]. Skew heaps were developed by Sleator and Tarjan [24]. Binomial queues were invented by Vuillemin [27]; Brown provided a detailed analysis and empirical study showing that they perform well in practice [4], if carefully implemented.

  Exercise 6.7(b–c) is taken from [17]. Exercise 6.10(c) is from [6]. A method for constructing binary heaps that uses about $1.52N$ comparisons on average is described in [23].

Lazy deletion in leftist heaps (Exercise 6.24) is from [10]. A solution to Exercise 6.36 can be found in [8].

Min-max heaps (Exercise 6.18) were originally described in [1]. A more efficient implementation of the operations is given in [18] and [25]. Alternative representations for double-ended priority queues are the *deap* and *diamond dequeue*. Details can be found in [5], [7], and [9]. Solutions to 6.18(e) are given in [12] and [20].

A theoretically interesting priority queue representation is the *Fibonacci heap* [16], which we will describe in Chapter 11. The Fibonacci heap allows all operations to be performed in $O(1)$ amortized time, except for deletions, which are $O(\log N)$. *Relaxed heaps* [13] achieve identical bounds in the worst case (with the exception of `merge`). The procedure of [3] achieves optimal worst-case bounds for all operations. Another interesting implementation is the *pairing heap* [15], which is described in Chapter 12. Finally, priority queues that work when the data consist of small integers are described in [2] and [26].

1. M. D. Atkinson, J. R. Sack, N. Santoro, and T. Strothotte, "Min-Max Heaps and Generalized Priority Queues," *Communications of the ACM,* 29 (1986), 996–1000.

2. J. D. Bright, "Range Restricted Mergeable Priority Queues," *Information Processing Letters,* 47 (1993), 159–164.

3. G. S. Brodal, "Worst-Case Efficient Priority Queues," *Proceedings of the Seventh Annual ACM-SIAM Symposium on Discrete Algorithms* (1996), 52–58.

4. M. R. Brown, "Implementation and Analysis of Binomial Queue Algorithms," *SIAM Journal on Computing,* 7 (1978), 298–319.

5. S. Carlsson, "The Deap—A Double-Ended Heap to Implement Double-Ended Priority Queues," *Information Processing Letters,* 26 (1987), 33–36.

6. S. Carlsson and J. Chen, "The Complexity of Heaps," *Proceedings of the Third Symposium on Discrete Algorithms* (1992), 393–402.

7. S. Carlsson, J. Chen, and T. Strothotte, "A Note on the Construction of the Data Structure 'Deap'," *Information Processing Letters,* 31 (1989), 315–317.

8. S. Carlsson, J. I. Munro, and P. V. Poblete, "An Implicit Binomial Queue with Constant Insertion Time," *Proceedings of First Scandinavian Workshop on Algorithm Theory* (1988), 1–13.

9. S. C. Chang and M. W. Due, "Diamond Deque: A Simple Data Structure for Priority Deques," *Information Processing Letters,* 46 (1993), 231–237.

10. D. Cheriton and R. E. Tarjan, "Finding Minimum Spanning Trees," *SIAM Journal on Computing,* 5 (1976), 724–742.

11. C. A. Crane, "Linear Lists and Priority Queues as Balanced Binary Trees," *Technical Report STAN-CS-72-259,* Computer Science Department, Stanford University, Stanford, Calif., 1972.

12. Y. Ding and M. A. Weiss, "The Relaxed Min-Max Heap: A Mergeable Double-Ended Priority Queue," *Acta Informatica,* 30 (1993), 215–231.

13. J. R. Driscoll, H. N. Gabow, R. Shrairman, and R. E. Tarjan, "Relaxed Heaps: An Alternative to Fibonacci Heaps with Applications to Parallel Computation," *Communications of the ACM,* 31 (1988), 1343–1354.

14. R. W. Floyd, "Algorithm 245: Treesort 3," *Communications of the ACM,* 7 (1964), 701.

15. M. L. Fredman, R. Sedgewick, D. D. Sleator, and R. E. Tarjan, "The Pairing Heap: A New Form of Self-adjusting Heap," *Algorithmica,* 1 (1986), 111–129.

16. M. L. Fredman and R. E. Tarjan, "Fibonacci Heaps and Their Uses in Improved Network Optimization Algorithms," *Journal of the ACM,* 34 (1987), 596–615.

17. G. H. Gonnet and J. I. Munro, "Heaps on Heaps," *SIAM Journal on Computing,* 15 (1986), 964–971.

18. A. Hasham and J. R. Sack, "Bounds for Min-max Heaps," *BIT,* 27 (1987), 315–323.

19. D. B. Johnson, "Priority Queues with Update and Finding Minimum Spanning Trees," *Information Processing Letters,* 4 (1975), 53–57.

20. C. M. Khoong and H. W. Leong, "Double-Ended Binomial Queues," *Proceedings of the Fourth Annual International Symposium on Algorithms and Computation* (1993), 128–137.

21. D. E. Knuth, *The Art of Computer Programming, Vol 3: Sorting and Searching,* 2d ed, Addison-Wesley, Reading, Mass., 1998.

22. A. LaMarca and R. E. Ladner, "The Influence of Caches on the Performance of Sorting," *Proceedings of the Eighth Annual ACM-SIAM Symposium on Discrete Algorithms,* (1997), 370–379.

23. C. J. H. McDiarmid and B. A. Reed, "Building Heaps Fast," *Journal of Algorithms,* 10 (1989), 352–365.

24. D. D. Sleator and R. E. Tarjan, "Self-adjusting Heaps," *SIAM Journal on Computing,* 15 (1986), 52–69.

25. T. Strothotte, P. Eriksson, and S. Vallner, "A Note on Constructing Min-max Heaps," *BIT,* 29 (1989), 251–256.

26. P. van Emde Boas, R. Kaas, and E. Zijlstra, "Design and Implementation of an Efficient Priority Queue," *Mathematical Systems Theory,* 10 (1977), 99–127.

27. J. Vuillemin, "A Data Structure for Manipulating Priority Queues," *Communications of the ACM,* 21 (1978), 309–314.

28. J. W. J. Williams, "Algorithm 232: Heapsort," *Communications of the ACM,* 7 (1964), 347–348.

CHAPTER 7

Sorting

In this chapter we discuss the problem of sorting an array of elements. To simplify matters, we will assume in our examples that the array contains only integers, although our code will once again allow more general objects. For most of this chapter, we will also assume that the entire sort can be done in main memory, so that the number of elements is relatively small (less than a few million). Sorts that cannot be performed in main memory and must be done on disk or tape are also quite important. This type of sorting, known as external sorting, will be discussed at the end of the chapter.

Our investigation of internal sorting will show that

- There are several easy algorithms to sort in $O(N^2)$, such as insertion sort.
- There is an algorithm, Shellsort, that is very simple to code, runs in $o(N^2)$, and is efficient in practice.
- There are slightly more complicated $O(N \log N)$ sorting algorithms.
- Any general-purpose sorting algorithm requires $\Omega(N \log N)$ comparisons.

The rest of this chapter will describe and analyze the various sorting algorithms. These algorithms contain interesting and important ideas for code optimization as well as algorithm design. Sorting is also an example where the analysis can be precisely performed. Be forewarned that where appropriate, we will do as much analysis as possible.

7.1. Preliminaries

The algorithms we describe will all be interchangeable. Each will be passed an array containing the elements; we assume all array positions contain data to be sorted. We will assume that N is the number of elements passed to our sorting routines.

The objects being sorted are of type `Comparable`, as described in Section 1.4. We thus use the `CompareTo` method to place a consistent ordering on the input. Besides (reference) assignments, this is the only operation allowed on the input data. Sorting under these conditions is known as *comparison-based* sorting.

7.2. Insertion Sort

7.2.1. The Algorithm

One of the simplest sorting algorithms is the *insertion sort*. Insertion sort consists of $N - 1$ passes. For pass $p = 1$ through $N - 1$, insertion sort ensures that the elements in positions 0 through p are in sorted order. Insertion sort makes use of the fact that elements in positions 0 through $p - 1$ are already known to be in sorted order. Figure 7.1 shows a sample array after each pass of insertion sort.

Figure 7.1 shows the general strategy. In pass p, we move the element in position p left until its correct place is found among the first $p + 1$ elements. The code in Figure 7.2 implements this strategy. Lines 2 through 5 implement that data movement without the explicit use of swaps. The element in position p is saved in **tmp**, and all larger elements (prior to position p) are moved one spot to the right. Then **tmp** is placed in the correct spot. This is the same technique that was used in the implementation of binary heaps.

7.2.2. Analysis of Insertion Sort

Because of the nested loops, each of which can take N iterations, insertion sort is $O(N^2)$. Furthermore, this bound is tight, because input in reverse order can achieve this bound.

Original	34	8	64	51	32	21	Positions Moved
After $p = 1$	8	34	64	51	32	21	1
After $p = 2$	8	34	64	51	32	21	0
After $p = 3$	8	34	51	64	32	21	1
After $p = 4$	8	32	34	51	64	21	3
After $p = 5$	8	21	32	34	51	64	4

Figure 7.1 Insertion sort after each pass

```
            /**
             * Simple insertion sort.
             * @param a an array of Comparable items.
             */
            public static void insertionSort( Comparable [ ] a )
            {
                int j;

/* 1*/          for( int p = 1; p < a.length; p++ )
                {
/* 2*/              Comparable tmp = a[ p ];

/* 3*/              for( j = p; j > 0 && tmp.compareTo( a[ j - 1 ] ) < 0; j-- )
/* 4*/                  a[ j ] = a[ j - 1 ];
/* 5*/              a[ j ] = tmp;
                }
            }
```

Figure 7.2 Insertion sort routine

A precise calculation shows that the test at line 3 can be executed at most $p + 1$ times for each value of p. Summing over all p gives a total of

$$\sum_{i=2}^{N} i = 2 + 3 + 4 + \cdots + N = \Theta(N^2)$$

On the other hand, if the input is presorted, the running time is $O(N)$, because the test in the inner **for** loop always fails immediately. Indeed, if the input is almost sorted (this term will be more rigorously defined in the next section), insertion sort will run quickly. Because of this wide variation, it is worth analyzing the average-case behavior of this algorithm. It turns out that the average case is $\Theta(N^2)$ for insertion sort, as well as for a variety of other sorting algorithms, as the next section shows.

7.3. A Lower Bound for Simple Sorting Algorithms

An *inversion* in an array of numbers is any ordered pair (i, j) having the property that $i < j$ but $a[i] > a[j]$. In the example of the last section, the input list 34, 8, 64, 51, 32, 21 had nine inversions, namely $(34, 8), (34, 32), (34, 21), (64, 51), (64, 32), (64, 21), (51, 32)$, $(51, 21)$, and $(32, 21)$. Notice that this is exactly the number of swaps that needed to be (implicitly) performed by insertion sort. This is always the case, because swapping two adjacent elements that are out of place removes exactly one inversion, and a sorted array has no inversions. Since there is $O(N)$ other work involved in the algorithm, the running time of insertion sort is $O(I + N)$, where I is the number of inversions in the original array. Thus, insertion sort runs in linear time if the number of inversions is $O(N)$.

We can compute precise bounds on the average running time of insertion sort by computing the average number of inversions in a permutation. As usual, defining *average* is a difficult proposition. We will assume that there are no duplicate elements (if we allow duplicates, it is not even clear what the average number of duplicates is). Using this assumption, we can assume that the input is some permutation of the first N integers (since only relative ordering is important) and that all are equally likely. Under these assumptions, we have the following theorem:

THEOREM 7.1.

The average number of inversions in an array of N distinct elements is $N(N - 1)/4$.

PROOF:

For any list, L, of elements, consider L_r, the list in reverse order. The reverse list of the example is 21, 32, 51, 64, 8, 34. Consider any pair of two elements in the list (x, y), with $y > x$. Clearly, in exactly one of L and L_r this ordered pair represents an inversion. The total number of these pairs in a list L and its reverse L_r is $N(N - 1)/2$. Thus, an average list has half this amount, or $N(N - 1)/4$ inversions.

This theorem implies that insertion sort is quadratic on average. It also provides a very strong lower bound about any algorithm that only exchanges adjacent elements.

THEOREM 7.2.

Any algorithm that sorts by exchanging adjacent elements requires $\Omega(N^2)$ time on average.

PROOF:

The average number of inversions is initially $N(N-1)/4 = \Omega(N^2)$. Each swap removes only one inversion, so $\Omega(N^2)$ swaps are required.

This is an example of a lower-bound proof. It is valid not only for insertion sort, which performs adjacent exchanges implicitly, but also for other simple algorithms such as bubble sort and selection sort, which we will not describe here. In fact, it is valid over an entire *class* of sorting algorithms, including those undiscovered, that perform only adjacent exchanges. Because of this, this proof cannot be confirmed empirically. Although this lower-bound proof is rather simple, in general proving lower bounds is much more complicated than proving upper bounds and in some cases resembles magic.

This lower bound shows us that in order for a sorting algorithm to run in subquadratic, or $o(N^2)$, time, it must do comparisons and, in particular, exchanges between elements that are far apart. A sorting algorithm makes progress by eliminating inversions, and to run efficiently, it must eliminate more than just one inversion per exchange.

7.4. Shellsort

Shellsort, named after its inventor, Donald Shell, was one of the first algorithms to break the quadratic time barrier, although it was not until several years after its initial discovery that a subquadratic time bound was proven. As suggested in the previous section, it works by comparing elements that are distant; the distance between comparisons decreases as the algorithm runs until the last phase, in which adjacent elements are compared. For this reason, Shellsort is sometimes referred to as *diminishing increment* sort.

Shellsort uses a sequence, $h_1, h_2, \ldots, h_t$, called the *increment sequence*. Any increment sequence will do as long as $h_1 = 1$, but some choices are better than others (we will discuss that issue later). After a *phase*, using some increment h_k, for every i, we have $a[i] \le a[i+h_k]$ (where this makes sense); all elements spaced h_k apart are sorted. The file is then said to be h_k-*sorted*. For example, Figure 7.3 shows an array after several phases of Shellsort. An important property of Shellsort (which we state without proof) is that an h_k-sorted file that is then h_{k-1}-sorted remains h_k-sorted. If this were not the case, the algorithm would likely be of little value, since work done by early phases would be undone by later phases.

Original	81	94	11	96	12	35	17	95	28	58	41	75	15
After 5-sort	35	17	11	28	12	41	75	15	96	58	81	94	95
After 3-sort	28	12	11	35	15	41	58	17	94	75	81	96	95
After 1-sort	11	12	15	17	28	35	41	58	75	81	94	95	96

Figure 7.3 Shellsort after each pass

```
        /**
         * Shellsort, using Shell's (poor) increments.
         * @param a an array of Comparable items.
         */
        public static void shellsort( Comparable [ ] a )
        {
/* 1*/      for( int gap = a.length / 2; gap > 0; gap /= 2 )
/* 2*/          for( int i = gap; i < a.length; i++ )
                {
/* 3*/              Comparable tmp = a[ i ];
/* 4*/              int j = i;

/* 5*/              for( ; j >= gap && tmp.compareTo( a[ j - gap ] ) < 0; j -= gap )
/* 6*/                  a[ j ] = a[ j - gap ];
/* 7*/              a[ j ] = tmp;
                }
        }
```

Figure 7.4 Shellsort routine using Shell's increments (better increments are possible)

The general strategy to h_k-sort is for each position, i, in $h_k, h_k + 1, \ldots, N - 1$, place the element in the correct spot among $i, i - h_k, i - 2h_k$, etc. Although this does not affect the implementation, a careful examination shows that the action of an h_k-sort is to perform an insertion sort on h_k independent subarrays. This observation will be important when we analyze the running time of Shellsort.

A popular (but poor) choice for increment sequence is to use the sequence suggested by Shell: $h_t = \lfloor N/2 \rfloor$, and $h_k = \lfloor h_{k+1}/2 \rfloor$. Figure 7.4 contains a method that implements Shellsort using this sequence. We shall see later that there are increment sequences that give a significant improvement in the algorithm's running time; even a minor change can drastically affect performance (Exercise 7.10).

The program in Figure 7.4 avoids the explicit use of swaps in the same manner as our implementation of insertion sort.

7.4.1. Worst-Case Analysis of Shellsort

Although Shellsort is simple to code, the analysis of its running time is quite another story. The running time of Shellsort depends on the choice of increment sequence, and the proofs can be rather involved. The average-case analysis of Shellsort is a long-standing open problem, except for the most trivial increment sequences. We will prove tight worst-case bounds for two particular increment sequences.

THEOREM 7.3.

The worst-case running time of Shellsort, using Shell's increments, is $\Theta(N^2)$.

PROOF:

The proof requires showing not only an upper bound on the worst-case running time but also showing that there exists some input that actually takes $\Omega(N^2)$ time to run. We prove the lower bound first, by constructing a bad case. First, we choose N to be a power of 2. This makes all the increments even, except for the last increment,

Start	1	9	2	10	3	11	4	12	5	13	6	14	7	15	8	16
After 8-sort	1	9	2	10	3	11	4	12	5	13	6	14	7	15	8	16
After 4-sort	1	9	2	10	3	11	4	12	5	13	6	14	7	15	8	16
After 2-sort	1	9	2	10	3	11	4	12	5	13	6	14	7	15	8	16
After 1-sort	1	2	3	4	5	6	7	8	9	10	11	12	13	14	15	16

Figure 7.5 Bad case for Shellsort with Shell's increments (positions are numbered 1 to 16)

which is 1. Now, we will give as input an array with the $N/2$ largest numbers in the even positions and the $N/2$ smallest numbers in the odd positions (for this proof, the first position is position 1). As all the increments except the last are even, when we come to the last pass, the $N/2$ largest numbers are still all in even positions and the $N/2$ smallest numbers are still all in odd positions. The ith smallest number ($i \leq N/2$) is thus in position $2i - 1$ before the beginning of the last pass. Restoring the ith element to its correct place requires moving it $i - 1$ spaces in the array. Thus, to merely place the $N/2$ smallest elements in the correct place requires at least $\sum_{i=1}^{N/2} i - 1 = \Omega(N^2)$ work. As an example, Figure 7.5 shows a bad (but not the worst) input when $N = 16$. The number of inversions remaining after the 2-sort is exactly $1+2+3+4+5+6+7 = 28$; thus, the last pass will take considerable time.

To finish the proof, we show the upper bound of $O(N^2)$. As we have observed before, a pass with increment h_k consists of h_k insertion sorts of about N/h_k elements. Since insertion sort is quadratic, the total cost of a pass is $O(h_k(N/h_k)^2) = O(N^2/h_k)$. Summing over all passes gives a total bound of $O(\sum_{i=1}^{t} N^2/h_i) = O(N^2 \sum_{i=1}^{t} 1/h_i)$. Because the increments form a geometric series with common ratio 2, and the largest term in the series is $h_1 = 1$, $\sum_{i=1}^{t} 1/h_i < 2$. Thus we obtain a total bound of $O(N^2)$.

The problem with Shell's increments is that pairs of increments are not necessarily relatively prime, and thus the smaller increment can have little effect. Hibbard suggested a slightly different increment sequence, which gives better results in practice (and theoretically). His increments are of the form $1, 3, 7, \ldots, 2^k - 1$. Although these increments are almost identical, the key difference is that consecutive increments have no common factors. We now analyze the worst-case running time of Shellsort for this increment sequence. The proof is rather complicated.

THEOREM 7.4.
The worst-case running time of Shellsort using Hibbard's increments is $\Theta(N^{3/2})$.

PROOF:
We will prove only the upper bound and leave the proof of the lower bound as an exercise. The proof requires some well-known results from additive number theory. References to these results are provided at the end of the chapter.

For the upper bound, as before, we bound the running time of each pass and sum over all passes. For increments $h_k > N^{1/2}$, we will use the bound $O(N^2/h_k)$ from the previous theorem. Although this bound holds for the other increments, it is too large to be useful. Intuitively, we must take advantage of the fact that *this* increment sequence is *special*. What we need to show is that for any element $a[p]$ in position p, when it is time to perform an h_k-sort, there are only a few elements to the left of position p that are larger than $a[p]$.

When we come to h_k-sort the input array, we know that it has already been h_{k+1}- and h_{k+2}-sorted. Prior to the h_k-sort, consider elements in positions p and $p - i$, $i \le p$. If i is a multiple of h_{k+1} or h_{k+2}, then clearly $a[p - i] < a[p]$. We can say more, however. If i is expressible as a linear combination (in nonnegative integers) of h_{k+1} and h_{k+2}, then $a[p - i] < a[p]$. As an example, when we come to 3-sort, the file is already 7- and 15-sorted. 52 is expressible as a linear combination of 7 and 15, because $52 = 1 * 7 + 3 * 15$. Thus, $a[100]$ cannot be larger than $a[152]$ because $a[100] \le a[107] \le a[122] \le a[137] \le a[152]$.

Now, $h_{k+2} = 2h_{k+1} + 1$, so h_{k+1} and h_{k+2} cannot share a common factor. In this case, it is possible to show that all integers that are at least as large as $(h_{k+1} - 1)(h_{k+2} - 1) = 8h_k^2 + 4h_k$ can be expressed as a linear combination of h_{k+1} and h_{k+2} (see the reference at the end of the chapter).

This tells us that the body of the innermost **for** loop can be executed at most $8h_k + 4 = O(h_k)$ times for each of the $N - h_k$ positions. This gives a bound of $O(Nh_k)$ per pass.

Using the fact that about half the increments satisfy $h_k < \sqrt{N}$, and assuming that t is even, the total running time is then

$$O\left(\sum_{k=1}^{t/2} Nh_k + \sum_{k=t/2+1}^{t} N^2/h_k \right) = O\left(N \sum_{k=1}^{t/2} h_k + N^2 \sum_{k=t/2+1}^{t} 1/h_k \right)$$

Because both sums are geometric series, and since $h_{t/2} = \Theta(\sqrt{N})$, this simplifies to

$$= O\left(Nh_{t/2} \right) + O\left(\frac{N^2}{h_{t/2}} \right) = O(N^{3/2})$$

The average-case running time of Shellsort, using Hibbard's increments, is thought to be $O(N^{5/4})$, based on simulations, but nobody has been able to prove this. Pratt has shown that the $\Theta(N^{3/2})$ bound applies to a wide range of increment sequences.

Sedgewick has proposed several increment sequences that give an $O(N^{4/3})$ worst-case running time (also achievable). The average running time is conjectured to be $O(N^{7/6})$ for these increment sequences. Empirical studies show that these sequences perform significantly better in practice than Hibbard's. The best of these is the sequence $\{1, 5, 19, 41, 109, \ldots\}$, in which the terms are either of the form $9 \cdot 4^i - 9 \cdot 2^i + 1$ or $4^i - 3 \cdot 2^i + 1$. This is most easily implemented by placing these values in an array. This increment sequence is the best known in practice, although there is a lingering possibility that some increment sequence might exist that could give a significant improvement in the running time of Shellsort.

There are several other results on Shellsort that (generally) require difficult theorems from number theory and combinatorics and are mainly of theoretical interest. Shellsort is a fine example of a very simple algorithm with an extremely complex analysis.

The performance of Shellsort is quite acceptable in practice, even for N in the tens of thousands. The simplicity of the code makes it the algorithm of choice for sorting up to moderately large input.

7.5. Heapsort

As mentioned in Chapter 6, priority queues can be used to sort in $O(N \log N)$ time. The algorithm based on this idea is known as *heapsort* and gives the best Big-Oh running time we have seen so far. In practice however, it is slower than a version of Shellsort that uses Sedgewick's increment sequence.

Recall, from Chapter 6, that the basic strategy is to build a binary heap of N elements. This stage takes $O(N)$ time. We then perform N `deleteMin` operations. The elements leave the heap smallest first, in sorted order. By recording these elements in a second array and then copying the array back, we sort N elements. Since each `deleteMin` takes $O(\log N)$ time, the total running time is $O(N \log N)$.

The main problem with this algorithm is that it uses an extra array. Thus, the memory requirement is doubled. This could be a problem in some instances. Notice that the extra time spent copying the second array back to the first is only $O(N)$, so that this is not likely to affect the running *time* significantly. The problem is space.

A clever way to avoid using a second array makes use of the fact that after each `deleteMin`, the heap shrinks by 1. Thus the cell that was last in the heap can be used to store the element that was just deleted. As an example, suppose we have a heap with six elements. The first `deleteMin` produces a_1. Now the heap has only five elements, so we can place a_1 in position 6. The next `deleteMin` produces a_2. Since the heap will now only have four elements, we can place a_2 in position 5.

Using this strategy, after the last `deleteMin` the array will contain the elements in *decreasing* sorted order. If we want the elements in the more typical *increasing* sorted order, we can change the ordering property so that the parent has a larger key than the child. Thus we have a *(max)*heap.

In our implementation, we will use a *(max)*heap, but avoid the actual ADT for the purposes of speed. As usual, everything is done in an array. The first step builds the heap in linear time. We then perform $N - 1$ `deleteMax`es by swapping the last element in the heap with the first, decrementing the heap size, and percolating down. When the algorithm terminates, the array contains the elements in sorted order. For instance, consider the input sequence 31, 41, 59, 26, 53, 58, 97. The resulting heap is shown in Figure 7.6.

Figure 7.7 shows the heap that results after the first `deleteMax`. As the figures imply, the last element in the heap is 31; 97 has been placed in a part of the heap array that is technically no longer part of the heap. After 5 more `deleteMax` operations, the heap will actually have only one element, but the elements left in the heap array will be in sorted order.

The code to perform heapsort is given in Figure 7.8. The slight complication is that, unlike the binary heap, where the data begin at array index 1, the array for heapsort contains data in position 0. Thus the code is a little different from the binary heap code. The changes are minor.

7.5.1. Analysis of Heapsort

As we saw in Chapter 6, the first phase, which constitutes the building of the heap, uses at most $2N$ comparisons. In the second phase, the ith `deleteMax` uses at most $2\lfloor \log i \rfloor$ comparisons, for a total of at most $2N \log N - O(N)$ comparisons (assuming $N \geq 2$). Consequently, in the worst case, at most $2N \log N - O(N)$ comparisons are used by heapsort.

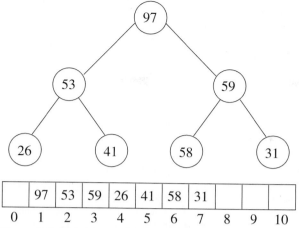

Figure 7.6 (*Max*) heap after `buildHeap` phase

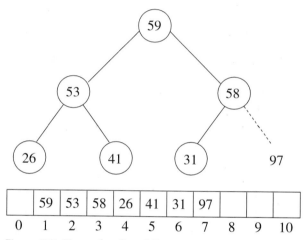

Figure 7.7 Heap after first `deleteMax`

Exercise 7.13 asks you to show that it is possible for all of the `deleteMax` operations to achieve their worst case simultaneously.

Experiments have shown that the performance of heapsort is extremely consistent: On average it uses only slightly fewer comparisons than the worst-case bound suggests. Until recently, however, nobody had been able to show nontrivial bounds on heapsort's average running time. The problem, it seems, is that successive `deleteMax` operations destroy the heap's randomness, making the probability arguments very complex. Recently another approach proved successful.

THEOREM 7.5.

The average number of comparisons used to heapsort a random permutation of N distinct items is $2N \log N - O(N \log \log N)$.

```java
/**
 * Internal method for heapsort.
 * @param i the index of an item in the heap.
 * @return the index of the left child.
 */
private static int leftChild( int i )
{
    return 2 * i + 1;
}

/**
 * Internal method for heapsort that is used in
 * deleteMax and buildHeap.
 * @param a an array of Comparable items.
 * @index i the position from which to percolate down.
 * @int n the logical size of the binary heap.
 */
private static void percDown( Comparable [ ] a, int i, int n )
{
    int child;
    Comparable tmp;

/* 1*/      for( tmp = a[ i ]; leftChild( i ) < n; i = child )
            {
/* 2*/          child = leftChild( i );
/* 3*/          if( child != n - 1 && a[ child ].compareTo( a[ child+1 ] ) < 0 )
/* 4*/              child++;
/* 5*/          if( tmp.compareTo( a[ child ] ) < 0 )
/* 6*/              a[ i ] = a[ child ];
                else
/* 7*/              break;
            }
/* 8*/      a[ i ] = tmp;
}

/**
 * Standard heapsort.
 * @param a an array of Comparable items.
 */
public static void heapsort( Comparable [ ] a )
{
/* 1*/      for( int i = a.length / 2; i >= 0; i-- )  /* buildHeap */
/* 2*/          percDown( a, i, a.length );
/* 3*/      for( int i = a.length - 1; i > 0; i-- )
            {
/* 4*/          swapReferences( a, 0, i );                    /* deleteMax */
/* 5*/          percDown( a, 0, i );
            }
}
```

Figure 7.8 Heapsort

PROOF:

The heap construction phase uses $\Theta(N)$ comparisons on average, and so we only need to prove the bound for the second phase. We assume a permutation of $\{1, 2, \ldots, N\}$.

Suppose the ith `deleteMax` pushes the root element down d_i levels. Then it uses $2d_i$ comparisons. For heapsort on any input, there is a cost sequence $D : d_1, d_2, \ldots, d_N$ that defines the cost of phase 2. That cost is given by $M_D = \sum_{i=1}^{N} d_i$; the number of comparisons used is thus $2M_D$.

Let $f(N)$ be the number of heaps of N items. One can show (Exercise 7.53) that $f(N) > (N/(4e))^N$ (where $e = 2.71828\ldots$). We will show that only an exponentially small fraction of these heaps (in particular $(N/16)^N$) have a cost smaller than $M = N(\log N - \log \log N - 4)$. When this is shown, it follows that the average value of M_D is at least M minus a term that is $o(1)$, and thus the average number of comparisons is at least $2M$. Consequently, our basic goal is to show that there are very few heaps that have small cost sequences.

Because level d_i has at most 2^{d_i} nodes, there are 2^{d_i} possible places that the root element can go for any d_i. Consequently, for any sequence D, the number of distinct corresponding `deleteMax` sequences is at most

$$S_D = 2^{d_1} 2^{d_2} \cdots 2^{d_N}$$

A simple algebraic manipulation shows that *for a given sequence D*

$$S_D = 2^{M_D}$$

Because each d_i can assume any value between 1 and $\lfloor \log N \rfloor$, there are at most $(\log N)^N$ possible sequences D. It follows that the number of distinct `deleteMax` sequences that require cost exactly M is at most the number of cost sequences of total cost M times the number of `deleteMax` sequences for each of these cost sequences. A bound of $(\log N)^N 2^M$ follows immediately.

The total number of heaps with cost sequence less than M is at most

$$\sum_{i=1}^{M-1} (\log N)^N 2^i < (\log N)^N 2^M$$

If we choose $M = N(\log N - \log \log N - 4)$, then the number of heaps that have cost sequence less than M is at most $(N/16)^N$, and the theorem follows from our earlier comments.

Using a more complex argument, it can be shown that heapsort always uses at least $N \log N - O(N)$ comparisons, and that there are inputs that can achieve this bound. It seems that the average case should also be $2N \log N - O(N)$ comparisons (rather than the nonlinear second term in Theorem 7.5); whether this is provable (or even true) is open.

7.6. Mergesort

We now turn our attention to *mergesort*. Mergesort runs in $O(N \log N)$ worst-case running time, and the number of comparisons used is nearly optimal. It is a fine example of a recursive algorithm.

The fundamental operation in this algorithm is merging two sorted lists. Because the lists are sorted, this can be done in one pass through the input, if the output is put in a third list. The basic merging algorithm takes two input arrays A and B, an output array C, and three counters, $Actr$, $Bctr$, and $Cctr$, which are initially set to the beginning of their respective arrays. The smaller of $A[Actr]$ and $B[Bctr]$ is copied to the next entry in C, and the appropriate counters are advanced. When either input list is exhausted, the remainder of the other list is copied to C. An example of how the merge routine works is provided for the following input.

If the array A contains 1, 13, 24, 26, and B contains 2, 15, 27, 38, then the algorithm proceeds as follows: First, a comparison is done between 1 and 2. 1 is added to C, and then 13 and 2 are compared.

2 is added to C, and then 13 and 15 are compared.

13 is added to C, and then 24 and 15 are compared. This proceeds until 26 and 27 are compared.

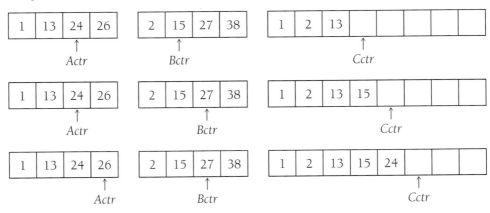

26 is added to C, and the A array is exhausted.

The remainder of the B array is then copied to C.

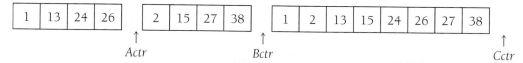

The time to merge two sorted lists is clearly linear, because at most $N - 1$ comparisons are made, where N is the total number of elements. To see this, note that every comparison adds an element to C, except the last comparison, which adds at least two.

The mergesort algorithm is therefore easy to describe. If $N = 1$, there is only one element to sort, and the answer is at hand. Otherwise, recursively mergesort the first half and the second half. This gives two sorted halves, which can then be merged together using the merging algorithm described above. For instance, to sort the eight-element array $24, 13, 26, 1, 2, 27, 38, 15$, we recursively sort the first four and last four elements, obtaining $1, 13, 24, 26, 2, 15, 27, 38$. Then we merge the two halves as above, obtaining the final list $1, 2, 13, 15, 24, 26, 27, 38$. This algorithm is a classic divide-and-conquer strategy. The problem is *divided* into smaller problems and solved recursively. The *conquering* phase consists of patching together the answers. Divide-and-conquer is a very powerful use of recursion that we will see many times.

An implementation of mergesort is provided in Figure 7.9. The public `mergeSort` is just a driver for the private recursive method `mergeSort`.

The `merge` routine is subtle. If a temporary array is declared locally for each recursive call of `merge`, then there could be $\log N$ temporary arrays active at any point. A close examination shows that since `merge` is the last line of `mergeSort`, there only needs to be one temporary array active at any point, and that the temporary array can be created in the public `mergeSort` driver. Further, we can use any part of the temporary array; we will use the same portion as the input array **a**. This allows the improvement described at the end of this section. Figure 7.10 implements the `merge` routine.

7.6.1. Analysis of Mergesort

Mergesort is a classic example of the techniques used to analyze recursive routines: we have to write a recurrence relation for the running time. We will assume that N is a power of 2, so that we always split into even halves. For $N = 1$, the time to mergesort is constant, which we will denote by 1. Otherwise, the time to mergesort N numbers is equal to the time to do two recursive mergesorts of size $N/2$, plus the time to merge, which is linear. The following equations say this exactly:

$$T(1) = 1$$
$$T(N) = 2T(N/2) + N$$

This is a standard recurrence relation, which can be solved several ways. We will show two methods. The first idea is to divide the recurrence relation through by N. The reason for doing this will become apparent soon. This yields

$$\frac{T(N)}{N} = \frac{T(N/2)}{N/2} + 1$$

```
/**
 * Internal method that makes recursive calls.
 * @param a an array of Comparable items.
 * @param tmpArray an array to place the merged result.
 * @param left the left-most index of the subarray.
 * @param right the right-most index of the subarray.
 */
private static void mergeSort( Comparable [ ] a, Comparable [ ] tmpArray,
              int left, int right )
{
    if( left < right )
    {
        int center = ( left + right ) / 2;
        mergeSort( a, tmpArray, left, center );
        mergeSort( a, tmpArray, center + 1, right );
        merge( a, tmpArray, left, center + 1, right );
    }
}


/**
 * Mergesort algorithm.
 * @param a an array of Comparable items.
 */
public static void mergeSort( Comparable [ ] a )
{
    Comparable [ ] tmpArray = new Comparable[ a.length ];

    mergeSort( a, tmpArray, 0, a.length - 1 );
}
```

Figure 7.9 Mergesort routines

This equation is valid for any N that is a power of 2, so we may also write

$$\frac{T(N/2)}{N/2} = \frac{T(N/4)}{N/4} + 1$$

and

$$\frac{T(N/4)}{N/4} = \frac{T(N/8)}{N/8} + 1$$

$$\vdots$$

$$\frac{T(2)}{2} = \frac{T(1)}{1} + 1$$

Now add up all the equations. This means that we add all of the terms on the left-hand side and set the result equal to the sum of all of the terms on the right-hand side. Observe that the term $T(N/2)/(N/2)$ appears on both sides and thus cancels. In fact, virtually all the

```
/**
 * Internal method that merges two sorted halves of a subarray.
 * @param a an array of Comparable items.
 * @param tmpArray an array to place the merged result.
 * @param leftPos the left-most index of the subarray.
 * @param rightPos the index of the start of the second half.
 * @param rightEnd the right-most index of the subarray.
 */
private static void merge( Comparable [ ] a, Comparable [ ] tmpArray,
        int leftPos, int rightPos, int rightEnd )
{
    int leftEnd = rightPos - 1;
    int tmpPos = leftPos;
    int numElements = rightEnd - leftPos + 1;

    // Main loop
    while( leftPos <= leftEnd && rightPos <= rightEnd )
        if( a[ leftPos ].compareTo( a[ rightPos ] ) <= 0 )
            tmpArray[ tmpPos++ ] = a[ leftPos++ ];
        else
            tmpArray[ tmpPos++ ] = a[ rightPos++ ];

    while( leftPos <= leftEnd )    // Copy rest of first half
        tmpArray[ tmpPos++ ] = a[ leftPos++ ];

    while( rightPos <= rightEnd )  // Copy rest of right half
        tmpArray[ tmpPos++ ] = a[ rightPos++ ];

    // Copy tmpArray back
    for( int i = 0; i < numElements; i++, rightEnd-- )
        a[ rightEnd ] = tmpArray[ rightEnd ];
}
```

Figure 7.10 merge routine

terms appear on both sides and cancel. This is called *telescoping* a sum. After everything is added, the final result is

$$\frac{T(N)}{N} = \frac{T(1)}{1} + \log N$$

because all of the other terms cancel and there are $\log N$ equations, and so all the 1s at the end of these equations add up to $\log N$. Multiplying through by N gives the final answer.

$$T(N) = N \log N + N = O(N \log N)$$

Notice that if we did not divide through by N at the start of the solutions, the sum would not telescope. This is why it was necessary to divide through by N.

An alternative method is to substitute the recurrence relation continually on the right-hand side. We have

$$T(N) = 2T(N/2) + N$$

Since we can substitute $N/2$ into the main equation,

$$2T(N/2) = 2(2(T(N/4)) + N/2) = 4T(N/4) + N$$

we have

$$T(N) = 4T(N/4) + 2N$$

Again, by substituting $N/4$ into the main equation, we see that

$$4T(N/4) = 4(2T(N/8) + N/4) = 8T(N/8) + N$$

So we have

$$T(N) = 8T(N/8) + 3N$$

Continuing in this manner, we obtain

$$T(N) = 2^k T(N/2^k) + k \cdot N$$

Using $k = \log N$, we obtain

$$T(N) = NT(1) + N \log N = N \log N + N$$

The choice of which method to use is a matter of taste. The first method tends to produce scrap work that fits better on a standard, $8\frac{1}{2} \times 11$ sheet of paper, leading to fewer mathematical errors, but it requires a certain amount of experience to apply. The second method is more of a brute-force approach.

Recall that we have assumed $N = 2^k$. The analysis can be refined to handle cases when N is not a power of 2. The answer turns out to be almost identical (this is usually the case).

Although mergesort's running time is $O(N \log N)$, it is hardly ever used for main memory sorts. The main problem is that merging two sorted lists uses linear extra memory,* and the additional work spent copying to the temporary array and back, throughout the algorithm, has the effect of slowing down the sort considerably. This copying can be avoided by judiciously switching the roles of `a` and `tmpArray` at alternate levels of the recursion. A variant of mergesort can also be implemented nonrecursively (Exercise 7.16), but even so, for serious internal sorting applications, the algorithm of choice is quicksort, which is described in the next section. Nevertheless, as we will see later in this chapter, the merging routine is the cornerstone of most external sorting algorithms.

7.7. Quicksort

As its name implies, *quicksort* is the fastest known sorting algorithm in practice. Its average running time is $O(N \log N)$. It is very fast, mainly due to a very tight and highly optimized inner loop. It has $O(N^2)$ worst-case performance, but this can be made exponentially unlikely with a little effort. The quicksort algorithm is simple to understand and prove correct, although for many years it had the reputation of being an algorithm that could in theory be

---

*It is theoretically possible to use less extra memory, but the resulting algorithm is complex and impractical.

highly optimized but in practice was impossible to code correctly. Like mergesort, quicksort is a divide-and-conquer recursive algorithm. The basic algorithm to sort an array S consists of the following four easy steps:

1. If the number of elements in S is 0 or 1, then return.
2. Pick any element v in S. This is called the *pivot*.
3. *Partition* $S - \{v\}$ (the remaining elements in S) into two disjoint groups: $S_1 = \{x \in S - \{v\}|x \leq v\}$, and $S_2 = \{x \in S - \{v\}|x \geq v\}$.
4. Return $\{$quicksort(S_1) followed by v followed by quicksort$(S_2)\}$.

Since the partition step ambiguously describes what to do with elements equal to the pivot, this becomes a design decision. Part of a good implementation is handling this case as efficiently as possible. Intuitively, we would hope that about half the keys that are equal to the pivot go into S_1 and the other half into S_2, much as we like binary search trees to be balanced.

Figure 7.11 shows the action of quicksort on a set of numbers. The pivot is chosen (by chance) to be 65. The remaining elements in the set are partitioned into two smaller sets. Recursively sorting the set of smaller numbers yields 0, 13, 26, 31, 43, 57 (by rule 3 of recursion). The set of large numbers is similarly sorted. The sorted arrangement of the entire set is then trivially obtained.

It should be clear that this algorithm works, but it is not clear why it is any faster than mergesort. Like mergesort, it recursively solves two subproblems and requires linear additional work (step 3), but, unlike mergesort, the subproblems are not guaranteed to be of equal size, which is potentially bad. The reason that quicksort is faster is that the partitioning step can actually be performed in place and very efficiently. This efficiency more than makes up for the lack of equal-sized recursive calls.

The algorithm as described so far lacks quite a few details, which we now fill in. There are many ways to implement steps 2 and 3; the method presented here is the result of extensive analysis and empirical study and represents a very efficient way to implement quicksort. Even the slightest deviations from this method can cause surprisingly bad results.

7.7.1. Picking the Pivot

Although the algorithm as described works no matter which element is chosen as pivot, some choices are obviously better than others.

A Wrong Way

The popular, uninformed choice is to use the first element as the pivot. This is acceptable if the input is random, but if the input is presorted or in reverse order, then the pivot provides a poor partition, because either all the elements go into S_1 or they go into S_2. Worse, this happens consistently throughout the recursive calls. The practical effect is that if the first element is used as the pivot and the input is presorted, then quicksort will take quadratic time to do essentially nothing at all, which is quite embarrassing. Moreover, presorted input (or input with a large presorted section) is quite frequent, so using the first element as pivot *is an absolutely horrible idea* and should be discarded immediately. An alternative is choosing the larger of the first two distinct elements as pivot, but this has the same bad properties as merely choosing the first element. Do not use that pivoting strategy either.

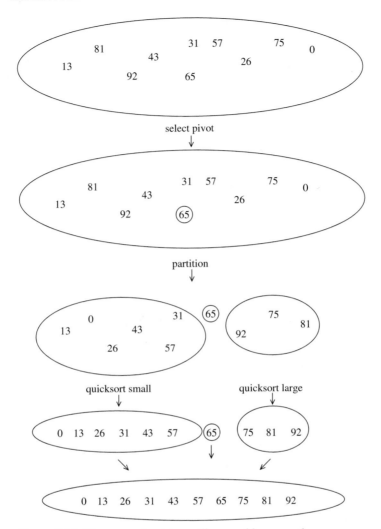

Figure 7.11 The steps of quicksort illustrated by example

A Safe Maneuver

A safe course is merely to choose the pivot randomly. This strategy is generally perfectly safe, unless the random number generator has a flaw (which is not as uncommon as you might think), since it is very unlikely that a random pivot would consistently provide a poor partition. On the other hand, random number generation is generally an expensive commodity and does not reduce the average running time of the rest of the algorithm at all.

Median-of-Three Partitioning

The median of a group of N numbers is the $\lceil N/2 \rceil$ th largest number. The best choice of pivot would be the median of the array. Unfortunately, this is hard to calculate and would slow down quicksort considerably. A good estimate can be obtained by picking three elements randomly and using the median of these three as pivot. The randomness turns out not to help much, so the common course is to use as pivot the median of the left, right, and center elements. For instance, with input 8, 1, 4, 9, 6, 3, 5, 2, 7, 0 as before, the left element is 8, the right element is 0 and the center (in position $\lfloor(left + right)/2\rfloor$) element is 6. Thus, the pivot would be $v = 6$. Using median-of-three partitioning clearly eliminates the bad case for sorted input (the partitions become equal in this case) and actually reduces the running time of quicksort by about 5 percent.

7.7.2. Partitioning Strategy

There are several partitioning strategies used in practice, but the one described here is known to give good results. It is very easy, as we shall see, to do this wrong or inefficiently, but it is safe to use a known method. The first step is to get the pivot element out of the way by swapping it with the last element. i starts at the first element and j starts at the next-to-last element. If the original input was the same as before, the following figure shows the current situation.

```
┌─────────────────────────────────────────────────┐
│                                                 │
│  8   1   4   9   0   3   5   2   7   6          │
│  ↑                           ↑                  │
│  i                           j                  │
│                                                 │
└─────────────────────────────────────────────────┘
```

For now we will assume that all the elements are distinct. Later on we will worry about what to do in the presence of duplicates. As a limiting case, our algorithm must do the proper thing if *all* of the elements are identical. It is surprising how easy it is to do the *wrong* thing.

What our partitioning stage wants to do is to move all the small elements to the left part of the array and all the large elements to the right part. "Small" and "large" are, of course, relative to the pivot.

While i is to the left of j, we move i right, skipping over elements that are smaller than the pivot. We move j left, skipping over elements that are larger than the pivot. When i and j have stopped, i is pointing at a large element and j is pointing at a small element. If i is to the left of j, those elements are swapped. The effect is to push a large element to the right and a small element to the left. In the example above, i would not move and j would slide over one place. The situation is as follows.

```
┌─────────────────────────────────────────────────┐
│                                                 │
│  8   1   4   9   0   3   5   2   7   6          │
│  ↑                       ↑                      │
│  i                       j                      │
│                                                 │
└─────────────────────────────────────────────────┘
```

We then swap the elements pointed to by i and j and repeat the process until i and j cross.

```
┌─────────────────────────────────────────────────┐
│              After First Swap                   │
├─────────────────────────────────────────────────┤
│  2   1   4   9   0   3   5   8   7   6          │
│  ↑                       ↑                      │
│  i                       j                      │
└─────────────────────────────────────────────────┘
```

Before Second Swap									
2	1	4	9	0	3	5	8	7	6
			↑			↑			
			i			j			

After Second Swap									
2	1	4	5	0	3	9	8	7	6
			↑			↑			
			i			j			

Before Third Swap									
2	1	4	5	0	3	9	8	7	6
					↑	↑			
					j	i			

At this stage, i and j have crossed, so no swap is performed. The final part of the partitioning is to swap the pivot element with the element pointed to by i.

After Swap with Pivot									
2	1	4	5	0	3	6	8	7	9
						↑			↑
						i			pivot

When the pivot is swapped with i in the last step, we know that every element in a position $p < i$ must be small. This is because either position p contained a small element to start with, or the large element originally in position p was replaced during a swap. A similar argument shows that elements in positions $p > i$ must be large.

One important detail we must consider is how to handle elements that are equal to the pivot. The questions are whether or not i should stop when it sees an element equal to the pivot and whether or not j should stop when it sees an element equal to the pivot. Intuitively, i and j ought to do the same thing, since otherwise the partitioning step is biased. For instance, if i stops and j does not, then all elements that are equal to the pivot will wind up in S_2.

To get an idea of what might be good, we consider the case where all the elements in the array are identical. If both i and j stop, there will be many swaps between identical elements. Although this seems useless, the positive effect is that i and j will cross in the middle, so when the pivot is replaced, the partition creates two nearly equal subarrays. The mergesort analysis tells us that the total running time would then be $O(N \log N)$.

If neither i nor j stops, and code is present to prevent them from running off the end of the array, no swaps will be performed. Although this seems good, a correct implementation would then swap the pivot into the last spot that i touched, which would be the next-to-last position (or last, depending on the exact implementation). This would create very uneven subarrays. If all the elements are identical, the running time is $O(N^2)$. The effect is the same as using the first element as a pivot for presorted input. It takes quadratic time to do nothing!

Thus, we find that it is better to do the unnecessary swaps and create even subarrays than to risk wildly uneven subarrays. Therefore, we will have both i and j stop if they encounter an element equal to the pivot. This turns out to be the only one of the four possibilities that does not take quadratic time for this input.

At first glance it may seem that worrying about an array of identical elements is silly. After all, why would anyone want to sort 5,000 identical elements? However, recall that quicksort is recursive. Suppose there are 100,000 elements, of which 5,000 are identical (or, more likely, complex elements whose sort keys are identical). Eventually, quicksort will make the recursive call on only these 5,000 elements. Then it really will be important to make sure that 5,000 identical elements can be sorted efficiently.

7.7.3. Small Arrays

For very small arrays ($N \leq 20$), quicksort does not perform as well as insertion sort. Furthermore, because quicksort is recursive, these cases will occur frequently. A common solution is not to use quicksort recursively for small arrays, but instead use a sorting algorithm that is efficient for small arrays, such as insertion sort. Using this strategy can actually save about 15 percent in the running time (over doing no cutoff at all). A good cutoff range is $N = 10$, although any cutoff between 5 and 20 is likely to produce similar results. This also saves nasty degenerate cases, such as taking the median of three elements when there are only one or two.

7.7.4. Actual Quicksort Routines

The driver for quicksort is shown in Figure 7.12.

The general form of the routines will be to pass the array and the range of the array (left and right) to be sorted. The first routine to deal with is pivot selection. The easiest way to do this is to sort a[left], a[right], and a[center] in place. This has the extra advantage that the smallest of the three winds up in a[left], which is where the partitioning step would put it anyway. The largest winds up in a[right], which is also the correct place, since it is larger than the pivot. Therefore, we can place the pivot in a[right-1] and initialize i and j to left+1 and right-2 in the partition phase. Yet another benefit is that because a[left] is smaller than the pivot, it will act as a sentinel for j. Thus, we do not

```
/**
 * Quicksort algorithm.
 * @param a an array of Comparable items.
 */
public static void quicksort( Comparable [ ] a )
{
    quicksort( a, 0, a.length - 1 );
}
```

Figure 7.12 Driver for quicksort

```
/**
 * Return median of left, center, and right.
 * Order these and hide the pivot.
 */
private static
Comparable median3( Comparable [ ] a, int left, int right )
{
    int center = ( left + right ) / 2;
    if( a[ center ].compareTo( a[ left ] ) < 0 )
        swapReferences( a, left, center );
    if( a[ right ].compareTo( a[ left ] ) < 0 )
        swapReferences( a, left, right );
    if( a[ right ].compareTo( a[ center ] ) < 0 )
        swapReferences( a, center, right );

        // Place pivot at position right - 1
    swapReferences( a, center, right - 1 );
    return a[ right - 1 ];
}
```

Figure 7.13 Code to perform median-of-three partitioning

need to worry about j running past the end. Since i will stop on elements equal to the pivot, storing the pivot in a[right-1] provides a sentinel for i. The code in Figure 7.13 does the median-of-three partitioning with all the side effects described. It may seem that it is only slightly inefficient to compute the pivot by a method that does not actually sort a[left], a[center], and a[right], but, surprisingly, this produces bad results (see Exercise 7.46).

The real heart of the quicksort routine is in Figure 7.14. It includes the partitioning and recursive calls. There are several things worth noting in this implementation. Line 3 initializes i and j to 1 past their correct values, so that there are no special cases to consider. This initialization depends on the fact that median-of-three partitioning has some side effects; this program will not work if you try to use it without change with a simple pivoting strategy, because i and j start in the wrong place and there is no longer a sentinel for j.

The swapping action at line 8 is sometimes written explicitly, for speed purposes. For the algorithm to be fast, it may be necessary to force the compiler to compile this code in-line. Many compilers will do this automatically if swapReferences is a final method, but for those that do not, the difference can be significant.

Finally, lines 5 and 6 show why quicksort is so fast. The inner loop of the algorithm consists of an increment/decrement (by 1, which is fast), a test, and a jump. There is no extra juggling as there is in mergesort. This code is still surprisingly tricky. It is tempting to replace lines 3 through 9 with the statements in Figure 7.15. This does not work, because there would be an infinite loop if a[i] = a[j] = pivot.

7.7.5. Analysis of Quicksort

Like mergesort, quicksort is recursive, and hence, its analysis requires solving a recurrence formula. We will do the analysis for a quicksort, assuming a random pivot (no median-of-three partitioning) and no cutoff for small arrays. We will take $T(0) = T(1) = 1$, as in mergesort. The running time of quicksort is equal to the running time of the two recursive

```
        /**
         * Internal quicksort method that makes recursive calls.
         * Uses median-of-three partitioning and a cutoff of 10.
         * @param a an array of Comparable items.
         * @param left the left-most index of the subarray.
         * @param right the right-most index of the subarray.
         */
        private static void quicksort( Comparable [ ] a, int left, int right )
        {
/* 1*/      if( left + CUTOFF <= right )
            {
/* 2*/          Comparable pivot = median3( a, left, right );

                // Begin partitioning
/* 3*/          int i = left, j = right - 1;
/* 4*/          for( ; ; )
                {
/* 5*/              while( a[ ++i ].compareTo( pivot ) < 0 ) { }
/* 6*/              while( a[ --j ].compareTo( pivot ) > 0 ) { }
/* 7*/              if( i < j )
/* 8*/                  swapReferences( a, i, j );
                    else
/* 9*/                  break;
                }

/*10*/          swapReferences( a, i, right - 1 );   // Restore pivot

/*11*/          quicksort( a, left, i - 1 );    // Sort small elements
/*12*/          quicksort( a, i + 1, right );   // Sort large elements
            }
            else  // Do an insertion sort on the subarray
/*13*/          insertionSort( a, left, right );
        }
```

Figure 7.14 Main quicksort routine

```
/* 3*/          int i = left + 1, j = right - 2;
/* 4*/          for( ; ; )
                {
/* 5*/              while( a[ i ].compareTo( pivot ) < 0 ) i++;
/* 6*/              while( a[ j ].compareTo( pivot ) > 0 ) j--;
/* 7*/              if( i < j )
/* 8*/                  swapReferences( a, i, j );
                    else
/* 9*/                  break;
                }
```

Figure 7.15 A small change to quicksort, which breaks the algorithm calls plus the linear time spent in the partition (the pivot selection takes only constant time). This gives the basic quicksort relation

$$T(N) = T(i) + T(N - i - 1) + cN \tag{7.1}$$

where $i = |S_1|$ is the number of elements in S_1. We will look at three cases.

Worst-Case Analysis

The pivot is the smallest element, all the time. Then $i = 0$ and if we ignore $T(0) = 1$, which is insignificant, the recurrence is

$$T(N) = T(N - 1) + cN, \quad N > 1 \tag{7.2}$$

We telescope, using Equation (7.2) repeatedly. Thus

$$T(N - 1) = T(N - 2) + c(N - 1) \tag{7.3}$$

$$T(N - 2) = T(N - 3) + c(N - 2) \tag{7.4}$$

$$\vdots$$

$$T(2) = T(1) + c(2) \tag{7.5}$$

Adding up all these equations yields

$$T(N) = T(1) + c\sum_{i=2}^{N} i = O(N^2) \tag{7.6}$$

as claimed earlier.

Best-Case Analysis

In the best case, the pivot is in the middle. To simplify the math, we assume that the two subarrays are each exactly half the size of the original, and although this gives a slight overestimate, this is acceptable because we are only interested in a Big-Oh answer.

$$T(N) = 2T(N/2) + cN \tag{7.7}$$

Divide both sides of Equation (7.7) by N.

$$\frac{T(N)}{N} = \frac{T(N/2)}{N/2} + c \tag{7.8}$$

We will telescope using this equation.

$$\frac{T(N/2)}{N/2} = \frac{T(N/4)}{N/4} + c \tag{7.9}$$

$$\frac{T(N/4)}{N/4} = \frac{T(N/8)}{N/8} + c \tag{7.10}$$

$$\vdots$$

$$\frac{T(2)}{2} = \frac{T(1)}{1} + c \tag{7.11}$$

We add all the equations from (7.7) to (7.11) and note that there are $\log N$ of them:

$$\frac{T(N)}{N} = \frac{T(1)}{1} + c\log N \tag{7.12}$$

which yields

$$T(N) = cN \log N + N = O(N \log N) \qquad (7.13)$$

Notice that this is the exact same analysis as mergesort, hence we get the same answer.

Average-Case Analysis

This is the most difficult part. For the average case, we assume that each of the sizes for S_1 is equally likely, and hence has probability $1/N$. This assumption is actually valid for our pivoting and partitioning strategy, but it is not valid for some others. Partitioning strategies that do not preserve the randomness of the subarrays cannot use this analysis. Interestingly, these strategies seem to result in programs that take longer to run in practice.

With this assumption, the average value of $T(i)$, and hence $T(N - i - 1)$, is $(1/N)\sum_{j=0}^{N-1} T(j)$. Equation (7.1) then becomes

$$T(N) = \frac{2}{N}\left[\sum_{j=0}^{N-1} T(j)\right] + cN \qquad (7.14)$$

If Equation (7.14) is multiplied by N, it becomes

$$NT(N) = 2\left[\sum_{j=0}^{N-1} T(j)\right] + cN^2 \qquad (7.15)$$

We need to remove the summation sign to simplify matters. We note that we can telescope with one more equation.

$$(N - 1)T(N - 1) = 2\left[\sum_{j=0}^{N-2} T(j)\right] + c(N - 1)^2 \qquad (7.16)$$

If we subtract Equation (7.16) from Equation (7.15), we obtain

$$NT(N) - (N - 1)T(N - 1) = 2T(N - 1) + 2cN - c \qquad (7.17)$$

We rearrange terms and drop the insignificant $-c$ on the right, obtaining

$$NT(N) = (N + 1)T(N - 1) + 2cN \qquad (7.18)$$

We now have a formula for $T(N)$ in terms of $T(N - 1)$ only. Again the idea is to telescope, but Equation (7.18) is in the wrong form. Divide Equation (7.18) by $N(N + 1)$:

$$\frac{T(N)}{N + 1} = \frac{T(N - 1)}{N} + \frac{2c}{N + 1} \qquad (7.19)$$

Now we can telescope.

$$\frac{T(N - 1)}{N} = \frac{T(N - 2)}{N - 1} + \frac{2c}{N} \qquad (7.20)$$

$$\frac{T(N - 2)}{N - 1} = \frac{T(N - 3)}{N - 2} + \frac{2c}{N - 1} \qquad (7.21)$$

$$\vdots$$

$$\frac{T(2)}{3} = \frac{T(1)}{2} + \frac{2c}{3} \qquad (7.22)$$

Adding Equations (7.19) through (7.22) yields

$$\frac{T(N)}{N+1} = \frac{T(1)}{2} + 2c \sum_{i=3}^{N+1} \frac{1}{i} \qquad (7.23)$$

The sum is about $\log_e(N+1) + \gamma - \frac{3}{2}$, where $\gamma \approx 0.577$ is known as Euler's constant, so

$$\frac{T(N)}{N+1} = O(\log N) \qquad (7.24)$$

And so

$$T(N) = O(N \log N) \qquad (7.25)$$

Although this analysis seems complicated, it really is not—the steps are natural once you have seen some recurrence relations. The analysis can actually be taken further. The highly optimized version that was described above has also been analyzed, and this result gets extremely difficult, involving complicated recurrences and advanced mathematics. The effect of equal elements has also been analyzed in detail, and it turns out that the code presented does the right thing.

7.7.6. A Linear-Expected-Time Algorithm for Selection

Quicksort can be modified to solve the *selection problem*, which we have seen in Chapters 1 and 6. Recall that by using a priority queue, we can find the kth largest (or smallest) element in $O(N + k \log N)$. For the special case of finding the median, this gives an $O(N \log N)$ algorithm.

Since we can sort the array in $O(N \log N)$ time, one might expect to obtain a better time bound for selection. The algorithm we present to find the kth smallest element in a set S is almost identical to quicksort. In fact, the first three steps are the same. We will call this algorithm *quickselect*. Let $|S_i|$ denote the number of elements in S_i. The steps of quickselect are

1. If $|S| = 1$, then $k = 1$ and return the element in S as the answer. If a cutoff for small arrays is being used and $|S| \leq$ CUTOFF, then sort S and return the kth smallest element.

2. Pick a pivot element, $v \in S$.

3. Partition $S - \{v\}$ into S_1 and S_2, as was done with quicksort.

4. If $k \leq |S_1|$, then the kth smallest element must be in S_1. In this case, return quickselect (S_1, k). If $k = 1 + |S_1|$, then the pivot is the kth smallest element and we can return it as the answer. Otherwise, the kth smallest element lies in S_2, and it is the $(k - |S_1| - 1)$st smallest element in S_2. We make a recursive call and return quickselect $(S_2, k - |S_1| - 1)$.

In contrast to quicksort, quickselect makes only one recursive call instead of two. The worst case of quickselect is identical to that of quicksort and is $O(N^2)$. Intuitively, this is because quicksort's worst case is when one of S_1 and S_2 is empty; thus, quickselect is not really saving a recursive call. The average running time, however, is $O(N)$. The analysis is similar to quicksort's and is left as an exercise.

The implementation of quickselect is even simpler than the abstract description might imply. The code to do this is shown in Figure 7.16. When the algorithm terminates, the kth smallest element is in position $k - 1$ (because arrays start at index 0). This destroys the original ordering; if this is not desirable, then a copy must be made.

Using a median-of-three pivoting strategy makes the chance of the worst case occurring almost negligible. By carefully choosing the pivot, however, we can eliminate the quadratic

```
            /**
             * Internal selection method that makes recursive calls.
             * Uses median-of-three partitioning and a cutoff of 10.
             * Places the kth smallest item in a[k-1].
             * @param a an array of Comparable items.
             * @param left the left-most index of the subarray.
             * @param right the right-most index of the subarray.
             * @param k the desired rank (1 is minimum) in the entire array.
             */
            private static void quickSelect( Comparable [ ] a, int left,
                                                      int right, int k )
            {
/* 1*/          if( left + CUTOFF <= right )
                {
/* 2*/              Comparable pivot = median3( a, left, right );

                        // Begin partitioning
/* 3*/              int i = left, j = right - 1;
/* 4*/              for( ; ; )
                    {
/* 5*/                  while( a[ ++i ].compareTo( pivot ) < 0 ) { }
/* 6*/                  while( a[ --j ].compareTo( pivot ) > 0 ) { }
/* 7*/                  if( i < j )
/* 8*/                      swapReferences( a, i, j );
                        else
/* 9*/                      break;
                    }

/*10*/              swapReferences( a, i, right - 1 );    // Restore pivot

/*11*/              if( k - 1 < i )
/*12*/                  quickSelect( a, left, i - 1, k );
/*13*/              else if( k - 1 > i )
/*14*/                  quickSelect( a, i + 1, right, k );
                }
                else  // Do an insertion sort on the subarray
/*15*/              insertionSort( a, left, right );
            }
```

Figure 7.16 Main quickselect routine

worst case and ensure an $O(N)$ algorithm. The overhead involved in doing this is considerable, so the resulting algorithm is mostly of theoretical interest. In Chapter 10, we will examine the linear-time worst-case algorithm for selection, and we shall also see an interesting technique of choosing the pivot that results in a somewhat faster selection algorithm in practice.

7.8. A General Lower Bound for Sorting

Although we have $O(N \log N)$ algorithms for sorting, it is not clear that this is as good as we can do. In this section, we prove that any algorithm for sorting that uses only comparisons requires $\Omega(N \log N)$ comparisons (and hence time) in the worst case, so that mergesort and heapsort are optimal to within a constant factor. The proof can be extended to show that $\Omega(N \log N)$ comparisons are required, even on average, for any sorting algorithm that uses only comparisons, which means that quicksort is optimal on average to within a constant factor.

Specifically, we will prove the following result: Any sorting algorithm that uses only comparisons requires $\lceil \log(N!) \rceil$ comparisons in the worst case and $\log(N!)$ comparisons on average. We will assume that all N elements are distinct, since any sorting algorithm must work for this case.

7.8.1. Decision Trees

A *decision tree* is an abstraction used to prove lower bounds. In our context, a decision tree is a binary tree. Each node represents a set of possible orderings, consistent with comparisons that have been made, among the elements. The results of the comparisons are the tree edges.

The decision tree in Figure 7.17 represents an algorithm that sorts the three elements a, b, and c. The initial state of the algorithm is at the root. (We will use the terms *state* and *node* interchangeably.) No comparisons have been done, so all orderings are legal. The first comparison that *this particular* algorithm performs compares a and b. The two results lead to two possible states. If $a < b$, then only three possibilities remain. If the algorithm reaches node 2, then it will compare a and c. Other algorithms might do different things; a different algorithm would have a different decision tree. If $a > c$, the algorithm enters state 5. Since there is only one ordering that is consistent, the algorithm can terminate and report that it has completed the sort. If $a < c$, the algorithm cannot do this, because there are two possible orderings and it cannot possibly be sure which is correct. In this case, the algorithm will require one more comparison.

Every algorithm that sorts by using only comparisons can be represented by a decision tree. Of course, it is only feasible to draw the tree for extremely small input sizes. The number of comparisons used by the sorting algorithm is equal to the depth of the deepest leaf. In our case, this algorithm uses three comparisons in the worst case. The average number of comparisons used is equal to the average depth of the leaves. Since a decision tree is large, it follows that there must be some long paths. To prove the lower bounds, all that needs to be shown are some basic tree properties.

LEMMA 7.1.
Let T be a binary tree of depth d. Then T has at most 2^d leaves.

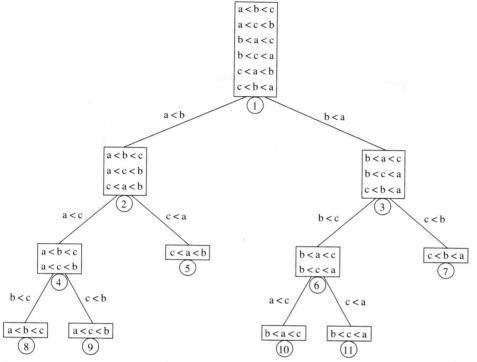

Figure 7.17 A decision tree for three-element insertion sort

PROOF:

The proof is by induction. If $d = 0$, then there is at most one leaf, so the basis is true. Otherwise, we have a root, which cannot be a leaf, and a left and right subtree, each of depth at most $d - 1$. By the induction hypothesis, they can each have at most 2^{d-1} leaves, giving a total of at most 2^d leaves. This proves the lemma.

LEMMA 7.2.

A binary tree with L leaves must have depth at least $\lceil \log L \rceil$.

PROOF:

Immediate from the preceding lemma.

THEOREM 7.6.

Any sorting algorithm that uses only comparisons between elements requires at least $\lceil \log(N!) \rceil$ comparisons in the worst case.

PROOF:

A decision tree to sort N elements must have $N!$ leaves. The theorem follows from the preceding lemma.

THEOREM 7.7.

Any sorting algorithm that uses only comparisons between elements requires $\Omega(N \log N)$ comparisons.

PROOF:

From the previous theorem, $\log(N!)$ comparisons are required.

$$
\begin{aligned}
\log(N!) &= \log(N(N-1)(N-2)\cdots(2)(1)) \\
&= \log N + \log(N-1) + \log(N-2) + \cdots + \log 2 + \log 1 \\
&\geq \log N + \log(N-1) + \log(N-2) + \cdots + \log(N/2) \\
&\geq \frac{N}{2}\log\frac{N}{2} \\
&\geq \frac{N}{2}\log N - \frac{N}{2} \\
&= \Omega(N\log N)
\end{aligned}
$$

This type of lower-bound argument, when used to prove a worst-case result, is sometimes known as an *information-theoretic* lower bound. The general theorem says that if there are P different possible cases to distinguish, and the questions are of the form YES/NO, then $\lceil \log P \rceil$ questions are always required in some case by any algorithm to solve the problem. It is possible to prove a similar result for the average-case running time of any comparison-based sorting algorithm. This result is implied by the following lemma, which is left as an exercise: Any binary tree with L leaves has an average depth of at least $\log L$.

7.9. Bucket Sort

Although we proved in the previous section that any general sorting algorithm that uses only comparisons requires $\Omega(N\log N)$ time in the worst case, recall that it is still possible to sort in linear time in some special cases.

A simple example is bucket sort. For bucket sort to work, extra information must be available. The input $A_1, A_2, \ldots, A_N$ must consist of only positive integers smaller than M. (Obviously extensions to this are possible.) If this is the case, then the algorithm is simple: Keep an array called **count**, of size M, which is initialized to all 0s. Thus, **count** has M cells, or buckets, which are initially empty. When A_i is read, increment **count**$[A_i]$ by 1. After all the input is read, scan the **count** array, printing out a representation of the sorted list. This algorithm takes $O(M+N)$; the proof is left as an exercise. If M is $O(N)$, then the total is $O(N)$.

Although this algorithm seems to violate the lower bound, it turns out that it does not because it uses a more powerful operation than simple comparisons. By incrementing the appropriate bucket, the algorithm essentially performs an M-way comparison in unit time. This is similar to the strategy used in extendible hashing (Section 5.6). This is clearly not in the model for which the lower bound was proven.

This algorithm does, however, question the validity of the model used in proving the lower bound. The model actually is a strong model, because a *general-purpose* sorting algorithm cannot make assumptions about the type of input it can expect to see, but must make decisions based on ordering information only. Naturally, if there is extra information available, we should expect to find a more efficient algorithm, since otherwise the extra information would be wasted.

Although bucket sort seems like much too trivial an algorithm to be useful, it turns out that there are many cases where the input is only small integers, so that using a method like quicksort is really overkill.

7.10. External Sorting

So far, all the algorithms we have examined require that the input fit into main memory. There are, however, applications where the input is much too large to fit into memory. This section will discuss *external sorting* algorithms, which are designed to handle very large inputs.

7.10.1. Why We Need New Algorithms

Most of the internal sorting algorithms take advantage of the fact that memory is directly addressable. Shellsort compares elements a[i] and a[i-h_k] in one time unit. Heapsort compares elements a[i] and a[i*2+1] in one time unit. Quicksort, with median-of-three partitioning, requires comparing a[left], a[center], and a[right] in a constant number of time units. If the input is on a tape, then all these operations lose their efficiency, since elements on a tape can only be accessed sequentially. Even if the data is on a disk, there is still a practical loss of efficiency because of the delay required to spin the disk and move the disk head.

To see how slow external accesses really are, create a random file that is large, but not too big to fit in main memory. Read the file in and sort it using an efficient algorithm. The time it takes to read the input is certain to be significant compared to the time to sort the input, even though sorting is an $O(N \log N)$ operation and reading the input is only $O(N)$.

7.10.2. Model for External Sorting

The wide variety of mass storage devices makes external sorting much more device-dependent than internal sorting. The algorithms that we will consider work on tapes, which are probably the most restrictive storage medium. Since access to an element on tape is done by winding the tape to the correct location, tapes can be efficiently accessed only in sequential order (in either direction).

We will assume that we have at least three tape drives to perform the sorting. We need two drives to do an efficient sort; the third drive simplifies matters. If only one tape drive is present, then we are in trouble: any algorithm will require $\Omega(N^2)$ tape accesses.

7.10.3. The Simple Algorithm

The basic external sorting algorithm uses the merging algorithm from mergesort. Suppose we have four tapes, T_{a1}, T_{a2}, T_{b1}, T_{b2}, which are two input and two output tapes. Depending on the point in the algorithm, the *a* and *b* tapes are either input tapes or output tapes. Suppose the data is initially on T_{a1}. Suppose further that the internal memory can hold (and sort) M records at a time. A natural first step is to read M records at a time from the input tape, sort the records internally, and then write the sorted records alternately to T_{b1}

and T_{b2}. We will call each set of sorted records a *run*. When this is done, we rewind all the tapes. Suppose we have the same input as our example for Shellsort.

T_{a1}	81	94	11	96	12	35	17	99	28	58	41	75	15
T_{a2}												
T_{b1}												
T_{b2}												

If $M = 3$, then after the runs are constructed, the tapes will contain the data indicated in the following figure.

T_{a1}							
T_{a2}							
T_{b1}	11	81	94	17	28	99	15
T_{b2}	12	35	96	41	58	75	

Now T_{b1} and T_{b2} contain a group of runs. We take the first run from each tape and merge them, writing the result, which is a run twice as long, onto T_{a1}. Recall that merging two sorted lists is simple; we need almost no memory, since the merge is performed as T_{b1} and T_{b2} advance. Then we take the next run from each tape, merge these, and write the result to T_{a2}. We continue this process, alternating between T_{a1} and T_{a2}, until either T_{b1} or T_{b2} is empty. At this point either both are empty or there is one run left. In the latter case, we copy this run to the appropriate tape. We rewind all four tapes, and repeat the same steps, this time using the a tapes as input and the b tapes as output. This will give runs of $4M$. We continue the process until we get one run of length N.

This algorithm will require $\lceil \log(N/M) \rceil$ passes, plus the initial run-constructing pass. For instance, if we have 10 million records of 128 bytes each, and four megabytes of internal memory, then the first pass will create 320 runs. We would then need nine more passes to complete the sort. Our example requires $\lceil \log 13/3 \rceil = 3$ more passes, which are shown in the following figures.

T_{a1}	11	12	35	81	94	96	15
T_{a2}	17	28	41	58	75	99	
T_{b1}							
T_{b2}							

T_{a1}												
T_{a2}												
T_{b1}	11	12	17	28	35	51	58	75	81	94	96	99
T_{b2}	15											

T_{a1}	11	12	15	17	28	35	41	58	75	81	94	96	99
T_{a2}													
T_{b1}													
T_{b2}													

7.10.4. Multiway Merge

If we have extra tapes, then we can expect to reduce the number of passes required to sort our input. We do this by extending the basic (two-way) merge to a k-way merge.

Merging two runs is done by winding each input tape to the beginning of each run. Then the smaller element is found, placed on an output tape, and the appropriate input tape is advanced. If there are k input tapes, this strategy works the same way, the only difference being that it is slightly more complicated to find the smallest of the k elements. We can find the smallest of these elements by using a priority queue. To obtain the next element to write on the output tape, we perform a `deleteMin` operation. The appropriate input tape is advanced, and if the run on the input tape is not yet completed, we `insert` the new element into the priority queue. Using the same example as before, we distribute the input onto the three tapes.

T_{a1}						
T_{a2}						
T_{a3}						
T_{b1}	11	81	94	41	58	75
T_{b2}	12	35	96	15		
T_{b3}	17	28	99			

We then need two more passes of three-way merging to complete the sort.

T_{a1}	11	12	17	28	35	81	94	96	99
T_{a2}	15	41	58	75					
T_{a3}									
T_{b1}									
T_{b2}									
T_{b3}									

T_{a1}													
T_{a2}													
T_{a3}													
T_{b1}	11	12	15	17	28	35	41	58	75	81	94	96	99
T_{b2}													
T_{b3}													

After the initial run construction phase, the number of passes required using k-way merging is $\lceil \log_k(N/M) \rceil$, because the runs get k times as large in each pass. For the example above, the formula is verified, since $\lceil \log_3(13/3) \rceil = 2$. If we have 10 tapes, then $k = 5$, and our large example from the previous section would require $\lceil \log_5 320 \rceil = 4$ passes.

7.10.5. Polyphase Merge

The k-way merging strategy developed in the last section requires the use of $2k$ tapes. This could be prohibitive for some applications. It is possible to get by with only $k + 1$ tapes. As an example, we will show how to perform two-way merging using only three tapes.

Suppose we have three tapes, T_1, T_2, and T_3, and an input file on T_1 that will produce 34 runs. One option is to put 17 runs on each of T_2 and T_3. We could then merge this result onto T_1, obtaining one tape with 17 runs. The problem is that since all the runs are on one tape, we must now put some of these runs on T_2 to perform another merge. The logical way to do this is to copy the first eight runs from T_1 onto T_2 and then perform the merge. This has the effect of adding an extra half pass for every pass we do.

An alternative method is to split the original 34 runs unevenly. Suppose we put 21 runs on T_2 and 13 runs on T_3. We would then merge 13 runs onto T_1 before T_3 was empty. At this point, we could rewind T_1 and T_3, and merge T_1, with 13 runs, and T_2, which has 8 runs, onto T_3. We could then merge 8 runs until T_2 was empty, which would leave 5 runs left on T_1 and 8 runs on T_3. We could then merge T_1 and T_3, and so on. The following table shows the number of runs on each tape after each pass.

	Run Const.	After $T_3 + T_2$	After $T_1 + T_2$	After $T_1 + T_3$	After $T_2 + T_3$	After $T_1 + T_2$	After $T_1 + T_3$	After $T_2 + T_3$
T_1	0	13	5	0	3	1	0	1
T_2	21	8	0	5	2	0	1	0
T_3	13	0	8	3	0	2	1	0

The original distribution of runs makes a great deal of difference. For instance, if 22 runs are placed on T_2, with 12 on T_3, then after the first merge, we obtain 12 runs on T_1 and 10 runs on T_2. After another merge, there are 10 runs on T_1 and 2 runs on T_3. At this point the going gets slow, because we can only merge two sets of runs before T_3 is exhausted. Then T_1 has 8 runs and T_2 has 2 runs. Again, we can only merge two sets of runs, obtaining T_1 with 6 runs and T_3 with 2 runs. After three more passes, T_2 has two runs and the other tapes are empty. We must copy one run to another tape, and then we can finish the merge.

It turns out that the first distribution we gave is optimal. If the number of runs is a Fibonacci number F_N, then the best way to distribute them is to split them into two Fibonacci numbers F_{N-1} and F_{N-2}. Otherwise, it is necessary to pad the tape with dummy runs in order to get the number of runs up to a Fibonacci number. We leave the details of how to place the initial set of runs on the tapes as an exercise.

We can extend this to a k-way merge, in which case we need kth order Fibonacci numbers for the distribution, where the kth order Fibonacci number is defined as $F^{(k)}(N) = F^{(k)}(N-1) + F^{(k)}(N-2) + \cdots + F^{(k)}(N-k)$, with the appropriate initial conditions $F^{(k)}(N) = 0, 0 \leq N \leq k - 2, F^{(k)}(k-1) = 1$.

7.10.6. Replacement Selection

The last item we will consider is construction of the runs. The strategy we have used so far is the simplest possible: We read as many records as possible and sort them, writing the result to some tape. This seems like the best approach possible, until one realizes that as soon as the first record is written to an output tape, the memory it used becomes available for another record. If the next record on the input tape is larger than the record we have just output, then it can be included in the run.

Using this observation, we can give an algorithm for producing runs. This technique is commonly referred to as *replacement selection*. Initially, M records are read into memory and placed in a priority queue. We perform a `deleteMin`, writing the smallest (valued) record to the output tape. We read the next record from the input tape. If it is larger than the record we have just written, we can add it to the priority queue. Otherwise, it cannot go into the current run. Since the priority queue is smaller by one element, we can store this new element in the dead space of the priority queue until the run is completed and use the element for the next run. Storing an element in the dead space is similar to what is done in heapsort. We continue doing this until the size of the priority queue is zero, at which point the run is over. We start a new run by building a new priority queue, using all the elements in the dead space. Figure 7.18 shows the run construction for the small example we have been using, with $M = 3$. Dead elements are indicated by an asterisk.

In this example, replacement selection produces only three runs, compared with the five runs obtained by sorting. Because of this, a three-way merge finishes in one pass instead of two. If the input is randomly distributed, replacement selection can be shown to produce runs of average length $2M$. For our large example, we would expect 160 runs instead of 320 runs, so a five-way merge would require four passes. In this case, we have not saved a pass, although we might if we get lucky and have 125 runs or less. Since external sorts take so long, every pass saved can make a significant difference in the running time.

	3 Elements In Heap Array			Output	Next Element Read
	h[1]	h[2]	h[3]		
Run 1	11	94	81	11	96
	81	94	96	81	12*
	94	96	12*	94	35*
	96	35*	12*	96	17*
	17*	35*	12*	End of Run.	Rebuild Heap
Run 2	12	35	17	12	99
	17	35	99	17	28
	28	99	35	28	58
	35	99	58	35	41
	41	99	58	41	15*
	58	99	15*	58	end of tape
	99		15*	99	
			15*	End of Run.	Rebuild Heap
Run 3	15			15	

Figure 7.18 Example of run construction

As we have seen, it is possible for replacement selection to do no better than the standard algorithm. However, the input is frequently sorted or nearly sorted to start with, in which case replacement selection produces only a few very long runs. This kind of input is common for external sorts and makes replacement selection extremely valuable.

SUMMARY

For most general internal sorting applications, either insertion sort, Shellsort, or quicksort will be the method of choice, and the decision of which to use will depend mostly on the size of the input. Figure 7.19 shows the running time obtained for each algorithm on various input sizes (on a relatively slow computer).

The data was chosen to be random permutations of N integers, and the times given include only the actual time to sort. The code given in Figure 7.2 was used for insertion sort. Shellsort used the code in Section 7.4 modified to run with Sedgewick's increments. Based on literally millions of sorts, ranging in size from 100 to 25 million, the expected running time of Shellsort with these increments is conjectured to be $O(N^{7/6})$. The heapsort routine is the same as in Section 7.5. Two versions of quicksort are given. The first uses a simple pivoting strategy and does not do a cutoff. Fortunately, the input was random. The second uses median-of-three partitioning and a cutoff of ten. Further optimizations were possible. We could have coded the median-of-three routine in-line instead of using a method, and we could have written quicksort nonrecursively. There are some other optimizations to the code that are fairly tricky to implement, and of course we could have used an assembly language. We have made an honest attempt to code all routines efficiently, but of course the performance can vary somewhat from machine to machine.

The highly optimized version of quicksort is as fast as Shellsort even for very small input sizes. The improved version of quicksort still has an $O(N^2)$ worst case (one exercise asks you to construct a small example), but the chances of this worst case appearing are so negligible as to not be a factor. If you need to sort large amounts of data, quicksort is the method of choice. But never, ever, take the easy way out and use the first element as pivot. It is just not safe to assume that the input will be random. If you do not want to worry about this, use Shellsort. Shellsort will give a small performance penalty but could also be acceptable, especially if simplicity is required. Its worst case is only $O(N^{4/3})$; the chance of that worst case occurring is likewise negligible.

Heapsort, although an $O(N \log N)$ algorithm with an apparently tight inner loop, is slower than Shellsort. A close examination of the algorithm reveals that in order to move

N	Insertion Sort $O(N^2)$	Shellsort $O(N^{7/6})(?)$	Heapsort $O(N \log N)$	Quicksort $O(N \log N)$	Quicksort (opt.) $O(N \log N)$
10	0.00044	0.00041	0.00057	0.00052	.00046
100	0.00675	0.00171	0.00420	0.00284	.00244
1000	0.59564	0.02927	0.05565	0.03153	.02587
10000	58.864	0.42998	0.71650	0.36765	.31532
100000	NA	5.7298	8.8591	4.2298	3.5882
1000000	NA	71.164	104.68	47.065	41.282

Figure 7.19 Comparison of different sorting algorithms (all times are in seconds)

data, heapsort does two comparisons. An improvement suggested by Floyd moves data with essentially only one comparison, but implementing this improvement makes the code somewhat longer. We leave it to the reader to decide whether the extra coding effort is worth the increased speed (Exercise 7.51).

Insertion sort is useful only for small or very nearly sorted inputs. We have not included mergesort, because its performance is not as good as quicksort for main memory sorts and it is not any simpler to code. We have seen, however, that merging is the central idea of external sorts.

EXERCISES

7.1 Sort the sequence 3, 1, 4, 1, 5, 9, 2, 6, 5 using insertion sort.

7.2 What is the running time of insertion sort if all elements are equal?

7.3 Suppose we exchange elements `a[i]` and `a[i+k]`, which were originally out of order. Prove that at least 1 and at most $2k - 1$ inversions are removed.

7.4 Show the result of running Shellsort on the input 9, 8, 7, 6, 5, 4, 3, 2, 1 using the increments $\{1, 3, 7\}$.

7.5 a. What is the running time of Shellsort using the two-increment sequence $\{1, 2\}$?

　　b. Show that for any N, there exists a three-increment sequence such that Shellsort runs in $O(N^{5/3})$ time.

　　c. Show that for any N, there exists a six-increment sequence such that Shellsort runs in $O(N^{3/2})$ time.

7.6 *a. Prove that the running time of Shellsort is $\Omega(N^2)$ using increments of the form 1, $c, c^2, \ldots, c^i$ for any integer c.

　**b. Prove that for these increments, the average running time is $\Theta(N^{3/2})$.

*7.7 Prove that if a k-sorted file is then h-sorted, it remains k-sorted.

**7.8 Prove that the running time of Shellsort, using the increment sequence suggested by Hibbard, is $\Omega(N^{3/2})$ in the worst case. *Hint:* You can prove the bound by considering the special case of what Shellsort does when all elements are either 0 or 1. Set `a[i]` $=$ 1 if i is expressible as a linear combination of $h_t, h_{t-1}, \ldots, h_{\lfloor t/2 \rfloor + 1}$ and 0 otherwise.

7.9 Determine the running time of Shellsort for

　a. sorted input

　*b. reverse-ordered input

7.10 Do either of the following modifications to the Shellsort routine coded in Fig. 7.4 affect the worst-case running time?

　a. Before line 2, subtract one from **gap** if it is even.

　b. Before line 2, add one to **gap** if it is even.

7.11 Show how heapsort processes the input 142, 543, 123, 65, 453, 879, 572, 434, 111, 242, 811, 102.

7.12 What is the running time of heapsort for presorted input?

*7.13 Show that there are inputs that force every **percolateDown** in heapsort to go all the way to a leaf. (*Hint:* Work backward.)

7.14 Rewrite heapsort so that it sorts only items that are in the range **low** to **high** which are passed as additional parameters.

7.15 Sort 3, 1, 4, 1, 5, 9, 2, 6 using mergesort.

7.16 How would you implement mergesort without using recursion?

7.17 Determine the running time of mergesort for
  a. sorted input
  b. reverse-ordered input
  c. random input

7.18 In the analysis of mergesort, constants have been disregarded. Prove that the number of comparisons used in the worst case by mergesort is $N\lceil \log N \rceil - 2^{\lceil \log N \rceil} + 1$.

7.19 Sort 3, 1, 4, 1, 5, 9, 2, 6, 5, 3, 5 using quicksort with median-of-three partitioning and a cutoff of 3.

7.20 Using the quicksort implementation in this chapter, determine the running time of quicksort for
  a. sorted input
  b. reverse-ordered input
  c. random input

7.21 Repeat Exercise 7.20 when the pivot is chosen as
  a. the first element
  b. the larger of the first two nondistinct elements
  c. a random element
  *d. the average of all elements in the set

7.22 a. For the quicksort implementation in this chapter, what is the running time when all keys are equal?
  b. Suppose we change the partitioning strategy so that neither i nor j stops when an element with the same key as the pivot is found. What fixes need to be made in the code to guarantee that quicksort works, and what is the running time, when all keys are equal?
  c. Suppose we change the partitioning strategy so that i stops at an element with the same key as the pivot, but j does not stop in a similar case. What fixes need to be made in the code to guarantee that quicksort works, and when all keys are equal, what is the running time of quicksort?

7.23 Suppose we choose the element in the middle position of the array as pivot. Does this make it unlikely that quicksort will require quadratic time?

7.24 Construct a permutation of 20 elements that is as bad as possible for quicksort using median-of-three partitioning and a cutoff of 3.

7.25 The quicksort in the text uses two recursive calls. Remove one of the calls as follows:
  a. Rewrite the code so that the second recursive call is unconditionally the last line in quicksort. Do this by reversing the if/else and returning after the call to insertionSort.
  b. Remove the tail recursion by writing a while loop and altering left.

7.26 Continuing from Exercise 7.25, after part (a),
  a. Perform a test so that the smaller subarray is processed by the first recursive call, while the larger subarray is processed by the second recursive call.

   b. Remove the tail recursion by writing a `while` loop and altering `left` or `right`, as necessary.

   c. Prove that the number of recursive calls is logarithmic in the worst case.

7.27 Suppose the recursive quicksort receives an `int` parameter, `depth`, from the driver that is initially approximately $2 \log N$.

   a. Modify the recursive quicksort to call `heapsort` on its current subarray if the level of recursion has reached `depth`. (*Hint:* Decrement `depth` as you make recursive calls; when it is 0, switch to heapsort.)

   b. Prove that the worst-case running time of this algorithm is $O(N \log N)$.

   c. Conduct experiments to determine how often `heapsort` gets called.

   d. Implement this technique in conjunction with tail-recursion removal in Exercise 7.25.

   e. Explain why the technique in Exercise 7.26 would no longer be needed.

7.28 When implementing quicksort, if the array contains lots of duplicates, it may be better to perform a three-way partition (into elements less than, equal to, and greater than the pivot), to make smaller recursive calls. Assume three-way comparisons, as provided by the `compareTo` method.

   a. Give an algorithm that performs a three-way in-place partition of an N-element subarray using only $N - 1$ three-way comparisons. If there are d items equal to the pivot, you may use d additional `Comparable` swaps, above and beyond the two-way partitioning algorithm. (*Hint:* As `i` and `j` move toward each other, maintain five groups of elements as shown below):

   EQUAL   SMALL   UNKNOWN   LARGE   EQUAL
                i   j

   b. Prove that using the algorithm above, sorting an N-element array that contains only d different values, takes $O(dN)$ time.

7.29 Write a program to implement the selection algorithm.

7.30 Solve the following recurrence: $T(N) = (1/N)\left[\sum_{i=0}^{N-1} T(i) \right] + cN, T(0) = 0$.

7.31 A sorting algorithm is *stable* if elements with equal keys are left in the same order as they occur in the input. Which of the sorting algorithms in this chapter are stable and which are not? Why?

7.32 Suppose you are given a sorted list of N elements followed by $f(N)$ randomly ordered elements. How would you sort the entire list if

   a. $f(N) = O(1)$?

   b. $f(N) = O(\log N)$?

   c. $f(N) = O(\sqrt{N})$?

   *d. How large can $f(N)$ be for the entire list still to be sortable in $O(N)$ time?

7.33 Prove that any algorithm that finds an element X in a sorted list of N elements requires $\Omega(\log N)$ comparisons.

7.34 Using Stirling's formula, $N! \approx (N/e)^N \sqrt{2\pi N}$, give a precise estimate for $\log(N!)$.

7.35 *a. In how many ways can two sorted arrays of N elements be merged?

   *b. Give a nontrivial lower bound on the number of comparisons required to merge two sorted lists of N elements.

7.36 Consider the following algorithm for sorting six numbers:

- Sort the first three numbers using Algorithm A.
- Sort the second three numbers using Algorithm B.
- Merge the two sorted groups using Algorithm C.

Show that this algorithm is suboptimal, regardless of the choices for Algorithms A, B, and C.

*7.37 Give a linear-time algorithm to sort N fractions, each of whose numerators and denominators are integers between 1 and N.

7.38 Suppose arrays A and B are both sorted and both contain N elements. Give an $O(\log N)$ algorithm to find the median of $A \cup B$.

7.39 Suppose you have an array of N elements containing only two distinct keys, **true** and **false**. Give an $O(N)$ algorithm to rearrange the list so that all **false** elements precede the **true** elements. You may use only constant extra space.

7.40 Suppose you have an array of N elements, containing three distinct keys, **true**, **false**, and **maybe**. Give an $O(N)$ algorithm to rearrange the list so that all **false** elements precede **maybe** elements, which in turn precede **true** elements. You may use only constant extra space.

7.41 a. Prove that any comparison-based algorithm to sort 4 elements requires 5 comparisons.

   b. Give an algorithm to sort 4 elements in 5 comparisons.

7.42 a. Prove that 7 comparisons are required to sort 5 elements using any comparison-based algorithm.

   *b. Give an algorithm to sort 5 elements with 7 comparisons.

7.43 Write an efficient version of Shellsort and compare performance when the following increment sequences are used:

   a. Shell's original sequence
   b. Hibbard's increments
   c. Knuth's increments: $h_i = \frac{1}{2}(3^i + 1)$
   d. Gonnet's increments: $h_t = \lfloor \frac{N}{2.2} \rfloor$, and $h_k = \lfloor \frac{h_{k+1}}{2.2} \rfloor$ (with $h_1 = 1$ if $h_2 = 2$)
   e. Sedgewick's increments.

7.44 Implement an optimized version of quicksort and experiment with combinations of the following:

   a. Pivot: first element, middle element, random element, median of three, median of five.
   b. Cutoff values from 0 to 20.

7.45 Write a routine that reads in two alphabetized files and merges them together, forming a third, alphabetized, file.

7.46 Suppose we implement the median of three routine as follows: Find the median of `a[left]`, `a[center]`, `a[right]`, and swap it with `a[right]`. Proceed with the normal partitioning step starting `i` at `left` and `j` at `right-1` (instead of `left+1` and `right-2`).

   a. Suppose the input is 2, 3, 4, ..., $N - 1$, N, 1. For this input, what is the running time of this version of quicksort?

b. Suppose the input is in reverse order. For this input, what is the running time of this version of quicksort?

7.47 Prove that any comparison-based sorting algorithm requires $\Omega(N \log N)$ comparisons on average.

7.48 We are given an array that contains N numbers. We want to determine if there are two numbers whose sum equals a given number K. For instance, if the input is 8, 4, 1, 6, and K is 10, then the answer is yes (4 and 6). A number may be used twice. Do the following:

a. Give an $O(N^2)$ algorithm to solve this problem.

b. Give an $O(N \log N)$ algorithm to solve this problem. (*Hint:* Sort the items first. After that is done, you can solve the problem in linear time.)

c. Code both solutions and compare the running times of your algorithms.

7.49 Repeat Exercise 7.48 for four numbers. Try to design an $O(N^2 \log N)$ algorithm. (*Hint:* Compute all possible sums of two elements. Sort these possible sums. Then proceed as in Exercise 7.48.)

7.50 Repeat Exercise 7.48 for three numbers. Try to design an $O(N^2)$ algorithm.

7.51 Consider the following strategy for **percolateDown.** We have a hole at node X. The normal routine is to compare X's children and then move the child up to X if it is larger (in the case of a (*max*)heap) than the element we are trying to place, thereby pushing the hole down; we stop when it is safe to place the new element in the hole. The alternative strategy is to move elements up and the hole down as far as possible, without testing whether the new cell can be inserted. This would place the new cell in a leaf and probably violate the heap order; to fix the heap order, percolate the new cell up in the normal manner. Write a routine to include this idea, and compare the running time with a standard implementation of heapsort.

7.52 Propose an algorithm to sort a large file using only two tapes.

7.53 a. Show that a lower bound of $N!/2^{2N}$ on the number of heaps is implied by the fact that **buildHeap** uses at most $2N$ comparisons.

b. Use Stirling's formula to expand this bound.

REFERENCES

Knuth's book [12] is a comprehensive reference for sorting. Gonnet and Baeza-Yates [5] has some more recent results, as well as a huge bibliography.

The original paper detailing Shellsort is [24]. The paper by Hibbard [6] suggested the use of the increments $2^k - 1$ and tightened the code by avoiding swaps. Theorem 7.4 is from [15]. Pratt's lower bound, which uses a more complex method than that suggested in the text, can be found in [17]. Improved increment sequences and upper bounds appear in [10], [23], and [26]; matching lower bounds have been shown in [27]. A recent result shows that no increment sequence gives an $O(N \log N)$ worst-case running time [16]. The average-case running time for Shellsort is still unresolved. Yao [29] has performed an extremely complex analysis for the three-increment case. The result has yet to be extended to more increments, but has recently been slightly improved [11]. Experiments with various increment sequences appear in [25].

Heapsort was invented by Williams [28]; Floyd [2] provided the linear-time algorithm for heap construction. Theorem 7.5 is from [18].

An exact average-case analysis of mergesort has been described in [4]. An algorithm to perform merging in linear time without extra space is described in [9].

Quicksort is from Hoare [7]. This paper analyzes the basic algorithm, describes most of the improvements, and includes the selection algorithm. A detailed analysis and empirical study was the subject of Sedgewick's dissertation [22]. Many of the important results appear in the three papers [19], [20], and [21]. [1] provides a detailed C implementation with some additional improvements, and points out that most implementations of the UNIX *qsort* library routine are easily driven to quadratic behavior. Exercise 7.27 is from [14].

Decision trees and sorting optimality are discussed in Ford and Johnson [3]. This paper also provides an algorithm that almost meets the lower bound in terms of number of comparisons (but not other operations). This algorithm was eventually shown to be slightly suboptimal by Manacher [13].

External sorting is covered in detail in [12]. Stable sorting, described in Exercise 7.31, has been addressed by Horvath [8].

1. J. L. Bentley and M. D. McElroy, "Engineering a Sort Function," *Software—Practice and Experience,* 23 (1993), 1249–1265.
2. R. W. Floyd, "Algorithm 245: Treesort 3," *Communications of the ACM,* 7 (1964), 701.
3. L. R. Ford and S. M. Johnson, "A Tournament Problem," *American Mathematics Monthly,* 66 (1959), 387–389.
4. M. Golin and R. Sedgewick, "Exact Analysis of Mergesort," *Fourth SIAM Conference on Discrete Mathematics,* 1988.
5. G. H. Gonnet and R. Baeza-Yates, *Handbook of Algorithms and Data Structures,* 2nd ed., Addison-Wesley, Reading, Mass., 1991.
6. T. H. Hibbard, "An Empirical Study of Minimal Storage Sorting," *Communications of the ACM,* 6 (1963), 206–213.
7. C. A. R. Hoare, "Quicksort," *Computer Journal,* 5 (1962), 10–15.
8. E. C. Horvath, "Stable Sorting in Asymptotically Optimal Time and Extra Space," *Journal of the ACM,* 25 (1978), 177–199.
9. B. Huang and M. Langston, "Practical In-place Merging," *Communications of the ACM,* 31 (1988), 348–352.
10. J. Incerpi and R. Sedgewick, "Improved Upper Bounds on Shellsort," *Journal of Computer and System Sciences,* 31 (1985), 210–224.
11. S. Janson and D. E. Knuth, "Shellsort with Three Increments," *Random Structures and Algorithms* 10 (1997), 125–142.
12. D. E. Knuth, *The Art of Computer Programming. Volume 3: Sorting and Searching,* 2d ed., Addison-Wesley, Reading, Mass., 1998.
13. G. K. Manacher, "The Ford-Johnson Sorting Algorithm Is Not Optimal," *Journal of the ACM,* 26 (1979), 441–456.
14. D. R. Musser, "Introspective Sorting and Selection Algorithms," *Software—Practice and Experience,* 27 (1997), 983–993.
15. A. A. Papernov and G. V. Stasevich, "A Method of Information Sorting in Computer Memories," *Problems of Information Transmission,* 1 (1965), 63–75.
16. C. G. Plaxton, B. Poonen, and T. Suel, "Improved Lower Bounds for Shellsort," Proceedings of the Thirty-third Annual Symposium on the Foundations of Computer Science (1992), 226–235.
17. V. R. Pratt, *Shellsort and Sorting Networks,* Garland Publishing, New York, 1979. (Originally presented as the author's Ph.D. thesis, Stanford University, 1971.)

18. R. Schaffer and R. Sedgewick, "The Analysis of Heapsort," *Journal of Algorithms,* 14 (1993), 76–100.

19. R. Sedgewick, "Quicksort with Equal Keys," *SIAM Journal on Computing,* 6 (1977), 240–267.

20. R. Sedgewick, "The Analysis of Quicksort Programs," *Acta Informatica,* 7 (1977), 327–355.

21. R. Sedgewick, "Implementing Quicksort Programs," *Communications of the ACM,* 21 (1978), 847–857.

22. R. Sedgewick, *Quicksort,* Garland Publishing, New York, 1978. (Originally presented as the author's Ph.D. thesis, Stanford University, 1975.)

23. R. Sedgewick, "A New Upper Bound for Shellsort," *Journal of Algorithms,* 7 (1986), 159–173.

24. D. L. Shell, "A High-Speed Sorting Procedure," *Communications of the ACM,* 2 (1959), 30–32.

25. M. A. Weiss, "Empirical Results on the Running Time of Shellsort," *Computer Journal,* 34 (1991), 88–91.

26. M. A. Weiss and R. Sedgewick, "More on Shellsort Increment Sequences," *Information Processing Letters,* 34 (1990), 267–270.

27. M. A. Weiss and R. Sedgewick, "Tight Lower Bounds for Shellsort," *Journal of Algorithms,* 11 (1990), 242–251.

28. J. W. J. Williams, "Algorithm 232: Heapsort," *Communications of the ACM,* 7 (1964), 347–348.

29. A. C. Yao, "An Analysis of $(h, k, 1)$ Shellsort," *Journal of Algorithms,* 1 (1980), 14–50.

CHAPTER 8

The Disjoint Set ADT

In this chapter, we describe an efficient data structure to solve the equivalence problem. The data structure is simple to implement. Each routine requires only a few lines of code, and a simple array can be used. The implementation is also extremely fast, requiring constant average time per operation. This data structure is also very interesting from a theoretical point of view, because its analysis is extremely difficult; the functional form of the worst case is unlike any we have yet seen. For the disjoint set ADT, we will

- Show how it can be implemented with minimal coding effort.
- Greatly increase its speed, using just two simple observations.
- Analyze the running time of a fast implementation.
- See a simple application.

8.1. Equivalence Relations

A *relation R* is defined on a set S if for every pair of elements (a, b), $a, b \in S$, $a R b$ is either true or false. If $a R b$ is true, then we say that a is related to b.

An *equivalence relation* is a relation R that satisfies three properties:

1. (*Reflexive*) $a R a$, for all $a \in S$.
2. (*Symmetric*) $a R b$ if and only if $b R a$.
3. (*Transitive*) $a R b$ and $b R c$ implies that $a R c$.

We will consider several examples.

The $\leq$ relationship is not an equivalence relationship. Although it is reflexive, since $a \leq a$, and transitive, since $a \leq b$ and $b \leq c$ implies $a \leq c$, it is not symmetric, since $a \leq b$ does not imply $b \leq a$.

Electrical connectivity, where all connections are by metal wires, is an equivalence relation. The relation is clearly reflexive, as any component is connected to itself. If a is electrically connected to b, then b must be electrically connected to a, so the relation is symmetric. Finally, if a is connected to b and b is connected to c, then a is connected to c. Thus electrical connectivity is an equivalence relation.

Two cities are related if they are in the same country. It is easily verified that this is an equivalence relation. Suppose town a is related to b if it is possible to travel from a to b by taking roads. This relation is an equivalence relation if all the roads are two-way.

8.2. The Dynamic Equivalence Problem

Given an equivalence relation $\sim$, the natural problem is to decide, for any a and b, if $a \sim b$. If the relation is stored as a two-dimensional array of Boolean variables, then, of course, this can be done in constant time. The problem is that the relation is usually not explicitly, but rather implicitly, defined.

As an example, suppose the equivalence relation is defined over the five-element set $\{a_1, a_2, a_3, a_4, a_5\}$. Then there are 25 pairs of elements, each of which is either related or not. However, the information $a_1 \sim a_2, a_3 \sim a_4, a_5 \sim a_1, a_4 \sim a_2$ implies that all pairs are related. We would like to be able to infer this quickly.

The *equivalence class* of an element $a \in S$ is the subset of S that contains all the elements that are related to a. Notice that the equivalence classes form a partition of S: every member of S appears in exactly one equivalence class. To decide if $a \sim b$, we need only to check whether a and b are in the same equivalence class. This provides our strategy to solve the equivalence problem.

The input is initially a collection of N sets, each with one element. This initial representation is that all relations (except reflexive relations) are false. Each set has a different element, so that $S_i \cap S_j = \varnothing$; this makes the sets *disjoint*.

There are two permissible operations. The first is find, which returns the name of the set (that is, the equivalence class) containing a given element. The second operation adds relations. If we want to add the relation $a \sim b$, then we first see if a and b are already related. This is done by performing finds on both a and b and checking whether they are in the same equivalence class. If they are not, then we apply **union**. This operation merges the two equivalence classes containing a and b into a new equivalence class. From a set point of view, the result of $\cup$ is to create a new set $S_k = S_i \cup S_j$, destroying the originals and preserving the disjointness of all the sets. The algorithm to do this is frequently known as the disjoint set *union/find algorithm* for this reason.

This algorithm is *dynamic* because, during the course of the algorithm, the sets can change via the **union** operation. The algorithm must also operate *on-line:* When a find is performed, it must give an answer before continuing. Another possibility would be an *off-line* algorithm. Such an algorithm would be allowed to see the entire sequence of unions and finds. The answer it provides for each find must still be consistent with all the unions that were performed up until the find, but the algorithm can give all its answers after it has seen *all* the questions. The difference is similar to taking a written exam (which is generally off-line—you only have to give the answers before time expires), and an oral exam (which is on-line, because you must answer the current question before proceeding to the next question).

Notice that we do not perform any operations comparing the relative values of elements, but merely require knowledge of their location. For this reason, we can assume that all the elements have been numbered sequentially from 0 to $N - 1$ and that the numbering can be determined easily by some hashing scheme. Thus, initially we have $S_i = \{i\}$ for $i = 0$ through $N - 1$.*

Our second observation is that the name of the set returned by find is actually fairly arbitrary. All that really matters is that find(a)==find(b) is true if and only if a and b are in the same set.

---

*This reflects the fact that array indices start at 0.

These operations are important in many graph theory problems and also in compilers which process equivalence (or type) declarations. We will see an application later.

There are two strategies to solve this problem. One ensures that the find instruction can be executed in constant worst-case time, and the other ensures that the union instruction can be executed in constant worst-case time. It has been shown that both cannot be done simultaneously in constant worst-case time.

We will now briefly discuss the first approach. For the find operation to be fast, we could maintain, in an array, the name of the equivalence class for each element. Then find is just a simple $O(1)$ lookup. Suppose we want to perform union(a,b). Suppose that a is in equivalence class i and b is in equivalence class j. Then we scan down the array, changing all i's to j. Unfortunately, this scan takes $\Theta(N)$. Thus, a sequence of $N - 1$ unions (the maximum, since then everything is in one set) would take $\Theta(N^2)$ time. If there are $\Omega(N^2)$ find operations, this performance is fine, since the total running time would then amount to $O(1)$ for each union or find operation over the course of the algorithm. If there are fewer finds, this bound is not acceptable.

One idea is to keep all the elements that are in the same equivalence class in a linked list. This saves time when updating, because we do not have to search through the entire array. This by itself does not reduce the asymptotic running time, because it is still possible to perform $\Theta(N^2)$ equivalence class updates over the course of the algorithm.

If we also keep track of the size of each equivalence class, and when performing unions we change the name of the smaller equivalence class to the larger, then the total time spent for $N - 1$ merges is $O(N \log N)$. The reason for this is that each element can have its equivalence class changed at most $\log N$ times, since every time its class is changed, its new equivalence class is at least twice as large as its old. Using this strategy, any sequence of M finds and up to $N - 1$ unions takes at most $O(M + N \log N)$ time.

In the remainder of this chapter, we will examine a solution to the union/find problem that makes unions easy but finds hard. Even so, the running time for any sequence of at most M finds and up to $N - 1$ unions will be only a little more than $O(M + N)$.

8.3. Basic Data Structure

Recall that the problem does not require that a find operation return any specific name, just that finds on two elements return the same answer if and only if they are in the same set. One idea might be to use a tree to represent each set, since each element in a tree has the same root. Thus, the root can be used to name the set. We will represent each set by a tree. (Recall that a collection of trees is known as a *forest*.) Initially, each set contains one element. The trees we will use are not necessarily binary trees, but their representation is easy, because the only information we will need is a parent link. The name of a set is given by the node at the root. Since only the name of the parent is required, we can assume that this tree is stored implicitly in an array: each entry s[i] in the array represents the parent of element i. If i is a root, then s[i] $= -1$. In the forest in Figure 8.1, s[i] $= -1$ for $0 \le i < 8$. As with binary heaps, we will draw the trees explicitly, with the understanding that an array is being used. Figure 8.1 shows the explicit representation. We will draw the root's parent link vertically for convenience.

To perform a union of two sets, we merge the two trees by making the parent link of one tree's root link to the root node of the other tree. It should be clear that this operation

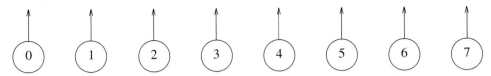

Figure 8.1 Eight elements, initially in different sets

takes constant time. Figures 8.2, 8.3, and 8.4 represent the forest after each of union(4,5), union(6,7), union(4,6), where we have adopted the convention that the new root after the union(x,y) is x. The implicit representation of the last forest is shown in Figure 8.5.

A find(x) on element x is performed by returning the root of the tree containing x. The time to perform this operation is proportional to the depth of the node representing x,

Figure 8.2 After union(4,5)

Figure 8.3 After union(6,7)

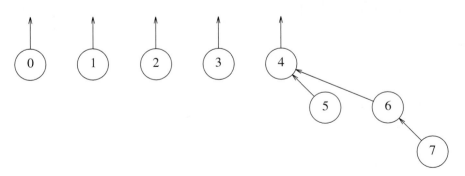

Figure 8.4 After union(4,6)

−1	−1	−1	−1	−1	4	4	6
0	1	2	3	4	5	6	7

Figure 8.5 Implicit representation of previous tree

assuming, of course, that we can find the node representing x in constant time. Using the strategy above, it is possible to create a tree of depth $N - 1$, so the worst-case running time of a find is $O(N)$. Typically, the running time is computed for a *sequence* of M intermixed instructions. In this case, M consecutive operations could take $O(MN)$ time in the worst case.

The code in Figures 8.6 through 8.9 represents an implementation of the basic algorithm, assuming that error checks have already been performed. In our routine, unions are performed on the roots of the trees. Sometimes the operation is performed

```
public class DisjSets
{
    public DisjSets( int numElements )
      { /* Figure 8.7 */ }
    public void union( int root1, int root2 )
      { /* Figures 8.8 and 8.13 */ }
    public int find( int x )
      { /* Figures 8.9 and 8.15 */ }

    private int [ ] s;
}
```

Figure 8.6 Disjoint set class skeleton

```
/**
 * Construct the disjoint sets object.
 * @param numElements the initial number of disjoint sets.
 */
public DisjSets( int numElements )
{
    s = new int [ numElements ];
    for( int i = 0; i < s.length; i++ )
        s[ i ] = -1;
}
```

Figure 8.7 Disjoint set initialization routine

```
/**
 * Union two disjoint sets.
 * For simplicity, we assume root1 and root2 are distinct
 * and represent set names.
 * @param root1 the root of set 1.
 * @param root2 the root of set 2.
 */
public void union( int root1, int root2 )
{
    s[ root2 ] = root1;
}
```

Figure 8.8 union (not the best way)

```
/**
 * Perform a find.
 * Error checks omitted again for simplicity.
 * @param x the element being searched for.
 * @return the set containing x.
 */
public int find( int x )
{
    if( s[ x ] < 0 )
        return x;
    else
        return find( s[ x ] );
}
```

Figure 8.9 A simple disjoint set `find` algorithm

by passing any two elements, and having the **union** perform two **find**s to determine the roots.

The average-case analysis is quite hard to do. The least of the problems is that the answer depends on how to define *average* (with respect to the **union** operation). For instance, in the forest in Figure 8.4, we could say that since there are five trees, there are $5 \cdot 4 = 20$ equally likely results of the next **union** (as any two different trees can be **union**ed). Of course, the implication of this model is that there is only a $\frac{2}{5}$ chance that the next **union** will involve the large tree. Another model might say that all **union**s between any two *elements* in different trees are equally likely, so a larger tree is more likely to be involved in the next **union** than a smaller tree. In the example above, there is an $\frac{8}{11}$ chance that the large tree is involved in the next **union**, since (ignoring symmetries) there are 6 ways in which to merge two elements in $\{0, 1, 2, 3\}$, and 16 ways to merge an element in $\{4, 5, 6, 7\}$ with an element in $\{0, 1, 2, 3\}$. There are still more models and no general agreement on which is the best. The average running time depends on the model; $\Theta(M)$, $\Theta(M \log N)$, and $\Theta(MN)$ bounds have actually been shown for three different models, although the latter bound is thought to be more realistic.

Quadratic running time for a sequence of operations is generally unacceptable. Fortunately, there are several ways of easily ensuring that this running time does not occur.

8.4. Smart Union Algorithms

The **union**s above were performed rather arbitrarily, by making the second tree a subtree of the first. A simple improvement is always to make the smaller tree a subtree of the larger, breaking ties by any method; we call this approach *union-by-size*. The three **union**s in the preceding example were all ties, and so we can consider that they were performed by size. If the next operation were **union(3, 4)**, then the forest in Figure 8.10 would form. Had the size heuristic not been used, a deeper tree would have been formed (Fig. 8.11).

We can prove that if **union**s are done by size, the depth of any node is never more than $\log N$. To see this, note that a node is initially at depth 0. When its depth increases as a

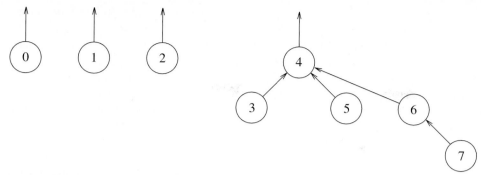

Figure 8.10 Result of union-by-size

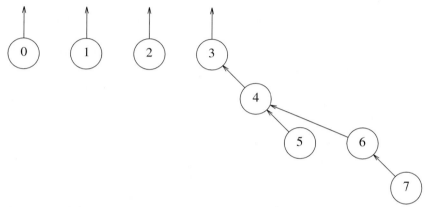

Figure 8.11 Result of an arbitrary union

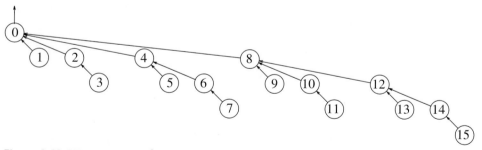

Figure 8.12 Worst-case tree for $N = 16$

result of a **union**, it is placed in a tree that is at least twice as large as before. Thus, its depth can be increased at most $\log N$ times. (We used this argument in the quick-find algorithm at the end of Section 8.2.) This implies that the running time for a **find** operation is $O(\log N)$, and a sequence of M operations takes $O(M \log N)$. The tree in Figure 8.12 shows the worst tree possible after 16 **union**s and is obtained if all **union**s are between equal-sized trees (the worst-case trees are binomial trees, discussed in Chapter 6).

To implement this strategy, we need to keep track of the size of each tree. Since we are really just using an array, we can have the array entry of each root contain the *negative* of the size of its tree. Thus, initially the array representation of the tree is all -1s. When a **union** is performed, check the sizes; the new size is the sum of the old. Thus, union-by-size is not at all difficult to implement and requires no extra space. It is also fast, on average. For virtually all reasonable models, it has been shown that a sequence of M operations requires $O(M)$ average time if union-by-size is used. This is because when random **union**s are performed, generally very small (usually one-element) sets are merged with large sets throughout the algorithm.

An alternative implementation, which also guarantees that all the trees will have depth at most $O(\log N)$, is *union-by-height*. We keep track of the height, instead of the size, of each tree and perform **union**s by making the shallow tree a subtree of the deeper tree. This is an easy algorithm, since the height of a tree increases only when two equally deep trees are joined (and then the height goes up by one). Thus, union-by-height is a trivial modification of union-by-size. Since heights of zero would not be negative, we actually store the negative of height, minus an additional 1. Initially, all entries are -1.

The following figures show a tree and its implicit representation for both union-by-size and union-by-height. The code in Figure 8.13 implements union-by-height.

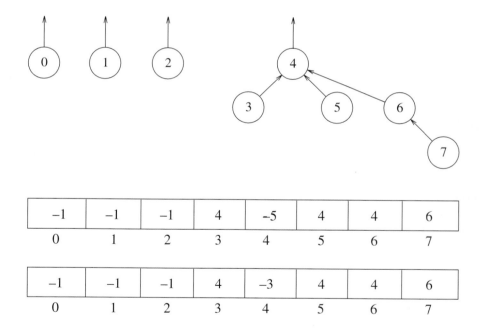

8.5. Path Compression

The union/find algorithm, as described so far, is quite acceptable for most cases. It is very simple and linear on average for a sequence of M instructions (under all models). However,

```
/**
 * Union two disjoint sets using the height heuristic.
 * For simplicity, we assume root1 and root2 are distinct
 * and represent set names.
 * @param root1 the root of set 1.
 * @param root2 the root of set 2.
 */
public void union( int root1, int root2 )
{
    if( s[ root2 ] < s[ root1 ] )  /* root2 is deeper */
        s[ root1 ] = root2;        /* Make root2 new root */
    else
    {
        if( s[ root1 ] == s[ root2 ] )
            s[ root1 ]--;          /* Update height if same */
        s[ root2 ] = root1;        /* Make root1 new root */
    }
}
```

Figure 8.13 Code for union-by-height (rank)

the worst case of $O(M \log N)$ can occur fairly easily and naturally. For instance, if we put all the sets on a queue and repeatedly dequeue the first two sets and enqueue the union, the worst case occurs. If there are many more finds than unions, this running time is worse than that of the quick-find algorithm. Moreover, it should be clear that there are probably no more improvements possible for the union algorithm. This is based on the observation that any method to perform the unions will yield the same worst-case trees, since it must break ties arbitrarily. Therefore, the only way to speed the algorithm up, without reworking the data structure entirely, is to do something clever on the find operation.

The clever operation is known as *path compression*. Path compression is performed during a find operation and is independent of the strategy used to perform unions. Suppose the operation is find(x). Then the effect of path compression is that *every* node on the path from x to the root has its parent changed to the root. Figure 8.14 shows the effect of path compression after find(14) on the generic worst tree of Figure 8.12.

The effect of path compression is that with an extra two link changes, nodes 12 and 13 are now one position closer to the root and nodes 14 and 15 are now two positions closer. Thus, the fast future accesses on these nodes will pay (we hope) for the extra work to do the path compression.

As the code in Figure 8.15 shows, path compression is a trivial change to the basic find algorithm. The only change to the find routine is that s[x] is made equal to the value returned by find; thus after the root of the set is found recursively, x's parent link references it. This occurs recursively to every node on the path to the root, so this implements path compression.

When unions are done arbitrarily, path compression is a good idea, because there is an abundance of deep nodes and these are brought near the root by path compression. It has been proven that when path compression is done in this case, a sequence of M operations

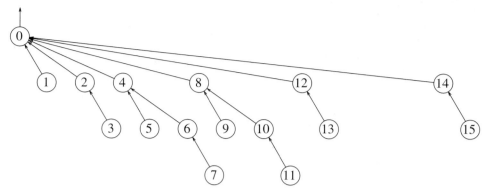

Figure 8.14 An example of path compression

```
/**
 * Perform a find with path compression.
 * Error checks omitted again for simplicity.
 * @param x the element being searched for.
 * @return the set containing x.
 */
public int find( int x )
{
    if( s[ x ] < 0 )
        return x;
    else
        return s[ x ] = find( s[ x ] );
}
```

Figure 8.15 Code for the disjoint set **find** with path compression

requires at most $O(M \log N)$ time. It is still an open problem to determine what the average-case behavior is in this situation.

Path compression is perfectly compatible with union-by-size, and thus both routines can be implemented at the same time. Since doing union-by-size by itself is expected to execute a sequence of M operations in linear time, it is not clear that the extra pass involved in path compression is worthwhile on average. Indeed, this problem is still open. However, as we shall see later, the combination of path compression and a smart union rule guarantees a very efficient algorithm in all cases.

Path compression is not entirely compatible with union-by-height, because path compression can change the heights of the trees. It is not at all clear how to recompute them efficiently. The answer is do not!! Then the heights stored for each tree become estimated heights (sometimes known as *ranks*), but it turns out that union-by-rank (which is what this has now become) is just as efficient in theory as union-by-size. Furthermore, heights are updated less often than sizes. As with union-by-size, it is not clear whether path compression is worthwhile on average. What we will show in the next section is that with either union heuristic, path compression significantly reduces the worst-case running time.

8.6. Worst Case for Union-by-Rank and Path Compression

When both heuristics are used, the algorithm is almost linear in the worst case. Specifically, the time required in the worst case is $\Theta(M\alpha(M,N))$ (provided $M \geq N$), where $\alpha(M,N)$ is a functional inverse of Ackermann's function, which is defined below:*

$$A(1,j) = 2^j \text{ for } j \geq 1$$
$$A(i,1) = A(i-1,2) \text{ for } i \geq 2$$
$$A(i,j) = A(i-1, A(i,j-1)) \text{ for } i,j \geq 2$$

From this, we define

$$\alpha(M,N) = \min\{i \geq 1 | A(i, \lfloor M/N \rfloor) > \log N\}$$

You may want to compute some values, but for all practical purposes, $\alpha(M,N) \leq 4$, which is all that is really important here. The single-variable inverse Ackerman function, sometimes written as $\log^* N$, is the number of times the logarithm of N needs to be applied until $N \leq 1$. Thus, $\log^* 65536 = 4$, because $\log\log\log\log 65536 = 1$. $\log^* 2^{65536} = 5$, but keep in mind that 2^{65536} is a 20,000-digit number. $\alpha(M,N)$ actually grows even slower then $\log^* N$. However, $\alpha(M,N)$ is not a constant, so the running time is not linear.

In the remainder of this section, we will prove a slightly weaker result. We will show that any sequence of $M = \Omega(N)$ union/find operations takes a total of $O(M\log^* N)$ running time. The same bound holds if union-by-rank is replaced with union-by-size. This analysis is probably the most complex in the book and one of the first truly complex worst-case analyses ever performed for an algorithm that is essentially trivial to implement.

8.6.1. Analysis of the Union/Find Algorithm

In this section we establish a fairly tight bound on the running time of a sequence of $M = \Omega(N)$ union/find operations. The **union**s and **find**s may occur in any order, but **union**s are done by rank and **find**s are done with path compression.

We begin by establishing some lemmas concerning the number of nodes of *rank r*. Intuitively, because of the union-by-rank rule, there are many more nodes of small rank than large rank. In particular, there can be at most one node of rank $\log N$. What we would like to do is to produce as precise a bound as possible on the number of nodes of any particular rank r. Since ranks only change when **union**s are performed (and then only when the two trees have the same rank), we can prove this bound by ignoring the path compression.

LEMMA 8.1.

When executing a sequence of **union** *instructions, a node of rank r must have at least 2^r descendants (including itself).*

---

*Ackermann's function is frequently defined with $A(1,j) = j + 1$ for $j \geq 1$. The form in this text grows faster; thus, the inverse grows more slowly.

PROOF:

By induction. The basis, $r = 0$, is clearly true. Let T be the tree of rank r with the fewest number of descendants and let X be T's root. Suppose the last **union** X was involved in was between T_1 and T_2. Suppose T_1's root was X. If T_1 had rank r, then T_1 would be a tree of height r with fewer descendants than T, which contradicts the assumption that T is the tree with the smallest number of descendants. Hence the rank of $T_1 \leq r - 1$. The rank of $T_2 \leq$ the rank of T_1. Since T has rank r and the rank could only increase because of T_2, it follows that the rank of $T_2 = r - 1$. Then the rank of $T_1 = r - 1$. By the induction hypothesis, each tree has at least 2^{r-1} descendants, giving a total of 2^r and establishing the lemma.

Lemma 8.1 tells us that if no path compression is performed, then any node of rank r must have at least 2^r descendants. Path compression can change this, of course, since it can remove descendants from a node. However, when **union**s are performed, even with path compression, we are using the ranks, which are estimated heights. These ranks behave as though there is no path compression. Thus, when bounding the *number* of nodes of rank r, path compression can be ignored.

Thus, the next lemma is valid with or without path compression.

LEMMA 8.2.
The number of nodes of rank r is at most $N/2^r$.

PROOF:

Without path compression, each node of rank r is the root of a subtree of at least 2^r nodes. No node in the subtree can have rank r. Thus all subtrees of nodes of rank r are disjoint. Therefore, there are at most $N/2^r$ disjoint subtrees and hence $N/2^r$ nodes of rank r.

The next lemma seems somewhat obvious but is crucial in the analysis.

LEMMA 8.3.
At any point in the union/find algorithm, the ranks of the nodes on a path from the leaf to a root increase monotonically.

PROOF:

The lemma is obvious if there is no path compression (see the example). If, after path compression, some node v is a descendant of w, then clearly v must have been a descendant of w when only **union**s were considered. Hence the rank of v is less than the rank of w.

Let us summarize the preliminary results. Lemma 8.2 tells us how many nodes can be assigned rank r. Because ranks are assigned only by **union**s, which have no idea of path compression, Lemma 8.2 is valid at any stage of the union/find algorithm—even in the midst of path compression. Figure 8.16 shows that while there are many nodes of ranks 0 and 1, there are fewer nodes of rank r as r gets larger.

Lemma 8.2 is tight, in the sense that it is possible for there to be $N/2^r$ nodes for any rank r. It is slightly loose, because it is not possible for the bound to hold for all ranks r

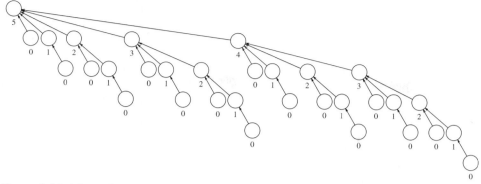

Figure 8.16 A large disjoint set tree (numbers below nodes are ranks)

simultaneously. While Lemma 8.2 describes the *number* of nodes in a rank r, Lemma 8.3 tells us their *distribution*. As one would expect, the rank of nodes is strictly increasing along the path from a leaf to the root.

We are now ready to prove the main theorem. Our basic idea is as follows: A **find** on any node v costs time proportional to the number of nodes on the path from v to the root. Let us, then, charge one unit of cost for every node on the path from v to the root for each **find**. To help us count the charges, we will deposit an imaginary penny into each node on the path. This is strictly an accounting gimmick, which is not part of the program. When the algorithm is over, we collect all the coins that have been deposited; this is the total cost.

As a further accounting gimmick, we deposit both American and Canadian pennies. We will show that during the execution of the algorithm, we can deposit only a certain number of American pennies during each **find**. We will also show that we can deposit only a certain number of Canadian pennies to each node. Adding these two totals gives us a bound on the total number of pennies that can be deposited.

We now sketch our accounting scheme in a little more detail. We will divide the nodes by their ranks. We then divide the ranks into rank groups. On each **find**, we will deposit some American coins into the general kitty and some Canadian coins into specific vertices.* To compute the total number of Canadian coins deposited, we will compute the deposits per node. By adding up all the deposits for each node in rank r, we will get the total deposits per rank r. Then we will add up all the deposits for each rank r in group g and thereby obtain the total deposits for each rank group g. Finally, we add up all the deposits for each rank group g to obtain the total number of Canadian coins deposited in the forest. Adding this to the number of American coins in the kitty gives us the answer.

We will partition ranks into groups. Rank r goes into group $G(r)$, and G will be determined later. The largest rank in any rank group g is $F(g)$, where $F = G^{-1}$ is the *inverse* of G. The number of ranks in any rank group, $g > 0$, is thus $F(g) - F(g - 1)$. Clearly $G(N)$ is a very loose upper bound on the largest rank group. As an example, suppose that we partitioned the ranks as in Figure 8.17. In this case, $G(r) = \lceil \sqrt{r} \rceil$. The largest rank in group g is $F(g) = g^2$, and observe that group $g > 0$ contains ranks $F(g - 1) + 1$ through $F(g)$ inclusive. This formula does not apply for rank group 0, so for convenience we will

---

*We use the terms *node* and *vertex* interchangeably.

Group	Rank
0	0
1	1
2	2,3,4
3	5 through 9
4	10 through 16
i	$(i-1)^2 + 1$ through i^2

Figure 8.17 Possible partitioning of ranks into groups

ensure that rank group 0 contains only elements of rank 0. Notice that the groups are made of consecutive ranks.

As mentioned before, each **union** instruction takes constant time, as long as each root keeps track of how big its subtrees are. Thus, **union**s are essentially free, as far as this proof goes.

Each **find(i)** takes time proportional to the number of vertices on the path from the vertex representing i to the root. We will thus deposit one penny for each vertex on the path. If this is all we do, however, we cannot expect much of a bound, because we are not taking advantage of path compression. Thus, we need to take advantage of path compression in our analysis. We will use fancy accounting.

For each vertex, v, on the path from the vertex representing i to the root, we deposit one penny under one of two accounts:

1. If v is the root, or if the parent of v is the root, or if the parent of v is in a different rank group from v, then charge one unit under this rule. This deposits an American penny into the kitty.

2. Otherwise deposit a Canadian penny into the vertex.

LEMMA 8.4.
For any **find(v)**, *the total number of pennies deposited, either into the kitty or into a vertex, is exactly equal to the number of nodes on the path from v to the root.*

PROOF:
Obvious.

Thus all we need to do is to sum all the American pennies deposited under rule 1 with all the Canadian pennies deposited under rule 2.

We are doing at most M **find**s. We need to bound the number of pennies that can be deposited into the kitty during a **find**.

LEMMA 8.5.
Over the entire algorithm, the total deposits of American pennies under rule 1 amount to at most $M(G(N) + 2)$.

PROOF:

This is easy. For any `find`, two American pennies are deposited, because of the root and its child. By Lemma 8.3, the vertices going up the path are monotonically increasing in rank, and since there are at most $G(N)$ rank groups, only $G(N)$ other vertices on the path can qualify as a rule 1 deposit for any particular `find`. Thus, during any one `find`, at most $G(N) + 2$ American pennies can be placed in the kitty. Thus, at most $M(G(N) + 2)$ American pennies can be deposited under rule 1 for a sequence of M `finds`.

To get a good estimate for all the Canadian deposits under rule 2, we will add up the deposits by vertices instead of by `find` instructions. If a coin is deposited into vertex v under rule 2, v will be moved by path compression and get a new parent of higher rank than its old parent. (This is where we are using the fact that path compression is being done.) Thus, a vertex v in rank group $g > 0$ can be moved at most $F(g) - F(g - 1)$ times before its parent gets pushed out of rank group g, since that is the size of the rank group.* After this happens, all future charges to v will go under rule 1.

LEMMA 8.6.

The number of vertices, $V(g)$, in rank group $g > 0$ is at most $N/2^{F(g-1)}$.

PROOF:

By Lemma 8.2, there are at most $N/2^r$ vertices of rank r. Summing over the ranks in group g, we obtain

$$V(g) \le \sum_{r=F(g-1)+1}^{F(g)} \frac{N}{2^r}$$

$$\le \sum_{r=F(g-1)+1}^{\infty} \frac{N}{2^r}$$

$$\le N \sum_{r=F(g-1)+1}^{\infty} \frac{1}{2^r}$$

$$\le \frac{N}{2^{F(g-1)+1}} \sum_{s=0}^{\infty} \frac{1}{2^s}$$

$$\le \frac{2N}{2^{F(g-1)+1}}$$

$$\le \frac{N}{2^{F(g-1)}}$$

LEMMA 8.7.

The maximum number of Canadian pennies deposited to all vertices in rank group g is at most $NF(g)/2^{F(g-1)}$.

---

*This can be reduced by 1. We do not for the sake of clarity; the bound is not improved by being more careful here.

PROOF:

Each vertex in the rank group can receive at most $F(g) - F(g-1) \leq F(g)$ Canadian pennies while its parent stays in its rank group, and Lemma 8.6 tells how many such vertices there are. The result is obtained by a simple multiplication.

LEMMA 8.8.

The total deposit under rule 2 is at most $N \sum_{g=1}^{G(N)} F(g)/2^{F(g-1)}$ Canadian pennies.

PROOF:

Because rank group 0 contains only elements of rank 0, it cannot contribute to rule 2 charges (it cannot have a parent in the same rank group). The bound is obtained by summing the other rank groups.

Thus we have the deposits under rules 1 and 2. The total is

$$M(G(N) + 2) + N \sum_{g=1}^{G(N)} F(g)/2^{F(g-1)} \tag{8.1}$$

We still have not specified $G(N)$ or its inverse $F(N)$. Obviously, we are free to choose virtually anything we want, but it makes sense to choose $G(N)$ to minimize the bound above. However, if $G(N)$ is too small, then $F(N)$ will be large, hurting the bound. An apparently good choice is to choose $F(i)$ to be the function recursively defined by $F(0) = 0$ and $F(i) = 2^{F(i-1)}$. This gives $G(N) = 1 + \lfloor \log^* N \rfloor$. Figure 8.18 shows how this partitions the ranks. Notice that group 0 contains only rank 0, which we required in the previous lemma. F is very similar to the single-variable Ackerman function, which differs only in the definition of the base case ($F(0) = 1$).

THEOREM 8.1.

*The running time of M **unions** and **finds** is $O(M \log^* N)$.*

PROOF:

Plug in the definitions of F and G into Equation (8.1). The total number of American pennies is $O(MG(N)) = O(M \log^* N)$. The total number of Canadian pennies is

Group	Rank
0	0
1	1
2	2
3	3,4
4	5 through 16
5	17 through 2^{16}
6	65537 through 2^{65536}
7	truly huge ranks

Figure 8.18 Actual partitioning of ranks into groups used in the proof

$N \sum_{g=1}^{G(N)} F(g)/2^{F(g-1)} = N \sum_{g=1}^{G(N)} 1 = NG(N) = O(N \log^* N)$. Since $M = \Omega(N)$, the bound follows.

What the analysis shows is that there are few nodes that could be moved frequently by path compression, and thus the total time spent is relatively small.

8.7. An Application

An example of the use of the union/find data structure is the generation of mazes, such as the one shown in Figure 8.19. In Figure 8.19, the starting point is the top-left corner, and the ending point is the bottom-right corner. We can view the maze as a 50-by-88 rectangle of cells in which the top-left cell is connected to the bottom-right cell, and cells are separated from their neighboring cells via walls.

A simple algorithm to generate the maze is to start with walls everywhere (except for the entrance and exit). We then continually choose a wall randomly, and knock it down if the cells that the wall separates are not already connected to each other. If we repeat this process until the starting and ending cells are connected, then we have a maze. It is actually better to continue knocking down walls until every cell is reachable from every other cell (this generates more false leads in the maze).

We illustrate the algorithm with a 5-by-5 maze. Figure 8.20 shows the initial configuration. We use the union/find data structure to represent sets of cells that are connected to each other. Initially, walls are everywhere, and each cell is in its own equivalence class.

Figure 8.21 shows a later stage of the algorithm, after a few walls have been knocked down. Suppose, at this stage, the wall that connects cells 8 and 13 is randomly targeted. Because 8 and 13 are already connected (they are in the same set), we would not remove

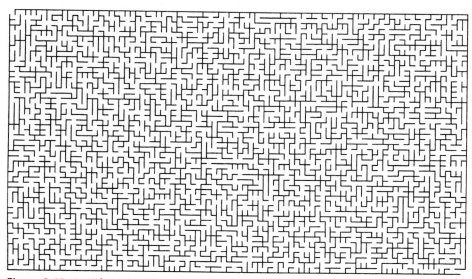

Figure 8.19 A 50-by-88 maze

0	1	2	3	4
5	6	7	8	9
10	11	12	13	14
15	16	17	18	19
20	21	22	23	24

{0} {1} {2} {3} {4} {5} {6} {7} {8} {9} {10} {11} {12} {13} {14} {15} {16} {17} {18} {19} {20} {21} {22} {23} {24}

Figure 8.20 Initial state: all walls up, all cells in their own set

0	1	2	3	4
5	6	7	8	9
10	11	12	13	14
15	16	17	18	19
20	21	22	23	24

{0, 1} {2} {3} {4, 6, 7, 8, 9, 13, 14} {5} {10, 11, 15} {12} {16, 17, 18, 22} {19} {20} {21} {23} {24}

Figure 8.21 At some point in the algorithm: several walls down, sets have merged.
If at this point the wall between squares 8 and 13 is randomly selected,
this wall is not knocked down, because 8 and 13 are already connected.

the wall, as it would simply trivialize the maze. Suppose that cells 18 and 13 are randomly targeted next. By performing two **find** operations, we see that these are in different sets; thus 18 and 13 are not already connected. therefore, we knock down the wall that separates them, as shown in Figure 8.22. Notice that as a result of this operation, the sets containing 18 and 13 are combined via a **union** operation. This is because everything that was connected to 18 is now connected to everything that was connected to 13. At the end of the algorithm, depicted in Figure 8.23, everything is connected, and we are done.

The running time of the algorithm is dominated by the union/find costs. The size of the union/find universe is equal to the number of cells. The number of **find** operations is proportional to the number of cells, since the number of removed walls is one less than the number of cells, while with care, we see that there only about twice the number of walls as cells in the first place. Thus, if N is the number of cells, since there are two finds per randomly targeted wall, this gives an estimate of between (roughly) $2N$ and $4N$ **find** operations throughout the algorithm. Therefore, the algorithm's running time can be taken as $O(N \log^* N)$, and this algorithm quickly generates a maze.

{0, 1} {2} {3} {4, 6, 7, 8, 9, 13, 14, 16, 17, 18, 22} {5} {10, 11, 15} {12} {19} {20} {21} {23} {24}

Figure 8.22 Wall between squares 18 and 13 is randomly selected in Figure 8.21. This wall is knocked down, because 18 and 13 are not already connected. Their sets are merged.

{0, 1, 2, 3, 4, 5, 6, 7, 8, 9, 10, 11, 12, 13, 14, 15, 16, 17, 18, 19, 20, 21, 22, 23, 24}

Figure 8.23 Eventually, 24 walls are knocked down. All elements are in the same set.

SUMMARY

We have seen a very simple data structure to maintain disjoint sets. When the **union** operation is performed, it does not matter, as far as correctness is concerned, which set retains its name. A valuable lesson that should be learned here is that it can be very important to consider the alternatives when a particular step is not totally specified. The **union** step is flexible; by taking advantage of this, we are able to get a much more efficient algorithm.

Path compression is one of the earliest forms of *self-adjustment*, which we have seen elsewhere (splay trees, skew heaps). Its use is extremely interesting, especially from a theoretical point of view, because it was one of the first examples of a simple algorithm with a not-so-simple worst-case analysis.

EXERCISES

8.1 Show the result of the following sequence of instructions: union(1,2), union(3,4), union(3,5), union(1,7), union(3,6), union(8,9), union(1,8), union(3,10), union

union(3,11), union(3,12), union(3,13), union(14,15), union(16,0), union(14,16), union(1,3), union(1,14) when the unions are:

    a. Performed arbitrarily.

    b. Performed by height.

    c. Performed by size.

8.2 For each of the trees in the previous exercise, perform a find with path compression on the deepest node.

8.3 Write a program to determine the effects of path compression and the various unioning strategies. Your program should process a long sequence of equivalence operations using all six of the possible strategies.

8.4 Show that if unions are performed by height, then the depth of any tree is $O(\log N)$.

8.5   a. Show that if $M = N^2$, then the running time of M union/find operations is $O(M)$.

    b. Show that if $M = N \log N$, then the running time of M union/find operations is $O(M)$.

   *c. Suppose $M = \Theta(N \log \log N)$. What is the running time of M union/find operations?

   *d. Suppose $M = \Theta(N \log^* N)$. What is the running time of M union/find operations?

8.6 Prove that for the mazes generated by the algorithm in Section 8.7, the path from the starting to ending points is unique.

8.7 Design an algorithm that generates a maze that contains no path from start to finish, but has the property that the removal of a **prespecified** wall creates a unique path.

*8.8 Suppose we want to add an extra operation, deunion, which undoes the last union operation that has not been already undone.

    a. Show that if we do union-by-height and finds without path compression, then deunion is easy and a sequence of M union, find, and deunion operations takes $O(M \log N)$ time.

    b. Why does path compression make deunion hard?

  **c. Show how to implement all three operations so that the sequence of M operations takes $O(M \log N/\log \log N)$ time.

*8.9 Suppose we want to add an extra operation, remove(x), which removes x from its current set and places it in its own. Show how to modify the union/find algorithm so that the running time of a sequence of M union, find, and remove operations is $O(M\alpha(M, N))$.

**8.10 Give an algorithm that takes as input an N-vertex tree and a list of N pairs of vertices and determines for each pair (v, w) the closest common ancestor of v and w. Your algorithm should run in $O(N \log^* N)$.

*8.11 Show that if all of the unions precede the finds, then the disjoint set algorithm with path compression requires linear time, even if the unions are done arbitrarily.

**8.12 Prove that if unions are done arbitrarily, but path compression is performed on the finds, then the worst-case running time is $\Theta(M \log N)$.

8.13 Prove that if unions are done by size and path compression is performed, the worst-case running time is $O(M \log^* N)$.

8.14 Suppose we implement partial path compression on `find(i)` by making every other node on the path from i to the root link to its grandparent (where this makes sense). This is known as *path halving*.

  a. Write a procedure to do this.

  b. Prove that if path halving is performed on the `find`s and either union-by-height or union-by-size is used, the worst-case running time is $O(M \log^* N)$.

8.15 Write a program that generates mazes of arbitrary size. Use the AWT to generate a maze similar to that in Figure 8.19.

REFERENCES

Various solutions to the union/find problem can be found in [6], [9], and [11]. Hopcroft and Ullman showed the $O(M \log^* N)$ bound of Section 8.6. Tarjan [15] obtained the bound $O(M\alpha(M, N))$. A more precise (but asymptotically identical) bound for $M < N$ appears in [2] and [18]. Various other strategies for path compression and **union**s also achieve the same bound; see [18] for details.

A lower bound showing that under certain restrictions $\Omega(M\alpha(M, N))$ time is required to process M union/find operations was given by Tarjan [16]. Identical bounds under less restrictive conditions have been shown in [7] and [14].

Applications of the union/find data structure appear in [1] and [10]. Certain special cases of the union/find problem can be solved in $O(M)$ time [8]. This reduces the running time of several algorithms, such as [1], graph dominance, and reducibility (see references in Chapter 9) by a factor of $\alpha(M, N)$. Others, such as [10] and the graph connectivity problem in this chapter, are unaffected. The paper lists 10 examples. Tarjan has used path compression to obtain efficient algorithms for several graph problems [17].

Average case results for the union/find problem appear in [5], [12], [21], and [3]. Results bounding the running time of any single operation (as opposed to the entire sequence) appear in [4] and [13].

Exercise 8.8 is solved in [20]. A general union/find structure, supporting more operations, is given in [19].

1. A. V. Aho, J. E. Hopcroft, and J. D. Ullman, "On finding Lowest Common Ancestors in Trees," *SIAM Journal on Computing,* 5 (1976), 115–132.

2. L. Banachowski, "A Complement to Tarjan's Result about the Lower Bound on the Complexity of the Set Union Problem," *Information Processing Letters,* 11 (1980), 59–65.

3. B. Bollobás and I. Simon, "Probabilistic Analysis of Disjoint Set Union Algorithms," *SIAM Journal on Computing,* 22 (1993), 1053–1086.

4. N. Blum, "On the Single-Operation Worst-Case Time Complexity of the Disjoint Set Union Problem," *SIAM Journal on Computing,* 15 (1986), 1021–1024.

5. J. Doyle and R. L. Rivest, "Linear Expected Time of a Simple Union Find Algorithm," *Information Processing Letters,* 5 (1976), 146–148.

6. M. J. Fischer, "Efficiency of Equivalence Algorithms," in *Complexity of Computer Computation* (eds. R. E. Miller and J. W. Thatcher), Plenum Press, New York 1972, 153–168.

7. M. L. Fredman and M. E. Saks, "The Cell Probe Complexity of Dynamic Data Structures," *Proceedings of the Twenty-first Annual Symposium on Theory of Computing* (1989), 345–354.

8. H. N. Gabow and R. E. Tarjan, "A Linear-Time Algorithm for a Special Case of Disjoint Set Union," *Journal of Computer and System Sciences,* 30 (1985), 209–221.

9. B. A. Galler and M. J. Fischer, "An Improved Equivalence Algorithm," *Communications of the ACM,* 7 (1964), 301–303.

10. J. E. Hopcroft and R. M. Karp, "An Algorithm for Testing the Equivalence of Finite Automata," *Technical Report TR-71-114,* Department of Computer Science, Cornell University, Ithaca, N.Y., 1971.

11. J. E. Hopcroft and J. D. Ullman, "Set Merging Algorithms," *SIAM Journal on Computing,* 2 (1973), 294–303.

12. D. E. Knuth and A. Schonhage, "The Expected Linearity of a Simple Equivalence Algorithm," *Theoretical Computer Science,* 6 (1978), 281–315.

13. J. A. LaPoutre, "New Techniques for the Union-Find Problem," *Proceedings of the First Annual ACM–SIAM Symposium on Discrete Algorithms* (1990), 54–63.

14. J. A. LaPoutre, "Lower Bounds for the Union-Find and the Split-Find Problem on Pointer Machines," *Proceedings of the Twenty-Second Annual ACM Symposium on Theory of Computing* (1990), 34–44.

15. R. E. Tarjan, "Efficiency of a Good but Not Linear Set Union Algorithm," *Journal of the ACM,* 22 (1975), 215–225.

16. R. E. Tarjan, "A Class of Algorithms Which Require Nonlinear Time to Maintain Disjoint Sets," *Journal of Computer and System Sciences,* 18 (1979), 110–127.

17. R. E. Tarjan, "Applications of Path Compression on Balanced Trees," *Journal of the ACM,* 26 (1979), 690–715.

18. R. E. Tarjan and J. van Leeuwen, "Worst Case Analysis of Set Union Algorithms," *Journal of the ACM,* 31 (1984), 245–281.

19. M. J. van Kreveld and M. H. Overmars, "Union-Copy Structures and Dynamic Segment Trees," *Journal of the ACM,* 40 (1993), 635–652.

20. J. Westbrook and R. E. Tarjan, "Amortized Analysis of Algorithms for Set Union with Backtracking," *SIAM Journal on Computing,* 18 (1989), 1–11.

21. A. C. Yao, "On the Average Behavior of Set Merging Algorithms," *Proceedings of Eighth Annual ACM Symposium on the Theory of Computation,* (1976), 192–195.

Graph Algorithms

In this chapter we discuss several common problems in graph theory. Not only are these algorithms useful in practice, they are interesting because in many real-life applications they are too slow unless careful attention is paid to the choice of data structures. We will

- Show several real-life problems, which can be converted to problems on graphs.
- Give algorithms to solve several common graph problems.
- Show how the proper choice of data structures can drastically reduce the running time of these algorithms.
- See an important technique, known as depth-first search, and show how it can be used to solve several seemingly nontrivial problems in linear time.

9.1. Definitions

A *graph* $G = (V, E)$ consists of a set of *vertices*, V, and a set of *edges*, E. Each edge is a pair (v, w), where $v, w \in V$. Edges are sometimes referred to as *arcs*. If the pair is ordered, then the graph is *directed*. Directed graphs are sometimes referred to as *digraphs*. Vertex w is *adjacent* to v if and only if $(v, w) \in E$. In an undirected graph with edge (v, w), and hence (w, v), w is adjacent to v and v is adjacent to w. Sometimes an edge has a third component, known as either a *weight* or a *cost*.

A *path* in a graph is a sequence of vertices $w_1, w_2, w_3, \ldots, w_N$ such that $(w_i, w_{i+1}) \in E$ for $1 \le i < N$. The *length* of such a path is the number of edges on the path, which is equal to $N - 1$. We allow a path from a vertex to itself; if this path contains no edges, then the path length is 0. This is a convenient way to define an otherwise special case. If the graph contains an edge (v, v) from a vertex to itself, then the path v, v is sometimes referred to as a *loop*. The graphs we will consider will generally be loopless. A *simple* path is a path such that all vertices are distinct, except that the first and last could be the same.

A *cycle* in a directed graph is a path of length at least 1 such that $w_1 = w_N$; this cycle is simple if the path is simple. For undirected graphs, we require that the edges be distinct. The logic of these requirements is that the path u, v, u in an undirected graph should not be considered a cycle, because (u, v) and (v, u) are the same edge. In a directed graph, these are different edges, so it makes sense to call this a cycle. A directed graph is *acyclic* if it has no cycles. A directed acyclic graph is sometimes referred to by its abbreviation, *DAG*.

An undirected graph is *connected* if there is a path from every vertex to every other vertex. A directed graph with this property is called *strongly connected*. If a directed graph is not strongly connected, but the underlying graph (without direction to the arcs) is connected, then the graph is said to be *weakly connected*. A *complete graph* is a graph in which there is an edge between every pair of vertices.

An example of a real-life situation that can be modeled by a graph is the airport system. Each airport is a vertex, and two vertices are connected by an edge if there is a nonstop flight from the airports that are represented by the vertices. The edge could have a weight, representing the time, distance, or cost of the flight. It is reasonable to assume that such a graph is directed, since it might take longer or cost more (depending on local taxes, for example) to fly in different directions. We would probably like to make sure that the airport system is strongly connected, so that it is always possible to fly from any airport to any other airport. We might also like to quickly determine the best flight between any two airports. "Best" could mean the path with the fewest number of edges or could be taken with respect to one, or all, of the weight measures.

Traffic flow can be modeled by a graph. Each street intersection represents a vertex, and each street is an edge. The edge costs could represent, among other things, a speed limit or a capacity (number of lanes). We could then ask for the shortest route or use this information to find the most likely location for bottlenecks.

In the remainder of this chapter, we will see several more applications of graphs. Many of these graphs can be quite large, so it is important that the algorithms we use be efficient.

9.1.1. Representation of Graphs

We will consider directed graphs (undirected graphs are similarly represented).

Suppose, for now, that we can number the vertices, starting at 1. The graph shown in Figure 9.1 represents 7 vertices and 12 edges.

One simple way to represent a graph is to use a two-dimensional array. This is known as an *adjacency matrix* representation. For each edge (u, v), we set $A[u][v]$ to **true**; otherwise

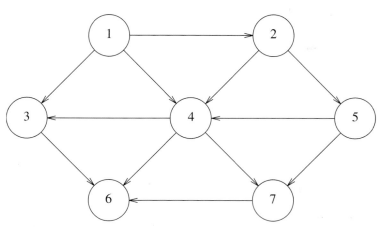

Figure 9.1 A directed graph

the entry in the array is **false**. If the edge has a weight associated with it, then we can set $A[u][v]$ equal to the weight and use either a very large or a very small weight as a sentinel to indicate nonexistent edges. For instance, if we were looking for the cheapest airplane route, we could represent nonexistent flights with a cost of ∞. If we were looking, for some strange reason, for the most expensive airplane route, we could use $-\infty$ (or perhaps 0) to represent nonexistent edges.

Although this has the merit of extreme simplicity, the space requirement is $\Theta(|V|^2)$, which can be prohibitive if the graph does not have very many edges. An adjacency matrix is an appropriate representation if the graph is *dense*: $|E| = \Theta(|V|^2)$. In most of the applications that we shall see, this is not true. For instance, suppose the graph represents a street map. Assume a Manhattan-like orientation, where almost all the streets run either north–south or east–west. Therefore, any intersection is attached to roughly four streets, so if the graph is directed and all streets are two-way, then $|E| \approx 4|V|$. If there are 3,000 intersections, then we have a 3,000-vertex graph with 12,000 edge entries, which would require an array of size 9,000,000. Most of these entries would contain zero. This is intuitively bad, because we want our data structures to represent the data that are actually there and not the data that are not present.

If the graph is not dense, in other words, if the graph is *sparse*, a better solution is an *adjacency list* representation. For each vertex, we keep a list of all adjacent vertices. The space requirement is then $O(|E|+|V|)$, which is linear in the size of the graph.* The leftmost structure in Figure 9.2 is merely an array of header cells. The representation should be clear from Figure 9.2. If the edges have weights, then this additional information is also stored in the cells.

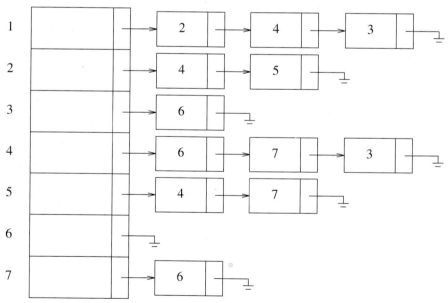

Figure 9.2 An adjacency list representation of a graph

---

*When we speak of linear-time graph algorithms, $O(|E| + |V|)$ is the running time we require.

Adjacency lists are the standard way to represent graphs. Undirected graphs can be similarly represented; each edge (u, v) appears in two lists, so the space usage essentially doubles. A common requirement in graph algorithms is to find all vertices adjacent to some given vertex v, and this can be done, in time proportional to the number of such vertices found, by a simple scan down the appropriate adjacency list.

Information about each vertex, including a list of its adjacent vertices, is stored in an object of type **Vertex**. In most real-life applications, the vertices have names, which are unknown at compile-time, and thus generally, we will need to provide a mapping of names to their corresponding **Vertex** object. The easiest way to do this is to use a hash table, in which we store a name (which serves as a key) and a reference to a **Vertex**. New **Vertex** objects are created as the graph is read. As each edge is input, we check whether each of the two vertices has already been seen. If so, we use the **Vertex** corresponding to it. Otherwise, we create a new **Vertex** object and insert the name and **Vertex** object as a pair into the hash table. Each **Vertex** entry will also need to store the vertex name, since eventually we will need to output these names.

The code that we present in this chapter will be pseudocode using ADTs as much as possible. We will do this to save space and, of course, to make the algorithmic presentation of the algorithms much clearer. Appendix B provides working code for the shortest-path algorithm discussed in Section 9.3.1. Two versions are provided: one using the Java Collections API and another using the data structures developed in earlier chapters.

9.2. Topological Sort

A *topological sort* is an ordering of vertices in a directed acyclic graph, such that if there is a path from v_i to v_j, then v_j appears *after* v_i in the ordering. The graph in Figure 9.3 represents

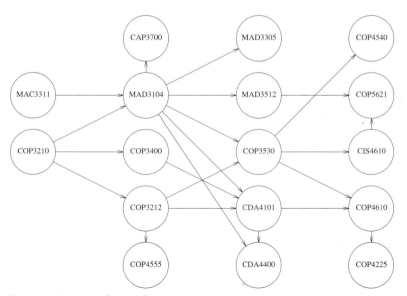

Figure 9.3 An acyclic graph representing course prerequisite structure

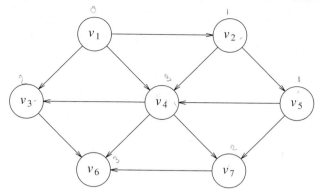

Figure 9.4 An acyclic graph

the course prerequisite structure at a state university in Miami. A directed edge (v, w) indicates that course v must be completed before course w may be attempted. A topological ordering of these courses is any course sequence that does not violate the prerequisite requirement.

It is clear that a topological ordering is not possible if the graph has a cycle, since for two vertices v and w on the cycle, v precedes w and w precedes v. Furthermore, the ordering is not necessarily unique; any legal ordering will do. In the graph in Figure 9.4, $v_1, v_2, v_5, v_4, v_3, v_7, v_6$ and $v_1, v_2, v_5, v_4, v_7, v_3, v_6$ are both topological orderings.

A simple algorithm to find a topological ordering is first to find any vertex with no incoming edges. We can then print this vertex, and remove it, along with its edges, from the graph. Then we apply this same strategy to the rest of the graph.

To formalize this, we define the *indegree* of a vertex v as the number of edges (u, v). We compute the indegrees of all vertices in the graph. Assuming that the indegree for each vertex is stored and that the graph is read into an adjacency list, we can then apply the algorithm in Figure 9.5 to generate a topological ordering.

```
void topsort( ) throws CycleFound
{
    Vertex v, w;

    for( int counter = 0; counter < NUM_VERTICES; counter++ )
    {
        v = findNewVertexOfDegreeZero( );
        if( v == null )
            throw new CycleFound( );
        v.topNum = counter;
        for each w adjacent to v
            w.indegree--;
    }
}
```

Figure 9.5 Simple topological sort pseudocode

The method `findNewVertexOfIndegreeZero` scans the array looking for a vertex with indegree 0 that has not already been assigned a topological number. It returns **null** if no such vertex exists; this indicates that the graph has a cycle.

Because `findNewVertexOfIndegreeZero` is a simple sequential scan of the array of vertices, each call to it takes $O(|V|)$ time. Since there are $|V|$ such calls, the running time of the algorithm is $O(|V|^2)$.

By paying more careful attention to the data structures, it is possible to do better. The cause of the poor running time is the sequential scan through the array of vertices. If the graph is sparse, we would expect that only a few vertices have their indegrees updated during each iteration. However, in the search for a vertex of indegree 0, we look at (potentially) all the vertices, even though only a few have changed.

We can remove this inefficiency by keeping all the (unassigned) vertices of indegree 0 in a special *box*. The `findNewVertexOfIndegreeZero` method then returns (and removes) any vertex in the box. When we decrement the indegrees of the adjacent vertices, we check each vertex and place it in the box if its indegree falls to 0.

To implement the box, we can use either a stack or a queue; we will use a queue. First, the indegree is computed for every vertex. Then all vertices of indegree 0 are placed on an initially empty queue. While the queue is not empty, a vertex v is removed, and all edges adjacent to v have their indegrees decremented. A vertex is put on the queue as soon as its indegree falls to 0. The topological ordering then is the order in which the vertices dequeue. Figure 9.6 shows the status after each phase.

A pseudocode implementation of this algorithm is given in Figure 9.7. As before, we will assume that the graph is already read into an adjacency list and that the indegrees are computed and stored with the vertices. We also assume each vertex has a field named `topNum`, in which to place its topological numbering.

The time to perform this algorithm is $O(|E| + |V|)$ if adjacency lists are used. This is apparent when one realizes that the body of the **for** loop is executed at most once per edge. The queue operations are done at most once per vertex, and the initialization steps also take time proportional to the size of the graph.

Vertex	Indegree Before Dequeue #						
	1	2	3	4	5	6	7
v_1	0	0	0	0	0	0	0
v_2	1	0	0	0	0	0	0
v_3	2	1	1	1	0	0	0
v_4	3	2	1	0	0	0	0
v_5	1	1	0	0	0	0	0
v_6	3	3	3	3	2	1	0
v_7	2	2	2	1	0	0	0
Enqueue	v_1	v_2	v_5	v_4	v_3, v_7		v_6
Dequeue	v_1	v_2	v_5	v_4	v_3	v_7	v_6

Figure 9.6 Result of applying topological sort to the graph in Figure 9.4

```
         void topsort( ) throws CycleFound
         {
             Queue q;
             int counter = 0;
             Vertex v, w;

/* 1*/       q = new Queue( );
/* 2*/       for each vertex v
/* 3*/           if( v.indegree == 0 )
/* 4*/               q.enqueue( v );

/* 5*/       while( !q.isEmpty( ) )
             {
/* 6*/           v = q.dequeue( );
/* 7*/           v.topNum = ++counter;   // Assign next number

/* 8*/           for each w adjacent to v
/* 9*/               if( --w.indegree == 0 )
/*10*/                   q.enqueue( w );
             }

/*11*/       if( counter != NUM_VERTICES )
/*12*/           throw new CycleFound( );
         }
```

Figure 9.7 Pseudocode to perform topological sort

9.3. Shortest-Path Algorithms

In this section we examine various shortest-path problems. The input is a weighted graph: associated with each edge (v_i, v_j) is a cost $c_{i,j}$ to traverse the edge. The cost of a path $v_1 v_2 \ldots v_N$ is $\sum_{i=1}^{N-1} c_{i,i+1}$. This is referred to as the *weighted path length*. The *unweighted path length* is merely the number of edges on the path, namely, $N - 1$.

SINGLE-SOURCE SHORTEST-PATH PROBLEM:
Given as input a weighted graph, $G = (V, E)$, and a distinguished vertex, s, find the shortest weighted path from s to every other vertex in G.

For example, in the graph in Figure 9.8, the shortest weighted path from v_1 to v_6 has a cost of 6 and goes from v_1 to v_4 to v_7 to v_6. The shortest unweighted path between these vertices is 2. Generally, when it is not specified whether we are referring to a weighted or an unweighted path, the path is weighted if the graph is. Notice also that in this graph there is no path from v_6 to v_1.

The graph in the preceding example has no edges of negative cost. The graph in Figure 9.9 shows the problems that negative edges can cause. The path from v_5 to v_4 has cost 1, but a shorter path exists by following the loop v_5, v_4, v_2, v_5, v_4, which has cost -5. This path is still not the shortest, because we could stay in the loop arbitrarily long. Thus, the shortest path between these two points is undefined. Similarly, the shortest path from

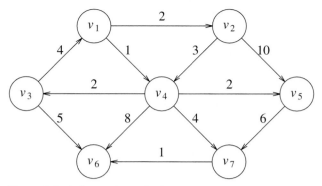

Figure 9.8 A directed graph G

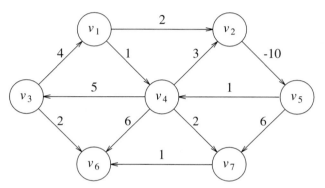

Figure 9.9 A graph with a negative-cost cycle

v_1 to v_6 is undefined, because we can get into the same loop. This loop is known as a *negative-cost cycle;* when one is present in the graph, the shortest paths are not defined. Negative-cost edges are not necessarily bad, as the cycles are, but their presence seems to make the problem harder. For convenience, in the absence of a negative-cost cycle, the shortest path from s to s is zero.

There are many examples where we might want to solve the shortest-path problem. If the vertices represent computers; the edges represent a link between computers; and the costs represent communication costs (phone bill per 1,000 bytes of data), delay costs (number of seconds required to transmit 1,000 bytes), or a combination of these and other factors, then we can use the shortest-path algorithm to find the cheapest way to send electronic news from one computer to a set of other computers.

We can model airplane or other mass transit routes by graphs and use a shortest-path algorithm to compute the best route between two points. In this and many practical applications, we might want to find the shortest path from one vertex, s, to only one other vertex, t. Currently there are no algorithms in which finding the path from s to one vertex is any faster (by more than a constant factor) than finding the path from s to all vertices.

We will examine algorithms to solve four versions of this problem. First, we will consider the unweighted shortest-path problem and show how to solve it in $O(|E| + |V|)$. Next, we will show how to solve the weighted shortest-path problem if we assume that there are no negative edges. The running time for this algorithm is $O(|E| \log |V|)$ when implemented with reasonable data structures.

If the graph has negative edges, we will provide a simple solution, which unfortunately has a poor time bound of $O(|E| \cdot |V|)$. Finally, we will solve the weighted problem for the special case of acyclic graphs in linear time.

9.3.1. Unweighted Shortest Paths

Figure 9.10 shows an unweighted graph, G. Using some vertex, s, which is an input parameter, we would like to find the shortest path from s to all other vertices. We are only interested in the number of edges contained on the path, so there are no weights on the edges. This is clearly a special case of the weighted shortest-path problem, since we could assign all edges a weight of 1.

For now, suppose we are interested only in the length of the shortest paths, not in the actual paths themselves. Keeping track of the actual paths will turn out to be a matter of simple bookkeeping.

Suppose we choose s to be v_3. Immediately, we can tell that the shortest path from s to v_3 is then a path of length 0. We can mark this information, obtaining the graph in Figure 9.11.

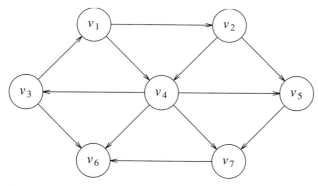

Figure 9.10 An unweighted directed graph G

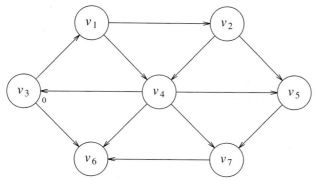

Figure 9.11 Graph after marking the start node as reachable in zero edges

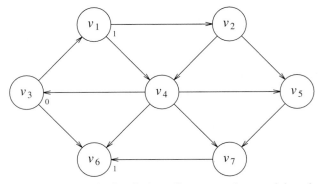

Figure 9.12 Graph after finding all vertices whose path length from s is 1

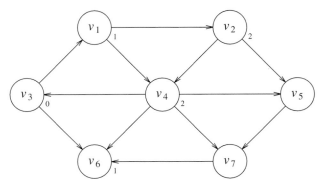

Figure 9.13 Graph after finding all vertices whose shortest path is 2

Now we can start looking for all vertices that are a distance 1 away from s. These can be found by looking at the vertices that are adjacent to s. If we do this, we see that v_1 and v_6 are one edge from s. This is shown in Figure 9.12.

We can now find vertices whose shortest path from s is exactly 2, by finding all the vertices adjacent to v_1 and v_6 (the vertices at distance 1), whose shortest paths are not already known. This search tells us that the shortest path to v_2 and v_4 is 2. Figure 9.13 shows the progress that has been made so far.

Finally we can find, by examining vertices adjacent to the recently evaluated v_2 and v_4, that v_5 and v_7 have a shortest path of three edges. All vertices have now been calculated, and so Figure 9.14 shows the final result of the algorithm.

This strategy for searching a graph is known as *breadth-first search*. It operates by processing vertices in layers: the vertices closest to the start are evaluated first, and the most distant vertices are evaluated last. This is much the same as a level-order traversal for trees.

Given this strategy, we must translate it into code. Figure 9.15 shows the initial configuration of the table that our algorithm will use to keep track of its progress.

For each vertex, we will keep track of three pieces of information. First, we will keep its distance from s in the entry d_v. Initially all vertices are unreachable except for s, whose

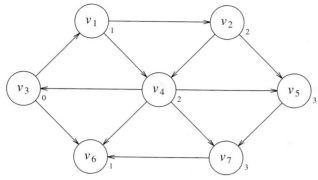

Figure 9.14 Final shortest paths

v	known	d_v	p_v
v_1	F	∞	0
v_2	F	∞	0
v_3	F	0	0
v_4	F	∞	0
v_5	F	∞	0
v_6	F	∞	0
v_7	F	∞	0

Figure 9.15 Initial configuration of table used in unweighted shortest-path computation

path length is 0. The entry in p_v is the bookkeeping variable, which will allow us to print the actual paths. The entry *known* is set to **true** after a vertex is processed. Initially, all entries are not *known*, including the start vertex. When a vertex is marked *known*, we have a guarantee that no cheaper path will ever be found, and so processing for that vertex is essentially complete.

The basic algorithm can be described in Figure 9.16. The algorithm in Figure 9.16 mimics the diagrams by declaring as *known* the vertices at distance $d = 0$, then $d = 1$, then $d = 2$, and so on, and setting all the adjacent vertices w that still have $d_w = \infty$ to a distance $d_w = d + 1$.

By tracing back through the p_v variable, the actual path can be printed. We will see how when we discuss the weighted case.

The running time of the algorithm is $O(|V|^2)$, because of the doubly nested **for** loops. An obvious inefficiency is that the outside loop continues until NUM_VERTICES $-$ 1, even if all the vertices become *known* much earlier. Although an extra test could be made to avoid this, it does not affect the worst-case running time, as can be seen by generalizing what happens when the input is the graph in Figure 9.17 with start vertex v_9.

We can remove the inefficiency in much the same way as was done for topological sort. At any point in time, there are only two types of *unknown* vertices that have $d_v \neq \infty$. Some have $d_v = $ currDist and the rest have $d_v = $ currDist $+$ 1. Because of this extra structure, it is very wasteful to search through the entire table to find a proper vertex at lines 3 and 4.

```
              void unweighted( Vertex s )
              {
                  Vertex v, w;

/* 1*/            s.dist = 0;
/* 2*/            for( int currDist = 0; currDist < NUM_VERTICES; currDist++ )
/* 3*/                for each vertex v
/* 4*/                    if( !v.known && v.dist == currDist )
                          {
/* 5*/                        v.known = true;
/* 6*/                        for each w adjacent to v
/* 7*/                            if( w.dist == INFINITY )
                                  {
/* 8*/                                w.dist = currDist + 1;
/* 9*/                                w.path = v;
                                  }
                          }
              }
```

Figure 9.16 Pseudocode for unweighted shortest-path algorithm

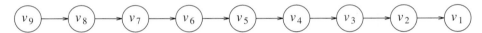

Figure 9.17 A bad case for unweighted shortest-path algorithm using Figure 9.16 (pseudocode)

A very simple but abstract solution is to keep two boxes. Box #1 will have the unknown vertices with $d_v =$ currDist, and box #2 will have $d_v =$ currDist + 1. The test at lines 3 and 4 can be replaced by finding any vertex in box #1. After line 9 (inside the innermost if block), we can add w to box #2. After the outermost for loop terminates, box #1 is empty, and box #2 can be transferred to box #1 for the next pass of the for loop.

We can refine this idea even further by using just one queue. At the start of the pass, the queue contains only vertices of distance currDist. When we add adjacent vertices of distance currDist + 1, since they enqueue at the rear, we are guaranteed that they will not be processed until after all the vertices of distance currDist have been processed. After the last vertex at distance currDist dequeues and is processed, the queue only contains vertices of distance currDist + 1, so this process perpetuates. We merely need to begin the process by placing the start node on the queue by itself.

The refined algorithm is shown in Figure 9.18. In the pseudocode, we have assumed that the start vertex, s, is passed as a parameter. Also, it is possible that the queue might empty prematurely, if some vertices are unreachable from the start node. In this case, a distance of INFINITY will be reported for these nodes, which is perfectly reasonable. Finally, the known field is not used; once a vertex is processed it can never enter the queue again, so the fact that it need not be reprocessed is implicitly marked. Thus, the known field can be discarded. Figure 9.19 shows how the values on the graph we have been using are changed during the algorithm. We keep the known field to make the table easier to follow and for consistency with the rest of this section.

```
              void unweighted( Vertex s )
              {
                  Queue q;
                  Vertex v, w;

/* 1*/            q = new Queue( );
/* 2*/            q.enqueue( s ); s.dist = 0;

/* 3*/            while( !q.isEmpty( ) )
                  {
/* 4*/                v = q.dequeue( );
/* 5*/                v.known = true;  // Not really needed anymore

/* 6*/                for each w adjacent to v
/* 7*/                    if( w.dist == INFINITY )
                          {
/* 8*/                        w.dist = v.dist + 1;
/* 9*/                        w.path = v;
/*10*/                        q.enqueue( w );
                          }
                  }
              }
```

Figure 9.18 Pseudocode for unweighted shortest-path algorithm

v	Initial State known	d_v	p_v	v_3 Dequeued known	d_v	p_v	v_1 Dequeued known	d_v	p_v	v_6 Dequeued known	d_v	p_v
v_1	F	∞	0	F	1	v_3	T	1	v_3	T	1	v_3
v_2	F	∞	0	F	∞	0	F	2	v_1	F	2	v_1
v_3	F	0	0	T	0	0	T	0	0	T	0	0
v_4	F	∞	0	F	∞	0	F	2	v_1	F	2	v_1
v_5	F	∞	0	F	∞	0	F	∞	0	F	∞	0
v_6	F	∞	0	F	1	v_3	F	1	v_3	T	1	v_3
v_7	F	∞	0	F	∞	0	F	∞	0	F	∞	0
Q :	v_3			v_1, v_6			v_6, v_2, v_4			v_2, v_4		

v	v_2 Dequeued known	d_v	p_v	v_4 Dequeued known	d_v	p_v	v_5 Dequeued known	d_v	p_v	v_7 Dequeued known	d_v	p_v
v_1	T	1	v_3	T	1	v_3	T	1	v_3	T	1	v_3
v_2	T	2	v_1	T	2	v_1	T	2	v_1	T	2	v_1
v_3	T	0	0	T	0	0	T	0	0	T	0	0
v_4	F	2	v_1	T	2	v_1	T	2	v_1	T	2	v_1
v_5	F	3	v_2	F	3	v_2	T	3	v_2	T	3	v_2
v_6	T	1	v_3	T	1	v_3	T	1	v_3	T	1	v_3
v_7	F	∞	0	F	3	v_4	F	3	v_4	T	3	v_4
Q :	v_4, v_5			v_5, v_7			v_7			empty		

Figure 9.19 How the data change during the unweighted shortest-path algorithm

Using the same analysis as was performed for topological sort, we see that the running time is $O(|E| + |V|)$, as long as adjacency lists are used.

9.3.2. Dijkstra's Algorithm

If the graph is weighted, the problem (apparently) becomes harder, but we can still use the ideas from the unweighted case.

We keep all of the same information as before. Thus, each vertex is marked as either *known* or *unknown*. A tentative distance d_v is kept for each vertex, as before. This distance turns out to be the shortest path length from s to v using only *known* vertices as intermediates. As before, we record p_v, which is the last vertex to cause a change to d_v.

The general method to solve the single-source shortest-path problem is known as *Dijkstra's algorithm*. This thirty-year-old solution is a prime example of a *greedy algorithm*. Greedy algorithms generally solve a problem in stages by doing what appears to be the best thing at each stage. For example, to make change in U.S. currency, most people count out the quarters first, then the dimes, nickels, and pennies. This greedy algorithm gives change using the minimum number of coins. The main problem with greedy algorithms is that they do not always work. The addition of a 12-cent piece breaks the coin-changing algorithm for returning 15 cents, because the answer it gives (one 12-cent piece and three pennies) is not optimal (one dime and one nickel).

Dijkstra's algorithm proceeds in stages, just like the unweighted shortest-path algorithm. At each stage, Dijkstra's algorithm selects a vertex v, which has the smallest d_v among all the *unknown* vertices, and declares that the shortest path from s to v is *known*. The remainder of a stage consists of updating the values of d_w.

In the unweighted case, we set $d_w = d_v + 1$ if $d_w = \infty$. Thus, we essentially lowered the value of d_w if vertex v offered a shorter path. If we apply the same logic to the weighted case, then we should set $d_w = d_v + c_{v,w}$ if this new value for d_w would be an improvement. Put simply, the algorithm decides whether or not it is a good idea to use v on the path to w. The original cost, d_w, is the cost without using v; the cost calculated above is the cheapest path using v (and only *known* vertices).

The graph in Figure 9.20 is our example. Figure 9.21 represents the initial configuration, assuming that the start node, s, is v_1. The first vertex selected is v_1, with path length 0. This vertex is marked *known*. Now that v_1 is *known*, some entries need to be adjusted.

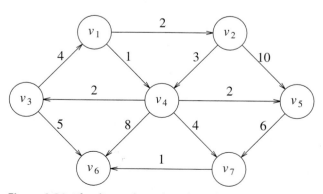

Figure 9.20 The directed graph G (again)

v	known	d_v	p_v
v_1	F	0	0
v_2	F	∞	0
v_3	F	∞	0
v_4	F	∞	0
v_5	F	∞	0
v_6	F	∞	0
v_7	F	∞	0

Figure 9.21 Initial configuration of table used in Dijkstra's algorithm

v	known	d_v	p_v
v_1	T	0	0
v_2	F	2	v_1
v_3	F	∞	0
v_4	F	1	v_1
v_5	F	∞	0
v_6	F	∞	0
v_7	F	∞	0

Figure 9.22 After v_1 is declared *known*

v	known	d_v	p_v
v_1	T	0	0
v_2	F	2	v_1
v_3	F	3	v_4
v_4	T	1	v_1
v_5	F	3	v_4
v_6	F	9	v_4
v_7	F	5	v_4

Figure 9.23 After v_4 is declared *known*

The vertices adjacent to v_1 are v_2 and v_4. Both these vertices get their entries adjusted, as indicated in Figure 9.22.

Next, v_4 is selected and marked *known*. Vertices v_3, v_5, v_6, and v_7 are adjacent, and it turns out that all require adjusting, as shown in Figure 9.23.

Next, v_2 is selected. v_4 is adjacent but already *known*, so no work is performed on it. v_5 is adjacent but not adjusted, because the cost of going through v_2 is $2 + 10 = 12$ and a path of length 3 is already known. Figure 9.24 shows the table after these vertices are selected.

v	known	d_v	p_v
v_1	T	0	0
v_2	T	2	v_1
v_3	F	3	v_4
v_4	T	1	v_1
v_5	F	3	v_4
v_6	F	9	v_4
v_7	F	5	v_4

Figure 9.24 After v_2 is declared *known*

v	known	d_v	p_v
v_1	T	0	0
v_2	T	2	v_1
v_3	T	3	v_4
v_4	T	1	v_1
v_5	T	3	v_4
v_6	F	8	v_3
v_7	F	5	v_4

Figure 9.25 After v_5 and then v_3 are declared *known*

v	known	d_v	p_v
v_1	T	0	0
v_2	T	2	v_1
v_3	T	3	v_4
v_4	T	1	v_1
v_5	T	3	v_4
v_6	F	6	v_7
v_7	T	5	v_4

Figure 9.26 After v_7 is declared *known*

The next vertex selected is v_5 at cost 3. v_7 is the only adjacent vertex, but it is not adjusted, because $3 + 6 > 5$. Then v_3 is selected, and the distance for v_6 is adjusted down to $3 + 5 = 8$. The resulting table is depicted in Figure 9.25.

Next v_7 is selected; v_6 gets updated down to $5 + 1 = 6$. The resulting table is Figure 9.26.

Finally, v_6 is selected. The final table is shown in Figure 9.27. Figure 9.28 graphically shows how edges are marked *known* and vertices updated during Dijkstra's algorithm.

To print out the actual path from a start vertex to some vertex v, we can write a recursive routine to follow the trail left in the p variables.

v	known	d_v	p_v
v_1	T	0	0
v_2	T	2	v_1
v_3	T	3	v_4
v_4	T	1	v_1
v_5	T	3	v_4
v_6	T	6	v_7
v_7	T	5	v_4

Figure 9.27 After v_6 is declared *known* and algorithm terminates

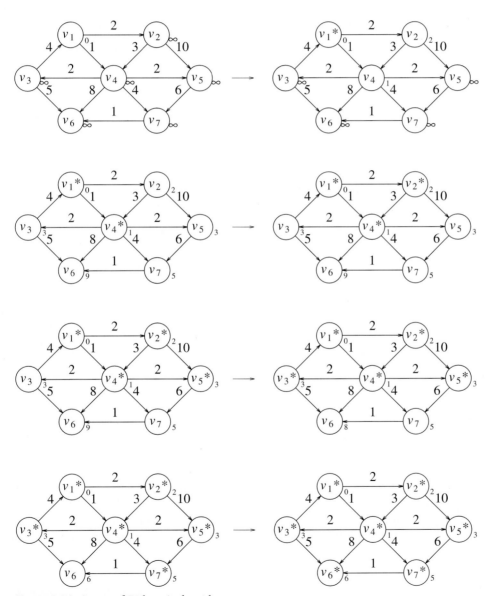

Figure 9.28 Stages of Dijkstra's algorithm

```
class Vertex
{
    public List    adj;      // Adjacency list
    public boolean known;
    public DistType dist;     // DistType is probably int
    public Vertex   path;
        // Other fields and methods as needed
}
```

Figure 9.29 Vertex class for Dijkstra's algorithm

```
        public Vertex [ ] createTable( )
        {
/* 1*/      Vertex [ ] t = readGraph( );  // Read graph somehow; fill in adj
/* 2*/      for( int i = 0; i < t.length; i++ )
            {
/* 3*/          t[ i ].known = false;
/* 4*/          t[ i ].dist = INFINITY;
/* 5*/          t[ i ].path = null;
            }
/* 6*/      NUM_VERTICES = t.length;
        }
```

Figure 9.30 Routine to return an array of Vertex

```
        /*
         * Print shortest path to v after dijkstra has run.
         * Assume that the path exists.
         */
        void printPath( Vertex v )
        {
            if( v.path != null )
            {
                printPath( v.path );
                System.out.print( " to " );
            }
            System.out.print( v );
        }
```

Figure 9.31 Routine to print the actual shortest path

We now give pseudocode to implement Dijkstra's algorithm. Each **Vertex** stores various data fields that are used in the algorithm. This is shown in Figure 9.29. We will assume that the graph can be read into an array of **Vertex**, with all adjacency lists constructed, by the routine **readGraph**. It is then a simple matter to initialize the other data fields, as shown in Figure 9.30.*

The path can be printed out using the recursive routine in Figure 9.31. The routine recursively prints the path all the way up to the vertex before *v* on the path, and then just prints *v*. This works because the path is simple.

---

*To run several algorithms on one graph, we would probably separate out lines 2–5 into a separate `initializePath` method. Since this is pseudocode, we opt not to do that here.

```
         void dijkstra( Vertex s )
         {
             Vertex v, w;

/* 1*/       s.dist = 0;

/* 2*/       for( ; ; )
             {
/* 3*/           v = smallest unknown distance vertex;
/* 4*/           if( v == null )
/* 5*/               break;
/* 6*/           v.known = true;

/* 7*/           for each w adjacent to v
/* 8*/               if( !w.known )
/* 9*/                   if( v.dist + cvw < w.dist )
                         {      // Update w
/*10*/                       decrease( w.dist to v.dist + cvw );
/*11*/                       w.path = v;
                         }
             }
         }
```

Figure 9.32 Pseudocode for Dijkstra's algorithm

Figure 9.32 shows the main algorithm, which is just a **for** loop to fill up the table using the greedy selection rule.

A proof by contradiction will show that this algorithm always works as long as no edge has a negative cost. If any edge has negative cost, the algorithm could produce the wrong answer (see Exercise 9.7a). The running time depends on how the vertices are manipulated, which we have yet to consider. If we use the obvious algorithm of scanning down the array of vertices to find the minimum d_v, each phase will take $O(|V|)$ time to find the minimum, and thus $O(|V|^2)$ time will be spent finding the minimum over the course of the algorithm. The time for updating d_w is constant per update, and there is at most one update per edge for a total of $O(|E|)$. Thus, the total running time is $O(|E| + |V|^2) = O(|V|^2)$. If the graph is dense, with $|E| = \Theta(|V|^2)$, this algorithm is not only simple but essentially optimal, since it runs in time linear in the number of edges.

If the graph is sparse, with $|E| = \Theta(|V|)$, this algorithm is too slow. In this case, the distances would need to be kept in a priority queue. There are actually two ways to do this; both are similar.

Lines 3 and 6 combine to form a **deleteMin** operation, since once the unknown minimum vertex is found, it is no longer unknown and must be removed from future consideration. The update at line 10 can be implemented two ways.

One way treats the update as a **decreaseKey** operation. The time to find the minimum is then $O(\log |V|)$, as is the time to perform updates, which amount to **decreaseKey** operations. This gives a running time of $O(|E| \log |V| + |V| \log |V|) = O(|E| \log |V|)$, an improvement over the previous bound for sparse graphs. Since priority queues do not efficiently support the **find** operation, the location in the priority queue of each value of d_i will need to be maintained and updated whenever d_i changes in the priority queue. If the priority queue is implemented by a binary heap, this will be messy. If a pairing heap (Chapter 12) is used, the code is not too bad.

An alternate method is to insert w and the new value d_w into the priority queue every time line 10 is executed. Thus, there may be more than one representative for each vertex in the priority queue. When the `deleteMin` operation removes the smallest vertex from the priority queue, it must be checked to make sure that it is not already *known*. Thus, line 3 becomes a loop performing `deleteMin`s until an *unknown* vertex emerges. Although this method is superior from a software point of view, and is certainly much easier to code, the size of the priority queue could get to be as large as $|E|$. This does not affect the asymptotic time bounds, since $|E| \leq |V|^2$ implies that $\log |E| \leq 2 \log |V|$. Thus, we still get an $O(|E| \log |V|)$ algorithm. However, the space requirement does increase, and this could be important in some applications. Moreover, because this method requires $|E|$ `deleteMin`s instead of only $|V|$, it is likely to be slower in practice.

Notice that for the typical problems, such as computer mail and mass transit commutes, the graphs are typically very sparse because most vertices have only a couple of edges, so it is important in many applications to use a priority queue to solve this problem.

There are better time bounds possible using Dijkstra's algorithm if different data structures are used. In Chapter 11, we will see another priority queue data structure called the Fibonacci heap. When this is used, the running time is $O(|E| + |V| \log |V|)$. Fibonacci heaps have good theoretical time bounds but a fair amount of overhead, so it is not clear whether using Fibonacci heaps is actually better in practice than Dijkstra's algorithm with binary heaps. To date, there are no meaningful average-case results for this problem.

9.3.3. Graphs with Negative Edge Costs

If the graph has negative edge costs, then Dijkstra's algorithm does not work. The problem is that once a vertex u is declared *known*, it is possible that from some other, *unknown* vertex v there is a path back to u that is very negative. In such a case, taking a path from s to v back to u is better than going from s to u without using v. Exercise 9.7(a) asks you to construct an explicit example.

A tempting solution is to add a constant Δ to each edge cost, thus removing negative edges, calculate a shortest path on the new graph, and then use that result on the original. The naive implementation of this strategy does not work because paths with many edges become more weighty than paths with few edges.

A combination of the weighted and unweighted algorithms will solve the problem, but at the cost of a drastic increase in running time. We forget about the concept of *known* vertices, since our algorithm needs to be able to change its mind. We begin by placing s on a queue. Then, at each stage, we dequeue a vertex v. We find all vertices w adjacent to v such that $d_w > d_v + c_{v,w}$. We update d_w and p_w, and place w on a queue if it is not already there. A bit can be set for each vertex to indicate presence in the queue. We repeat the process until the queue is empty. Figure 9.33 (almost) implements this algorithm.

Although the algorithm works if there are no negative-cost cycles, it is no longer true that the code in lines 6 through 10 is executed once per edge. Each vertex can dequeue at most $|V|$ times, so the running time is $O(|E| \cdot |V|)$ if adjacency lists are used (Exercise 9.7(b)). This is quite an increase from Dijkstra's algorithm, so it is fortunate that, in practice, edge costs are nonnegative. If negative-cost cycles are present, then the algorithm as written will loop indefinitely. By stopping the algorithm after any vertex has dequeued $|V| + 1$ times, we can guarantee termination.

```
              void weightedNegative( Vertex s )
              {
                  Queue q;
                  Vertex v, w;

/* 1*/            q = new Queue( );
/* 2*/            q.enqueue( s ); // Enqueue the start vertex s

/* 3*/            while( !q.isEmpty( ) )
                  {
/* 4*/                v = q.dequeue( );
/* 5*/                for each w adjacent to v
/* 6*/                    if( v.dist + cvw < w.dist )
                          {
                              // Update w
/* 7*/                        w.dist = v.dist + cvw;
/* 8*/                        w.path = v;
/* 9*/                        if( w is not already in q )
/*10*/                            q.enqueue( w );
                          }
                  }
              }
```

Figure 9.33 Pseudocode for weighted shortest-path algorithm with negative edge costs

9.3.4. Acyclic Graphs

If the graph is known to be acyclic, we can improve Dijkstra's algorithm by changing the order in which vertices are declared *known*, otherwise known as the vertex selection rule. The new rule is to select vertices in topological order. The algorithm can be done in one pass, since the selections and updates can take place as the topological sort is being performed.

This selection rule works because when a vertex v is selected, its distance, d_v, can no longer be lowered, since by the topological ordering rule it has no incoming edges emanating from *unknown* nodes.

There is no need for a priority queue with this selection rule; the running time is $O(|E| + |V|)$, since the selection takes constant time.

An acyclic graph could model some downhill skiing problem—we want to get from point a to b, but can only go downhill, so clearly there are no cycles. Another possible application might be the modeling of (nonreversible) chemical reactions. We could have each vertex represent a particular state of an experiment. Edges would represent a transition from one state to another, and the edge weights might represent the energy released. If only transitions from a higher energy state to a lower are allowed, the graph is acyclic.

A more important use of acyclic graphs is *critical path analysis*. The graph in Figure 9.34 will serve as our example. Each node represents an activity that must be performed, along with the time it takes to complete the activity. This graph is thus known as an *activity-node* graph. The edges represent precedence relationships: An edge (v, w) means that activity v must be completed before activity w may begin. Of course, this implies that the graph must be acyclic. We assume that any activities that do not depend (either directly or indirectly) on each other can be performed in parallel by different servers.

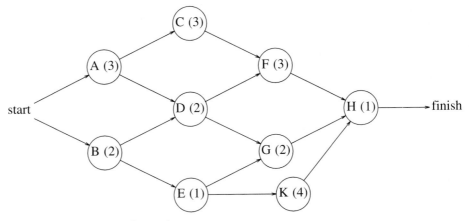

Figure 9.34 Activity-node graph

This type of a graph could be (and frequently is) used to model construction projects. In this case, there are several important questions which would be of interest to answer. First, what is the earliest completion time for the project? We can see from the graph that 10 time units are required along the path *A, C, F, H*. Another important question is to determine which activities can be delayed, and by how long, without affecting the minimum completion time. For instance, delaying any of *A, C, F,* or *H* would push the completion time past 10 units. On the other hand, activity *B* is less critical and can be delayed up to two time units without affecting the final completion time.

To perform these calculations, we convert the activity-node graph to an *event-node* graph. Each event corresponds to the completion of an activity and all its dependent activities. Events reachable from a node *v* in the event-node graph may not commence until after the event *v* is completed. This graph can be constructed automatically or by hand. Dummy edges and nodes may need to be inserted in the case where an activity depends on several others. This is necessary in order to avoid introducing false dependencies (or false lack of dependencies). The event-node graph corresponding to the graph in Figure 9.34 is shown in Figure 9.35.

To find the earliest completion time of the project, we merely need to find the length of the *longest* path from the first event to the last event. For general graphs, the longest-path problem generally does not make sense, because of the possibility of *positive-cost cycles*. These are the equivalent of negative-cost cycles in shortest-path problems. If positive-cost

Figure 9.35 Event-node graph

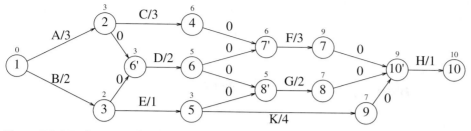

Figure 9.36 Earliest completion times

cycles are present, we could ask for the longest *simple* path, but no satisfactory solution is known for this problem. Since the event-node graph is acyclic, we need not worry about cycles. In this case, it is easy to adapt the shortest-path algorithm to compute the earliest completion time for all nodes in the graph. If EC_i is the earliest completion time for node i, then the applicable rules are

$$EC_1 = 0$$
$$EC_w = \max_{(v,w)\in E} (EC_v + c_{v,w})$$

Figure 9.36 shows the earliest completion time for each event in our example event-node graph.

We can also compute the latest time, LC_i, that each event can finish without affecting the final completion time. The formulas to do this are

$$LC_n = EC_n$$
$$LC_v = \min_{(v,w)\in E} (LC_w - c_{v,w})$$

These values can be computed in linear time by maintaining, for each vertex, a list of all adjacent and preceding vertices. The earliest completion times are computed for vertices by their topological order, and the latest completion times are computed by reverse topological order. The latest completion times are shown in Figure 9.37.

The *slack* time for each edge in the event-node graph represents the amount of time that the completion of the corresponding activity can be delayed without delaying the overall completion. It is easy to see that

$$Slack_{(v,w)} = LC_w - EC_v - c_{v,w}$$

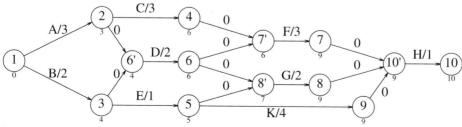

Figure 9.37 Latest completion times

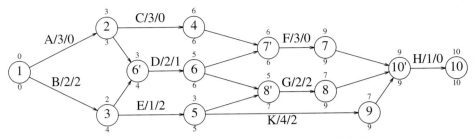

Figure 9.38 Earliest completion time, latest completion time, and slack

Figure 9.38 shows the slack (as the third entry) for each activity in the event-node graph. For each node, the top number is the earliest completion time and the bottom entry is the latest completion time.

Some activities have zero slack. These are critical activities, which must finish on schedule. There is at least one path consisting entirely of zero-slack edges; such a path is a *critical path*.

9.3.5. All-Pairs Shortest Path

Sometimes it is important to find the shortest paths between all pairs of vertices in the graph. Although we could just run the appropriate single-source algorithm $|V|$ times, we might expect a somewhat faster solution, especially on a dense graph, if we compute all the information at once.

In Chapter 10, we will see an $O(|V|^3)$ algorithm to solve this problem for weighted graphs. Although, for dense graphs, this is the same bound as running a simple (non–priority queue) Dijkstra's algorithm $|V|$ times, the loops are so tight that the specialized all-pairs algorithm is likely to be faster in practice. On sparse graphs, of course, it is faster to run $|V|$ Dijkstra's algorithms coded with priority queues.

9.4. Network Flow Problems

Suppose we are given a directed graph $G = (V, E)$ with edge capacities $c_{v,w}$. These capacities could represent the amount of water that could flow through a pipe or the amount of traffic that could flow on a street between two intersections. We have two vertices: s, which we call the *source*, and t, which is the *sink*. Through any edge, (v, w), at most $c_{v,w}$ units of "flow" may pass. At any vertex, v, that is not either s or t, the total flow coming in must equal the total flow going out. The maximum flow problem is to determine the maximum amount of flow that can pass from s to t. As an example, for the graph in Figure 9.39 on the left the maximum flow is 5, as indicated by the graph on the right.

As required by the problem statement, no edge carries more flow than its capacity. Vertex a has three units of flow coming in, which it distributes to c and d. Vertex d takes three units of flow from a and b and combines this, sending the result to t. A vertex can combine and distribute flow in any manner that it likes, as long as edge capacities are not violated and as long as flow conservation is maintained (what goes in must come out).

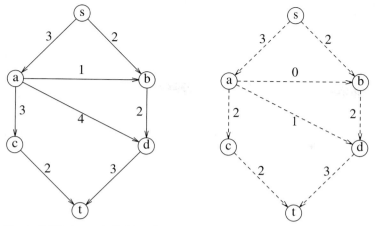

Figure 9.39 A graph (left) and its maximum flow

9.4.1. A Simple Maximum-Flow Algorithm

A first attempt to solve the problem proceeds in stages. We start with our graph, G, and construct a flow graph G_f. G_f tells the flow that has been attained at any stage in the algorithm. Initially all edges in G_f have no flow, and we hope that when the algorithm terminates, G_f contains a maximum flow. We also construct a graph, G_r, called the *residual* graph. G_r tells, for each edge, how much more flow can be added. We can calculate this by subtracting the current flow from the capacity for each edge. An edge in G_r is known as a *residual* edge.

At each stage, we find a path in G_r from s to t. This path is known as an *augmenting path*. The minimum edge on this path is the amount of flow that can be added to every edge on the path. We do this by adjusting G_f and recomputing G_r. When we find no path from s to t in G_r, we terminate. This algorithm is nondeterministic, in that we are free to choose *any* path from s to t; obviously some choices are better than others, and we will address this issue later. We will run this algorithm on our example. The graphs below are G, G_f, G_r, respectively. Keep in mind that there is a slight flaw in this algorithm. The initial configuration is in Figure 9.40.

There are many paths from s to t in the residual graph. Suppose we select s, b, d, t. Then we can send two units of flow through every edge on this path. We will adopt the

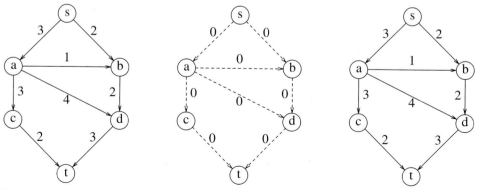

Figure 9.40 Initial stages of the graph, flow graph, and residual graph

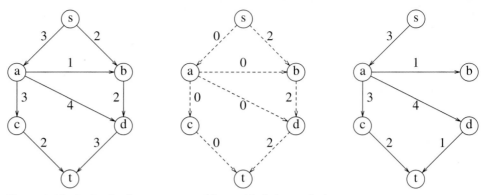

Figure 9.41 G, G_f, G_r after two units of flow added along s, b, d, t

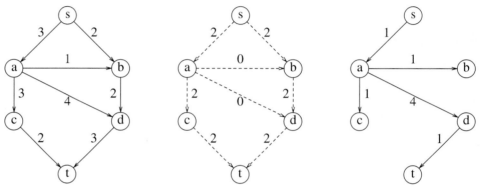

Figure 9.42 G, G_f, G_r after two units of flow added along s, a, c, t

convention that once we have filled (*saturated*) an edge, it is removed from the residual graph. We then obtain Figure 9.41.

Next, we might select the path s, a, c, t, which also allows two units of flow. Making the required adjustments gives the graphs in Figure 9.42.

The only path left to select is s, a, d, t, which allows one unit of flow. The resulting graphs are shown in Figure 9.43.

The algorithm terminates at this point, because t is unreachable from s. The resulting flow of 5 happens to be the maximum. To see what the problem is, suppose that with our initial graph, we chose the path s, a, d, t. This path allows three units of flow and thus seems to be a good choice. The result of this choice, however, is that there is now no longer any path from s to t in the residual graph, and thus, our algorithm has failed to find an optimal solution. This is an example of a greedy algorithm that does not work. Figure 9.44 shows why the algorithm fails.

In order to make this algorithm work, we need to allow the algorithm to change its mind. To do this, for every edge (v, w) with flow $f_{v,w}$ in the flow graph, we will add an edge in the residual graph (w, v) of capacity $f_{v,w}$. In effect, we are allowing the algorithm to undo its decisions by sending flow back in the opposite direction. This is best seen by example. Starting from our original graph and selecting the augmenting path s, a, d, t, we obtain the graphs in Figure 9.45.

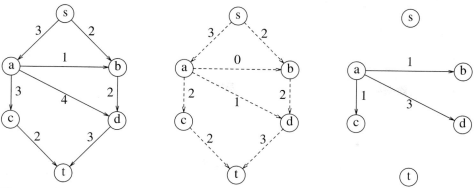

Figure 9.43 G, G_f, G_r after one unit of flow added along s, a, d, t—algorithm terminates

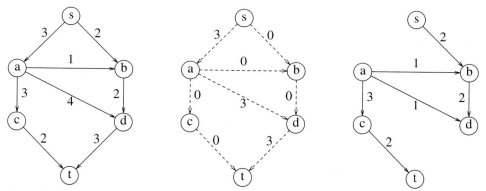

Figure 9.44 G, G_f, G_r if initial action is to add three units of flow along s, a, d, t—algorithm terminates with suboptimal solution

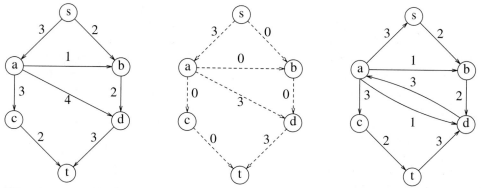

Figure 9.45 Graphs after three units of flow added along s, a, d, t using correct algorithm

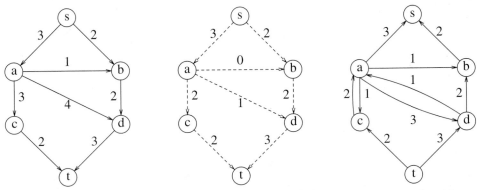

Figure 9.46 Graphs after two units of flow added along s, b, d, a, c, t using correct algorithm

Notice that in the residual graph, there are edges in both directions between a and d. Either one more unit of flow can be pushed from a to d, or up to three units can be pushed back—we can undo flow. Now the algorithm finds the augmenting path s, b, d, a, c, t, of flow 2. By pushing two units of flow from d to a, the algorithm takes two units of flow away from the edge (a, d) and is essentially changing its mind. Figure 9.46 shows the new graphs.

There is no augmenting path in this graph, so the algorithm terminates. Surprisingly, it can be shown that if the edge capacities are rational numbers, this algorithm always terminates with a maximum flow. This proof is somewhat difficult and is beyond the scope of this text. Although the example happened to be acyclic, this is not a requirement for the algorithm to work. We have used acyclic graphs merely to keep things simple.

If the capacities are all integers and the maximum flow is f, then, since each augmenting path increases the flow value by at least 1, f stages suffice, and the total running time is $O(f \cdot |E|)$, since an augmenting path can be found in $O(|E|)$ time by an unweighted shortest-path algorithm. The classic example of why this is a bad running time is shown by the graph in Figure 9.47.

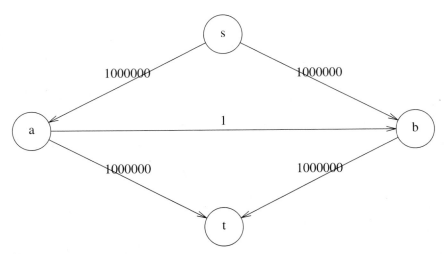

Figure 9.47 The classic bad case for augmenting

The maximum flow is seen by inspection to be 2,000,000 by sending 1,000,000 down each side. Random augmentations could continually augment along a path that includes the edge connected by a and b. If this were to occur repeatedly, 2,000,000 augmentations would be required, when we could get by with only 2.

A simple method to get around this problem is always to choose the augmenting path that allows the largest increase in flow. Finding such a path is similar to solving a weighted shortest-path problem and a single-line modification to Dijkstra's algorithm will do the trick. If cap_{max} is the maximum edge capacity, then one can show that $O(|E| \log cap_{max})$ augmentations will suffice to find the maximum flow. In this case, since $O(|E| \log |V|)$ time is used for each calculation of an augmenting path, a total bound of $O(|E|^2 \log |V| \log cap_{max})$ is obtained. If the capacities are all small integers, this reduces to $O(|E|^2 \log |V|)$.

Another way to choose augmenting paths is always to take the path with the least number of edges, with the plausible expectation that by choosing a path in this manner, it is less likely that a small, flow-restricting edge will turn up on the path. Using this rule, it can be shown that $O(|E| \cdot |V|)$ augmenting steps are required. Each step takes $O(|E|)$, again using an unweighted shortest-path algorithm, yielding an $O(|E|^2|V|)$ bound on the running time.

Further data structure improvements are possible to this algorithm, and there are several, more complicated, algorithms. A long history of improved bounds has lowered the current best-known bound for this problem. Although no $O(|E||V|)$ algorithm has been reported yet, algorithms with $O(|E||V| \log(|V|^2/|E|))$ and $O(|E||V| + |V|^{2+\varepsilon})$ bounds have been discovered (see the references). There are also a host of very good bounds for special cases. For instance, $O(|E||V|^{1/2})$ time finds a maximum flow in a graph, having the property that all vertices except the source and sink have either a single incoming edge of capacity 1 or a single outgoing edge of capacity 1. These graphs occur in many applications.

The analyses required to produce these bounds are rather intricate, and it is not clear how the worst-case results relate to the running times encountered in practice. A related, even more difficult problem is the *min-cost flow* problem. Each edge has not only a capacity but a cost per unit of flow. The problem is to find, among all maximum flows, the one flow of minimum cost. Both of these problems are being actively researched.

9.5. Minimum Spanning Tree

The next problem we will consider is that of finding a *minimum spanning tree* in an undirected graph. The problem makes sense for directed graphs but appears to be more difficult. Informally, a minimum spanning tree of an undirected graph G is a tree formed from graph edges that connects all the vertices of G at lowest total cost. A minimum spanning tree exists if and only if G is connected. Although a robust algorithm should report the case that G is unconnected, we will assume that G is connected and leave the issue of robustness as an exercise to the reader.

In Figure 9.48 the second graph is a minimum spanning tree of the first (it happens to be unique, but this is unusual). Notice that the number of edges in the minimum spanning tree is $|V| - 1$. The minimum spanning tree is a *tree* because it is acyclic, it is *spanning* because it covers every vertex, and it is *minimum* for the obvious reason. If we need to wire a house with a minimum of cable (assuming no other electrical constraints), then a minimum spanning tree problem needs to be solved.

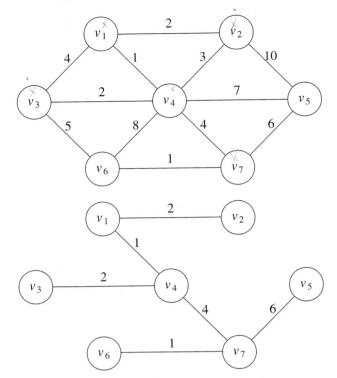

Figure 9.48 A graph G and its minimum spanning tree

For any spanning tree T, if an edge e that is not in T is added, a cycle is created. The removal of any edge on the cycle reinstates the spanning tree property. The cost of the spanning tree is lowered if e has lower cost than the edge that was removed. If, as a spanning tree is created, the edge that is added is the one of minimum cost that avoids creation of a cycle, then the cost of the resulting spanning tree cannot be improved, because any replacement edge would have cost at least as much as an edge already in the spanning tree. This shows that greed works for the minimum spanning tree problem. The two algorithms we present differ in how a minimum edge is selected.

9.5.1. Prim's Algorithm

One way to compute a minimum spanning tree is to grow the tree in successive stages. In each stage, one node is picked as the root, and we add an edge, and thus an associated vertex, to the tree.

At any point in the algorithm, we can see that we have a set of vertices that have already been included in the tree; the rest of the vertices have not. The algorithm then finds, at each stage, a new vertex to add to the tree by choosing the edge (u, v) such that the cost of (u, v) is the smallest among all edges where u is in the tree and v is not. Figure 9.49 shows how this algorithm would build the minimum spanning tree, starting from v_1. Initially, v_1 is in the tree as a root with no edges. Each step adds one edge and one vertex to the tree.

We can see that Prim's algorithm is essentially identical to Dijkstra's algorithm for shortest paths. As before, for each vertex we keep values d_v and p_v and an indication of whether

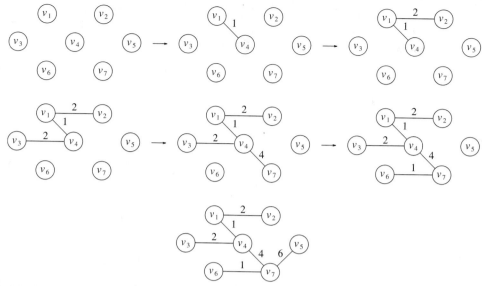

Figure 9.49 Prim's algorithm after each stage

v	known	d_v	p_v
v_1	F	0	0
v_2	F	∞	0
v_3	F	∞	0
v_4	F	∞	0
v_5	F	∞	0
v_6	F	∞	0
v_7	F	∞	0

Figure 9.50 Initial configuration of table used in Prim's algorithm

it is *known* or *unknown*. d_v is the weight of the shortest edge connecting v to a *known* vertex, and p_v, as before, is the last vertex to cause a change in d_v. The rest of the algorithm is exactly the same, with the exception that since the definition of d_v is different, so is the update rule. For this problem, the update rule is even simpler than before: After a vertex v is selected, for each *unknown* w adjacent to v, $d_w = \min(d_w, c_{w,v})$.

The initial configuration of the table is shown in Figure 9.50. v_1 is selected, and v_2, v_3, and v_4 are updated. The table resulting from this is shown in Figure 9.51. The next vertex selected is v_4. Every vertex is adjacent to v_4. v_1 is not examined, because it is *known*. v_2 is unchanged, because it has $d_v = 2$ and the edge cost from v_4 to v_2 is 3; all the rest are updated. Figure 9.52 shows the resulting table. The next vertex chosen is v_2 (arbitrarily breaking a tie). This does not affect any distances. Then v_3 is chosen, which affects the distance in v_6, producing Figure 9.53. Figure 9.54 results from the selection of v_7, which forces v_6 and v_5 to be adjusted. v_6 and then v_5 are selected, completing the algorithm.

v	known	d_v	p_v
v_1	T	0	0
v_2	F	2	v_1
v_3	F	4	v_1
v_4	F	1	v_1
v_5	F	∞	0
v_6	F	∞	0
v_7	F	∞	0

Figure 9.51 The table after v_1 is declared *known*

v	known	d_v	p_v
v_1	T	0	0
v_2	F	2	v_1
v_3	F	2	v_4
v_4	T	1	v_1
v_5	F	7	v_4
v_6	F	8	v_4
v_7	F	4	v_4

Figure 9.52 The table after v_4 is declared *known*

v	known	d_v	p_v
v_1	T	0	0
v_2	T	2	v_1
v_3	T	2	v_4
v_4	T	1	v_1
v_5	F	7	v_4
v_6	F	5	v_3
v_7	F	4	v_4

Figure 9.53 The table after v_2 and then v_3 are declared *known*

v	known	d_v	p_v
v_1	T	0	0
v_2	T	2	v_1
v_3	T	2	v_4
v_4	T	1	v_1
v_5	F	6	v_7
v_6	F	1	v_7
v_7	T	4	v_4

Figure 9.54 The table after v_7 is declared *known*

v	known	d_v	p_v
v_1	T	0	0
v_2	T	2	v_1
v_3	T	2	v_4
v_4	T	1	v_1
v_5	T	6	v_7
v_6	T	1	v_7
v_7	T	4	v_4

Figure 9.55 The table after v_6 and v_5 are selected
(Prim's algorithm terminates)

The final table is shown in Figure 9.55. The edges in the spanning tree can be read from the table: (v_2, v_1), (v_3, v_4), (v_4, v_1), (v_5, v_7), (v_6, v_7), (v_7, v_4). The total cost is 16.

The entire implementation of this algorithm is virtually identical to that of Dijkstra's algorithm, and everything that was said about the analysis of Dijkstra's algorithm applies here. Be aware that Prim's algorithm runs on undirected graphs, so when coding it, remember to put every edge in two adjacency lists. The running time is $O(|V|^2)$ without heaps, which is optimal for dense graphs, and $O(|E| \log |V|)$ using binary heaps, which is good for sparse graphs.

9.5.2. Kruskal's Algorithm

A second greedy strategy is continually to select the edges in order of smallest weight and accept an edge if it does not cause a cycle. The action of the algorithm on the graph in the preceding example is shown in Figure 9.56.

Formally, Kruskal's algorithm maintains a forest—a collection of trees. Initially, there are $|V|$ single-node trees. Adding an edge merges two trees into one. When the algorithm terminates, there is only one tree, and this is the minimum spanning tree. Figure 9.57 shows the order in which edges are added to the forest.

Edge	Weight	Action
(v_1, v_4)	1	Accepted
(v_6, v_7)	1	Accepted
(v_1, v_2)	2	Accepted
(v_3, v_4)	2	Accepted
(v_2, v_4)	3	Rejected
(v_1, v_3)	4	Rejected
(v_4, v_7)	4	Accepted
(v_3, v_6)	5	Rejected
(v_5, v_7)	6	Accepted

Figure 9.56 Action of Kruskal's algorithm on G

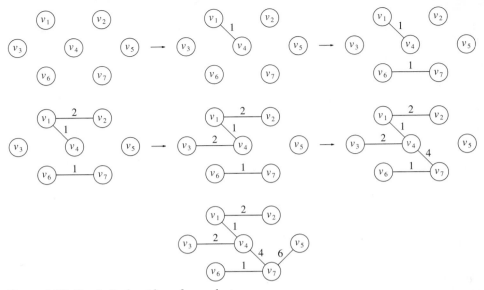

Figure 9.57 Kruskal's algorithm after each stage

```
public void kruskal( )
{
    int edgesAccepted;
    DisjSet s;
    PriorityQueue h;
    Vertex u, v;
    SetType uset, vset;
    Edge e;

/* 1*/    h = readGraphIntoHeapArray( );
/* 2*/    h.buildHeap( );
/* 3*/    s = new DisjSet( NUM_VERTICES );

/* 4*/    edgesAccepted = 0;
/* 5*/    while( edgesAccepted < NUM_VERTICES - 1 )
          {
/* 6*/        e = h.deleteMin( );   // Edge e = (u,v)
/* 7*/        uset = s.find( u );
/* 8*/        vset = s.find( v );
/* 9*/        if( uset != vset )
              {
                  // Accept the edge
/*10*/            edgesAccepted++;
/*11*/            s.union( uset, vset );
              }
          }
}
```

Figure 9.58 Pseudocode for Kruskal's algorithm

The algorithm terminates when enough edges are accepted. It turns out to be simple to decide whether edge (u, v) should be accepted or rejected. The appropriate data structure is the union/find algorithm of the previous chapter.

The invariant we will use is that at any point in the process, two vertices belong to the same set if and only if they are connected in the current spanning forest. Thus, each vertex is initially in its own set. If u and v are in the same set, the edge is rejected, because since they are already connected, adding (u, v) would form a cycle. Otherwise, the edge is accepted, and a **union** is performed on the two sets containing u and v. It is easy to see that this maintains the set invariant, because once the edge (u, v) is added to the spanning forest, if w was connected to u and x was connected to v, then x and w must now be connected, and thus belong in the same set.

The edges could be sorted to facilitate the selection, but building a heap in linear time is a much better idea. Then **deleteMin**s give the edges to be tested in order. Typically, only a small fraction of the edges need to be tested before the algorithm can terminate, although it is always possible that all the edges must be tried. For instance, if there was an extra vertex v_8 and edge (v_5, v_8) of cost 100, all the edges would have to be examined. Method **kruskal** in Figure 9.58 finds a minimum spanning tree.

The worst-case running time of this algorithm is $O(|E| \log |E|)$, which is dominated by the heap operations. Notice that since $|E| = O(|V|^2)$, this running time is actually $O(|E| \log |V|)$. In practice, the algorithm is much faster than this time bound would indicate.

9.6. Applications of Depth-First Search

Depth-first search is a generalization of preorder traversal. Starting at some vertex, v, we process v and then recursively traverse all vertices adjacent to v. If this process is performed on a tree, then all tree vertices are systematically visited in a total of $O(|E|)$ time, since $|E| = \Theta(|V|)$. If we perform this process on an arbitrary graph, we need to be careful to avoid cycles. To do this, when we visit a vertex v, we *mark* it visited, since now we have been there, and recursively call depth-first search on all adjacent vertices that are not already marked. We implicitly assume that for undirected graphs every edge (v, w) appears twice in the adjacency lists: once as (v, w) and once as (w, v). The procedure in Figure 9.59 performs a depth-first search (and does absolutely nothing else) and is a template for the general style.

For each vertex, the field **visited** is initialized to **false**. By recursively calling the procedures only on nodes that have not been visited, we guarantee that we do not loop

```
void dfs( Vertex v )
{
    v.visited = true;
    for each w adjacent to v
        if( !w.visited )
            dfs( w );
}
```

Figure 9.59 Template for depth-first search

indefinitely. If the graph is undirected and not connected, or directed and not strongly connected, this strategy might fail to visit some nodes. We then search for an unmarked node, apply a depth-first traversal there, and continue this process until there are no unmarked nodes.[*] Because this strategy guarantees that each edge is encountered only once, the total time to perform the traversal is $O(|E| + |V|)$, as long as adjacency lists are used.

9.6.1. Undirected Graphs

An undirected graph is connected if and only if a depth-first search starting from any node visits every node. Because this test is so easy to apply, we will assume that the graphs we deal with are connected. If they are not, then we can find all the connected components and apply our algorithm on each of these in turn.

As an example of depth-first search, suppose in the graph of Figure 9.60 we start at vertex A. Then we mark A as visited and call **dfs(B)** recursively. **dfs(B)** marks B as visited and calls **dfs(C)** recursively. **dfs(C)** marks C as visited and calls **dfs(D)** recursively. **dfs(D)** sees both A and B, but both of these are marked, so no recursive calls are made. **dfs(D)** also sees that C is adjacent but marked, so no recursive call is made there, and **dfs(D)** returns back to **dfs(C)**. **dfs(C)** sees B adjacent, ignores it, finds a previously unseen vertex E adjacent, and thus calls **dfs(E)**. **dfs(E)** marks E, ignores A and C, and returns to **dfs(C)**. **dfs(C)** returns to **dfs(B)**. **dfs(B)** ignores both A and D and returns. **dfs(A)** ignores both D and E and returns. (We have actually touched every edge twice, once as (v, w) and again as (w, v), but this is really once per adjacency list entry.)

We graphically illustrate these steps with a *depth-first spanning tree*. The root of the tree is A, the first vertex visited. Each edge (v, w) in the graph is present in the tree. If, when we process (v, w), we find that w is unmarked, or if, when we process (w, v), we find that v is

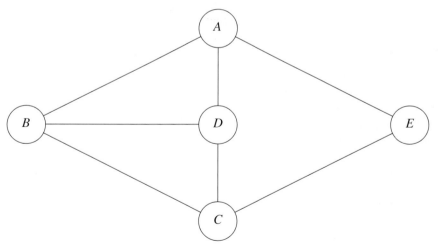

Figure 9.60 An undirected graph

---

[*]An efficient way of implementing this is to begin the depth-first search at v_1. If we need to restart the depth-first search, we examine the sequence $v_k, v_{k+1}, \ldots$ for an unmarked vertex, where v_{k-1} is the vertex where the last depth-first search was started. This guarantees that throughout the algorithm, only $O(|V|)$ is spent looking for vertices where new depth-first search trees can be started.

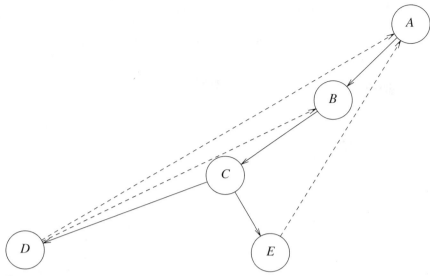

Figure 9.61 Depth-first search of previous graph

unmarked, we indicate this with a tree edge. If, when we process (v, w), we find that w is already marked, and when processing (w, v), we find that v is already marked, we draw a dashed line, which we will call a *back edge,* to indicate that this "edge" is not really part of the tree. The depth-first search of the graph in Figure 9.60 is shown in Figure 9.61.

The tree will simulate the traversal we performed. A preorder numbering of the tree, using only tree edges, tells us the order in which the vertices were marked. If the graph is not connected, then processing all nodes (and edges) requires several calls to dfs, and each generates a tree. This entire collection is a *depth-first spanning forest.*

9.6.2. Biconnectivity

A connected undirected graph is *biconnected* if there are no vertices whose removal disconnects the rest of the graph. The graph in the example above is biconnected. If the nodes are computers and the edges are links, then if any computer goes down, network mail is unaffected, except, of course, at the down computer. Similarly, if a mass transit system is biconnected, users always have an alternate route should some terminal be disrupted.

If a graph is not biconnected, the vertices whose removal would disconnect the graph are known as *articulation points.* These nodes are critical in many applications. The graph in Figure 9.62 is not biconnected: C and D are articulation points. The removal of C would disconnect G, and the removal of D would disconnect E and F, from the rest of the graph.

Depth-first search provides a linear-time algorithm to find all articulation points in a connected graph. First, starting at any vertex, we perform a depth-first search and number the nodes as they are visited. For each vertex v, we call this preorder number $Num(v)$. Then, for every vertex v in the depth-first search spanning tree, we compute the lowest-numbered vertex, which we call $Low(v)$, that is reachable from v by taking zero or more tree edges and then possibly one back edge (in that order). The depth-first search tree in Figure 9.63 shows the preorder number first, and then the lowest-numbered vertex reachable under the rule described above.

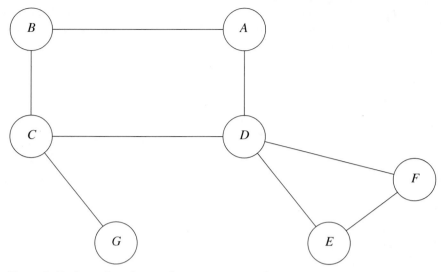

Figure 9.62 A graph with articulation points *C* and *D*

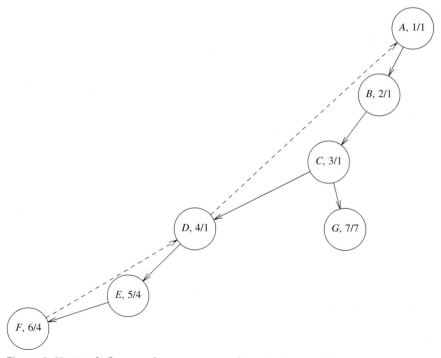

Figure 9.63 Depth-first tree for previous graph, with *Num* and *Low*

The lowest-numbered vertex reachable by A, B, and C is vertex 1 (A), because they can all take tree edges to D and then one back edge back to A. We can efficiently compute *Low* by performing a postorder traversal of the depth-first spanning tree. By the definition of *Low*, $Low(v)$ is the minimum of

1. $Num(v)$
2. the lowest $Num(w)$ among all back edges (v, w)
3. the lowest $Low(w)$ among all tree edges (v, w)

The first condition is the option of taking no edges, the second way is to choose no tree edges and a back edge, and the third way is to choose some tree edges and possibly a back edge. This third method is succinctly described with a recursive call. Since we need to evaluate *Low* for all the children of v before we can evaluate $Low(v)$, this is a postorder traversal. For any edge (v, w), we can tell whether it is a tree edge or a back edge merely by checking $Num(v)$ and $Num(w)$. Thus, it is easy to compute $Low(v)$: we merely scan down v's adjacency list, apply the proper rule, and keep track of the minimum. Doing all the computation takes $O(|E| + |V|)$ time.

All that is left to do is to use this information to find articulation points. The root is an articulation point if and only if it has more than one child, because if it has two children, removing the root disconnects nodes in different subtrees, and if it has only one child, removing the root merely disconnects the root. Any other vertex v is an articulation point if and only if v has some child w such that $Low(w) \geq Num(v)$. Notice that this condition is always satisfied at the root; hence the need for a special test.

The *if* part of the proof is clear when we examine the articulation points that the algorithm determines, namely, C and D. D has a child E, and $Low(E) \geq Num(D)$, since both are 4. Thus, there is only one way for E to get to any node above D, and that is by going through D. Similarly, C is an articulation point, because $Low(G) \geq Num(C)$. To prove that this algorithm is correct, one must show that the *only if* part of the assertion is true (that is, this finds *all* articulation points). We leave this as an exercise. As a second example, we show (Fig. 9.64) the result of applying this algorithm on the same graph, starting the depth-first search at C.

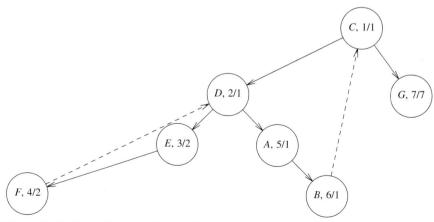

Figure 9.64 Depth-first tree that results if depth-first search starts at C

We close by giving pseudocode to implement this algorithm. We will assume that **Vertex** contains the data fields `visited` (initialized to `false`), `num`, `low`, and `parent`. We will also keep a (**Graph**) class variable called `counter`, which is initialized to 1, to assign the preorder traversal numbers, `num`. We also leave out the easily implemented test for the root.

As we have already stated, this algorithm can be implemented by performing a preorder traversal to compute *Num* and then a postorder traversal to compute *Low*. A third traversal can be used to check which vertices satisfy the articulation point criteria. Performing three traversals, however, would be a waste. The first pass is shown in Figure 9.65.

```
        // Assign Num and compute parents

        void assignNum( Vertex v )
        {
            Vertex w;

/* 1*/      v.num = counter++;
/* 2*/      v.visited = true;
/* 3*/      for each w adjacent to v
/* 4*/          if( !w.visited )
                {
/* 5*/              w.parent = v;
/* 6*/              assignNum( w );
                }
        }
```

Figure 9.65 Routine to assign *Num* to vertices (pseudocode)

```
        // Assign low; also check for articulation points.

        void assignLow( Vertex v )
        {
            Vertex w;

/* 1*/      v.low = v.num;  // Rule 1
/* 2*/      for each w adjacent to v
            {
/* 3*/          if( w.num > v.num )  // Forward edge
                {
/* 4*/              assignLow( w );
/* 5*/              if( w.low >= v.num )
/* 6*/                  System.out.println( v + " is an articulation point" );
/* 7*/              v.low = min( v.low, w.low );  // Rule 3
                }
                else
/* 8*/          if( v.parent != w )  // Back edge
/* 9*/              v.low = min( v.low, w.num );  // Rule 2
            }
        }
```

Figure 9.66 Pseudocode to compute *Low* and to test for articulation points (test for the root is omitted)

```
         void findArt( Vertex v )
         {
             Vertex w;

/* 1*/       v.visited = true;
/* 2*/       v.low = v.num = counter++;   // Rule 1
/* 3*/       for each w adjacent to v
             {
/* 4*/           if( !w.visited )  // Forward edge
                 {
/* 5*/               w.parent = v;
/* 6*/               findArt( w );
/* 7*/               if( w.low >= v.num )
/* 8*/                   System.out.println( v + " is an articulation point" );
/* 9*/               v.low = min( v.low, w.low );  // Rule 3
                 }
                 else
/*10*/           if( v.parent != w )  // Back edge
/*11*/               v.low = min( v.low, w.num );  // Rule 2
             }
         }
```

Figure 9.67 Testing for articulation points in one depth-first search (test for the root is omitted) (pseudocode)

The second and third passes, which are postorder traversals, can be implemented by the code in Figure 9.66. Line 8 handles a special case. If *w* is adjacent to *v*, then the recursive call to *w* will find *v* adjacent to *w*. This is not a back edge, only an edge that has already been considered and needs to be ignored. Otherwise, the procedure computes the minimum of the various **low** and **num** entries, as specified by the algorithm.

There is no rule that a traversal must be either preorder or postorder. It is possible to do processing both before and after the recursive calls. The procedure in Figure 9.67 combines the two routines **assignNum** and **assignLow** in a straightforward manner to produce the procedure **findArt**.

9.6.3. Euler Circuits

Consider the three figures in Figure 9.68. A popular puzzle is to reconstruct these figures using a pen, drawing each line exactly once. The pen may not be lifted from the paper while the drawing is being performed. As an extra challenge, make the pen finish at the

Figure 9.68 Three drawings

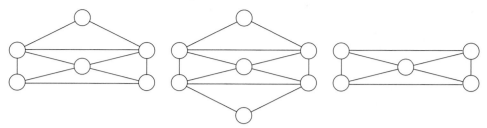

Figure 9.69 Conversion of puzzle to graph

same point at which it started. This puzzle has a surprisingly simple solution. Stop reading if you would like to try to solve it.

The first figure can be drawn only if the starting point is the lower left- or right-hand corner, and it is not possible to finish at the starting point. The second figure is easily drawn with the finishing point the same as the starting point, but the third figure cannot be drawn at all within the parameters of the puzzle.

We can convert this problem to a graph theory problem by assigning a vertex to each intersection. Then the edges can be assigned in the natural manner, as in Figure 9.69.

After this conversion is performed, we must find a path in the graph that visits every edge exactly once. If we are to solve the "extra challenge," then we must find a cycle that visits every edge exactly once. This graph problem was solved in 1736 by Euler and marked the beginning of graph theory. The problem is thus commonly referred to as an *Euler path* (sometimes *Euler tour*) or *Euler circuit problem,* depending on the specific problem statement. The Euler tour and Euler circuit problems, though slightly different, have the same basic solution. Thus, we will consider the Euler circuit problem in this section.

The first observation that can be made is that an Euler circuit, which must end on its starting vertex, is possible only if the graph is connected and each vertex has an even degree (number of edges). This is because, on the Euler circuit, a vertex is entered and then left. If any vertex v has odd degree, then eventually we will reach the point where only one edge into v is unvisited, and taking it will strand us at v. If exactly two vertices have odd degree, an Euler tour, which must visit every edge but need not return to its starting vertex, is still possible if we start at one of the odd-degree vertices and finish at the other. If more than two vertices have odd degree, then an Euler tour is not possible.

The observations of the preceding paragraph provide us with a necessary condition for the existence of an Euler circuit. It does not, however, tell us that all connected graphs that satisfy this property must have an Euler circuit, nor does it give us guidance on how to find one. It turns out that the necessary condition is also sufficient. That is, any connected graph, all of whose vertices have even degree, must have an Euler circuit. Furthermore, a circuit can be found in linear time.

We can assume that we know that an Euler circuit exists, since we can test the necessary and sufficient condition in linear time. Then the basic algorithm is to perform a depth-first search. There are a surprisingly large number of "obvious" solutions that do not work. Some of these are presented in the exercises.

The main problem is that we might visit a portion of the graph and return to the starting point prematurely. If all the edges coming out of the start vertex have been used up, then part of the graph is untraversed. The easiest way to fix this is to find the first vertex on this path that has an untraversed edge, and perform another depth-first search. This will give

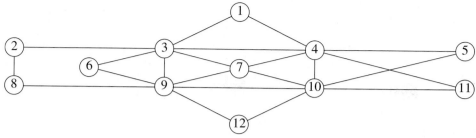

Figure 9.70 Graph for Euler circuit problem

another circuit, which can be spliced into the original. This is continued until all edges have been traversed.

As an example, consider the graph in Figure 9.70. It is easily seen that this graph has an Euler circuit. Suppose we start at vertex 5, and traverse the circuit 5, 4, 10, 5. Then we are stuck, and most of the graph is still untraversed. The situation is shown in Figure 9.71.

We then continue from vertex 4, which still has unexplored edges. A depth-first search might come up with the path 4, 1, 3, 7, 4, 11, 10, 7, 9, 3, 4. If we splice this path into the previous path of 5, 4, 10, 5, then we get a new path of 5, 4, 1, 3, 7, 4, 11, 10, 7, 9, 3, 4, 10, 5.

The graph that remains after this is shown in Figure 9.72. Notice that in this graph all the vertices must have even degree, so we are guaranteed to find a cycle to add. The remaining graph might not be connected, but this is not important. The next vertex on the

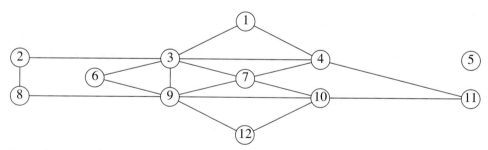

Figure 9.71 Graph remaining after 5, 4, 10, 5

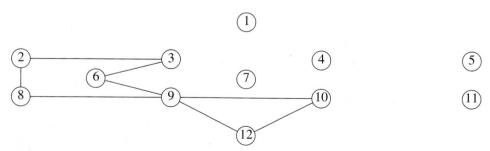

Figure 9.72 Graph after the path 5, 4, 1, 3, 7, 4, 11, 10, 7, 9, 3, 4, 10, 5

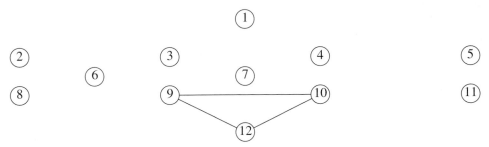

Figure 9.73 Graph remaining after the path 5, 4, 1, 3, 2, 8, 9, 6, 3, 7, 4, 11, 10, 7, 9, 3, 4, 10, 5

path that has untraversed edges is vertex 3. A possible circuit would then be 3, 2, 8, 9, 6, 3. When spliced in, this gives the path 5, 4, 1, 3, 2, 8, 9, 6, 3, 7, 4, 11, 10, 7, 9, 3, 4, 10, 5.

The graph that remains is in Figure 9.73. On this path, the next vertex with an untraversed edge is 9, and the algorithm finds the circuit 9, 12, 10, 9. When this is added to the current path, a circuit of 5, 4, 1, 3, 2, 8, 9, 12, 10, 9, 6, 3, 7, 4, 11, 10, 7, 9, 3, 4, 10, 5 is obtained. As all the edges are traversed, the algorithm terminates with an Euler circuit.

To make this algorithm efficient, we must use appropriate data structures. We will sketch some of the ideas, leaving the implementation as an exercise. To make splicing simple, the path should be maintained as a linked list. To avoid repetitious scanning of adjacency lists, we must maintain, for each adjacency list, the last edge scanned. When a path is spliced in, the search for a new vertex from which to perform the next depth-first search must begin at the start of the splice point. This guarantees that the total work performed on the vertex search phase is $O(|E|)$ during the entire life of the algorithm. With the appropriate data structures, the running time of the algorithm is $O(|E| + |V|)$.

A very similar problem is to find a simple cycle, in an undirected graph, that visits every vertex. This is known as the *Hamiltonian cycle problem*. Although it seems almost identical to the Euler circuit problem, no efficient algorithm for it is known. We shall see this problem again in Section 9.7.

9.6.4. Directed Graphs

Using the same strategy as with undirected graphs, directed graphs can be traversed in linear time, using depth-first search. If the graph is not strongly connected, a depth-first search starting at some node might not visit all nodes. In this case we repeatedly perform depth-first searches, starting at some unmarked node, until all vertices have been visited. As an example, consider the directed graph in Figure 9.74.

We arbitrarily start the depth-first search at vertex *B*. This visits vertices *B*, *C*, *A*, *D*, *E*, and *F*. We then restart at some unvisited vertex. Arbitrarily, we start at *H*, which visits *I* and *J*. Finally, we start at *G*, which is the last vertex that needs to be visited. The corresponding depth-first search tree is shown in Figure 9.75.

The dashed arrows in the depth-first spanning forest are edges (*v*, *w*) for which *w* was already marked at the time of consideration. In undirected graphs, these are always back edges, but, as we can see, there are three types of edges that do not lead to new vertices. First, there are *back edges*, such as (*A*, *B*) and (*I*, *H*). There are also *forward edges*, such as (*C*, *D*) and (*C*, *E*), that lead from a tree node to a descendant. Finally, there are *cross edges*, such as (*F*, *C*) and (*G*, *F*), which connect two tree nodes that are not directly related.

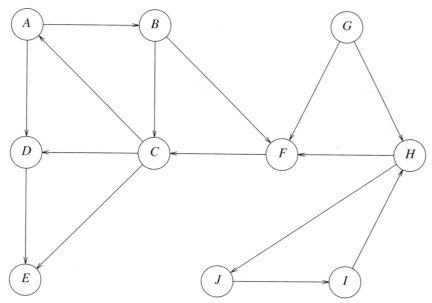

Figure 9.74 A directed graph

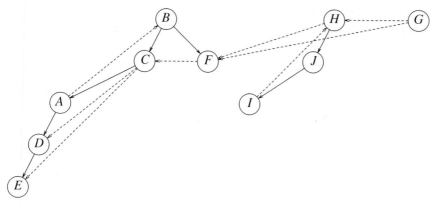

Figure 9.75 Depth-first search of previous graph

Depth-first search forests are generally drawn with children and new trees added to the forest from left to right. In a depth-first search of a directed graph drawn in this manner, cross edges always go from right to left.

Some algorithms that use depth-first search need to distinguish between the three types of nontree edges. This is easy to check as the depth-first search is being performed, and it is left as an exercise.

One use of depth-first search is to test whether or not a directed graph is acyclic. The rule is that a directed graph is acyclic if and only if it has no back edges. (The graph above has back edges, and thus is not acyclic.) The reader may remember that a topological sort can also be used to determine whether a graph is acyclic. Another way to perform topological sorting is to assign the vertices topological numbers $N, N - 1, \ldots, 1$ by postorder traversal of the depth-first spanning forest. As long as the graph is acyclic, this ordering will be consistent.

9.6.5. Finding Strong Components

By performing two depth-first searches, we can test whether a directed graph is strongly connected, and if it is not, we can actually produce the subsets of vertices that are strongly connected to themselves. This can also be done in only one depth-first search, but the method used here is much simpler to understand.

First, a depth-first search is performed on the input graph G. The vertices of G are numbered by a postorder traversal of the depth-first spanning forest, and then all edges in G are reversed, forming G_r. The graph in Figure 9.76 represents G_r for the graph G shown in Figure 9.74; the vertices are shown with their numbers.

The algorithm is completed by performing a depth-first search on G_r, always starting a new depth-first search at the highest-numbered vertex. Thus, we begin the depth-first search of G_r at vertex G, which is numbered 10. This leads nowhere, so the next search is started at H. This call visits I and J. The next call starts at B and visits A, C, and F. The next calls after this are **dfs(D)** and finally **dfs(E)**. The resulting depth-first spanning forest is shown in Figure 9.77.

Each of the trees (this is easier to see if you completely ignore all nontree edges) in this depth-first spanning forest forms a strongly connected component. Thus, for our example, the strongly connected components are $\{G\}$, $\{H, I, J\}$, $\{B, A, C, F\}$, $\{D\}$, and $\{E\}$.

To see why this algorithm works, first note that if two vertices v and w are in the same strongly connected component, then there are paths from v to w and from w to v in the original graph G, and hence also in G_r. Now, if two vertices v and w are not in the

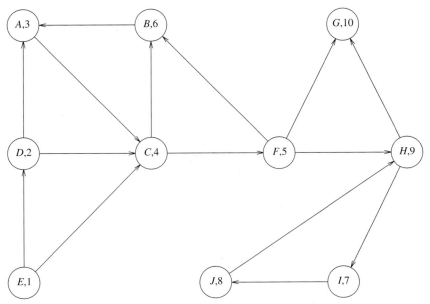

Figure 9.76 G_r numbered by postorder traversal of G (from Fig. 9.74)

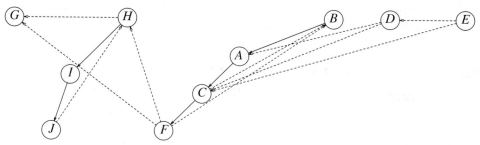

Figure 9.77 Depth-first search of G_r—strong components are $\{G\}, \{H, I, J\}, \{B, A, C, F\}, \{D\}, \{E\}$

same depth-first spanning tree of G_r, clearly they cannot be in the same strongly connected component.

To prove that this algorithm works, we must show that if two vertices v and w are in the same depth-first spanning tree of G_r, there must be paths from v to w and from w to v. Equivalently, we can show that if x is the root of the depth-first spanning tree of G_r containing v, then there is a path from x to v and from v to x. Applying the same logic to w would then give a path from x to w and from w to x. These paths would imply paths from v to w and w to v (going through x).

Since v is a descendant of x in G_r's depth-first spanning tree, there is a path from x to v in G_r and thus a path from v to x in G. Furthermore, since x is the root, x has the higher postorder number from the first depth-first search. Therefore, during the first depth-first search, all the work processing v was completed before the work at x was completed. Since there is a path from v to x, it follows that v must be a descendant of x in the spanning tree for G—otherwise v would finish *after* x. This implies a path from x to v in G and completes the proof.

9.7. Introduction to NP-Completeness

In this chapter, we have seen solutions to a wide variety of graph theory problems. All these problems have polynomial running times, and with the exception of the network flow problem, the running time is either linear or only slightly more than linear ($O(|E| \log |E|)$). We have also mentioned, in passing, that for some problems certain variations seem harder than the original.

Recall that the Euler circuit problem, which finds a path that touches every edge exactly once, is solvable in linear time. The Hamiltonian cycle problem asks for a simple cycle that contains every vertex. No linear algorithm is known for this problem.

The single-source unweighted shortest-path problem for directed graphs is also solvable in linear time. No linear-time algorithm is known for the corresponding longest-simple-path problem.

The situation for these problem variations is actually much worse than we have described. Not only are no linear algorithms known for these variations, but there are no known algorithms that are guaranteed to run in polynomial time. The best known algorithms for these problems could take exponential time on some inputs.

In this section we will take a brief look at this problem. This topic is rather complex, so we will only take a quick and informal look at it. Because of this, the discussion may be (necessarily) somewhat imprecise in places.

We will see that there are a host of important problems that are roughly equivalent in complexity. These problems form a class called the *NP-complete* problems. The exact complexity of these *NP*-complete problems has yet to be determined and remains the foremost open problem in theoretical computer science. Either all these problems have polynomial-time solutions or none of them do.

9.7.1. Easy vs. Hard

When classifying problems, the first step is to examine the boundaries. We have already seen that many problems can be solved in linear time. We have also seen some $O(\log N)$ running times, but these either assume some preprocessing (such as input already being read or a data structure already being built) or occur on arithmetic examples. For instance, the *gcd* algorithm, when applied on two numbers M and N, takes $O(\log N)$ time. Since the numbers consist of $\log M$ and $\log N$ bits respectively, the *gcd* algorithm is really taking time that is linear in the *amount* or *size* of input. Thus, when we measure running time, we will be concerned with the running time as a function of the amount of input. Generally, we cannot expect better than linear running time.

At the other end of the spectrum lie some truly hard problems. These problems are so hard that they are *impossible*. This does not mean the typical exasperated moan, which means that it would take a genius to solve the problem. Just as real numbers are not sufficient to express a solution to $x^2 < 0$, one can prove that computers cannot solve every problem that happens to come along. These "impossible" problems are called *undecidable* problems.

One particular undecidable problem is the *halting problem*. Is it possible to have your Java compiler have an extra feature that not only detects syntax errors but also all infinite loops? This seems like a hard problem, but one might expect that if some very clever programmers spent enough time on it, they could produce this enhancement.

The intuitive reason that this problem is undecidable is that such a program might have a hard time checking itself. For this reason, these problems are sometimes called *recursively undecidable*.

If an infinite loop–checking program could be written, surely it could be used to check itself. We could then produce a program called *LOOP*. *LOOP* takes as input a program P and runs P on itself. It prints out the phrase *YES* if P loops when run on itself. If P terminates when run on itself, a natural thing to do would be to print out *NO*. Instead of doing that, we will have *LOOP* go into an infinite loop.

What happens when *LOOP* is given itself as input? Either *LOOP* halts, or it does not halt. The problem is that both these possibilities lead to contradictions, in much the same way as does the phrase "This sentence is a lie."

By our definition, *LOOP*(P) goes into an infinite loop if $P(P)$ terminates. Suppose that when $P = LOOP$, $P(P)$ terminates. Then, according to the *LOOP* program, *LOOP*(P) is obligated to go into an infinite loop. Thus, we must have *LOOP*(LOOP) terminating *and* entering an infinite loop, which is clearly not possible. On the other hand, suppose that when $P = LOOP$, $P(P)$ enters an infinite loop. Then *LOOP*(P) must terminate, and we arrive at the same set of contradictions. Thus, we see that the program *LOOP* cannot possibly exist.

9.7.2. The Class NP

A few steps down from the horrors of undecidable problems lies the class *NP*. *NP* stands for *nondeterministic polynomial-time*. A deterministic machine, at each point in time, is executing an instruction. Depending on the instruction, it then goes to some next instruction, which is unique. A nondeterministic machine has a choice of next steps. It is free to choose any that it wishes, and if one of these steps leads to a solution, it will always choose the correct one. A nondeterministic machine thus has the power of extremely good (optimal) guessing. This probably seems like a ridiculous model, since nobody could possibly build a nondeterministic computer, and because it would seem to be an incredible upgrade to your standard computer (every problem might now seem trivial). We will see that nondeterminism is a very useful theoretical construct. Furthermore, nondeterminism is not as powerful as one might think. For instance, undecidable problems are still undecidable, even if nondeterminism is allowed.

A simple way to check if a problem is in *NP* is to phrase the problem as a yes/no question. The problem is in *NP* if, in polynomial time, we can prove that any "yes" instance is correct. We do not have to worry about "no" instances, since the program always makes the right choice. Thus, for the Hamiltonian cycle problem, a "yes" instance would be any simple circuit in the graph that includes all the vertices. This is in *NP*, since, given the path, it is a simple matter to check that it is really a Hamiltonian cycle. Appropriately phrased questions, such as "Is there a simple path of length $> K$?" can also easily be checked and are in *NP*. Any path that satisfies this property can be checked trivially.

The class *NP* includes all problems that have polynomial-time solutions, since obviously the solution provides a check. One would expect that since it is so much easier to check an answer than to come up with one from scratch, there would be problems in *NP* that do not have polynomial-time solutions. To date no such problem has been found, so it is entirely possible, though not considered likely by experts, that nondeterminism is not such an important improvement. The problem is that proving exponential lower bounds is an extremely difficult task. The information theory bound technique, which we used to show that sorting requires $\Omega(N \log N)$ comparisons, does not seem to be adequate for the task, because the decision trees are not nearly large enough.

Notice also that not all decidable problems are in *NP*. Consider the problem of determining whether a graph *does not* have a Hamiltonian cycle. To prove that a graph has a Hamiltonian cycle is a relatively simple matter—we just need to exhibit one. Nobody knows how to show, in polynomial time, that a graph does not have a Hamiltonian cycle. It seems that one must enumerate all the cycles and check them one by one. Thus the Non–Hamiltonian cycle problem is not known to be in *NP*.

9.7.3. NP-Complete Problems

Among all the problems known to be in *NP*, there is a subset, known as the *NP-complete* problems, which contains the hardest. An *NP*-complete problem has the property that any problem in *NP* can be *polynomially reduced* to it.

A problem P_1 can be reduced to P_2 as follows: Provide a mapping so that any instance of P_1 can be transformed to an instance of P_2. Solve P_2, and then map the answer back to the original. As an example, numbers are entered into a pocket calculator in decimal. The decimal numbers are converted to binary, and all calculations are performed in binary. Then the final answer is converted back to decimal for display. For P_1 to be polynomially reducible to P_2, all the work associated with the transformations must be performed in polynomial time.

The reason that NP-complete problems are the hardest NP problems is that a problem that is NP-complete can essentially be used as a subroutine for *any* problem in NP, with only a polynomial amount of overhead. Thus, if any NP-complete problem has a polynomial-time solution, then *every* problem in NP must have a polynomial-time solution. This makes the NP-complete problems the hardest of all NP problems.

Suppose we have an NP-complete problem P_1. Suppose P_2 is known to be in NP. Suppose further that P_1 polynomially reduces to P_2, so that we can solve P_1 by using P_2 with only a polynomial time penalty. Since P_1 is NP-complete, every problem in NP polynomially reduces to P_1. By applying the closure property of polynomials, we see that every problem in NP is polynomially reducible to P_2: We reduce the problem to P_1 and then reduce P_1 to P_2. Thus, P_2 is NP-complete.

As an example, suppose that we already know that the Hamiltonian cycle problem is NP-complete. The *traveling salesman problem* is as follows.

TRAVELING SALESMAN PROBLEM:
Given a complete graph $G = (V, E)$, with edge costs, and an integer K, is there a simple cycle that visits all vertices and has total cost $\le K$?

The problem is different from the Hamiltonian cycle problem, because all $|V|(|V|-1)/2$ edges are present and the graph is weighted. This problem has many important applications. For instance, printed circuit boards need to have holes punched so that chips, resistors, and other electronic components can be placed. This is done mechanically. Punching the hole is a quick operation; the time-consuming step is positioning the hole puncher. The time required for positioning depends on the distance traveled from hole to hole. Since we would like to punch every hole (and then return to the start for the next board), and minimize the total amount of time spent traveling, what we have is a traveling salesman problem.

The traveling salesman problem is NP-complete. It is easy to see that a solution can be checked in polynomial time, so it is certainly in NP. To show that it is NP-complete, we polynomially reduce the Hamiltonian cycle problem to it. To do this we construct a new graph G'. G' has the same vertices as G. For G', each edge (v, w) has a weight of 1 if $(v, w) \in G$, and 2 otherwise. We choose $K = |V|$. See Figure 9.78.

It is easy to verify that G has a Hamiltonian cycle if and only if G' has a Traveling Salesman tour of total weight $|V|$.

There is now a long list of problems known to be NP-complete. To prove that some new problem is NP-complete, it must be shown to be in NP, and then an appropriate NP-complete problem must be transformed into it. Although the transformation to a traveling salesman problem was rather straightforward, most transformations are actually quite involved and require some tricky constructions. Generally, several different NP-complete problems are considered before the problem that actually provides the reduction. As we are only interested in the general ideas, we will not show any more transformations; the interested reader can consult the references.

The alert reader may be wondering how the first NP-complete problem was actually proven to be NP-complete. Since proving that a problem is NP-complete requires transforming it from another NP-complete problem, there must be some NP-complete problem for which this strategy will not work. The first problem that was proven to be NP-complete

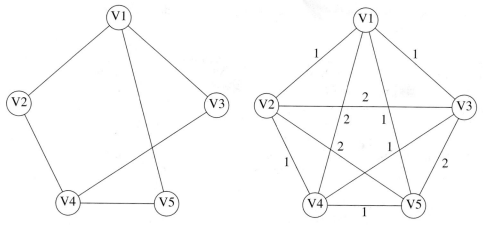

Figure 9.78 Hamiltonian cycle problem transformed to traveling salesman problem

was the *satisfiability* problem. The satisfiability problem takes as input a Boolean expression and asks whether the expression has an assignment to the variables that gives a value of `true`.

Satisfiability is certainly in *NP*, since it is easy to evaluate a Boolean expression and check whether the result is true. In 1971, Cook showed that satisfiability was *NP*-complete by directly proving that all problems that are in *NP* could be transformed to satisfiability. To do this, he used the one known fact about every problem in *NP*: Every problem in *NP* can be solved in polynomial time by a nondeterministic computer. The formal model for a computer is known as a *Turing machine*. Cook showed how the actions of this machine could be simulated by an extremely complicated and long, but still polynomial, Boolean formula. This Boolean formula would be true if and only if the program which was being run by the Turing machine produced a "yes" answer for its input.

Once satisfiability was shown to be *NP*-complete, a host of new *NP*-complete problems, including some of the most classic problems, were also shown to be *NP*-complete.

In addition to the satisfiability, Hamiltonian circuit, traveling salesman, and longest-path problems, which we have already examined, some of the more well-known *NP*-complete problems which we have not discussed are *bin packing, knapsack, graph coloring,* and *clique.* The list is quite extensive and includes problems from operating systems (scheduling and security), database systems, operations research, logic, and especially graph theory.

SUMMARY

In this chapter we have seen how graphs can be used to model many real-life problems. Many of the graphs that occur are typically very sparse, so it is important to pay attention to the data structures that are used to implement them.

We have also seen a class of problems that do not seem to have efficient solutions. In Chapter 10, some techniques for dealing with these problems will be discussed.

EXERCISES

9.1 Find a topological ordering for the graph in Figure 9.79.

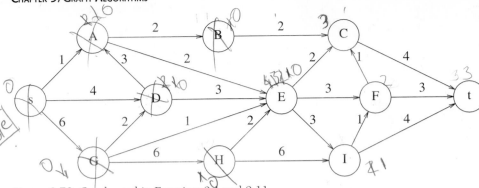

Figure 9.79 Graph used in Exercises 9.1 and 9.11

9.2 If a stack is used instead of a queue for the topological sort algorithm in Section 9.1, does a different ordering result? Why might one data structure give a "better" answer?

9.3 Write a program to perform a topological sort on a graph.

9.4 An adjacency matrix requires $O(|V|^2)$ merely to initialize using a standard double loop. Propose a method that stores a graph in an adjacency matrix (so that testing for the existence of an edge is $O(1)$) but avoids the quadratic running time.

9.5 a. Find the shortest path from A to all other vertices for the graph in Figure 9.80.

 b. Find the shortest unweighted path from B to all other vertices for the graph in Figure 9.80.

9.6 What is the worst-case running time of Dijkstra's algorithm when implemented with d-heaps (Section 6.5)?

9.7 a. Give an example where Dijkstra's algorithm gives the wrong answer in the presence of a negative edge but no negative-cost cycle.

 **b. Show that the weighted shortest-path algorithm suggested in Section 9.3.3 works if there are negative-weight edges, but no negative-cost cycles, and that the running time of this algorithm is $O(|E| \cdot |V|)$.

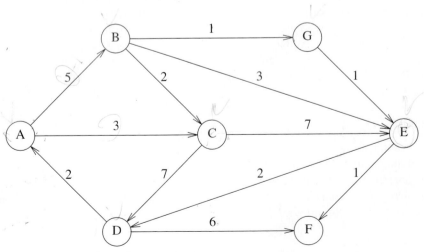

Figure 9.80 Graph used in Exercise 9.5

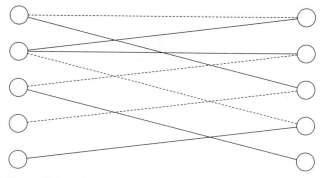

Figure 9.81 A bipartite graph

*9.8 Suppose all the edge weights in a graph are integers between 1 and $|E|$. How fast can Dijkstra's algorithm be implemented?

9.9 Write a program to solve the single-source shortest-path problem.

9.10 a. Explain how to modify Dijkstra's algorithm to produce a count of the number of different minimum paths from v to w.

   b. Explain how to modify Dijkstra's algorithm so that if there is more than one minimum path from v to w, a path with the fewest number of edges is chosen.

9.11 Find the maximum flow in the network of Figure 9.79.

9.12 Suppose that $G = (V, E)$ is a tree, s is the root, and we add a vertex t and edges of infinite capacity from all leaves in G to t. Give a linear-time algorithm to find a maximum flow from s to t.

9.13 A bipartite graph, $G = (V, E)$, is a graph such that V can be partitioned into two subsets V_1 and V_2 and no edge has both its vertices in the same subset.

   a. Give a linear algorithm to determine whether a graph is bipartite.

   b. The bipartite matching problem is to find the largest subset E' of E such that no vertex is included in more than one edge. A matching of four edges (indicated by dashed edges) is shown in Figure 9.81. There is a matching of five edges, which is maximum.

   Show how the bipartite matching problem can be used to solve the following problem: We have a set of instructors, a set of courses, and a list of courses that each instructor is qualified to teach. If no instructor is required to teach more than one course, and only one instructor may teach a given course, what is the maximum number of courses that can be offered?

   c. Show that the network flow problem can be used to solve the bipartite matching problem.

   d. What is the time complexity of your solution to part (b)?

9.14 Give an algorithm to find an augmenting path that permits the maximum flow.

9.15 a. Find a minimum spanning tree for the graph in Figure 9.82 using both Prim's and Kruskal's algorithms.

   b. Is this minimum spanning tree unique? Why?

9.16 Does either Prim's or Kruskal's algorithm work if there are negative edge weights?

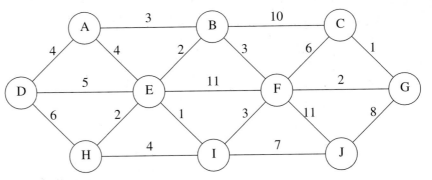

Figure 9.82 Graph used in Exercise 9.15

9.17 Show that a graph of V vertices can have V^{V-2} minimum spanning trees.

9.18 Write a program to implement Kruskal's algorithm.

9.19 If all of the edges in a graph have weights between 1 and $|E|$, how fast can the minimum spanning tree be computed?

9.20 Give an algorithm to find a *maximum* spanning tree. Is this harder than finding a minimum spanning tree?

9.21 Find all the articulation points in the graph in Figure 9.83. Show the depth-first spanning tree and the values of *Num* and *Low* for each vertex.

9.22 Prove that the algorithm to find articulation points works.

9.23 a. Give an algorithm to find the minimum number of edges that need to be removed from an undirected graph so that the resulting graph is acyclic.

   *b. Show that this problem is *NP*-complete for directed graphs.

9.24 Prove that in a depth-first spanning forest of a directed graph, all cross edges go from right to left.

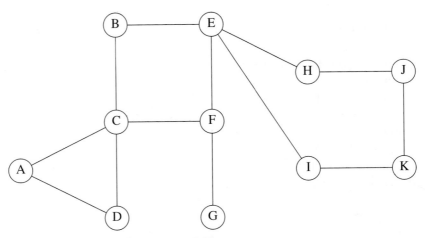

Figure 9.83 Graph used in Exercise 9.21

Figure 9.84 Graph used in Exercise 9.26

9.25 Give an algorithm to decide whether an edge (v, w) in a depth-first spanning forest of a directed graph is a tree, back, cross, or forward edge.

9.26 Find the strongly connected components in the graph of Figure 9.84.

9.27 Write a program to find the strongly connected components in a digraph.

*9.28 Give an algorithm that finds the strongly connected components in only one depth-first search. Use an algorithm similar to the biconnectivity algorithm.

9.29 The *biconnected components* of a graph G is a partition of the edges into sets such that the graph formed by each set of edges is biconnected. Modify the algorithm in Figure 9.67 to find the biconnected components instead of the articulation points.

9.30 Suppose we perform a breadth-first search of an undirected graph and build a breadth-first spanning tree. Show that all edges in the tree are either tree edges or cross edges.

9.31 Give an algorithm to find in an undirected (connected) graph a path that goes through every edge exactly once in each direction.

9.32 a. Write a program to find an Euler circuit in a graph if one exists.

  b. Write a program to find an Euler tour in a graph if one exists.

9.33 An Euler circuit in a directed graph is a cycle in which every edge is visited exactly once.

  *a. Prove that a directed graph has an Euler circuit if and only if it is strongly connected and every vertex has equal indegree and outdegree.

  *b. Give a linear-time algorithm to find an Euler circuit in a directed graph where one exists.

9.34 a. Consider the following solution to the Euler circuit problem: Assume that the graph is biconnected. Perform a depth-first search, taking back edges only as a last resort. If the graph is not biconnected, apply the algorithm recursively on the biconnected components. Does this algorithm work?

  b. Suppose that when taking back edges, we take the back edge to the nearest ancestor. Does the algorithm work?

9.35 A planar graph is a graph that can be drawn in a plane without any two edges intersecting.

  *a. Show that neither of the graphs in Figure 9.85 is planar.

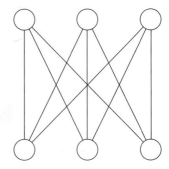

Figure 9.85 Graph used in Exercise 9.35

b. Show that in a planar graph, there must exist some vertex which is connected to no more than five nodes.

**c. Show that in a planar graph, $|E| \le 3|V| - 6$.

9.36 A *multigraph* is a graph in which multiple edges are allowed between pairs of vertices. Which of the algorithms in this chapter work without modification for multigraphs? What modifications need to be done for the others?

*9.37 Let $G = (V, E)$ be an undirected graph. Use depth-first search to design a linear algorithm to convert each edge in G to a directed edge such that the resulting graph is strongly connected, or determine that this is not possible.

9.38 You are given a set of N sticks, which are lying on top of each other in some configuration. Each stick is specified by its two endpoints; each endpoint is an ordered triple giving its x, y, and z coordinates; no stick is vertical. A stick may be picked up only if there is no stick on top of it.

a. Explain how to write a routine that takes two sticks a and b and reports whether a is above, below, or unrelated to b. (This has nothing to do with graph theory.)

b. Give an algorithm that determines whether it is possible to pick up all the sticks, and if so, provides a sequence of stick pickups that accomplishes this.

9.39 A graph is k-colorable if each vertex can be given one of k colors, and no edge connects identically colored vertices. Give a linear-time algorithm to test a graph for two-colorability. Assume graphs are stored in adjacency list format; you must specify any additional data structures that are needed.

9.40 Give a polynomial-time algorithm that finds $\lceil V/2 \rceil$ vertices that collectively cover at least three-fourths (3/4) of the edges in an arbitrary undirected graph.

9.41 Show how to modify the topological sort algorithm so that if the graph is not acyclic, the algorithm will print out some cycle. You may not use depth-first search.

9.42 Let G be a directed graph with N vertices. A vertex s is called a *sink* if, for every v in V such that $s \ne v$, there is an edge (v, s), and there are no edges of the form (s, v). Give an $O(N)$ algorithm to determine whether or not G has a sink, assuming that G is given by its $N \times N$ adjacency matrix.

9.43 When a vertex and its incident edges are removed from a tree, a collection of subtrees remains. Give a linear-time algorithm that finds a vertex whose removal from an N vertex tree leaves no subtree with more than $N/2$ vertices.

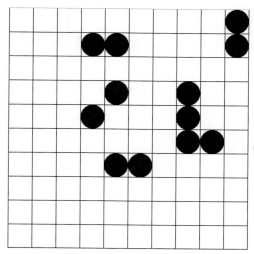

Figure 9.86 Grid for Exercise 9.45

9.44 Give a linear-time algorithm to determine the longest unweighted path in an acyclic undirected graph (that is, a tree).

9.45 Consider an N-by-N grid in which some squares are occupied by black circles. Two squares belong to the same group if they share a common edge. In Figure 9.86, there is one group of four occupied squares, three groups of two occupied squares, and two individual occupied squares. Assume that the grid is represented by a two-dimensional array. Write a program that does the following:

a. Computes the size of a group when a square in the group is given.

b. Computes the number of different groups.

c. Lists all groups.

9.46 Section 8.7 described the generating of mazes. Suppose we want to output the path in the maze. Assume that the maze is represented as a matrix; each cell in the matrix stores information about what walls are present (or absent).

a. Write a program that computes enough information to output a path in the maze. Give output in the form **SEN...** (representing go south, then east, then north, etc.).

b. Write a program that uses the AWT to draw the maze and, at the press of a button, draws the path.

9.47 Suppose that walls in the maze can be knocked down, with a penalty of P squares. P is specified as a parameter to the algorithm. (If the penalty is 0, then the problem is trivial.) Describe an algorithm to solve this version of the problem. What is the running time of your algorithm?

9.48 Suppose that the maze may or may not have a solution.

a. Describe a linear-time algorithm that determines the minimum number of walls that need to be knocked down to create a solution. (*Hint:* Use a double-ended queue.)

b. Describe an algorithm (not necessarily linear-time) that finds a shortest path after knocking down the minimum number of walls. Note that the solution to part (a) would give no information about which walls would be the best to knock down. (*Hint:* Use Exercise 9.47.)

Explain how each of the following problems (Exercises 9.49–9.53) can be solved by applying a shortest-path algorithm. Then design a mechanism for representing an input, and write a program that solves the problem.

9.49 The input is a list of league game scores (and there are no ties). If all teams have at least one win and a loss, we can generally prove, by a silly transitivity argument, that any team is better than any other. For instance, in the six-team league where everyone plays three games, suppose we have the following results: *A* beat *B* and *C*; *B* beat *C* and *F*; *C* beat *D*; *D* beat *E*; *E* beat *A*; *F* beat *D* and *E*. Then we can prove that *A* is better than *F*, because *A* beat *B*, who in turn beat *F*. Similarly, we can prove that *F* is better than *A* because *F* beat *E* and *E* beat *A*. Given a list of game scores and two teams *X* and *Y*, either find a proof (if one exists) that *X* is better than *Y*, or indicate that no proof of this form can be found.

9.50 A word can be changed to another word by a 1-character substitution. Assume that a dictionary of 5-letter words exists. Give an algorithm to determine if a word *A* can be transformed to a word *B* by a series of 1-character substitutions, and if so, output the corresponding sequence of words. Note that all intermediate words must be in the dictionary. As an example, `bleed` converts to `blood` by the sequence `bleed`, `blend`, `blond`, `blood`.

9.51 The input is a collection of currencies and their exchange rates. Is there a sequence of exchanges that makes money instantly? For instance, if the currencies are *X*, *Y*, and *Z* and the exchange rate is 1 *X* equals 2 *Y*s, 1 *Y* equals 2 *Z*s, and 1 *X* equals 3 *Z*s, then 300 *Z*s will buy 100 *X*s, which in turn will buy 200 *Y*s, which in turn will buy 400 *Z*s. We have thus made a profit of 33 percent.

9.52 A student needs to take a certain number of courses to graduate, and these courses have prerequisites that must be followed. Assume that all courses are offered every semester and that the student can take an unlimited number of courses. Given a list of courses and their prerequisites, compute a schedule that requires the minimum number of semesters.

9.53 The object of the *Kevin Bacon Game* is to link a movie actor to Kevin Bacon via shared movie roles. The minimum number of links is an actor's *Bacon number.* For instance, Tom Hanks has a Bacon number of 1; he was in *Apollo 13* with Kevin Bacon. Sally Field has a Bacon number of 2, because she was in *Forrest Gump* with Tom Hanks, who was in *Apollo 13* with Kevin Bacon. Almost all well-known actors have a Bacon number of 1 or 2. Assume that you have a comprehensive list of actors, with roles,[1] and do the following:

a. Explain how to find an actor's Bacon number.

b. Explain how to find the actor with the highest Bacon number.

c. Explain how to find the minimum number of links between two arbitrary actors.

9.54 The *clique* problem can be stated as follows: Given an undirected graph $G = (V, E)$ and an integer *K*, does *G* contain a complete subgraph of at least *K* vertices?

---

[1]For instance, see the *Internet Movie Database* files `actors.list.gz` and `actresses.list.gz` at `ftp://uiarchive.cso.uiuc.edu/pub/info/imdb/`.

The *vertex cover* problem can be stated as follows: Given an undirected graph $G = (V, E)$ and an integer K, does G contain a subset $V' \subset V$ such that $|V'| \leq K$ and every edge in G has a vertex in V'? Show that the clique problem is polynomially reducible to vertex cover.

9.55 Assume that the Hamiltonian cycle problem is *NP*-complete for undirected graphs.

   a. Prove that the Hamiltonian cycle problem is *NP*-complete for directed graphs.

   b. Prove that the unweighted simple longest-path problem is *NP*-complete for directed graphs.

9.56 The *baseball card collector* problem is as follows: Given packets $P_1, P_2, \ldots, P_M$, each of which contains a subset of the year's baseball cards, and an integer K, is it possible to collect all the baseball cards by choosing $\leq K$ packets? Show that the baseball card collector problem is *NP*-complete.

REFERENCES

Good graph theory textbooks include [8], [13], [22], and [37]. More advanced topics, including the more careful attention to running times, are covered in [39], [41], and [48].

Use of adjacency lists was advocated in [24]. The topological sort algorithm is from [29], as described in [34]. Dijkstra's algorithm appeared in [9]. The improvements using d-heaps and Fibonacci heaps are described in [28] and [15], respectively. The shortest-path algorithm with negative edge weights is due to Bellman [3]; Tarjan [48] describes a more efficient way to guarantee termination.

Ford and Fulkerson's seminal work on network flow is [14]. The idea of augmenting along shortest paths or on paths admitting the largest flow increase is from [12]. Other approaches to the problem can be found in [10], [32], [21], [6], and [33]. An algorithm for the min-cost flow problem can be found in [19].

An early minimum spanning tree algorithm can be found in [4]. Prim's algorithm is from [42]; Kruskal's algorithm appears in [35]. Two $O(|E| \log \log |V|)$ algorithms are [5] and [49]. The theoretically best-known algorithms appear in [15], [17], and [30]. An empirical study of these algorithms suggests that Prim's algorithm, implemented with **decreaseKey**, is best in practice on most graphs [40].

The algorithm for biconnectivity is from [44]. The first linear-time strong components algorithm (Exercise 9.28) appears in the same paper. The algorithm presented in the text is due to Kosaraju (unpublished) and Sharir [43]. Other applications of depth-first search appear in [25], [26], [45], and [46] (as mentioned in Chapter 8, the results in [45] and [46] have been improved, but the basic algorithm is unchanged).

The classic reference work for the theory of *NP*-complete problems is [20]. Additional material can be found in [1]. The *NP*-completeness of satisfiability is shown in [7]. The other seminal paper is [31], which showed the *NP*-completeness of 21 problems. An excellent survey of complexity theory is [47]. An approximation algorithm for the traveling salesman problem, which generally gives nearly optimal results, can be found in [38].

A solution to Exercise 9.8 can be found in [2]. Solutions to the bipartite matching problem in Exercise 9.13 can be found in [23] and [36]. The problem can be generalized by adding weights to the edges and removing the restriction that the graph is bipartite. Efficient solutions for the unweighted matching problem for general graphs are quite complex. Details can be found in [11], [16], and [18].

Exercise 9.35 deals with planar graphs, which commonly arise in practice. Planar graphs are very sparse, and many difficult problems are easier on planar graphs. An example is the graph isomorphism problem, which is solvable in linear time for planar graphs [27]. No polynomial time algorithm is known for general graphs.

1. A. V. Aho, J. E. Hopcroft, and J. D. Ullman, *The Design and Analysis of Computer Algorithms,* Addison-Wesley, Reading, Mass., 1974.

2. R. K. Ahuja, K. Melhorn, J. B. Orlin, and R. E. Tarjan, "Faster Algorithms for the Shortest Path Problem," *Journal of the ACM,* 37 (1990), 213–223.

3. R. E. Bellman, "On a Routing Problem," *Quarterly of Applied Mathematics,* 16 (1958), 87–90.

4. O. Borůvka, "Ojistém problému minimálním (On a Minimal Problem)," *Práca Moravské Přirodo-vědecké Společnosti,* 3 (1926), 37–58.

5. D. Cheriton and R. E. Tarjan, "Finding Minimum Spanning Trees," *SIAM Journal on Computing,* 5 (1976), 724–742.

6. J. Cheriyan and T. Hagerup, "A Randomized Maximum-Flow Algorithm," *SIAM Journal on Computing,* 24 (1995), 203–226.

7. S. Cook, "The Complexity of Theorem Proving Procedures," *Proceedings of the Third Annual ACM Symposium on Theory of Computing* (1971), 151–158.

8. N. Deo, *Graph Theory with Applications to Engineering and Computer Science,* Prentice Hall, Englewood Cliffs, N.J., 1974.

9. E. W. Dijkstra, "A Note on Two Problems in Connexion with Graphs," *Numerische Mathematik,* 1 (1959), 269–271.

10. E. A. Dinic, "Algorithm for Solution of a Problem of Maximum Flow in Networks with Power Estimation," *Soviet Mathematics Doklady,* 11 (1970), 1277–1280.

11. J. Edmonds, "Paths, Trees, and Flowers," *Canadian Journal of Mathematics,* 17 (1965) 449–467.

12. J. Edmonds and R. M. Karp, "Theoretical Improvements in Algorithmic Efficiency for Network Flow Problems," *Journal of the ACM,* 19 (1972), 248–264.

13. S. Even, *Graph Algorithms,* Computer Science Press, Potomac, Md., 1979.

14. L. R. Ford, Jr., and D. R. Fulkerson, *Flows in Networks,* Princeton University Press, Princeton, N.J., 1962.

15. M. L. Fredman and R. E. Tarjan, "Fibonacci Heaps and Their Uses in Improved Network Optimization Algorithms," *Journal of the ACM,* 34 (1987), 596–615.

16. H. N. Gabow, "Data Structures for Weighted Matching and Nearest Common Ancestors with Linking," *Proceedings of First Annual ACM-SIAM Symposium on Discrete Algorithms* (1990), 434–443.

17. H. N. Gabow, Z. Galil, T. H. Spencer, and R. E. Tarjan, "Efficient Algorithms for Finding Minimum Spanning Trees on Directed and Undirected Graphs," *Combinatorica,* 6 (1986), 109–122.

18. Z. Galil, "Efficient Algorithms for Finding Maximum Matchings in Graphs," *ACM Computing Surveys,* 18 (1986), 23–38.

19. Z. Galil and E. Tardos, "An $O(n^2(m + n \log n) \log n)$ Min-Cost Flow Algorithm," *Journal of the ACM,* 35 (1988), 374–386.

20. M. R. Garey and D. S. Johnson, *Computers and Intractability: A Guide to the Theory of NP-Completeness,* Freeman, San Francisco, 1979.

21. A. V. Goldberg and R. E. Tarjan, "A New Approach to the Maximum-Flow Problem," *Journal of the ACM,* 35 (1988), 921–940.

22. F. Harary, *Graph Theory,* Addison-Wesley, Reading, Mass., 1969.

23. J. E. Hopcroft and R. M. Karp, "An $n^{5/2}$ Algorithm for Maximum Matchings in Bipartite Graphs," *SIAM Journal on Computing,* 2 (1973), 225–231.

24. J. E. Hopcroft and R. E. Tarjan, "Algorithm 447: Efficient Algorithms for Graph Manipulation," *Communications of the ACM,* 16 (1973), 372–378.

25. J. E. Hopcroft and R. E. Tarjan, "Dividing a Graph into Triconnected Components," *SIAM Journal on Computing,* 2 (1973), 135–158.

26. J. E. Hopcroft and R. E. Tarjan, "Efficient Planarity Testing," *Journal of the ACM,* 21 (1974), 549–568.

27. J. E. Hopcroft and J. K. Wong, "Linear Time Algorithm for Isomorphism of Planar Graphs," *Proceedings of the Sixth Annual ACM Symposium on Theory of Computing* (1974), 172–184.

28. D. B. Johnson, "Efficient Algorithms for Shortest Paths in Sparse Networks," *Journal of the ACM,* 24 (1977), 1–13.

29. A. B. Kahn, "Topological Sorting of Large Networks," *Communications of the ACM,* 5 (1962), 558–562.

30. D. R. Karger, P. N. Klein, and R. E. Tarjan, "A Randomized Linear-Time Algorithm to Find Minimum Spanning Trees," *Journal of the ACM,* 42 (1995), 321–328.

31. R. M. Karp, "Reducibility among Combinatorial Problems," *Complexity of Computer Computations* (eds. R. E. Miller and J. W. Thatcher), Plenum Press, New York, 1972, 85–103.

32. A. V. Karzanov, "Determining the Maximal Flow in a Network by the Method of Preflows," *Soviet Mathematics Doklady,* 15 (1974), 434–437.

33. V. King, S. Rao, and R. E. Tarjan, "A Faster Deterministic Maximum Flow Algorithm," *Journal of Algorithms,* 17 (1994), 447–474.

34. D. E. Knuth, *The Art of Computer Programming, Vol. 1: Fundamental Algorithms,* 3d. ed., Addison-Wesley, Reading, Mass., 1997.

35. J. B. Kruskal, Jr., "On the Shortest Spanning Subtree of a Graph and the Traveling Salesman Problem," *Proceedings of the American Mathematical Society,* 7 (1956), 48–50.

36. H. W. Kuhn, "The Hungarian Method for the Assignment Problem," *Naval Research Logistics Quarterly,* 2 (1955), 83–97.

37. E. L. Lawler, *Combinatorial Optimization: Networks and Matroids,* Holt, Reinhart, and Winston, New York, 1976.

38. S. Lin and B. W. Kernighan, "An Effective Heuristic Algorithm for the Traveling Salesman Problem," *Operations Research,* 21 (1973), 498–516.

39. K. Melhorn, *Data Structures and Algorithms 2: Graph Algorithms and NP-completeness,* Springer-Verlag, Berlin, 1984.

40. B. M. E. Moret and H. D. Shapiro, "An Empirical Analysis of Algorithms for Constructing a Minimum Spanning Tree," *Proceedings of the Second Workshop on Algorithms and Data Structures* (1991), 400–411.

41. C. H. Papadimitriou and K. Steiglitz, *Combinatorial Optimization: Algorithms and Complexity,* Prentice Hall, Englewood Cliffs, N.J., 1982.

42. R. C. Prim, "Shortest Connection Networks and Some Generalizations," *Bell System Technical Journal,* 36 (1957), 1389–1401.

43. M. Sharir, "A Strong-Connectivity Algorithm and Its Application in Data Flow Analysis," *Computers and Mathematics with Applications,* 7 (1981), 67–72.

44. R. E. Tarjan, "Depth First Search and Linear Graph Algorithms," *SIAM Journal on Computing,* 1 (1972), 146–160.

45. R. E. Tarjan, "Testing Flow Graph Reducibility," *Journal of Computer and System Sciences,* 9 (1974), 355–365.

46. R. E. Tarjan, "Finding Dominators in Directed Graphs," *SIAM Journal on Computing,* 3 (1974), 62–89.

47. R. E. Tarjan, "Complexity of Combinatorial Algorithms," *SIAM Review,* 20 (1978), 457–491.

48. R. E. Tarjan, *Data Structures and Network Algorithms,* Society for Industrial and Applied Mathematics, Philadelphia, 1983.

49. A. C. Yao, "An $O(|E| \log \log |V|)$ Algorithm for Finding Minimum Spanning Trees," *Information Processing Letters,* 4 (1975), 21–23.

CHAPTER **10**

Algorithm Design Techniques

So far, we have been concerned with the efficient implementation of algorithms. We have seen that when an algorithm is given, the actual data structures need not be specified. It is up to the programmer to choose the appropriate data structure in order to make the running time as small as possible.

In this chapter, we switch our attention from the *implementation* of algorithms to the *design* of algorithms. Most of the algorithms that we have seen so far are straightforward and simple. Chapter 9 contains some algorithms that are much more subtle, and some require an argument (in some cases lengthy) to show that they are indeed correct. In this chapter, we will focus on five of the common types of algorithms used to solve problems. For many problems, it is quite likely that at least one of these methods will work. Specifically, for each type of algorithm we will

- See the general approach.
- Look at several examples (the exercises at the end of the chapter provide many more examples).
- Discuss, in general terms, the time and space complexity, where appropriate.

10.1. Greedy Algorithms

The first type of algorithm we will examine is the *greedy algorithm*. We have already seen three greedy algorithms in Chapter 9: Dijkstra's, Prim's, and Kruskal's algorithms. Greedy algorithms work in phases. In each phase, a decision is made that appears to be good, without regard for future consequences. Generally, this means that some *local optimum* is chosen. This "take what you can get now" strategy is the source of the name for this class of algorithms. When the algorithm terminates, we hope that the local optimum is equal to the *global optimum*. If this is the case, then the algorithm is correct; otherwise, the algorithm has produced a suboptimal solution. If the absolute best answer is not required, then simple greedy algorithms are sometimes used to generate approximate answers, rather than using the more complicated algorithms generally required to generate an exact answer.

There are several real-life examples of greedy algorithms. The most obvious is the coin-changing problem. To make change in U.S. currency, we repeatedly dispense the largest denomination. Thus, to give out seventeen dollars and sixty-one cents in change, we give out a ten-dollar bill, a five-dollar bill, two one-dollar bills, two quarters, one dime, and one penny. By doing this, we are guaranteed to minimize the number of bills and coins. This algorithm does not work in all monetary systems, but fortunately, we can prove that it does work in the American monetary system. Indeed, it works even if two-dollar bills and fifty-cent pieces are allowed.

Traffic problems provide an example where making locally optimal choices does not always work. For example, during certain rush hour times in Miami, it is best to stay off the prime streets even if they look empty, because traffic will come to a standstill a mile down the road, and you will be stuck. Even more shocking, it is better in some cases to make a temporary detour in the direction opposite your destination in order to avoid all traffic bottlenecks.

In the remainder of this section, we will look at several applications that use greedy algorithms. The first application is a simple scheduling problem. Virtually all scheduling problems are either *NP*-complete (or of similar difficult complexity) or are solvable by a greedy algorithm. The second application deals with file compression and is one of the earliest results in computer science. Finally, we will look at an example of a greedy approximation algorithm.

10.1.1. A Simple Scheduling Problem

We are given jobs $j_1, j_2, \ldots, j_N$, all with known running times $t_1, t_2, \ldots, t_N$, respectively. We have a single processor. What is the best way to schedule these jobs in order to minimize the average completion time? In this entire section, we will assume *nonpreemptive scheduling*: Once a job is started, it must run to completion.

As an example, suppose we have the four jobs and associated running times shown in Figure 10.1. One possible schedule is shown in Figure 10.2. Because j_1 finishes in 15 (time units), j_2 in 23, j_3 in 26, and j_4 in 36, the average completion time is 25. A better schedule, which yields a mean completion time of 17.75, is shown in Figure 10.3.

The schedule given in Figure 10.3 is arranged by shortest job first. We can show that this will always yield an optimal schedule. Let the jobs in the schedule be $j_{i_1}, j_{i_2}, \ldots, j_{i_N}$. The first job finishes in time t_{i_1}. The second job finishes after $t_{i_1} + t_{i_2}$, and the third job finishes after $t_{i_1} + t_{i_2} + t_{i_3}$. From this, we see that the total cost, C, of the schedule is

Job	Time
j_1	15
j_2	8
j_3	3
j_4	10

Figure 10.1 Jobs and times

Figure 10.2 Schedule #1

Figure 10.3 Schedule #2 (optimal)

$$C = \sum_{k=1}^{N} (N - k + 1) t_{i_k} \qquad (10.1)$$

$$C = (N + 1) \sum_{k=1}^{N} t_{i_k} - \sum_{k=1}^{N} k \cdot t_{i_k} \qquad (10.2)$$

Notice that in Equation (10.2), the first sum is independent of the job ordering, so only the second sum affects the total cost. Suppose that in an ordering there exists some $x > y$ such that $t_{i_x} < t_{i_y}$. Then a calculation shows that by swapping j_{i_x} and j_{i_y}, the second sum increases, decreasing the total cost. Thus, any schedule of jobs in which the times are not monotonically nondecreasing must be suboptimal. The only schedules left are those in which the jobs are arranged by smallest running time first, breaking ties arbitrarily.

This result indicates the reason the operating system scheduler generally gives precedence to shorter jobs.

The Multiprocessor Case

We can extend this problem to the case of several processors. Again we have jobs $j_1, j_2, \ldots, j_N$, with associated running times $t_1, t_2, \ldots, t_N$, and a number P of processors. We will assume without loss of generality that the jobs are ordered, shortest running time first. As an example, suppose $P = 3$, and the jobs are as shown in Figure 10.4.

Figure 10.5 shows an optimal arrangement to minimize mean completion time. Jobs $j_1, j_4,$ and j_7 are run on Processor 1. Processor 2 handles $j_2, j_5,$ and j_8, and Processor 3 runs the remaining jobs. The total time to completion is 165, for an average of $\frac{165}{9} = 18.33$.

The algorithm to solve the multiprocessor case is to start jobs in order, cycling through processors. It is not hard to show that no other ordering can do better, although if the number of processors P evenly divides the number of jobs N, there are many optimal orderings. This is obtained by, for each $0 \le i < N/P$, placing each of the jobs j_{iP+1} through $j_{(i+1)P}$ on a different processor. In our case, Figure 10.6 shows a second optimal solution.

Even if P does not divide N exactly, there can still be many optimal solutions, even if all the job times are distinct. We leave further investigation of this as an exercise.

Minimizing the Final Completion Time

We close this section by considering a very similar problem. Suppose we are only concerned with when the last job finishes. In our two examples above, these completion times are 40

Job	Time
j_1	3
j_2	5
j_3	6
j_4	10
j_5	11
j_6	14
j_7	15
j_8	18
j_9	20

Figure 10.4 Jobs and times

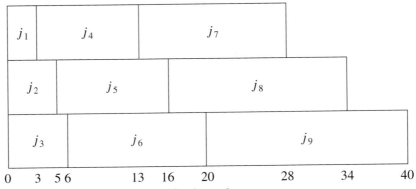

Figure 10.5 An optimal solution for the multiprocessor case

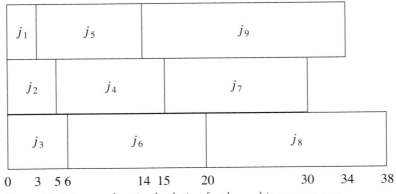

Figure 10.6 A second optimal solution for the multiprocessor case

and 38, respectively. Figure 10.7 shows that the minimum final completion time is 34, and this clearly cannot be improved, because every processor is always busy.

Although this schedule does not have minimum mean completion time, it has merit in that the completion time of the entire sequence is earlier. If the same user owns all these jobs, then this is the preferable method of scheduling. Although these problems are very

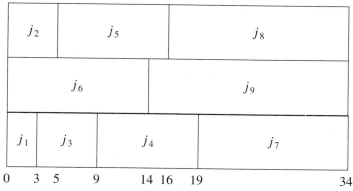

Figure 10.7 Minimizing the final completion time

similar, this new problem turns out to be *NP*-complete; it is just another way of phrasing the knapsack or bin-packing problems, which we will encounter later in this section. Thus, minimizing the final completion time is apparently much harder than minimizing the mean completion time.

10.1.2. Huffman Codes

In this section, we consider a second application of greedy algorithms, known as *file compression*.

The normal ASCII character set consists of roughly 100 "printable" characters. In order to distinguish these characters, $\lceil \log 100 \rceil = 7$ bits are required. Seven bits allow the representation of 128 characters, so the ASCII character set adds some other "nonprintable" characters. An eighth bit is added as a parity check. The important point, however, is that if the size of the character set is C, then $\lceil \log C \rceil$ bits are needed in a standard encoding.

Suppose we have a file that contains only the characters *a, e, i, s, t,* plus blank spaces and *newline*s. Suppose further, that the file has ten *a*'s, fifteen *e*'s, twelve *i*'s, three *s*'s, four *t*'s, thirteen blanks, and one *newline*. As the table in Figure 10.8 shows, this file requires 174 bits to represent, since there are 58 characters and each character requires three bits.

Character	Code	Frequency	Total Bits
a	000	10	30
e	001	15	45
i	010	12	36
s	011	3	9
t	100	4	12
space	101	13	39
newline	110	1	3
Total			174

Figure 10.8 Using a standard coding scheme

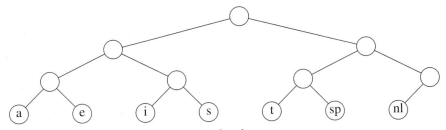

Figure 10.9 Representation of the original code in a tree

In real life, files can be quite large. Many of the very large files are output of some program and there is usually a big disparity between the most frequent and least frequent characters. For instance, many large data files have an inordinately large amount of digits, blanks, and *newlines*, but few *q*'s and *x*'s. We might be interested in reducing the file size in the case where we are transmitting it over a slow phone line. Also, since on virtually every machine, disk space is precious, one might wonder if it would be possible to provide a better code and reduce the total number of bits required.

The answer is that this is possible, and a simple strategy achieves 25 percent savings on typical large files and as much as 50 to 60 percent savings on many large data files. The general strategy is to allow the code length to vary from character to character and to ensure that the frequently occurring characters have short codes. Notice that if all the characters occur with the same frequency, then there are not likely to be any savings.

The binary code that represents the alphabet can be represented by the binary tree shown in Figure 10.9.

The tree in Figure 10.9 has data only at the leaves. The representation of each character can be found by starting at the root and recording the path, using a 0 to indicate the left branch and a 1 to indicate the right branch. For instance, *s* is reached by going left, then right, and finally right. This is encoded as 011. This data structure is sometimes referred to as a *trie*. If character c_i is at depth d_i and occurs f_i times, then the *cost* of the code is equal to $\sum d_i f_i$.

A better code than the one given in Figure 10.9 can be obtained by noticing that the *newline* is an only child. By placing the *newline* symbol one level higher at its parent, we obtain the new tree in Figure 10.10. This new tree has cost of 173, but is still far from optimal.

Notice that the tree in Figure 10.10 is a *full tree*: All nodes either are leaves or have two children. An optimal code will always have this property, since otherwise, as we have already seen, nodes with only one child could move up a level.

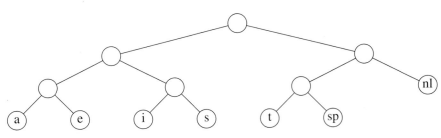

Figure 10.10 A slightly better tree

If the characters are placed only at the leaves, any sequence of bits can always be decoded unambiguously. Suppose the encoded string is 01001111000101100010000111, for example. 0 is not a character code, 01 is not a character code, but 010 represents i, so the first character is i. Then 011 follows, giving an s. Then 11 follows, which is a *newline*. The remainder of the code is a, *space*, t, i, e, and *newline*. Thus, it does not matter if the character codes are different lengths, as long as no character code is a prefix of another character code. Such an encoding is known as a *prefix code*. Conversely, if a character is contained in a nonleaf node, it is no longer possible to guarantee that the decoding will be unambiguous.

Putting these facts together, we see that our basic problem is to find the full binary tree of minimum total cost (as defined above), where all characters are contained in the leaves. The tree in Figure 10.11 shows the optimal tree for our sample alphabet. As can be seen in Figure 10.12, this code uses only 146 bits.

Notice that there are many optimal codes. These can be obtained by swapping children in the encoding tree. The main unresolved question, then, is how the coding tree is constructed. The algorithm to do this was given by Huffman in 1952. Thus, this coding system is commonly referred to as a Huffman code.

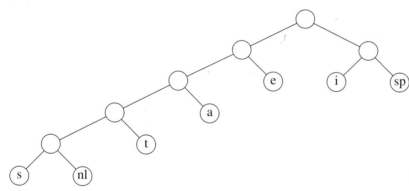

Figure 10.11 Optimal prefix code

Character	Code	Frequency	Total Bits
a	001	10	30
e	01	15	30
i	10	12	24
s	00000	3	15
t	0001	4	16
space	11	13	26
newline	00001	1	5
Total			146

Figure 10.12 Optimal prefix code

Figure 10.13 Initial stage of Huffman's algorithm

Figure 10.14 Huffman's algorithm after the first merge

Huffman's Algorithm

Throughout this section we will assume that the number of characters is C. Huffman's algorithm can be described as follows: We maintain a forest of trees. The *weight* of a tree is equal to the sum of the frequencies of its leaves. $C - 1$ times, select the two trees, T_1 and T_2, of smallest weight, breaking ties arbitrarily, and form a new tree with subtrees T_1 and T_2. At the beginning of the algorithm, there are C single-node trees—one for each character. At the end of the algorithm there is one tree, and this is the optimal Huffman coding tree.

A worked example will make the operation of the algorithm clear. Figure 10.13 shows the initial forest; the weight of each tree is shown in small type at the root. The two trees of lowest weight are merged together, creating the forest shown in Figure 10.14. We will name the new root $T1$, so that future merges can be stated unambiguously. We have made s the left child arbitrarily; any tiebreaking procedure can be used. The total weight of the new tree is just the sum of the weights of the old trees, and can thus be easily computed. It is also a simple matter to create the new tree, since we merely need to get a new node, set the left and right links, and record the weight.

Figure 10.15 Huffman's algorithm after the second merge

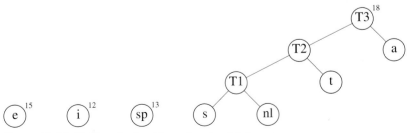

Figure 10.16 Huffman's algorithm after the third merge

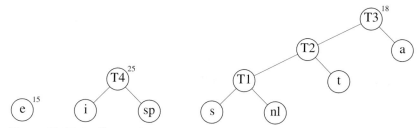

Figure 10.17 Huffman's algorithm after the fourth merge

Now there are six trees, and we again select the two trees of smallest weight. These happen to be $T1$ and t, which are then merged into a new tree with root $T2$ and weight 8. This is shown in Figure 10.15. The third step merges $T2$ and a, creating $T3$, with weight $10 + 8 = 18$. Figure 10.16 shows the result of this operation.

After the third merge is completed, the two trees of lowest weight are the single-node trees representing i and the blank space. Figure 10.17 shows how these trees are merged into the new tree with root $T4$. The fifth step is to merge the trees with roots e and $T3$, since these trees have the two smallest weights. The result of this step is shown in Figure 10.18.

Finally, the optimal tree, which was shown in Figure 10.11, is obtained by merging the two remaining trees. Figure 10.19 shows this optimal tree, with root $T6$.

We will sketch the ideas involved in proving that Huffman's algorithm yields an optimal code; we will leave the details as an exercise. First, it is not hard to show by contradiction that the tree must be full, since we have already seen how a tree that is not full is improved.

Next, we must show that the two least frequent characters α and β must be the two deepest nodes (although other nodes may be as deep). Again, this is easy to show by contradiction, since if either α or β is not a deepest node, then there must be some γ that is (recall that the tree is full). If α is less frequent than γ, then we can improve the cost by swapping them in the tree.

We can then argue that the characters in any two nodes at the same depth can be swapped without affecting optimality. This shows that an optimal tree can always be found that contains the two least frequent symbols as siblings; thus the first step is not a mistake.

The proof can be completed by using an induction argument. As trees are merged, we consider the new character set to be the characters in the roots. Thus, in our example, after four merges, we can view the character set as consisting of e and the metacharacters $T3$ and $T4$. This is probably the trickiest part of the proof; you are urged to fill in all of the details.

The reason that this is a greedy algorithm is that at each stage we perform a merge without regard to global considerations. We merely select the two smallest trees.

If we maintain the trees in a priority queue, ordered by weight, then the running time is $O(C \log C)$, since there will be one **buildHeap**, $2C - 2$ **deleteMins**, and $C - 2$ **inserts**, on a priority queue that never has more than C elements. A simple implementation of the priority queue, using a linked list, would give an $O(C^2)$ algorithm. The choice of priority queue implementation depends on how large C is. In the typical case of an ASCII character set, C is small enough that the quadratic running time is acceptable. In such an application, virtually all the running time will be spent on the disk I/O required to read the input file and write out the compressed version.

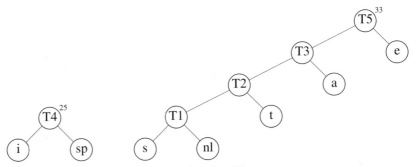

Figure 10.18 Huffman's algorithm after the fifth merge

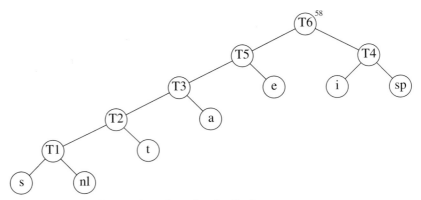

Figure 10.19 Huffman's algorithm after the final merge

There are two details that must be considered. First, the encoding information must be transmitted at the start of the compressed file, since otherwise it will be impossible to decode. There are several ways of doing this; see Exercise 10.4. For small files, the cost of transmitting this table will override any possible savings in compression, and the result will probably be file expansion. Of course, this can be detected and the original left intact. For large files, the size of the table is not significant.

The second problem is that as described, this is a two-pass algorithm. The first pass collects the frequency data and the second pass does the encoding. This is obviously not a desirable property for a program dealing with large files. Some alternatives are described in the references.

10.1.3. Approximate Bin Packing

In this section, we will consider some algorithms to solve the *bin packing* problem. These algorithms will run quickly but will not necessarily produce optimal solutions. We will prove, however, that the solutions that are produced are not too far from optimal.

We are given N items of sizes $s_1, s_2, \ldots, s_N$. All sizes satisfy $0 < s_i \leq 1$. The problem is to pack these items in the fewest number of bins, given that each bin has unit capacity. As an example, Figure 10.20 shows an optimal packing for an item list with sizes 0.2, 0.5, 0.4, 0.7, 0.1, 0.3, 0.8.

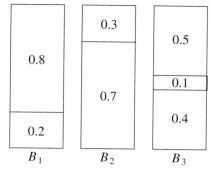

Figure 10.20 Optimal packing for 0.2, 0.5, 0.4, 0.7, 0.1, 0.3, 0.8

There are two versions of the bin packing problem. The first version is *on-line* bin packing. In this version, each item must be placed in a bin before the next item can be processed. The second version is the *off-line* bin packing problem. In an off-line algorithm, we do not need to do anything until all the input has been read. The distinction between on-line and off-line algorithms was discussed in Section 8.2.

On-line Algorithms

The first issue to consider is whether or not an on-line algorithm can actually always give an optimal answer, even if it is allowed unlimited computation. Remember that even though unlimited computation is allowed, an on-line algorithm must place an item before processing the next item and cannot change its decision.

To show that an on-line algorithm cannot always give an optimal solution, we will give it particularly difficult data to work on. Consider an input sequence I_1 of M small items of weight $\frac{1}{2} - \epsilon$ followed by M large items of weight $\frac{1}{2} + \epsilon$, $0 < \epsilon < 0.01$. It is clear that these items can be packed in M bins if we place one small item and one large item in each bin. Suppose there were an optimal on-line algorithm A that could perform this packing. Consider the operation of algorithm A on the sequence I_2, consisting of only M small items of weight $\frac{1}{2} - \epsilon$. I_2 can be packed in $\lceil M/2 \rceil$ bins. However, A will place each item in a separate bin, since A must yield the same results on I_2 as it does for the first half of I_1, and the first half of I_1 is exactly the same input as I_2. This means that A will use twice as many bins as is optimal for I_2. What we have proven is that there is no optimal algorithm for on-line bin packing.

What the argument above shows is that an on-line algorithm never knows when the input might end, so any performance guarantees it provides must hold at every instant throughout the algorithm. If we follow the foregoing strategy, we can prove the following.

THEOREM 10.1.

There are inputs that force any on-line bin-packing algorithm to use at least $\frac{4}{3}$ the optimal number of bins.

PROOF:

Suppose otherwise, and suppose for simplicity that M is even. Consider any on-line algorithm A running on the input sequence I_1, above. Recall that this sequence consists of M small items followed by M large items. Let us consider what the algorithm A has done after processing the Mth item. Suppose A has already used b bins. At this point in the algorithm, the optimal number of bins is $M/2$, because we can place two elements in each bin. Thus we know that $2b/M < \frac{4}{3}$, by our assumption of a better-than-$\frac{4}{3}$ performance guarantee.

Now consider the performance of algorithm A after all items have been packed. All bins created after the bth bin must contain exactly one item, since all small items are placed in the first b bins, and two large items will not fit in a bin. Since the first b bins can have at most two items each, and the remaining bins have one item each, we see that packing $2M$ items will require at least $2M - b$ bins. Since the $2M$ items can be optimally packed using M bins, our performance guarantee assures us that $(2M - b)/M < \frac{4}{3}$.

The first inequality implies that $b/M < \frac{2}{3}$, and the second inequality implies that $b/M > \frac{2}{3}$, which is a contradiction. Thus, no on-line algorithm can guarantee that it will produce a packing with less than $\frac{4}{3}$ the optimal number of bins.

There are three simple algorithms that guarantee that the number of bins used is no more than twice optimal. There are also quite a few more complicated algorithms with better guarantees.

Next Fit

Probably the simplest algorithm is *next fit*. When processing any item, we check to see whether it fits in the same bin as the last item. If it does, it is placed there; otherwise, a new bin is created. This algorithm is incredibly simple to implement and runs in linear time. Figure 10.21 shows the packing produced for the same input as Figure 10.20.

Not only is next fit simple to program, its worst-case behavior is also easy to analyze.

THEOREM 10.2.

Let M be the optimal number of bins required to pack a list I of items. Then next fit never uses more than $2M$ bins. There exist sequences such that next fit uses $2M - 2$ bins.

PROOF:

Consider any adjacent bins B_j and B_{j+1}. The sum of the sizes of all items in B_j and B_{j+1} must be larger than 1, since otherwise all of these items would have been placed in B_j. If we apply this result to all pairs of adjacent bins, we see that at most half of the space is wasted. Thus next fit uses at most twice the optimal number of bins.

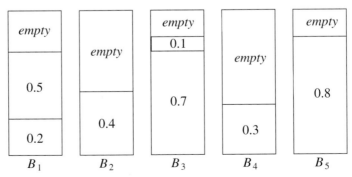

Figure 10.21 Next fit for 0.2, 0.5, 0.4, 0.7, 0.1, 0.3, 0.8

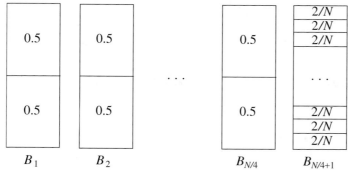

Figure 10.22 Optimal packing for 0.5, 2/N, 0.5, 2/N, 0.5, 2/N, . . .

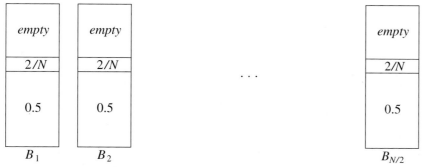

Figure 10.23 Next fit packing for 0.5, 2/N, 0.5, 2/N, 0.5, 2/N, . . .

To see that this bound is tight, suppose that the N items have size $s_i = 0.5$ if i is odd and $s_i = 2/N$ if i is even. Assume N is divisible by 4. The optimal packing, shown in Figure 10.22, consists of $N/4$ bins, each containing 2 elements of size 0.5, and one bin containing the $N/2$ elements of size $2/N$, for a total of $(N/4) + 1$. Figure 10.23 shows that next fit uses $N/2$ bins. Thus, next fit can be forced to use almost twice as many bins as optimal.

First Fit

Although next fit has a reasonable performance guarantee, it performs poorly in practice, because it creates new bins when it does not need to. In the sample run, it could have placed the item of size 0.3 in either B_1 or B_2, rather than create a new bin.

The *first fit* strategy is to scan the bins in order and place the new item in the first bin that is large enough to hold it. Thus, a new bin is created only when the results of previous placements have left no other alternative. Figure 10.24 shows the packing that results from first fit on our standard input.

A simple method of implementing first fit would process each item by scanning down the list of bins sequentially. This would take $O(N^2)$. It is possible to implement first fit to run in $O(N \log N)$; we leave this as an exercise.

A moment's thought will convince you that at any point, at most one bin can be more than half empty, since if a second bin were also half empty, its contents would fit into the first bin. Thus, we can immediately conclude that first fit guarantees a solution with at most twice the optimal number of bins.

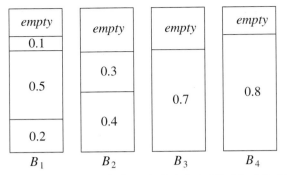

Figure 10.24 First fit for 0.2, 0.5, 0.4, 0.7, 0.1, 0.3, 0.8

On the other hand, the bad case that we used in the proof of next fit's performance bound does not apply for first fit. Thus, one might wonder if a better bound can be proven. The answer is yes, but the proof is complicated.

THEOREM 10.3.
Let M be the optimal number of bins required to pack a list I of items. Then first fit never uses more than $\lceil \frac{17}{10} M \rceil$ bins. There exist sequences such that first fit uses $\frac{17}{10}(M - 1)$ bins.

PROOF:
See the references at the end of the chapter.

An example where first fit does almost as poorly as the previous theorem would indicate is shown in Figure 10.25. The input consists of 6M items of size $\frac{1}{7} + \epsilon$, followed by 6M items of size $\frac{1}{3} + \epsilon$, followed by 6M items of size $\frac{1}{2} + \epsilon$. One simple packing places one item of each size in a bin and requires 6M bins. First fit requires 10M bins.

When first fit is run on a large number of items with sizes uniformly distributed between 0 and 1, empirical results show that first fit uses roughly 2 percent more bins than optimal. In many cases, this is quite acceptable.

Best Fit

The third on-line strategy we will examine is *best fit*. Instead of placing a new item in the first spot that is found, it is placed in the tightest spot among all bins. A typical packing is shown in Figure 10.26.

Notice that the item of size 0.3 is placed in B_3, where it fits perfectly, instead of B_2. One might expect that since we are now making a more educated choice of bins, the performance guarantee would improve. This is not the case, because the generic bad cases are the same. Best fit is never more than roughly 1.7 times as bad as optimal, and there are inputs for which it (nearly) achieves this bound. Nevertheless, best fit is also simple to code, especially if an $O(N \log N)$ algorithm is required, and it does perform better for random inputs.

Off-line Algorithms

If we are allowed to view the entire item list before producing an answer, then we should expect to do better. Indeed, since we can eventually find the optimal packing by exhaustive search, we already have a theoretical improvement over the on-line case.

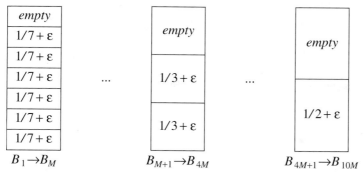

Figure 10.25 A case where first fit uses 10M bins instead of 6M

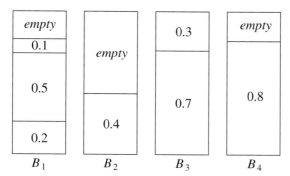

Figure 10.26 Best fit for 0.2, 0.5, 0.4, 0.7, 0.1, 0.3, 0.8

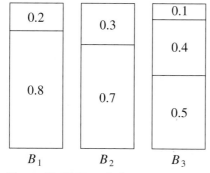

Figure 10.27 First fit for 0.8, 0.7, 0.5, 0.4, 0.3, 0.2, 0.1

   The major problem with all the on-line algorithms is that it is hard to pack the large items, especially when they occur late in the input. The natural way around this is to sort the items, placing the largest items first. We can then apply first fit or best fit, yielding the algorithms *first fit decreasing* and *best fit decreasing,* respectively. Figure 10.27 shows that in our case this yields an optimal solution (although, of course, this is not true in general).

   In this section, we will deal with first fit decreasing. The results for best fit decreasing are almost identical. Since it is possible that the item sizes are not distinct, some authors prefer to call the algorithm *first fit nonincreasing*. We will stay with the original name. We will also assume, without loss of generality, that input sizes are already sorted.

The first remark we can make is that the bad case, which showed first fit using 10M bins instead of 6M bins, does not apply when the items are sorted. We will show that if an optimal packing uses M bins, then first fit decreasing never uses more than $(4M + 1)/3$ bins.

The result depends on two observations. First, all the items with weight larger than $\frac{1}{3}$ will be placed in the first M bins. This implies that all the items in the extra bins have weight at most $\frac{1}{3}$. The second observation is that the number of items in the extra bins can be at most $M - 1$. Combining these two results, we find that at most $\lceil (M - 1)/3 \rceil$ extra bins can be required. We now prove these two observations.

LEMMA 10.1.

Let the N items have (sorted in decreasing order) input sizes $s_1, s_2, \ldots, s_N$, respectively, and suppose that the optimal packing is M bins. Then all items that first fit decreasing places in extra bins have size at most $\frac{1}{3}$.

PROOF:

Suppose the ith item is the first placed in bin $M + 1$. We need to show that $s_i \leq \frac{1}{3}$. We will prove this by contradiction. Assume $s_i > \frac{1}{3}$.

It follows that $s_1, s_2, \ldots, s_{i-1} > \frac{1}{3}$, since the sizes are arranged in sorted order. From this it follows that all bins $B_1, B_2, \ldots, B_M$ have at most two items each.

Consider the state of the system after the $i - 1$st item is placed in a bin, but before the ith item is placed. We now want to show that (under the assumption that $s_i > \frac{1}{3}$) the first M bins are arranged as follows: First there are some bins with exactly one element, and then the remaining bins have two elements.

Suppose there were two bins B_x and B_y, such that $1 \leq x < y \leq M$, B_x has two items, and B_y has one item. Let x_1 and x_2 be the two items in B_x, and let y_1 be the item in B_y. $x_1 \geq y_1$, since x_1 was placed in the earlier bin. $x_2 \geq s_i$, by similar reasoning. Thus, $x_1 + x_2 \geq y_1 + s_i$. This implies that s_i could be placed in B_y. By our assumption this is not possible. Thus, if $s_i > \frac{1}{3}$, then, at the time that we try to process s_i, the first M bins are arranged such that the first j have one element and the next $M - j$ have two elements.

To prove the lemma we will show that there is no way to place all the items in M bins, which contradicts the premise of the lemma.

Clearly, no two items $s_1, s_2, \ldots, s_j$ can be placed in one bin, by any algorithm, since if they could, first fit would have done so too. We also know that first fit has not placed any of the items of size $s_{j+1}, s_{j+2}, \ldots, s_i$ into the first j bins, so none of them fit. Thus, in any packing, specifically the optimal packing, there must be j bins that do not contain these items. It follows that the items of size $s_{j+1}, s_{j+2}, \ldots, s_{i-1}$ must be contained in some set of $M - j$ bins, and from previous considerations, the total number of such items is $2(M - j)$.*

The proof is completed by noting that if $s_i > \frac{1}{3}$, there is no way for s_i to be placed in one of these M bins. Clearly, it cannot go in one of the j bins, since if it could, then

---

*Recall that first fit packed these elements into $M - j$ bins and placed two items in each bin. Thus, there are $2(M - j)$ items.

first fit would have done so too. To place it in one of the remaining $M - j$ bins requires distributing $2(M - j) + 1$ items into the $M - j$ bins. Thus, some bin would have to have three items, each of which is larger than $\frac{1}{3}$, a clear impossibility.

This contradicts the fact that all the sizes can be placed in M bins, so the original assumption must be incorrect. Thus, $s_i \le \frac{1}{3}$.

LEMMA 10.2.
The number of objects placed in extra bins is at most $M - 1$.

PROOF:
Assume that there are at least M objects placed in extra bins. We know that $\sum_{i=1}^{N} s_i \le M$, since all the objects fit in M bins. Suppose that B_j is filled with W_j total weight for $1 \le j \le M$. Suppose the first M extra objects have sizes $x_1, x_2, \ldots, x_M$. Then, since the items in the first M bins plus the first M extra items are a subset of all the items, it follows that

$$\sum_{i=1}^{N} s_i \ge \sum_{j=1}^{M} W_j + \sum_{j=1}^{M} x_j \ge \sum_{j=1}^{M} (W_j + x_j)$$

Now $W_j + x_j > 1$, since otherwise the item corresponding to x_j would have been placed in B_j. Thus

$$\sum_{i=1}^{N} s_i > \sum_{j=1}^{M} 1 > M$$

But this is impossible if the N items can be packed in M bins. Thus, there can be at most $M - 1$ extra items.

THEOREM 10.4.
Let M be the optimal number of bins required to pack a list I of items. Then first fit decreasing never uses more than $(4M + 1)/3$ bins.

PROOF:
There are $M - 1$ extra items, of size at most $\frac{1}{3}$. Thus, there can be at most $\lceil (M - 1)/3 \rceil$ extra bins. The total number of bins used by first fit decreasing is thus at most $\lceil (4M - 1)/3 \rceil \le (4M + 1)/3$.

It is possible to prove a much tighter bound for both first fit decreasing and next fit decreasing.

THEOREM 10.5.
Let M be the optimal number of bins required to pack a list I of items. Then first fit decreasing never uses more than $\frac{11}{9}M + 4$ bins. There exist sequences such that first fit decreasing uses $\frac{11}{9}M$ bins.

PROOF:
The upper bound requires a very complicated analysis. The lower bound is exhibited by a sequence consisting of $6M$ elements of size $\frac{1}{2} + \epsilon$, followed by $6M$ elements of

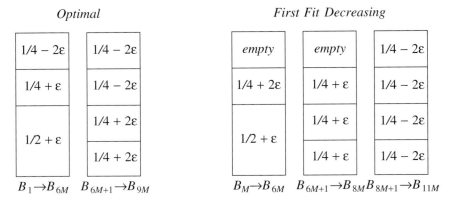

Figure 10.28 Example where first fit decreasing uses 11M bins, but only 9M bins are required

size $\frac{1}{4} + 2\epsilon$, followed by 6M elements of size $\frac{1}{4} + \epsilon$, followed by 12M elements of size $\frac{1}{4} - 2\epsilon$. Figure 10.28 shows that the optimal packing requires 9M bins, but first fit decreasing uses 11M bins.

In practice, first fit decreasing performs extremely well. If sizes are chosen uniformly over the unit interval, then the expected number of extra bins is $\Theta(\sqrt{M})$. Bin packing is a fine example of how simple greedy heuristics can give good results.

10.2. Divide and Conquer

Another common technique used to design algorithms is *divide and conquer*. Divide and conquer algorithms consist of two parts:

Divide: Smaller problems are solved recursively (except, of course, base cases).

Conquer: The solution to the original problem is then formed from the solutions to the subproblems.

Traditionally, routines in which the text contains at least two recursive calls are called divide and conquer algorithms, while routines whose text contains only one recursive call are not. We generally insist that the subproblems be disjoint (that is, essentially nonoverlapping). Let us review some of the recursive algorithms that have been covered in this text.

We have already seen several divide and conquer algorithms. In Section 2.4.3, we saw an $O(N \log N)$ solution to the maximum subsequence sum problem. In Chapter 4, we saw linear-time tree traversal strategies. In Chapter 7, we saw the classic examples of divide and conquer, namely mergesort and quicksort, which have $O(N \log N)$ worst-case and average-case bounds, respectively.

We have also seen several examples of recursive algorithms that probably do not classify as divide and conquer, but merely reduce to a single simpler case. In Section 1.3, we saw a simple routine to print a number. In Chapter 2, we used recursion to perform efficient exponentiation. In Chapter 4, we examined simple search routines for binary search trees. In Section 6.6, we saw simple recursion used to merge leftist heaps. In Section 7.7, an algorithm was given for selection that takes linear average time. The disjoint set `find` operation was written recursively in Chapter 8. Chapter 9 showed routines to recover the shortest path in Dijkstra's algorithm and other procedures to perform depth-first search in graphs. None of these algorithms are really divide and conquer algorithms, because only one recursive call is performed.

We have also seen, in Section 2.4, a very bad recursive routine to compute the Fibonacci numbers. This could be called a divide and conquer algorithm, but it is terribly inefficient, because the problem really is not divided at all.

In this section, we will see more examples of the divide and conquer paradigm. Our first application is a problem in *computational geometry*. Given N points in a plane, we will show that the closest pair of points can be found in $O(N \log N)$ time. The exercises describe some other problems in computational geometry which can be solved by divide and conquer. The remainder of the section shows some extremely interesting, but mostly theoretical, results. We provide an algorithm that solves the selection problem in $O(N)$ worst-case time. We also show that 2 N-bit numbers can be multiplied in $o(N^2)$ operations and that two $N \times N$ matrices can be multiplied in $o(N^3)$ operations. Unfortunately, even though these algorithms have better worst-case bounds than the conventional algorithms, none are practical except for very large inputs.

10.2.1. Running Time of Divide and Conquer Algorithms

All the efficient divide and conquer algorithms we will see divide the problems into sub-problems, each of which is some fraction of the original problem, and then perform some additional work to compute the final answer. As an example, we have seen that mergesort operates on two problems, each of which is half the size of the original, and then uses $O(N)$ additional work. This yields the running time equation (with appropriate initial conditions)

$$T(N) = 2T(N/2) + O(N)$$

We saw in Chapter 7 that the solution to this equation is $O(N \log N)$. The following theorem can be used to determine the running time of most divide and conquer algorithms.

THEOREM 10.6.

The solution to the equation $T(N) = aT(N/b) + \Theta(N^k)$, where $a \geq 1$ and $b > 1$, is

$$T(N) = \begin{cases} O(N^{\log_b a}) & \text{if } a > b^k \\ O(N^k \log N) & \text{if } a = b^k \\ O(N^k) & \text{if } a < b^k \end{cases}$$

PROOF:

Following the analysis of mergesort in Chapter 7, we will assume that N is a power of b; thus, let $N = b^m$. Then $N/b = b^{m-1}$ and $N^k = (b^m)^k = b^{mk} = b^{km} = (b^k)^m$. Let us assume $T(1) = 1$, and ignore the constant factor in $\Theta(N^k)$. Then we have

$$T(b^m) = aT(b^{m-1}) + (b^k)^m$$

If we divide through by a^m, we obtain the equation

$$\frac{T(b^m)}{a^m} = \frac{T(b^{m-1})}{a^{m-1}} + \left\{ \frac{b^k}{a} \right\}^m \tag{10.3}$$

We can apply this equation for other values of m, obtaining

$$\frac{T(b^{m-1})}{a^{m-1}} = \frac{T(b^{m-2})}{a^{m-2}} + \left\{\frac{b^k}{a}\right\}^{m-1} \tag{10.4}$$

$$\frac{T(b^{m-2})}{a^{m-2}} = \frac{T(b^{m-3})}{a^{m-3.}} + \left\{\frac{b^k}{a}\right\}^{m-2} \tag{10.5}$$

$$\cdots$$

$$\frac{T(b^1)}{a^1} = \frac{T(b^0)}{a^0} + \left\{\frac{b^k}{a}\right\}^1 \tag{10.6}$$

We use our standard trick of adding up the telescoping equations (10.3) through (10.6). Virtually all the terms on the left cancel the leading terms on the right, yielding

$$\frac{T(b^m)}{a^m} = 1 + \sum_{i=1}^{m}\left\{\frac{b^k}{a}\right\}^i \tag{10.7}$$

$$= \sum_{i=0}^{m}\left\{\frac{b^k}{a}\right\}^i \tag{10.8}$$

Thus

$$T(N) = T(b^m) = a^m \sum_{i=0}^{m}\left\{\frac{b^k}{a}\right\}^i \tag{10.9}$$

If $a > b^k$, then the sum is a geometric series with ratio smaller than 1. Since the sum of infinite series would converge to a constant, this finite sum is also bounded by a constant, and thus Equation (10.10) applies:

$$T(N) = O(a^m) = O(a^{\log_b N}) = O(N^{\log_b a}) \tag{10.10}$$

If $a = b^k$, then each term in the sum is 1. Since the sum contains $1 + \log_b N$ terms and $a = b^k$ implies that $\log_b a = k$,

$$T(N) = O(a^m \log_b N) = O(N^{\log_b a} \log_b N) = O(N^k \log_b N)$$
$$= O(N^k \log N) \tag{10.11}$$

Finally, if $a < b^k$, then the terms in the geometric series are larger than 1, and the second formula in Section 1.2.3 applies. We obtain

$$T(N) = a^m \frac{(b^k/a)^{m+1} - 1}{(b^k/a) - 1} = O(a^m(b^k/a)^m) = O((b^k)^m) = O(N^k) \tag{10.12}$$

proving the last case of the theorem.

As an example, mergesort has $a = b = 2$ and $k = 1$. The second case applies, giving the answer $O(N \log N)$. If we solve three problems, each of which is half the original size, and combine the solutions with $O(N)$ additional work, then $a = 3$, $b = 2$, and $k = 1$.

Case 1 applies here, giving a bound of $O(N^{\log_2 3}) = O(N^{1.59})$. An algorithm that solved three half-sized problems, but required $O(N^2)$ work to merge the solution, would have an $O(N^2)$ running time, since the third case would apply.

There are two important cases that are not covered by Theorem 10.6. We state two more theorems, leaving the proofs as exercises. Theorem 10.7 generalizes the previous theorem.

THEOREM 10.7.
The solution to the equation $T(N) = aT(N/b) + \Theta(N^k \log^p N)$, where $a \geq 1$, $b > 1$, and $p \geq 0$ is

$$T(N) = \begin{cases} O(N^{\log_b a}) & \text{if } a > b^k \\ O(N^k \log^{p+1} N) & \text{if } a = b^k \\ O(N^k \log^p N) & \text{if } a < b^k \end{cases}$$

THEOREM 10.8.
If $\sum_{i=1}^{k} \alpha_i < 1$, then the solution to the equation $T(N) = \sum_{i=1}^{k} T(\alpha_i N) + O(N)$ is $T(N) = O(N)$.

10.2.2. Closest-Points Problem

The input to our first problem is a list P of points in a plane. If $p_1 = (x_1, y_1)$ and $p_2 = (x_2, y_2)$, then the Euclidean distance between p_1 and p_2 is $[(x_1 - x_2)^2 + (y_1 - y_2)^2]^{1/2}$. We are required to find the closest pair of points. It is possible that two points have the same position; in that case that pair is the closest, with distance zero.

If there are N points, then there are $N(N - 1)/2$ pairs of distances. We can check all of these, obtaining a very short program, but at the expense of an $O(N^2)$ algorithm. Since this approach is just an exhaustive search, we should expect to do better.

Let us assume that the points have been sorted by x coordinate. At worst, this adds $O(N \log N)$ to the final time bound. Since we will show an $O(N \log N)$ bound for the entire algorithm, this sort is essentially free, from a complexity standpoint.

Figure 10.29 shows a small sample point set P. Since the points are sorted by x coordinate, we can draw an imaginary vertical line that partitions the point set into two halves, P_L and P_R. This is certainly simple to do. Now we have almost exactly the same situation

Figure 10.29 A small point set

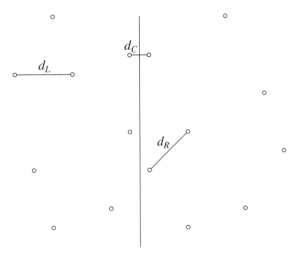

Figure 10.30 P partitioned into P_L and P_R; shortest distances are shown

as we saw in the maximum subsequence sum problem in Section 2.4.3. Either the closest points are both in P_L, or they are both in P_R, or one is in P_L and the other is in P_R. Let us call these distances d_L, d_R, and d_C. Figure 10.30 shows the partition of the point set and these three distances.

We can compute d_L and d_R recursively. The problem, then, is to compute d_C. Since we would like an $O(N \log N)$ solution, we must be able to compute d_C with only $O(N)$ additional work. We have already seen that if a procedure consists of two half-sized recursive calls and $O(N)$ additional work, then the total time will be $O(N \log N)$.

Let $\delta = \min(d_L, d_R)$. The first observation is that we only need to compute d_C if d_C improves on δ. If d_C is such a distance, then the two points that define d_C must be within δ of the dividing line; we will refer to this area as a *strip*. As shown in Figure 10.31,

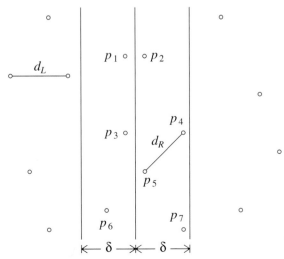

Figure 10.31 Two-lane strip, containing all points considered for d_C strip

```
// Points are all in the strip

for( i = 0; i < numPointsInStrip; i++ )
    for( j = i + 1; j < numPointsInStrip; j++ )
        if( dist(pᵢ, pⱼ) < δ )
            δ = dist(pᵢ, pⱼ);
```

Figure 10.32 Brute force calculation of $min(\delta, d_C)$

```
// Points are all in the strip and sorted by y coordinate

for( i = 0; i < numPointsInStrip; i++ )
    for( j = i + 1; j < numPointsInStrip; j++ )
        if( pᵢ and pⱼ 's coordinates differ by more than δ )
            break;        // Go to next pᵢ .
        else
        if( dist(pᵢ, pⱼ) < δ )
            δ = dist(pᵢ, pⱼ);
```

Figure 10.33 Refined calculation of $min(\delta, d_C)$

this observation limits the number of points that need to be considered (in our case, $\delta = d_R$).

There are two strategies that can be tried to compute d_C. For large point sets that are uniformly distributed, the number of points that are expected to be in the strip is very small. Indeed, it is easy to argue that only $O(\sqrt{N})$ points are in the strip on average. Thus, we could perform a brute force calculation on these points in $O(N)$ time. The pseudocode in Figure 10.32 implements this strategy, assuming the Java convention that the points are indexed starting at 0.

In the worst case, all the points could be in the strip, so this strategy does not always work in linear time. We can improve this algorithm with the following observation: The y coordinates of the two points that define d_C can differ by at most δ. Otherwise, $d_C > \delta$. Suppose that the points in the strip are sorted by their y coordinates. Therefore, if p_i and p_j's y coordinates differ by more than δ, then we can proceed to p_{i+1}. This simple modification is implemented in Figure 10.33.

This extra test has a significant effect on the running time, because for each p_i only a few points p_j are examined before p_i's and p_j's y coordinates differ by more than δ and force an exit from the inner **for** loop. Figure 10.34 shows, for instance, that for point p_3, only the two points p_4 and p_5 lie in the strip within δ vertical distance.

In the worst case, for any point p_i, at most 7 points p_j are considered. This is because these points must lie either in the δ by δ square in the left half of the strip or in the δ by δ square in the right half of the strip. On the other hand, all the points in each δ by δ square are separated by at least δ. In the worst case, each square contains four points, one at each corner. One of these points is p_i, leaving at most seven points to be considered. This worst-case situation is shown in Figure 10.35. Notice that even though p_{L2} and p_{R1} have the same coordinates, they could be different points. For the actual analysis, it is only important that the number of points in the λ by 2λ rectangle be $O(1)$, and this much is certainly clear.

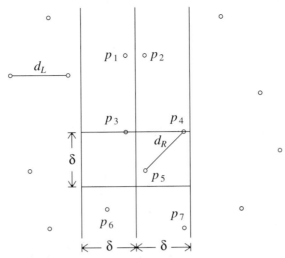

Figure 10.34 Only p_4 and p_5 are considered in the second **for** loop

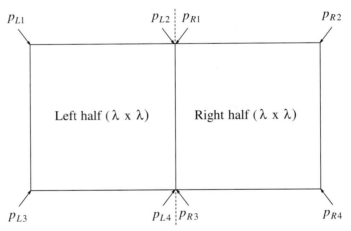

Figure 10.35 At most eight points fit in the rectangle; there are two coordinates shared by two points each

Because at most seven points are considered for each p_i, the time to compute a d_C that is better than δ is $O(N)$. Thus, we appear to have an $O(N \log N)$ solution to the closest-points problem, based on the two half-sized recursive calls plus the linear extra work to combine the two results. However, we do not quite have an $O(N \log N)$ solution yet.

The problem is that we have assumed that a list of points sorted by y coordinate is available. If we perform this sort for each recursive call, then we have $O(N \log N)$ extra work: this gives an $O(N \log^2 N)$ algorithm. This is not all that bad, especially when compared to the brute force $O(N^2)$. However, it is not hard to reduce the work for each recursive call to $O(N)$, thus ensuring an $O(N \log N)$ algorithm.

We will maintain two lists. One is the point list sorted by x coordinate, and the other is the point list sorted by y coordinate. We will call these lists P and Q, respectively. These can be obtained by a preprocessing sorting step at cost $O(N \log N)$ and thus does not affect the time bound. P_L and Q_L are the lists passed to the left-half recursive call, and P_R and Q_R are the lists passed to the right-half recursive call. We have already seen that P is easily split in the middle. Once the dividing line is known, we step through Q sequentially, placing each element in Q_L or Q_R as appropriate. It is easy to see that Q_L and Q_R will be automatically sorted by y coordinate. When the recursive calls return, we scan through the Q list and discard all the points whose x coordinates are not within the strip. Then Q contains only points in the strip, and these points are guaranteed to be sorted by their y coordinates.

This strategy ensures that the entire algorithm is $O(N \log N)$, because only $O(N)$ extra work is performed.

10.2.3. The Selection Problem

The *selection problem* requires us to find the kth smallest element in a collection S of N elements. Of particular interest is the special case of finding the median. This occurs when $k = \lceil N/2 \rceil$.

In Chapters 1, 6, and 7 we have seen several solutions to the selection problem. The solution in Chapter 7 uses a variation of quicksort and runs in $O(N)$ average time. Indeed, it is described in Hoare's original paper on quicksort.

Although this algorithm runs in linear average time, it has a worst case of $O(N^2)$. Selection can easily be solved in $O(N \log N)$ worst-case time by sorting the elements, but for a long time it was unknown whether or not selection could be accomplished in $O(N)$ worst-case time. The *quickselect* algorithm outlined in Section 7.7.6 is quite efficient in practice, so this was mostly a question of theoretical interest.

Recall that the basic algorithm is a simple recursive strategy. Assuming that N is larger than the cutoff point where elements are simply sorted, an element v, known as the pivot, is chosen. The remaining elements are placed into two sets, S_1 and S_2. S_1 contains elements that are guaranteed to be no larger than v, and S_2 contains elements that are no smaller than v. Finally, if $k \leq |S_1|$, then the kth smallest element in S can be found by recursively computing the kth smallest element in S_1. If $k = |S_1| + 1$, then the pivot is the kth smallest element. Otherwise, the kth smallest element in S is the $(k - |S_1| - 1)$st smallest element in S_2. The main difference between this algorithm and quicksort is that there is only one subproblem to solve instead of two.

In order to obtain a linear algorithm, we must ensure that the subproblem is only a fraction of the original and not merely only a few elements smaller than the original. Of course, we can always find such an element if we are willing to spend some time to do so. The difficult problem is that we cannot spend too much time finding the pivot.

For quicksort, we saw that a good choice for pivot was to pick three elements and use their median. This gives some expectation that the pivot is not too bad, but does not provide a guarantee. We could choose 21 elements at random, sort them in constant time, use the 11th largest as pivot, and get a pivot that is even more likely to be good. However, if these 21 elements were the 21 largest, then the pivot would still be poor. Extending this, we could use up to $O(N/\log N)$ elements, sort them using heapsort in $O(N)$ total time, and be almost certain, from a statistical point of view, of obtaining a good pivot. In the worst case, however, this does not work because we might select the $O(N/\log N)$ largest elements, and then the pivot would be the $[N - O(N/\log N)]$th largest element, which is not a constant fraction of N.

The basic idea is still useful. Indeed, we will see that we can use it to improve the expected number of comparisons that quickselect makes. To get a good worst case, however, the key idea is to use one more level of indirection. Instead of finding the median from a sample of random elements, we will find the median from a *sample of medians*.

The basic pivot selection algorithm is as follows:

1. Arrange the N elements into $\lfloor N/5 \rfloor$ groups of five elements, ignoring the (at most four) extra elements.
2. Find the median of each group. This gives a list M of $\lfloor N/5 \rfloor$ medians.
3. Find the median of M. Return this as the pivot, v.

We will use the term *median-of-median-of-five partitioning* to describe the quickselect algorithm that uses the pivot selection rule given above. We will now show that median-of-median-of-five partitioning guarantees that each recursive sub-problem is at most roughly 70 percent as large as the original. We will also show that the pivot can be computed quickly enough to guarantee an $O(N)$ running time for the entire selection algorithm.

Let us assume for the moment that N is divisible by 5, so there are no extra elements. Suppose also that $N/5$ is odd, so that the set M contains an odd number of elements. This provides some symmetry, as we shall see. We are thus assuming, for convenience, that N is of the form $10k + 5$. We will also assume that all the elements are distinct. The actual algorithm must make sure to handle the case where this is not true. Figure 10.36 shows how the pivot might be chosen when $N = 45$.

In Figure 10.36, v represents the element which is selected by the algorithm as pivot. Since v is the median of nine elements, and we are assuming that all elements are distinct, there must be four medians that are larger than v and four that are smaller. We denote these by L and S, respectively. Consider a group of five elements with a large median (type L). The median of the group is smaller than two elements in the group and larger than two

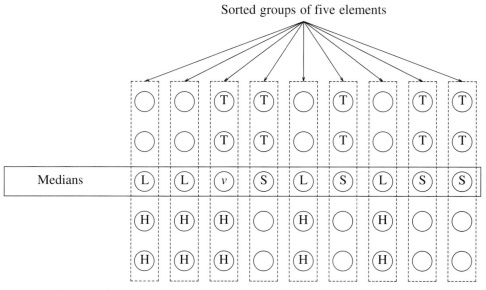

Figure 10.36 How the pivot is chosen

elements in the group. We will let H represent the *huge* elements. These are elements that are known to be larger than a large median. Similarly, T represents the *tiny* elements, which are smaller than a small median. There are 10 elements of type H: Two are in each of the groups with an L type median, and two elements are in the same group as v. Similarly, there are 10 elements of type T.

Elements of type L or H are guaranteed to be larger than v, and elements of type S or T are guaranteed to be smaller than v. There are thus guaranteed to be 14 large and 14 small elements in our problem. Therefore, a recursive call could be on at most $45 - 14 - 1 = 30$ elements.

Let us extend this analysis to general N of the form $10k + 5$. In this case, there are k elements of type L and k elements of type S. There are $2k + 2$ elements of type H, and also $2k + 2$ elements of type T. Thus, there are $3k + 2$ elements that are guaranteed to be larger than v and $3k + 2$ elements that are guaranteed to be smaller. Thus, in this case, the recursive call can contain at most $7k + 2 < 0.7N$ elements. If N is not of the form $10k + 5$, similar arguments can be made without affecting the basic result.

It remains to bound the running time to obtain the pivot element. There are two basic steps. We can find the median of five elements in constant time. For instance, it is not hard to sort five elements in eight comparisons. We must do this $\lfloor N/5 \rfloor$ times, so this step takes $O(N)$ time. We must then compute the median of a group of $\lfloor N/5 \rfloor$ elements. The obvious way to do this is to sort the group and return the element in the middle. But this takes $O(\lfloor N/5 \rfloor \log \lfloor N/5 \rfloor) = O(N \log N)$ time, so this does not work. The solution is to call the selection algorithm recursively on the $\lfloor N/5 \rfloor$ elements.

This completes the description of the basic algorithm. There are still some details that need to be filled in if an actual implementation is desired. For instance, duplicates must be handled correctly, and the algorithm needs a cutoff large enough to ensure that the recursive calls make progress. There is quite a large amount of overhead involved, and this algorithm is not practical at all, so we will not describe any more of the details that need to be considered. Even so, from a theoretical standpoint, the algorithm is a major breakthrough, because, as the following theorem shows, the running time is linear in the worst case.

THEOREM 10.9.

The running time of quickselect using median-of-median-of-five partitioning is $O(N)$.

PROOF:

The algorithm consists of two recursive calls of size $0.7N$ and $0.2N$, plus linear extra work. By Theorem 10.8, the running time is linear. ∎

Reducing the Average Number of Comparisons

Divide and conquer can also be used to reduce the expected number of comparisons required by the selection algorithm. Let us look at a concrete example. Suppose we have a group S of 1,000 numbers and are looking for the 100th smallest number, which we will call X. We choose a subset S' of S consisting of 100 numbers. We would expect that the value of X is similar in size to the 10th smallest number in S'. More specifically, the fifth smallest number in S' is almost certainly less than X, and the 15th smallest number in S' is almost certainly greater than X.

More generally, a sample S' of s elements is chosen from the N elements. Let δ be some number, which we will choose later so as to minimize the average number of comparisons used by the procedure. We find the $(v_1 = ks/N - \delta)$th and $(v_2 = ks/N + \delta)$th smallest elements in S'. Almost certainly, the kth smallest element in S will fall between v_1 and v_2, so we are left with a selection problem on 2δ elements. With low probability, the kth smallest element does not fall in this range, and we have considerable work to do. However, with a good choice of s and δ, we can ensure, by the laws of probability, that the second case does not adversely affect the total work.

If an analysis is performed, we find that if $s = N^{2/3} \log^{1/3} N$ and $\delta = N^{1/3} \log^{2/3} N$, then the expected number of comparisons is $N + k + O(N^{2/3} \log^{1/3} N)$, which is optimal except for the low-order term. (If $k > N/2$, we can consider the symmetric problem of finding the $(N - k)$th largest element.)

Most of the analysis is easy to do. The last term represents the cost of performing the two selections to determine v_1 and v_2. The average cost of the partitioning, assuming a reasonably clever strategy, is equal to N plus the expected rank of v_2 in S, which is $N + k + O(N\delta/s)$. If the kth element winds up in S', the cost of finishing the algorithm is equal to the cost of selection on S', namely, $O(s)$. If the kth smallest element doesn't wind up in S', the cost is $O(N)$. However, s and δ have been chosen to guarantee that this happens with very low probability $o(1/N)$, so the expected cost of this possibility is $o(1)$, which is a term that goes to zero as N gets large. An exact calculation is left as Exercise 10.21.

This analysis shows that finding the median requires about $1.5N$ comparisons on average. Of course, this algorithm requires some floating-point arithmetic to compute s, which can slow down the algorithm on some machines. Even so, experiments have shown that if correctly implemented, this algorithm compares favorably with the quickselect implementation in Chapter 7.

10.2.4. Theoretical Improvements for Arithmetic Problems

In this section we describe a divide and conquer algorithm that multiplies two N-digit numbers. Our previous model of computation assumed that multiplication was done in constant time, because the numbers were small. For large numbers, this assumption is no longer valid. If we measure multiplication in terms of the size of numbers being multiplied, then the natural multiplication algorithm takes quadratic time. The divide and conquer algorithm runs in subquadratic time. We also present the classic divide and conquer algorithm that multiplies two N by N matrices in subcubic time.

Multiplying Integers

Suppose we want to multiply two N-digit numbers X and Y. If exactly one of X and Y is negative, then the answer is negative; otherwise it is positive. Thus, we can perform this check and then assume that $X, Y \geq 0$. The algorithm that almost everyone uses when multiplying by hand requires $\Theta(N^2)$ operations, because each digit in X is multiplied by each digit in Y.

If $X = 61,438,521$ and $Y = 94,736,407$, $XY = 5,820,464,730,934,047$. Let us break X and Y into two halves, consisting of the most significant and least significant digits, respectively. Then $X_L = 6,143$, $X_R = 8,521$, $Y_L = 9,473$, and $Y_R = 6,407$. We also have $X = X_L 10^4 + X_R$ and $Y = Y_L 10^4 + Y_R$. It follows that

$$XY = X_L Y_L 10^8 + (X_L Y_R + X_R Y_L)10^4 + X_R Y_R$$

Notice that this equation consists of four multiplications, $X_L Y_L$, $X_L Y_R$, $X_R Y_L$, and $X_R Y_R$, which are each half the size of the original problem ($N/2$ digits). The multiplications by 10^8 and 10^4 amount to the placing of zeros. This and the subsequent additions add only $O(N)$ additional work. If we perform these four multiplications recursively using this algorithm, stopping at an appropriate base case, then we obtain the recurrence

$$T(N) = 4T(N/2) + O(N)$$

From Theorem 10.6, we see that $T(N) = O(N^2)$, so, unfortunately, we have not improved the algorithm. To achieve a subquadratic algorithm, we must use less than four recursive calls. The key observation is that

$$X_L Y_R + X_R Y_L = (X_L - X_R)(Y_R - Y_L) + X_L Y_L + X_R Y_R$$

Thus, instead of using two multiplications to compute the coefficient of 10^4, we can use one multiplication, plus the result of two multiplications that have already been performed. Figure 10.37 shows how only three recursive subproblems need to be solved.

It is easy to see that now the recurrence equation satisfies

$$T(N) = 3T(N/2) + O(N)$$

and so we obtain $T(N) = O(N^{\log_2 3}) = O(N^{1.59})$. To complete the algorithm, we must have a base case, which can be solved without recursion.

Function	Value	Computational Complexity
X_L	6,143	Given
X_R	8,521	Given
Y_L	9,473	Given
Y_R	6,407	Given
$D_1 = X_L - X_R$	$-2,378$	$O(N)$
$D_2 = Y_R - Y_L$	$-3,066$	$O(N)$
$X_L Y_L$	58,192,639	$T(N/2)$
$X_R Y_R$	54,594,047	$T(N/2)$
$D_1 D_2$	7,290,948	$T(N/2)$
$D_3 = D_1 D_2 + X_L Y_L + X_R Y_R$	120,077,634	$O(N)$
$X_R Y_R$	54,594,047	Computed above
$D_3 10^4$	1,200,776,340,000	$O(N)$
$X_L Y_L 10^8$	5,819,263,900,000,000	$O(N)$
$X_L Y_L 10^8 + D_3 10^4 + X_R Y_R$	5,820,464,730,934,047	$O(N)$

Figure 10.37 The divide and conquer algorithm in action

```
/**
 * Standard matrix multiplication.
 * Arrays start at 0.
 * Assumes a and b are square.
 */
public static int [ ][ ] multiply( int [ ][ ] a, int [ ][ ] b )
{
    int n = a.length;
    int [ ][ ] c = new int[ n ][ n ];

    for( int i = 0; i < n; i++ )    // Initialization
        for( int j = 0; j < n; j++ )
            c[ i ][ j ] = 0;

    for( int i = 0; i < n; i++ )
        for( int j = 0; j < n; j++ )
            for( int k = 0; k < n; k++ )
                c[ i ][ j ] += a[ i ][ k ] * b[ k ][ j ];

    return c;
}
```

Figure 10.38 Simple $O(N^3)$ matrix multiplication

When both numbers are one-digit, we can do the multiplication by table lookup. If one number has zero digits, then we return zero. In practice, if we were to use this algorithm, we would choose the base case to be that which is most convenient for the machine.

Although this algorithm has better asymptotic performance than the standard quadratic algorithm, it is rarely used, because for small N the overhead is significant, and for larger N there are even better algorithms. These algorithms also make extensive use of divide and conquer.

Matrix Multiplication

A fundamental numerical problem is the multiplication of two matrices. Figure 10.38 gives a simple $O(N^3)$ algorithm to compute $\mathbf{C} = \mathbf{AB}$, where $\mathbf{A}$, $\mathbf{B}$, and $\mathbf{C}$ are $N \times N$ matrices. The algorithm follows directly from the definition of matrix multiplication. To compute $C_{i,j}$, we compute the dot product of the ith row in $\mathbf{A}$ with the jth column in $\mathbf{B}$. As usual, arrays begin at index 0.

For a long time it was assumed that $\Omega(N^3)$ was required for matrix multiplication. However, in the late sixties Strassen showed how to break the $\Omega(N^3)$ barrier. The basic idea of Strassen's algorithm is to divide each matrix into four quadrants, as shown in Figure 10.39. Then it is easy to show that

$$\begin{bmatrix} A_{1,1} & A_{1,2} \\ A_{2,1} & A_{2,2} \end{bmatrix} \begin{bmatrix} B_{1,1} & B_{1,2} \\ B_{2,1} & B_{2,2} \end{bmatrix} = \begin{bmatrix} C_{1,1} & C_{1,2} \\ C_{2,1} & C_{2,2} \end{bmatrix}$$

Figure 10.39 Decomposing $\mathbf{AB} = \mathbf{C}$ into four quadrants

$$C_{1,1} = A_{1,1}B_{1,1} + A_{1,2}B_{2,1}$$
$$C_{1,2} = A_{1,1}B_{1,2} + A_{1,2}B_{2,2}$$
$$C_{2,1} = A_{2,1}B_{1,1} + A_{2,2}B_{2,1}$$
$$C_{2,2} = A_{2,1}B_{1,2} + A_{2,2}B_{2,2}$$

As an example, to perform the multiplication **AB**

$$\mathbf{AB} = \begin{bmatrix} 3 & 4 & 1 & 6 \\ 1 & 2 & 5 & 7 \\ 5 & 1 & 2 & 9 \\ 4 & 3 & 5 & 6 \end{bmatrix} \begin{bmatrix} 5 & 6 & 9 & 3 \\ 4 & 5 & 3 & 1 \\ 1 & 1 & 8 & 4 \\ 3 & 1 & 4 & 1 \end{bmatrix}$$

we define the following eight $N/2$ by $N/2$ matrices:

$$A_{1,1} = \begin{bmatrix} 3 & 4 \\ 1 & 2 \end{bmatrix} \quad A_{1,2} = \begin{bmatrix} 1 & 6 \\ 5 & 7 \end{bmatrix} \quad B_{1,1} = \begin{bmatrix} 5 & 6 \\ 4 & 5 \end{bmatrix} \quad B_{1,2} = \begin{bmatrix} 9 & 3 \\ 3 & 1 \end{bmatrix}$$

$$A_{2,1} = \begin{bmatrix} 5 & 1 \\ 4 & 3 \end{bmatrix} \quad A_{2,2} = \begin{bmatrix} 2 & 9 \\ 5 & 6 \end{bmatrix} \quad B_{2,1} = \begin{bmatrix} 1 & 1 \\ 3 & 1 \end{bmatrix} \quad B_{2,2} = \begin{bmatrix} 8 & 4 \\ 4 & 1 \end{bmatrix}$$

We could then perform eight $N/2$ by $N/2$ matrix multiplications and four $N/2$ by $N/2$ matrix additions. The matrix additions take $O(N^2)$ time. If the matrix multiplications are done recursively, then the running time satisfies

$$T(N) = 8T(N/2) + O(N^2)$$

From Theorem 10.6, we see that $T(N) = O(N^3)$, so we do not have an improvement. As we saw with integer multiplication, we must reduce the number of subproblems below 8. Strassen used a strategy similar to the integer multiplication divide and conquer algorithm and showed how to use only seven recursive calls by carefully arranging the computations. The seven multiplications are

$$M_1 = (A_{1,2} - A_{2,2})(B_{2,1} + B_{2,2})$$
$$M_2 = (A_{1,1} + A_{2,2})(B_{1,1} + B_{2,2})$$
$$M_3 = (A_{1,1} - A_{2,1})(B_{1,1} + B_{1,2})$$
$$M_4 = (A_{1,1} + A_{1,2})B_{2,2}$$
$$M_5 = A_{1,1}(B_{1,2} - B_{2,2})$$
$$M_6 = A_{2,2}(B_{2,1} - B_{1,1})$$
$$M_7 = (A_{2,1} + A_{2,2})B_{1,1}$$

Once the multiplications are performed, the final answer can be obtained with eight more additions.

$$C_{1,1} = M_1 + M_2 - M_4 + M_6$$
$$C_{1,2} = M_4 + M_5$$
$$C_{2,1} = M_6 + M_7$$
$$C_{2,2} = M_2 - M_3 + M_5 - M_7$$

It is straightforward to verify that this tricky ordering produces the desired values. The running time now satisfies the recurrence

$$T(N) = 7T(N/2) + O(N^2)$$

The solution of this recurrence is $T(N) = O(N^{\log_2 7}) = O(N^{2.81})$.

As usual, there are details to consider, such as the case when N is not a power of 2, but these are basically minor nuisances. Strassen's algorithm is worse than the straightforward algorithm until N is fairly large. It does not generalize for the case where the matrices are sparse (contain many zero entries), and it does not easily parallelize. When run with floating-point entries, it is less stable numerically than the classic algorithm. Thus, it has only limited applicability. Nevertheless, it represents an important theoretical milestone and certainly shows that in computer science, as in many other fields, even though a problem seems to have an intrinsic complexity, nothing is certain until proven.

10.3. Dynamic Programming

In the previous section, we saw that a problem that can be mathematically expressed recursively can also be expressed as a recursive algorithm, in many cases yielding a significant performance improvement over a more naïve exhaustive search.

Any recursive mathematical formula could be directly translated to a recursive algorithm, but the underlying reality is that often the compiler will not do justice to the recursive algorithm, and an inefficient program results. When we suspect that this is likely to be the case, we must provide a little more help to the compiler, by rewriting the recursive algorithm as a nonrecursive algorithm that systematically records the answers to the subproblems in a table. One technique that makes use of this approach is known as *dynamic programming*.

10.3.1. Using a Table Instead of Recursion

In Chapter 2, we saw that the natural recursive program to compute the Fibonacci numbers is very inefficient. Recall that the program shown in Figure 10.40 has a running time $T(N)$ that satisfies $T(N) \geq T(N-1) + T(N-2)$. Since $T(N)$ satisfies the same recurrence relation as the Fibonacci numbers and has the same initial conditions, $T(N)$ in fact grows at the same rate as the Fibonacci numbers, and is thus exponential.

```
/**
 * Compute Fibonacci numbers as described in Chapter 1.
 */
public static int fib( int n )
{
    if( n <= 1 )
        return 1;
    else
        return fib( n - 1 ) + fib( n - 2 );
}
```

10.40 Inefficient algorithm to compute Fibonacci numbers

```
/**
 * Compute Fibonacci numbers as described in Chapter 1.
 */
public static int fibonacci( int n )
{
    if( n <= 1 )
        return 1;

    int last = 1;
    int nextToLast = 1;
    int answer = 1;
    for( int i = 2; i <= n; i++ )
    {
        answer = last + nextToLast;
        nextToLast = last;
        last = answer;
    }
    return answer;
}
```

Figure 10.41 Linear algorithm to compute Fibonacci numbers

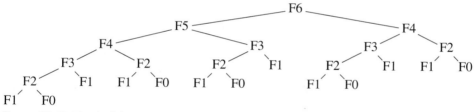

Figure 10.42 Trace of the recursive calculation of Fibonacci numbers

On the other hand, since to compute F_N, all that is needed is F_{N-1} and F_{N-2}, we only need to record the two most recently computed Fibonacci numbers. This yields the $O(N)$ algorithm in Figure 10.41.

The reason that the recursive algorithm is so slow is because of the algorithm used to simulate recursion. To compute F_N, there is one call to F_{N-1} and F_{N-2}. However, since F_{N-1} recursively makes a call to F_{N-2} and F_{N-3}, there are actually two separate calls to compute F_{N-2}. If one traces out the entire algorithm, then we can see that F_{N-3} is computed three times, F_{N-4} is computed five times, F_{N-5} is computed eight times, and so on. As Figure 10.42 shows, the growth of redundant calculations is explosive. If the compiler's recursion simulation algorithm were able to keep a list of all precomputed values and not make a recursive call for an already solved subproblem, then this exponential explosion would be avoided. This is why the program in Figure 10.41 is so much more efficient.

As a second example, we saw in Chapter 7 how to solve the recurrence $C(N) = (2/N)\sum_{i=0}^{N-1} C(i)+N$, with $C(0) = 1$. Suppose that we want to check, numerically, whether the solution we obtained is correct. We could then write the simple program in Figure 10.43 to evaluate the recursion.

```
public static double eval( int n )
{
    if( n == 0 )
        return 1.0;
    else
    {
        double sum = 0.0;
        for( int i = 0; i < n; i++ )
            sum += eval( i );
        return 2.0 * sum / n + n;
    }
}
```

Figure 10.43 Recursive method to evaluate $C(N) = 2/N \sum_{i=0}^{N-1} C(i) + N$

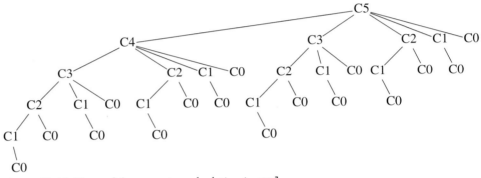

Figure 10.44 Trace of the recursive calculation in eval

```
public static double eval( int n )
{
    double [ ] c = new double [ n + 1 ];

    c[ 0 ] = 1.0;
    for( int i = 1; i <= n; i++ )
    {
        double sum = 0.0;
        for( int j = 0; j < i; j++ )
            sum += c[ j ];
        c[ i ] = 2.0 * sum / i + i;
    }

    return c[ n ];
}
```

Figure 10.45 Evaluating $C(N) = 2/N \sum_{i=0}^{N-1} C(i) + N$ with a table

Once again, the recursive calls duplicate work. In this case, the running time $T(N)$ satisfies $T(N) = \sum_{i=0}^{N-1} T(i) + N$, because, as shown in Figure 10.44, there is one (direct) recursive call of each size from 0 to $N - 1$, plus $O(N)$ additional work (where else have we seen the tree shown in Figure 10.44?). Solving for $T(N)$, we find that it grows exponentially. By using a table, we obtain the program in Figure 10.45. This program avoids the redundant recursive calls and runs in $O(N^2)$. It is not a perfect program; as an exercise, you should make the simple change that reduces its running time to $O(N)$.

10.3.2. Ordering Matrix Multiplications

Suppose we are given four matrices, **A**, **B**, **C**, and **D**, of dimensions $\mathbf{A} = 50 \times 10$, $\mathbf{B} = 10 \times 40$, $\mathbf{C} = 40 \times 30$, and $\mathbf{D} = 30 \times 5$. Although matrix multiplication is not commutative, it is associative, which means that the matrix product **ABCD** can be parenthesized, and thus evaluated, in any order. The obvious way to multiply two matrices of dimensions $p \times q$ and $q \times r$, respectively, uses pqr scalar multiplications. (Using a theoretically superior algorithm such as Strassen's algorithm does not significantly alter the problem we will consider, so we will assume this performance bound.) What is the best way to perform the three matrix multiplications required to compute **ABCD**?

In the case of four matrices, it is simple to solve the problem by exhaustive search, since there are only five ways to order the multiplications. We evaluate each case below:

- (**A**((**BC**)**D**)): Evaluating **BC** requires $10 \times 40 \times 30 = 12{,}000$ multiplications. Evaluating (**BC**)**D** requires the 12,000 multiplications to compute **BC**, plus an additional $10 \times 30 \times 5 = 1{,}500$ multiplications, for a total of 13,500. Evaluating (**A**((**BC**)**D**)) requires 13,500 multiplications for (**BC**)**D**, plus an additional $50 \times 10 \times 5 = 2{,}500$ multiplications, for a grand total of 16,000 multiplications.

- (**A**(**B**(**CD**))): Evaluating **CD** requires $40 \times 30 \times 5 = 6{,}000$ multiplications. Evaluating **B**(**CD**) requires the 6,000 multiplications to compute **CD**, plus an additional $10 \times 40 \times 5 = 2{,}000$ multiplications, for a total of 8,000. Evaluating (**A**(**B**(**CD**))) requires 8,000 multiplications for **B**(**CD**), plus an additional $50 \times 10 \times 5 = 2{,}500$ multiplications, for a grand total of 10,500 multiplications.

- ((**AB**)(**CD**)): Evaluating **CD** requires $40 \times 30 \times 5 = 6{,}000$ multiplications. Evaluating **AB** requires $50 \times 10 \times 40 = 20{,}000$ multiplications. Evaluating ((**AB**)(**CD**)) requires 6,000 multiplications for **CD**, 20,000 multiplications for **AB**, plus an additional $50 \times 40 \times 5 = 10{,}000$ multiplications for a grand total of 36,000 multiplications.

- (((**AB**)**C**)**D**): Evaluating **AB** requires $50 \times 10 \times 40 = 20{,}000$ multiplications. Evaluating (**AB**)**C** requires the 20,000 multiplications to compute **AB**, plus an additional $50 \times 40 \times 30 = 60{,}000$ multiplications, for a total of 80,000. Evaluating (((**AB**)**C**)**D**) requires 80,000 multiplications for (**AB**)**C**, plus an additional $50 \times 30 \times 5 = 7{,}500$ multiplications, for a grand total of 87,500 multiplications.

- ((**A**(**BC**))**D**): Evaluating **BC** requires $10 \times 40 \times 30 = 12{,}000$ multiplications. Evaluating **A**(**BC**) requires the 12,000 multiplications to compute **BC**, plus an additional $50 \times 10 \times 30 = 15{,}000$ multiplications, for a total of 27,000. Evaluating ((**A**(**BC**))**D**) requires 27,000 multiplications for **A**(**BC**), plus an additional $50 \times 30 \times 5 = 7{,}500$ multiplications, for a grand total of 34,500 multiplications.

The calculations show that the best ordering uses roughly one-ninth the number of multiplications as the worst ordering. Thus, it might be worthwhile to perform a few calculations to determine the optimal ordering. Unfortunately, none of the obvious greedy strategies seems to work. Moreover, the number of possible orderings grows quickly. Suppose we define $T(N)$ to be this number. Then $T(1) = T(2) = 1$, $T(3) = 2$, and $T(4) = 5$, as we have seen. In general,

$$T(N) = \sum_{i=1}^{N-1} T(i)T(N - i)$$

To see this, suppose that the matrices are $\mathbf{A}_1$, $\mathbf{A}_2, \ldots, \mathbf{A}_N$, and the last multiplication performed is $(\mathbf{A}_1\mathbf{A}_2 \cdots \mathbf{A}_i)(\mathbf{A}_{i+1}\mathbf{A}_{i+2} \cdots \mathbf{A}_N)$. Then there are $T(i)$ ways to compute $(\mathbf{A}_1\mathbf{A}_2 \cdots \mathbf{A}_i)$ and $T(N-i)$ ways to compute $(\mathbf{A}_{i+1}\mathbf{A}_{i+2} \cdots \mathbf{A}_N)$. Thus, there are $T(i)T(N-i)$ ways to compute $(\mathbf{A}_1\mathbf{A}_2 \cdots \mathbf{A}_i)(\mathbf{A}_{i+1}\mathbf{A}_{i+2} \cdots \mathbf{A}_N)$ for each possible i.

The solution of this recurrence is the well-known *Catalan numbers,* which grow exponentially. Thus, for large N, an exhaustive search through all possible orderings is useless. Nevertheless, this counting argument provides a basis for a solution that is substantially better than exponential. Let c_i be the number of columns in matrix $\mathbf{A}_i$ for $1 \leq i \leq N$. Then $\mathbf{A}_i$ has c_{i-1} rows, since otherwise the multiplications are not valid. We will define c_0 to be the number of rows in the first matrix, $\mathbf{A}_1$.

Suppose $m_{Left,Right}$ is the number of multiplications required to multiply $\mathbf{A}_{Left}\mathbf{A}_{Left+1} \cdots \mathbf{A}_{Right-1}\mathbf{A}_{Right}$. For consistency, $m_{Left,Left} = 0$. Suppose the last multiplication is $(\mathbf{A}_{Left} \cdots \mathbf{A}_i)(\mathbf{A}_{i+1} \cdots \mathbf{A}_{Right})$, where $Left \leq i < Right$. Then the number of multiplications used is $m_{Left,i} + m_{i+1,Right} + c_{Left-1}c_i c_{Right}$. These three terms represent the multiplications required to compute $(\mathbf{A}_{Left} \cdots \mathbf{A}_i)$, $(\mathbf{A}_{i+1} \cdots \mathbf{A}_{Right})$, and their product, respectively.

If we define $M_{Left,Right}$ to be the number of multiplications required in an *optimal* ordering, then, if $Left < Right$,

$$M_{Left,Right} = \min_{Left \leq i < Right} \{M_{Left,i} + M_{i+1,Right} + c_{Left-1}c_i c_{Right}\}$$

This equation implies that if we have an optimal multiplication arrangement of $\mathbf{A}_{Left} \cdots \mathbf{A}_{Right}$, the subproblems $\mathbf{A}_{Left} \cdots \mathbf{A}_i$ and $\mathbf{A}_{i+1} \cdots \mathbf{A}_{Right}$ cannot be performed suboptimally. This should be clear, since otherwise we could improve the entire result by replacing the suboptimal computation by an optimal computation.

The formula translates directly to a recursive program, but, as we have seen in the last section, such a program would be blatantly inefficient. However, since there are only approximately $N^2/2$ values of $M_{Left,Right}$ that ever need to be computed, it is clear that a table can be used to store these values. Further examination shows that if $Right - Left = k$, then the only values $M_{x,y}$ that are needed in the computation of $M_{Left,Right}$ satisfy $y - x < k$. This tells us the order in which we need to compute the table.

If we want to print out the actual ordering of the multiplications in addition to the final answer $M_{1,N}$, then we can use the ideas from the shortest-path algorithms in Chapter 9. Whenever we make a change to $M_{Left,Right}$, we record the value of i that is responsible. This gives the simple program shown in Figure 10.46.

Although the emphasis of this chapter is not coding, it is worth noting that many programmers tend to shorten variable names to a single letter. c, i, and k are used as single-letter variables because this agrees with the names we have used in the description of the algorithm, which is very mathematical. However, it is generally best to avoid l as a variable name, because l looks too much like 1 and can make for very difficult debugging if you make a transcription error.

```
/**
 * Compute optimal ordering of matrix multiplication.
 * c contains the number of columns for each of the n matrices.
 * c[ 0 ] is the number of rows in matrix 1.
 * The minimum number of multiplications is left in m[ 1 ][ n ].
 * Actual ordering is computed via another procedure using lastChange.
 * m and lastChange are indexed starting at 1, instead of 0.
 * Note: Entries below main diagonals of m and lastChange
 * are meaningless and uninitialized.
 */
public static void optMatrix( int [ ] c,
                             long [ ][ ] m, int [ ][ ] lastChange )
{
    int n = c.length - 1;

    for( int left = 1; left <= n; left++ )
        m[ left ][ left ] = 0;
    for( int k = 1; k < n; k++ )    // k is right - left
        for( int left = 1; left <= n - k; left++ )
        {
            // For each position
            int right = left + k;
            m[ left ][ right ] = INFINITY;
            for( int i = left; i < right; i++ )
            {
                long thisCost = m[ left ][ i ] + m[ i + 1 ][ right ]
                    + c[ left - 1 ] * c[ i ] * c[ right ];
                if( thisCost < m[ left ][ right ] )  // Update min
                {
                    m[ left ][ right ] = thisCost;
                    lastChange[ left ][ right ] = i;
                }
            }
        }
}
```

Figure 10.46 Program to find optimal ordering of matrix multiplications

Returning to the algorithmic issues, this program contains a triply nested loop and is easily seen to run in $O(N^3)$ time. The references describe a faster algorithm, but since the time to perform the actual matrix multiplication is still likely to be much larger than the time to compute the optimal ordering, this algorithm is still quite practical.

10.3.3. Optimal Binary Search Tree

Our second dynamic programming example considers the following input: We are given a list of words, $w_1, w_2, \ldots, w_N$, and *fixed* probabilities $p_1, p_2, \ldots, p_N$ of their occurrence. The problem is to arrange these words in a binary search tree in a way that minimizes the expected total access time. In a binary search tree, the number of comparisons needed to

Word	Probability
a	0.22
am	0.18
and	0.20
egg	0.05
if	0.25
the	0.02
two	0.08

Figure 10.47 Sample input for optimal binary search tree problem

access an element at depth d is $d + 1$, so if w_i is placed at depth d_i, then we want to minimize $\sum_{i=1}^{N} p_i(1 + d_i)$.

As an example, Figure 10.47 shows seven words along with their probability of occurrence in some context. Figure 10.48 shows three possible binary search trees. Their searching costs are shown in Figure 10.49.

The first tree was formed using a greedy strategy. The word with the highest probability of being accessed was placed at the root. The left and right subtrees were then formed

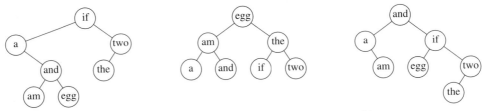

Figure 10.48 Three possible binary search trees for data in previous table

Input		Tree #1		Tree #2		Tree #3	
Word w_i	Probability p_i	Access Cost Once	Sequence	Access Cost Once	Sequence	Access Cost Once	Sequence
a	0.22	2	0.44	3	0.66	2	0.44
am	0.18	4	0.72	2	0.36	3	0.54
and	0.20	3	0.60	3	0.60	1	0.20
egg	0.05	4	0.20	1	0.05	3	0.15
if	0.25	1	0.25	3	0.75	2	0.50
the	0.02	3	0.06	2	0.04	4	0.08
two	0.08	2	0.16	3	0.24	3	0.24
Totals	1.00		2.43		2.70		2.15

Figure 10.49 Comparison of the three binary search trees

recursively. The second tree is the perfectly balanced search tree. Neither of these trees is optimal, as demonstrated by the existence of the third tree. From this we can see that neither of the obvious solutions works.

This is initially surprising, since the problem appears to be very similar to the construction of a Huffman encoding tree, which, as we have already seen, can be solved by a greedy algorithm. Construction of an optimal binary search tree is harder, because the data are not constrained to appear only at the leaves, and also because the tree must satisfy the binary search tree property.

A dynamic programming solution follows from two observations. Once again, suppose we are trying to place the (sorted) words $w_{Left}, w_{Left+1}, \ldots, w_{Right-1}, w_{Right}$ into a binary search tree. Suppose the optimal binary search tree has w_i as the root, where $Left \leq i \leq Right$. Then the left subtree must contain $w_{Left}, \ldots, w_{i-1}$, and the right subtree must contain $w_{i+1}, \ldots, w_{Right}$ (by the binary search tree property). Further, both of these subtrees must also be optimal, since otherwise they could be replaced by optimal subtrees, which would give a better solution for $w_{Left}, \ldots, w_{Right}$. Thus, we can write a formula for the cost $C_{Left,Right}$ of an optimal binary search tree. Figure 10.50 may be helpful.

If $Left > Right$, then the cost of the tree is 0; this is the `null` case, which we always have for binary search trees. Otherwise, the root costs p_i. The left subtree has a cost of $C_{Left,i-1}$, relative to its root, and the right subtree has a cost of $C_{i+1,Right}$ relative to its root. As Figure 10.50 shows, each node in these subtrees is one level deeper from w_i than from their respective roots, so we must add $\sum_{j=Left}^{i-1} p_j$ and $\sum_{j=i+1}^{Right} p_j$. This gives the formula

$$
C_{Left,Right} = \min_{Left \leq i \leq Right} \left\{ p_i + C_{Left,i-1} + C_{i+1,Right} + \sum_{j=Left}^{i-1} p_j + \sum_{j=i+1}^{Right} p_j \right\}
$$

$$
= \min_{Left \leq i \leq Right} \left\{ C_{Left,i-1} + C_{i+1,Right} + \sum_{j=Left}^{Right} p_j \right\}
$$

From this equation, it is straightforward to write a program to compute the cost of the optimal binary search tree. As usual, the actual search tree can be maintained by saving the value of i that minimizes $C_{Left,Right}$. The standard recursive routine can be used to print the actual tree.

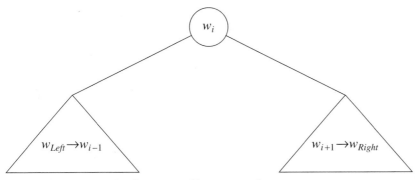

Figure 10.50 Structure of an optimal binary search tree

	Left=1		Left=2		Left=3		Left=4		Left=5		Left=6		Left=7	
Iteration=1	a..a		am..am		and..and		egg..egg		if..if		the..the		two..two	
	.22	a	.18	am	.20	and	.05	egg	.25	if	.02	the	.08	two
Iteration=2	a..am		am..and		and..egg		egg..if		if..the		the..two			
	.58	a	.56	and	.30	and	.35	if	.29	if	.12	two		
Iteration=3	a..and		am..egg		and..if		egg..the		if..two					
	1.02	am	.66	and	.80	if	.39	if	.47	if				
Iteration=4	a..egg		am..if		and..the		egg..two							
	1.17	am	1.21	and	.84	if	.57	if						
Iteration=5	a..if		am..the		and..two									
	1.83	and	1.27	and	1.02	if								
Iteration=6	a..the		am..two											
	1.89	and	1.53	and										
Iteration=7	a..two													
	2.15	and												

Figure 10.51 Computation of the optimal binary search tree for sample input

Figure 10.51 shows the table that will be produced by the algorithm. For each subrange of words, the cost and root of the optimal binary search tree are maintained. The bottommost entry computes the optimal binary search tree for the entire set of words in the input. The optimal tree is the third tree shown in Figure 10.48.

The precise computation for the optimal binary search tree for a particular subrange, namely, *am..if*, is shown in Figure 10.52. It is obtained by computing the minimum-cost

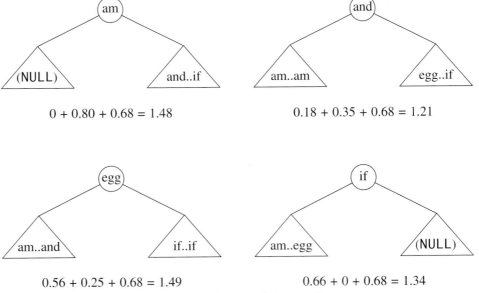

Figure 10.52 Computation of table entry (1.21, *and*) for *am..if*

tree obtained by placing *am, and, egg,* and *if* at the root. For instance, when *and* is placed at the root, the left subtree contains *am..am* (of cost 0.18, via previous calculation), the right subtree contains *egg..if* (of cost 0.35), and $p_{am} + p_{and} + p_{egg} + p_{if} = 0.68$, for a total cost of 1.21.

The running time of this algorithm is $O(N^3)$, because when it is implemented, we obtain a triple loop. An $O(N^2)$ algorithm for the problem is sketched in the exercises.

10.3.4. All-Pairs Shortest Path

Our third and final dynamic programming application is an algorithm to compute shortest weighted paths between every pair of points in a directed graph $G = (V, E)$. In Chapter 9, we saw an algorithm for the *single-source shortest-path* problem, which finds the shortest path from some arbitrary vertex s to all others. That algorithm (Dijkstra's) runs in $O(|V|^2)$ time on dense graphs, but substantially faster on sparse graphs. We will give a short algorithm to solve the all-pairs problem for dense graphs. The running time of the algorithm is $O(|V|^3)$, which is not an asymptotic improvement over $|V|$ iterations of Dijkstra's algorithm but could be faster on a very dense graph, because its loops are tighter. The algorithm also performs correctly if there are negative edge costs, but no negative-cost cycles; Dijkstra's algorithm fails in this case.

Let us recall the important details of Dijkstra's algorithm (the reader may wish to review Section 9.3). Dijkstra's algorithm starts at a vertex s and works in stages. Each vertex in the graph is eventually selected as an intermediate vertex. If the current selected vertex is v, then for each $w \in V$, we set $d_w = \min(d_w, d_v + c_{v,w})$. This formula says that the best distance to w (from s) is either the previously known distance to w from s, or the result of going from s to v (optimally) and then directly from v to w.

Dijkstra's algorithm provides the idea for the dynamic programming algorithm: we select the vertices in sequential order. We will define $D_{k,i,j}$ to be the weight of the shortest path from v_i to v_j that uses only $v_1, v_2, \ldots, v_k$ as intermediates. By this definition, $D_{0,i,j} = c_{i,j}$, where $c_{i,j}$ is ∞ if (v_i, v_j) is not an edge in the graph. Also, by definition, $D_{|V|,i,j}$ is the shortest path from v_i to v_j in the graph.

As Figure 10.53 shows, when $k > 0$ we can write a simple formula for $D_{k,i,j}$. The shortest path from v_i to v_j that uses only $v_1, v_2, \ldots, v_k$ as intermediates is the shortest path that either does not use v_k as an intermediate at all, or consists of the merging of the two paths $v_i \rightarrow v_k$ and $v_k \rightarrow v_j$, each of which uses only the first $k - 1$ vertices as intermediates. This leads to the formula

$$D_{k,i,j} = \min\left\{ D_{k-1,i,j}, D_{k-1,i,k} + D_{k-1,k,j} \right\}$$

The time requirement is once again $O(|V|^3)$. Unlike the two previous dynamic programming examples, this time bound has not been substantially lowered by another approach.

Because the kth stage depends only on the $(k - 1)$th stage, it appears that only two $|V| \times |V|$ matrices need to be maintained. However, using k as an *intermediate* vertex on a path that starts or finishes with k does not improve the result unless there is a negative cycle. Thus, only one matrix is necessary, because $D_{k-1,i,k} = D_{k,i,k}$ and $D_{k-1,k,j} = D_{k,k,j}$, which implies that none of the terms on the right change values and need to be saved. This observation leads to the simple program in Figure 10.53, which numbers vertices starting at zero to conform with Java's conventions.

On a complete graph, where every pair of vertices is connected (in both directions), this algorithm is almost certain to be faster than $|V|$ iterations of Dijkstra's algorithm, because

```
            /**
             * Compute all-shortest paths.
             * a contains the adjacency matrix with
             * a[ i ][ i ] presumed to be zero.
             * d contains the values of the shortest path.
             * Vertices are numbered starting at 0; all arrays
             * have equal dimension. A negative cycle exists if
             * d[ i ][ i ] is set to a negative value.
             * Actual path can be computed using path.
             * NOT_A_VERTEX is -1
             */
            public static void allPairs( int [ ][ ] a,
                            int [ ][ ] d, int [ ][ ] path )
            {
                int n = a.length;

                // Initialize d and path
/* 1*/          for( int i = 0; i < n; i++ )
/* 2*/              for( int j = 0; j < n; j++ )
                    {
/* 3*/                  d[ i ][ j ] = a[ i ][ j ];
/* 4*/                  path[ i ][ j ] = NOT_A_VERTEX;
                    }

/* 5*/          for( int k = 0; k < n; k++ )
                    // Consider each vertex as an intermediate
/* 6*/              for( int i = 0; i < n; i++ )
/* 7*/                  for( int j = 0; j < n; j++ )
/* 8*/                      if( d[ i ][ k ] + d[ k ][ j ] < d[ i ][ j ] )
                            {
                                // Update shortest path
/* 9*/                          d[ i ][ j ] = d[ i ][ k ] + d[ k ][ j ];
/*10*/                          path[ i ][ j ] = k;
                            }
            }
```

Figure 10.53 All-pairs shortest path

the loops are so tight. Lines 1 through 4 can be executed in parallel, as can lines 6 through 10. Thus, this algorithm seems to be well suited for parallel computation.

Dynamic programming is a powerful algorithm design technique, which provides a starting point for a solution. It is essentially the divide and conquer paradigm of solving simpler problems first, with the important difference being that the simpler problems are not a clear division of the original. Because subproblems are repeatedly solved, it is important to record their solutions in a table rather than recompute them. In some cases, the solution can be improved (although it is certainly not always obvious and frequently difficult), and in other cases, the dynamic programming technique is the best approach known.

In some sense, if you have seen one dynamic programming problem, you have seen them all. More examples of dynamic programming can be found in the exercises and references.

10.4. Randomized Algorithms

Suppose you are a professor who is giving weekly programming assignments. You want to make sure that the students are doing their own programs or, at the very least, understand the code they are submitting. One solution is to give a quiz on the day that each program is due. On the other hand, these quizzes take time out of class, so it might only be practical to do this for roughly half of the programs. Your problem is to decide when to give the quizzes.

Of course, if the quizzes are announced in advance, that could be interpreted as an implicit license to cheat for the 50 percent of the programs that will not get a quiz. One could adopt the unannounced strategy of giving quizzes on alternate programs, but students would figure out the strategy before too long. Another possibility is to give quizzes on what seem like the important programs, but this would likely lead to similar quiz patterns from semester to semester. Student grapevines being what they are, this strategy would probably be worthless after a semester.

One method that seems to eliminate these problems is to use a coin. A quiz is made for every program (making quizzes is not nearly as time-consuming as grading them), and at the start of class, the professor will flip a coin to decide whether the quiz is to be given. This way, it is impossible to know before class whether or not the quiz will occur, and these patterns do not repeat from semester to semester. Thus, the students will have to expect that a quiz will occur with 50 percent probability, regardless of previous quiz patterns. The disadvantage is that it is possible that there is no quiz for an entire semester. This is not a likely occurrence, unless the coin is suspect. Each semester, the expected number of quizzes is half the number of programs, and with high probability, the number of quizzes will not deviate much from this.

This example illustrates what we call *randomized algorithms*. At least once during the algorithm, a random number is used to make a decision. The running time of the algorithm depends not only on the particular input, but also on the random numbers that occur.

The worst-case running time of a randomized algorithm is often the same as the worst-case running time of the nonrandomized algorithm. The important difference is that a good randomized algorithm has no bad inputs, but only bad random numbers (relative to the particular input). This may seem like only a philosophical difference, but actually it is quite important, as the following example shows.

Consider two variants of quicksort. Variant A uses the first element as pivot, while variant B uses a randomly chosen element as pivot. In both cases, the worst-case running time is $\Theta(N^2)$, because it is possible at each step that the largest element is chosen as pivot. The difference between these worst cases is that there is a particular input that can always be presented to variant A to cause the bad running time. Variant A will run in $\Theta(N^2)$ time every single time it is given an already-sorted list. If variant B is presented with the same input twice, it will have two different running times, depending on what random numbers occur.

Throughout the text, in our calculations of running times, we have assumed that all inputs are equally likely. This is not true, because nearly sorted input, for instance, occurs much more often than is statistically expected, and this causes problems, particularly for quicksort and binary search trees. By using a randomized algorithm, the particular input is no longer important. The random numbers are important, and we can get an *expected* running time, where we now average over all possible random numbers instead of over all possible inputs. Using quicksort with a random pivot gives an $O(N \log N)$-expected-time algorithm. This means that for any input, including already-sorted input, the running time is expected to be $O(N \log N)$, based on the statistics of random numbers. An expected running time bound is somewhat stronger than an average-case bound but, of course, is weaker than the corresponding worst-case bound. On the other hand, as we saw in the selection problem, solutions that obtain the worst-case bound are frequently not as practical as their average-case counterparts. Randomized algorithms usually are.

In this section we will examine two uses of randomization. First, we will see a novel scheme for supporting the binary search tree operations in $O(\log N)$ expected time. Once again, this means that there are no bad inputs, just bad random numbers. From a theoretical point of view, this is not terribly exciting, since balanced search trees achieve this bound in the worst case. Nevertheless, the use of randomization leads to relatively simple algorithms for searching, inserting, and especially deleting.

Our second application is a randomized algorithm to test the primality of large numbers. No efficient polynomial-time nonrandomized algorithms are known for this problem. The algorithm we present runs quickly but occasionally makes an error. The probability of error can, however, be made negligibly small.

10.4.1. Random Number Generators

Since our algorithms require random numbers, we must have a method to generate them. Actually, true randomness is virtually impossible to do on a computer, since these numbers will depend on the algorithm, and thus cannot possibly be random. Generally, it suffices to produce *pseudorandom* numbers, which are numbers that appear to be random. Random numbers have many known statistical properties; pseudorandom numbers satisfy most of these properties. Surprisingly, this too is much easier said than done.

Suppose we only need to flip a coin; thus, we must generate a 0 (for heads) or 1 (for tails) randomly. One way to do this is to examine the system clock. The clock might record time as an integer that counts the number of seconds since some starting time. We could then use the lowest bit. The problem is that this does not work well if a sequence of random numbers is needed. One second is a long time, and the clock might not change at all while the program is running. Even if the time was recorded in units of microseconds, if the program was running by itself the sequence of numbers that would be generated would be far from random, since the time between calls to the generator would be essentially identical on every program invocation. We see, then, that what is really needed is a *sequence* of random numbers.[*] These numbers should appear independent. If a coin is flipped and heads appears, the next coin flip should still be equally likely to come up heads or tails.

The simplest method to generate random numbers is the linear congruential generator, which was first described by Lehmer in 1951. Numbers $x_1, x_2, \ldots$ are generated satisfying

$$x_{i+1} = A x_i \bmod M$$

To start the sequence, some value of x_0 must be given. This value is known as the *seed*. If $x_0 = 0$, then the sequence is far from random, but if A and M are correctly chosen, then any other $1 \le x_0 < M$ is equally valid. If M is prime, then x_i is never 0. As an example, if $M = 11$, $A = 7$, and $x_0 = 1$, then the numbers generated are

$$7, 5, 2, 3, 10, 4, 6, 9, 8, 1, 7, 5, 2, \ldots$$

---

[*]We will use random in place of pseudorandom in the rest of this section.

Notice that after $M - 1 = 10$ numbers, the sequence repeats. Thus, this sequence has a period of $M - 1$, which is as large as possible (by the pigeonhole principle). If M is prime, there are always choices of A that give a full period of $M - 1$. Some choices of A do not; if $A = 5$ and $x_0 = 1$, the sequence has a short period of 5.

$$5, 3, 4, 9, 1, 5, 3, 4, \ldots$$

If M is chosen to be a large, 31-bit prime, the period should be significantly large for most applications. Lehmer suggested the use of the 31-bit prime $M = 2^{31} - 1 = 2,147,483,647$. For this prime, $A = 48,271$ is one of the many values that gives a full-period generator. Its use has been well studied and is recommended by experts in the field. We will see later that with random number generators, tinkering usually means breaking, so one is well advised to stick with this formula until told otherwise.

This seems like a simple routine to implement. Generally, a class variable is used to hold the current value in the sequence of x's. When debugging a program that uses random numbers, it is probably best to set $x_0 = 1$, so that the same random sequence occurs all the time. When the program seems to work, either the system clock can be used or the user can be asked to input a value for the seed.

It is also common to return a random real number in the open interval $(0, 1)$ (0 and 1 are not possible values); this can be done by dividing by M. From this, a random number in any closed interval $[\alpha, \beta]$ can be computed by normalizing. This yields the "obvious" class in Figure 10.54 which, unfortunately, is erroneous.

The problem with this class is that the multiplication could overflow; although this is not an error, it affects the result and thus the pseudorandomness. Even though we could use 64-bit `long`s, this would slow down the computation. Schrage gave a procedure in which all of the calculations can be done on a 32-bit machine without overflow. We compute the quotient and remainder of M/A and define these as Q and R, respectively. In our case, $Q = 44,488$, $R = 3,399$, and $R < Q$. We have

$$x_{i+1} = A x_i \bmod M = A x_i - M \left\lfloor \frac{A x_i}{M} \right\rfloor$$

$$= A x_i - M \left\lfloor \frac{x_i}{Q} \right\rfloor + M \left\lfloor \frac{x_i}{Q} \right\rfloor - M \left\lfloor \frac{A x_i}{M} \right\rfloor$$

$$= A x_i - M \left\lfloor \frac{x_i}{Q} \right\rfloor + M \left(\left\lfloor \frac{x_i}{Q} \right\rfloor - \left\lfloor \frac{A x_i}{M} \right\rfloor \right)$$

Since $x_i = Q \lfloor \frac{x_i}{Q} \rfloor + x_i \bmod Q$, we can replace the leading $A x_i$ and obtain

$$x_{i+1} = A \left(Q \left\lfloor \frac{x_i}{Q} \right\rfloor + x_i \bmod Q \right) - M \left\lfloor \frac{x_i}{Q} \right\rfloor + M \left(\left\lfloor \frac{x_i}{Q} \right\rfloor - \left\lfloor \frac{A x_i}{M} \right\rfloor \right)$$

$$= (AQ - M) \left\lfloor \frac{x_i}{Q} \right\rfloor + A(x_i \bmod Q) + M \left(\left\lfloor \frac{x_i}{Q} \right\rfloor - \left\lfloor \frac{A x_i}{M} \right\rfloor \right)$$

Since $M = AQ + R$, it follows that $AQ - M = -R$. Thus, we obtain

$$x_{i+1} = A(x_i \bmod Q) - R \left\lfloor \frac{x_i}{Q} \right\rfloor + M \left(\left\lfloor \frac{x_i}{Q} \right\rfloor - \left\lfloor \frac{A x_i}{M} \right\rfloor \right)$$

```
public class Random
{
    private static final int A = 48271;
    private static final int M = 2147483647;

    public Random( )
    {
        state = System.currentTimeMillis( ) % Integer.MAX_VALUE;
    }

    /**
     * Return a pseudorandom int, and change the
     * internal state. DOES NOT WORK.
     * @return the pseudorandom int.
     */
    public int randomIntWRONG( )
    {
        return state = ( A * state ) % M;
    }

    /**
     * Return a pseudorandom double in the open range 0..1
     * and change the internal state.
     * @return the pseudorandom double.
     */
    public double random0_1( )
    {
        return (double) randomInt( ) / M;
    }

    private int state;
}
```

Figure 10.54 Random number generator that does not work

The term $\delta(x_i) = \lfloor \frac{x_i}{Q} \rfloor - \lfloor \frac{Ax_i}{M} \rfloor$ is either 0 or 1, because both terms are integers and their difference lies between 0 and 1. Thus, we have

$$x_{i+1} = A(x_i \bmod Q) - R \left\lfloor \frac{x_i}{Q} \right\rfloor + M\delta(x_i)$$

A quick check shows that because $R < Q$, all the remaining terms can be calculated without overflow (this is one of the reasons for choosing $A = 48{,}271$). Furthermore, $\delta(x_i) = 1$ only if the remaining terms evaluate to less than zero. Thus $\delta(x_i)$ does not need to be explicitly computed but can be determined by a simple test. This leads to the revisions in Figure 10.55.

One might be tempted to assume that all machines have a random number generator at least as good as the one in Figure 10.55 in their standard library. Sadly, this is not true. Many libraries have generators based on the function

$$x_{i+1} = (A x_i + C) \bmod 2^B$$

```
public class Random
{
    private static final int A = 48271;
    private static final int M = 2147483647;
    private static final int Q = M / A;
    private static final int R = M % A;

    /**
     * Return a pseudorandom int, and change the internal state.
     * @return the pseudorandom int.
     */
    public int randomInt( )
    {
        int tmpState = A * ( state % Q ) - R * ( state / Q );

        if( tmpState >= 0 )
            state = tmpState;
        else
            state = tmpState + M;

        return state;
    }

    // Remainder of this class is the same as Figure 10.54
}
```

Figure 10.55 Random number generator that does not overflow

where B is chosen to match the number of bits in the machine's integer, and C is odd. Unfortunately, these generators always produce values of x_i that alternate between even and odd—hardly a desirable property. Indeed, the lower k bits cycle with period 2^k (at best). Many other random number generators have much smaller cycles than the one provided in Figure 10.55. These are not suitable for the case where long sequences of random numbers are needed. The Java library and the UNIX **drand48** function use a generator of this form. However, they use a 48-bit linear congruential generator and return only the high 32 bits, thus avoiding the cycling problem in the low-order bits. The constants are $A = 25{,}214{,}903{,}917$, $B = 48$, and $C = 13$. Finally, it may seem that we can get a better random number generator by adding a constant to the equation. For instance, it seems that

$$x_{i+1} = (48{,}271x_i + 1) \bmod (2^{31} - 1)$$

would somehow be even more random. This illustrates how fragile these generators are.

$$[48{,}271(179{,}424{,}105) + 1] \bmod (2^{31} - 1) = 179{,}424{,}105$$

so if the seed is 179,424,105, the generator gets stuck in a cycle of period 1.

10.4.2. Skip Lists

Our first use of randomization is a data structure that supports both searching and insertion in $O(\log N)$ expected time. As mentioned in the introduction to this section, this means that

Figure 10.56 Simple linked list

Figure 10.57 Linked list with links to two cells ahead

the running time for each operation on *any input sequence* has expected value $O(\log N)$, where the expectation is based on the random number generator. It is possible to add deletion and all the operations that involve ordering and obtain expected time bounds that match the average time bounds of binary search trees.

The simplest possible data structure to support searching is the linked list. Figure 10.56 shows a simple linked list. The time to perform a search is proportional to the number of nodes that have to be examined, which is at most N.

Figure 10.57 shows a linked list in which every other node has an additional link to the node two ahead of it in the list. Because of this, at most $\lceil N/2 \rceil + 1$ nodes are examined in the worst case.

We can extend this idea and obtain Figure 10.58. Here, every fourth node has a link to the node four ahead. Only $\lceil N/4 \rceil + 2$ nodes are examined.

The limiting case of this argument is shown in Figure 10.59. Every 2^i th node has a link to the node 2^i ahead of it. The total number of links has only doubled, but now at most $\lceil \log N \rceil$ nodes are examined during a search. It is not hard to see that the total time spent for a search is $O(\log N)$, because the search consists of either advancing to a new node or dropping to a lower link in the same node. Each of these steps consumes at most $O(\log N)$ total time during a search. Notice that the search in this data structure is essentially a binary search.

The problem with this data structure is that it is much too rigid to allow efficient insertion. The key to making this data structure usable is to relax the structure conditions slightly. We define a *level k node* to be a node that has k links. As Figure 10.59 shows, the ith link in any level k node ($k \geq i$) links to the next node with at least i levels. This is an easy

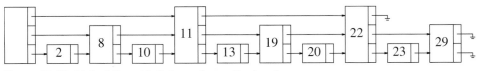

Figure 10.58 Linked list with links to four cells ahead

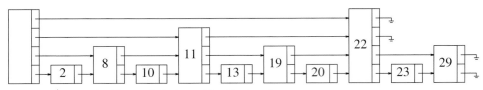

Figure 10.59 Linked list with links to 2^i cells ahead

Figure 10.60 A skip list

property to maintain; however, Figure 10.59 shows a more restrictive property than this. We thus drop the restriction that the ith link links to the node 2^i ahead, and we replace it with the less restrictive condition above.

When it comes time to insert a new element, we allocate a new node for it. We must at this point decide what level the node should be. Examining Figure 10.59, we find that roughly half the nodes are level 1 nodes, roughly a quarter are level 2, and, in general, approximately $1/2^i$ nodes are level i. We choose the level of the node randomly, in accordance with this probability distribution. The easiest way to do this is to flip a coin until a head occurs and use the total number of flips as the node level. Figure 10.60 shows a typical skip list.

Given this, the skip list algorithms are simple to describe. To perform a **find**, we start at the highest link at the header. We traverse along this level until we find that the next node is larger than the one we are looking for (or **null**). When this occurs, we go to the next lower level and continue the strategy. When progress is stopped at level 1, either we are in front of the node we are looking for, or it is not in the list. To perform an **insert**, we proceed as in a **find**, and keep track of each point where we switch to a lower level. The new node, whose level is determined randomly, is then spliced into the list. This operation is shown in Figure 10.61.

A cursory analysis shows that since the expected number of nodes at each level is unchanged from the original (nonrandomized) algorithm, the total amount of work that is expected to be performed traversing to nodes on the same level is unchanged. This tells us that these operations have $O(\log N)$ *expected* costs. Of course, a more formal proof is required, but it is not much different from this.

Skip lists are similar to hash tables, in that they require an estimate of the number of elements that will be in the list (so that the number of levels can be determined). If an estimate is not available, we can assume a large number or use a technique similar to

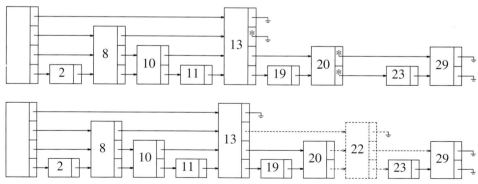

Figure 10.61 Before and after an insertion

rehashing. Experiments have shown that skip lists are as efficient as many balanced search tree implementations and are certainly much simpler to implement in many languages.

10.4.3. Primality Testing

In this section we examine the problem of determining whether or not a large number is prime. As was mentioned at the end of Chapter 2, some cryptography schemes depend on the difficulty of factoring a large, 200-digit number into two 100-digit primes. In order to implement this scheme, we need a method of generating these two primes. The problem is of major theoretical interest, because nobody now knows how to test whether a d-digit number N is prime in time polynomial in d. For instance, the obvious method of testing for the divisibility by odd numbers from 3 to $\sqrt{N}$ requires roughly $\frac{1}{2}\sqrt{N}$ divisions, which is about $10^{d/2}$. On the other hand, this problem is not thought to be NP-complete; thus, it is one of the few problems on the fringe—its complexity is unknown at the time of this writing.

In this section, we will give a polynomial-time algorithm that can test for primality. If the algorithm declares that the number is not prime, we can be certain that the number is not prime. If the algorithm declares that the number is prime, then, with high probability but not 100 percent certainty, the number is prime. The error probability does not depend on the particular number that is being tested but instead depends on random choices made by the algorithm. Thus, this algorithm occasionally makes a mistake, but we will see that the error ratio can be made arbitrarily negligible.

The key to the algorithm is a well-known theorem due to Fermat.

THEOREM 10.10.
Fermat's Lesser Theorem: If P is prime, and $0 < A < P$, then $A^{P-1} \equiv 1 (\bmod P)$.

PROOF:
A proof of this theorem can be found in any textbook on number theory.

For instance, since 67 is prime, $2^{66} \equiv 1 (\bmod 67)$. This suggests an algorithm to test whether a number N is prime. Merely check whether $2^{N-1} \equiv 1 (\bmod N)$. If $2^{N-1} \not\equiv 1 (\bmod N)$, then we can be certain that N is not prime. On the other hand, if the equality holds, then N is probably prime. For instance, the smallest N that satisfies $2^{N-1} \equiv 1 (\bmod N)$ but is not prime is $N = 341$.

This algorithm will occasionally make errors, but the problem is that it will always make the same errors. Put another way, there is a fixed set of N for which it does not work. We can attempt to randomize the algorithm as follows: Pick $1 < A < N - 1$ at random. If $A^{N-1} \equiv 1 (\bmod N)$, declare that N is probably prime, otherwise declare that N is definitely not prime. If $N = 341$, and $A = 3$, we find that $3^{340} \equiv 56 (\bmod 341)$. Thus, if the algorithm happens to choose $A = 3$, it will get the correct answer for $N = 341$.

Although this seems to work, there are numbers that fool even this algorithm for most choices of A. One such set of numbers is known as the *Carmichael numbers*. These are not prime but satisfy $A^{N-1} \equiv 1 (\bmod N)$ for *all* $0 < A < N$ that are relatively prime to N. The smallest such number is 561. Thus, we need an additional test to improve the chances of not making an error.

In Chapter 7, we proved a theorem related to quadratic probing. A special case of this theorem is the following:

THEOREM 10.11.

If P is prime and $0 < X < P$, the only solutions to $X^2 \equiv 1 \pmod{P}$ are $X = 1, P - 1$.

PROOF:

$X^2 \equiv 1 \pmod{P}$ implies that $X^2 - 1 \equiv 0 \pmod{P}$. This implies $(X - 1)(X + 1) \equiv 0 \pmod{P}$. Since P is prime, $0 < X < P$, and P must divide either $(X - 1)$ or $(X + 1)$, the theorem follows.

Therefore, if at any point in the computation of $A^{N-1} \pmod{N}$ we discover a violation of this theorem, we can conclude that N is definitely not prime. If we use `power`, from Section 2.4.4, we see that there will be several opportunities to apply this test. We modify this routine to perform operations mod N, and apply the test of Theorem 10.11. This strategy is implemented in the pseudocode shown in Figure 10.62.

Recall that if `witness` returns anything but 1, it has *proven* that N cannot be prime. The proof is nonconstructive, because it gives no method of actually finding the factors. It has been shown that for any (sufficiently large) N, at most $(N - 9)/4$ values of A fool this algorithm. Thus, if A is chosen at random, and the algorithm answers that N is (probably) prime, then the algorithm is correct at least 75 percent of the time. Suppose `witness` is run 50 times. The probability that the algorithm is fooled once is at most $\frac{1}{4}$. Thus, the probability that 50 independent random trials fool the algorithm is never more than $1/4^{50} = 2^{-100}$. This is actually a very conservative estimate, which holds for only a few choices of N. Even so, one is more likely to see a hardware error than an incorrect claim of primality.

10.5. Backtracking Algorithms

The last algorithm design technique we will examine is *backtracking*. In many cases, a backtracking algorithm amounts to a clever implementation of exhaustive search, with generally unfavorable performance. This is not always the case, however, and even so, in some cases, the savings over a brute force exhaustive search can be significant. Performance is, of course, relative: an $O(N^2)$ algorithm for sorting is pretty bad, but an $O(N^5)$ algorithm for the traveling salesman (or any *NP*-complete) problem would be a landmark result.

A practical example of a backtracking algorithm is the problem of arranging furniture in a new house. There are many possibilities to try, but typically only a few are actually considered. Starting with no arrangement, each piece of furniture is placed in some part of the room. If all the furniture is placed and the owner is happy, then the algorithm terminates. If we reach a point where all subsequent placement of furniture is undesirable, we have to undo the last step and try an alternative. Of course, this might force another undo, and so forth. If we find that we undo all possible first steps, then there is no placement of furniture that is satisfactory. Otherwise, we eventually terminate with a satisfactory arrangement. Notice that although this algorithm is essentially brute force, it does not try all possibilities directly. For instance, arrangements that consider placing the sofa in the kitchen are never tried. Many other bad arrangements are discarded early, because an undesirable subset of the arrangement is detected. The elimination of a large group of possibilities in one step is known as *pruning*.

```
/**
 * Method that implements the basic primality test.
 * If witness does not return 1, n is definitely composite.
 * Do this by computing a^i (mod n) and looking for
 * nontrivial square roots of 1 along the way.
 */
private static long witness( long a, long i, long n )
{
    if( i == 0 )
        return 1;

    long x = witness( a, i / 2, n );
    if( x == 0 )    // If n is recursively composite, stop
        return 0;

    // n is not prime if we find a nontrivial square root of 1
    long y = ( x * x ) % n;
    if( y == 1 && x != 1 && x != n - 1 )
        return 0;

    if( i % 2 != 0 )
        y = ( a * y ) % n;

    return y;
}

/**
 * The number of witnesses queried in randomized primality test.
 */
public static final int TRIALS = 5;

/**
 * Randomized primality test.
 * Adjust TRIALS to increase confidence level.
 * @param n the number to test.
 * @return if false, n is definitely not prime.
 *     If true, n is probably prime.
 */
public static boolean isPrime( long n )
{
    Random r = new Random( );

    for( int counter = 0; counter < TRIALS; counter++ )
        if( witness( r.randomLong( 2, n - 2 ), n - 1, n ) != 1 )
            return false;

    return true;
}
```

Figure 10.62 A probabilistic primality testing algorithm (pseudocode)

We will see two examples of backtracking algorithms. The first is a problem in computational geometry. Our second example shows how computers select moves in games, such as chess and checkers.

10.5.1. The Turnpike Reconstruction Problem

Suppose we are given N points, $p_1, p_2, \ldots, p_N$, located on the x-axis. x_i is the x coordinate of p_i. Let us further assume that $x_1 = 0$ and the points are given from left to right. These N points determine $N(N-1)/2$ (not necessarily unique) distances $d_1, d_2, \ldots, d_N$ between every pair of points of the form $|x_i - x_j|$ $(i \neq j)$. It is clear that if we are given the set of points, it is easy to *construct* the set of distances in $O(N^2)$ time. This set will not be sorted, but if we are willing to settle for an $O(N^2 \log N)$ time bound, the distances can be sorted, too. The *turnpike reconstruction problem* is to reconstruct a point set from the distances. This finds applications in physics and molecular biology (see the references for pointers to more specific information). The name derives from the analogy of points to turnpike exits on East Coast highways. Just as factoring seems harder than multiplication, the reconstruction problem seems harder than the construction problem. Nobody has been able to give an algorithm that is guaranteed to work in polynomial time. The algorithm that we will present generally runs in $O(N^2 \log N)$ but can take exponential time in the worst case.

Of course, given one solution to the problem, an infinite number of others can be constructed by adding an offset to all the points. This is why we insist that the first point is anchored at 0 and that the point set that constitutes a solution is output in nondecreasing order.

Let D be the set of distances, and assume that $|D| = M = N(N-1)/2$. As an example, suppose that

$$D = \{1, 2, 2, 2, 3, 3, 3, 4, 5, 5, 5, 6, 7, 8, 10\}$$

Since $|D| = 15$, we know that $N = 6$. We start the algorithm by setting $x_1 = 0$. Clearly, $x_6 = 10$, since 10 is the largest element in D. We remove 10 from D. The points that we have placed and the remaining distances are as shown in the following figure.

$$x_1 = 0 \qquad\qquad\qquad\qquad\qquad\qquad\qquad\qquad x_6 = 10$$
$$D = \{1, 2, 2, 2, 3, 3, 3, 4, 5, 5, 5, 6, 7, 8\}$$

The largest remaining distance is 8, which means that either $x_2 = 2$ or $x_5 = 8$. By symmetry, we can conclude that the choice is unimportant, since either both choices lead to solutions (which are mirror images of each other), or neither do, so we can set $x_5 = 8$ without affecting the solution. We then remove the distances $x_6 - x_5 = 2$ and $x_5 - x_1 = 8$ from D, obtaining

$$x_1 = 0 \qquad\qquad\qquad\qquad\qquad\qquad x_5 = 8 \qquad x_6 = 10$$
$$D = \{1, 2, 2, 3, 3, 3, 4, 5, 5, 5, 6, 7\}$$

The next step is not obvious. Since 7 is the largest value in D, either $x_4 = 7$ or $x_2 = 3$. If $x_4 = 7$, then the distances $x_6 - 7 = 3$ and $x_5 - 7 = 1$ must also be present in D. A quick check shows that indeed they are. On the other hand, if we set $x_2 = 3$, then $3 - x_1 = 3$ and $x_5 - 3 = 5$ must be present in D. These distances are also in D, so we have no guidance on which choice to make. Thus, we try one and see if it leads to a solution. If it turns out that it does not, we can come back and try the other. Trying the first choice, we set $x_4 = 7$, which leaves

$$x_1 = 0 \qquad\qquad x_4 = 7 \; x_5 = 8 \quad x_6 = 10$$
$$D = \{2, 2, 3, 3, 4, 5, 5, 5, 6\}$$

At this point, we have $x_1 = 0, x_4 = 7, x_5 = 8$, and $x_6 = 10$. Now the largest distance is 6, so either $x_3 = 6$ or $x_2 = 4$. But if $x_3 = 6$, then $x_4 - x_3 = 1$, which is impossible, since 1 is no longer in D. On the other hand, if $x_2 = 4$ then $x_2 - x_0 = 4$, and $x_5 - x_2 = 4$. This is also impossible, since 4 only appears once in D. Thus, this line of reasoning leaves no solution, so we backtrack.

Since $x_4 = 7$ failed to produce a solution, we try $x_2 = 3$. If this also fails, we give up and report no solution. We now have

$$x_1 = 0 \qquad x_2 = 3 \qquad\qquad x_5 = 8 \quad x_6 = 10$$
$$D = \{1, 2, 2, 3, 3, 4, 5, 5, 6\}$$

Once again, we have to choose between $x_4 = 6$ and $x_3 = 4$. $x_3 = 4$ is impossible, because D only has one occurrence of 4, and two would be implied by this choice. $x_4 = 6$ is possible, so we obtain

$$x_1 = 0 \qquad x_2 = 3 \qquad x_4 = 6 \quad x_5 = 8 \quad x_6 = 10$$
$$D = \{1, 2, 3, 5, 5\}$$

The only remaining choice is to assign $x_3 = 5$; this works because it leaves D empty, and so we have a solution.

$$x_1 = 0 \qquad x_2 = 3 \quad x_3 = 5 \; x_4 = 6 \quad x_5 = 8 \quad x_6 = 10$$
$$D = \{\}$$

Figure 10.63 shows a decision tree representing the actions taken to arrive at the solution. Instead of labeling the branches, we have placed the labels in the branches' destination nodes. A node with an asterisk indicates that the points chosen are inconsistent with the given distances; nodes with two asterisks have only impossible nodes as children, and thus represent an incorrect path.

The pseudocode to implement this algorithm is mostly straightforward. The driving routine, **turnpike**, is shown in Figure 10.64. It receives the point array **x** (which need not be initialized) and the distance set D and N.* If a solution is discovered, then **true** will be returned, the answer will be placed in **x**, and D will be empty. Otherwise, **false** will be returned, **x** will be undefined, and the distance set D will be untouched. The routine sets x_1, x_{N-1}, and x_N, as described above, alters D, and calls the backtracking algorithm **place**

---

*We have used one-letter variable names, which is generally poor style, for consistency with the worked example. We also, for simplicity, do not give the type of variables. Finally, we index arrays starting at 1, instead of 0.

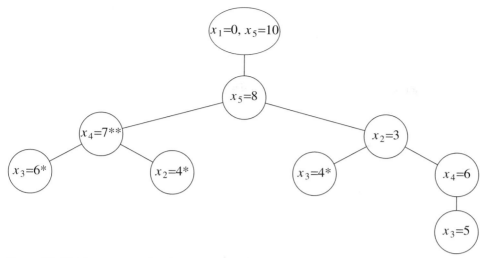

Figure 10.63 Decision tree for the worked turnpike reconstruction example

```
           boolean turnpike( int [ ] x, DistSet d, int n )
           {
/* 1*/         x[ 1 ] = 0;
/* 2*/         x[ n ] = d.deleteMax( );
/* 3*/         x[ n - 1 ] = d.deleteMax( );
/* 4*/         if( x[ n ] - x[ n - 1 ] ∈ d )
               {
/* 5*/             d.remove( x[ n ] - x[ n - 1 ] );
/* 6*/             return place( x, d, n, 2, n - 2 );
               }
               else
/* 7*/             return false;
           }
```

Figure 10.64 Turnpike reconstruction algorithm: driver routine (pseudocode)

to place the other points. We presume that a check has already been made to ensure that $|D| = N(N - 1)/2$.

The more difficult part is the backtracking algorithm, which is shown in Figure 10.65. Like most backtracking algorithms, the most convenient implementation is recursive. We pass the same arguments plus the boundaries *Left* and *Right*; $x_{Left}, \ldots, x_{Right}$ are the x coordinates of points that we are trying to place. If D is empty (or *Left* > *Right*), then a solution has been found, and we can return. Otherwise, we first try to place $x_{Right} = D_{max}$. If all the appropriate distances are present (in the correct quantity), then we tentatively place this point, remove these distances, and try to fill from *Left* to *Right* − 1. If the distances are not present, or the attempt to fill *Left* to *Right* − 1 fails, then we try setting $x_{Left} = x_N - d_{max}$, using a similar strategy. If this does not work, then there is no solution; otherwise a solution has been found, and this information is eventually passed back to **turnpike** by the **return** statement and **x** array.

```
         /**
          * Backtracking algorithm to place the points x[left] ... x[right].
          * x[1]...x[left-1] and x[right+1]...x[n] are already tentatively placed.
          * If place returns true, then x[left]...x[right] will have values.
          */
         boolean place( int [ ] x, DistSet d, int n, int left, int right )
         {
             int dmax;
             boolean found = false;

/* 1*/       if( d.isEmpty( ) )
/* 2*/           return true;

/* 3*/       dmax = d.findMax( );

             // Check if setting x[right] = dmax is feasible
/* 4*/       if( | x[j] - dmax | ∈ d for all 1 ≤  j < left and right < j ≤  n )
             {
/* 5*/           x[right] = dmax;               // Try x[right]=dmax
/* 6*/           for( 1 ≤  j < left, right < j ≤  n )
/* 7*/               d.remove( | x[j] - dmax | );
/* 8*/           found = place( x, d, n, left, right-1 );

/* 9*/           if( !found )    // Backtrack
/*10*/               for( 1 ≤  j < left, right < j ≤  n )     // Undo the deletion
/*11*/                   d.insert( | x[j] - dmax | );
             }
             // If first attempt failed, try to see if setting
             // x[left] = x[n] - dmax is feasible
/*12*/       if( !found && ( | x[n] - dmax - x[j] | ∈ d
/*13*/                           for all 1 ≤  j < left and right < j≤  n) )
             {
/*14*/           x[ left ] = x[n] - dmax;                // Same logic as before
/*15*/           for( 1 ≤  j < left, right < j ≤  n )
/*16*/               d.remove( | x[n] - dmax - x[j] | );
/*17*/           found = place( x, d, n, left+1, right );

/*18*/           if( !found )    // Backtrack
/*19*/               for( 1 ≤  j < left, right < j ≤  n )     // Undo the deletion
/*20*/                   d.insert( | x[n] - dmax - x[j] | );
             }

/*21*/       return found;
         }
```

Figure 10.65 Turnpike reconstruction algorithm: backtracking steps (pseudocode)

The analysis of the algorithm involves two factors. Suppose lines 9 through 11 and 18 through 20 are never executed. We can maintain D as a balanced binary search (or splay) tree (this would require a code modification, of course). If we never backtrack, there are at most $O(N^2)$ operations involving D, such as deletion and the **find**s implied at lines 4 and 12 to 13. This claim is obvious for deletions, since D has $O(N^2)$ elements and no element is ever reinserted. Each call to **place** uses at most $2N$ **find**s, and since **place** never backtracks in this analysis, there can be at most $2N^2$ **find**s. Thus, if there is no backtracking, the running time is $O(N^2 \log N)$.

Of course, backtracking happens, and if it happens repeatedly, then the performance of the algorithm is affected. This can be forced to happen by construction of a pathological case. Experiments have shown that if the points have integer coordinates distributed uniformly and randomly from $[0, D_{\max}]$, where $D_{\max} = \Theta(N^2)$, then, almost certainly, at most one backtrack is performed during the entire algorithm.

10.5.2. Games

As our last application, we will consider the strategy that a computer might use to play a strategic game, such as checkers or chess. We will use, as an example, the much simpler game of tic-tac-toe, because it makes the points easier to illustrate.

Tic-tac-toe is a draw if both sides play optimally. By performing a careful case-by-case analysis, it is not a difficult matter to construct an algorithm that never loses and always wins when presented the opportunity. This can be done, because certain positions are known traps and can be handled by a lookup table. Other strategies, such as taking the center square when it is available, make the analysis simpler. If this is done, then by using a table we can always choose a move based only on the current position. Of course, this strategy requires the programmer, and not the computer, to do most of the thinking.

Minimax Strategy

The more general strategy is to use an evaluation function to quantify the "goodness" of a position. A position that is a win for a computer might get the value of $+1$; a draw could get 0; and a position that the computer has lost would get a -1. A position for which this assignment can be determined by examining the board is known as a *terminal* position.

If a position is not terminal, the value of the position is determined by recursively assuming optimal play by both sides. This is known as a *minimax* strategy, because one player (the human) is trying to minimize the value of the position, while the other player (the computer) is trying to maximize it.

A *successor position* of P is any position P_s that is reachable from P by playing one move. If the computer is to move when in some position P, it recursively evaluates the value of all the successor positions. The computer chooses the move with the largest value; this is the value of P. To evaluate any successor position P_s, all of P_s's successors are recursively evaluated, and the smallest value is chosen. This smallest value represents the most favorable reply for the human player.

The code in Figure 10.66 makes the computer's strategy more clear. Lines 1 through 4 evaluate immediate wins or draws. If neither of these cases apply, then the position is nonterminal. Recalling that **value** should contain the maximum of all possible successor positions, line 5 initializes it to the smallest possible value, and the loop in lines 6 through 13 searches for improvements. Each successor position is recursively evaluated in turn by lines 8 through 10. This is recursive, because, as we will see, **findHumanMove** calls **findCompMove**. If the human's response to a move leaves the computer with a more favorable position than

```
         public class MoveInfo
         {
             public int move;
             public int value;

             public MoveInfo( int m, int v )
               { move = m; value = v; }
         }

         /**
          * Recursive method to find best move for computer.
          * MoveInfo.move returns a number from 1-9 indicating square.
          * Possible evaluations satisfy COMP_LOSS < DRAW < COMP_WIN.
          * Complementary method findHumanMove is Figure 10.67.
          */
         public MoveInfo findCompMove( )
         {
             int i, responseValue;
             int value, bestMove = 1;
             MoveInfo quickWinInfo;

/* 1*/       if( fullBoard( ) )
/* 2*/           value = DRAW;
             else
/* 3*/       if( ( quickWinInfo = immediateCompWin( ) ) != null )
/* 4*/           return quickWinInfo;
             else
             {
/* 5*/           value = COMP_LOSS;
/* 6*/           for( i = 1; i <= 9; i++ )  // Try each square
                 {
/* 7*/               if( isEmpty( i ) )
                     {
/* 8*/                   place( i, COMP );
/* 9*/                   responseValue = findHumanMove( ).value;
/*10*/                   unplace( i );   // Restore board

/*11*/                   if( responseValue > value )
                         {
                             // Update best move
/*12*/                       value = responseValue;
/*13*/                       bestMove = i;
                         }
                     }
                 }
             }
/*14*/       return new MoveInfo( bestMove, value );
         }
```

Figure 10.66 Minimax tic-tac-toe algorithm: computer selection

```
          public MoveInfo findHumanMove( )
          {
              int i, responseValue;
              int value, bestMove = 1;
              MoveInfo quickWinInfo;

/* 1*/        if( fullBoard( ) )
/* 2*/            value = DRAW;
          else
/* 3*/        if( ( quickWinInfo = immediateHumanWin( ) ) != null )
/* 4*/            return quickWinInfo;
          else
              {
/* 5*/            value = COMP_WIN;
/* 6*/            for( i = 1; i <= 9; i++ )  // Try each square
                  {
/* 7*/                if( isEmpty( i ) )
                      {
/* 8*/                    place( i, HUMAN );
/* 9*/                    responseValue = findCompMove( ).value;
/*10*/                    unplace( i );  // Restore board

/*11*/                    if( responseValue < value )
                          {
                              // Update best move
/*12*/                        value = responseValue;
/*13*/                        bestMove = i;
                          }
                      }
                  }
              }
/*14*/        return new MoveInfo( bestMove, value );
          }
```

Figure 10.67 Minimax tic-tac-toe algorithm: human selection

that obtained with the previously best computer move, then the **value** and **bestMove** are updated. Figure 10.67 shows the method for the human's move selection. The logic is virtually identical, except that the human player chooses the move that leads to the lowest-valued position. Indeed, it is not difficult to combine these two procedures into one by passing an extra variable, which indicates whose turn it is to move. This does make the code somewhat less readable, so we have stayed with separate routines.

Since these routines must pass back both the value of the position and the best move, we pass these two variables in a **MoveInfo** object.

We leave supporting routines as an exercise. The most costly computation is the case where the computer is asked to pick the opening move. Since at this stage the game is a forced draw, the computer selects square 1.* A total of 97,162 positions were examined, and

---

*We numbered the squares starting from the top left and moving right. However, this is only important for the supporting routines.

the calculation took a few seconds. No attempt was made to optimize the code. When the computer moves second, the number of positions examined is 5,185 if the human selects the center square, 9,761 when a corner square is selected, and 13,233 when a noncorner edge square is selected.

For more complex games, such as checkers and chess, it is obviously infeasible to search all the way to the terminal nodes.* In this case, we have to stop the search after a certain depth of recursion is reached. The nodes where the recursion is stopped become terminal nodes. These terminal nodes are evaluated with a function that estimates the value of the position. For instance, in a chess program, the evaluation function measures such variables as the relative amount and strength of pieces and positional factors. The evaluation function is crucial for success, because the computer's move selection is based on maximizing this function. The best computer chess programs have surprisingly sophisticated evaluation functions.

Nevertheless, for computer chess, the single most important factor seems to be number of moves of look-ahead the program is capable of. This is sometimes known as *ply*; it is equal to the depth of the recursion. To implement this, an extra parameter is given to the search routines.

The basic method to increase the look-ahead factor in game programs is to come up with methods that evaluate fewer nodes without losing any information. One method which we have already seen is to use a table to keep track of all positions that have been evaluated. For instance, in the course of searching for the first move, the program will examine the positions in Figure 10.68. If the values of the positions are saved, the second occurrence of a position need not be recomputed; it essentially becomes a terminal position. The data structure that records this is known as a *transposition table*; it is almost always implemented by hashing. In many cases, this can save considerable computation. For instance, in a chess endgame, where there are relatively few pieces, the time savings can allow a search to go several levels deeper.

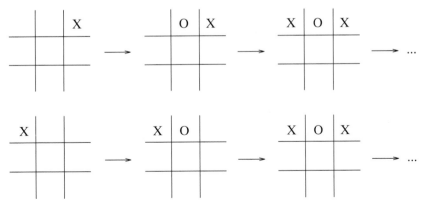

Figure 10.68 Two searches that arrive at identical position

---

*It is estimated that if this search were conducted for chess, at least 10^{100} positions would be examined for the first move. Even if the improvements described later in this section were incorporated, this number could not be reduced to a practical level.

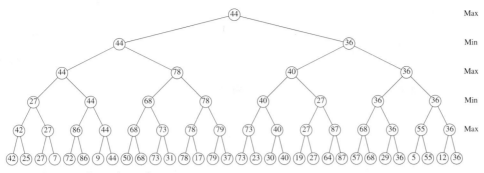

Figure 10.69 A hypothetical game tree

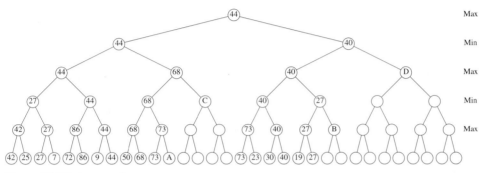

Figure 10.70 A pruned game tree

$\alpha-\beta$ Pruning

Probably the most significant improvement one can obtain in general is known as $\alpha-\beta$ pruning. Figure 10.69 shows the trace of the recursive calls used to evaluate some hypothetical position in a hypothetical game. This is commonly referred to as a *game tree*. (We have avoided the use of this term until now, because it is somewhat misleading: no tree is actually constructed by the algorithm. The game tree is just an abstract concept.) The value of the game tree is 44.

Figure 10.70 shows the evaluation of the same game tree, with several unevaluated nodes. Almost half of the terminal nodes have not been checked. We show that evaluating them would not change the value at the root.

First, consider node D. Figure 10.71 shows the information that has been gathered when it is time to evaluate D. At this point, we are still in `findHumanMove` and are contemplating a call to `findCompMove` on D. However, we already know that `findHumanMove` will return at most 40, since it is a *min* node. On the other hand, its *max* node parent has already found a sequence that guarantees 44. Nothing that D does can possibly increase this value. Therefore, D does not need to be evaluated. This pruning of the tree is known as α pruning. An identical situation occurs at node B. To implement α pruning, `findCompMove` passes its tentative maximum (α) to `findHumanMove`. If the tentative minimum of `findHumanMove` falls below this value, then `findHumanMove` returns immediately.

A similar thing happens at nodes A and C. This time, we are in the middle of a `findCompMove` and are about to make a call to `findHumanMove` to evaluate C. Figure 10.72

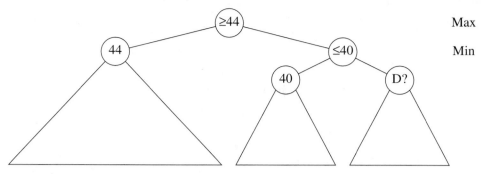

Figure 10.71 The node marked ? is unimportant

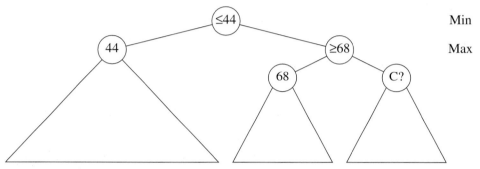

Figure 10.72 The node marked ? is unimportant

shows the situation that is encountered at node C. However, the findHumanMove, at the *min* level, which has called findCompMove, has already determined that it can force a value of at most 44 (recall that low values are good for the human side). Since findCompMove has a tentative maximum of 68, nothing that C does will affect the result at the *min* level. Therefore, C should not be evaluated. This type of pruning is known as β pruning; it is the symmetric version of α pruning. When both techniques are combined, we have α–β pruning.

Implementing α–β pruning requires surprisingly little code. Figure 10.73 shows half of the α–β pruning scheme (minus type declarations); you should have no trouble coding the other half.

To take full advantage of α–β pruning, game programs usually try to apply the evaluation function to nonterminal nodes in an attempt to place the best moves early in the search. The result is even more pruning than one would expect from a random ordering of the nodes. Other techniques, such as searching deeper in more active lines of play, are also employed.

In practice, α–β pruning limits the searching to only $O(\sqrt{N})$ nodes, where N is the size of the full game tree. This is a huge saving and means that searches using α–β pruning can go twice as deep as compared to an unpruned tree. Our tic-tac-toe example is not ideal, because there are so many identical values, but even so, the initial search of 97,162 nodes is reduced to 4,493 nodes. (These counts include nonterminal nodes).

In many games, computers are among the best players in the world. The techniques used are very interesting, and can be applied to more serious problems. More details can be found in the references.

```
          /**
           * Same as before, but perform alpha-beta pruning.
           * The main routine should make the call with
           * alpha = COMP_LOSS and beta = COMP_WIN.
           */
          public MoveInfo findCompMove( int alpha, int beta )
          {
              int i, responseValue;
              int value, bestMove = 1;
              MoveInfo quickWinInfo;

/* 1*/        if( fullBoard( ) )
/* 2*/            value = DRAW;
              else
/* 3*/        if( ( quickWinInfo = immediateCompWin( ) ) != null )
/* 4*/            return quickWinInfo;
              else
              {
/* 5*/            value = alpha;
/* 6*/            for( i = 1; i <= 9 && value < beta; i++ )  // Try each square
                  {
/* 7*/                if( isEmpty( i ) )
                      {
/* 8*/                    place( i, COMP );
/* 9*/                    responseValue = findHumanMove( value, beta ).value;
/*10*/                    unplace( i );   // Restore board

/*11*/                    if( responseValue > value )
                          {
                              // Update best move
/*12*/                        value = responseValue;
/*13*/                        bestMove = i;
                          }
                      }
                  }
              }
/*14*/        return new MoveInfo( bestMove, value );
          }
```

Figure 10.73 Minimax tic-tac-toe algorithm with $\alpha-\beta$ pruning: computer selection

SUMMARY

This chapter illustrates five of the most common techniques found in algorithm design. When confronted with a problem, it is worthwhile to see if any of these methods apply. A proper choice of algorithm, combined with judicious use of data structures, can often lead quickly to efficient solutions.

EXERCISES

10.1 Show that the greedy algorithm to minimize the mean completion time for multi-processor job scheduling works.

10.2 The input is a set of jobs $j_1, j_2, \ldots, j_N$, each of which takes one time unit to complete. Each job j_i earns d_i dollars if it is completed by the time limit t_i, but no money if completed after the time limit.

    a. Give an $O(N^2)$ greedy algorithm to solve the problem.

    **b. Modify your algorithm to obtain an $O(N \log N)$ time bound. (*Hint:* The time bound is due entirely to sorting the jobs by money. The rest of the algorithm can be implemented, using the disjoint set data structure, in $o(N \log N)$.)

10.3 A file contains only colons, spaces, newlines, commas, and digits in the following frequency: colon (100), space (605), newline (100), comma (705), 0 (431), 1 (242), 2 (176), 3 (59), 4 (185), 5 (250), 6 (174), 7 (199), 8 (205), 9 (217). Construct the Huffman code.

10.4 Part of the encoded file must be a header indicating the Huffman code. Give a method for constructing the header of size at most $O(N)$ (in addition to the symbols), where N is the number of symbols.

10.5 Complete the proof that Huffman's algorithm generates an optimal prefix code.

10.6 Show that if the symbols are sorted by frequency, Huffman's algorithm can be implemented in linear time.

10.7 Write a program to implement file compression (and uncompression) using Huffman's algorithm.

*10.8 Show that any on-line bin-packing algorithm can be forced to use at least $\frac{3}{2}$ the optimal number of bins, by considering the following sequence of items: N items of size $\frac{1}{6} - 2\epsilon$, N items of size $\frac{1}{3} + \epsilon$, N items of size $\frac{1}{2} + \epsilon$.

10.9 Explain how to implement first fit and best fit in $O(N \log N)$ time.

10.10 Show the operation of all of the bin-packing strategies discussed in Section 10.1.3 on the input 0.42, 0.25, 0.27, 0.07, 0.72, 0.86, 0.09, 0.44, 0.50, 0.68, 0.73, 0.31, 0.78, 0.17, 0.79, 0.37, 0.73, 0.23, 0.30.

10.11 Write a program that compares the performance (both in time and number of bins used) of the various bin packing heuristics.

10.12 Prove Theorem 10.7.

10.13 Prove Theorem 10.8.

*10.14 N points are placed in a unit square. Show that the distance between the closest pair is $O(N^{-1/2})$.

*10.15 Argue that for the closest-points algorithm, the average number of points in the strip is $O(\sqrt{N})$. (*Hint:* Use the result of the previous exercise.)

10.16 Write a program to implement the closest-pair algorithm.

10.17 What is the asymptotic running time of quickselect, using a median-of-median-of-three partitioning strategy?

10.18 Show that quickselect with median-of-median-of-seven partitioning is linear. Why is median-of-median-of-seven partitioning not used in the proof?

10.19 Implement the quickselect algorithm in Chapter 7, quickselect using median-of-median-of-five partitioning, and the sampling algorithm at the end of Section 10.2.3. Compare the running times.

10.20 Much of the information used to compute the median-of-median-of-five is thrown away. Show how the number of comparisons can be reduced by more careful use of the information.

*10.21 Complete the analysis of the sampling algorithm described at the end of Section 10.2.3, and explain how the values of δ and s are chosen.

10.22 Show how the recursive multiplication algorithm computes XY, where $X = 1234$ and $Y = 4321$. Include all recursive computations.

10.23 Show how to multiply two complex numbers $X = a + bi$ and $Y = c + di$ using only three multiplications.

10.24 a. Show that

$$X_L Y_R + X_R Y_L = (X_L + X_R)(Y_L + Y_R) - X_L Y_L - X_R Y_R$$

b. This gives an $O(N^{1.59})$ algorithm to multiply N-bit numbers. Compare this method to the solution in the text.

10.25 *a. Show how to multiply two numbers by solving five problems that are roughly one-third of the original size.

**b. Generalize this problem to obtain an $O(N^{1+\epsilon})$ algorithm for any constant $\epsilon > 0$.

c. Is the algorithm in part (b) better than $O(N \log N)$?

10.26 Why is it important that Strassen's algorithm does not use commutativity in the multiplication of 2×2 matrices?

10.27 Two 70×70 matrices can be multiplied using 143,640 multiplications. Show how this can be used to improve the bound given by Strassen's algorithm.

10.28 What is the optimal way to compute $A_1 A_2 A_3 A_4 A_5 A_6$, where the dimensions of the matrices are: $A_1 : 10 \times 20$, $A_2 : 20 \times 1$, $A_3 : 1 \times 40$, $A_4 : 40 \times 5$, $A_5 : 5 \times 30$, $A_6 : 30 \times 15$?

10.29 Show that none of the following greedy algorithms for chained matrix multiplication work. At each step

a. Compute the cheapest multiplication.

b. Compute the most expensive multiplication.

c. Compute the multiplication between the two matrices M_i and M_{i+1}, such that the number of columns in M_i is minimized (breaking ties by one of the rules above).

10.30 Write a program to compute the best ordering of matrix multiplication. Include the routine to print out the actual ordering.

10.31 Show the optimal binary search tree for the following words, where the frequency of occurrence is in parentheses: a (0.18), and (0.19), I (0.23), it (0.21), or (0.19).

*10.32 Extend the optimal binary search tree algorithm to allow for unsuccessful searches. In this case, q_j, for $1 \leq j < N$, is the probability that a search is performed for any word W satisfying $w_j < W < w_{j+1}$. q_0 is the probability of performing a search for $W < w_1$, and q_N is the probability of performing a search for $W > w_N$. Notice that $\sum_{i=1}^{N} p_i + \sum_{j=0}^{N} q_j = 1$.

*10.33 Suppose $C_{i,i} = 0$ and that otherwise

$$C_{i,j} = W_{i,j} + \min_{i < k \leq j} (C_{i,k-1} + C_{k,j})$$

Suppose that W satisfies the *quadrangle inequality*, namely, for all $i \leq i' \leq j \leq j'$,

$$W_{i,j} + W_{i',j'} \leq W_{i',j} + W_{i,j'}$$

```
CoinSide flip( )
{
    if( ( random( ) % 2 ) == 0 )
        return HEADS;
    else
        return TAILS;
}
```

Figure 10.74 Questionable coin flipper

Suppose further, that **W** is *monotone:* If $i \leq i'$ and $j \leq j'$, then $W_{i,j} \leq W_{i',j'}$.

a. Prove that **C** satisfies the quadrangle inequality.

b. Let $R_{i,j}$ be the largest k that achieves the minimum $C_{i,k-1} + C_{k,j}$. (That is, in case of ties, choose the largest k). Prove that

$$R_{i,j} \leq R_{i,j+1} \leq R_{i+1,j+1}$$

c. Show that **R** is nondecreasing along each row and column.

d. Use this to show that all entries in **C** can be computed in $O(N^2)$ time.

e. Which of the dynamic programming algorithms can be solved in $O(N^2)$ using these techniques?

10.34 Write a routine to reconstruct the shortest paths from the algorithm in Section 10.3.4.

10.35 The binomial coefficients $C(N, k)$ can be defined recursively as follows: $C(N, 0) = 1$, $C(N, N) = 1$, and, for $0 < k < N, C(N, k) = C(N-1, k) + C(N-1, k-1)$. Write a method and give an analysis of the running time to compute the binomial coefficients as follows:

a. recursively

b. using dynamic programming

10.36 Write the routines to perform insertion, deletion, and searching in skip lists.

10.37 Give a formal proof that the expected time for the skip list operations is $O(\log N)$.

10.38 Figure 10.74 shows a routine to flip a coin, assuming that **random** returns an integer (which is prevalent in many systems). What is the expected performance of the skip list algorithms if the random number generator uses a modulus of the form $M = 2^B$ (which is unfortunately prevalent on many systems)?

10.39 a. Use the exponentiation algorithm to prove that $2^{340} \equiv 1 \pmod{341}$.

b. Show how the randomized primality test works for $N = 561$ with several choices of A.

10.40 Implement the turnpike reconstruction algorithm.

10.41 Two point sets are *homometric* if they yield the same distance set and are not rotations of each other. The following distance set gives two distinct point sets: { 1, 2, 3, 4, 5, 6, 7, 8, 9, 10, 11, 12, 13, 16, 17 }. Find the two point sets.

10.42 Extend the reconstruction algorithm to find *all* homometric point sets given a distance set.

10.43 Show the result of α–β pruning of the tree in Figure 10.75.

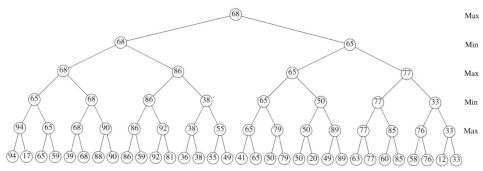

Figure 10.75 Game tree, which can be pruned

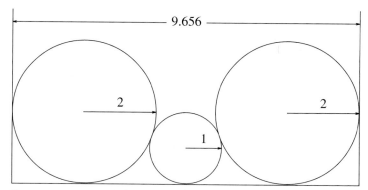

Figure 10.76 Sample for circle packing problem

10.44 a. Does the code in Figure 10.73 implement α pruning or β pruning?

b. Implement the complementary routine.

10.45 Write the remaining procedures for tic-tac-toe.

10.46 The *one-dimensional circle packing problem* is as follows: You have N circles of radii $r_1, r_2, \ldots, r_N$. These circles are packed in a box such that each circle is tangent to the bottom of the box, and are arranged in the original order. The problem is to find the width of the minimum-sized box. Figure 10.76 shows an example with circles of radii 2, 1, 2 respectively. The minimum-sized box has width $4 + 4\sqrt{2}$.

*10.47 Suppose that the edges in an undirected graph G satisfy the triangle inequality: $c_{u,v} + c_{v,w} \geq c_{u,w}$. Show how to compute a traveling salesman tour of cost at most twice optimal. (*Hint:* Construct a minimum spanning tree.)

*10.48 You are a tournament director and need to arrange a round robin tournament among $N = 2^k$ players. In this tournament, everyone plays exactly one game each day; after $N - 1$ days, a match has occurred between every pair of players. Give a recursive algorithm to do this.

10.49 *a. Prove that in a round robin tournament it is always possible to arrange the players in an order $p_{i_1}, p_{i_2}, \ldots, p_{i_N}$ such that for all $1 \leq j < N$, p_{i_j} has won the match against $p_{i_{j+1}}$.

b. Give an $O(N \log N)$ algorithm to find one such arrangement. Your algorithm may serve as a proof for part (a).

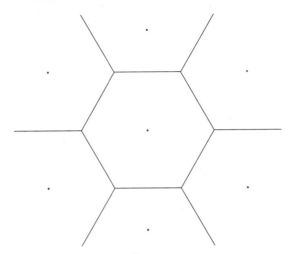

Figure 10.77 Voronoi diagram

*10.50 We are given a set $P = p_1, p_2, \ldots, p_N$ of N points in a plane. A *Voronoi diagram* is a partition of the plane into N regions R_i such that all points in R_i are closer to p_i than any other point in P. Figure 10.77 shows a sample Voronoi diagram for seven (nicely arranged) points. Give an $O(N \log N)$ algorithm to construct the Voronoi diagram.

*10.51 A *convex polygon* is a polygon with the property that any line segment whose endpoints are on the polygon lies entirely within the polygon. The *convex hull* problem consists of finding the smallest (area) convex polygon that encloses a set of points in the plane. Figure 10.78 shows the convex hull for a set of 40 points. Give an $O(N \log N)$ algorithm to find the convex hull.

*10.52 Consider the problem of right-justifying a paragraph. The paragraph contains a sequence of words $w_1, w_2, \ldots, w_N$ of length $a_1, a_2, \ldots, a_N$, which we wish to break into lines of length L. Words are separated by blanks whose ideal length is b (millimeters), but blanks can stretch or shrink as necessary (but must be >0), so that a line $w_i w_{i+1} \ldots w_j$ has length exactly L. However, for each blank b' we charge $|b' - b|$ *ugliness points*. The exception to this is the last line, for which we charge only if $b' < b$ (in other words, we charge only for shrinking), since the last line does not need to be justified. Thus, if b_i is the length of the blank between a_i and a_{i+1}, then the *ugliness* of

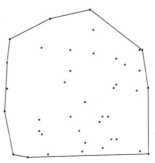

Figure 10.78 Example of a convex hull

setting any line (but the last) $w_i w_{i+1} \ldots w_j$ for $j > i$ is $\sum_{k=i}^{j-1} |b_k - b| = (j-i)|b' - b|$, where b' is the average size of a blank on this line. This is true of the last line only if $b' < b$, otherwise the last line is not ugly at all.

   a. Give a dynamic programming algorithm to find the least ugly setting of w_1, w_2, $\ldots, w_N$ into lines of length L. (*Hint:* For $i = N, N - 1, \ldots, 1$, compute the best way to set $w_i, w_{i+1}, \ldots, w_N$.)

   b. Give the time and space complexities for your algorithm (as a function of the number of words, N).

   c. Consider the special case where we are using a fixed-width font, and assume the optimal value of b is 1 (space). In this case, no shrinking of blanks is allowed, since the next smallest blank space would be 0. Give a linear-time algorithm to generate the least ugly setting for this case.

*10.53 The *longest increasing subsequence* problem is as follows: Given numbers $a_1, a_2, \ldots$ $, a_N$, find the maximum value of k such that $a_{i_1} < a_{i_2} < \cdots < a_{i_k}$, and $i_1 < i_2 < \cdots < i_k$. As an example, if the input is 3, 1, 4, 1, 5, 9, 2, 6, 5, the maximum increasing subsequence has length four (1, 4, 5, 9 among others). Give an $O(N^2)$ algorithm to solve the longest increasing subsequence problem.

*10.54 The *longest common subsequence* problem is as follows: Given two sequences $A = a_1, a_2, \ldots, a_M$, and $B = b_1, b_2, \ldots, b_N$, find the length, k, of the longest sequence $C = c_1, c_2, \ldots, c_k$ such that C is a subsequence of both A and B. As an example, if

$$A = d, y, n, a, m, i, c$$

and

$$B = p, r, o, g, r, a, m, m, i, n, g,$$

then the longest common subsequence is a,m and has length 2. Give an algorithm to solve the longest common subsequence problem. Your algorithm should run in $O(MN)$ time.

*10.55 The *pattern matching problem* is as follows: Given a string S of text, and a pattern P, find the first occurrence of P in S. *Approximate pattern matching* allows k mismatches of three types:

   1. A character can be in S that is not in P.

   2. A character can be in P that is not in S.

   3. P and S can differ in a position.

As an example, if we are searching for the pattern "textbook" with at most three mismatches in the string "data structures txtborpk", we find a match (insert an e, change an r to an o, delete a p). Give an $O(MN)$ algorithm to solve the approximate string matching problem, where $M = |P|$ and $N = |S|$.

*10.56 One form of the *knapsack problem* is as follows: We are given a set of integers $A = a_1, a_2, \ldots, a_N$ and an integer K. Is there a subset of A whose sum is exactly K?

   a. Give an algorithm that solves the knapsack problem in $O(NK)$ time.

   b. Why does this not show that $P = NP$?

*10.57 You are given a currency system with coins of (decreasing) value $c_1, c_2, \ldots, c_N$ cents.

   a. Give an algorithm that computes the minimum number of coins required to give K cents in change.

b. Give an algorithm that computes the number of different ways to give K cents in change.

*10.58 Consider the problem of placing eight queens on an (eight by eight) chess board. Two queens are said to attack each other if they are on the same row, column, or (not necessarily main) diagonal.

a. Give a randomized algorithm to place eight nonattacking queens on the board.

b. Give a backtracking algorithm to solve the same problem.

c. Implement both algorithms and compare the running time.

*10.59 In the game of chess, a knight in row R and column C may move to row $1 \leq R' \leq B$ and column $1 \leq C' \leq B$ (where B is the size of the board) provided that either

$$|R - R'| = 2 \text{ and } |C - C'| = 1$$

or

$$|R - R'| = 1 \text{ and } |C - C'| = 2$$

A *knight's tour* is a sequence of moves that visits all squares exactly once before returning to the starting point.

a. If B is odd, show that a knight's tour cannot exist.

b. Give a backtracking algorithm to find a knight's tour.

10.60 Consider the recursive algorithm in Figure 10.79 for finding the shortest weighted path in an acyclic graph, from s to t.

a. Why does this algorithm not work for general graphs?

b. Prove that this algorithm terminates for acyclic graphs.

c. What is the worst-case running time of the algorithm?

10.61 Let A be an N-by-N matrix of zeros and ones. A submatrix S of A is any group of *contiguous* entries that forms a square.

```
Distance shortest( s, t )
{
    Distance dₜ, tmp;

    if( s == t )
        return 0;

    dₜ = ∞;
    for each vertex v adjacent to s
    {
        tmp = shortest( v, t );
        if( c_{s,v} + tmp < Dₜ )
            dₜ = c_{s,v} + tmp;
    }
    return dₜ;
}
```

Figure 10.79 Recursive shortest path algorithm

a. Design an $O(N^2)$ algorithm that determines the size of the largest submatrix of ones in A. For instance, in the matrix below, the largest submatrix is a 4-by-4 square.

```
10111000
00010100
00111000
00111010
00111111
01011110
01011110
00011110
```

**b. Repeat part (a) if S is allowed to be a rectangle instead of a square. *Largest* is measured by area.

10.62 Even if the computer has a move that gives an immediate win, it may not make it if it detects another move that is also guaranteed to win. Some early chess programs were problematic in that they would get into a repetition of position when a forced win was detected, thereby allowing the opponent to claim a draw. In tic-tac-toe, this is not a problem, because the program eventually will win. Modify the tic-tac-toe algorithm so that when a winning position is found, the move that leads to the shortest win is always taken. You can do this by adding `9-depth` to `COMP_WIN` so that the quickest win gives the highest value.

10.63 Write a program to play 5-by-5 tic-tac-toe, where 4 in a row wins. Can you search to terminal nodes?

10.64 The game of Boggle consists of a grid of letters and a word list. The object is to find words in the grid that are subject to the constraint that two adjacent letters must be adjacent in the grid (that is, north, south, east, or west of each other), and each item in the grid can be used, at most, once per word. Write a program to play Boggle.

10.65 Write a program to play MAXIT. The board is represented as an N-by-N grid of numbers randomly placed at the start of the game. One position is designated as the initial current position. Two players alternate turns. At each turn, a player must select a grid element in the current row or column. The value of the selected position is added to the player's score, and that position becomes the current position and cannot be selected again. Players alternate until all grid elements in the current row and column are already selected, at which point the game ends and the player with the highest score wins.

10.66 Othello played on a 6-by-6 board is a forced win for black. Prove this by writing a program. What is the final score if play on both sides is optimal?

REFERENCES

The original paper on Huffman codes is [22]. Variations on the algorithm are discussed in [30], [33], and [34]. Another popular compression scheme is Ziv–Lempel encoding [60], [61]. Here the codes have a fixed length but represent strings instead of characters. [8] and [36] are good surveys of the common compression schemes.

The analysis of bin-packing heuristics first appeared in Johnson's Ph.D. thesis and was published in [23]. The improved lower bound for on-line bin packing given in Exercise 10.8 is from [57]; this result has been improved further in [37] and [55]. [49] describes another approach to on-line bin packing.

Theorem 10.7 is from [7]. The closest points algorithm appeared in [50]. [52] describes the turnpike reconstruction problem and its applications. The exponential worst case input was given by [59]. Two older books on the relatively new field of computational geometry are [14] and [45]. [41] and [42] contain more recent results. [2] contains the lecture notes for a computational geometry course taught at MIT; it includes an extensive bibliography.

The linear-time selection algorithm appeared in [9]. [17] discusses the sampling approach that finds the median in $1.5N$ expected comparisons. The $O(N^{1.59})$ multiplication is from [24]. Generalizations are discussed in [10] and [26]. Strassen's algorithm appears in the short paper [53]. The paper states the results and not much else. Pan [43] gives several divide and conquer algorithms, including the one in Exercise 10.27. The best known bound is $O(N^{2.376})$, which is due to Coppersmith and Winograd [13].

The classic references on dynamic programming are the books [5] and [6]. The matrix ordering problem was first studied in [19]. It was shown in [21] that the problem can be solved in $O(N \log N)$ time.

An $O(N^2)$ algorithm was provided for the construction of optimal binary search trees by Knuth [27]. The all-pairs shortest-path algorithm is from Floyd [16]. A theoretically better $O(N^3(\log \log N/\log N)^{1/3})$ algorithm is given by Fredman [18], but not surprisingly, it is not practical. A slightly improved bound (with 1/2 instead of 1/3) is given in [54]; see also [3] for related results. Under certain conditions, the running time of dynamic programs can automatically be improved by a factor of N or more. This is discussed in Exercise 10.33, [15], and [58].

The discussion of random number generators is based on [44]. Park and Miller attribute the portable implementation to Schrage [51]. Skip lists are discussed by Pugh in [46]. An alternative, namely the *treap,* is discussed in Chapter 12. The randomized primality-testing algorithm is due to Miller [38] and Rabin [48]. The theorem that at most $(N - 9)/4$ values of A fool the algorithm is from Monier [39]. Other randomized algorithms are discussed in [47]. More examples of randomization techniques can be found in [21], [25], and [40].

More information on α–β pruning can be found in [1], [28], and [31]. The top programs that play chess, checkers, Othello, and backgammon have all achieved world class status. [35] describes an Othello program. The paper appears in a special issue on computer games (mostly chess); this issue is a gold mine of ideas. One of the papers describes the use of dynamic programming to solve chess endgames completely when only a few pieces are left on the board. Related research has resulted in the change of the 50-move rule in certain cases.

Exercise 10.41 is solved in [8]. Determining whether a homometric point set with no duplicate distances exists for $N > 6$ is open. Christofides [12] gives a solution to Exercise 10.47, and also an algorithm that generates a tour at most $\frac{3}{2}$ optimal. Exercise 10.52 is discussed in [29]. Exercise 10.55 is solved in [56]. An $O(kN)$ algorithm is given in [32]. Exercise 10.57 is discussed in [11], but do not be misled by the title of the paper.

1. B. Abramson, "Control Strategies for Two-Player Games," *ACM Computing Surveys,* 21 (1989), 137–161.
2. A. Aggarwal and J. Wein, *Computational Geometry: Lecture Notes for 18.409,* MIT Laboratory for Computer Science, 1988.
3. N. Alon, Z. Galil, and O. Margalit, "On the Exponent of the All-Pairs Shortest Path Problem," *Proceedings of the Thirty-Second Annual Symposium on the Foundations of Computer Science,* (1991), 569–575.

4. T. Bell, I. H. Witten, and J. G. Cleary, "Modeling for Text Compression," *ACM Computing Surveys,* 21 (1989), 557–591.

5. R. E. Bellman, *Dynamic Programming,* Princeton University Press, Princeton, N.J., 1957.

6. R. E. Bellman and S. E. Dreyfus, *Applied Dynamic Programming,* Princeton University Press, Princeton, N.J., 1962.

7. J. L. Bentley, D. Haken, and J. B. Saxe, "A General Method for Solving Divide-and-Conquer Recurrences," *SIGACT News,* 12 (1980), 36–44.

8. G. S. Bloom, "A Counterexample to the Theorem of Piccard," *Journal of Combinatorial Theory A* (1977), 378–379.

9. M. Blum, R. W. Floyd, V. R. Pratt, R. L. Rivest, and R. E. Tarjan, "Time Bounds for Selection," *Journal of Computer and System Sciences,* 7 (1973), 448–461.

10. A. Borodin and J. I. Munro, *The Computational Complexity of Algebraic and Numerical Problems,* American Elsevier, New York, 1975.

11. L. Chang and J. Korsh, "Canonical Coin Changing and Greedy Solutions," *Journal of the ACM,* 23 (1976), 418–422.

12. N. Christofides, "Worst-case Analysis of a New Heuristic for the Traveling Salesman Problem," *Management Science Research Report #388,* Carnegie-Mellon University, Pittsburgh, Pa. 1976.

13. D. Coppersmith and S. Winograd, "Matrix Multiplication via Arithmetic Progressions," *Proceedings of the Nineteenth Annual ACM Symposium on the Theory of Computing* (1987), 1–6.

14. H. Edelsbrunner, *Algorithms in Combinatorial Geometry,* Springer-Verlag, Berlin, 1987.

15. D. Eppstein, Z. Galil, and R. Giancarlo, "Speeding up Dynamic Programming," *Proceedings of the Twenty-ninth Annual IEEE Symposium on the Foundations of Computer Science,* (1988), 488–495.

16. R. W. Floyd, "Algorithm 97: Shortest Path," *Communications of the ACM,* 5 (1962), 345.

17. R. W. Floyd and R. L. Rivest, "Expected Time Bounds for Selection," *Communications of the ACM,* 18 (1975), 165–172.

18. M. L. Fredman, "New Bounds on the Complexity of the Shortest Path Problem," *SIAM Journal on Computing,* 5 (1976), 83–89.

19. S. Godbole, "On Efficient Computation of Matrix Chain Products," *IEEE Transactions on Computers,* 9 (1973), 864–866.

20. R. Gupta, S. A. Smolka, and S. Bhaskar, "On Randomization in Sequential and Distributed Algorithms," *ACM Computing Surveys,* 26 (1994), 7–86.

21. T. C. Hu and M. R. Shing, "Computations of Matrix Chain Products, Part I," *SIAM Journal on Computing,* 11 (1982), 362–373.

22. D. A. Huffman, "A Method for the Construction of Minimum Redundancy Codes," *Proceedings of the IRE,* 40 (1952), 1098–1101.

23. D. S. Johnson, A. Demers, J. D. Ullman, M. R. Garey, and R. L. Graham, "Worst-case Performance Bounds for Simple One-Dimensional Packing Algorithms," *SIAM Journal on Computing,* 3 (1974), 299–325.

24. A. Karatsuba and Y. Ofman, "Multiplication of Multi-digit Numbers on Automata," *Doklady Akademii Nauk SSSR,* 145 (1962), 293–294.

25. D. R. Karger, "Random Sampling in Graph Optimization Problems," Ph. D. thesis, Stanford University, 1995.

26. D. E. Knuth, *The Art of Computer Programming, Vol 2: Seminumerical Algorithms,* 3d ed., Addison-Wesley, Reading, Mass., 1998.

27. D. E. Knuth, "Optimum Binary Search Trees," *Acta Informatica,* 1 (1971), 14–25.

28. D. E. Knuth, "An Analysis of Alpha-Beta Cutoffs," *Artificial Intelligence,* 6 (1975), 293–326.

29. D. E. Knuth, *T_EX and Metafont, New Directions in Typesetting,* Digital Press, Bedford, Mass., 1981.

30. D. E. Knuth, "Dynamic Huffman Coding," *Journal of Algorithms,* 6 (1985), 163–180.

31. D. E. Knuth and R. W. Moore, "Estimating the Efficiency of Backtrack Programs," *Mathematics of Computation,* 29 (1975), 121–136.

32. G. M. Landau and U. Vishkin, "Introducing Efficient Parallelism into Approximate String Matching and a New Serial Algorithm," *Proceedings of the Eighteenth Annual ACM Symposium on Theory of Computing* (1986), 220–230.

33. L. L. Larmore, "Height-Restricted Optimal Binary Trees," *SIAM Journal on Computing,* 16 (1987), 1115–1123.

34. L. L. Larmore and D. S. Hirschberg, "A Fast Algorithm for Optimal Length-Limited Huffman Codes," *Journal of the ACM,* 37 (1990), 464–473.

35. K. Lee and S. Mahajan, "The Development of a World Class Othello Program," *Artificial Intelligence,* 43 (1990), 21–36.

36. D. A. Lelewer and D. S. Hirschberg, "Data Compression," *ACM Computing Surveys,* 19 (1987), 261–296.

37. F. M. Liang, "A Lower Bound for On-line Bin Packing," *Information Processing Letters,* 10 (1980), 76–79.

38. G. L. Miller, "Riemann's Hypothesis and Tests for Primality," *Journal of Computer and System Sciences,* 13 (1976), 300–317.

39. L. Monier, "Evaluation and Comparison of Two Efficient Probabilistic Primality Testing Algorithms," *Theoretical Computer Science,* 12 (1980), 97–108.

40. R. Motwani and P. Raghavan, *Randomized Algorithms,* Cambridge University Press, New York (1995).

41. K. Mulmuley, *Computational Geometry: An Introduction Through Randomized Algorithms,* Prentice–Hall, Englewood Cliffs, N.J. (1994).

42. J. O'Rourke, *Computational Geometry in C,* Cambridge University Press, New York (1994).

43. V. Pan, "Strassen's Algorithm is Not Optimal," *Proceedings of the Nineteenth Annual IEEE Symposium on the Foundations of Computer Science* (1978), 166–176.

44. S. K. Park and K. W. Miller, "Random Number Generators: Good Ones are Hard To Find," *Communications of the ACM,* 31 (1988), 1192–1201. (See also *Technical Correspondence,* in 36 (1993) 105–110).

45. F. P. Preparata and M. I. Shamos, *Computational Geometry: An Introduction,* Springer-Verlag, New York, 1985.

46. W. Pugh, "Skip Lists: A Probabilistic Alternative to Balanced Trees," *Communications of the ACM,* 33 (1990), 668–676.

47. M. O. Rabin, "Probabilistic Algorithms," in *Algorithms and Complexity, Recent Results and New Directions* (J. F. Traub, ed.), Academic Press, New York, 1976, 21–39.

48. M. O. Rabin, "Probabilistic Algorithms for Testing Primality," *Journal of Number Theory,* 12 (1980), 128–138.

49. P. Ramanan, D. J. Brown, C. C. Lee, and D. T. Lee, "On-line Bin Packing in Linear Time," *Journal of Algorithms,* 10 (1989), 305–326.

50. M. I. Shamos and D. Hoey, "Closest-Point Problems," *Proceedings of the Sixteenth Annual IEEE Symposium on the Foundations of Computer Science* (1975), 151–162.

51. L. Schrage, "A More Portable FORTRAN Random Number Generator," *ACM Transactions on Mathematics Software,* 5 (1979), 132–138.

52. S. S. Skiena, W. D. Smith, and P. Lemke, "Reconstructing Sets From Interpoint Distances," *Proceedings of the Sixth Annual ACM Symposium on Computational Geometry* (1990), 332–339.

53. V. Strassen, "Gaussian Elimination is Not Optimal," *Numerische Mathematik,* 13 (1969), 354–356.

54. T. Takaoka, "A New Upper Bound on the Complexity of the All-Pairs Shortest Path Problem," *Information Processing Letters,* 43 (1992), 195–199.

55. A. van Vleit, "An Improved Lower Bound for On-Line Bin Packing Algorithms," *Information Processing Letters,* 43 (1992), 277–284.

56. R. A. Wagner and M. J. Fischer, "The String-to-String Correction Problem," *Journal of the ACM,* 21 (1974), 168–173.

57. A. C. Yao, "New Algorithms for Bin Packing," *Journal of the ACM,* 27 (1980), 207–227.

58. F. F. Yao, "Efficient Dynamic Programming Using Quadrangle Inequalities," *Proceedings of the Twelfth Annual ACM Symposium on the Theory of Computing* (1980), 429–435.

59. Z. Zhang, "An Exponential Example for a Partial Digest Mapping Algorithm," *Journal of Computational Molecular Biology,* 1 (1994), 235–239.

60. J. Ziv and A. Lempel, "A Universal Algorithm for Sequential Data Compression," *IEEE Transactions on Information Theory* IT23 (1977), 337–343.

61. J. Ziv and A. Lempel, "Compression of Individual Sequences via Variable-rate Coding," *IEEE Transactions on Information Theory* IT24 (1978), 530–536.

CHAPTER 11

Amortized Analysis

In this chapter, we will analyze the running times for several of the advanced data structures that have been presented in Chapters 4 and 6. In particular, we will consider the worst-case running time for any sequence of M operations. This contrasts with the more typical analysis, in which a worst-case bound is given for any *single* operation.

As an example, we have seen that AVL trees support the standard tree operations in $O(\log N)$ worst-case time per operation. AVL trees are somewhat complicated to implement, not only because there are a host of cases, but also because height balance information must be maintained and updated correctly. The reason that AVL trees are used is that a sequence of $\Theta(N)$ operations on an unbalanced search tree could require $\Theta(N^2)$ time, which would be expensive. For search trees, the $O(N)$ worst-case running time of an operation is not the real problem. The major problem is that this could happen repeatedly. Splay trees offer a pleasant alternative. Although any operation can still require $\Theta(N)$ time, this degenerate behavior cannot occur repeatedly, and we can prove that any sequence of M operations takes $O(M \log N)$ worst-case time (total). Thus, in the long run this data structure behaves as though each operation takes $O(\log N)$. We call this an *amortized time bound*.

Amortized bounds are weaker than the corresponding worst-case bounds, because there is no guarantee for any single operation. Since this is generally not important, we are willing to sacrifice the bound on a single operation, if we can retain the same bound for the sequence of operations and at the same time simplify the data structure. Amortized bounds are stronger than the equivalent average-case bound. For instance, binary search trees have $O(\log N)$ average time per operation, but it is still possible for a sequence of M operations to take $O(MN)$ time.

Because deriving an amortized bound requires us to look at an entire sequence of operations instead of just one, we expect that the analysis will be more tricky. We will see that this expectation is generally realized.

In this chapter we shall

- Analyze the binomial queue operations.
- Analyze skew heaps.
- Introduce and analyze the Fibonacci heap.
- Analyze splay trees.

11.1. An Unrelated Puzzle

Consider the following puzzle: Two kittens are placed on opposite ends of a football field, 100 yards apart. They walk toward each other at the speed of 10 yards per minute. At the same time, their mother is at one end of the field. She can run at 100 yards per minute. The mother runs from one kitten to the other, making turns with no loss of speed, until the kittens (and thus the mother) meet at midfield. How far does the mother run?

It is not hard to solve this puzzle with a brute-force calculation. We leave the details to you, but one expects that this calculation will involve computing the sum of an infinite geometric series. Although this straightforward calculation will lead to an answer, it turns out that a much simpler solution can be arrived at by introducing an extra variable, namely, time.

Because the kittens are 100 yards apart and approach each other at a combined velocity of 20 yards per minute, it takes them five minutes to get to midfield. Since the mother runs 100 yards per minute, her total is 500 yards.

This puzzle illustrates the point that sometimes it is easier to solve a problem indirectly than directly. The amortized analyses that we will perform will use this idea. We will introduce an extra variable, known as the *potential,* to allow us to prove results that seem very difficult to establish otherwise.

11.2. Binomial Queues

The first data structure we will look at is the binomial queue of Chapter 6, which we now review briefly. Recall that a *binomial tree* B_0 is a one-node tree, and for $k > 0$, the binomial tree B_k is built by melding two binomial trees B_{k-1} together. Binomial trees B_0 through B_4 are shown in Figure 11.1.

B_0 B_1 B_2 B_3

B_4

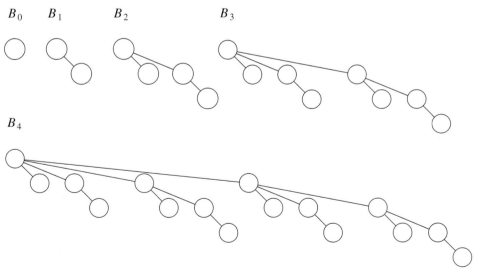

Figure 11.1 Binomial trees B_0, B_1, B_2, B_3, and B_4

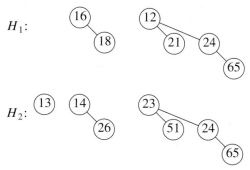

Figure 11.2 Two binomial queues H_1 and H_2

The *rank* of a node in a binomial tree is equal to the number of children; in particular, the rank of the root of B_k is k. A *binomial queue* is a collection of heap-ordered binomial trees, in which there can be at most one binomial tree B_k for any k. Two binomial queues, H_1 and H_2, are shown in Figure 11.2.

The most important operation is `merge`. To merge two binomial queues, an operation similar to addition of binary integers is performed: At any stage we may have zero, one, two, or possibly three B_k trees, depending on whether or not the two priority queues contain a B_k tree and whether or not a B_k tree is carried over from the previous step. If there is zero or one B_k tree, it is placed as a tree in the resultant binomial queue. If there are two B_k trees, they are melded into a B_{k+1} tree and carried over; if there are three B_k trees, one is placed as a tree in the binomial queue and the other two are melded and carried over. The result of merging H_1 and H_2 is shown in Figure 11.3.

Insertion is performed by creating a one-node binomial queue and performing a `merge`. The time to do this is $M + 1$, where M represents the smallest type of binomial tree B_M not present in the binomial queue. Thus, insertion into a binomial queue that has a B_0 tree but no B_1 tree requires two steps. Deletion of the minimum is accomplished by removing the minimum and splitting the original binomial queue into two binomial queues, which are then merged. A less terse explanation of these operations is given in Chapter 6.

We consider a very simple problem first. Suppose we want to build a binomial queue of N elements. We know that building a binary heap of N elements can be done in $O(N)$, so we expect a similar bound for binomial queues.

CLAIM:
A binomial queue of N elements can be built by N successive insertions in $O(N)$ time.

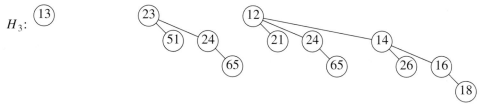

Figure 11.3 Binomial queue H_3: the result of merging H_1 and H_2

The claim, if true, would give an extremely simple algorithm. Since the worst-case time for each insertion is $O(\log N)$, it is not obvious that the claim is true. Recall that if this algorithm were applied to binary heaps, the running time would be $O(N \log N)$.

To prove the claim, we could do a direct calculation. To measure the running time, we define the cost of each insertion to be one time unit plus an extra unit for each linking step. Summing this cost over all insertions gives the total running time. This total is N units plus the total number of linking steps. The 1st, 3rd, 5th, and all odd-numbered steps require no linking steps, since there is no B_0 present at the time of insertion. Thus, half of the insertions require no linking steps. A quarter of the insertions require only one linking step (2nd, 6th, 10th, and so on). An eighth require two, and so on. We could add this all up and bound the number of linking steps by N, proving the claim. This brute-force calculation will not help when we try to analyze a sequence of operations that include more than just insertions, so we will use another approach to prove this result.

Consider the result of an insertion. If there is no B_0 tree present at the time of the insertion, then the insertion costs a total of one unit, using the same accounting as above. The result of the insertion is that there is now a B_0 tree, and thus we have added one tree to the forest of binomial trees. If there is a B_0 tree but no B_1 tree, then the insertion costs two units. The new forest will have a B_1 tree but will no longer have a B_0 tree, so the number of trees in the forest is unchanged. An insertion that costs three units will create a B_2 tree but destroy a B_0 and B_1 tree, yielding a net loss of one tree in the forest. In fact, it is easy to see that, in general, an insertion that costs c units results in a net increase of $2 - c$ trees in the forest, because a B_{c-1} tree is created but all B_i trees $0 \le i < c - 1$ are removed. Thus, expensive insertions remove trees, while cheap insertions create trees.

Let C_i be the cost of the ith insertion. Let T_i be the number of trees *after* the ith insertion. $T_0 = 0$ is the number of trees initially. Then we have the invariant

$$C_i + (T_i - T_{i-1}) = 2 \tag{11.1}$$

We then have

$$C_1 + (T_1 - T_0) = 2$$
$$C_2 + (T_2 - T_1) = 2$$
$$\vdots$$
$$C_{N-1} + (T_{N-1} - T_{N-2}) = 2$$
$$C_N + (T_N - T_{N-1}) = 2$$

If we add all these equations, most of the T_i terms cancel, leaving

$$\sum_{i=1}^{N} C_i + T_N - T_0 = 2N$$

or equivalently,

$$\sum_{i=1}^{N} C_i = 2N - (T_N - T_0)$$

Recall that $T_0 = 0$ and T_N, the number of trees after the N insertions, is certainly not negative, so $(T_N - T_0)$ is not negative. Thus

$$\sum_{i=1}^{N} C_i \leq 2N$$

which proves the claim.

During the `buildBinomialQueue` routine, each insertion had a worst-case time of $O(\log N)$, but since the entire routine used at most $2N$ units of time, the insertions behaved as though each used no more than two units each.

This example illustrates the general technique we will use. The state of the data structure at any time is given by a function known as the *potential*. The potential function is not maintained by the program, but rather is an accounting device that will help with the analysis. When operations take less time than we have allocated for them, the unused time is "saved" in the form of a higher potential. In our example, the potential of the data structure is simply the number of trees. In the analysis above, when we have insertions that use only one unit instead of the two units that are allocated, the extra unit is saved for later by an increase in potential. When operations occur that exceed the allotted time, then the excess time is accounted for by a decrease in potential. One may view the potential as representing a savings account. If an operation uses less than its allotted time, the difference is saved for use later on by more expensive operations. Figure 11.4 shows the cumulative running time used by `buildBinomialQueue` over a sequence of insertions. Observe that the running time never exceeds $2N$ and that the potential in the binomial queue after any insertion measures the amount of savings.

Once a potential function is chosen, we write the main equation:

$$T_{actual} + \Delta Potential = T_{amortized} \tag{11.2}$$

T_{actual}, the *actual time* of an operation, represents the exact (observed) amount of time required to execute a particular operation. In a binary search tree, for example, the actual

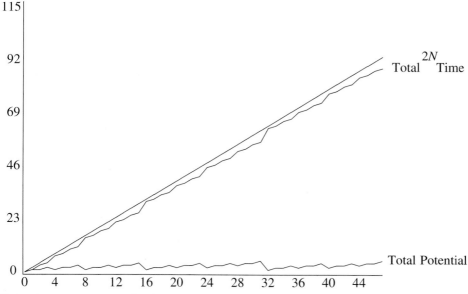

Figure 11.4 A sequence of N inserts

time to perform a find(x) is 1 plus the depth of the node containing x. If we sum the basic equation over the entire sequence, and if the final potential is at least as large as the initial potential, then the amortized time is an upper bound on the actual time used during the execution of the sequence. Notice that while T_{actual} varies from operation to operation, $T_{\text{amortized}}$ is stable.

Picking a potential function that proves a meaningful bound is a very tricky task; there is no one method that is used. Generally, many potential functions are tried before the one that works is found. Nevertheless, the discussion above suggests a few rules, which tell us the properties that good potential functions have. The potential function should

- Always assume its minimum at the start of the sequence. A popular method of choosing potential functions is to ensure that the potential function is initially 0, and always nonnegative. All of the examples that we will encounter use this strategy.

- Cancel a term in the actual time. In our case, if the actual cost was c, then the potential change was $2 - c$. When these are added, an amortized cost of 2 is obtained. This is shown in Figure 11.5.

We can now perform a complete analysis of binomial queue operations.

THEOREM 11.1.
The amortized running times of insert, deleteMin, *and* merge *are* $O(1)$, $O(\log N)$, *and* $O(\log N)$, *respectively, for binomial queues.*

PROOF:
The potential function is the number of trees. The initial potential is 0, and the potential is always nonnegative, so the amortized time is an upper bound on the actual time. The analysis for insert follows from the argument above. For merge, assume the two trees have N_1 and N_2 nodes with T_1 and T_2 trees, respectively. Let $N = N_1 + N_2$. The actual time to perform the merge is $O(\log(N_1) + \log(N_2)) = O(\log N)$. After the merge,

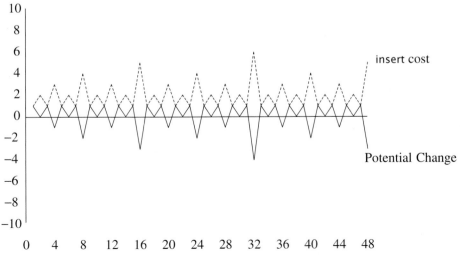

Figure 11.5 The insertion cost and potential change for each operation in a sequence

there can be at most $\log N$ trees, so the potential can increase by at most $O(\log N)$. This gives an amortized bound of $O(\log N)$. The `deleteMin` bound follows in a similar manner.

11.3. Skew Heaps

The analysis of binomial queues is a fairly easy example of an amortized analysis. We now look at skew heaps. As is common with many of our examples, once the right potential function is found, the analysis is easy. The difficult part is choosing a meaningful potential function.

Recall that for skew heaps, the key operation is merging. To merge two skew heaps, we merge their right paths and make this the new left path. For each node on the new path, except the last, the old left subtree is attached as the right subtree. The last node on the new left path is known to not have a right subtree, so it is silly to give it one. The bound does not depend on this exception, and if the routine is coded recursively, this is what will happen naturally. Figure 11.6 shows the result of merging two skew heaps.

Suppose we have two heaps, H_1 and H_2, and there are r_1 and r_2 nodes on their respective right paths. Then the actual time to perform the merge is proportional to $r_1 + r_2$, so we will drop the Big-Oh notation and charge one unit of time for each node on the paths. Since the heaps have no structure, it is possible that all the nodes in both heaps lie on the right path, and this would give a $\Theta(N)$ worst-case bound to merge the heaps (Exercise 11.3 asks you to construct an example). We will show that the amortized time to merge two skew heaps is $O(\log N)$.

What is needed is some sort of a potential function that captures the effect of skew heap operations. Recall that the effect of a `merge` is that every node on the right path is moved to the left path, and its old left child becomes the new right child. One idea might be to classify each node as a right node or left node, depending on whether or not it is a right child, and use the number of right nodes as a potential function. Although the potential is initially 0 and always nonnegative, the problem is that the potential does not decrease after a merge and thus does not adequately reflect the savings in the data structure. The result is that this potential function cannot be used to prove the desired bound.

A similar idea is to classify nodes as either heavy or light, depending on whether or not the right subtree of any node has more nodes than the left subtree.

DEFINITION: A node p is *heavy* if the number of descendants of p's right subtree is at least half of the number of descendants of p, and *light* otherwise. Note that the number of descendants of a node includes the node itself.

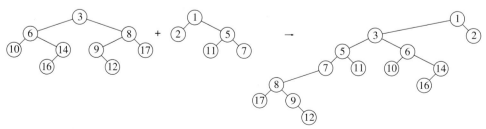

Figure 11.6 Merging of two skew heaps

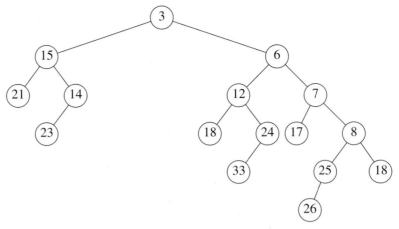

Figure 11.7 Skew heap—heavy nodes are 3, 6, 7, 12, and 15

As an example, Figure 11.7 shows a skew heap. The nodes with values 15, 3, 6, 12, and 7 are heavy, and all other nodes are light.

The potential function we will use is the number of heavy nodes in the (collection) of heaps. This seems like a good choice, because a long right path will contain an inordinate number of heavy nodes. Because nodes on this path have their children swapped, these nodes will be converted to light nodes as a result of the merge.

THEOREM 11.2.
The amortized time to merge two skew heaps is $O(\log N)$.

PROOF:
Let H_1 and H_2 be the two heaps, with N_1 and N_2 nodes respectively. Suppose the right path of H_1 has l_1 light nodes and h_1 heavy nodes, for a total of $l_1 + h_1$. Likewise, H_2 has l_2 light and h_2 heavy nodes on its right path, for a total of $l_2 + h_2$ nodes.

If we adopt the convention that the cost of merging two skew heaps is the total number of nodes on their right paths, then the actual time to perform the merge is $l_1 + l_2 + h_1 + h_2$. Now the only nodes whose heavy/light status can change are nodes that are initially on the right path (and wind up on the left path), since no other nodes have their subtrees altered. This is shown by the example in Figure 11.8.

If a heavy node is initially on the right path, then after the merge it must become a light node. The other nodes that were on the right path were light and may or may

Figure 11.8 Change in heavy/light status after a merge

not become heavy, but since we are proving an upper bound, we will have to assume the worst, which is that they become heavy and increase the potential. Then the net change in the number of heavy nodes is at most $l_1 + l_2 - h_1 - h_2$. Adding the actual time and the potential change (Equation (11.2)) gives an amortized bound of $2(l_1 + l_2)$.

Now we must show that $l_1 + l_2 = O(\log N)$. Since l_1 and l_2 are the number of light nodes on the original right paths, and the right subtree of a light node is less than half the size of the tree rooted at the light node, it follows directly that the number of light nodes on the right path is at most $\log N_1 + \log N_2$, which is $O(\log N)$.

The proof is completed by noting that the initial potential is 0 and that the potential is always nonnegative. It is important to verify this, since otherwise the amortized time does not bound the actual time and is meaningless.

Since the **insert** and **deleteMin** operations are basically just **merge**s, they also have $O(\log N)$ amortized bounds.

11.4. Fibonacci Heaps

In Section 9.3.2, we showed how to use priority queues to improve on the naïve $O(|V|^2)$ running time of Dijkstra's shortest-path algorithm. The important observation was that the running time was dominated by $|E|$ **decreaseKey** operations and $|V|$ **insert** and **deleteMin** operations. These operations take place on a set of size at most $|V|$. By using a binary heap, all these operations take $O(\log |V|)$ time, so the resulting bound for Dijkstra's algorithm can be reduced to $O(|E| \log |V|)$.

In order to lower this time bound, the time required to perform the **decreaseKey** operation must be improved. d-heaps, which were described in Section 6.5, give an $O(\log_d |V|)$ time bound for the **decreaseKey** operation as well as for **insert**, but an $O(d \log_d |V|)$ bound for **deleteMin**. By choosing d to balance the costs of $|E|$ **decreaseKey** operations with $|V|$ **deleteMin** operations, and remembering that d must always be at least 2, we see that a good choice for d is

$$d = \max(2, \lfloor |E|/|V| \rfloor)$$

This improves the time bound for Dijkstra's algorithm to

$$O(|E| \log_{(2+\lfloor |E|/|V| \rfloor)} |V|)$$

The *Fibonacci heap* is a data structure that supports all the basic heap operations in $O(1)$ amortized time, with the exception of **deleteMin** and **delete**, which take $O(\log N)$ amortized time. It immediately follows that the heap operations in Dijkstra's algorithm will require a total of $O(|E| + |V| \log |V|)$ time.

Fibonacci heaps* generalize binomial queues by adding two new concepts:

A different implementation of **decreaseKey**: The method we have seen before is to percolate the element up toward the root. It does not seem reasonable to expect an $O(1)$ amortized bound for this strategy, so a new method is needed.

---

*The name comes from a property of this data structure, which we will prove later in the section.

Lazy merging: Two heaps are merged only when it is required to do so. This is similar to lazy deletion. For lazy merging, `merge`s are cheap, but because lazy merging does not actually combine trees, the `deleteMin` operation could encounter lots of trees, making that operation expensive. Any one `deleteMin` could take linear time, but it is always possible to charge the time to previous `merge` operations. In particular, an expensive `deleteMin` must have been preceded by a large number of unduly cheap `merge`s, which were able to store up extra potential.

11.4.1. Cutting Nodes in Leftist Heaps

In binary heaps, the `decreaseKey` operation is implemented by lowering the value at a node and then percolating it up toward the root until heap order is established. In the worst case, this can take $O(\log N)$ time, which is the length of the longest path toward the root in a balanced tree.

This strategy does not work if the tree that represents the priority queue does not have $O(\log N)$ depth. As an example, if this strategy is applied to leftist heaps, then the `decreaseKey` operation could take $\Theta(N)$ time, as the example in Figure 11.9 shows.

We see that for leftist heaps, another strategy is needed for the `decreaseKey` operation. Our example will be the leftist heap in Figure 11.10. Suppose we want to decrease the key with value 9 down to 0. If we make the change, we find that we have created a violation of heap order, which is indicated by a dashed line in Figure 11.11.

We do not want to percolate the 0 to the root, because, as we have seen, there are cases where this could be expensive. The solution is to *cut* the heap along the dashed line, thus creating two trees, and then merge the two trees back into one. Let X be the node to which the `decreaseKey` operation is being applied, and let P be its parent. After the cut, we have two trees, namely, H_1 with root X, and T_2, which is the original tree with H_1 removed. The situation is shown in Figure 11.12.

If these two trees were both leftist heaps, then they could be merged in $O(\log N)$ time, and we would be done. It is easy to see that H_1 is a leftist heap, since none of its nodes have had any changes in their descendants. Thus, since all of its nodes originally satisfied the leftist property, they still must.

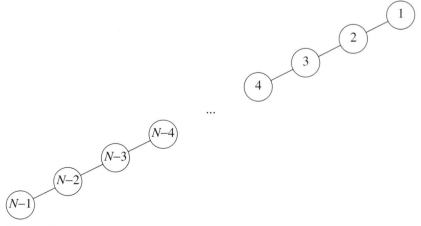

Figure 11.9 Decreasing $N - 1$ to 0 via percolate up would take $\Theta(N)$ time

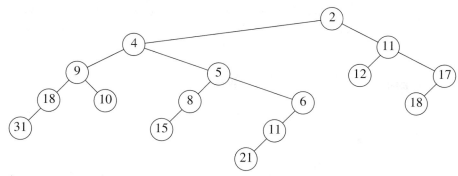

Figure 11.10 Sample leftist heap H

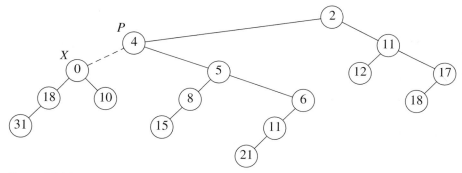

Figure 11.11 Decreasing 9 to 0 creates a heap order violation

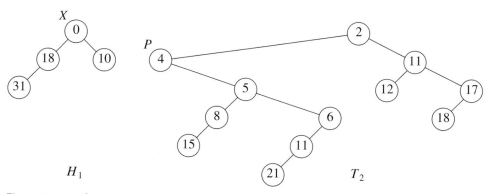

Figure 11.12 The two trees after the cut

Nevertheless, it seems that this scheme will not work, because T_2 is not necessarily leftist. However, it is easy to reinstate the leftist heap property by using two observations:

- Only nodes on the path from P to the root of T_2 can be in violation of the leftist heap property; these can be fixed by swapping children.
- Since the maximum right path length has at most $\lfloor \log(N + 1) \rfloor$ nodes, we only need to check the first $\lfloor \log(N + 1) \rfloor$ nodes on the path from P to the root of T_2. Figure 11.13 shows H_1 and T_2 after T_2 is converted to a leftist heap.

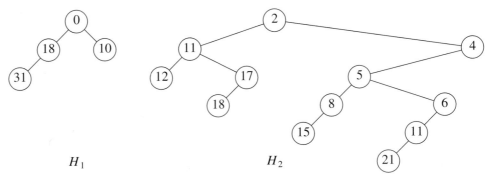

H_1 H_2

Figure 11.13 T_2 converted to the leftist heap H_2

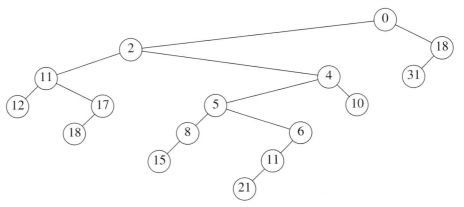

Figure 11.14 decreaseKey$(X, 9)$ completed by merging H_1 and H_2

Because we can convert T_2 to the leftist heap H_2 in $O(\log N)$ steps, and then merge H_1 and H_2, we have an $O(\log N)$ algorithm for performing the **decreaseKey** operation in leftist heaps. The heap that results in our example is shown in Figure 11.14.

11.4.2. Lazy Merging for Binomial Queues

The second idea that is used by Fibonacci heaps is *lazy merging*. We will apply this idea to binomial queues and show that the amortized time to perform a **merge** operation (as well as insertion, which is a special case) is $O(1)$. The amortized time for **deleteMin** will still be $O(\log N)$.

The idea is as follows: To merge two binomial queues, merely concatenate the two lists of binomial trees, creating a new binomial queue. This new queue may have several trees of the same size, so it violates the binomial queue property. We will call this a *lazy binomial queue* in order to maintain consistency. This is a fast operation that always takes constant (worst-case) time. As before, an insertion is done by creating a one-node binomial queue and merging. The difference is that the **merge** is lazy.

The **deleteMin** operation is much more painful, because it is where we finally convert the lazy binomial queue back into a standard binomial queue, but, as we will show, it is still $O(\log N)$ amortized time—but not $O(\log N)$ worst-case time, as before. To perform a

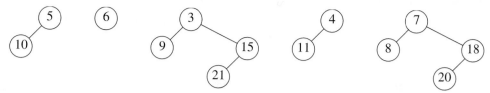

Figure 11.15 Lazy binomial queue

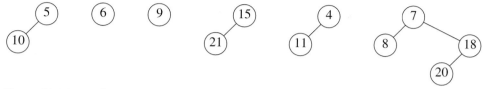

Figure 11.16 Lazy binomial queue after removing the smallest element (3)

```
/* 1*/   for( R = 0; R <= ⌊log N⌋; R++ )
/* 2*/       while( |L_R| >= 2 )
           {
/* 3*/         Remove two trees from L_R;
/* 4*/         Merge the two trees into a new tree;
/* 5*/         Add the new tree to L_{R+1};
           }
```

Figure 11.17 Procedure to reinstate a binomial queue

deleteMin, we find (and eventually return) the minimum element. As before, we delete it from the queue, making each of its children new trees. We then merge all the trees into a binomial queue by merging two equal-sized trees until it is no longer possible.

As an example, Figure 11.15 shows a lazy binomial queue. In a lazy binomial queue, there can be more than one tree of the same size. To perform the deleteMin, we remove the smallest element, as before, and obtain the tree in Figure 11.16.

We now have to merge all the trees and obtain a standard binomial queue. A standard binomial queue has at most one tree of each rank. In order to do this efficiently, we must be able to perform the merge in time proportional to the number of trees present (T) (or $\log N$, whichever is larger). To do this, we form an array of lists, $L_0, L_1, \ldots, L_{R_{max}+1}$, where R_{max} is the rank of the largest tree. Each list L_R contains all of the trees of rank R. The procedure in Figure 11.17 is then applied.

Each time through the loop, at lines 3 through 5, the total number of trees is reduced by 1. This means that this part of the code, which takes constant time per execution, can only be performed $T - 1$ times, where T is the number of trees. The for loop counters and tests at the end of the while loop take $O(\log N)$ time, so the running time is $O(T + \log N)$, as required. Figure 11.18 shows the execution of this algorithm on the previous collection of binomial trees.

Amortized Analysis of Lazy Binomial Queues

To carry out the amortized analysis of lazy binomial queues, we will use the same potential function that was used for standard binomial queues. Thus, the potential of a lazy binomial queue is the number of trees.

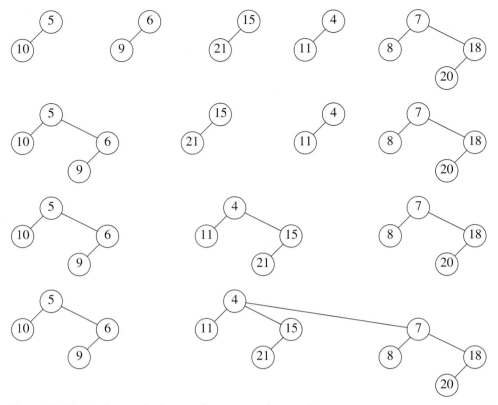

Figure 11.18 Combining the binomial trees into a binomial queue

THEOREM 11.3.
The amortized running times of **merge** *and* **insert** *are both $O(1)$ for lazy binomial queues. The amortized running time of* **deleteMin** *is $O(\log N)$.*

PROOF:
The potential function is the number of trees in the collection of binomial queues. The initial potential is 0, and the potential is always nonnegative. Thus, over a sequence of operations, the total amortized time is an upper bound on the total actual time.

For the **merge** operation, the actual time is constant, and the number of trees in the collection of binomial queues is unchanged, so, by Equation (11.2), the amortized time is $O(1)$.

For the **insert** operation, the actual time is constant, and the number of trees can increase by at most 1, so the amortized time is $O(1)$.

The **deleteMin** operation is more complicated. Let R be the rank of the tree that contains the minimum element, and let T be the number of trees. Thus, the potential at the start of the **deleteMin** operation is T. To perform a **deleteMin**, the children of the smallest node are split off into separate trees. This creates $T + R$ trees, which must be merged into a standard binomial queue. The actual time to perform this is $T + R + \log N$, if we ignore the constant in the Big-Oh notation, by the argument above.* On the other hand, once this is done, there can be at most $\log N$ trees remaining, so the potential function can increase by at most $(\log N) - T$. Adding the actual time and the change in potential gives an amortized bound of $2 \log N + R$. Since all the trees are binomial trees, we know that $R \leq \log N$. Thus we arrive at an $O(\log N)$ amortized time bound for the deleteMin operation.

11.4.3. The Fibonacci Heap Operations

As we mentioned before, the Fibonacci heap combines the leftist heap decreaseKey operation with the lazy binomial queue merge operation. Unfortunately, we cannot use both operations without a slight modification. The problem is that if arbitrary cuts are made in the binomial trees, the resulting forest will no longer be a collection of binomial trees. Because of this, it will no longer be true that the rank of every tree is at most $\lfloor \log N \rfloor$. Since the amortized bound for deleteMin in lazy binomial queues was shown to be $2 \log N + R$, we need $R = O(\log N)$ for the deleteMin bound to hold.

In order to ensure that $R = O(\log N)$, we apply the following rules to all nonroot nodes:

- Mark a (nonroot) node the first time that it loses a child (because of a cut).
- If a marked node loses another child, then cut it from its parent. This node now becomes the root of a separate tree and is no longer marked. This is called a *cascading cut,* because several of these could occur in one decreaseKey operation.

Figure 11.19 shows one tree in a Fibonacci heap prior to a decreaseKey operation. When the node with key 39 is changed to 12, the heap order is violated. Therefore, the node is cut from its parent, becoming the root of a new tree. Since the node containing 33 is marked, this is its second lost child, and thus it is cut from its parent (10). Now 10 has lost its second child, so it is cut from 5. The process stops here, since 5 was unmarked. The node 5 is now marked. The result is shown in Figure 11.20.

Notice that 10 and 33, which used to be marked nodes, are no longer marked, because they are now root nodes. This will be a crucial observation in our proof of the time bound.

11.4.4. Proof of the Time Bound

Recall that the reason for marking nodes is that we needed to bound the rank (number of children) R of any node. We will now show that any node with N descendants has rank $O(\log N)$.

LEMMA 11.1.
Let X be any node in a Fibonacci heap. Let c_i be the ith youngest child of X. Then the rank of c_i is at least $i - 2$.

PROOF:
At the time when c_i was linked to X, X already had (older) children $c_1, c_2, \ldots, c_{i-1}$. Thus, X had at least $i - 1$ children when it linked to c_i. Since nodes are linked only

---

*We can do this because we can place the constant implied by the Big-Oh notation in the potential function and still get the cancellation of terms, which is needed in the proof.

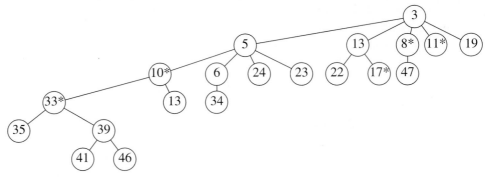

Figure 11.19 A tree in the Fibonacci heap prior to decreasing 39 to 12

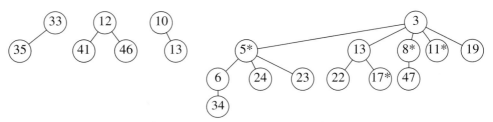

Figure 11.20 The resulting segment of the Fibonacci heap after the **decreaseKey** operation

if they have the same rank, it follows that at the time that c_i was linked to X, c_i had at least $i - 1$ children. Since that time, it could have lost at most one child, or else it would have been cut from X. Thus, c_i has at least $i - 2$ children.

From Lemma 11.1, it is easy to show that any node of rank R must have a lot of descendants.

LEMMA 11.2.

Let F_k be the Fibonacci numbers defined (in Section 1.2) by $F_0 = 1$, $F_1 = 1$, and $F_k = F_{k-1} + F_{k-2}$. Any node of rank $R \geq 1$ has at least F_{R+1} descendants (including itself).

PROOF:

Let S_R be the smallest tree of rank R. Clearly, $S_0 = 1$ and $S_1 = 2$. By Lemma 11.1, a tree of rank R must have subtrees of rank at least $R - 2$, $R - 3$, ..., 1, and 0, plus another subtree, which has at least one node. Along with the root of S_R itself, this gives a minimum value for $S_{R>1}$ of $S_R = 2 + \sum_{i=0}^{R-2} S_i$. It is easy to show that $S_R = F_{R+1}$ (Exercise 1.9a).

Because it is well known that the Fibonacci numbers grow exponentially, it immediately follows that any node with s descendants has rank at most $O(\log s)$. Thus, we have

LEMMA 11.3.

The rank of any node in a Fibonacci heap is $O(\log N)$.

PROOF:

Immediate from the discussion above.

If all we were concerned about were the time bounds for the `merge`, `insert`, and `deleteMin` operations, then we could stop here and prove the desired amortized time bounds. Of course, the whole point of Fibonacci heaps is to obtain an $O(1)$ time bound for `decreaseKey` as well.

The actual time required for a `decreaseKey` operation is 1 plus the number of cascading cuts that are performed during the operation. Since the number of cascading cuts could be much more than $O(1)$, we will need to pay for this with a loss in potential. If we look at Figure 11.20, we see that the number of trees actually increases with each cascading cut, so we will have to enhance the potential function to include something that decreases during cascading cuts. Notice that we cannot just throw out the number of trees from the potential function, since then we will not be able to prove the time bound for the `merge` operation. Looking at Figure 11.20 again, we see that a cascading cut causes a decrease in the number of marked nodes, because each node that is the victim of a cascading cut becomes an unmarked root. Since each cascading cut costs 1 unit of actual time and increases the tree potential by 1, we will count each marked node as two units of potential. This way, we have a chance of canceling out the number of cascading cuts.

THEOREM 11.4

The amortized time bounds for Fibonacci heaps are $O(1)$ for `insert`, `merge`, and `decreaseKey` and $O(\log N)$ for `deleteMin`.

PROOF:

The potential is the number of trees in the collection of Fibonacci heaps plus twice the number of marked nodes. As usual, the initial potential is 0 and is always nonnegative. Thus, over a sequence of operations, the total amortized time is an upper bound on the total actual time.

For the `merge` operation, the actual time is constant, and the number of trees and marked nodes is unchanged, so, by Equation (11.2), the amortized time is $O(1)$.

For the `insert` operation, the actual time is constant, the number of trees increases by 1, and the number of marked nodes is unchanged. Thus, the potential increases by at most 1, so the amortized time is $O(1)$.

For the `deleteMin` operation, let R be the rank of the tree that contains the minimum element, and let T be the number of trees before the operation. To perform a `deleteMin`, we once again split the children of a tree, creating an additional R new trees. Notice that, although this can remove marked nodes (by making them unmarked roots), this cannot create any additional marked nodes. These R new trees, along with the other T trees, must now be merged, at a cost of $T + R + \log N = T + O(\log N)$, by Lemma 11.3. Since there can be at most $O(\log N)$ trees, and the number of marked nodes cannot increase, the potential change is at most $O(\log N) - T$. Adding the actual time and potential change gives the $O(\log N)$ amortized bound for `deleteMin`.

Finally, for the **decreaseKey** operation, let C be the number of cascading cuts. The actual cost of a **decreaseKey** is $C + 1$, which is the total number of cuts performed. The first (noncascading) cut creates a new tree and thus increases the potential by 1. Each cascading cut creates a new tree, but converts a marked node to an unmarked (root) node, for a net loss of one unit per cascading cut. The last cut also can convert an unmarked node (in Fig. 11.20 it is node 5) into a marked node, thus increasing the potential by 2. The total change in potential is thus at most $3 - C$. Adding the actual time and the potential change gives a total of 4, which is $O(1)$.

11.5. Splay Trees

As a final example, we analyze the running time of splay trees. Recall, from Chapter 4, that after an access of some item X is performed, a splaying step moves X to the root by a series of three operations: *zig, zig-zag,* and *zig-zig.* These tree rotations are shown in Figure 11.21. We adopt the convention that if a tree rotation is being performed at node X, then prior to the rotation P is its parent and (if X is not a child of the root) G is its grandparent.

Recall that the time required for any tree operation on node X is proportional to the number of nodes on the path from the root to X. If we count each *zig* operation as one rotation and each *zig-zig* or *zig-zag* as two rotations, then the cost of any access is equal to 1 plus the number of rotations.

In order to show an $O(\log N)$ amortized bound for the splaying step, we need a potential function that can increase by at most $O(\log N)$ over the entire splaying step but that

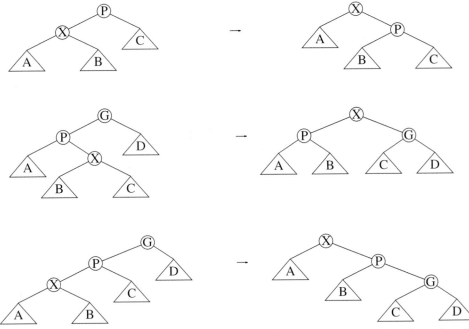

Figure 11.21 *zig, zig-zag,* and *zig-zig* operations; each has a symmetric case (not shown)

will also cancel out the number of rotations performed during the step. It is not at all easy to find a potential function that satisfies these criteria. A simple first guess at a potential function might be the sum of the depths of all the nodes in the tree. This does not work, because the potential can increase by $\Theta(N)$ during an access. A canonical example of this occurs when elements are inserted in sequential order.

A potential function Φ that does work is defined as

$$\Phi(T) = \sum_{i \in T} \log S(i)$$

where $S(i)$ represents the number of descendants of i (including i itself). The potential function is the sum, over all nodes i in the tree T, of the logarithm of $S(i)$.

To simplify the notation, we will define

$$R(i) = \log S(i)$$

This makes

$$\Phi(T) = \sum_{i \in T} R(i)$$

$R(i)$ represents the *rank* of node i. The terminology is similar to what we used in the analysis of the disjoint set algorithm, binomial queues, and Fibonacci heaps. In all these data structures, the meaning of *rank* is somewhat different, but the rank is generally meant to be on the order (magnitude) of the logarithm of the size of the tree. For a tree T with N nodes, the rank of the root is simply $R(T) = \log N$. Using the sum of ranks as a potential function is similar to using the sum of heights as a potential function. The important difference is that while a rotation can change the heights of many nodes in the tree, only X, P, and G can have their ranks changed.

Before proving the main theorem, we need the following lemma.

LEMMA 11.4.
If $a + b \leq c$, and a and b are both positive integers, then

$$\log a + \log b \leq 2 \log c - 2$$

PROOF:
By the arithmetic-geometric mean inequality,

$$\sqrt{ab} \leq (a + b)/2$$

Thus

$$\sqrt{ab} \leq c/2$$

Squaring both sides gives

$$ab \leq c^2/4$$

Taking logarithms of both sides proves the lemma.

With the preliminaries taken care of, we are ready to prove the main theorem.

THEOREM 11.5

The amortized time to splay a tree with root T at node X is at most $3(R(T) - R(X)) + 1 = O(\log N)$.

PROOF:

The potential function is the sum of the ranks of the nodes in T.

If X is the root of T, then there are no rotations, so there is no potential change. The actual time is 1 to access the node; thus, the amortized time is 1 and the theorem is true. Thus, we may assume that there is at least one rotation.

For any splaying step, let $R_i(X)$ and $S_i(X)$ be the rank and size of X before the step, and let $R_f(X)$ and $S_f(X)$ be the rank and size of X immediately after the splaying step. We will show that the amortized time required for a *zig* is at most $3(R_f(X) - R_i(X)) + 1$ and that the amortized time for either a *zig-zag* or *zig-zig* is at most $3(R_f(X) - R_i(X))$. We will show that when we add over all steps, the sum telescopes to the desired time bound.

Zig step: For the *zig* step, the actual time is 1 (for the single rotation), and the potential change is $R_f(X) + R_f(P) - R_i(X) - R_i(P)$. Notice that the potential change is easy to compute, because only X's and P's trees change size. Thus

$$AT_{\text{zig}} = 1 + R_f(X) + R_f(P) - R_i(X) - R_i(P)$$

From Figure 11.21 we see that $S_i(P) \geq S_f(P)$; thus, it follows that $R_i(P) \geq R_f(P)$. Thus,

$$AT_{\text{zig}} \leq 1 + R_f(X) - R_i(X)$$

Since $S_f(X) \geq S_i(X)$, it follows that $R_f(X) - R_i(X) \geq 0$, so we may increase the right side, obtaining

$$AT_{\text{zig}} \leq 1 + 3(R_f(X) - R_i(X))$$

Zig-zag step: For the *zig-zag* case, the actual cost is 2, and the potential change is $R_f(X) + R_f(P) + R_f(G) - R_i(X) - R_i(P) - R_i(G)$. This gives an amortized time bound of

$$AT_{\text{zig-zag}} = 2 + R_f(X) + R_f(P) + R_f(G) - R_i(X) - R_i(P) - R_i(G)$$

From Figure 11.21 we see that $S_f(X) = S_i(G)$, so their ranks must be equal. Thus, we obtain

$$AT_{\text{zig-zag}} = 2 + R_f(P) + R_f(G) - R_i(X) - R_i(P)$$

We also see that $S_i(P) \geq S_i(X)$. Consequently, $R_i(X) \leq R_i(P)$. Making this substitution gives

$$AT_{\text{zig-zag}} \leq 2 + R_f(P) + R_f(G) - 2R_i(X)$$

From Figure 11.21 we see that $S_f(P) + S_f(G) \leq S_f(X)$. If we apply Lemma 11.4, we obtain

$$\log S_f(P) + \log S_f(G) \leq 2 \log S_f(X) - 2$$

By the definition of *rank*, this becomes

$$R_f(P) + R_f(G) \leq 2R_f(X) - 2$$

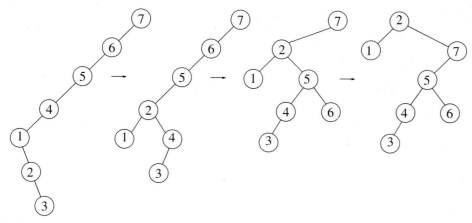

Figure 11.22 The splaying steps involved in splaying at node 2

Substituting this, we obtain

$$AT_{\text{zig-zag}} \leq 2R_f(X) - 2R_i(X)$$
$$\leq 2(R_f(X) - R_i(X))$$

Since $R_f(X) \geq R_i(X)$, we obtain

$$AT_{\text{zig-zag}} \leq 3(R_f(X) - R_i(X))$$

Zig-zig step: The third case is the *zig-zig*. The proof of this case is very similar to the *zig-zag* case. The important inequalities are $R_f(X) = R_i(G)$, $R_f(X) \geq R_f(P)$, $R_i(X) \leq R_i(P)$, and $S_i(X) + S_f(G) \leq S_f(X)$. We leave the details as Exercise 11.8.

The amortized cost of an entire splay is the sum of the amortized costs of each splay step. Figure 11.22 shows the steps that are performed in a splay at node 2. Let $R_1(2)$, $R_2(2)$, $R_3(2)$, and $R_4(2)$ be the rank of node 2 in each of the four trees. The cost of the first step, which is a *zig-zag*, is at most $3(R_2(2) - R_1(2))$. The cost of the second step, which is a *zig-zig*, is $3(R_3(2) - R_2(2))$. The last step is a *zig* and has cost no larger than $3(R_4(2) - R_3(2)) + 1$. The total cost thus telescopes to $3(R_4(2) - R_1(2)) + 1$.

In general, by adding up the amortized costs of all the rotations, of which at most one can be a *zig*, we see that the total amortized cost to splay at node X is at most $3(R_f(X) - R_i(X)) + 1$, where $R_i(X)$ is the rank of X before the first splaying step and $R_f(X)$ is the rank of X after the last splaying step. Since the last splaying step leaves X at the root, we obtain an amortized bound of $3(R_f(T) - R_i(X)) + 1$, which is $O(\log N)$.

Because every operation on a splay tree requires a splay, the amortized cost of any operation is within a constant factor of the amortized cost of a splay. Thus, all splay tree operations take $O(\log N)$ amortized time. By using a more general potential function, it is possible to show that splay trees have several remarkable properties. This is discussed in more detail in the exercises.

SUMMARY

In this chapter, we have seen how an amortized analysis can be used to apportion charges among operations. To perform the analysis, we invent a fictitious potential function. The potential function measures the state of the system. A high-potential data structure is volatile, having been built on relatively cheap operations. When the expensive bill comes for an operation, it is paid for by the savings of previous operations. One can view potential as standing for *potential for disaster,* in that very expensive operations can occur only when the data structure has a high potential and has used considerably less time than has been allocated.

Low potential in a data structure means that the cost of each operation has been roughly equal to the amount allocated for it. Negative potential means debt; more time has been spent than has been allocated, so the allocated (or amortized) time is not a meaningful bound.

As expressed by Equation (11.2), the amortized time for an operation is equal to the sum of the actual time and potential change. Taken over an entire sequence of operations, the amortized time for the sequence is equal to the total sequence time plus the net change in potential. As long as this net change is positive, then the amortized bound provides an *upper bound* for the actual time spent and is meaningful.

The keys to choosing a potential function are to guarantee that the minimum potential occurs at the beginning of the algorithm, and to have the potential increase for cheap operations and decrease for expensive operations. It is important that the excess or saved time be measured by an opposite change in potential. Unfortunately, this is sometimes easier said than done.

EXERCISES

11.1 When do M consecutive insertions into a binomial queue take less than $2M$ time units?

11.2 Suppose a binomial queue of $N = 2^k - 1$ elements is built. Alternately perform M **insert** and **deleteMin** pairs. Clearly, each operation takes $O(\log N)$ time. Why does this not contradict the amortized bound of $O(1)$ for insertion?

*11.3 Show that the amortized bound of $O(\log N)$ for the skew heap operations described in the text cannot be converted to a worst-case bound, by giving a sequence of operations that lead to a **merge** requiring $\Theta(N)$ time.

*11.4 Show how to merge two skew heaps with one top-down pass and reduce the **merge** cost to $O(1)$ amortized time.

11.5 Extend skew heaps to support the **decreaseKey** operation in $O(\log N)$ amortized time.

11.6 Implement Fibonacci heaps and compare their performance with that of binary heaps when used in Dijkstra's algorithm.

11.7 A standard implementation of Fibonacci heaps requires four links per node (parent, child, and two siblings). Show how to reduce the number of links, at the cost of at most a constant factor in the running time.

11.8 Show that the amortized time of a zig-zig splay is at most $3(R_f(X) - R_i(X))$.

11.9 By changing the potential function, it is possible to prove different bounds for splaying. Let the *weight function* $W(i)$ be some function assigned to each node in the tree, and let $S(i)$ be the sum of the weights of all the nodes in the subtree rooted at i, including i itself. The special case $W(i) = 1$ for all nodes corresponds to the function used in the proof of the splaying bound. Let N be the number of nodes in the tree, and let M be the number of accesses. Prove the following two theorems:

   a. The total access time is $O(M + (M + N)\log N)$.

*b. If q_i is the number of times that item i is accessed, and $q_i > 0$ for all i, then the total access time is

$$O\left(M + \sum_{i=1}^{N} q_i \log(M/q_i)\right)$$

11.10 a. Show how to implement the **merge** operation on splay trees so that any sequence of $N - 1$ **merge**s starting from N single-element trees takes $O(N \log^2 N)$ time.

   *b. Improve the bound to $O(N \log N)$.

11.11 In Chapter 5, we described *rehashing*: When a table becomes more than half full, a new table twice as large is constructed, and the entire old table is rehashed. Give a formal amortized analysis, with potential function, to show that the amortized cost of an insertion is still $O(1)$.

11.12 Show that if deletions are not allowed, then any sequence of M insertions into an N-node 2–3 tree produces $O(M + N)$ node splits.

11.13 A *deque* with *heap order* is a data structure consisting of a list of items, on which the following operations are possible:

   push(x): Insert item **x** on the front end of the deque.

   pop(): Remove the front item from the deque and return it.

   inject(x): Insert item **x** on the rear end of the deque.

   eject(): Remove the rear item from the deque and return it.

   findMin(): Return the smallest item from the deque (breaking ties arbitrarily).

   a. Describe how to support these operations in constant amortized time per operation.

   **b. Describe how to support these operations in constant worst-case time per operation.

11.14 Show that the binomial queues actually support merging in $O(1)$ amortized time. Define the potential of a binomial queue to be the number of trees plus the rank of the largest tree.

11.15 Suppose that in an attempt to save time, we splay on every second tree operation. Does the amortized cost remain logarithmic?

11.16 Using the potential function in the proof of the splay tree bound, what is the maximum and minimum potential of a splay tree? By how much can the potential function decrease in one splay? By how much can the potential function increase in one splay? You may give Big-Oh answers.

11.17 As a result of a splay, most of the nodes on the access path are moved halfway towards the root, while a couple of nodes on the path move down one level. This suggests using the sum over all nodes of the logarithm of each node's depth as a potential function.

   a. What is the maximum value of the potential function?

   b. What is the minimum value of the potential function?

   c. The difference in the answers to parts (a) and (b) gives some indication that this potential function isn't too good. Show that a splaying operation could increase the potential by $\Theta(N/\log N)$.

11.18 What is the maximum depth of a Fibonacci heap?

REFERENCES

An excellent survey of amortized analysis is provided in [10].

Most of the references below duplicate citations in earlier chapters. We cite them again for convenience and completeness. Binomial queues were first described in [11] and analyzed in [1]. Solutions to Exercises 11.3 and 11.4 appear in [9]. Fibonacci heaps are described in [3]. Exercise 11.9(a) shows that splay trees are optimal, to within a constant factor of the best static search trees. Exercise 11.9(b) shows that splay trees are optimal, to within a constant factor of the best optimal search trees. These, as well as two other strong results, are proved in the original splay tree paper [7].

The **merge** operation for splay trees is described in [6]. Exercise 11.12 is solved, with an implicit use of amortization, in [2]. The paper also shows how to merge 2–3 trees efficiently. A solution to Exercise 11.13 can be found in [4]. Exercise 11.14 is from [5].

Amortized analysis is used in [8] to design an on-line algorithm that processes a series of queries in time only a constant factor larger than any off-line algorithm in its class.

1. M. R. Brown, "Implementation and Analysis of Binomial Queue Algorithms," *SIAM Journal on Computing,* 7 (1978), 298–319.
2. M. R. Brown and R. E. Tarjan, "Design and Analysis of a Data Structure for Representing Sorted Lists," *SIAM Journal on Computing,* 9 (1980), 594–614.
3. M. L. Fredman and R. E. Tarjan, "Fibonacci Heaps and Their Uses in Improved Network Optimization Algorithms," *Journal of the ACM,* 34 (1987), 596–615.
4. H. Gajewska and R. E. Tarjan, "Deques with Heap Order," *Information Processing Letters,* 22 (1986), 197–200.
5. C. M. Khoong and H. W. Leong, "Double-Ended Binomial Queues," *Proceedings of the Fourth Annual International Symposium on Algorithms and Computation* (1993), 128–137.
6. G. Port and A. Moffat, "A Fast Algorithm for Melding Splay Trees," *Proceedings of First Workshop on Algorithms and Data Structures* (1989), 450–459.
7. D. D. Sleator and R. E. Tarjan, "Self-adjusting Binary Search Trees," *Journal of the ACM,* 32 (1985), 652–686.
8. D. D. Sleator and R. E. Tarjan, "Amortized Efficiency of List Update and Paging Rules," *Communications of the ACM,* 28 (1985), 202–208.
9. D. D. Sleator and R. E. Tarjan, "Self-adjusting Heaps," *SIAM Journal on Computing,* 15 (1986), 52–69.
10. R. E. Tarjan, "Amortized Computational Complexity," *SIAM Journal on Algebraic and Discrete Methods,* 6 (1985), 306–318.
11. J. Vuillemin, "A Data Structure for Manipulating Priority Queues," *Communications of the ACM,* 21 (1978), 309–314.

Advanced Data Structures and Implementation

In this chapter, we discuss seven data structures with an emphasis on practicality. We begin by examining alternatives to the AVL tree discussed in Chapter 4. These include an optimized version of the splay tree, the red-black tree, a deterministic form of the skip list (previously discussed in Chapter 10), the AA-tree, and the treap.

We then examine a data structure that can be used for multidimensional data. In this case, each item may have several keys. The k-d tree allows searching relative to any key.

Finally, we examine the pairing heap, which seems to be the most practical alternative to the Fibonacci heap.

Recurring themes include

- Nonrecursive, top-down (instead of bottom-up) search tree implementations when appropriate.

- Detailed, optimized implementations that make use of, among other things, sentinel nodes.

12.1. Top-Down Splay Trees

In Chapter 4, we discussed the basic splay tree operation. When an item X is inserted as a leaf, a series of tree rotations, known as a *splay*, makes X the new root of the tree. A splay is also performed during searches, and if an item is not found, a splay is performed on the last node on the access path. In Chapter 11, we showed that the *amortized* cost of a splay tree operation is $O(\log N)$.

A direct implementation of this strategy requires a traversal from the root down the tree, and then a bottom-up traversal to implement the splaying step. This can be done either by maintaining parent links, or by storing the access path on a stack. Unfortunately, both methods require a substantial amount of overhead, and both must handle many special cases. In this section, we show how to perform rotations on the initial access path. The result is a procedure that is faster in practice, uses only $O(1)$ extra space, but retains the $O(\log N)$ amortized time bound.

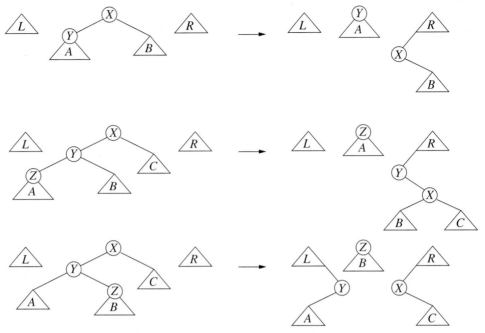

Figure 12.1 Top-down splay rotations: *zig, zig-zig,* and *zig-zag*

Figure 12.1 shows the rotations for the *zig, zig-zig,* and *zig-zag* cases. (As is customary, three symmetric rotations are omitted.) At any point in the access, we have a current node *X* that is the root of its subtree; this is represented in our diagrams as the "middle" tree.* Tree *L* stores nodes in the tree *T* that are less than *X*, but not in *X*'s subtree; similarly tree *R* stores nodes in the tree *T* that are larger than *X*, but not in *X*'s subtree. Initially, *X* is the root of *T*, and *L* and *R* are empty.

If the rotation should be a *zig,* then the tree rooted at *Y* becomes the new root of the middle tree. *X* and subtree *B* are attached as a left child of the smallest item in *R*; *X*'s left child is logically made null.† As a result, *X* is the new smallest item in *R*. Note carefully that *Y* does not have to be a leaf for the *zig* case to apply. If we are searching for an item that is smaller than *Y*, and *Y* has no left child (but does have a right child), then the *zig* case will apply.

For the *zig-zig* case, we have a similar dissection. The crucial point is that a rotation between *X* and *Y* is performed. The *zig-zag* case brings the bottom node *Z* to the top in the middle tree, and attaches subtrees *X* and *Y* to *R* and *L*, respectively. Note that *Y* is attached to, and then becomes, the largest item in *L*.

The *zig-zag* step can be simplified somewhat because no rotations are performed. Instead of making *Z* the root of the middle tree, we make *Y* the root. This is shown in Figure 12.2. This simplifies the coding because the action for the *zig-zag* case becomes identical to the *zig* case. This would seem advantageous because testing for a host of

---

*For simplicity we don't distinguish between a "node" and the item in the node.
†In the code, the smallest node in *R* does not have a null left link because there is no need for it. This means that printTree(r) will include some items that logically are not in *R*.

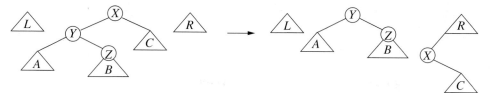

Figure 12.2 Simplified top-down *zig-zag*

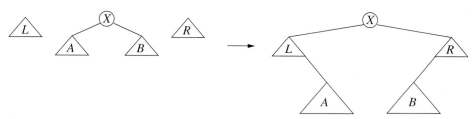

Figure 12.3 Final arrangement for top-down splaying

cases is time-consuming. The disadvantage is that by descending only one level, we have more iterations in the splaying procedure.

Once we have performed the final splaying step, Figure 12.3 shows how L, R, and the middle tree are arranged to form a single tree. Note carefully that the result is different from bottom-up splaying. The crucial fact is that the $O(\log N)$ amortized bound is preserved (Exercise 12.1).

An example of the top-down splaying algorithm is shown in Figure 12.4. We attempt to access 19 in the tree. The first step is a *zig-zag*. In accordance with (a symmetric version of) Figure 12.2, we bring the subtree rooted at 25 to the root of the middle tree, and attach 12 and its left subtree to L.

Next we have a *zig-zig*: 15 is elevated to the root of the middle tree, and a rotation between 20 and 25 is performed, with the resulting subtree being attached to R. The search for 19 then results in a terminal *zig*. The middle tree's new root is 18, and 15 and its left subtree are attached as a right child of L's largest node. The reassembly, in accordance with Figure 12.3, terminates the splay step.

We will use a header with left and right links to eventually reference the roots of the left and right trees. Since these trees are initially empty, a header is used to correspond to the min or max node of the right or left tree, respectively, in this initial state. This way the code can avoid checking for empty trees. The first time the left tree becomes nonempty, the right link will get initialized and will not change in the future; thus it will contain the root of the right tree at the end of the top-down search. Similarly, the left link will eventually contain the root of the right tree.

The **SplayTree** class, whose skeleton is shown in Figure 12.5, includes a *static initializer* that is used to allocate the **nullNode** sentinel. We use the sentinel **nullNode** to represent logically a **null** reference. We will repeatedly use this technique to simplify the code (and consequently make the code somewhat faster). Figure 12.6 (shown on page 458) gives the code for the splaying procedure. The **header** node allows us to be certain that we can attach

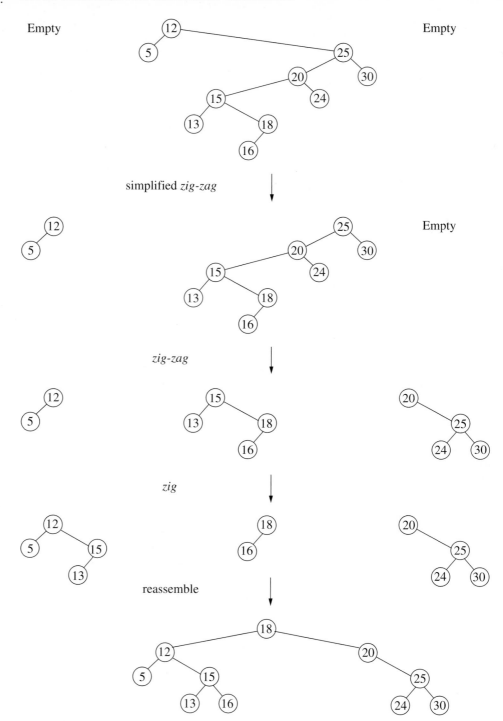

Figure 12.4 Steps in top-down splay (access 19 in top tree)

```java
public class SplayTree
{
    public SplayTree( )
    {
        root = nullNode;
    }

    private BinaryNode splay( Comparable x, BinaryNode t )
      { /* Figure 12.6 */ }
    public void insert( Comparable x )
      { /* Figure 12.7 */ }
    public void remove( Comparable x )
      { /* Figure 12.8 */ }

    public Comparable findMin( )
      { /* See online code */ }
    public Comparable findMax( )
      { /* See online code */ }
    public Comparable find( Comparable x )
      { /* See online code */ }
    public void makeEmpty( )
      { /* See online code */ }
    public boolean isEmpty( )
      { /* See online code */ }
    public void printTree( )
      { /* See online code */ }
    static BinaryNode rotateWithLeftChild( BinaryNode k2 )
      { /* See online code */ }
    static BinaryNode rotateWithRightChild( BinaryNode k1 )
      { /* See online code */ }
    private void printTree( BinaryNode t )
      { /* See online code */ }

    private BinaryNode root;
    private static BinaryNode nullNode;
        static           // Static initializer for nullNode
        {
            nullNode = new BinaryNode( null );
            nullNode.left = nullNode.right = nullNode;
        }

    private static BinaryNode newNode = null;  // Used between different inserts
    private static BinaryNode header = new BinaryNode( null ); // For splay
}
```

Figure 12.5 Splay trees: class skeleton

```
/**
 * Internal method to perform a top-down splay.
 * The last accessed node becomes the new root.
 * @param x the target item to splay around.
 * @param t the root of the subtree to splay.
 * @return the subtree after the splay.
 */
private BinaryNode splay( Comparable x, BinaryNode t )
{
    BinaryNode leftTreeMax, rightTreeMin;

    header.left = header.right = nullNode;
    leftTreeMax = rightTreeMin = header;

    nullNode.element = x;    // Guarantee a match

    for( ; ; )
        if( x.compareTo( t.element ) < 0 )
        {
            if( x.compareTo( t.left.element ) < 0 )
                t = rotateWithLeftChild( t );
            if( t.left == nullNode )
                break;
            // Link Right
            rightTreeMin.left = t;
            rightTreeMin = t;
            t = t.left;
        }
        else if( x.compareTo( t.element ) > 0 )
        {
            if( x.compareTo( t.right.element ) > 0 )
                t = rotateWithRightChild( t );
            if( t.right == nullNode )
                break;
            // Link Left
            leftTreeMax.right = t;
            leftTreeMax = t;
            t = t.right;
        }
        else
            break;

    leftTreeMax.right = t.left;
    rightTreeMin.left = t.right;
    t.left = header.right;
    t.right = header.left;
    return t;
}
```

Figure 12.6 Top-down splaying method

```
/**
 * Insert into the tree.
 * @param x the item to insert.
 */
public void insert( Comparable x )
{
    if( newNode == null )
        newNode = new BinaryNode( null );
    newNode.element = x;

    if( root == nullNode )
    {
        newNode.left = newNode.right = nullNode;
        root = newNode;
    }
    else
    {
        root = splay( x, root );
        if( x.compareTo( root.element ) < 0 )
        {
            newNode.left = root.left;
            newNode.right = root;
            root.left = nullNode;
            root = newNode;
        }
        else
        if( x.compareTo( root.element ) > 0 )
        {
            newNode.right = root.right;
            newNode.left = root;
            root.right = nullNode;
            root = newNode;
        }
        else
            return;
    }
    newNode = null;    // So next insert will call new
}
```

Figure 12.7 Top-down splay tree insert

X to the largest node in R without having to worry that R might be empty (and similarly for the symmetric case dealing with L).

As we mentioned above, before the reassembly at the end of the splay, header.left and header.right reference the roots of R and L, respectively (this is not a typo—follow the links). Except for this detail, the code is relatively straightforward.

Figure 12.7 shows the method to insert an item into a tree. A new node is allocated (if necessary), and if the tree is empty, a one-node tree is created. Otherwise we splay root around the inserted value x. If the data in the new root is equal to x, we have a duplicate; instead of reinserting x, we preserve newNode for a future insertion and return immediately. If

```
/**
 * Remove from the tree.
 * @param x the item to remove.
 */
public void remove( Comparable x )
{
    BinaryNode newTree;

        // If x is found, it will be at the root
    root = splay( x, root );
    if( root.element.compareTo( x ) != 0 )
        return;   // Item not found; do nothing

    if( root.left == nullNode )
        newTree = root.right;
    else
    {
        // Find the maximum in the left subtree
        // Splay it to the root; and then attach right child
        newTree = root.left;
        newTree = splay( x, newTree );
        newTree.right = root.right;
    }
    root = newTree;
}
```

Figure 12.8 Top-down deletion procedure

the new root contains a value larger than **x**, then the new root and its right subtree become a right subtree of **newNode**, and **root**'s left subtree becomes the left subtree of **newNode**. Similar logic applies if **root**'s new root contains a value smaller than **x**. In either case, **newNode** becomes the new root.

In Chapter 4, we showed that deletion in splay trees is easy, because a splay will place the target of the deletion at the root. We close by showing the deletion routine in Figure 12.8. It is indeed rare that a deletion procedure is shorter than the corresponding insertion procedure.

12.2. Red-Black Trees

A historically popular alternative to the AVL tree is the *red-black* tree. Operations on red-black trees take $O(\log N)$ time in the worst case, and, as we will see, a careful nonrecursive implementation (for insertion) can be done relatively effortlessly (compared with AVL trees).

A red-black tree is a binary search tree with the following coloring properties:

1. Every node is colored either red or black.
2. The root is black.
3. If a node is red, its children must be black.

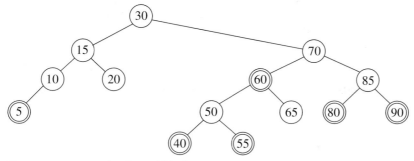

Figure 12.9 Example of a red-black tree (insertion sequence is: 10, 85, 15, 70, 20, 60, 30, 50, 65, 80, 90, 40, 5, 55)

4. Every path from a node to a `null` reference must contain the same number of black nodes.

A consequence of the coloring rules is that the height of a red-black tree is at most $2 \log(N + 1)$. Consequently, searching is guaranteed to be a logarithmic operation. Figure 12.9 shows a red-black tree. Red nodes are shown with double circles.

The difficulty, as usual, is inserting a new item into the tree. The new item, as usual is placed as a leaf in the tree. If we color this item black, then we are certain to violate condition 4, because we will create a longer path of black nodes. Thus the item must be colored red. If the parent is black, we are done. If the parent is already red, then we will violate condition 3 by having consecutive red nodes. In this case, we have to adjust the tree to ensure that condition 3 is enforced (without introducing a violation of condition 4). The basic operations that are used to do this are color changes and tree rotations.

12.2.1. Bottom-Up Insertion

As we have already mentioned, if the parent of the newly inserted item is black, we are done. Thus insertion of 25 into the tree in Figure 12.9 is trivial.

There are several cases (each with a mirror image symmetry) to consider if the parent is red. First, suppose that the sibling of the parent is black (we adopt the convention that `null` nodes are black). This would apply for an insertion of 3 or 8, but not for the insertion of 99. Let X be the newly added leaf, P be its parent, S be the sibling of the parent (if it exists), and G be the grandparent. Only X and P are red in this case; G is black, because otherwise there would be two consecutive red nodes *prior* to the insertion, in violation of red-black rules. Adopting the splay tree terminology, X, P, and G can form either a *zig-zig* chain or a *zig-zag* chain (in either of two directions). Figure 12.10 shows how we can rotate the tree for the case where P is a left child (note there is a symmetric case). Even though X is a leaf, we have drawn a more general case that allows X to be in the middle of the tree. We will use this more general rotation later.

The first case corresponds to a single rotation between P and G, and the second case corresponds to a double rotation, first between X and P and then between X and G. When we write the code, we have to keep track of the parent, the grandparent, and, for reattachment purposes, the great-grandparent.

In both cases, the subtree's new root is colored black, and so even if the original great-grandparent was red, we removed the possibility of two consecutive red nodes. Equally

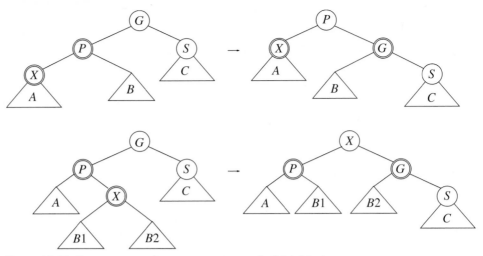

Figure 12.10 *Zig* rotation and *zig-zag* rotation work if S is black

important, the number of black nodes on the paths into A, B, and C has remained unchanged as a result of the rotations.

So far so good. But what happens if S is red, as is the case when we attempt to insert 79 in the tree in Figure 12.9? In that case, initially there is one black node on the path from the subtree's root to C. After the rotation, there must still be only one black node. But in both cases, there are three nodes (the new root, G, and S) on the path to C. Since only one may be black, and since we cannot have consecutive red nodes, it follows that we'd have to color both S and the subtree's new root red, and G (and our fourth node) black. That's great, but what happens if the great-grandparent is also red? In that case, we could percolate this procedure up toward the root as is done for B-trees and binary heaps, until we no longer have two consecutive red nodes, or we reach the root (which will be recolored-black).

12.2.2. Top-Down Red-Black Trees

Implementing the percolation would require maintaining the path using a stack or parent links. We saw that splay trees are more efficient if we use a top-down procedure, and it turns out that we can apply a top-down procedure to red-black trees that guarantees that S won't be red.

The procedure is conceptually easy. On the way down, when we see a node X that has two red children, we make X red and the two children black. Figure 12.11 shows this color flip. This will induce a red-black violation only if X's parent P is also red. But in that

Figure 12.11 Color flip: only if X's parent is red do we continue with a rotation

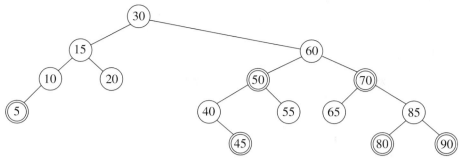

Figure 12.12 Insertion of 45 into Figure 12.9

case, we can apply the appropriate rotations in Figure 12.10. What if X's parent's sibling is red? This possibility has been removed by our actions on the way down, and so X's parent's sibling can't be red! Specifically, if on the way down the tree we see a node Y that has two red children, we know that Y's grandchildren must be black, and that since Y's children are made black too, even after the rotation that may occur, we won't see another red node for two levels. Thus when we see X, if X's parent is red, it is not possible for X's parent's sibling to be red also.

As an example, suppose we want to insert 45 into the tree in Figure 12.9. On the way down the tree, we see node 50, which has two red children. Thus, we perform a color flip, making 50 red, and 40 and 55 black. Now 50 and 60 are both red. We perform the single rotation between 60 and 70, making 60 the black root of 30's right subtree, and 70 and 50 both red. We then continue, performing an identical action if we see other nodes on the path that contain two red children. When we get to the leaf, we insert 45 as a red node, and since the parent is black, we are done. The resulting tree is shown in Figure 12.12.

As Figure 12.12 shows, the red-black tree that results is frequently very well balanced. Experiments suggest that the average red-black tree is about as deep as an average AVL tree and that, consequently, the searching times are typically near optimal. The advantage of red-black trees is the relatively low overhead required to perform insertion, and the fact that in practice rotations occur relatively infrequently.

An actual implementation is complicated not only by the host of possible rotations, but also by the possibility that some subtrees (such as 10's right subtree) might be empty, and the special case of dealing with the root (which among other things, has no parent). Thus, we use two sentinel nodes: one for the root, and `nullNode`, which indicates a `null` reference, as it did for splay trees. The root sentinel will store the key $-\infty$ and a right link to the real root. Because of this, the searching and printing procedures need to be adjusted. The recursive routines are trickiest. Figure 12.13 shows how the inorder traversal is re-written.

Figure 12.14 shows the `RedBlackTree` skeleton, along with the constructors and static initializers. Next, Figure 12.15 shows the routine to perform a single rotation. Because the resultant tree must be attached to a parent, `rotate` takes the parent node as a parameter. Rather than keeping track of the type of rotation as we descend the tree, we pass `item` as a parameter. Since we expect very few rotations during the insertion procedure, it turns out that it is not only simpler, but actually faster, to do it this way. `rotate` simply returns the result of performing an appropriate single rotation.

```java
/**
 * Print the tree contents in sorted order.
 */
public void printTree( )
{
    if( isEmpty( ) )
        System.out.println( "Empty tree" );
    else
        printTree( header.right );
}

/**
 * Internal method to print a subtree in sorted order.
 * @param t the node that roots the tree.
 */
private void printTree( RedBlackNode t )
{
    if( t != nullNode )
    {
        printTree( t.left );
        System.out.println( t.element );
        printTree( t.right );
    }
}
```

Figure 12.13 Inorder traversal for tree with two sentinels

Figure 12.14 Class skeleton and initialization routines

```java
class RedBlackNode
{
        // Constructors
    RedBlackNode( Comparable theElement )
    {
        this( theElement, null, null );
    }

    RedBlackNode( Comparable theElement, RedBlackNode lt, RedBlackNode rt )
    {
        element = theElement;
        left    = lt;
        right   = rt;
        color   = RedBlackTree.BLACK;
    }

        // Friendly data; accessible by other package routines
    Comparable   element;    // The data in the node
    RedBlackNode left;       // Left child
    RedBlackNode right;      // Right child
    int          color;      // Color
}
```

(continues)

(continued)

```java
    // RedBlackTree initialization routines
class RedBlackTree
{
    /**
     * Construct the tree.
     * @param negInf a value less than or equal to all others.
     */
    public RedBlackTree( Comparable negInf )
    {
        header        = new RedBlackNode( negInf );
        header.left = header.right = nullNode;
    }

    private RedBlackNode header;
    private static RedBlackNode nullNode;
        static            // Static initializer for nullNode
        {
            nullNode = new RedBlackNode( null );
            nullNode.left = nullNode.right = nullNode;
        }
}
```

Figure 12.14 Class skeleton and initialization routines

```java
    /**
     * Internal routine that performs a single or double rotation.
     * Because the result is attached to the parent, there are four cases.
     * Called by handleReorient.
     * @param item the item in handleReorient.
     * @param parent the parent of the root of the rotated subtree.
     * @return the root of the rotated subtree.
     */
    private RedBlackNode rotate( Comparable item, RedBlackNode parent )
    {
        if( item.compareTo( parent.element ) < 0 )
            return parent.left = item.compareTo( parent.left.element ) < 0 ?
                rotateWithLeftChild( parent.left )  :  // LL
                rotateWithRightChild( parent.left ) ;  // LR
        else
            return parent.right = item.compareTo( parent.right.element ) < 0 ?
                rotateWithLeftChild( parent.right ) :  // RL
                rotateWithRightChild( parent.right );  // RR
    }
```

Figure 12.15 rotate method

Figure 12.16 Insertion procedure

```
      // Used in insert routine and its helpers
private static RedBlackNode current;
private static RedBlackNode parent;
private static RedBlackNode grand;
private static RedBlackNode great;

/**
 * Internal routine that is called during an insertion
 * if a node has two red children. Performs flip and rotations.
 * @param item the item being inserted.
 */
private void handleReorient( Comparable item )
{
       // Do the color flip
    current.color = RED;
    current.left.color = BLACK;
    current.right.color = BLACK;

    if( parent.color == RED )    // Have to rotate
    {
        grand.color = RED;
        if( ( item.compareTo( grand.element ) < 0 ) !=
            ( item.compareTo( parent.element ) < 0 ) )
            parent = rotate( item, grand );  // Start dbl rotate
        current = rotate( item, great );
        current.color = BLACK;
    }
    header.right.color = BLACK; // Make root black
}

/**
 * Insert into the tree. Does nothing if item already present.
 * @param item the item to insert.
 */
public void insert( Comparable item )
{
    current = parent = grand = header;
    nullNode.element = item;

    while( current.element.compareTo( item ) != 0 )
    {
        great = grand; grand = parent; parent = current;
        current = item.compareTo( current.element ) < 0 ?
                    current.left : current.right;

            // Check if two red children; fix if so
        if( current.left.color == RED && current.right.color == RED )
            handleReorient( item );
    }

        // Insertion fails if already present
    if( current != nullNode )
```

(continued)

```
            return;
    current = new RedBlackNode( item, nullNode, nullNode );

        // Attach to parent
    if( item.compareTo( parent.element ) < 0 )
        parent.left = current;
    else
        parent.right = current;
    handleReorient( item );
}
```

Figure 12.16 Insertion procedure

Finally, we provide the insertion procedure in Figure 12.16. The routine `handleReorient` is called when we encounter a node with two red children, and also when we insert a leaf. The most tricky part is the observation that a double rotation is really two single rotations, and is done only when branching to X (represented in the `insert` method by `current`) takes opposite directions. As we mentioned in the earlier discussion, `insert` must keep track of the parent, grandparent, and great-grandparent as the tree is descended. Since these are shared with `handleReorient`, we make these (`static`) class members. Note that after a rotation, the values stored in the grandparent and great-grandparent are no longer correct. However, we are assured that they will be restored by the time they are next needed.

12.2.3. Top-Down Deletion

Deletion in red-black trees can also be performed top-down. Everything boils down to being able to delete a leaf. This is because to delete a node that has two children, we replace it with the smallest node in the right subtree; that node, which must have at most one child, is then deleted. Nodes with only a right child can be deleted in the same manner, while nodes with only a left child can be deleted by replacement with the largest node in the left subtree, and subsequent deletion of that node. Note that for red-black trees, we don't want to use the strategy of bypassing for the case of a node with one child because that may connect two red nodes in the middle of the tree, making enforcement of the red-black condition difficult.

Deletion of a red leaf is, of course, trivial. If a leaf is black, however, the deletion is more complicated because removal of a black node will violate condition 4. The solution is to ensure during the top-down pass that the leaf is red.

Throughout this discussion, let X be the current node, T be its sibling, and P be their parent. We begin by coloring the root red. As we traverse down the tree, we attempt to ensure that X is red. When we arrive at a new node, we are certain that P is red (inductively, by the invariant we are trying to maintain), and that X and T are black (because we can't have two consecutive red nodes). There are two main cases.

First, suppose X has two black children. Then there are three subcases, which are shown in Figure 12.17. If T also has two black children, we can flip the colors of X, T, and P to maintain the invariant. Otherwise, one of T's children is red. Depending on which one it is,* we can apply the rotation shown in the second and third cases of Figure 12.17.

---

*If both children are red, we can apply either rotation. As usual, there are symmetric rotations for the case when X is a right child that are not shown.

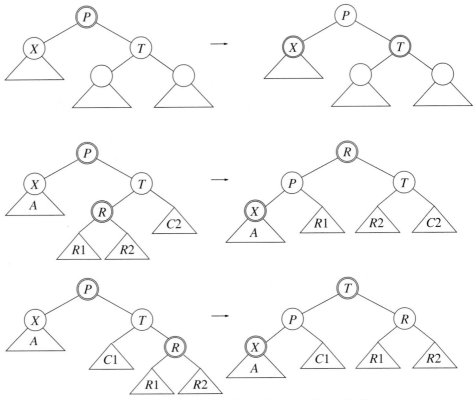

Figure 12.17 Three cases when X is a left child and has two black children

Note carefully that this case will apply for the leaf, because `nullNode` is considered to be black.

Otherwise, one of X's children is red. In this case, we fall through to the next level, obtaining new X, T, and P. If we're lucky, X will land on the red child, and we can continue onward. If not, we know that T will be red, and X and P will be black. We can rotate T and P, making X's new parent red; X and its grandparent will, of course, be black. At this point we can go back to the first main case.

12.3. Deterministic Skip Lists

The ideas that we saw used for red-black trees can be applied to skip lists to ensure logarithmic worst-case operation. In this section, we describe the simplest implementation of the resulting data structure, the *1-2-3 deterministic skip list*.

Recall from Chapter 10 that nodes in a skip list have randomly assigned heights. A node of height h contains h forward links $p_1, p_2, \ldots, p_h$; p_i links to the next node of height i or larger. The probability that a node has height h is 0.5^h (0.5 can be replaced by any number between 0 and 1.0, to implement time/space trade-offs). As a consequence, we expect to process only a few forward links until we drop down a level; since we will have roughly $\log N$ levels, we obtain $O(\log N)$ expected running time per operation.

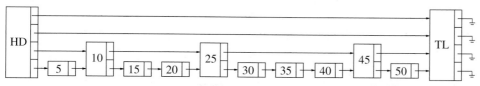

Figure 12.18 A 1-2-3 deterministic skip list

Figure 12.19 Insertion of 27: first, a gap of three height 2 nodes is split by raising 25

To make this bound a worst-case bound, we need to guarantee that only a constant number of forward links need to be examined until we can drop down to a lower level. To do this, we add a balancing condition. First we need two definitions.

DEFINITION: Two elements are *linked* if there exists at least one link going from one to another.

DEFINITION: The *gap size* between two elements linked at height h is equal to the number of elements of height $h - 1$ between them.

A 1-2-3 deterministic skip list satisfies the property that every gap (except possibly the zero gap between the header and tail) is of size 1, 2, or 3. As an example, Figure 12.18 shows a 1-2-3 deterministic skip list. There are two gaps of size 3: The first is the three elements of height 1 that are between 25 and 45, and the second is the three elements of height 2 between the list header and tail. The tail node contains ∞; its presence simplifies the algorithms and also makes it easier to define the notion of a gap at the end of the list.

Clearly, only a constant number of links are traversed along any level before we drop to a lower level. Consequently, the searching time is $O(\log N)$ in the worst case.

To perform insertion, we must make sure that when a new node of height h is added, it doesn't create a gap of four height h nodes. This turns out to be simple. We adopt a top-down strategy that is similar to what was done with red-black trees.

Let us suppose we are on level L and are about to drop one level. If the gap we are about to drop into has size 3, then we raise the middle item in the gap to have height L, thereby forming two gaps of size 1. Since this eliminates gaps of size 3 on the way toward the insertion, we know that the insertion is safe, as is any increase of middle item heights.

As an example, Figure 12.19 shows the insertion of item 27 into the deterministic skip list in Figure 12.18. At the header node, we are about to drop from level 3 to level 2. Since the drop would be into a 3 gap, the middle item (25) is raised to height 3 and spliced in. The search at level 2 takes us to 25, at which point we need to drop to level 1. Again we see a 3 gap, so 35 is raised to height 2. The result is shown in Figure 12.20. When it is time to insert 27, it is spliced into the list, as shown in Figure 12.21.

Difficulty in deletion occurs with gaps of size 1. When we see that we are about to drop into a 1 gap, we enlarge it, either by borrowing from a neighbor (if it is not a 1 gap) or by lowering the height of the node that separates the gap from the neighbor. Since both

Figure 12.20 Insertion of 27: next, a gap of three height 1 nodes is split by raising 35

Figure 12.21 Insertion of 27: finally, 27 is inserted as height 1 node

of these are gaps of size 1, the result is a 3 gap. The code is a bit more complex than this description because there are several cases to deal with.

How is all of this implemented? After we describe all the details, we will see that the amount of code is actually quite small.

The first important detail is that when we promote a height h node to height $h + 1$, we can't spend the $O(h)$ time that would be used to copy h links to a new array. Otherwise, the time bound would be $O(\log^2 N)$ for insertion. A reasonable method is to represent the h forward links in a height h node by a linked list. Since we go down levels, the linked list for a node would start with the level h forward link and end with the level 1 forward link.

The second optimization is more tricky, and could cost space. Instead of storing a node as an item and a linked list of forward links, we store a linked list of forward link, forward item pairs. The easiest way to see what this means is to look at Figure 12.22, which is another representation of Figure 12.21. We'll use the term *abstract* or *logical* representation to describe Figure 12.21 and refer to Figure 12.22 as the (actual) implementation.

First, notice that the skyline (i.e., heights as we scan from left to right) of both the abstract representation and actual implementation are identical except that the tail node has been removed. In our implementation, each node maintains a link that allows us to descend a level, a link to the next node on the same level, and the item that is logically stored in that next item (as shown in our original abstract description).

Figure 12.22 Linked list implementation of 1-2-3 deterministic skip list in Figure 12.21

Notice that some items appear more than once: for instance, 25 appears in three places. Indeed, if a node has height h in the abstract representation, its item will appear in h places in our actual implementation. There are important consequences and surprising results that we will explain after we provide an implementation.

The basic node consists of an item and two links. To make the coding faster and more simple, we have used the tail node; if it is impossible or undesirable to assign ∞, then some other mechanism must be used. We'll also have a sentinel for the header, and a sentinel for the bottom, to replace the `null` links. The `SkipNode` class and `DSL` constructor are shown in Figure 12.23.

The searching function is the same as for randomized skip lists. Figure 12.24 shows that if we don't have a match, then we either go down or right, depending on the result of a comparison. Insertion, shown in Figure 12.25, is greatly simplified by the sentinels. As we can see by some of the outrageous link trails, if we had to test each link against `null`, we would easily triple the size of the code.

As Figure 12.25 indicates, the code for deterministic skip list insertion is somewhat shorter, with many fewer cases than for the red-black tree. The price we pay seems to be space: In the worst case we have $2N$ nodes that contain two links and an item. For a red-black tree, we have N nodes that contain two links, an item, and a color bit. So we might be using twice as much space. However, things aren't necessarily that bad. First, experiments suggest that on average the deterministic skip list has about $1.57N$ nodes. Second, in some cases, the deterministic skip list actually uses less space than the red-black tree.

Here is a real-life example that applies in C or C++. On a 32-bit machine, links and integers are 4 bytes. On some systems, including some versions of UNIX, memory is allocated in chunks that are powers of 2, but 4 bytes of that chunk are used by the memory management routines. Thus a request for 12 bytes is filled by a 16-byte chunk: 12 bytes for the user and 4 bytes overhead. A request for 13 bytes, however, must be filled by a 32-byte chunk. So, in this case, a deterministic skip list will use 16 bytes per node, and on average there are $1.57N$ nodes, so the total is typically about $25N$ bytes. The red-black tree uses $32N$ bytes! This illustrates that on some machines an extra bit is very expensive; this is one of the attractions of self-organizing structures.

The performance of deterministic skip lists seems to compare favorably with red-black trees. When looking for improvement in the insertion time, the line of code that contains the logical test

```
if( current.down.right.right.element.compareTo( current.element ) < 0 )
```

seems to stand out;* if we store items in an array of up to three elements, the access of the third item could be direct, rather than through two `right` links. Figure 12.26 (on page 474) shows the resulting structure, which, ironically, bears strong resemblance to the B-tree discussed in Chapter 4. This is known as the *horizontal array implementation* of the 1-2-3 deterministic skip list. Just as there are higher-order B-trees, we can have higher-order deterministic skip lists, in both linked list and horizontal array forms. Which of these methods is best remains to be studied, and may well depend on the particular system and application.

---

*Indeed, the more "obvious" test
```
if( current.down.right.right.right.element.compareTo( current.element ) == 0 )
```
takes 20 percent longer on some systems!

```java
class SkipNode
{
        // Constructors
    SkipNode( Comparable theElement )
    {
        this( theElement, null, null );
    }

    SkipNode( Comparable theElement, SkipNode rt, SkipNode dt )
    {
        element = theElement;
        right   = rt;
        down    = dt;
    }


        // Friendly data; accessible by other package routines
    Comparable element;        // The data in the node
    SkipNode   right;          // Right link
    SkipNode   down;           // Down link
}


        // Data members and initialization
public class DSL
{
    /**
     * Construct the DSL.
     * @param inf the largest Comparable.
     */
    public DSL( Comparable inf )
    {
        infinity = inf;
        bottom = new SkipNode( null );
        bottom.right = bottom.down = bottom;
        tail   = new SkipNode( infinity );
        tail.right = tail;
        header = new SkipNode( infinity, tail, bottom );
    }

    private Comparable infinity;

    private SkipNode header;
    private SkipNode bottom = null;
    private SkipNode tail   = null;
}
```

Figure 12.23 Deterministic skip list: SkipNode class and DSL initialization

```
/**
 * Find an item in the DSL.
 * @param x the item to search for.
 * @return the matching item, or null if not found.
 */
public Comparable find( Comparable x )
{
    SkipNode current = header;

    bottom.element = x;
    for( ; ; )
        if( x.compareTo( current.element ) < 0 )
            current = current.down;
        else if( x.compareTo( current.element ) > 0 )
            current = current.right;
        else
            return elementAt( current );
}

/**
 * Internal method to get element field.
 * @param t the node.
 * @return the element field, or null if t is null.
 */
private Comparable elementAt( SkipNode t )
{
    return t == bottom ? null : t.element;
}
```

Figure 12.24 Deterministic skip list: find routine

Figure 12.25 Deterministic skip list: insertion procedure

```
/**
 * Insert into the DSL.
 * @param x the item to insert.
 */
public void insert( Comparable x )
{
    SkipNode current = header;
    SkipNode newNode = null;

    bottom.element = x;
    while( current != bottom )
    {
        while( current.element.compareTo( x ) < 0 )
            current = current.right;
```

(continues)

(*continued*)

```
                // If gap size is 3 or at bottom level and
                // must insert, then promote middle element
                if( current.down.right.right.element.compareTo( current.element )
                    < 0 )
                {
                    newNode = new SkipNode( current.element, current.right,
                                          current.down.right.right );
                    current.right = newNode;
                    current.element = current.down.right.element;
                }
                else
                    current = current.down;
        }

        // Raise height of DSL if necessary
        if( header.right != tail )
            header = new SkipNode( infinity, tail, header );
    }
```

Figure 12.25 Deterministic skip list: insertion procedure

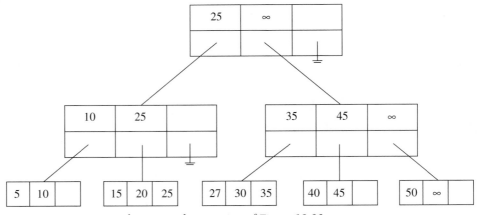

Figure 12.26 Horizontal array implementation of Figure 12.22

12.4. AA-Trees

Because of a host of possible rotations, the red-black tree is fairly tricky to code, especially for deletion. The deterministic skip list requires somewhat less code, but it is still quite tricky, as indicated by the three sentinels that are required. Deletion in a deterministic skip list is certainly a nontrivial task. In this section we describe a simple but competitive implementation of the *binary B-tree*, known as a BB-tree. A BB-tree is a red-black tree with one extra condition: A node may have at most one red child. To make coding easier, we adopt a few rules.

1. First, we add the condition that only right children can be red. This eliminates about half of the possible restructuring cases. It also eliminates an annoying case in the deletion algorithm: if an internal node has only one child, the child must be a right child (that happens to be red), because a black left child would violate condition 4 for red-black trees. Thus, we can always replace an internal node with the smallest node in its right subtree.

2. We code our procedures recursively.

3. Instead of storing a color bit with each node, we store information in a small integer (for instance, eight bits). This information is the *level* of a node. The level of a node is

   - One if the node is a leaf.

   - The level of its parent, if the node is red.

   - One less than the level of its parent, if the node is black.

The result is an AA-tree. Figure 12.27 shows the type declarations that are used for an AA-tree. Once again, we use a sentinel to represent `null`.

If we translate the AA structure requirements from colors to levels, we see that the left child must be exactly one level lower than its parent, and the right child may be zero or one level lower than its parent (but not more).

A *horizontal link* is a connection between a node and a child of equal levels; the structure requirements mandate that horizontal links are right links, and that there may not be two consecutive horizontal links. Figure 12.28 shows a sample AA-tree. Searching is done using the usual algorithm. Insertion of a new item is always done at the bottom level. However, two problems can result: insertion of a 2 would generate a left horizontal link, while insertion of 45 would create two consecutive right horizontal links.

In both cases a single rotation fixes the problem: we remove left horizontal links by right rotations, and consecutive right horizontal links by a left rotation. These procedures are called **skew** and **split**, respectively. Figure 12.29 shows the code for these primitives. A **skew** removes a left horizontal link, but may create consecutive right horizontal links; thus we process **skew** first, and then **split**. After a **split**, the middle node R increases in level. This may cause problems for the original parent of X by creating either a left horizontal node or consecutive right horizontal nodes; both problems can be fixed by percolating up the **skew/split** strategy. This is done automatically if we use recursion. Figure 12.30 depicts both methods.

The actions taken to insert 45 in the AA-tree in Figure 12.28 are shown in Figures 12.31 through 12.35 (on page 478). The insertion procedure is then only two lines longer than an unbalanced implementation, as shown in Figure 12.36 (on page 479).

Deletion is, of course, more complex, but since we removed many of the special cases, the code is actually pretty reasonable. Recall, first of all, that if a node is not a leaf, then it must have a right child. This means that when deleting a node, we can always replace the node with the smallest child in the right subtree, which is guaranteed to be at level 1.

To help us out, we keep two **static** class variables **deletedNode** and **lastNode**. These must be **static** because **remove** is a recursive method. When we traverse a right link, we adjust **deletedNode**; because we call **remove** recursively until we reach the bottom (we don't test for equality on the way down), we are guaranteed that if the item to be removed is in

```
class AANode
{
        // Constructors
    AANode( Comparable theElement )
    {
        this( theElement, null, null );
    }

    AANode( Comparable theElement, AANode lt, AANode rt )
    {
        element = theElement;
        left    = lt;
        right   = rt;
        level   = 1;
    }

        // Friendly data; accessible by other package routines
    Comparable element;        // The data in the node
    AANode     left;           // Left child
    AANode     right;          // Right child
    int        level;          // Level
}

public class AATree
{
    /**
     * Construct the tree.
     */
    public AATree( )
    {
        root = nullNode;
    }


    private AANode root;
    private static AANode nullNode;
        static             // static initializer for NullNode
        {
            nullNode = new AANode( null );
            nullNode.left = nullNode.right = nullNode;
            nullNode.level = 0;
        }
}
```

Figure 12.27 AA-trees: node class and AATree initialization

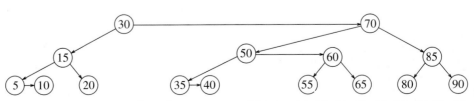

Figure 12.28 AA-tree resulting from insertion of 10, 85, 15, 70, 20, 60, 30, 50, 65, 80, 90, 40, 5, 55, 35

```
/**
 * Skew primitive for AA-trees.
 * @param t the node that roots the tree.
 * @return the new root after the rotation.
 */
private AANode skew( AANode t )
{
    if( t.left.level == t.level )
        t = rotateWithLeftChild( t );
    return t;
}

/**
 * Split primitive for AA-trees.
 * @param t the node that roots the tree.
 * @return the new root after the rotation.
 */
private AANode split( AANode t )
{
    if( t.right.right.level == t.level )
    {
        t = rotateWithRightChild( t );
        t.level++;
    }
    return t;
}
```

Figure 12.29 AA-trees: skew and split methods

Figure 12.30 skew and split. Note that R's level increases in a split

the tree, deletedNode will be referencing the node that contains it.* lastNode references the leaf at which the search terminates. Because we don't stop until we reach the bottom, if the

---

*This technique can be used in the find method to replace the three-way comparisons done at each node with two-way comparisons at each node, plus one extra equality test at the bottom.

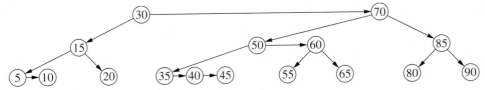

Figure 12.31 After inserting 45 into sample tree

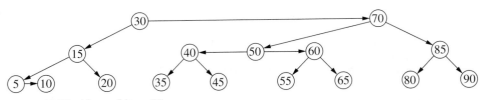

Figure 12.32 After split at 35

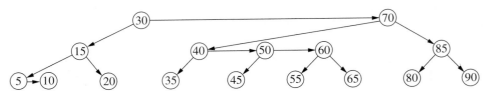

Figure 12.33 After skew at 50

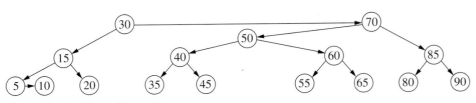

Figure 12.34 After split at 40

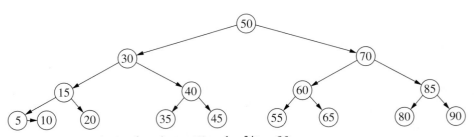

Figure 12.35 Final tree after skew at 70 and split at 30

```
/**
 * Internal method to insert into a subtree.
 * @param x the item to insert.
 * @param t the node that roots the tree.
 * @return the new root.
 */
private AANode insert( Comparable x, AANode t )
{
    if( t == nullNode )
        t = new AANode( x, nullNode, nullNode );
    else if( x.compareTo( t.element ) < 0 )
        t.left = insert( x, t.left );
    else if( x.compareTo( t.element ) > 0 )
        t.right = insert( x, t.right );
    else
        return t;

    t = skew( t );
    t = split( t );
    return t;
}
```

Figure 12.36 AA-trees: insertion method

item is in the tree, `lastNode` will reference the level 1 node that contains the replacement value, and must be removed from the tree.

When we reach the bottom of the tree, we perform step 2, which copies the level 1 node value into the internal node and then bypasses the level 1 node.

Nonleaf nodes check to see if their levels have been destroyed by a recursive call. Let T be the current node. If the deletion has lowered the level of one of T's children (only the child entered by the recursive call could actually be affected, but for simplicity, we don't keep track of it) to two less than T's level, then T's level needs to be lowered also. Furthermore, if T has a right red child, T's right child must also have its level lowered. At this point, we could have six nodes on the same level: T, T's right red child R, R's two children, and those children's right red children. Figure 12.37 shows the simplest possible scenario.

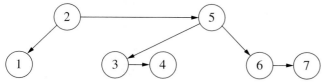

Figure 12.37 When 1 is deleted, all nodes become level 1, introducing horizontal left links. Getting links to point right is accomplished by three calls to skew. Two calls to `split` remove consecutive horizontal links.

```
/**
 * Internal method to remove from a subtree.
 * @param x the item to remove.
 * @param t the node that roots the tree.
 * @return the new root.
 */
private AANode remove( Comparable x, AANode t )
{
    if( t != nullNode )
    {
        // Step 1: Search down the tree and set lastNode and deletedNode
        lastNode = t;
        if( x.compareTo( t.element ) < 0 )
            t.left = remove( x, t.left );
        else
        {
            deletedNode = t;
            t.right = remove( x, t.right );
        }

        // Step 2: If at the bottom of the tree and
        //         x is present, we remove it
        if( t == lastNode )
        {
            if( deletedNode == nullNode ||
                    x.compareTo( deletedNode.element ) != 0 )
                return t;    // Item not found; do nothing
            deletedNode.element = t.element;
            t = t.right;
        }

        // Step 3: Otherwise, we are not at the bottom; rebalance
        else
        if( t.left.level < t.level - 1 || t.right.level < t.level - 1 )
        {
            if( t.right.level > --t.level )
                t.right.level = t.level;
            t = skew( t );
            t.right = skew( t.right );
            t.right.right = skew( t.right.right );
            t = split( t );
            t.right = split( t.right );
        }
    }
    return t;
}
```

Figure 12.38 AA-Trees: deletion procedure

After node 1 is removed, node 2 and thus node 5 become level 1 nodes. First we must fix the left horizontal link that is now introduced between nodes 5 and 3. This essentially requires two rotations (one between nodes 5 and 3, and then one between nodes 5 and 4).

In this case, the current node, T, is not involved. But if a deletion came from the right side, then T's left node could suddenly become horizontal; that would also require a similar double rotation (starting at T). To avoid testing all these cases, we call skew three times. Once that's done, two calls to split suffice to rearrange the horizontal edges. The entire deletion routine is shown in Figure 12.38. All in all, this is a relatively simple data structure to code.

12.5. Treaps

Our last type of binary search tree, known as the *treap*, is probably the simplest of all. Like the skip list, it uses random numbers and gives $O(\log N)$ expected time behavior for any input. Searching time is identical to an unbalanced binary search tree (and thus slower than balanced search trees), while insertion time is only slightly slower than a recursive unbalanced binary search tree implementation. Although deletion is much slower, it is still $O(\log N)$ expected time.

The treap is so simple that we can describe it without a picture. Each node in the tree stores an item, a left and right link, and a priority that is randomly assigned when the node is created. A treap is a binary search tree with the property that the node priorities satisfy heap order: any node's priority must be at least as large as its parent's.

A collection of distinct items each of which has a distinct priority can only be represented by one treap. This is easily deduced by induction, since the node with the lowest priority must be the root. Consequently, the tree is formed on the basis of the $N!$ possible arrangements of priority instead of the $N!$ item orderings. The node declarations are straightforward, requiring only the addition of the priority field, as shown in Figure 12.39. The

```java
class TreapNode
{
        // Constructors
    TreapNode( Comparable theElement )
    {
        this( theElement, null, null );
    }

    TreapNode( Comparable theElement, TreapNode lt, TreapNode rt )
    {
        element  = theElement;
        left     = lt;
        right    = rt;
        priority = randomObj.randomInt( );
    }


        // Friendly data; accessible by other package routines
    Comparable element;      // The data in the node
    TreapNode  left;         // Left child
    TreapNode  right;        // Right child
    int        priority;     // Priority

    private static Random randomObj = new Random( );
}
```

Figure 12.39 Node declaration for treaps

```
/**
 * Internal method to insert into a subtree.
 * @param x the item to insert.
 * @param t the node that roots the tree.
 * @return the new root.
 */
private TreapNode insert( Comparable x, TreapNode t )
{
    if( t == nullNode )
        t = new TreapNode( x, nullNode, nullNode );
    else if( x.compareTo( t.element ) < 0 )
    {
        t.left = insert( x, t.left );
        if( t.left.priority < t.priority )
            t = rotateWithLeftChild( t );
    }
    else if( x.compareTo( t.element ) > 0 )
    {
        t.right = insert( x, t.right );
        if( t.right.priority < t.priority )
            t = rotateWithRightChild( t );
    }
    // Otherwise, it's a duplicate; do nothing

    return t;
}
```

Figure 12.40 Treaps: insertion routine

sentinel **nullNode** will have priority of ∞. A single, shared, **Random** object generates random priorities.

Insertion into the treap is simple: After an item is added as a leaf, we rotate it up the treap until its priority satisfies heap order. It can be shown that the expected number of rotations is less than 2. After the item to be deleted has been found, it can be deleted by increasing its priority to ∞ and rotating it down through the path of low-priority children. Once it is a leaf, it can be removed. The routines in Figure 12.40 and Figure 12.41 implement these strategies using recursion. A nonrecursive implementation is left for the reader (Exercise 12.17). For deletion, note that when the node is logically a leaf, it still has **nullNode** as both its left and right children. Consequently, it is rotated with the right child. After the rotation, **t** is **nullNode**, and the left child stores the item that is to be deleted. Thus we change **t.left** to reference the **nullNode** sentinel. Note also that our implementation assumes that there are no duplicates; if this is not true, then the **remove** could fail (why?).

The treap is particularly easy to implement because we never have to worry about adjusting the **priority** field. One of the difficulties of the balanced tree approaches is that it is difficult to track down errors that result from failing to update balance information in the course of an operation. In terms of total lines for a reasonable insertion and deletion package, the treap, especially a nonrecursive implementation, seems like the hands-down winner.

```
/**
 * Internal method to remove from a subtree.
 * @param x the item to remove.
 * @param t the node that roots the tree.
 * @return the new root.
 */
private TreapNode remove( Comparable x, TreapNode t )
{
    if( t != nullNode )
    {
        if( x.compareTo( t.element ) < 0 )
            t.left = remove( x, t.left );
        else if( x.compareTo( t.element ) > 0 )
            t.right = remove( x, t.right );
        else
        {
            // Match found
            if( t.left.priority < t.right.priority )
                t = rotateWithLeftChild( t );
            else
                t = rotateWithRightChild( t );

            if( t != nullNode )      // Continue on down
                t = remove( x, t );
            else
                t.left = nullNode;  // Fix nullNode after final rotation
        }
    }
    return t;
}
```

Figure 12.41 Treaps: deletion procedure

12.6. *k*-d Trees

Suppose that an advertising company maintains a database and needs to generate mailing labels for certain constituencies. A typical request might require sending out a mailing to people who are between the ages of 34 and 49 and whose annual income is between $100,000 and $150,000. This problem is known as a two-dimensional range query. In one dimension, the problem can be solved by a simple recursive algorithm in $O(M + \log N)$ average time, by traversing a preconstructed binary search tree. Here M is the number of matches reported by the query. We would like to obtain a similar bound for two or more dimensions.

The two-dimensional search tree has the simple property that branching on odd levels is done with respect to the first key, and branching on even levels is done with respect to the second key. The root is arbitrarily chosen to be an odd level. Figure 12.42 shows a 2-d tree. Insertion into a 2-d tree is a trivial extension of insertion into a binary search tree: as we go down the tree, we need to maintain the current level. To keep our code simple, we assume

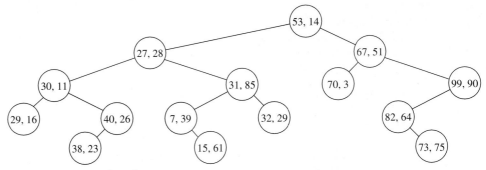

Figure 12.42 Sample 2-d tree

```
public void insert( Comparable [ ] x )
{
    root = insert( x, root, 0 );
}

private KdNode insert( Comparable [ ] x, KdNode t, int level )
{
    if( t == null )
        t = new KdNode( x );
    else if( x[ level ].compareTo( t.data[ level ] ) < 0 )
        t.left = insert( x, t.left, 1 - level );
    else
        t.right = insert( x, t.right, 1 - level );
    return t;
}
```

Figure 12.43 Insertion into 2-d trees

that a basic item is an array of two elements. We then need to toggle the level between 0 and 1. Figure 12.43 shows the code to perform an insertion. We use recursion in this section; a nonrecursive implementation that would be used in practice is straightforward and left as Exercise 12.23. One difficulty is duplicates, particularly since several items can agree in one key. Our code allows duplicates, and always places them in right branches; clearly this can be a problem if there are too many duplicates.

A moment's thought will convince you that a randomly constructed 2-d tree has the same structural properties as a random binary search tree: the height is $O(\log N)$ on average, but $O(N)$ in the worst case.

Unlike binary search trees, for which clever $O(\log N)$ worst-case variants exist, there are no schemes that are known to guarantee a balanced 2-d tree. The problem is that such a scheme would likely be based on tree rotations, and tree rotations don't work in 2-d trees. The best one can do is to periodically rebalance the tree by reconstructing a subtree, as described in the exercises. Similarly, there are no deletion algorithms beyond the obvious lazy deletion strategy. If all of the items arrive before we need to process queries, then we can construct a perfectly balanced 2-d tree in $O(N \log N)$ time; we leave this as Exercise 12.21c.

```
/**
 * Print items satisfying
 * low[ 0 ] <= x[ 0 ] <= high[ 0 ] and
 * low[ 1 ] <= x[ 1 ] <= high[ 1 ].
 */
public void printRange( Comparable [ ] low, Comparable [ ] high )
{
    printRange( low, high, root, 0 );
}

private void printRange( Comparable [ ] low, Comparable [ ] high,
                         KdNode t, int level )
{
    if( t != null )
    {
        if( low[ 0 ].compareTo( t.data[ 0 ] ) <= 0 &&
                low[ 1 ].compareTo( t.data[ 1 ] ) <= 0 &&
                high[ 0 ].compareTo( t.data[ 0 ] ) >= 0 &&
                high[ 1 ].compareTo( t.data[ 1 ] ) >= 0 )
            System.out.println( "(" + t.data[ 0 ] + ","
                                    + t.data[ 1 ] + ")" );

        if( low[ level ].compareTo( t.data[ level ] ) <= 0 )
            printRange( low, high, t.left, 1 - level );
        if( high[ level ].compareTo( t.data[ level ] ) >= 0 )
            printRange( low, high, t.right, 1 - level );
    }
}
```

Figure 12.44 2-d trees: range search

Several kinds of queries are possible on a 2-d tree. We can ask for an exact match, or a match based on one of the two keys; the latter type of request is a *partial match query*. Both of these are special cases of an (orthogonal) *range query*.

An orthogonal range query gives all items whose first key is between a specified set of values and whose second key is between another specified set of values. This is exactly the problem that was described in the introduction to this section. A range query is easily solved by a recursive tree traversal, as shown in Figure 12.44. By testing before making a recursive call, we can avoid unnecessarily visiting all nodes.

To find a specific item, we can set **low** equal to **high** equal to the item we are searching for. To perform a partial match query, we set the range for the key not involved in the match to $-\infty$ to ∞. The other range is set with the low and high point equal to the value of the key involved in the match.

An insertion or exact match search in a 2-d tree takes time that is proportional to the depth of the tree, namely, $O(\log N)$ on average and $O(N)$ in the worst case. The running time of a range search depends on how balanced the tree is, whether or not a partial match is requested, and how many items are actually found. We mention three results that have been shown.

For a perfectly balanced tree, a range query could take $O(M + \sqrt{N})$ time in the worst case, to report M matches. At any node, we may have to visit two of the four grandchildren, leading to the equation $T(N) = 2T(N/4) + O(1)$. In practice, however, these searches tend to be very efficient, and even the worst case is not poor because for typical N, the difference between $\sqrt{N}$ and $\log N$ is compensated by the smaller constant that is hidden in the Big-Oh notation.

For a randomly constructed tree, the average running time of a partial match query is $O(M + N^\alpha)$, where $\alpha = (-3 + \sqrt{17})/2$ (see below). A recent, and somewhat surprising, result is that this essentially describes the average running time of a range search of a random 2-d tree.

For k dimensions, the same algorithm works; we just cycle through the keys at each level. However, in practice the balance starts getting worse because typically the effect of duplicates and nonrandom inputs becomes more pronounced. We leave the coding details as an exercise for the reader, and mention the analytical results: For a perfectly balanced tree, the worst-case running time of a range query is $O(M + kN^{1-1/k})$. In a randomly constructed k-d tree, a partial match query that involves p of the k keys takes $O(M + N^\alpha)$, where α is the (only) positive root of

$$(2 + \alpha)^p(1 + \alpha)^{k-p} = 2^k$$

Computation of α for various p and k is left as an exercise; the value for $k = 2$ and $p = 1$ is reflected in the result stated above for partial matching in random 2-d trees.

Although there are several exotic structures that support range searching, the k-d tree is probably the simplest such structure that achieves respectable running times.

12.7. Pairing Heaps

The last data structure we examine is the *pairing heap*. The analysis of the pairing heap is still open, but when **decreaseKey** operations are needed, it seems to outperform other heap structures. The most likely reason for its efficiency is its simplicity. The pairing heap is represented as a heap-ordered tree. Figure 12.45 shows a sample pairing heap.

The actual pairing heap implementation uses a left child, right sibling representation as discussed in Chapter 4. The **decreaseKey** operation, as we will see, requires that each node contain an additional link. A node that is a leftmost child contains a link to its parent; otherwise the node is a right sibling, and contains a link to its left sibling. We'll refer to this field as the **prev** field. The class skeleton and pairing heap node declaration are omitted for brevity; they are completely straightforward. Figure 12.46 shows the actual representation of the pairing heap in Figure 12.45.

We begin by sketching the basic operations. To merge two pairing heaps, we make the heap with the larger root a left child of the heap with the smaller root. Insertion is, of course, a special case of merging. To perform a **decreaseKey**, we lower the value in the requested node. Because we are not maintaining parent links for all nodes, we don't know if this violates the heap order. Thus we cut the adjusted node from its parent and complete the **decreaseKey** by merging the two heaps that result. To perform a **deleteMin**, we remove the root, creating a collection of heaps. If there are c children of the root, then $c - 1$ calls to the merge procedure will reassemble the heap. The most important detail is the method used to perform the merge and how the $c - 1$ merges are applied.

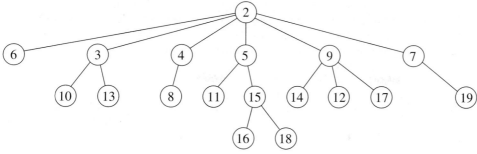

Figure 12.45 Sample pairing heap: abstract representation

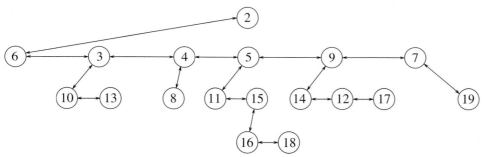

Figure 12.46 Actual representation of previous pairing heap

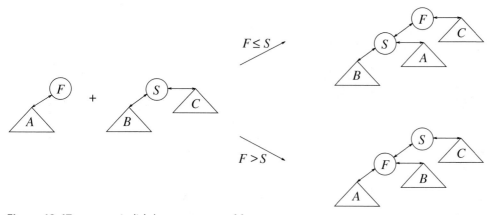

Figure 12.47 `compareAndLink` merges two subheaps

Figure 12.47 shows how two subheaps are combined. The procedure is generalized to allow the second subheap to have siblings. As we mentioned earlier, the subheap with the larger root is made a leftmost child of the other subheap. The code is straightforward and shown in Figure 12.48. Notice that we have several instances in which a node reference is tested against **null** before assigning its **prev** field; this suggests that perhaps it would

```
/**
 * Internal method that is the basic operation to maintain order.
 * Links first and second together to satisfy heap order.
 * @param first root of tree 1, which may not be null.
 *     first.nextSibling MUST be null on entry.
 * @param second root of tree 2, which may be null.
 * @return result of the tree merge.
 */
private PairNode compareAndLink( PairNode first, PairNode second )
{
    if( second == null )
        return first;

    if( second.element.compareTo( first.element ) < 0 )
    {
        // Attach first as leftmost child of second
        second.prev = first.prev;
        first.prev = second;
        first.nextSibling = second.leftChild;
        if( first.nextSibling != null )
            first.nextSibling.prev = first;
        second.leftChild = first;
        return second;
    }
    else
    {
        // Attach second as leftmost child of first
        second.prev = first;
        first.nextSibling = second.nextSibling;
        if( first.nextSibling != null )
            first.nextSibling.prev = first;
        second.nextSibling = first.leftChild;
        if( second.nextSibling != null )
            second.nextSibling.prev = second;
        first.leftChild = second;
        return first;
    }
}
```

Figure 12.48 Pairing heaps: routine to merge two subheaps

be useful to have a nullNode sentinel, which was customary in this chapter's search tree implementations.

The insert and decreaseKey operations are, then, simple implementations of the abstract description. decreaseKey requires a *position* object, which is just a PairNode reference. Since this is determined (irrevocably) when an item is first inserted, insert returns the PairNode reference back to the caller. The code is shown in Figure 12.49. Our routine

```
/**
 * Insert into the priority queue, and return a PairNode
 * that can be used by decreaseKey.
 * Duplicates are allowed.
 * @param x the item to insert.
 * @return the node containing the newly inserted item.
 */
public PairNode insert( Comparable x )
{
    PairNode newNode = new PairNode( x );

    if( root == null )
        root = newNode;
    else
        root = compareAndLink( root, newNode );
    return newNode;
}


/**
 * Change the value of the item stored in the pairing heap.
 * Does nothing if newVal is larger than the currently stored value.
 * @param p any node returned by addItem.
 * @param newVal the new value, which must be smaller
 *     than the currently stored value.
 */
public void decreaseKey( PairNode p, Comparable newVal )
{
    if( p.element.compareTo( newVal ) < 0 )
        return;     // newVal cannot be bigger
    p.element = newVal;
    if( p != root )
    {
        if( p.nextSibling != null )
            p.nextSibling.prev = p.prev;
        if( p.prev.leftChild == p )
            p.prev.leftChild = p.nextSibling;
        else
            p.prev.nextSibling = p.nextSibling;

        p.nextSibling = null;
        root = compareAndLink( root, p );
    }
}
```

Figure 12.49 Pairing heaps: insert and decreaseKey

for decreaseKey returns immediately if the new value is not smaller than the old; otherwise, the resulting structure might not obey heap order. The basic deleteMin procedure follows directly from the abstract description and is shown in Figure 12.50.

Figure 12.50 Pairing heap deleteMin

```java
/**
 * Remove the smallest item from the priority queue.
 * @return the smallest item, or null if empty.
 */
public Comparable deleteMin( )
{
    if( isEmpty( ) )
        return null;

    Comparable x = findMin( );
    if( root.leftChild == null )
        root = null;
    else
        root = combineSiblings( root.leftChild );

    return x;
}
```

Figure 12.51 Pairing heaps: two-pass merging

```java
private PairNode [ ] doubleIfFull( PairNode [ ] array, int index )
{
    if( index == array.length )
    {
        PairNode [ ] oldArray = array;

        array = new PairNode[ index * 2 ];
        for( int i = 0; i < index; i++ )
            array[ i ] = oldArray[ i ];
    }
    return array;
}

    // The array of trees for combineSiblings
PairNode [ ] treeArray = new PairNode[ 5 ];

/**
 * Internal method that implements two-pass merging.
 * @param firstSibling the root of the conglomerate;
 *     assumed not null.
 */
private PairNode combineSiblings( PairNode firstSibling )
{
    if( firstSibling.nextSibling == null )
        return firstSibling;

        // Store the subtrees in an array
    int numSiblings = 0;
    for( ; firstSibling != null; numSiblings++ )
    {
```

(continues)

(*continued*)

```
                    treeArray = doubleIfFull( treeArray, numSiblings );
                    treeArray[ numSiblings ] = firstSibling;
                    firstSibling.prev.nextSibling = null;  // break links
                    firstSibling = firstSibling.nextSibling;
                }
                treeArray = doubleIfFull( treeArray, numSiblings );
                treeArray[ numSiblings ] = null;

                    // Combine subtrees two at a time, going left to right
                int i = 0;
                for( ; i + 1 < numSiblings; i += 2 )
                    treeArray[ i ] = compareAndLink( treeArray[ i ], treeArray[ i + 1 ] );

                    // j has the result of last compareAndLink.
                    // If an odd number of trees, get the last one.
                int j = i - 2;
                if( j == numSiblings - 3 )
                    treeArray[ j ] = compareAndLink( treeArray[ j ], treeArray[ j + 2 ] );

                    // Now go right to left, merging last tree with
                    // next to last. The result becomes the new last.
                for( ; j >= 2; j -= 2 )
                    treeArray[ j - 2 ] = compareAndLink( treeArray[ j - 2 ], treeArray[ j ] );

                return treeArray[ 0 ];
            }
```

Figure 12.51 Pairing heaps: two-pass merging

The devil, of course, is in the details: How is **combineSiblings** implemented? Several variants have been proposed, but none has been shown to provide the same amortized bounds as the Fibonacci heap. It has recently been shown that almost all of the proposed methods are in fact theoretically less efficient than the Fibonacci heap. Even so, the method coded in Figure 12.51 always seems to perform as well as or better than other heap structures, including the binary heap, for the typical graph theory uses that involve a host of **decreaseKey** operations.

This method, known as *two-pass merging,* is the simplest and most practical of the many variants that have been suggested. We first scan left to right, merging pairs of children.* After the first scan, we have half as many trees to merge. A second scan is then performed, right to left. At each step we merge the rightmost tree remaining from the first scan with the current merged result. As an example, if we have eight children, c_1 through c_8, the first scan performs the merges c_1 and c_2, c_3 and c_4, c_5 and c_6, and c_7 and c_8. As a result we obtain d_1, d_2, d_3, and d_4. We perform the second pass by merging d_3 and d_4; d_2 is then merged with that result, and then d_1 is merged with the result of the previous merge.

Our implementation requires an array to store the subtrees. In the worst case, $N - 1$ items could be children of the root, but declaring an array of size N inside of **combineSiblings** would give an $O(N)$ algorithm. So we use an expanding array instead.

---

*We must be careful if there is an odd number of children. When that happens, we merge the last child with the result of the rightmost merge to complete the first scan.

Other merging strategies are discussed in the exercises. The only simple merging strategy that is easily seen to be poor is a left-to-right single-pass merge (Exercise 12.35). The pairing heap is a good example of "simple is better" and seems to be the method of choice for serious applications requiring the **decreaseKey** or **merge** operation.

SUMMARY

In this chapter, we've seen several efficient variations of the binary search tree. The top-down splay tree provides $O(\log N)$ amortized performance, the treap gives $O(\log N)$ randomized performance, and the red-black tree, deterministic skip list, and AA-tree all give $O(\log N)$ worst-case performance for the basic operations. The trade-offs between the various structures involve code complexity, ease of deletion, and differing searching and insertion costs. It is difficult to say that any one structure is a clear winner. Recurring themes include tree rotations and the use of sentinel nodes to eliminate many of the annoying tests for **null** references that would otherwise be necessary. The k-d tree provides a practical method for performing range searches, even though the theoretical bounds are not optimal.

Finally, we described and coded the pairing heap, which seems to be the most practical mergeable priority queue, especially when **decreaseKey** operations are required, even though it is theoretically less efficient than the Fibonacci heap.

EXERCISES

12.1 Prove that the amortized cost of a top-down splay is $O(\log N)$.

**12.2 Prove that there exist access sequences that require $2 \log N$ rotations per access for bottom-up splaying. Show that a similar result holds for top-down splaying.

12.3 Modify the splay tree to support queries for the kth smallest item. How would this be done in a deterministic skip list?

12.4 Compare, empirically, the simplified top-down splay with the originally described top-down splay.

12.5 Write the deletion procedure for red-black trees.

12.6 Prove that the height of a red-black tree is at most $2 \log N$, and that this bound cannot be substantially lowered.

12.7 Show that every AVL tree can be colored as a red-black tree. Are all red-black trees AVL?

12.8 Show that a 1-2-3 deterministic skip list can be represented as a 2-3-4 tree, with items at internal nodes as well as leaves.

12.9 What happens if we try to insert an item that is already in the deterministic skip list?

12.10 Show that at most $2N$ nodes are used in a 1-2-3 deterministic skip list.

*12.11 In Java, we can represent each abstract node as a dynamically allocated array of forward links, instead of a linked list of node references. Show how to implement a 1-2-3 deterministic skip list in this scheme and maintain the $O(\log N)$ bound for each operation.

12.12 Write the deletion procedure for a 1-2-3 deterministic skip list.

12.13 Prove that the algorithm for deletion in AA-trees is correct.

12.14 Give a nonrecursive top-down implementation of AA-trees. Compare the implementation with the text's for simplicity and efficiency.

12.15 Write the **skew** and **split** procedures recursively, so that only one call of each is need for deletion.

12.16 How many fewer lines of code than the BB-tree does the AA-tree use? Does this make AA-trees faster?

12.17 Implement the insertion routine for treaps nonrecursively by maintaining a stack. Is it worth the effort?

12.18 We can make treaps self-adjusting by using the number of accesses as a priority and performing rotations as needed after each access. Compare this method with the randomized strategy. Alternatively, generate a random number each time an item X is accessed. If this number is smaller than X's current priority, use it as X's new priority (performing the appropriate rotation).

**12.19 Show that if the items are sorted, then a treap can be constructed in linear time, even if the priorities are not sorted.

12.20 Implement some of the tree structures without using the **nullNode** sentinel. How much coding effort is saved by using the sentinel?

12.21 Suppose we store, for each node, the number of **null** links in its subtree; call this the node's *weight*. Adopt the following strategy: If the left and right subtrees have weights that are not within a factor of 2 of each other, then completely rebuild the subtree rooted at the node. Show the following:

  a. We can rebuild a node in $O(S)$, where S is the weight of the node.

  b. The algorithm has amortized cost of $O(\log N)$ per insertion.

  c. We can rebuild a node in a k-d tree in $O(S \log S)$ time, where S is the weight of the node.

  d. We can apply the algorithm to k-d trees, at a cost of $O(\log^2 N)$ per insertion.

12.22 Suppose we call **rotateWithLeftChild** on an arbitrary 2-d tree. Explain in detail all the reasons that the result is no longer a usable 2-d tree.

12.23 Implement the insertion and range search for the k-d tree. Do not use recursion.

12.24 Determine the time for partial match query for values of p corresponding to $k = 3$, 4, and 5.

12.25 For a perfectly balanced k-d tree, derive the worst-case running time of a range query that is quoted in the text (see p. 486).

12.26 The *2-d heap* is a data structure that allows each item to have two individual keys. **deleteMin** can be performed with respect to either of these keys. The 2-d heap is a complete binary tree with the following order property: For any node X at even depth, the item stored at X has the smallest key #1 in its subtree, while for any node X at odd depth, the item stored at X has the smallest key #2 in its subtree.

  a. Draw a possible 2-d heap for the items (1,10), (2,9), (3,8), (4,7), (5,6).

  b. How do we find the item with minimum key #1?

  c. How do we find the item with minimum key #2?

  d. Give an algorithm to insert a new item into the 2-d heap.

  e. Give an algorithm to perform **deleteMin** with respect to either key.

  f. Give an algorithm to perform **buildHeap** in linear time.

12.27 Generalize the preceding exercise to obtain a *k-d heap*, in which each item can have k individual keys. You should be able to obtain the following bounds: `insert` in $O(\log N)$, `deleteMin` in $O(2^k \log N)$, and `buildHeap` in $O(kN)$.

12.28 Show that the k-d heap can be used to implement a double-ended priority queue.

12.29 Abstractly, generalize the k-d heap so that only levels that branch on key #1 have two children (all others have one).

 a. Do we need links?

 b. Clearly, the basic algorithms still work; what are the new time bounds?

12.30 Use a k-d tree to implement `deleteMin`. What would you expect the average running time to be for a random tree?

12.31 Use a k-d heap to implement a *deque* (Exercise 3.28) that also supports `deleteMin`.

12.32 Implement the pairing heap with a `nullNode` sentinel.

**12.33 Show that the amortized cost of each operation is $O(\log N)$ for the pairing heap algorithm in the text.

12.34 An alternative method for `combineSiblings` is to place all of the siblings on a queue, and repeatedly `dequeue` and merge the first two items on the queue, placing the result at the end of the queue. Implement this variation.

12.35 Show that using a stack instead of a queue in the previous exercise is bad, by giving a sequence that leads to $\Omega(N)$ cost per operation. This is the left-to-right single-pass merge.

12.36 Without `decreaseKey`, we can remove parent links. How competitive is the result with the skew heap?

12.37 Assume that each of the following is represented as a tree with child and parent references. Explain how to implement a `decreaseKey` operation.

 a. Binary heap

 b. Splay tree

12.38 When viewed graphically, each node in a 2-d tree *partitions the plane* into regions. For instance, Figure 12.52 shows the first five insertions into the 2-d tree in Figure 12.42. The first insertion, of $p1$, splits the plane into a left part and a right part. The second insertion, of $p2$, splits the left part into a top part and a bottom part, and so on.

 a. For a given set of N items, does the order of insertion affect the final partition?

 b. If two different insertion sequences result in the same tree, is the same partition produced?

 c. Give a formula for the number of regions that result from the partition after N insertions.

 d. Show the final partition for the 2-d tree in Figure 12.42.

Figure 12.52 The plane partitioned by a 2-d tree after the insertion of $p1 = (53, 14)$, $p2 = (27, 28)$, $p3 = (30, 11)$, $p4 = (67, 51)$, $p5 = (70, 3)$

Figure 12.53 The plane partitioned by a quad tree after the insertion of $p1 = (53, 14), p2 = (27, 28), p3 = (30, 11), p4 = (67, 51), p5 = (70, 3)$

12.39 An alternative to the 2-d tree is the *quad tree*. Figure 12.53 shows how a plane is partitioned by a quad tree. Initially we have a region (which is often a square, but need not be). Each region may store one point. If a second point is inserted into a region, then the region is split into four equal-sized quadrants (northeast, southeast, southwest, and northwest). If this places the points in different quadrants (as when $p2$ is inserted), we are done; otherwise, we continue splitting recursively (as is done when $p5$ is inserted).

   a. For a given set of N items, does the order of insertion affect the final partition?

   b. Show the final partition if the same elements that were in the 2-d tree in Figure 12.42 are inserted into the quad tree.

12.40 A tree data structure can store the quad tree. We maintain the bounds of the original region. The tree root represents the original region. Each node is either a leaf that stores an inserted item, or has exactly four children, representing four quadrants. To perform a search, we begin at the root and repeatedly branch to an appropriate quadrant until a leaf (or **null** entry) is reached.

   a. Draw the quad tree that corresponds to Figure 12.53.

   b. What factors influence how deep the (quad) tree will be?

   c. Describe an algorithm that performs an orthogonal range query in a quad tree.

REFERENCES

Top-down splay trees were described in the original splay tree paper [29]. A similar strategy, but without the crucial rotation, was described in [31]. The top-down red-black tree algorithm is from [17]; a more accessible description can be found in [28]. An implementation of top-down red-black trees without sentinel nodes is given in [14]; this provides a convincing demonstration of the usefulness of **nullNode**. Deterministic skip lists and their variants are discussed in [23] and [26]. Symmetric binary B-trees are from [6]; the AA-tree implementation shown in the text is adapted from the description in [1] and [3]. Treaps [4] are based on the *Cartesian tree* described in [32]. A related data structure is the *priority search tree* [21].

   The *k*-d tree was first presented in [7]. Other range-searching algorithms are described in [8]. The worst case for range searching in a balanced *k*-d tree was obtained in [19], and the average-case results cited in the text are from [13] and [10].

   The pairing heap and the alternatives suggested in the exercises were described in [16]. The study [18] suggests that the splay tree is the priority queue of choice when the **decreaseKey** operation is not required. Another study [30] suggests that the pairing heap achieves the same asymptotic bounds as the Fibonacci heap, with better performance in practice. However, a related study [22] using priority queues to implement minimum spanning tree algorithms suggests that the amortized cost of **decreaseKey** is not $O(1)$. M. Fredman [15] has settled the issue of optimality by proving that there are sequences for which the amortized cost of a **decreaseKey** operation is suboptimal (in fact, at least $\Omega(\log \log N)$). However, he has also shown that when used to implement Prim's minimum spanning tree algorithm, the pairing heap is optimal if the graph is slightly dense (that is, the number of edges in the graph is $O(N^{(1+\varepsilon)})$ for any ε). However, complete analysis of the pairing heap is still open.

The solutions to most of the exercises can be found in the primary references. Exercise 12.21 represents a "lazy" balancing strategy that has become somewhat popular. [20], [5], [11], and [9] describe specific strategies; [2] shows how to implement all of these strategies in one framework. A tree that satisfies the property in Exercise 12.21 is *weight-balanced*. These trees can also be maintained by rotations [24]. Part (d) is from [25]. A solution to Exercises 12.26 to 12.28 can be found in [12]. Quad trees are described in [27].

1. A. Andersson, "A Note on Searching a Binary Search Tree," *Software—Practice and Experience*, 21 (1991), 1125–1128.
2. A. Andersson, "General Balanced Trees," *Journal of Algorithms*, to appear.
3. A. Andersson, "Balanced Search Trees Made Simple," *Proceedings on the Third Workshop on Algorithms and Data Structures* (1993), 61–71.
4. C. Aragon and R. Seidel, "Randomized Search Trees," *Proceedings of the Thirtieth Annual Symposium on Foundations of Computer Science* (1989), 540–545.
5. J. L. Baer and B. Schwab, "A Comparison of Tree-Balancing Algorithms," *Communications of the ACM*, 20 (1977), 322–330.
6. R. Bayer, "Symmetric Binary B-Trees: Data Structure and Maintenance Algorithms," *Acta Informatica*, 1 (1972), 290–306.
7. J. L. Bentley, "Multidimensional Binary Search Trees Used for Associative Searching," *Communications of the ACM*, 18 (1975), 509–517.
8. J. L. Bentley and J. H. Friedman, "Data Structures for Range Searching," *Computing Surveys*, 11 (1979), 397–409.
9. H. Chang and S. S. Iyengar, "Efficient Algorithms to Globally Balance a Binary Search Tree," *Communications of the ACM*, 27 (1984), 695–702.
10. P. Chanzy, "Range Search and Nearest Neighbor Search," *Master's Thesis*, McGill University (1993).
11. A. C. Day, "Balancing a Binary Tree," *Computer Journal*, 19 (1976), 360–361.
12. Y. Ding and M. A. Weiss, "The k-d Heap: An Efficient Multi-Dimensional Priority Queue," *Proceedings of the Third Workshop on Algorithms and Data Structures* (1993), 302–313.
13. P. Flajolet and C. Puech, "Partial Match Retrieval of Multidimensional Data," *Journal of the ACM*, 33 (1986), 371–407.
14. B. Flamig, *Practical Data Structures in C++*, John Wiley, New York (1994).
15. M. Fredman, "Information Theoretic Implications for Pairing Heaps," *Proceedings of the Thirtieth Annual ACM Symposium on the Theory of Computing* (1998), 319–326.
16. M. L Fredman, R. Sedgewick, D. D. Sleator, and R. E. Tarjan, "The Pairing Heap: A New Form of Self-Adjusting Heap," *Algorithmica*, 1 (1986), 111–129.
17. L. J. Guibas and R. Sedgewick, "A Dichromatic Framework for Balanced Trees," *Proceedings of the Nineteenth Annual Symposium on Foundations of Computer Science* (1978), 8–21.
18. D. W. Jones, "An Empirical Comparison of Priority-Queue and Event-Set Implementations," *Communications of the ACM*, 29 (1986), 300–311.
19. D. T. Lee and C. K. Wong, "Worst-Case Analysis for Region and Partial Region Searches in Multidimensional Binary Search Trees and Balanced Quad Trees," *Acta Informatica*, 9 (1977), 23–29.

20. W. A. Martin and D. N. Ness, "Optimizing Binary Trees Grown with a Sorting Algorithm," *Communications of the ACM,* 15 (1972), 88–93.

21. E. McCreight, "Priority Search Trees," *SIAM Journal of Computing,* 14 (1985), 257–276.

22. B. M. E. Moret and H. D. Shapiro, "An Empirical Analysis of Algorithms for Constructing a Minimum Spanning Tree," *Proceedings of the Second Workshop on Algorithms and Data Structures,* (1991), 400–411.

23. J. I. Munro, T. Papadakis, and R. Sedgewick, "Deterministic Skip Lists," *Proceedings of the Third Annual Symposium of Discrete Algorithms* (1992), 367–375.

24. J. Nievergelt and E. M. Reingold, "Binary Search Trees of Bounded Balance," *SIAM Journal on Computing,* 2 (1973), 33–43.

25. M. H. Overmars and J. van Leeuwen, "Dynamic Multidimensional Data Structures Based on Quad and K-D Trees," *Acta Informatica,* 17 (1982), 267–285.

26. T. Papadakis, *Skip Lists and Probabilistic Analysis of Algorithms,* Ph.D. Dissertation, University of Waterloo (1993).

27. A. H. Samet, "The Quadtree and Related Hierarchical Data Structures," *Computing Surveys,* 16 (1984), 187–260.

28. R. Sedgewick, *Algorithms in C,* Addison-Wesley, Reading, Mass. (1990).

29. D. D. Sleator and R. E. Tarjan, "Self Adjusting Binary Search Trees," *Journal of the ACM,* 32 (1985), 652–686.

30. J. T. Stasko and J. S. Vitter, "Pairing Heaps: Experiments and Analysis," *Communications of the ACM,* 30 (1987), 234–249.

31. C. J. Stephenson, "A Method for Constructing Binary Search Trees by Making Insertions at the Root," *International Journal of Computer and Information Science,* 9 (1980), 15–29.

32. J. Vuillemin, "A Unifying Look at Data Structures," *Communications of the ACM,* 23 (1980), 229–239.

Some Library Routines

This appendix lists some of the Java library classes. For each class, a brief description is provided, as well as some of the commonly used members. A complete description of these classes is in the *JDK API Documentation*.

A.1. Classes in Package `java.lang`

This is the standard package that is automatically imported by all Java programs.

A.1.1. Character

The `Character` class wraps a value of the primitive type `char` in an object. An object of type `Character` contains a single field whose type is `char`. This class also provides several methods for determining the type of a character and converting characters from uppercase to lowercase and vice versa.

Important Methods

`Character( char value )`

constructs a `Character` object and initializes it so that it represents the primitive value argument.

`char charValue( )`

returns the value of this `Character` object.

`boolean equals( Object obj )`

compares this `Character` object against the specified object. The result is `true` if and only if the argument is not `null` and is a `Character` object that represents the same `char` value as this object.

`String toString( )`

returns a `String` object representing this `Character` object's value. The result is a `String` whose length is 1. The `String`'s sole component is the primitive `char` value represented by this object.

`static boolean isDigit( char ch )`

returns true if and only if the specified character is a digit.

`static boolean isDefined( char ch )`

returns true if and only if the specified character has a defined meaning in Unicode.

`static boolean isLetter( char ch )`

returns true if and only if the specified character is a letter.

`static boolean isLetterOrDigit( char ch )`

returns true if and only if the specified character is a letter or digit.

`static boolean isLowerCase( char ch )`

returns true if and only if the specified character is a lowercase character.

`static boolean isUpperCase( char ch )`

returns true if and only if the specified character is an uppercase character.

`static boolean isWhitespace( char ch )`

returns true if and only if the specified character is a Java whitespace character.

`static char toLowerCase( char ch )`

returns the lowercase equivalent of the specified character, if any; otherwise, returns the character itself.

`static char toUpperCase( char ch )`

returns the uppercase equivalent of the specified character, if any; otherwise, returns the character itself.

`static boolean isJavaIdentifierStart( char ch )`

returns true if and only if the specified character is permissible as the first character in a Java identifier. (New to Java 1.1.)

`static boolean isJavaIdentifierPart( char ch )`

returns true if and only if the specified character may be part of a Java identifier as other than the first character. (New to Java 1.1.)

A.1.2. Integer

The Integer class wraps a value of the primitive type int in an object. An object of type Integer contains a single field whose type is int. This class also provides several methods for converting an int to a String and a String to an int, as well as other constants and methods useful when dealing with an int.

Important Data Members

`static final int MAX_VALUE`

The largest value of type int.

`static final int MIN_VALUE`

The smallest value of type `int`.

Important Methods

`Integer( int val )`

constructs a newly allocated `Integer` object that represents the primitive `int` argument.

`int intValue( )`

returns the value of this `Integer` object as an `int`.

`boolean equals( Object obj )`

returns `true` if and only if the argument is not `null` and is an `Integer` object that contains the same `int` value as this object.

`static int parseInt( String str )`

parses the `String` argument as a signed decimal integer. Throws `NumberFormatException`.

`static int parseInt( String str, int radix )`

parses the `String` argument as a signed integer in the radix specified by the second argument. Throws `NumberFormatException`.

`String toString( )`

returns a `String` object representing this `Integer`'s value.

`static String toString( int theInt )`

returns a `String` object representing the specified integer.

`static String toString( int theInt, int radix )`

creates a `String` object representing the first argument in the radix specified by the second argument.

A.1.3. Object

Class `Object` is the root of the class hierarchy. Every class has `Object` as a superclass. All objects, including arrays, implement the methods of this class.

Important Methods

`Object( )`

constructs an object; rarely is it called directly.

`boolean equals( Object obj )`

compares two `Object`s for equality. The `equals` method for class `Object` implements the most discriminating possible test on objects. That is, for any reference values x and y, `x.equals(y)` returns `true` if and only if x and y refer to the same object (x==y has the value `true`).

```
String toString( )
```

returns a string representation of the object. The result should be a concise but informative representation that is easy for a person to read.

A.1.4. String

The `String` class represents character strings. All string literals in Java programs, such as "abc", are implemented as instances of this class. `String`s are constant—their values cannot be changed after they are created. String buffers (Section A.1.5) support mutable strings. The class `String` includes a host of methods, some of which are described in this section.

The Java language provides special support for the string concatenation operator (+) and for conversion of other objects to strings. `String` conversions are implemented through the method `toString`, defined by `Object`, and inherited by all classes in Java.

Important Methods

```
String( )
```

allocates a new `String` containing no characters.

```
String( String anotherStr )
```

allocates a new `String` that contains the same sequence of characters as the `String` argument.

```
char charAt( int index )
```

returns the character at the specified index. An `index` ranges from 0 to `length( )-1`. Throws `StringIndexOutOfBoundsException` if the index is out of range.

```
boolean equals( Object obj )
```

compares this `String` to the specified object. The result is `true` if and only if the argument is not `null` and is a `String` object that represents the same sequence of characters as this object.

```
int compareTo( String str )
```

compares two `String`s lexicographically. The comparison is based on the Unicode value of each character in the `String`s. Returns the value 0 if the argument `String` is equal to this `String`; a value less than 0 if this `String` is lexicographically less than the `String` argument; and a value greater than 0 if this `String` is lexicographically greater than the `String` argument.

```
int length( )
```

returns the length of this `String`.

```
boolean startsWith( String prefix )
```

returns `true` if and only if this `String` starts with the specified prefix.

```
boolean endsWith( String suffix )
```

returns `true` if and only if this `String` ends with the specified suffix.

```
String substring( int beginIdx, int endIdx )
```

Returns a new String that is a substring of this String. The substring begins at the specified beginIdx and extends to the character at index endIdx-1. Throws StringIndexOutOfBounds-Exception if beginIdx or endIdx is out of range.

A.1.5. StringBuffer

Because Strings are immutable, minor changes to the contents of a String can be expensive. Specifically, the += operator is very inefficient. For instance, str+='A' is implemented as str=str+'A'. This implies that a new String is created whose value is the result of str+'A', and then str references the new String. As a result, the cost of concatenating a single character is not a constant (as it logically should be). Instead, it is proportional to the length of the String being operated on. If there are repeated concatenations to a String, this cost can be prohibitive.

An example is the straightforward method in Figure A.1 that generates a String of N As. Tacking on the ith character costs time proportional to i, since as we just discussed, a new String of length i is created. The total cost of the routine is given by $1+2+3+\cdots+N$, which is quadratic. As an extreme case, running this method for $N = 64,000$ takes over a minute on a Pentium computer.

For efficient String operations, you would have to manipulate the characters on your own and then construct a single String containing the desired result after the manipulation is complete. This is what the StringBuffer does.

A StringBuffer can be constructed with any String or as an empty String. You can then apply operations that manipulate the StringBuffer, including **append**, which adds to the end; **setChar**, which changes a single character; and **insert**, which adds to the middle (sliding characters over, as needed). The compiler uses the StringBuffer to generate efficient code for trivial concatenation. For nontrivial operations, such as the example in Figure A.1, you must do it yourself. Figure A.2 shows how the StringBuffer can be used to generate a String of N As efficiently. This method is linear and runs in 1.5 sec for $N = 64,000$.

By the way, the StringBuffer uses array doubling to ensure that its capacity can expand as needed. The default initial capacity is 16 characters.

Important Methods

```
StringBuffer( )
```

constructs a string buffer with no characters in it and an initial capacity of 16 characters.

```
        // Quadratic method that generates a String of n As
    static String badLongString( int n )
    {
        String result = "";
        for( int i = 0; i < n; i++ )
            result += 'A';
        return result;
    }
```

Figure A.1 An inefficient method to generate a String of N As

```
                  // Linear method that generates a String of n As
              static String goodLongString( int n )
              {
                  StringBuffer result = new StringBuffer( );

                  for( int i = 0; i < n; i++ )
                      result.append( 'A' );

                  return new String( result );
              }
```

Figure A.2 An efficient method to generate a String of N As

StringBuffer(String str)

constructs a string buffer so that it represents the same sequence of characters as the String argument. The initial capacity of the string buffer is 16 plus the length of the argument.

int length( )

returns the length (character count) of this string buffer.

char charAt(int index)

returns the character at a specific index in this string buffer. The first character of a string buffer is at index 0, the next at index 1, and so on, for array indexing. Throws a StringIndex-OutOfBoundsException if the index is invalid.

void setCharAt(int index, char ch)

The character at the specified index of this string buffer is set to ch. Throws a StringIndexOut-OfBoundsException if the index is invalid.

StringBuffer append(Object obj)

appends the String representation of the Object argument to this string buffer. The argument is converted to a String, and the characters of that String are then appended to this string buffer. This string buffer is returned, so it can be used in a chain of operations. There are other append operations available for all the primitive types, as well as character arrays.

StringBuffer insert(int offset, Object obj)

inserts the String representation of the Object argument into this string buffer. The second argument is converted to a String, and the characters of that String are then inserted into this string buffer at the indicated offset. This string buffer is returned, so it can be used in a chain of operations. There are other insert operations available for all the primitive types, as well as character arrays. Throws a StringIndexOutOfBoundsException if the offset is invalid.

StringBuffer reverse( )

The character sequence contained in this string buffer is replaced by the reverse of the sequence. This string buffer is returned, so it can be used in a chain of operations.

`String toString( )`

converts to a string representing the data in this string buffer. A new `String` object is allocated and initialized to contain the character sequence currently represented by this string buffer. This `String` is then returned. Subsequent changes to the string buffer do not affect the contents of the `String`.

A.1.6. System

The `System` class contains several useful class fields and methods. It cannot be instantiated. Among the facilities provided by the `System` class are standard input, standard output, and error output streams; an `exit` method; and many system methods that are not used in this text.

Important Data Members

`static final InputStream in`

the standard input stream. This stream is already open and ready to supply input data. Typically, this stream corresponds to keyboard input or another input source specified by the host environment or user.

`static final PrintStream out`

the standard output stream. This stream is already open and ready to accept output data. Typically, this stream corresponds to display output or another output destination specified by the host environment or user.

`static final PrintStream err`

the standard error output stream. This stream is already open and ready to accept output data. Typically, this stream corresponds to display output or another output destination specified by the host environment or user. By convention, this output stream is used to display error messages or other information that should come to the immediate attention of a user, even if the principal output stream, the value of the variable `out`, has been redirected to a file or other destination that is typically not continuously monitored.

Important Methods

`static long currentTimeMillis( )`

returns the current time in milliseconds.

`static String getProperty( String key )`

gets the system property indicated by the specified key.

`static void exit( int status )`

terminates the program. The argument serves as a status code; by convention, a nonzero status code indicates abnormal termination. This method never returns normally and may not be called from an applet.

`static void gc( )`

runs the garbage collector. Calling the `gc` method suggests that the run-time system should expend effort toward recycling unused objects in order to make the memory those objects currently occupy available for quick reuse. When control returns from the method call, the system has made a best effort to reclaim space from all unused objects.

A.1.7. Throwable

The Throwable class is the superclass of all errors and exceptions in the Java language. Only objects that are instances of this class (or of one of its subclasses) are thrown. Similarly, only this class or one of its subclasses can be the argument type in a catch clause. A Throwable class contains a snapshot of the execution stack of its thread at the time it was created. It can also contain a message string that gives more information about the error.

Important Methods

Throwable( )

constructs a new Throwable with no detail message. The stack trace is automatically filled in.

Throwable(String message)

constructs a new Throwable with the specified detail message. The stack trace is automatically filled in.

String getMessage( )

returns the detail message of this throwable object.

String getLocalizedMessage( )

returns a localized description of this Throwable. Subclasses may override this method in order to produce a locale-specific message. For subclasses that do not override this method, the default implementation returns the same result as getMessage.

String toString( )

returns a short description of this throwable object.

void printStackTrace( )

prints this Throwable and its backtrace to the standard error stream.

A.2. Classes in Package java.io

This package contains classes that manipulate files and I/O streams. Except for File, the classes discussed here are new in Java 1.1.

A.2.1. BufferedReader

Reads text from a character-input stream, buffering characters so as to provide for the efficient reading of characters, arrays, and lines. The buffer size may be specified, or the default size may be used. The default is large enough for most purposes. In general, each read request made of a Reader causes a corresponding read request to be made of the underlying character or byte stream. It is therefore advisable to wrap a BufferedReader around any Reader whose read operations may be costly, such as a FileReader and an InputStreamReader.

Important Methods

BufferedReader(Reader in)

creates a buffering character-input stream that uses a default-sized input buffer.

int read( )

reads a single character. It throws an IOException if an I/O error occurs. The character is returned as an int. Thus typical use will require a type conversion to char.

String readLine( )

reads a line of text. A line is considered to be terminated by any one of a line feed ('\n'), a carriage return ('\r'), or a carriage return followed immediately by a linefeed. It returns a String containing the contents of the line, not including any line-termination characters, or null, if the end of the stream has been reached. It throws an IOException if an I/O error occurs.

boolean ready( )

tells whether this stream is ready to be read. A buffered character stream is ready if the buffer is not empty or if the underlying character stream is ready. It throws an IOException if an I/O error occurs.

void close( )

closes the stream. It throws an IOException if an I/O error occurs.

A.2.2. BufferedWriter

BufferedWriter writes text to a character-output stream, buffering characters so as to provide for the efficient writing of characters, arrays, and lines. The buffer size may be specified, or the default size may be used. The default is large enough for most purposes. In general, each write request made of a Writer causes a corresponding write request to be made of the underlying character or byte stream. It is therefore advisable to wrap a BufferedWriter around any Writer whose write operations may be costly, such as a FileWriter and an OutputStreamWriter. The BufferedWriter can be used to construct a PrintWriter object that supports the familiar print and println.

Important Methods

BufferedWriter(Writer out)

Creates a buffering character-output stream that uses a default-sized input buffer.

A.2.3. File

The File class is intended to provide an abstraction that deals with most of the machine-dependent complexities of files and pathnames in a machine-independent fashion. It is used to implement the pseudocode in Figures 4.6 and 4.9 (the online code has an example).

Important Data Members

static final char separatorChar

The system-dependent path separator string. This character separates the directory and file components in a filename.

Important Methods

File(String name)

creates a `File` instance that represents the file whose pathname is given by name.

String getName( )

returns the name of the file represented by this `File` object. The name is everything in the pathname after the last occurrence of the separator character.

String getPath( )

returns the pathname of the file represented by this `File` object.

boolean exists( )

returns `true` if and only if the file specified by this `File` object exists.

boolean isDirectory( )

returns `true` if and only if the file specified by this `File` object is a directory.

long length( )

returns the length of the file represented by this `File` object.

String [ ] list( )

returns an array of filenames in this `File` object's directory. This list does not include the current directory or the parent directory ("." and ".." on UNIX systems).

A.2.4. FileReader

`FileReader` is a convenience class for reading character files. This class extends the abstract class `Reader`, but its methods should not be used directly. Instead, wrap the object in a `BufferedReader` for efficiency and the ability to call `readLine`.

Important Method

FileReader(String fileName)

constructs a `FileReader` object from a given filename. It throws `FileNotFoundException` if the file cannot be opened.

A.2.5. FileWriter

`FileWriter` is a convenience class for writing character files. This class extends the abstract class `Writer`, but its methods should not be used directly. Instead, wrap the object in a `BufferedWriter` for efficiency, and wrap that in a `PrintWriter` for the ability to call `println`.

Important Method

FileWriter(String fileName)

constructs a FileWriter object from a given filename. It throws IOException if the file cannot be opened or created.

A.2.6. InputStreamReader

An InputStreamReader is a bridge from byte streams to character streams: It reads bytes and translates them into characters. Its primary use is construction with System.in as a parameter. This class extends the abstract class Reader, but its methods should not be used directly. Instead, wrap the object in a BufferedReader for efficiency and the ability to call readLine.

Important Method

InputStreamReader(InputStream in)

creates an InputStreamReader from a given InputStream. A typical InputStream is System.in.

A.2.7. PrintWriter

A PrintWriter prints formatted representations of objects to a text-output stream. It contains methods such as print and println.

Important Methods

PrintWriter(Writer out)

creates a PrintWriter from a given Writer (such as a BufferedWriter).

PrintWriter(OutputStream out)

creates a PrintWriter from a given OutputStream. A typical OutputStream is System.out.

boolean checkError( )

flushes the stream and checks its error state. Errors are cumulative; once the stream encounters an error, this routine returns true on all successive calls.

void print(String str)

prints a String.

void println(String str)

prints a String; then finishes the line. (The particular newline sequence is machine dependent).

void close( )

closes the stream. It throws an IOException if an I/O error occurs.

A.2.8. PushbackReader

PushbackReader implements a character-stream reader that allows characters to be pushed back into the stream.

Important Methods

PushbackReader(Reader in)

creates a new pushback reader with a 1-character pushback buffer.

PushbackReader(Reader in, int bufferSize)

creates a new pushback reader with a multicharacter pushback buffer whose capacity is specified by the second parameter.

int read( )

reads a single character; returns the character read, or −1, if the end of the stream has been reached. It throws an IOException if an I/O error occurs. The character is returned as an int. Thus typical use will require a type conversion to char.

void unread(int ch)

pushes back a single character, ch. The parameter has type int. Thus typical use will require a type conversion to char. It throws an IOException if the pushback buffer is full, or if some other I/O error occurs.

void unread(char [ ] cbuf)

pushes back an array of characters by copying it to the front of the pushback buffer. After this method returns, the next character to be read will have the value cbuf[0], the character after that will have the value cbuf[1], and so forth. It throws IOException, if there is insufficient room in the pushback buffer, or if some other I/O error occurs.

A.3. Classes in Package `java.util`

This package defines several useful classes, including some data structures. It also provides support for dates and times. Two useful classes are described next.

A.3.1. Random

An instance of this class is used to generate a stream of pseudorandom numbers. The class uses a 48-bit seed, which is modified by using a linear congruential formula (given at the end of Section 10.4.1). If two instances of Random are created with the same seed, and the same sequence of method calls is made for each, they will generate and return identical sequences of numbers.

Important Methods

Random( )

creates a new random-number generator. Its seed is initialized to a value based on the current time.

Random(long seed)

creates a new random-number generator by using a single long seed.

int nextInt( )

returns the next pseudorandom, uniformly distributed `int` value from this random-number generator's sequence.

long nextLong( )

returns the next pseudorandom, uniformly distributed `long` value from this random-number generator's sequence.

double nextDouble( )

returns the next pseudorandom, uniformly distributed `double` value between 0.0 and 1.0 from this random-number generator's sequence.

double nextGaussian( )

returns the next pseudorandom, Gaussian-distributed `double` value with mean 0.0 and standard deviation 1.0 from this random-number generator's sequence.

A.3.2. StringTokenizer

The `StringTokenizer` class allows an application to break a string into tokens. The set of delimiters (the characters that separate tokens) may be specified either at creation time or on a per-token basis. An instance of `StringTokenizer` behaves in one of two ways, depending on whether it was created with the `returnTokens` flag having the value `true` or `false`. If the flag is `false`, delimiter characters serve to separate tokens. A token is a maximal sequence of consecutive characters that are not delimiters. If the flag is `true`, delimiter characters are considered to be tokens. A token is either one delimiter character or a maximal sequence of consecutive characters that are not delimiters.

Important Methods

StringTokenizer(String str)

constructs a string tokenizer for the specified string. The tokenizer uses the default delimiter set, which is " \t\n\r": the space character, the tab character, the newline character, and the carriage-return character.

StringTokenizer(String str, String delim)

constructs a string tokenizer for the specified string. The characters in the `delim` argument are the delimiters for separating tokens.

StringTokenizer(String str, String delim, boolean returnTokens)

constructs a string tokenizer for the specified string. The characters in the `delim` argument are the delimiters for separating tokens. If the `returnTokens` flag is `true`, then the delimiter characters are also returned as tokens. Each delimiter is returned as a string of length one. If the flag is `false`, the delimiter characters are skipped and serve only as separators between tokens.

boolean hasMoreTokens( )

returns `true` if and only if there are more tokens available from this tokenizer's string.

String nextToken( )

returns the next token from this string tokenizer. It throws a NoSuchElementException if there are no more tokens in this tokenizer's string.

String nextToken(String delim)

returns the next token from this string tokenizer, using delim as the delimiter set. The new delimiter set remains the default after this call. Throws a NoSuchElementException if there are no more tokens in this tokenizer's string.

int countTokens( )

returns the number of tokens remaining in the string, using the current delimiter set.

APPENDIX B

The Collections Library

Java Version 1.2 introduces, among other things, a data-structures library known as the *Collections* API. Future versions of Java will no doubt expand the functionality of the library, and may deprecate some of its features. Even so, it is interesting to examine the library in its 1.2 state, because it illustrates many of the concepts that have been explored in this text. We will also see that even though the data-structures package developed in this text has only basic methods, using it is very similar to using a more robust package, such as the Collections API.

In this appendix, we

- Describe the organization of the Collections API, and its integration with the rest of the language.
- Examine its lists, sets, and maps.
- Provide two Java programs that use the Collections API, including an implementation of the unweighted shortest-path algorithm.
- Reimplement the two Java programs, using the data structures package developed in Chapters 1 to 12.

B.1. Introduction

The Collections API, introduced in Java Version 1.2, contains implementations of some of the data structures that have been described in this text. Specifically, there is a doubly linked list class, with an associated iterator, data structures that make use of red-black trees, and (open addressing) hash tables. As expected, the functionality of these classes is somewhat different from the classes written in this text; however, the basic concepts, algorithms, and running times are the same. In the first version of the API, there is no priority queue data structure and no union/find data structure. There is a binary search algorithm and a quicksort algorithm.

Version 1.2 seems incomplete, especially compared to the STL that accompanies C++. It is likely that future releases will add classes and functionality, perhaps making the API as powerful as the STL. Because the Collections API is part of the Java library, it is likely to undergo extensive testing and optimization, and to survive use by legions of programmers around the world. Thus, in general, it will be preferable to use it, rather than provide an alternate implementation.

B.2. Basic Classes

The Collections API uses inheritance to achieve a large amount of abstraction. Four interfaces are new to Java 1.2: Collection, Iterator, Comparable, and Comparator. Except for Comparable, all are in java.util.

B.2.1. Collection

The Collection interface represents a group of objects, known as its elements. Different implementations of the Collection, however, may place restrictions on the kinds of elements in the interface. For instance, some implementations, such as linked lists, allow duplicates. Others, such as sets, do not. Some implementations may impose an order; others may not. All Collections support the following operations:

boolean contains(Object element)

returns true if this Collection contains element; false otherwise.

boolean isEmpty( )

returns true if this Collection contains no elements; false otherwise.

Iterator iterator( )

returns an Iterator over the elements in this Collection.

int size( )

returns the number of elements in this Collection.

The most interesting of these methods is iterator. The operations that can be performed by an Iterator are described in Section B.2.2.

B.2.2. Iterator

The Iterator interface provides three methods:

boolean hasNext( )

returns true if the iteration has more elements.

Object next( )

returns the next element in the iteration.

void remove( )

removes from the underlying Collection the last element returned by the Iterator.

As an example, the routine in Figure B.1 prints each element in any collection. If the collection is an ordered set, its elements are output in sorted order.

```
// Print the contents of Collection C
static void printCollection( Collection C )
{
    Iterator itr = C.iterator( );
    while( itr.hasNext( ) )
        System.out.println( itr.next( ) );
}
```

Figure B.1 Print the contents of any `Collection`

B.2.3. Comparable

Java 1.2 defines the `Comparable` interface in `java.lang` with a single method:

int compareTo(Object rhs) throws ClassCastException

compares this `Object` with `rhs` for order. Returns negative if this `Object` is less than `rhs`, zero if they are equal, and positive if this `Object` is greater than `rhs`. Throws `ClassCastException` if `rhs` is not comparable to this `Object`.

Objects that implement the `Comparable` interface can be manipulated by sorting and searching algorithms that require order, such as quicksort, the binary search, and red-black trees.

Note that in Java 1.2, `String` and the wrapper classes such as `Integer` all implement the `Comparable` interface. Thus they can be directly inserted into sorted containers.

B.2.4. Comparator

Java 1.2 defines an interface, `Comparator`, also with only a single method:

int compare(Object lhs, Object rhs)

Compares its two arguments for order, using the same rules as `compareTo`.

Collection algorithms that require an ordering property can generally provide an object that implements a `Comparator` interface; the `compare` method of that object will be used to specify an ordering. This is most useful when the natural ordering is not exactly what is needed. For instance, we may want to sort a list of strings, but ignore case distinctions. Or for a simpler example, we may want to sort the strings by their length. An example is shown in Figure B.2.

```
static void sortListOfStringsByLength( List L )
{
    class Comp implements Comparator
    {
        public int compare( Object lhs, Object rhs )
          { return ((String)lhs).length( ) - ((String)rhs).length( ); }
    }

    Collections.sort( L, new Comp( ) );
}
```

Figure B.2 A sorting algorithm using a `Comparator`

This example assumes that `java.util` is imported. It also uses an *inner class* (whose scope is valid only inside the method in which it is declared). The inner class, `Comp`, implements `Comparator`, using a common technique for comparing small-valued integers. An object of type `Comp` is then used to guide the sort. To sort using the normal `String` order, we would call `sort`, with only the `List` as a parameter.

B.3. Lists

A `List` is an ordered `Collection` (also known as a sequence). The user has precise control over where in the `List` each element is inserted. The user can access elements by their position in the `List`, and search for elements in the `List`. The position is specified as an integer index (starting at 0, like arrays). However, since these operations are likely to take time proportional to the index of the position, many of these operations are not practical for large lists. We refer the reader to the JDK documentation for further details on operations that use indices; iterators, previously described, can be used for most of the important list operations.

B.3.1. ArrayList vs. LinkedList

The Collections API provides two `List` implementations: an array-based and a doubly linked list-based version. The array-based version can be appropriate if a maximum capacity is known and insertions are performed only at the high end of the array, for the reasons discussed in Chapter 3. The Collections API efficiently expands the array if an insertion at the high end would exceed capacity, and is likely to be faster than the `LinkedList` in those cases. However, only the `LinkedList` efficiently supports double-ended access. Some of the efficient `LinkedList` methods (in addition to those guaranteed by the `Collection` interface) are:

void addFirst(Object element)

inserts `element` at the beginning of this `List`.

void addLast(Object element)

appends `element` to the end of this `List`.

void clear( )

removes all the elements from this `List`.

Object getFirst( )

returns the first element in this `List`.

Object getLast( )

returns the last element in this `List`.

Object removeFirst( )

returns and removes the first element from this `List`.

`Object removeLast( )`

returns and removes the last element from this `List`.

`ListIterator listIterator( int index )`

returns a `ListIterator` of the elements in this `List` (in proper sequence), starting at the specified position in the list.

B.3.2. Stacks and Queues

Java 1.2 provides a `Stack` class, but not a `Queue` class. However, it should be clear from the previous section, that both classes, as well as a double-ended queue, are directly supported by the `LinkedList` class.

B.3.3. ListIterator

The `ListIterator`, returned by method `listIterator`, is like an iterator, but supports bidirectional traversal. Thus there are methods `hasPrevious` and `previous`.

B.4. Sets

The `Set` extends `Collection`. It allows no duplicates. Two versions are provided: `TreeSet` and `HashSet`. The `TreeSet` uses a red-black tree, while a `HashSet` uses a hash table. In addition to the required `contains`, `iterator`, `size`, and `isEmpty`, both versions provide:

`boolean add( Object element )`

adds `element` to the set if it is not already present. Returns `true` if the set did not already contain `element`; otherwise, returns `false`.

`boolean remove( Object element )`

removes `element` from the set if it is present. Returns `true` if the set contained `element`; otherwise, returns `false`.

Hash tables require a hash function. Each object inherits a `hashCode` method. `Object`s such as `String` and `Integer` already have one defined. If you provide an `equals` method for an `Object`, then you may need to provide a consistent `hashCode`, too.

B.5. Maps

A `Map` is used to store a collection of entries that consists of *keys* and their *values*. The `Map` maps keys to values. Keys must be unique, but several keys can map to the same values. Thus values need not be unique. The `Map` is implemented by `HashMap` and `TreeMap`. The `TreeMap` uses a red-black tree to obtain logarithmic search times.

B.5.1. put, get, remove, and contains

Four methods are used for basic insertion, deletion, and access:

Object get(Object key)

returns the value to which this Map maps key. Returns null if key is not mapped, or if key is mapped to null.

Object put(Object key, Object value)

associates value with the specified key in this Map. Returns the prior mapped value.

Object containsKey(Object key)

returns true if this Map contains a mapping for key; otherwise, returns false.

boolean remove(Object key)

removes the mapping for key from this Map, if present. Returns true, if key was present; otherwise, returns false.

These methods are for the most part self-explanatory. A tricky point is that null is a valid value, so simply testing to see if the result of get is null does not always tell you if a key is in the map. Thus containsKey is provided. Notice, by the way, that a TreeMap can be used to implement a TreeSet by inserting keys with null values. The reverse is also true: a Map can be implemented by a Set, by storing (key, value) pairs in the Set, and by basing equality on only the key portion.

B.5.2. Getting a Collection from the Map

The collection of keys (which must be a set, since duplicate keys are disallowed), values, or (key, value) pairs can all be obtained by method calls shown below. The return values are all collections, and thus an iterator can be obtained from it by calling iterator.

Set keySet( )

returns a Set view of the keys contained in this Map.

Set entries( )

returns a Set view of the mappings contained in this Map.

Collection values( )

returns a Collection view of the values contained in this Map.

B.5.3. Map.Entry Pairs

The entries method returns a Set of Map.Entry pairs. The key and value in a Map.Entry pair is accessed by these two methods:

Object getKey( )

returns the key corresponding to this Map.Entry.

Object getValue( )

returns the value corresponding to this Map.Entry.

B.6. Example: Generating a Concordance

A concordance of a file is a listing that contains all the words in a file, with the line number on which the word occurs. Using the Collections API, we can write a program that produces a concordance. We assume that a word is any sequence of consecutive nonwhitespace characters.

The basic idea is to use a TreeMap, to map words to a linked list of lines on which the word occurs. Thus each key is a word, and its value is a linked list. When we see a word, we check to see if it is already in the map. If it is, then we simply add the current line number to the linked list of lines that corresponds to the word. If it is not, we add to the map the word, along with a linked list containing the current line number. After we have read all the words, we can iterate through the map. This generates the map entries in key-sorted order, so the words will appear in sorted order. For each map entry, we output the word, and then we go through the linked list of line numbers and output them.

B.6.1. Collections API Version

The code that uses the Collections API is shown in Figure B.3. We open a file at line 1 and create a TreeMap at line 2. In the for loop, we repeatedly read one line at a time, maintaining the current line number. The StringTokenizer is used to extract whitespace-delimited tokens from the line (it has the same look and feel as an iterator). At line 7, we have a word. We use get at line 8 to find its linked list of line numbers. If the list is null, we create an empty list and insert the word and its empty list as a pair into the map. At line 13, we add the new line number into the word's list of line numbers. When the first for loop ends, the file has been read, and the map has been built. Lines 14 and 15 then use an iterator to go through the map and print out each map entry.

The printEntry method simply prints the word on one line, and the list of line numbers on the next line. The word is obtained by calling getKey (line 18); the list of line numbers is obtained by calling getValue (line 19). We can print that list by obtaining an iterator (also line 19) and using the standard hasNext, next idiom. The code treats the first line number as a special case (it is not preceded by a comma, but is preceded by a tab); it is otherwise similar to the code in Figure B.1. Note that printEntry assumes that the linked list of line numbers is not empty, which is guaranteed by the rest of the code.

B.6.2. Version Using Package DataStructures

An implementation that uses the DataStructures package is similar to the implementation that uses the Collections API implementation. However, there are three basic differences:

1. The DataStructures package does not have a map. Instead, we must use a search tree containing entries that store a String and a LinkedList, with the String as the key. This entity will be a WordEntry object that implements the DataStructures.Comparable interface.

2. The LinkedList class is singly linked and does not have a built-in method to insert at the end. Thus the WordEntry will need to maintain an iterator that represents the last entry in its linked list.

3. There is no tree iterator (although an exercise asks you to write one). However, there is a printTree method. This requires that the WordEntry object provide a toString method.

```
import java.util.*;
import java.io.*;
class Concordance
{
         // A main routine that reads a file containing strings (from args[0])
         // and prints each string, and the lines on which it occurs.
     public static void main( String [ ] args )
     {
         try
         {
/* 1*/       BufferedReader inFile = new BufferedReader( new FileReader( args[0] ) );
/* 2*/       TreeMap wordMap = new TreeMap( );
/* 3*/       String oneLine;

                 // Read the words; add them to wordMap
/* 4*/       for( int lineNum = 1; (oneLine = inFile.readLine( )) != null; lineNum++ )
             {
/* 5*/           StringTokenizer st = new StringTokenizer( oneLine );
/* 6*/           while( st.hasMoreTokens( ) )
                 {
/* 7*/               String word = st.nextToken( );
/* 8*/               LinkedList lines = (LinkedList) wordMap.get( word );
/* 9*/               if( lines == null )
                     {
/*10*/                   lines = new LinkedList( );
/*11*/                   wordMap.put( word, lines );
/*12*/               }
/*13*/               lines.addLast( new Integer( lineNum ) );
                 }
             }
                 // Go through the word map
/*14*/       for( Iterator itr = wordMap.entries( ).iterator( ); itr.hasNext( ); )
/*15*/           printEntry( (Map.Entry) itr.next( ) );
         }
/*16*/   catch( Exception e )
/*17*/     { System.err.println( e ); }
     }

     public static void printEntry( Map.Entry entry )
     {
             // Print the word
/*18*/   System.out.println( entry.getKey( ) + ":" );

             // Now print the line numbers
/*19*/   Iterator itr = ( (LinkedList)(entry.getValue( )) ).iterator( );
/*20*/   System.out.print( "\t" + itr.next( ) );
/*21*/   while( itr.hasNext( ) )
/*22*/       System.out.print( ", " + itr.next( ) );
/*23*/   System.out.println( );
     }
}
```

Figure B.3 Concordance program using the Collections API

```java
import java.util.*;
import java.io.*;
import DataStructures.*;
import DataStructures.Comparable;
import DataStructures.LinkedList;

class WordEntry implements Comparable
{
    String        word;
    LinkedList    lines;
    LinkedListItr listEnd;

    public int compareTo( Comparable rhs )
      { return word.compareTo( ((WordEntry)rhs).word ); }

    public String toString( )
    {
        StringBuffer theString = new StringBuffer( );

            // Print the word
        theString.append( word + ":" );

            // Now print the line numbers
        if( lines != null && !lines.isEmpty( ) )
        {
            LinkedListItr itr = lines.first( );
            theString.append( "\t" + itr.retrieve( ) );
            for( itr.advance( ); !itr.isPastEnd( ); itr.advance( ) )
                theString.append( ", " + itr.retrieve( ) );
        }
        return new String( theString );
    }
}
```

Figure B.4 Concordance program using the `DataStructures` package (Part I)

The revised code is shown in two parts. First, Figure B.4 shows the `import` directives and the `WordEntry` class. `LinkedList` and `Comparable` are fully qualified to avoid ambiguity with identically named classes in the Collections API. As explained above, `WordEntry` contains three data members: the word, the list of lines, and an iterator representing the last position in the list of lines. The `compareTo` method simply calls the `compareTo` method on the word components. The `toString` method uses logic that is similar to what was done in `printEntry` (in Figure B.3): it gets the word and uses an iterator to obtain line numbers. Instead of printing these, it forms a `String` that can itself be printed.

The technical issue is that, although string concatenation can be performed with +, each + creates a new string. Thus each concatenation would take time proportional to the length of the resulting string, rather than time proportional to the number of characters added. For the case of repeated concatenations, in which P line numbers are concatenated, the result is that it would take $O(P^2)$ time to perform the P concatenations. Although P is unlikely to be large enough for this to be a problem, it is still best to be safe. Thus, a

```
class Concordance
{
        // A main routine that reads a file containing strings (from args[0])
        // and prints each string, and the lines on which it occurs.
        public static void main( String [ ] args )
        {
            try
            {
/* 0*/          WordEntry entry = new WordEntry( );
/* 1*/          BufferedReader inFile = new BufferedReader( new FileReader( args[0] ) );
/* 2*/          AvlTree wordMap = new AvlTree( );
/* 3*/          String oneLine;

                // Read the words; add them to wordMap
/* 4*/          for( int lineNum = 1; (oneLine = inFile.readLine( )) != null; lineNum++ )
                {
/* 5*/              StringTokenizer st = new StringTokenizer( oneLine );
/* 6*/              while( st.hasMoreTokens( ) )
                    {
/* 7*/                  entry.word = st.nextToken( );
/* 8*/                  WordEntry match = (WordEntry) wordMap.find( entry );
/* 9*/                  if( match == null )
                        {
/*10*/                      match = new WordEntry( );
/*11*/                      match.word = entry.word;
/*12*/                      match.lines = new LinkedList( );
/*13*/                      match.listEnd = match.lines.zeroth( );
/*14*/                      wordMap.insert( match );
                        }
/*15*/                  match.lines.insert( new Integer( lineNum ), match.listEnd );
/*16*/                  match.listEnd.advance( );
                    }
                }
/*17*/          wordMap.printTree( );
            }
            catch( Exception e )
              { System.err.println( "Error: " + e ); }
        }
}
```

Figure B.5 Concordance program using the DataStructures package (Part II)

StringBuffer is used, and its final result is used to form a String object, resulting in $O(P)$ performance.

     The main routine is shown in Figure B.5 and is similar to the main routine in Figure B.3. In the new version, entry is a WordEntry object that is used in the search (it is constructed once in the algorithm for performance reasons). To perform a lookup of the word in the word map, we set entry.word to be the search String, and perform a find. The result of the find is match, and will represent the matched WordEntry object. If match is null, this is a new word. In that case, we construct a new WordEntry object, insert it into the word map, and use it as `match`. Thus when we reach line 15, we simply add the current line number to the end of the list of lines for the matched `WordEntry` object, and then update the iterator that denotes the last position in the list.

B.7. Example: Shortest-Path Calculation

As a second example, we provide implementations of the unweighted shortest-path algorithm. We do not provide a main program (you can find one in the online code). We do provide all the class methods that are needed to write a `main` routine: methods to add edges to a graph, compute a shortest path, and print out a shortest path. The vertices are expressed externally as `String` types, but mapped internally to a `Vertex` (using a `HashMap` in the `Collections` implementation and a `QuadraticProbingHashTable` in the `DataStructures` package implementation).

Our code follows the pseudocode of Chapter 9 almost verbatim. The fact that the pseudocode is so similar to the Java code, while avoiding Java language details, justifies the use of pseudocode in that chapter, and also illustrates the power and convenience of prepackaged data structures.

For starters, the `Vertex` class, shown in Figure B.6, is almost identical to the pseudocode in Figure 9.29. The only difference is that we provide a constructor and a method to initialize the `dist` and `path` fields. The `LinkedList` implementation that is used is determined by the import directives, since both the Collections API and our `DataStructures` package define a `LinkedList` class.

B.7.1. Collections API Implementation

Figure B.7 is the `Graph` class. We provide three public methods. `addEdge` inserts a new edge into the graph. `unweighted` and `printPath` are identical to the pseudocode routines in Chapter 9. As mentioned earlier, a `HashMap` converts a `String` to a `Vertex`. We provide a private method that returns the `Vertex` that corresponds to a `String` (creating a new `Vertex` if needed). `printPath` and `clearAll` are similar to routines already seen in Chapter 9.

We can now look at the implementations of these methods. We begin by examining the new methods: those that deal with `String`s. `getVertex` is shown in Figure B.8. We consult the map to get the `Vertex` entry. If the `Vertex` does not exist, we create a new `Vertex` and update the map. `addEdge`, shown in Figure B.9, is almost trivial. We get the corresponding `Vertex` entries and then update an adjacency list. Also shown in Figure B.9 is the public `printPath`. We get the destination `Vertex`, verify that it exists and is reachable, and then call the recursive routine.

Prior to running the shortest-path calculation, we must reset the distances to infinity and clear the `path` entries (it is not enough to do this once; we must do it before each new calculation). This is the equivalent of the pseudocode in Figure 9.30. To do this, we must call the `reset` method for each `Vertex`. Figure B.10 shows how we do this: we use `values` to get the collection of `Vertex` entries from the map. Once we have the collection, we simply iterate over it in the usual style.

The `printPath` method is shown in Figure B.11. It is identical to the pseudocode in Figure 9.31.

```
class Vertex
{
    String      name;   // Vertex name
    LinkedList  adj;    // Adjacent vertices
    int         dist;   // Cost
    Vertex      path;   // Previous vertex on shortest path

    public Vertex( String nm )
      { name = nm; adj = new LinkedList( ); reset( ); }
    public void reset( )
      { dist = Graph.INFINITY; path = null; }
}
```

Figure B.6 The Vertex class (equivalent to Fig. 9.29)

```
public class Graph
{
    public static final int INFINITY = Integer.MAX_VALUE;

    public void addEdge( String sourceName, String destName )
      { /* Implementation in Figure B.9 */ }
    public void printPath( String destName ) throws NoSuchElementException
      { /* Implementation in Figure B.9 */ }
    public void unweighted( String startName ) throws NoSuchElementException
      { /* Implementation in Figure B.12 */ }

    private HashMap vertexMap = new HashMap( ); // Maps vertices to internal Vertex

    private Vertex getVertex( String vertexName )
      { /* Implementation in Figure B.8 */ }
    private void clearAll( )
      { /* Implementation in Figure B.10 */ }
    private void printPath( Vertex dest )
      { /* Implementation in Figure B.11 */ }
}
```

Figure B.7 Skeleton for Graph class (Collections API implementation)

```
    // If vertexName is not present, add it to vertexMap
    // In either case, return the Vertex
    private Vertex getVertex( String vertexName )
    {
        Vertex v = (Vertex) vertexMap.get( vertexName );
        if( v == null )
        {
            v = new Vertex( vertexName );
            vertexMap.put( vertexName, v );
        }
        return v;
    }
```

Figure B.8 Consult vertexMap to get reference to a Vertex (Collections API implementation)

```java
public void addEdge( String sourceName, String destName )
{
    Vertex v = getVertex( sourceName );
    Vertex w = getVertex( destName );
    v.adj.add( w );
}

public void printPath( String destName ) throws NoSuchElementException
{
    Vertex w = (Vertex) vertexMap.get( destName );
    if( w == null )
        throw new NoSuchElementException( "Destination vertex not found" );
    else if( w.dist == INFINITY )
        System.out.println( destName + " is unreachable" );
    else
    {
        printPath( w );
        System.out.println( );
    }
}
```

Figure B.9 Public methods to add a new edge and print a path (Collections API implementation); printPath calls a private recursive routine

```java
private void clearAll( )
{
    for( Iterator itr = vertexMap.values( ).iterator( ); itr.hasNext( ); )
        ( (Vertex)itr.next( ) ).reset( );
}
```

Figure B.10 Initialize distances (Collections API implementation, equivalent to Fig. 9.30)

```java
private void printPath( Vertex dest )
{
    if( dest.path != null )
    {
        printPath( dest.path );
        System.out.print( " to " );
    }
    System.out.print( dest.name );
}
```

Figure B.11 Routine to print actual shortest path (Collections API implementation, equivalent to Fig. 9.31)

Last, but not least, is the **unweighted** method shown in Figure B.12. This code is based on the pseudocode in Figure 9.18. Notice that we use a **LinkedList**, with **removeFirst** and **addLast**, to implement the queue. As mentioned earlier, an **ArrayList** would not have acceptable performance. The code itself illustrates little that is new. The iteration uses the same technique that we have already seen repeatedly.

```
public void unweighted( String startName ) throws NoSuchElementException
{
    clearAll( );
    Vertex start = (Vertex) vertexMap.get( startName );
    if( start == null )
        throw new NoSuchElementException( "Start vertex not found" );

    LinkedList q = new LinkedList( );
    q.addLast( start ); start.dist = 0;

    while( !q.isEmpty( ) )
    {
        Vertex v = (Vertex) q.removeFirst( );

        for( Iterator itr = v.adj.iterator( ); itr.hasNext( ); )
        {
            Vertex w = (Vertex) itr.next( );
            if( w.dist == INFINITY )
            {
                w.dist = v.dist + 1;
                w.path = v;
                q.addLast( w );
            }
        }
    }
}
```

Figure B.12 Unweighted shortest-path calculation (Collections API implementation, equivalent to Fig. 9.18)

B.7.2. Version Using Package DataStructures

The implementation using the **DataStructures** package is similar, but requires more work because the Collections API has more built-in functionality. The required changes include:

1. Once again, because there is no map in our package, we need to use a hash table class instead of a **HashMap**. This means that the hash table will store **MapEntry** objects consisting of the vertex name (as a **String**) and the **Vertex** it maps to. The hash table will use the vertex name as the key.

2. The **HashMap** in the Collections API returns a collection of **Vertex** objects that can be used by the **clearAll** method. When using the **DataStructures** package, we will need to maintain the collection of **Vertex** objects ourselves. The easiest way to do this is to use a **LinkedList**.

3. The unweighted shortest-path algorithm will use a queue; since the queue class in the **DataStructures** package requires the specification of a capacity, we keep track of how many vertices are in the graph. (The exercises in Chapter 3 suggested writing both a linked-list version and an array-doubling version of the queue. With either of those implementations, or if the hash table class provided a method to determine the number of items it stores, we would not need to maintain the vertex count.)

```
class MapEntry implements Hashable
{
    String vertexName;
    Vertex storedVertex;

    public MapEntry( String name )
      { vertexName = new String( name ); storedVertex = null; }
    public int hash( int tableSize )
      { return QuadraticProbingHashTable.hash( vertexName, tableSize ); }
    public boolean equals( Object rhs )
      { return rhs instanceof MapEntry &&
              vertexName.equals( ((MapEntry)rhs).vertexName ); }
}
```

Figure B.13 MapEntry class that is used to store map pairs in the hash table for the DataStructures implementation of Graph

Figure B.13 shows the `MapEntry` class. It contains a constructor, a hash function, and an `equals` method. Both the hash function and `equals` method use the `vertexName` field as the key.

The skeleton for the `Graph` class is shown in Figure B.14. The only differences between it and the skeleton that uses the Collections API implementation are that a hash table is used instead of a map, and a list and count of the `Vertex` entries are maintained. Of the six methods, all but the private `printPath` need to be rewritten.

```
class Graph
{
    public static final int INFINITY = Integer.MAX_VALUE;

    public void addEdge( String sourceName, String destName )
      { /* Implementation in Figure B.16 */ }
    public void printPath( String destName ) throws NoSuchElementException
      { /* Implementation in Figure B.16 */ }
    public void unweighted( String startName ) throws NoSuchElementException
      { /* Implementation in Figure B.18 */ }

    private Vertex getVertex( String vertexName )
      { /* Implementation in Figure B.15 */ }
    private void printPath( Vertex dest )
      { /* Implementation in Figure B.11 */ }
    private void clearAll( )
      { /* Implementation in Figure B.17 */ }

    private QuadraticProbingHashTable vertexMap =
        new QuadraticProbingHashTable( );     // Maps vertices to internal Vertex

    private LinkedList allVertices = new LinkedList( );  // List of vertices
    private int numVertices = 0;
}
```

Figure B.14 Skeleton for Graph class (DataStructures implementation)

```
        // If vertexName is not present, add it to vertexMap.
        // In either case, return the Vertex.
        // entry is made global to avoid repeated calls to new.
    MapEntry entry = new MapEntry( "" );
    private Vertex getVertex( String vertexName )
    {
        entry.vertexName = vertexName;
        MapEntry match = (MapEntry) vertexMap.find( entry );
        if( match == null )
        {
            match = new MapEntry( vertexName );
            match.storedVertex = new Vertex( vertexName );
            vertexMap.insert( match );
            allVertices.insert( match.storedVertex, allVertices.zeroth( ) );
            numVertices++;
        }
        return match.storedVertex;
    }
```

Figure B.15 Consult `vertexMap` to get reference to a `Vertex` (`DataStructures` implementation)

getVertex, shown in Figure B.15, uses the same technique seen in Section B.6.2. We maintain an **entry** object, fill in its key, and consult the hash table to obtain a MapEntry match. In the case of the graph application, if **match** is **null**, we have a new vertex that must be added to the hash table. We also have the additional two lines of code that inserts the Vertex into the linked list, allVertices, and then increments numVertices.

```
    public void addEdge( String sourceName, String destName )
    {
        Vertex v = getVertex( sourceName );
        Vertex w = getVertex( destName );
        v.adj.insert( w, v.adj.zeroth( ) );
    }


    public void printPath( String destName ) throws NoSuchElementException
    {
        MapEntry match = (MapEntry) vertexMap.find( new MapEntry( destName ) );
        if( match == null )
            throw new NoSuchElementException( "Destination vertex not found" );
        Vertex w = match.storedVertex;
        if( w.dist == INFINITY )
            System.out.println( destName + " is unreachable" );
        else
        {
            printPath( w );
            System.out.println( );
        }
    }
```

Figure B.16 Public methods to add a new edge and print a path (`DataStructures` implementation); `printPath` calls private recursive routine

Figure B.16 shows **addEdge** and the public **printPath**; these are virtually identical to the implementations in Figure B.9 that use the Collections API. Here, however, **addEdge** inserts w at the front of v's adjacency list, instead of at the end.

In Figure B.17, we see that **clearAll** uses a simple iteration to apply the **reset** method to each **Vertex**. The shortest-path calculation, shown in Figure B.18, closely mirrors both the pseudocode in Chapter 9 and the Collections API implementation in Figure B.12.

```java
private void clearAll( )
{
    LinkedListItr itr = allVertices.first( );
    for( ; !itr.isPastEnd( ); itr.advance( ) )
        ( (Vertex)itr.retrieve( ) ).reset( );
}
```

Figure B.17 Initialize distances (**DataStructures** implementation, equivalent to Fig. 9.30)

```java
public void unweighted( String startName ) throws NoSuchElementException
{
    clearAll( );
    MapEntry match = (MapEntry) vertexMap.find( new MapEntry( startName ) );
    if( match == null )
        throw new NoSuchElementException( "Start vertex not found" );
    Vertex start = match.storedVertex;

    try
    {
        QueueAr q = new QueueAr( numVertices );
        q.enqueue( start ); start.dist = 0;

        while( !q.isEmpty( ) )
        {
            Vertex v = (Vertex) q.dequeue( );

            LinkedListItr itr = v.adj.first( );
            for( ; !itr.isPastEnd( ); itr.advance( ) )
            {
                Vertex w = (Vertex) itr.retrieve( );
                if( w.dist == INFINITY )
                {
                    w.dist = v.dist + 1;
                    w.path = v;
                    q.enqueue( w );
                }
            }
        }
    }
    catch( Overflow e )
      { System.out.println( "Queue capacity exceeded unexpectedly!" ); }
}
```

Figure B.18 Unweighted shortest-path calculation (**DataStructures** implementation, equivalent to Fig. 9.18)

B.8. Priority Queues

There is no priority queue in the Collections API. It seems that a priority queue could be implemented by using a **TreeSet**. However, the **Set** cannot contain duplicates, so we would need to have the **TreeSet** store, for each key, a list of values that have that key, using the **keySet** method to maintain a reference to the underlying **Set**. This complicates things enough to suggest that a priority queue ought to appear in a future release.

Summary

The Collections API is a work-in-progress. Even in its current state, it can still be very useful for many applications. We have discussed only the bare-bones basics. The JDK documentation has all the details and technicalities.

A

α-β pruning, 413–415, 424
AA-trees, 474–481
Abramson, B., 424
Abstract data types (ADTS):
  defined, 55–56
  disjoint set, 269–287
  hash table, 155–177
  list, 56–75
  polynomial, 64–66
  queue, 88–94
  stack, 75–88
Ackerman function, 279
Activation record, 87
Acyclic graph, 292, 294–297, 311–314, 319
Adelson-Velskii, G. M., 152
Adjacency list, 293–294
Adjacency matrix, 292–293
Aggarwal, A., 424
Aho, A. V., 54, 152, 289, 350
Ahuja, R. K., 350
Albertson, M. O., 27
Algorithm analysis, 29–49
  amortized analysis, 273–279, 429–450
  average-case analysis, 116–118, 249–250
  basic rules, 32–34
  empirical confirmation, 48
  logarithmic running times, 43–47
  lower bound proofs, 48, 227–228,
    252–254
  recursive procedures, 37–43, 237–240,
    246–250, 371–373
Algorithm design:
  approximation algorithms 339–340, 341,
    362–370
  backtracking algorithms, 403–415
  divide-and-conquer strategy, 39, 43, 237,
    370–384
  dynamic programming, 384–394
  greedy algorithms, 304, 353–370
  randomized algorithms, 395–403

Alias test, 22
Allen, B., 152
Alon, N., 424
Amortized analysis, 130–138, 279–285,
    429–450
  binomial queue, 430–435
  disjoint set algorithm, 279–285
  Fibonacci heap, 437–446
  lazy binomial queue, 440
  potential function, 430–435
  skew heap, 435–437
  splay tree, 446–449
Andersson, A., 496
Approximation algorithm:
  bin packing, 341, 362–370
  traveling salesman problem, 340–341
Aragon, C., 496
Array implementation:
  of lists, 56–57
  of queues, 89–92
  of stacks, 78–81
ArrayList, 516–517
Articulation point, 322–326
Atkinson, M. D., 223
auf der Heide, F. Meyer, 181
AVL tree, 118–130, 453, 492
  deletion, 130
  double rotation, 120, 123–130
  insertion, 119, 124–127
  properties, 118–119
  single rotation, 120–123, 129

B

B-tree, 139–144, 174–176
B*-tree, 149
Backtracking algorithms, 403–415
  games, 409–415
    α-β pruning, 413–415, 424
    minimax algorithm, 409–412
  principles of, 403
  turnpike reconstruction, 405–409

Baer, J. L., 496

Baeza-Yates, R. A., 152, 153, 181, 266

Balance condition, 118

Banachowski, L., 289

Baseball card collector problem, 349

Bavel, Z., 27

Bayer, R., 152, 496

Bell, T., 182, 425

Bellman, R. E., 350, 425

Bentley, J. L., 54, 152, 266, 425, 496

Bhaskar, S., 425

Biconnectivity, 327–334

Big-Oh notation, 29–32, 35

Big-Omega notation, 29–32

Bin packing, 341, 362–370
  best fit, 366
  best fit decreasing, 366
  first fit, 365–366
  first fit decreasing, 367
  lower bound for on-line algorithms, 363–364
  next fit, 364–365

Binary heap, 184–195
  `deleteMin` operation, 189–191, 192
  heap order, 186–187
  insertion, 188–189
  miscellaneous operations, 192–195
  structure, 185–186

Binary search, 43–45

Binary search tree, 99, 109–118
  average running time, 116–118
  basic operations, 109–116
  deletion, 113–116
  vs. hash table, 177
  k-d tree, 483–486, 492, 495
  optimal, 389–393
  (*see also* Search trees)

Binary tree, 105–108
  Huffman code, 357–362

Binomial queue, 208–215
  amortized analysis of, 430–435
  `deleteMin` operation, 212, 215
  implementation of, 212–215
  insertion, 212–215
  lazy merging, 438, 440–443
  merging, 208–213, 213, 209, 431
  miscellaneous operations, 215
  structure, 208

Binomial tree, 208, 213, 430–431

Bipartite graph, 343

Bitner, J. R., 152

Bloom, G. S., 425

Blum, M., 425

Blum, N., 289

Bollobás, B., 289

Borodin, A., 425

Boruvka, O., 350

Boyer, R. S., 181

Breadth-first search, 299–304

Bright, J. D., 223

Brodal, G. S., 223

Brown, D. J., 426

Brown, M. R., 223, 452

Brualdi, R. A., 27

Bucket sort, 66, 254–255

`BufferedReader`, 506–507

`BufferedWriter`, 507

C

Carlsson, S., 223

Carmichael numbers, 402

Carter, J. L., 181

Cartesian tree, 495

Catalan numbers, 388

Chang, H., 496

Chang, L., 424

Chang, S. C., 223

Chanzy, P., 496

Chen, J., 223

Cheriton, D., 223, 350

Cheriyan, J., 350

Chess (*see* Backtracking algorithm, games)

Christofides, N., 425

`Character`, 499–500

Classes in Package:
  `java.io`, 506–510
  `java.lang`, 499–506
  `java.util`, 510–512

Cleary, J. G., 425

Clique, 337, 348

Closest points, 373–377, 420

Clustering, 162–171
  primary, 163
  secondary, 166

Code organization, 24–25

Coin changing problem, 304, 353–354, 421–422
Collections Library, 513–530
  Basic classes, 514–516
  examples, 519–529
  lists, 516–517
  maps, 517–518
  sets, 517
Collision resolution, 162–169
Coloring, 341
Comer, D., 152
Comparable, 515
Comparator, 515–516
Compression (*see* File compression)
Computational geometry, 369, 371–373, 405–409
  closest points, 373–377, 419
  convex hull, 420
  k-d tree, 483–486, 492, 495
  turnpike reconstruction, 405–409
  Voronoi diagram, 420
Concordance creation, 519–523
Connectivity, 269 329–331
Constructors, 11
Convex hull, 420
Cook, S., 350
Cook's theorem, 341
Coppersmith, D., 425
Cornell, G., 27
Crane, C. A., 223
Critical path analysis, 311–314
Cryptography, 48–49, 402–403
Culberson, J., 152
Culik, K., 152
Cursor implementation, 69–75

D
d-heap, 198, 342, 437
Day, A. C., 496
Deap, 223
Decision tree, 252–254
Demers, A., 425
Dense graph, 293
Deo, N., 350
Depth-first search, 325–337
  directed graph, 334–336
  undirected graph, 326–327
Deque, 97, 451

Dereference, 78
Deterministic skip lists; 468–473
Dietzfelbinger, M., 181
Digraphs, 291
  (*see also* Directed graphs)
Dijkstra, E. W., 27, 350
Dijkstra's algorithm, 304–310, 320, 437
Diminishing increment sort, 228
  (*see also* Shellsort)
Ding, Y., 223, 496
Dinic, E. A., 350
Directed acyclic graph (DAG), 292
Directed graph, 291, 334–336
Disjoint sets, 48, 269–287, 323–325
  analysis, 279–285
  deunion operation, 288
  dynamic equivalence problem, 270–271
  equivalence relations, 269
  Kruskal's algorithm, 323–325
  quick find algorithms, 270–271
  quick union algorithms, 270–278
    implementation of basic algorithm, 271–274
    path compression, 276–278, 285
    path halving, 281
    union heuristics, 273–279
Divide and conquer, 370–384
  analysis of general case, 371–373
  closest points, 373–377
  integers, multiplication of, 380–382
  matrix multiplication, 382–384
  maximum subsequence sum, 33, 37–43
  mergesort, 235–240
  principles of, 370–371
  quicksort, 240–252
  selection, 377–380
Double-ended queue (*see* Deque)
Doyle, J., 289
Dreyfus, S. E., 425
Driscoll, J. R., 223
Du, H. C., 181
Due, M. W., 223
Dynamic equivalence problem, 270–271
Dynamic programming, 384–394
  all-pairs shortest path, 393–394
  chained matrix multiplication, 387–389
  optimal binary search tree, 389–393
  principles of, 384–387

E

Edelsbrunner, H., 425
Edmonds, J., 350
Efficiency considerations, 24–25
Eight queens problem, 422
Eisenbath, B., 152
Enbody, R. J., 181
Eppinger, J. L., 153
Eppstein, D., 425
Equivalence class, 270–271
Equivalence problem, 270–271
Equivalence relations, 269
Eriksson, P., 224
Euclid's algorithm, 45
Euler circuit, 331–334, 337, 345
Euler's constant, 5
Even, S., 350
Event simulation, 94, 196–197
Exceptions, 16–19
   checked, 17
   standard, 17
Exponentiation, 46–47
Exponents, formulas for, 2
Expression tree, 106–108
Extendible hashing, 174–176
   performance of, 176
External sorting, 255–260, 266
   multiway merge, 257–258
   polyphase merge, 254
   replacement selection, 259–260
   run construction, 256–257, 259–260
   simple merging, 256–257

F

Fagin, R., 181
Fermat's lesser theorem, 402
Fibonacci heap, 437–445
   amortized analysis of, 441–443
   basic operations, 443–444
   cascading cut, 443
   Dijkstra's algorithm, 310
   marking nodes, 438–440
Fibonacci numbers, 444
   bad use of recursion, 37, 385
   kth order, 258
   polyphase merge, 258
   properties of, 5, 10, 444

`File`, 507–508
File compression, 357–362
`FileReader`, 508
`FileWriter`, 508–509
File system, 89–92
Fischer, M. J., 289, 290, 427
Flajolet, P., 153, 181, 496
Flamig, B., 496
Flanagan, D., 27
Floyd, R. W., 223, 266, 425
Ford, L. R., 266, 350
Fredman, M. L., 181, 223, 289, 350, 425, 452, 496
Fulkerson, D. R., 350
Fuller, S. H., 153

G

Gabow, H. N., 223, 289, 350
Gajewska, H., 452
Galil, Z., 350, 424, 425
Galler, B. A., 290
Game tree, 413
Garey, M. R., 350, 425
GCD (*see* Euclid's algorithm)
Giancarlo, R., 425
Godbole, S., 425
Goldberg, A. V., 350
Golin, M., 266
Gonnet, G. H., 152, 153, 181, 223, 266
Gosling, J., 28
Graham, R. L., 28, 425
Graph, 291–341
   acyclic, 292, 294–297, 319
      test for, 296, 335
   biconnectivity, 327–331
   bipartite, 343
   breadth-first search, 299–304
   clique, 341, 348
   colorability, 341
   complete, 292
   cycle, 291–292
      negative cost, 297
   definitions, 291–292
   dense, 293
   depth-first search, 325–337
   directed, 334–336
   Euler circuit, 331–334

Hamiltonian cycle, 334, 339
isomorphism, 150
longest path, 339, 341
matching, 343
minimum spanning tree, 319–325
multigraph, 346
planar, 345–346
representation, 292–294
shortest path, 297–314, 319, 393–394
    acyclic graph, 311–314
    all-pairs, 314, 393–394
    negative edge costs, 310
    single source unweighted, 297–304
    single source weighted, 304–310
sparse, 293, 296, 309
strong components, 336–337
topological sort, 294–297
traveling salesman, 340, 419
vertex cover, 349
Greedy algorithms, 353–370
    approximate bin packing, 362–370
    coin changing, 353–354
    Huffman codes, 357–362
    minimum spanning tree, 319–325
    processor scheduling, 354–357
    shortest path, 304–310
Gries, D., 28
Growth rate:
    exponential, 37
    of functions, 30–32
Gudes, E., 153
Guibas, L. J., 153, 182, 496
Gupta, R., 425

H

Hagerup, T., 350
Haken, D., 425
Halting problem, 338
Hamiltonian cycle, 334, 340
Harary, F., 350
Harries, R., 182
Hash table (*see* Hashing)
Hasham, A., 223
Hashing, 155–177
    binary search tree, compared to, 177
    closed (open addressing), 162–171
        analysis of, 162–164

clustering, 162–171
    deletion, 166
collision resolution, 162–169
double, 170–171
extendible, 174–176
hash function, 155, 156–158
linear probing, 162–164
load factor, 162
open (separate chaining), 158–162, 176
quadratic probing, 164–166
random collision resolution, 163
rehashing, 171–174, 451
table size, 155, 176–179, 401–402
Heap (*see* Priority queue)
Heap order property, 186–187
Heapsort, 196, 232–235, 260–261, 265
Hibbard, T. H., 153, 266
Hirschberg, D. S., 426
Hoare, C. A. R., 266
Hoey, D., 426
Hopcroft, J. E., 54, 152, 289, 290, 350, 351
Horner's rule, 51
Horstmann, C. S., 27
Horvath, E. C., 266
Hu, T. C., 425
Huang, B., 266
Huffman, D. A., 425
Huffman codes, 357–362
Hutchinson, J. P., 27

I

Incerpi, J., 266
Infix expression, 84
Infix to postfix conversion, 84–86
Information hiding, 11
Inline optimizations, 25
Inorder traversal, 106, 138
Input and output, 19–23
InputStreamReader, 509
Insertion sort, 226–227
    analysis, 226–227
    implementation, 226
Integer, 500-501
Integers, multiplication of, 380–382
Interface, 14
Inversion, 227–228
Iterator, 514–515

Iterator class, 60
Iyengar, S. S., 496

J

Janson, S. 266
Johnson, D. B., 224, 351
Johnson, D. S., 350, 425
Johnson, S. M., 266
Jonassen, A. T., 153
Jones, D. W., 496
Josephus problem, 96
Joy, B., 28

K

k-d heaps, 494
k-d tree, 483–486
Kaas, R., 224
Kaehler, E. B., 153
Kahn, A. B., 351
Karatsuba, A., 425
Karger, D. R., 351, 425
Karlin, A. R., 181
Karlton, P. L., 153
Karp, R. M., 182, 290, 350, 351
Karzanov, A. V., 351
Kernighan, B. W., 28, 351
Khoong, C. M., 224, 452
King, V., 351
Klein, P. N., 351
Knapsack problem, 341, 421
Knight's tour, 422
Knuth, D. E., 28, 54, 153, 182, 224, 266,
    290, 351, 425, 426
Komlos, J., 181
Korsh, J., 425
Kruskal, J. B., Jr., 351
Kruskal's algorithm, 323–325
    (*see also* Greedy algorithms)
Kuhn, H. W., 351

L

Ladner, R. E., 224
LaMarca, a., 224
Landau, G. M., 426
Landis, E. M., 152
Langston, M., 266
LaPoutre, J. A., 290

Larmore, L. L., 426
Lawler, E. L., 351
Lazy binomial queue, 440–443
Lazy deletion
    AVL tree, 130
    binary search trees, 113–116
    closed hash table, 162
    leftist heap, 220
    linked lists, 87
Lazy merging, 438, 440–443
Lee, C. C., 426
Lee, D. T., 426, 496
Lee, K., 426
Leftist heap, 198–206, 438–440
    cutting nodes, 438–440
    deleteMin operation, 202
    implementation of, 198–200
    insertion, 202
    merging, 198–200
    structure, 198
Lehmer, D., 396
Lelewer, D. A., 426
Lemke, P., 426
Lempel, A., 427
Leong, H. W., 224, 452
Level-order traversal, 139
Lewis, J., 28
Lewis, T. G., 182
Liang, F. M., 426
Lin, S., 351
Line printer queue, 92
Linear congruential generator,
    396–399
Linear function, 31
Linear probing, 162–164
Linked list, 57, 213, 399–402, 516–517
    adjacency, 293
    circularly linked list, 63
    cursor implementation, 69–74
    doubly linked list, 63
    header cell, 58–63
    implementation of, 64–69
    multilist, 68–69
    for polynomial arithmetic, 64–66
    skip list, 399–402
    stack, implementation of, 76–81
List, 516

Lists:
    array implementation, 56–57
    (*see also* Linked list)
List Iterator, 517
Load factor, 162
Loftus, W., 28
Logarithms:
    formulas for, 3
    in running time, 43–47
Longest common subsequence problem, 421
Longest increasing subsequence problem, 421
Lower bound:
    information theoretic, 254
    on-line bin packing, 363–364
    proof, 228, 252–254
    sorting, 228–229, 252–254
Lueker, G., 182

M
Mahajan, S, 426
Majority problem, 52–53
Manacher, G. K., 266
Maps, 517–518
Margalit, O., 426
Martin, W. A., 498
Matrix multiplication:
    chained, 387–389
    Strassen's algorithm, 382–384
Maurer, W. D., 182
Maximum subsequence sum problem, 33, 37–43, 54
Mazes, 285–286, 347
McCreight, E. M., 152, 496
McDiarmid, C. J. H., 224
McElroy, M. D., 266
McKenzie, B. J., 182
Median of three partitioning, 242–243, 251
Melhorn, K., 152, 153, 181, 350, 351
Merge/find algorithm (*see* Disjoint sets)
Mergesort, 235–240
    analysis, 237–240
    implementation, 237
    merging, 235–240
Merging:
    binomial queues, 208–213, 213, 430–435
    lazy, 438, 440–443

multiway, 257–258
polyphase, 258
skew heaps, 435
Method calls, 13
Miller, G. L., 426
Miller, K. W., 426
Minimax algorithm, 409–412
Minimum spanning tree, 319–325, 419
Modular arithmetic, 5, 164–166, 403, 404, 405–406
Moffat, A., 452
Molodowitch, M., 182
Monier, L., 426
Moore, J. S., 181
Moore, R. W., 426
Moret, B. M. E., 351, 496
Morris, J. H., 182
Motwani, R., 426
Mulmuley, K., 426
Multigraph, 346
Multilists, 68–69
Multiway merge, 257–258
Munro, J. I., 152, 223, 425, 496, 497
Musser, D. R., 266

N
Negative cost cycles, 297
Ness, D. N., 496
Network flow, 314–319
Next fit, 364–365
Nievergelt, J., 153, 181, 497
Nondeterminism, 339
Nonpreemptive scheduling, 354–357
NP problems, 339–340
NP-completeness, 338–341, 349

O
object, 501–502
Object creation, 13
Odlyzko, A., 153
Off-line algorithms, 270, 366–370
Ofman, Y., 425
One-dimensional circle packing problem, 419
On-line algorithms:
    bin packing, 362–370
    disjoint sets algorithm, 269–287
    graph connectivity, 269

On-line algorithms (*continued*)
  maximum subsequence sum problem, 33, 37–43, 54
  symbol balancing, 81
Optimal binary search tree, 389–393
Orlin, J. B., 350
O'Rourke, J., 426
Ottman, T., 152
Overmars, M. H., 290, 497

P

Packages, 24
Package friendly, 58–60
Pairing heaps, 486–491
Pan, V., 426
Papadakis, T., 497
Papadimitriou, C. H., 351
Papernov, A. A., 266
Paragraphing problem, 420–421
Park, S. K., 426
Parse tree, 144
Patashnik, O., 28
Path compression, 276–278
Path halving, 289
Pattern matching, 179, 421
Perlis, A. J., 153
Peterson, W. W., 182
Pippenger, N., 181
Planar graph, 345–346
Plauger, P. J., 28
Plaxton, C. G., 266
Poblete, P. V., 223
Polynomial ADT, 64–66
Polyphase merge, 258
Poonen, B., 266
Port, G., 452
Positive-cost cycles, 312
Postfix expression, 81–84
  evaluation of, 84
Postorder traversal, 102, 104, 106, 139
Potential, 430, 433, 450
Pratt, V. R., 182, 266, 425
Prefix code, 359
Prefix form, 105
Preorder traversal, 102, 107, 139, 325
Preparata, F. P., 426
Prim, R. C., 351

Prim's algorithm, 320–323
  (*see also* Greedy algorithms)
Primality test, 402–403
`PrintWriter`, 509
Priority queue, 183–218, 309, 326, 361, 530
  basic operations, 188–191
  binary heap, 184–195
  binomial queue, 208–215
  d-heap, 198
  deap, 223
  Dijkstra's algorithm, 310, 437
  external sorting, 255–260
  Fibonacci heap, 437–446
  heapsort, 196, 232–235, 260–261
  Huffman code, 361
  k-d heaps, 494
  Kruskal's algorithm, 323–325
  leftist heap, 198–206, 438–440
  min-max heap, 220
  pairing heaps, 486–491
  Prim's algorithm, 320–323
  simple implementations, 184
  simulation, 196–197
  skew heap, 206–208, 435–437
Probing:
  linear, 162–164
  quadratic, 164–169
Proofs:
  by contradiction, 7
  by counterexample, 6
  by induction, 5–6, 10
  lower-bound, 227–228, 252–254
Pruning, 403, 413–415
Puech, C., 496
Pugh, W., 426
`PushbackReader`, 509–510

Q

Quadratic probing, 164–169
Quad tree, 495
Queue, 88–94, 183–184, 517
  array implementation of, 89–92
  basic operations, 88
  breadth-first search, 300–302
  double-ended (deque), 97, 451
  line printer, 92
  topological sort, 294–297

Queueing theory, 94
Quickselect, 250, 377
Quicksort, 240–252, 260, 262
    analysis, 246–250
    basic algorithm, 241
    cutoff for small files, 245
    dealing with duplicates, 243
    implementation, 245–246
    partitioning, 243–245
    picking the pivot, 241–243
    pitfalls, 243–245

R

Rabin, M. O., 182, 426
Radix sort, 66–68
Raghavan, P., 426
Ramanan, P., 426
Random, 510–511
Random number generator, 396–399
Random permutation generator, 50
Randomized algorithm, 395–403
    primality test, 402
    principles of, 395–396
    quicksort, 242
    selection, 379–380
    skip list, 399–402
Rank(s), 278, 431, 441
Rao, S., 351
Recurrence relations:
    solution of, 237–240, 246–250, 371–373
Recursion:
    backtracking algorithm, 403–415
    bad uses of, 87–88, 385
    depth-first search, 325–337
    exponentiation, 46–47
    four basic rules, 8, 10
    leftist heap, 198–206
    path compression, 276–278
    principles of, 7–10
    printing out numbers, 9
    recovering shortest path, 313, 314
    selection, 250–252
    skew heap, 206–208
    tail recursion, 88
    trees, 99–145
    (see also Divide and conquer)
Recursively undecidable problems, 338

Red-black trees, 152, 460–468
    bottom-up insertion, 461–462
    properties, 460–461
    top-down deletion, 467–468
    top-down insertion, 454–456
Reduction, 339–341
Reed, B. A., 224
Reflexive relation, 269
Rehashing, 171–174, 451
Reingold, E. M., 153, 497
Relation, 269
Replacement selection, 259–260
Reverse Polish notation, 82
Rivest, R. L., 289, 425
Rohnert, H., 181
Roberts, F. S., 28
Rotation:
    double, 123–130
    single, 120–123
Run construction, 256–257, 259–260
Running time:
    calculations, 35–48
    checking analysis of, 47
    of divide-and-conquer algorithms, 371–373
    examples of, 32–34, 35
    general rules, 35–37
    growth rates of, 34
    as an issue in large inputs, 2, 31
    logarithms in, 43–47
    over-estimates of, 48
    solutions for maximum subsequence sum problem, 37–43

S

Sack, J. R., 223
Saks, M. E., 289
Samet, H., 497
Santoro, N., 223
Saxe, J. B., 425
Schaffer, R., 267
Scheduler, operating system, 183
Scheduling, 354–357
Schonhage, A., 290
Schrage, L., 426
Schwab, B., 496
Scroggs, R. E., 153

Search trees:
  AA-trees, 474–481
  AVL tree, 118–130, 453
  k-d trees, 483–486, 493, 494, 495
  red black trees, 152, 460–468
  splay trees, 130–138, 446–449, 453–460
  treaps, 482–485
Sedgewick, R., 153, 223, 266, 267, 496, 497
Seidel, R., 496
Selection problem:
  in linear worst-case time, 377–379
  inefficient algorithms for, 1
  priority queue solution, 190–191
  quickselect, 250
  sampling algorithm, 379–380
Self-adjusting data structure:
  disjoint sets algorithm, 269–287
  list, 94, 451
  skew heap, 206–208, 435–437
  splay tree, 130–138, 446–449
Sentinel, 189, 226
Sequential files, 20–23
Series, 3–5
  arithmetic, 4
  geometric, 4
  harmonic, 5
  sum of kth power, 4
Sequential scan, 11
Sets, 517
Shamos, M. I., 426
Shapiro, H. D., 351, 496
Sharir, M., 351
Shell, D. L., 267
Shellsort, 48, 228–231, 260, 265
  analysis, 229–231
    Hibbard's increments, 230–231
    Shell's increments, 229–230
  average running time, 231, 260
  implementation, 229
Shing, M. R., 425
Short-circuit operation, 61
Shortest-path algorithms, 297–314, 348
Shortest-path calculation, 523–529
Shrairman, R., 223
Sieve of Erastothenes, 52
Simon, I., 289
Simulation, 94, 196, 197

Sink, 346
Skew heap, 206–208, 435–437
  amortized analysis of, 435–437
Skiena, S. S., 426
Skip list, 399–402
Sleator, D. D., 153, 223, 224, 452, 496, 497
Smith, H. F., 153
Smith, W. D., 426
Smolka, S. A., 425
Sorting, 225–261
  algorithms, compared, 260–261
  bucket sort, 66, 254–255
  comparison-based, 225
  external, 255–260, 266
  heapsort, 232–235, 260–261
  insertion sort, 226–227
  lower bounds, 227–228, 252–254
  mergesort, 235–240
  quicksort, 240–252, 266
  Shellsort, 48, 228–231, 260, 265
  stable, 266
  topological, 294–297
  tree sort, 145
Sparse graph, 293, 296, 309
Spelling checker, 177
Spencer, T. H., 350
Splay tree, 130–138, 446–449, 453–460
  amortized analysis of, 446–449
  analysis of, 138
  deletion, 138
  merging, 443
  self-adjustment, 130–138
  splay steps: implementation of, 133–138
  top-down implementation, 453–460
  zig, 446, 448
  zig-zag, 133–134, 446, 448–449
  zig-zig, 133–134, 446, 449
Stack, 75–88, 296, 517
  array implementation, 78–81
  balancing parenthesis, 81
  fundamental operations, 75
  list implementation, 76–78
  and recursion, 84–86
  topological sort, 296
Stack frame, 77
Stasevich, G. V., 266
Stasko, J. T., 497

Static initializer, 69
Steele, G., 28
Steiglitz, K., 351
Stephenson, C. J., 497
Stirling's formula, 263
Strassen, V., 427
Strassen's algorithm, 382–384
String, 502–503
Stringbuffer, 503–505
StringTokenizer, 511–512
Strong components, 336–337
Strong, H. R., 181
Strothotte, T., 223, 224
Successor position, 409
Suel, T., 266
Symbol table, 177
Symmetric binary B-tree (*see* AA-trees)
Symmetric relation, 269
System, 505–506
Szemeredi, E., 181, 182

T

Tail recursion, 88
Takaoka, T., 427
Tardos, E., 350
Tarjan, R. E., 153, 181, 223, 224, 289,
        290, 350, 351, 352, 425, 452,
        496, 497
Telescoping, 239
Theta notation, 29–32
Thornton, C., 153
Threaded tree, 150
Throwable, 506
Thurston, W. P., 153
Tic-tac-toe, 409–412, 414
Topological sort, 294–297
Transitive relation, 269
Transposition table, 177, 412
Traveling salesman, 340–341
Treaps, 481–483
Tree(s), 99–153
    AA, 474–481
    AVL, 118–129, 429, 453, 492
    B-tree, 139–144, 174
    B*-tree, 149
    binary, 105–108, 357–362
    binary search, 99, 109–118

complete binary, 185
decision, 252–254
definitions, 99–100
game, 412
k-d, 483–486
left child/right sibling implementation,
        213
minimum spanning, 319–325, 419
red-black, 152, 460–468
splay tree, 130–138, 446–449, 453–460
threaded, 150
traversals, 101–104, 138–139
trie, 358
2-3, 451
weight-balanced, 152
Trie, 358
Tsur, S., 153
Tucker, A., 28
Turing machine, 341
Turnpike reconstruction, 405–409
2–3 tree, 451
Type-independent, 11

U

Ullman, J. D., 54, 152, 289, 290, 350, 425
Undecidability, 338
Undirected graph, 326–327
Union/find algorithm (*see* Disjoint sets)

V

Vallner, S., 224
van Emde Boas, P., 224
van Kreveld, M. J., 290
van Leeuwen, J., 290, 497
van Vleit, A., 427
Vertex cover problem, 349
Vishkin, U., 426
Visibility specifier, 11
Vitter, J. S., 181, 497
Voronoi diagram, 420
Vuillemin, J., 224, 452, 497

W

Wagner, R. A., 427
Wegman, M. N., 181
Weight-balanced tree, 495–496
Wein, J., 424

Weiss, M. A., 28, 223, 267, 496
Westbrook, J., 290
Williams, J. W. J., 224, 267
Winograd, S., 425
Witten, I. H., 424
Wong, C. K., 496
Wong, J. K., 351
Wood, D., 152
Wrapper classes, 14

Y

Yao, A. C., 153, 182, 267, 290, 352, 427
Yao, F. F., 427

Z

Zhang, Z., 427
Zijlstra, E., 224
Ziv, J., 427
Ziviana, N., 152